T0355680

The RISE and FALL of the SECOND AMERICAN REPUBLIC

ALSO BY MANISHA SINHA

The Slave's Cause: A History of Abolition

The Counterrevolution of Slavery:
Politics and Ideology in Antebellum South Carolina

"And Not This Man?"

Thomas Nast, *Harper's Weekly*, August 5, 1865. *Library of Congress*

The RISE and FALL of the SECOND AMERICAN REPUBLIC

RECONSTRUCTION, 1860–1920

MANISHA SINHA

Liveright Publishing Corporation

A Division of W. W. Norton & Company
Independent Publishers Since 1923

For information about permission to reproduce selections from this book, write to
Permissions, Liveright Publishing Corporation, a division of W. W. Norton & Company, Inc.,
500 Fifth Avenue, New York, NY 10110

For information about special discounts for bulk purchases, please contact
W. W. Norton Special Sales at specialsales@wwnorton.com or 800-233-4830

Manufacturing by Lakeside Book Company
Book design by Chris Welch
Production manager: Lauren Abbate

ISBN 978-1-63149-844-2

Liveright Publishing Corporation, 500 Fifth Avenue, New York, N.Y. 10110
www.wwnorton.com

W. W. Norton & Company Ltd., 15 Carlisle Street, London W1D 3BS

1 2 3 4 5 6 7 8 9 0

For my sons

Sheel and Shiv
Citizens of the American Republic

According to the best testimony now, the population of the earth—embracing Caucasians, Mongolians, Malays, Africans, and Americans—is about thirteen hundred millions, of whom only three hundred and seventy five millions are "white men," or less than one-fourth, so that, in claiming exclusive rights for "white men," you degrade nearly three-quarters of the Human Family, made in the "image of God" and declared to be "one blood," while you sanction a Caste offensive to religion, an Oligarchy inconsistent with Republican Government, and a Monopoly which has the whole world as its footstool.

—CHARLES SUMNER, 1866

CONTENTS

The Great Contest

Our Republic is itself a strong argument
in favor of composite nationality.

—FREDERICK DOUGLASS, 1869

"Uncle Sam's Thanksgiving Dinner," *Harper's Weekly*, November 20, 1869.
(While this image includes Native Americans, the New England holiday of
Thanksgiving, which Lincoln made into a national holiday, glosses over their
dispossession.) *Library of Congress*

On February 20, 1868, Amy Circuit, a freedwoman in Newberry, South Carolina, was murdered in cold blood by two white men. Her case was duly recorded in the Field Office Records of the South Carolina Freedmen's Bureau by a federal agent. The killers were Samuel Rudd, who worked "on the premises" of John G. Lifford, and Lifford himself. They invaded the Circuit home in search of Amy's husband, referred to in the records variously as Charles or Coleman. Coleman testified that he had earlier confronted Rudd for whipping his son for being "sassy to him." When the two white men later entered his home, Rudd shot Amy. For their attempts to protect their son from being treated like a slave, Amy lost her life and Coleman was arrested: the local magistrate, J. E. Peterson, known to the Bureau for his involvement in many "outrages" against freedpeople, detained Coleman for assault. But the Bureau agent intervened and arrested Rudd and Lifford for Amy's murder. After a few days, Coleman retracted his statement after being "visited" by the Rudd and Lifford families, who dropped charges of assault against him. Amy's death, Coleman now stated, could have been "accidental." It is not clear what pressure was brought to bear on the new widower. What is clear is that Rudd and Lifford were released and Amy's murder went unpunished.

Like countless freedpeople, the Circuits paid dearly for their freedom. The story of Amy's death could be the history of southern Reconstruction after the Civil War in microcosm: the attempt of freedpeople to breathe meaning into their freedom; the attempt of the Freedmen's Bureau, a stand-in for the federal government, to intervene in a miscarriage of justice; and the reassertion of the authority of local white elites to act with impunity and defy the rule of law. As the activist-scholar W. E. B. DuBois observed in 1935, "The slave went free; stood for a brief moment in the sun; and then moved back again toward slavery." Building on DuBois, who wrote the first great history of Reconstruction, this book narrates the rise and fall of what I call the Second American Republic.[1] Amy Circuit was murdered at the start of Reconstruction, when black men attained the right to vote and hold political office. In the following decades, when southern states started systematically overthrowing Reconstruction governments, things got even worse in the region. Where I depart from most historians of Reconstruction is in my attempt to link such developments in the South with others across the nation.

Daniel and Caroline Grant moved from Massachusetts to Wisconsin in the 1850s. Daniel was always coming up with get-rich-quick schemes, whining and begging his wife and her family for money and looking out for financial opportunities in the Southwest, especially after the Civil War, whether that meant taking advantage of poorly paid southern black labor or setting himself up in Indian country. Nothing bothered him more than seeing dispossessed indigenous nations living on reservations and supported, however meagerly, by the federal government. He blamed them for his own failure to succeed. Daniel Grant and other settlers conveniently repurposed their criticism of freedpeople during Reconstruction as "wards" of the government to Indians, who were then blamed for their own poverty, viewed as lazy and dependent people who were not fit for self-government or equal citizenship. Daniel complained about the reservations: "The Indian must have a large amount of land and then fed at Government expense and many whites forbidden at getting a living at their own expense. What folly. But 'so mote it be.'" His jaundiced view did not capture the full history of indigenous people, especially those who navigated settler society and politics to survive in its "political economy of plunder."[2]

While benefitting from homestead legislation and the military campaigns against western indigenous nations, settlers like Daniel Grant developed an antigovernment politics that was also voiced by reactionary southern elites during Reconstruction. Despite being the principal beneficiary of government handouts, men like him propagated the myth of individual success. The final conquest of the West and destruction of indigenous sovereignties paralleled the overthrow of southern Reconstruction and pointed the way to the rise of an overseas American empire, as the US government was fully diverted from emancipatory to imperial aims.

During the Great Railroad Strike of 1877, the Workingmen's Party organized mass rallies of the "Grand Army of Starvation," an allusion to the Grand Army of the Republic, a fraternal organization of Union army veterans, in Chicago. Conservatives, however, designated the party a "communist organization" and deemed the workers mere foreigners—German, Irish, and "half-savage Bohemians." One of the speakers at such a gathering was Albert Parsons, a repentant onetime Confederate from Texas who had married a former slave, Lucy Parsons, a labor leader in her own right, and supported Reconstruction. Both had escaped racist terror in Texas and resettled in Chicago, their trajectory revealing the connections between the fight for democracy in the South and the North. As Parsons put it, "My enemies in the southern states consisted of those who oppressed the black slave. My enemies in the North are among those who would perpetuate the slavery of the wage workers."[3]

Women activists like Lucy Parsons are central to the history of the Second American Republic. Reconstruction not only inaugurated the women's suffrage movement in the United States, it also unleashed broad emancipatory goals for American women. While freedwomen like Amy Circuit sought to protect a "homegrown citizenship" against violent assaults in the postwar South, abolitionist feminists demanded the social and gendered reconstruction of American democracy. Histories of Reconstruction are riddled with simplistic racial dualisms of northern white teachers and black freedpeople. But relatively forgotten northern black abolitionist teachers like Ellen Garrison Jackson and Rebecca Primus left behind a record of their work with freedpeople, the racist abuse they suffered, and their efforts to expand the boundaries of American democracy in fighting for black and women's rights simultaneously. In her letter to her parents in Hartford, Connecticut, Primus detailed the harassment she and other "colored teachers" suffered at the hands of "secesh" and "copperhead" whites in Royal Oak, Maryland. She hailed, however, the passage of the Civil Rights Act of 1866, the first federal civil rights law in US history, as promising "impartial justice" so that "rights which are so unjustly withheld from us now, have been obtained."

In a subsequent letter, Primus referred to Jackson's suit against the stationmaster in Baltimore for throwing her and another black teacher, Mary Anderson, out of the ladies room while they were waiting for their train, under the new civil rights law. When the stationmaster, Adam Smyzer, tried to settle the case, Jackson wrote to the American Missionary Association's Reverend S. Hunt, "We could not agree to compromise just then and no other time unless we can have all our rights conceded to." She recalled the southern white woman who "had first insulted us" and how Smyzer had "grasped my arm so tightly" that "I felt compelled to cry out, let me alone, take your hand off me." Engaging in the suit, Jackson confessed, required "a great degree of moral courage, to act in the matter it is no trifling subject." She wrote how all the "colored people" in the area rallied around her and aided her in her lawsuit. Jackson viewed the struggle for equal rights during Reconstruction as a peculiarly women's fight. She noted, "Our soldiers went forth with sword and bayonet to contend for right and justice. We could not do that. But we contend against outrage and oppression wherever we find it, firmly standing and giving away for the rudest shocks."[4]

Black women like Primus and Jackson unveiled a new understanding of American democracy during Reconstruction, where black and women's rights were not competing but overlapping struggles. They refused to heed the siren call of some suffragists who would pit one against the other. Their Reconstruction vision encompassed women's suffrage as well as freedpeople's rights. In this book, I argue that the history of Reconstruction is also women's history.

The Rise and Fall of the Second American Republic narrates the achievements and the violent overthrow of Reconstruction. Expanding the usual temporal bounds of Reconstruction, which is customarily understood to have begun in 1865 and to have ended in 1877, it moves from the election of Abraham Lincoln in 1860 to the passage of the Nineteenth Amendment in 1920, which, I argue, should be seen as the last Reconstruction amendment. The book aims to depict a "great contest" for and against interracial democracy that played out not just in the South, but in the North and West and even beyond American shores. The main concern of Reconstruction was the plight of the formerly enslaved, but its fall affected other groups as well, from women and workers to immigrants and Native Americans. The defeat of black freedom was the defeat of American democracy.

The crucial question of Reconstruction is this: How did interracial democracy progress under the revolutionary impetus of the war and emancipation, and why did that effort unravel by the end of the nine-teenth century? Reconstruction birthed a national citizenship, expand-ing the boundaries of political belonging, rights, and claims on the nation-state. Building a "composite nation," as the self-emancipated abolitionist Frederick Douglass argued, was the greatest challenge of the Second American Republic. It was a fraught and contested project. Nearly 750,000 Americans perished in the Civil War and nearly a hun-dred thousand indigenous people were killed in wars, on reservations, and in assimilation campaigns during the second half of the nineteenth century. Around four million enslaved won their freedom and citizen-ship rights, only to be subject to a new regime of racist terror after the destruction of Reconstruction. Despite the emergence of the suffrage movement, women remained disfranchised. Asian immigrants were systematically excluded and strikes by workers of all ethnicities vio-lently put down.

Within this larger frame, the book focuses on the debate over who is a citizen and the role of the state in expanding or constricting rights and indigenous sovereignty. Its primary theme is the ongoing tension between democracy and capitalism, with the latter's historical entan-glement in slavery and imperialism. After the industrial take-off in the United States, the reconstruction of capitalism proved to be success-ful even as its reconstruction of democracy faltered. Democracy in the United States has always been rigorously challenged by forces of polit-ical and economic reaction. The rapid industrialization of the country and the dismal conditions of labor that followed Reconstruction made a mockery of the free labor ideology of the victorious North. New wars and imperial dreams of empire, inspired by the regime of racist apart-heid in the postwar South and the conquest of western Indian nations, further hobbled American democracy at home and abroad. By the end of the nineteenth century, a formal US empire would subject people from the Caribbean to the Philippines to colonial rule. The demise of the Second American Republic inaugurated an era of hierarchy and inequality—racial, ethnic, gendered, and economic—rather than one of equal citizenship promised by the war for emancipation and Recon-struction.[5] Connecting the struggle for black citizenship with debates over ethnicity, gender, economic autonomy, and sovereignty that raged at the same time, I aim to show that we have missed much by confining our vision of the end of Reconstruction to the South.

It is not only the chronology and scope of this book but its interpretation that is thus at odds with conventional narratives, which have emphasized how the United States was able to develop a unique and long-lasting experiment in republican government by expanding democracy, incrementally but consistently, to groups previously denied inclusion. In the prevailing view, the Anglo-American tradition of liberal democracy is distinct from the more volatile histories of continental Europe. Or so the story goes. From simplistic stories of American exceptionalism to more sophisticated analyses of democracy in the Western world, the old consensus cannot, in fact, explain the violent upheavals of the mid to late nineteenth century in the United States. As President Abraham Lincoln put it in December 1862, "Fellow-Citizens, *we* cannot escape history."[6] The Civil War resulted in the destruction of the "first" American republic and birthed the second. My notion of a "second" republic comes from the history of French republicanism. In borrowing that terminology to describe events in the United States, I seek to highlight the growth of reactionary authoritarianism in the postwar South, a type of politics we often associate with Europe or the rest of the Americas.

Put simply, the long afterlives of slavery and imperialism are as important to understanding US history as are more familiar, ameliorative tales about the abolition of slavery and the expansion of democracy and citizenship rights during Reconstruction. The story of the contest between the two is designed to capture an essential and ongoing theme in the United States, which was never all one or the other. Not only that, but the history of the unmaking of Reconstruction reveals the global significance of the first abortive experiment to transform the slaveholders' republic into an interracial democracy. My goal is to put Reconstruction in a broad transnational context, and to thereby demonstrate that its long death has as much to tell us as its short-lived triumph.[7]

Other recent work has expanded Reconstruction's chronological and spatial boundaries, yet unlike these histories, this book emphasizes disjuncture rather than continuity. The reconstruction of the West was not a process parallel to southern Reconstruction but rather must be understood apiece with its downfall. To view the bold experiment in interracial democracy, recounted in Eric Foner's canonical *Reconstruction*, as the same political process that led to the subjugation of indigenous nations, nativism, and the triumph of industrial capitalism and imperialism, is to completely miss the contestation that shaped this era.[8] I argue that these events must be viewed as part of the long overthrow of Reconstruction and of the abolitionist aims of the American Civil War, and not as their consequence.

Where some see the seamless expansion of the American nation-state, I show change and open conflict over democracy, citizenship, sovereignty, and political economy.[9] Central to this history is the truly emancipatory moment represented by the new civic democracy of Reconstruction and its significant legacy of progressive constitutionalism and democratic governance, the novel notion that the government is responsible for expanding rights and maintaining the welfare of all its citizens regardless of race and previous condition of servitude. Debates on the nature of governance—whether all citizens and noncitizens are equally rights-bearing individuals and claimants before the state—defined the Second American Republic.

Another interpretative thread concerns capitalism and democracy, which were not born as conjoined twins in the United States or the rest of the world. To see them as such is to root one's claims in ideology, not history. More often than not, the aims of one were antagonistic to the goals of the other. It would be the defeat of the interracial democracy and the antislavery state of Reconstruction that paved the way for the reign of capital and the narrowing of emancipation to contract freedom and the triumph of laissez-faire liberalism—what we call political conservatism today. In this historical process, government activism on behalf of its citizens, former slaves, farmers, women, immigrants, and labor came to be seen as misguided, if not horrifying. Instead, the full military and coercive powers of the government were deployed to repress indigenous nations, immigrants, and labor. A neo-Confederate political vision—a fundamentally antidemocratic racist ideology combined with anti–big government rhetoric—was reborn. It went not only national but international. Dressed up in fundamentalist religious idiom, racism "redeemed" the South and the West and provided the rationale for American colonialism.[10] The Lost Cause mythology of the South was not just nostalgic window dressing for sordid industrialization. It became its ideological handmaiden.

There can be no doubt that the destruction of racial slavery and the reconstruction of the misbegotten southern Confederacy fundamentally remade the entire republic. That revolution transformed the US Constitution. Long before historians did so, the abolitionist William Goodell proclaimed in 1861 in his newspaper, the *Principia*, that the Civil War was "the Second American Revolution" that portended the national abolition of all inequalities. The abolitionist feminist Angelina Grimke Weld, in her 1863 "Address of the Woman's National Loyal League to the Soldiers of Our Second American Revolution," argued that the southern "slavocracy" threatened the freedom of all American citizens and sought to enslave workingmen of all colors. They were both right, in a way, though Goodell's prophecy has yet to come to pass. The massive economic and political dislocations of the Gilded Age that followed Reconstruction were not just the product of the changes wrought by the Civil War and Reconstruction; they were also a result of the defeat of the prior era's emancipatory legacy. They represented, to borrow the words of a historian of modern Europe, Arno J. Mayer, "the persistence of the old regime," a virulently antidemocratic, hierarchical politics that justified the new global political economy of industrial capitalism and imperialism.[11]

As the above quotation suggests, the international scene is important to this history, and its importance goes beyond terminology. It is often claimed that the American republic was the only one to grant citizenship rights, including voting for adult men, to the formerly enslaved after the abolition of slavery. In fact, France, which has an equally long democratic republican tradition, preceded the United States in granting voting rights to black freedmen in the colonies when the Second French

Republic abolished slavery in 1848.[12] (After the French Revolution, the first republic had also briefly enfranchised free black male citizens, just as propertied black men in the United States enjoyed the right to vote after the American Revolution. Black American men retained the right to vote only in a handful of New England states before the Civil War.) In both cases, political equality was imperfect, to say the least, and in the American South black citizenship was undermined by racist terror and draconian legal mechanisms for another hundred years after the downfall of Reconstruction.

In employing the Second American Republic framework, this book draws its inspiration not only from the history of French republicanism but also from the rest of the Americas, where republics rose and then fell to the forces of reaction and authoritarianism. The American experiment in democratic republicanism, abolition, and black citizenship was not unique but part of a broader global transition from slavery to freedom, from racial privilege to emancipation to a conservative backlash. In the Americas, one can discern a broader "Atlantic Reconstruction" that included Cuba and Brazil, two countries where the "second" slavery of the nineteenth century crumbled after slavery was destroyed in the US South.[13]

Along similar lines, the emergence of a strong nation-state in the United States in the 1870s paralleled the national unification of Germany and Italy. Universalist republican ideals that powered emancipation and democratic movements eventually came into conflict with authoritarian nationalisms that posited national homogeneity: one people, one language, one culture, one religion, and, most tragically, one "race." It is no coincidence that the rise of formal American empire occurred simultaneously with the "Scramble for Africa" among European powers and the heyday of imperialism at the turn of the century. Imperialist nationalisms, fueled further by the first military-industrial complex, led to the Great War of 1914–1918.

The rise and fall of the Second American Republic, in fact, had global consequences. The defeat of the "Slave Power" in the Civil War inspired the enslaved and abolitionists in Spain, Cuba, and Brazil, but the demise of interracial democracy in the United States also contributed to the unchecked emergence of imperialism and later, fascism. By the early twentieth century, the United States was not just the city upon a hill, an unprecedented experiment in democratic republicanism, but it now could serve as a barbaric model of racist oppression. The Jim Crow South and genocidal warfare against Indians would inspire the Nazis in Germany, as well as the apartheid state of South Africa.[14]

Another international comparison sheds light on the demise of Reconstruction. The more successful reconstructions undertaken by the United States and its allies of Germany and Japan after the Second World War reveal that the key ingredient for a long-lasting reconstruction is not indefinite military rule, but a genuine acceptance of defeat and moral culpability by the losers, or at least most of them. Much of the American South and its conservative political allies in the rest of the nation never came to terms with the destruction of slavery. They continued to resist black citizenship as well as Reconstruction laws and constitutional amendments. The Jim Crow South spun victory out of defeat with the enduring myth of the "Lost Cause" to justify the overthrow of Reconstruction. The actual history of the Confederacy as an antidemocratic, proslavery project in open rebellion against the American republic and its founding ideals was buried under a comforting narrative of national reconciliation between the North and the South—a reconciliation challenged by Union veterans as well as black people and their allies, who demanded an end to racial segregation, economic servitude, and disfranchisement, as well as full equality for all citizens regardless of color, as promised by Reconstruction. Some Americans, not only southerners, continue to espouse these pernicious ideas from the late nineteenth century, and to support the authoritarianism that undergirds them.[15]

This book opens in 1860, with the birth of the Second American Republic, when Abraham Lincoln was elected and South Carolina seceded from the Union. Lincoln was the first Reconstruction president. From his administration's first actions to reconstruct the Union during the Civil War, the book moves to the classic period of Reconstruction, which witnessed the failure of Andrew Johnson's presidential restoration in 1865 and the implementation of congressional Reconstruction, or "abolition democracy," in 1866–1870. Not only conceptions of national citizenship but also the modern welfare state were born during this moment. Freedpeople and their abolitionist allies raised questions of political economy that propelled state formation and seeded the idea of a social democracy.

The book centers the lives, labors, and trials of antislavery activists, federal agents, and soldiers—and, most importantly, freedpeople—in exploring what happened to the abolitionist project after emancipation. It examines grassroots freedom struggles and black political power at the local, state, and national levels—what I call "Grassroots Reconstruction." It privileges the voices of abolitionist and radical critics of mainstream society and politics that are seldom heard. I also try to capture how tenuous the experiment in interracial democracy was in the South: it was always under sustained attack from racist terrorists and ideologies about who was fit to be a rights-bearing citizen and who was fit to govern.

The mobilization of northern antislavery women, black and white, during the Civil War and Reconstruction advanced the idea of women's citizenship. Reconstruction did not bequeath only a history of failure for women, though it did do that; its legacy also opened new possibilities for suffrage through constitutional change. Freedwomen, in particular, connected women's emancipation with black liberation. Perhaps the most obvious intervention this book makes in the existing literature on Reconstruction is in its emphasis on women, whether within the suffrage movement or not. For many decades, even the best works on Reconstruction have not paid enough attention to gender. I hope that my narrative demonstrates why gender was an essential dimension to the freedom struggles of the era.

After Grassroots Reconstruction came the "American Thermidor" (to borrow another term from French history), or the downfall of the Second American Republic between the 1870s and the 1890s, a period that witnessed the simultaneous overthrow of Reconstruction and the

violent suppression of labor upheavals. For freedpeople the reign of capital meant brutal work conditions: convict lease labor, sharecropping,
and debt peonage in a revived plantation and manufacturing economy
of the "New South." The successful reconstruction of American capitalism doomed the reconstruction of American democracy. The use of the
federal army and courts, no longer to expand rights but to restrict them,
signaled the triumph of political reaction and industrial capital.

The conquest of the West through the so-called Indian wars, better referred to as "wars against Indians," lasted well until the end of
the nineteenth century and set the stage for the establishment of an
overseas US empire after the Spanish-Cuban-American War of 1898,
the annexation of Hawaii, and the colonization of the Philippines. The
unmaking of Reconstruction was completed legally only in the 1890s,
with black disfranchisement in the South and the establishment of
racial segregation, legitimized by a mostly reactionary Supreme Court
that emasculated Reconstruction laws and amendments. The ascendancy of "Jim Crow colonialism" marked the triumph of the vision of
the defeated South in the nation and abroad. There was no reflexive or
automatic transition from the antislavery nation-state to a racist, imperialist nation-state; rather, one political project had to be violently displaced by the other.[16]

The book closes with the struggle for women's emancipation at the
turn of the century. In treating the Nineteenth Amendment, which gave
women the right to vote in 1920, not just as a Progressive Era reform but
as the last of the Reconstruction amendments, I show how it was modeled after the Fifteenth Amendment that gave black men the right to
vote in 1870. As far as southern black, indigenous, and colonized women
were concerned, the amendment meant little. Yet at the same time,
black and white women's activism went well beyond the demand for suffrage, to include a broad array of demands on the state, from pensions to
government regulation of the economy. Such demands should properly
be seen as feminist ideas about the social state that were first developed
during Reconstruction. Some suffragists, who opposed Reconstruction, made expedient compromises with southern racists, but a new

generation of social and black feminists revived the old intersectional vision of abolitionist feminists—of the links between black, labor, and women's rights.[17]

To write this book I have drawn on a wide variety of sources, including government documents, congressional proceedings, manuscripts, letters, pamphlets, and newspapers. The voluminous Freedmen's Bureau papers and the thirteen-volume Report of the Joint Select Committee of Congress into the Condition of Affairs in the Late Insurrectionary States are especially valuable in recovering the testimony of freedpeople and are central to any history of Reconstruction. I have paid particular attention to abolitionist and suffragist material, published and unpublished, privileging the perspectives of those who are not well represented in the historical literature. My research method has been selective rather than comprehensive, but I have not neglected any major source for the period. I have balanced stories of resistance and achievement with the dismal history of oppression and violence. Indeed, this contest emerged from the sources themselves.

By the end of the nineteenth century, the Second American Republic's project of interracial democracy was in tatters. Yet its ideals, and the freedom claims of the disfranchised, animated the social movements and struggles for equality that followed. These alternative democratic visions were the product of Reconstruction and its discontents. Which is to say that the triumph of industrial capitalism by the end of the nineteenth century was itself contested. Resistance to it would bear fruit in the Populist and labor movements, during the Progressive Era, and later in the New Deal. Later still in the twentieth century, the civil rights movement inaugurated the second reconstruction of American democracy. Today, the attempt by conservatives to unravel the New Deal state and civil rights laws—and the advent of a new Gilded Age—reveal that the great contest between democracy and capitalism, equality and inequality, interracialism and racist authoritarianism, feminism and patriarchy, is far from over.[18] Democracy itself, the history of Reconstruction reveals, can be systematically overthrown and repressed for long periods in US history. As then, so too today: democracy's viability and future lie in the hands of ordinary citizens.

A Note on Terminology

In this book, "Reconstruction" refers to southern Reconstruction. The verb "to reconstruct," meanwhile, describes other struggles for citizenship and sovereignty by disparate groups: women, workers, immigrants, and indigenous people. When I refer to the "reconstruction" of the West and of capitalism, both of which coincided with the dismantling of southern Reconstruction, I do not capitalize the term. I dislike generic terms for the period, including "postwar," that have been advocated by some historians recently.

The book eschews traditional terms that perpetuate false understandings of Reconstruction, such as "carpetbagger," "scalawag," and "redemption."[19] I refer to Andrew Johnson's plans not as "Presidential Reconstruction," but more accurately as a brief yet consequential restoration of antebellum southern hierarchy that lay outside the actual process of Reconstruction. I prefer the term "interracial" to "biracial" or "multiracial," as the former suggests true interconnectedness and engagement, the abolitionist dream of interchange and fellow feeling. I use the gender-neutral term "freedpeople" rather than the conventional "freedmen," which leaves out freedwomen, to refer to the formerly enslaved—and I avoid when possible the word "slave," which is especially out of place in a book on Reconstruction, when black people proved that "slave" is not an identity but a temporary condition. "Enslaved" is preferred but I do use the word "slave" or "former slave" or "ex-slave" interchangeably at times. I also use former and ex-slaveholder and ex-master along with the more proactive "enslaver." I refer to native peoples and nations by their proper names or collectively as Native Americans, Indians, or indigenous.

PART ONE

THE MIDWIFE
OF REVOLUTION,
1860–1870

"Sic Semper Tyrannis, 22th Regt US Colored
Troops," by David Bustill Bowser. *Library of Congress*

CHAPTER ONE

Wartime Reconstruction

As our case is new, so we must think anew,
and act anew. We must disenthrall ourselves,
and then we shall save our country.

—ABRAHAM LINCOLN, 1862

"African Americans fording the Rappahannock River, VA,"
by Timothy O'Sullivan. *Library of Congress*

E nslaved people viewed Abraham Lincoln as their liberator before
he saw himself in that role. The presidential election of 1860 and
the ascendancy of the antislavery Republican Party was a political revolution, and both enslaved people and those who had been advocating the secession of the slave South from the republic were quick to
recognize it. Southern secessionists soon launched a counterrevolution
for the perpetuity and expansion of slavery.[1] And the war came.

The steady destruction of slavery during the Civil War laid the basis
for the reconstruction of American democracy. Emancipation meant
freedom for nearly four million slaves, and it also freed the country from
slavery, as Lincoln recognized. Yet the path to emancipation was neither straightforward nor free of obstacles. It took the combined determination of an antislavery Republican Congress and president, the
might of the Union army, the agitation of abolitionist men and women,

and, above all, the persistence of the "freedom dreams" of the enslaved to make it a reality.[2]

Liberty was not cheap, costing the blood of patriots as well as the blood of those who committed treason against the republic in defense of slavery. The greatest price, however, had already been paid by generations of the enslaved, most of whom now suffered disease and dislocation in the chaos of war. But the result of the just war against slavery was not only death and destruction, the gruesome outcome of all wars.

Abolitionists, many of whom were bona fide pacifists, welcomed the war against slavery, which they viewed as a state of war against black people. The long and brutal war against generations of enslaved Americans remains invisible to many today, dwarfed by the casualties and the landscapes of ruin produced by the Civil War. More Americans died in that war than all subsequent ones fought by the United States, including the two world wars and the Korean and Vietnam Wars. But for four million slaves and their descendants, the conflict meant freedom.[3] In their stories of endurance lay the true significance of the Civil War.

The war witnessed the destruction of slavery, the arming of black men, and the first tentative steps toward an interracial democracy, a political project that the abolition movement had long envisioned and that the enslaved would bring to life in countless everyday struggles. The war must be seen not just as the precondition for Reconstruction but also as a part of it; hence this book opens with "wartime reconstruction." If the Civil War proved to be the midwife of the Second American Republic, the enslaved and their antislavery allies were its founders. The creation of a strong central state—the idea that the federal government was responsible for protecting the freedom and well-being of freedpeople— was its product. But the main force behind wartime reconstruction was the enslaved and their abolitionist allies who learned from them, who together conducted a series of reconstruction experiments in Union-occupied parts of the Confederacy.

Historians typically locate the origins of Reconstruction at either the end of the Civil War in 1865 or the issuing of the Emancipation

Proclamation in 1863. The reconstruction of American democracy began not with the Civil War but even earlier, at the moment Lincoln, an antislavery Republican, was elected to the presidency. November 6, 1860, marked the start of revolutionary time. As Senator Charles Sumner, the Massachusetts Radical Republican, put it, "Every four years we choose a new President; but it rarely happens that we choose a new government, as was done yesterday." The Republican Party, founded in 1854—the last time a successful third party was created in US history—won the second presidential election it contested, sweeping the North, except New Jersey, even as it was barred from the ballot in much of the slave South. In the mid-nineteenth century, the Republican Party was the liberal party of antislavery and big government, and the Democratic Party was the conservative party of slavery and states' rights. Secessionists viewed the Republican platform, which aimed to block the extension of slavery into western territories, as the first step in strangling slavery to death. For Sumner, the political victory of antislavery made the American republic "more precious by consecration to Human Rights."[4]

Rather than accept the results of the presidential election, the Deep South states chose to leave the Union. South Carolina led the quick departure of the seven lower South states during the "secession winter" of 1860–1861 on December 20. All attempts at compromise failed in Congress, when Lincoln and the Republicans refused to repudiate the platform on which they were elected, the non-extension of slavery. In February 1861, the southern Confederacy created a government founded on counterrevolution. Confederate vice president Alexander Stephens proclaimed that its "foundations are laid, its cornerstone rests, upon the great truth that the negro is not equal to the white man; that slavery, subordination to the superior race, is his natural and moral condition." The ideal of human equality proclaimed in the Declaration of Independence was, according to Stephens, a lie.

The Confederacy waged war on the republic's founding ideals. Even the compromiser Charles Francis Adams Sr., son and grandson of presidents, wrote that "A collision in my mind seems inevitable." Confederates fired the first shot of the Civil War on Fort Sumter off South Carolina's coast on April 12, 1861. The South, as abolitionist Wendell Phillips put it pithily, had "made war upon the nation." The attack precipitated the secession of four more upper South slave states led by Virginia. Four border slave states— Maryland, Delaware, Kentucky, and Missouri—remained in the Union, and became a thorn in the side of the Lincoln administration. Northern conservatives failed to maintain the slaveholding republic, though not for lack of trying. Its death was irreversible. Sumner explained, "Thus far the National Government has been inspired by Slavery. It has seemed to exist for Slavery only. All is now changed."[5]

As Americans tried to make sense of this rapid succession of events, the enslaved voted with their feet. They defected to federal forts at the first inkling of conflict. Seventeen slaves in Petersburg, Virginia left their plantation on the day of Lincoln's inauguration, claiming to be free. A black woman in Baltimore said, "Wait till the Fourth of March [Inauguration Day] and then won't I slap my missus' face!" Even before the war started, an enslaved boy at Sumter speculated that slaves would rise and "assist" federal troops. Eight runaways arrived at Fort Pickens in Florida "entertaining the idea," according to its commander, that federal forces "were placed here to protect them and grant them freedom."[6]

Enslaved people's freedom claims initiated the emancipation process. Facing a continuous trickle of slaves to Fortress Monroe, Virginia, Union general Benjamin Butler, a northern Democrat from Massachusetts, declared them "contraband of war," subject to confiscation as enemy property according to the laws of war, in May 1861. Lincoln approved of "Butler's fugitive slave law." In July, the Republican-dominated House of Representatives declared that it was "no part of the duty of the soldiers of the United States to capture and return fugitive slaves," a deterrent to proslavery officers in the Union army who still upheld the 1850 Fugitive Slave Act.

Runaways created a political problem for the Lincoln administration and a logistical one for the army, propelling emancipation. Virginian fugitive John Washington observed after the First Battle of Bull Run in July 1861, "It had now become a well known fact that slaves were daily making their Escape into the union lines." A month later, Congress passed the First Confiscation Act, freeing all slaves used for military labor by the Confederacy. In practice, some Union commanders liberally interpreted the act to apply to all fleeing slaves, including those in border slave states still in the Union. The trickle, with federal encouragement, became a flood, and the enslaved became the architects of their own liberation.

Many enslaved people who made it to Union lines—especially those who escaped from Confederate frontlines—brought valuable military information. "Self-emancipated slaves," as leading abolitionist William Lloyd Garrison called them, also provided military labor in Union camps, with women employed to cook and do laundry. The scarred backs of desperate runaways and the arrogance of their enslavers, who attempted to hunt them down during the war, converted many a northern farm boy into an emancipationist.[7]

The humanitarian, political, and military arguments for emancipation were not mutually exclusive but rather reinforcing. In his speech, "The Death of Slavery is the Salvation of the Republic," Representative Owen Lovejoy of Illinois, a Lincoln confidant and brother of the murdered abolitionist editor Elijah Lovejoy, pronounced emancipation a "national necessity." Abolitionists and antislavery Republicans helped shape the course of wartime emancipation. Experienced at assisting fugitive slaves and defending them in northern courts, they were particularly attuned to their wartime travails. Abolitionist David Lee Child argued that the federal government could emancipate contraband slaves under the laws of war. Harriet Tubman predicted that God would not let Lincoln win the war until he freed the slaves.

In November 1861, Garrison formed the Emancipation League to demand immediate abolition as a "measure of justice" and "as a military necessity," vindicating his old maxim, "No Union with Slaveholders." Sumner asked Garrison to revive "antislavery sentiment" so that he might take *practical measures* in Congress "to clean the statute-book of all support of slavery." Preeminent abolitionist orators like Frederick Douglass barnstormed the North with speeches advocating emancipation. Phillips's most popular speech was on Toussaint Louverture, the leader of the Haitian Revolution (1791–1804), the successful slave rebellion that led to the founding of the black nation. The American Civil War should also result in the revolutionary overthrow of slavery, he recommended.

At the end of 1861, Charles Francis Adams Sr., now serving as Lincoln's American minister in London, wrote: "A memorable year indeed in the history of the world! The terrible explosion of the sad moral volcano of American slavery!" Radicals revived the argument of his antislavery father, John Quincy Adams, former president and congressman from Massachusetts. Before he died in 1848, Quincy Adams wrote,

> I lay this down as the law of nations. I say that the military authority takes the place of municipal institutions, Slavery among the rest. Under that state of things, so far from its being true that the States where Slavery exists have the exclusive management of the subject, not only the President of the United States, but the Commander of the army has the power to order the universal emancipation of the slaves.

This quotation graced the masthead of both *Douglass' Monthly* and Garrison's *The Liberator* throughout the war. Douglass also invoked the South American republics that had abolished slavery in their wars for independence. At every opportunity, Sumner importuned Lincoln to use his war powers to act against slavery.[8]

Abolitionist ideas made their way into the Union army. Generals John C. Fremont and David Hunter, who issued military proclamations of emancipation for their departments, are often portrayed as hotheads who acted prematurely. The reality is more complex. Fremont had been the first Republican presidential candidate in 1856; known as the "Pathfinder of the West," he had perpetrated Indian massacres. Now heading the Department of Missouri in St. Louis, Fremont surrounded himself with staunch unionists and socialist German emigres from the European revolutions of 1848.

In his proclamation of emancipation of August 1861, and at the prompting of the German radicals, Fremont declared martial law, hoping thereby to stamp out vicious guerilla warfare by Confederate sympathizers in the area. Those who took up arms against the government would be disarmed, court-martialed, and shot as traitors, their property confiscated and their slaves freed. Yet Lincoln balked at these revolutionary measures, nervous that he would lose the border slave states, even as abolitionists and Republicans applauded them. He cautioned Fremont that he should not jump ahead of the First Confiscation Act passed by Congress. In a letter to Orville Browning, a conservative Republican who defended Fremont, Lincoln wrote that no general or president could constitutionally issue an emancipation proclamation. In his annual address to Congress in December, he expressed his worry over the war "degenerat[ing] into a violent and remorseless revolutionary struggle."

Fremont's wife, Jesse—daughter of the old Jacksonian Democrat Thomas Hart Benton, who had broken with the extreme proslavery wing of his party—was an antislavery advocate in her own right and pleaded her husband's case in Washington. She is often portrayed as an ambitious woman who stepped out of her "proper sphere," but women had long been essential to antislavery politics. Abolitionist Gerrit Smith wrote to Lincoln that Fremont's actions were well within Quincy Adams's understanding of martial law and emancipation. House Republicans passed a resolution supporting Fremont's proclamation, while in the Senate, Lyman Trumbull of Illinois introduced a bill to free the slaves of all rebel slaveholders. The president took note of the widespread Republican support for Fremont's strong measures.[9]

Like Fremont's proclamation, Hunter's proclamation was not an early misstep but rather a precedent for emancipation, even though Lincoln revoked both orders and relieved Fremont of his command. In March 1862, Hunter, a man of abolitionist conviction, took command of the Department of the South. In April, he started recruiting black men into the army in the Union-occupied South Carolina Sea Islands and liberated slaves in the recaptured Fort Pulaski. In May, he issued an emancipation proclamation covering the entire Department of the South, South Carolina, Georgia, and Florida, declaring slavery incompatible with martial law. Lincoln's secretary of the treasury, Salmon P. Chase, founder of the abolitionist Liberty Party as well as the antislavery Free Soil and Republican Parties before the war, supported the general, though Lincoln believed that he, too, had overstepped his authority. The president, however, now reserved the power to free slaves in rebel areas to himself as commander-in-chief. Lincoln stated that he could constitutionally issue an emancipation proclamation, using his war powers. And unlike Fremont, Hunter retained his confidence. As abolitionist Henry C. Wright put it, what antislavery generals including Hunter and General John W. Phelps, who like Hunter had armed slaves, made local, the president and Congress made national.[10]

As a first step toward emancipation, Lincoln tried to persuade the four border slave states in the Union to accept compensated emancipation coupled with the colonization of freed blacks outside the country. But even Delaware, where 90 percent of the black population was already free, rejected his proposals. Still, Lincoln urged the passage of a congressional resolution for compensated emancipation, putting the federal government on record for abolition. Republican congressmen introduced resolutions and bills demanding immediate military emancipation and the recruitment of black soldiers. In April 1862, Congress abolished slavery in the District of Columbia, long demanded by prewar abolitionist petitions and proposed by Lincoln when he was an Illinois representative in 1849. But Congress and the president tacked on money for colonization and compensation for slaveholders, to the ire of abolitionists, who argued that if anyone deserved compensation, it was the enslaved themselves, for generations of unpaid labor. *The Christian Recorder,* the newspaper of the African Methodist Episcopal Church and the only black newspaper published throughout the war, however, called DC emancipation a "great moral victory" that "denationalizes slavery." Sumner, employing established abolitionist logic that justified buying individual slaves, argued that it was a ransom paid to kidnappers.

Abolishing slavery in Washington partially fulfilled Republicans' project of divorcing the federal government from slavery and making it stand, instead, for freedom. In June 1862, Congress followed through by excluding slavery from federal territories. In July, it passed the Second Confiscation Act, which freed the slaves of all rebel slaveholders, not just the enslaved coerced by the Confederacy for military labor. Though the law endorsed colonization and laid out a cumbersome judicial process, it opened the road to wider emancipation. Trumbull, chairman of the Senate Judiciary Committee, and the author of some of the most consequential Reconstruction laws and amendments, made clear that the act was intended to "give freedom to the slaves." A moderate antislavery lawyer who had assisted fugitive slaves before the war, Trumbull argued that the law was in line with the Constitution as well as international law. Senator Henry Wilson of Massachusetts said that the law made slavery and treason "synonymous words." Congress also passed the Militia Act, allowing black men to enlist in the Union army, a long-standing abolitionist demand.

During that same critical July, Lincoln announced his intention to issue an emancipation proclamation to his cabinet. On the advice of Secretary of State William Seward, the president would await a major Union victory before making his plans public. A series of battlefield losses had resulted in a military stalemate on the eastern front in the first two years of the war. In the West, however, the Army of West Tennessee under Maj. Gen. Ulysses S. Grant won victories in Tennessee and Mississippi, while the Union navy gained footholds on the Carolina coastline and in New Orleans, Louisiana. In September 1862, the Union army repulsed Confederate general Robert E. Lee's invasion of Antietam, Maryland, allowing Lincoln to act.[11]

The Lincoln administration took several antislavery steps before the president's decision to issue the Emancipation Proclamation. It strengthened the implementation of the laws against the African slave trade; the first American slave trader indicted for piracy was hanged in 1862. Black abolitionists who had waged a battle against the illegal international trade in New York City hailed the news. On the urging of Sumner, chairman of the Senate Foreign Relations Committee, the administration recognized the independent black nations of Haiti and Liberia. Seward would soon receive Haitian diplomats at the capital, to the delight of African Americans and abolitionists.

On September 22, 1862, Lincoln issued the Preliminary Emancipation Proclamation announcing that he, as commander-in-chief of the army and navy, would free all slaves in states that were in rebellion against the United States on January 1, 1863. He quoted the Second Confiscation Act at length and again asked rebel slave states to consider abolition, assuring them that the federal government would assist them financially and colonize "persons of African descent, with their consent, upon this continent or elsewhere." Meeting with black leaders a month earlier, he lectured them for causing the war and promoted colonization. Garrison called the meeting "insulting." Like other attendees, Reverend T. Strother noted to the president that slavery, not African Americans, was the cause of the war. Emancipation would not endanger white labor, nor would black people flood the north, as some argued so as to gin up racist fear.

Lincoln admitted that racist sentiment against "free colored persons remaining in the country" was "largely imaginary, if not sometimes malicious." Later in the year, in his annual address to Congress, Lincoln acknowledged that "Spanish American republics" had rejected his plans for colonizing black people in their territories and suggested Haiti and Liberia as alternatives. He also admitted that African Americans "do not seem so willing to migrate to those countries." Criticism from abolitionists and the failure of ill-conceived schemes—especially the disastrous expedition of black migrants to Ille de Vache, or Cow Island, off the coast of Haiti—finally prompted Lincoln to give up on colonization.[12]

The final Emancipation Proclamation contained no provision for colonization. Just the opposite, in a sense: in sanctioning black military service, it opened a path to citizenship for black men. Lincoln called emancipation the "central act of my administration." Douglass said it was "the greatest event in our nation's history." As promised, Lincoln issued the proclamation on January 1, 1863—the day the black republic of Haiti was founded in 1804, the only other instance of immediate, wartime emancipation; and the day Britain and the United States had abolished the African slave trade in 1808. Abolitionists held a "watch night" on New Year's Eve until news of the proclamation came down the telegraph wires. Black abolitionists led an interracial celebration in Tremont Temple in Boston, where Douglass sang the hymn "Blow ye trumpet, blow!" January 1 was observed in black communities as the Day of Jubilee or "Jubilo," from the Bible when God freed his chosen people, later Emancipation Day. William Cooper Nell, the black abolitionist, wrote, "New Year's Day—proverbially known throughout the

South as 'Heart-Break Day'" when enslavers sold their enslaved, was now "invested with new significance and imperishable glory in the calendar of time."

Lincoln's proclamation declared all enslaved Americans in the rebel states free but did not apply to the four border slave states in the Union and also exempted the newly created state of West Virginia, which had broken from Virginia and reentered the Union, as well as parts of Union-held Virginia, Louisiana, and Tennessee. But it went further than the Second Confiscation Act, freeing *all* slaves in the rebel states, even if their masters were unionists, and became effective immediately as a tool of war. Lincoln could constitutionally proclaim emancipation as a military necessity only in the Confederacy. Despite criticisms of the exceptions to the Proclamation's purview, everyone knew that if slavery were abolished in Mississippi, it would not last in Missouri. The enslaved continued to defect to Union lines regardless of the loyalty of their enslavers and states. The Proclamation directly addressed those freed, asking them to "abstain from all violence, unless in necessary self-defense"–which prompted slaveholders to accuse Lincoln of fomenting rebellion—and to "labor faithfully for reasonable wages."[13]

Lincoln's Proclamation ended all talk of European nations formally recognizing the Confederacy. During the *Trent* affair of 1861, when the Union navy intercepted Confederate diplomats, Britain came close to intervening in the war. Now, with emancipation, the Union became identified with the global cause of democracy and human rights, as the Italian revolutionary Giuseppe Garibaldi argued. The workingmen of London wrote to Lincoln on New Year's Eve that the proclamation would uphold "the brotherhood, freedom, and equality of all men." Despite the successful Union blockade of Confederate ports that prevented raw cotton from reaching Manchester's textile mills, many if not most British workers who lost their jobs as a result still supported the Union. British abolitionist George Thompson's son-in-law, Frederick W. Chesson, wrote to Garrison: "The working classes also have proved sound to the core, whenever their opinion has been tested." Their employers, especially Tories or British conservatives, tended to be pro-Confederate, but they were rendered "mute" by the proclamation, wrote Thompson. Karl Marx, who had been a foreign correspondent for the antislavery *New York Tribune*, congratulated Lincoln on behalf of the International Workingmen's Association: "The working classes of Europe understood at once, even before the fanatic partisanship of the upper classes for the Confederate gentry had given its dismal warning, that the slaveholders' rebellion was to sound the tocsin for a general holy crusade of property against labour."

The Confederacy, meanwhile, drew support from the ancien régime. Louis Napoleon Bonaparte, who had overthrown the Second French Republic, sympathized with the Confederacy, as did his puppet emperor Maximilian in Mexico—but liberal Mexicans such as ex-president Benito Juarez sought aid from the Union. Lincoln's old opposition to the Mexican War in 1846 and his administration's support for the Juarez government endeared him to Mexican republicans. Wartime abolition in the United States served as a warning to the remaining slave societies in the Americas: Brazil, Cuba, and Puerto Rico.[14]

Emancipation was the most consequential result of the Civil War. By the end of the conflict, nearly half a million slaves had fled to the Union. Historians have referred to this mass flight as, variously, a "general strike" and the "largest slave rebellion in modern history." The enslaved rejected the "domestic enemy" label that slaveholders had foisted on them. Instead, they revealed that their enslavers were the true internal enemies of the republic, while they rallied to its defense. As the eloquent slave turned soldier Corporal Prince Lambkin said, "Our mas'rs dey hab lib under de flag, dey got dere wealth under it, and ebryting beautiful for dere chilen. Under it dey hab grind us up, and put us in dere pocket for money. But de fus' minute dey tink dat ole flag mean freedom for we colored people, dey pull it right down, and run up de rag on dere own. But we'll never desert de ole flag, boys, never:

we hab lib under it for *eighteen hundred and sixty-two years,* and we'll die for it now." The enslaved proved Thomas Jefferson's old claims wrong: It was American slaveholders, rather than American slaves, who lacked political virtue and *amor patriae,* or love of country. If Lincoln could align his reverence for the Union and Constitution with antislavery during the Civil War, the enslaved could align their love of freedom with that of country. As another black Union soldier wrote, "we can and will be a wall of fire and death to the enemies of this country, our birth-place."[15]

The Union army became an army of liberation, regardless of the opinions of individual officers and soldiers, which ran the gamut. Emancipation and the military successes that followed made 1863 the turning point in the Civil War. Grant wrote that emancipation and the recruitment of black men constituted "the heaviest blow" to the slaveholders' rebellion. In July 1863, Lee's ill-considered invasion of Pennsylvania, a strategic blunder that resulted in his army's defeat at Gettysburg, sealed the connection between the freedom of the slaves and American democracy. Union victory was immortalized in Lincoln's Gettysburg Address as a "new birth of freedom" and a vow that government of the people, by the people, and for the people shall not perish from this earth. For its part, the retreating Confederate army killed and enslaved free black men, women, and children, carrying its captives back south. It was literally an army of enslavement.

With the recruitment of African American men, the Union army became not just an army of liberation, but a revolutionary army. Of the nearly 200,000 black men who ended up serving in the Union army and navy, an overwhelming majority were ex-slaves. They donned blue uniforms and took up arms against former masters. Some volunteered for the "love of liberty," as the motto of one black South Carolina regiment proclaimed; others were summarily impressed into military service. In the border slave states still in the Union, military service was the only way for enslaved men to gain their and their family's freedom. Black men's military service soon became an avenue for the freedom struggles of their wives and children during and after the Civil War. As in the

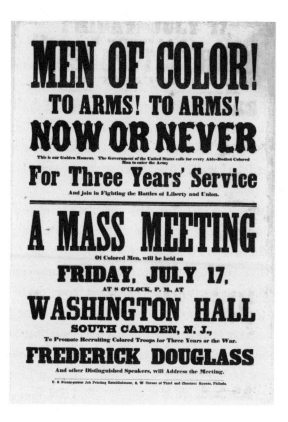

"Men of Color! To Arms! To Arms! Now or Never." *Library Company of Philadelphia*

American Revolution, some enslavers received bounties for the enlistment of their enslaved. But most border state slaveholders, unionist or
otherwise, opposed the recruitment of slaves.[16]

The first soldiers of color in the Union army were around three hundred enslaved and free Afro-Native Americans from Indian territory
in Oklahoma. They fought for the Union in 1861 against slaveholding
southeastern Indian nations that had signed treaties with the Confederacy. By 1862, the Union army mustered the First Indian Home Guard.
Senator James H. Lane, veteran of the Kansas wars against the expansion of slavery and an advocate of Indian enlistment, started recruiting black men, as did other antislavery generals including Phelps in
Louisiana and Hunter in South Carolina. Lane was uncompromising,

advocating that "every traitor who has to die, die by the hand of his own slave."

When the Union navy captured New Orleans, many in the First Louisiana Native Guards—composed of creole free blacks, who had a long history of militia service going back to the eighteenth century—joined the Union army. Like other free blacks in South Carolina, they had first volunteered for the Confederate army as an act of self-preservation—some southern states had threatened to reenslave free blacks on the eve of the war—but were disbanded by the Louisiana legislature as a threat to the Confederacy. Once they joined the Union army, their numbers quickly swelled with runaways from nearby plantations.

The enslaved who defected to Union lines risked their lives in the act. The "sight of warships of the Union" in Mobile Bay convinced one Alabama slave, Wallace Turnage, to brave the waters for freedom. The most spectacular case was that of Robert Smalls, an enslaved pilot who, with his family and an enslaved crew, daringly steered the Confederate steamer *Planter* to the Union blockade off the Carolina coast, while its officers were on shore.[17]

Abolitionists spearheaded the effort to recruit black men. In August 1862, Secretary of War Edwin Stanton authorized an antislavery general in South Carolina, Rufus Saxton, to recruit five thousand black soldiers and later dispatched Adjutant General Lorenzo Thomas to the Mississippi valley to raise black regiments. Owing in large part to the appeals of the abolitionist Governor John Andrew, Stanton also authorized the formation of black regiments from Massachusetts. Andrew assigned the task of black recruitment to George L. Stearns, one of the "Secret Six" who had supported John Brown's raid on Harpers Ferry in 1859. Stearns in turn secured the services of prominent black abolitionists to recruit black men from all over the North for the Fifty-Fourth and Fifty-Fifth Massachusetts Regiments. A few of the men who volunteered were born in Africa, the Caribbean, and the slave South. In his famous recruiting speech evoking the memory of slave rebels, "Men of Color, to Arms!," Douglass urged black men "to fly to arms, and smite with death the power that would bury the government and your liberty in the same hopeless grave." Other efforts were already afoot. In

1862, the Militia Act allowed for the recruitment of black soldiers and laborers into the Union army. In January 1863, Thaddeus Stevens, the Radical Republican congressman from Pennsylvania, who had recommended arming the enslaved early in the war, proposed a bill to enlist 150,000 black soldiers. In May, the War Department established the Bureau of Colored Troops. By 1865, black men comprised 10 percent of the Union army.[18]

Nothing illustrated the revolutionary nature of the war better than armed black men marching to abolitionist anthems such as "John Brown's Body," which became the basis of "The Battle Hymn of the Republic," composed by abolitionist feminist Julia Ward Howe. The First Arkansas Colored Regiment put their own words into the stanzas:

> We are going out of slavery; we're bound for freedom's light
> We mean to show Jeff Davis how the Africans can fight
> As we go marching on

The Colored Division of the Ninth Army Corps called itself "Louverture," after the leader of the Haitian Revolution. The battle colors of the Twenty-Second United States Colored Troops (USCT), designed by the black artist David Bustill Bowser, showed a prostrate Confederate soldier before a standing black soldier, the latter holding a rifle with a bayonet beneath the motto "Sic Semper Tyrannis" ("Thus Always to Tyrants"). A black soldier confronted his former enslaver, a Confederate prisoner of war: "Hello, massa; bottom rail on top dis time." Commanding officers of USCT regiments were often abolitionists like Thomas Wentworth Higginson. He wrote: "I had been an abolitionist too long, and had known and loved John Brown too well, not to feel a thrill of joy at last on finding myself in the position where he only wished to be." The Hallowell brothers, "fighting Quakers" who put antislavery above their pacifist principles, served as officers in the Fifty-Fourth and Fifty-Fifth Massachusetts. A surgeon in a black artillery regiment wrote, "*We are all Abolitionists.*"[19]

Black heroism at Port Hudson and Milliken's Bend in Louisiana, and in the assault on Fort Wagner, South Carolina (a story told in the

1989 film *Glory*), was celebrated throughout the North. The Confederacy likewise understood the revolutionary significance of black soldiers and resolved to treat any captured as slave rebels rather than prisoners of war, subjecting them to execution or reenslavement. Lincoln condemned this policy as "a relapse into barbarism," and General Order 252 in July 1863 halted the exchange of prisoners of war until the Confederates agreed to include black soldiers, which they finally did in the winter of 1864–1865.

According to George Washington Williams, a black veteran and pioneering historian, "The slave system made the entire South brutal, and many soldiers of the Confederate army were exceedingly cruel to prisoners." The appalling conditions in the infamous prisoner of war camp in Andersonville, Georgia, where thirteen thousand Union soldiers died, led to the postwar execution of its commandant, Henry Wirz, for war crimes, a concept popularized during the Civil War. Williams noted that Confederates were particularly hostile to black and southern Union soldiers, of whom there were about 100,000, mostly from the nonslaveholding areas of the upper South states and West Virginia.

The Confederate massacre of over five hundred mostly black Union soldiers and civilians who had surrendered at Fort Pillow, Tennessee in 1864 was one of the worst atrocities of a war that also saw massacres of Native Americans in the West. The report of the Joint Committee on the Conduct of the War in Congress, which included the testimony of numerous eyewitnesses, is still the best account of it. It stated that the massacre was the result of the deliberate "intention of rebel authorities not to recognize the officers and men of our colored regiments" and displayed "the malignity and barbarity of Forrest"—the commanding Confederate general Nathan Bedford Forrest, a former slave trader, "and his followers." Unlike Wirz, Forrest escaped punishment for his crimes; statues of him adorned public places in Tennessee until 2021.

Such barbaric conduct violated Lincoln's Code of War, which Francis Leiber, a German political thinker, had written for the Union army once emancipation became settled policy. Lincoln's code justified a "hard war," including destruction of property—he had earlier suspended habeas corpus for rebels "not adequately restrained by the ordinary processes of law"—but prohibited torture and the killing of surrendering soldiers. More significantly, it stated that "the law of nations knows no distinction of color," challenging the very foundation of the Confederacy's existence. The Union army displayed remarkable restraint, which it did not show indigenous nations in the West, in its dealing with the southern civilian population even after Confederate atrocities. When the Confederacy finally, in desperation, passed a law to enlist black men in 1865, it did not even offer emancipation as a reward for military service. Confederate general Howell Cobb of Georgia admitted, "And if slaves seem good soldiers our whole theory of slavery is wrong." No "Black Confederates" were recruited, but a pernicious myth of black Confederate soldiers—who allegedly supported the South—was born.[20]

For all their bravery and success, the story of black soldiers was not a simple one of triumph. They were generally treated worse than white soldiers, and their protest over racist inequities prepared African Americans for the long struggle for citizenship. They fought in segregated units and were barred from officer ranks, were assigned fatigue duty more frequently, and most egregiously, were paid considerably less than their white counterparts. Black soldiers received $10, the same pay as military laborers, from which $3 was deducted for their uniforms, while white soldiers received $13 and an additional $3 for their uniforms.

While some black soldiers, like white soldiers, deserted for various reasons, resistance was a more common reaction to unequal conditions. Widespread protest in black regiments resulted in some refusing pay altogether, something their families could ill afford. James Henry Gooding of the Fifty-Fifth Massachusetts wrote to the president demanding a soldier's salary for a soldier's duty. It was not the money but the principle of inequality, argued one of the many black soldiers whose letters flooded *The Christian Recorder*. William Walker of the Third South Carolina was court-martialed and shot for leading his company in mutiny: they had stacked their guns to protest unequal pay. Congress, on the initiative of abolitionist officers like Higginson and Senators Sumner and

Wilson, passed an act equalizing pay scales retroactive from January 1, 1864. In 1865, it passed another law granting retroactive pay to all black soldiers from the time of their enlistment. By the end of the war, African Americans were commissioned as officers, though a majority were from Louisiana's Native Guards or served as chaplains. After the war, black veterans and their widows continued the struggle for pensions and recognition.[21]

The black military experience was an important aspect of wartime reconstruction. For it was in the ranks of the Union army that many soldiers, especially the formerly enslaved, learned to read and write and bear arms. Black soldiering conformed to gendered notions of republican male citizenship: they were independent, virtuous citizens, heads of their own households, who through their military service earned the freedom of their families. The ideal of independent republican citizenship was far from reality for many American men, yet it remained a powerful political aspiration. At a time when women could not vote and lacked other rights too, black women fought for recognition of their labor and rights in army camps. In 1862, Attorney General Edward Bates, in a letter to Secretary of Treasury Salmon Chase, qualified the *Dred Scott* (1857) Supreme Court decision, in which Chief Justice Roger Taney declaimed that black men were not entitled to any rights that a "white man is bound to respect." African Americans *could* be citizens, Bates maintained; the question was whether they now would be.

Abolitionists demanded black male suffrage and equal rights. Before the war, only a handful of New England states granted adult black men the right to vote. In New York, property-holding qualifications for voting were retained for black men, and abolitionist campaigns to remove them had been repeatedly defeated, though by progressively smaller margins. If that fact suggested progress, there was reason for pessimism. New York City had witnessed the horrific draft riot of 1863 against emancipation and conscription. Legitimate grievances of the urban immigrant working class were undermined by this ugly demonstration of visceral racism that left hundreds of African Americans lynched and assaulted.

Victorious Union troops returning from Gettysburg were deployed to quell the mob in what was the largest domestic insurrection since the slaveholders' rebellion.

Yet the significance of black military service could not be denied, as Lincoln grasped. The war "educated" Lincoln, the black abolitionist H. Ford Douglas wrote, out of his colonization views. Like Grant, Lincoln believed that "the emancipation policy, and the use of colored troops, constitute the heaviest blow to the rebellion; and that at least one of these important successes could not have been achieved when it was, but for the aid of black soldiers." When peace comes, he wrote in a public letter to James C. Conkling in 1863, "there will be some black men who can remember that, with silent tongue, and clenched teeth, and steady eye, and well-poised bayonet, they have helped mankind onto this great consummation; while, I fear, there will be some white ones, unable to forget that, with malignant heart, and deceitful speech they have strove to hinder it."[22]

Some recent scholarship on emancipation views ex-slaves primarily as victims of the upheavals of war, emphasizing violence, death, disease, and dislocation. But it was in the turmoil generated by the conflict that the newly free developed a politics of survival, care, endurance, solidarity, and rights-making. They showed considerable acumen in navigating the changing politics of war and military occupation, enlisting the federal government on their own behalf. In Union-occupied territory and border slave states, African Americans demanded military intervention against the petty tyranny of their enslavers and economic autonomy.[23]

But a majority of enslaved people—who constituted nearly 40 percent of the southern population—remained stuck on the plantations and farms of the Confederacy. Nearly 75 percent of slaves lived far from the front lines, simply unable to feasibly make a run for freedom. They nevertheless found ways to shape their fate, actively working for the defeat of their enslavers. Not only did they refuse to work, at pain of whipping, but enslaved women, in particular, made slaveholding households "a critical site for wartime slave rebellion." They refused to endure any longer the routine cruelties of their mistresses; they talked back and acted in self-defense. It was a "war within" the southern home. In the waning days of the war, mistresses visited terror on slaves, selling their human property with impunity. The struggles over labor, land, and rights after the war had their origins in these everyday confrontations between the enslaved and their enslavers in the crumbling Confederacy.[24]

The Union's "contraband camps" in the slave states became the staging grounds for wartime reconstruction. They also served as a field of service for black women—a complementary, though lesser known, story to the military service of black men. Just as the origins of the emancipation process can be traced to the actions of the enslaved, the origins of wartime reconstruction can be found in the grassroots struggles of former slaves and their allies. In the "Citizen camps," ex-slaves redefined their legal status; no longer human property, they made claims as citizens. Today, scholars refer to self-emancipated slaves as wartime "refugees." In contemporary parlance, however, the term *refugee* was used for those slaves forcibly "refugeed" by their owners fleeing the Union army into the interior of the Confederacy, to Texas in particular. Black people felt that refugee was a more "honorable word" than contraband. Garrison refused to use "contraband," which implied that freedpeople were still property. Conditions in contraband camps resembled modern refugee camps, with their makeshift tents, rampant disease, food scarcity, hardship, and at times abuse by soldiers and officers.

In the camps, ex-slaves reconstructed families, communities, and their own forms of religious worship. One of the first things new arrivals did was to hunt for long lost family members sold by their enslavers. In 1865, Milford Thompson, after escaping to Union lines, posted one of the hundreds of "Information Wanted" advertisements, for his wife Eliza and their six children, ranging from age four to sixteen, who had been sold "down south" from Virginia. Long after emancipation, African Americans would still be advertising for family members lost in slavery. In 1871, Harriet Carrington, probably using up her scarce resources, advertised for information about her twenty-year old son Patrick Finch in the *Richmond Daily Dispatch*.

Many also sought official certificates for marriages, which were not recognized under slavery. "Group marriages," legalizing or securing state recognition, and entirely new marriages became common in camps. The American Tract Society, an organization devoted to the dissemination of Bibles and religious literature, was assiduous in promoting marriage, nuclear families, punctuality, work, and Christian beliefs among freedpeople. Legal protections for marriages and families, though, were not simply bourgeois domestic norms imposed on former slaves by northerners. Such protections emerged as demands from communities of freedpeople for whom the sundering of family and extended kin bonds was the primary trial of slavery. That said, black people relied on their own distinct definitions of marriage, family, and kinship, many of which differed from mainstream mores.[25]

Women refugees used their war service to negotiate rights, shelter, and provisions. The camp populations were largely female, in fact, making the experience and concerns of black women central to wartime reconstruction. At times the victims of sexual abuse by soldiers, they were able to secure redress through military discipline, their rapists court-martialed and cashiered. Before the war, southern states defined rape as a crime that could only be committed against white women. An exception was an 1860 Mississippi law that criminalized the rape of black girls under the age of ten. It is not clear whether it was ever enforced. But rape, without racial distinction, was punishable by Lincoln's Code of War. Over four hundred cases of rape were prosecuted by the Union army, with black women frequently the targets of sexual violence. In Port Royal, South Carolina, a northern physician, Dr. Esther Hawks, wrote: "No colored woman or girl is safe from the brutal lusts of the soldiers—and by soldiers I mean officers and men." General Rufus Saxton, she noted approvingly, put a stop to the abuse of black women and children. For the first time freedwomen had "access to the protective power of the federal state." In doing so, they "acted and identified as citizens."[26]

The War Department established and supervised over five hundred contraband camps, appointing superintendents who oversaw them directly. Union army chaplain Colonel John Eaton, appointed by Grant in 1862 as superintendent of the contraband camps for the Department of Tennessee and the State of Arkansas in the Mississippi valley, remarked of the slave refugees, "their own interests were identical, they felt, with the objects of our armies" and "they put themselves under the protection of our armies." While military aims and fortunes could easily upend the safety of refugee camps, they still attracted antislavery Quakers, sympathetic federal officials, and agents of numerous abolitionist freedmen's aid societies, which funneled clothing, food, school supplies, teachers, and ministers to them.

By the end of the war, freedpeople and their allies built permanent structures in what became, in some cases, freedmen's villages. After emancipation, Garrison contended that the most important duty of abolitionists was to address the travails faced by freedpeople. The American Missionary Association (AMA), formed in 1846 by black and white abolitionists in reaction to the proslavery, racist practices of mainstream missionary societies, was more of an antislavery than a missionary organization. It began its work with freedpeople in Fortress Monroe or "Freedom Fortress" in 1861, establishing "schools following the armies" and distributing relief in food and clothing. One AMA teacher, who hoped that freedpeople would become "the ruling race" of the South, observed that a "nation had been born in a day." The AMA sent hundreds of black and white teachers to the camps. The freedpeople, camp superintendent Edward L. Pierce wrote, expressed "a widespread desire to learn to read." Fortress Monroe and a second refugee camp in Hampton, also in Virginia, had eighteen schools in total. Hampton Institute, now Hampton University, became one of the first historically black schools established during Reconstruction. It was poetic justice that these camps were built in precisely that area where the first Africans had arrived in mainland British North America. The AMA hired a free black woman, Mary Smith Peake, who had run a clandestine school before the war. In her "multiplied labors," she exhibited "a martyr spirit, of the true type," wrote the admiring AMA minister Lewis C. Lockwood.

Wartime refugees and their abolitionist allies demanded that the federal government assume responsibility for their well-being, laying the foundations for the concept of a welfare state. Responding to their complaints of ill-treatment by the army, jurisdiction for freedpeople was

"Hampton, Virginia. 'Slabtown.' " *Library of Congress*

transferred from the War Department to Treasury, headed by the anti-slavery Salmon Chase, in 1863. Chase divided the South into five districts, and tasked treasury agents with taking charge of abandoned plantations, collecting taxes, and supervising black labor. This was the origin of the five southern military districts of Reconstruction. James Yeatman of the Western Sanitary Commission complained of nonpayment of wages by the army as well as by northern lessees of abandoned plantations. Based on his recommendations, the Treasury Department issued *Rules and Regulations for Leasing Abandoned Plantations and Employing Freedmen,* setting monthly wages ranging from $10 to $25, also payable through crop shares, with workers getting the first lien or right on the harvested crop.

Abolitionist and Quaker teachers became conduits for freedpeople's concerns, often reporting abusive practices of officers in the northern press and their own newspapers. The AMA found that "the condition of most of the colored people, driven from their homes, with neither food nor raiment, was pitiable in the extreme, especially in the West. Hundreds, if not thousands perished, and a large share of the efforts of the missionaries was employed in physical relief." Eaton was grateful for the presence of these "philanthropic" men and women. He had to ensure that freedpeople laboring on plantations that had been abandoned received just recompense, as "the price of cotton was then mounting, and speculation ran high." The aim, Eaton said, was to put freedpeople on the path to "self-respecting citizenship." A cohort of "preachers and exhorters," whose

numbers amazed Eaton—who was not immune to racial paternalism—
were quick to take over teaching from northerners and federal agents. In
Union-occupied Memphis, freedpeople preferred "their own teachers."[27]

While slaves fled toward the Union army, slaveholders fled in the
opposite direction, often forcing enslaved people to go with them. The
enslaved on the Sea Islands, though, who comprised over 80 percent of
the islands' population, refused to leave with their enslavers when the
Union navy landed in November 1861. One man, Cupid—slaveholders
foisted names from antiquity on their slaves to mock them—reported
that his master wanted to "sweep us up in a heap, an' put us in de
boat...Jus as if I was gwine to be sich a goat!" The enslaved instead
sacked the town of Beaufort, helping themselves to the fineries their
unpaid labor had made possible, even before the navy arrived. On seeing the destruction, Union commodore Samuel F. Du Pont remarked on
how South Carolinian slaveholders had deluded themselves by assuming enslaved people's loyalty. Some enslavers had even shot slaves dead
when they refused to be "refugeed." One planter burned his entire store
of corn and cotton, compelling his slaves to follow him or starve. After
the war, southerners bemoaned Union depredations and the perfidy of
their slaves, conveniently forgetting their own role in desolating their
property and violently targeting the enslaved.

With the slaveholders' flight, wartime reconstruction on the Sea
Islands began. The "Port Royal Experiment," supported by Garrisonian abolitionists in the Boston Educational Commission for Freedmen
and the Port Royal Relief Committee of Philadelphia, brought together
around ten thousand former slaves; "Gideonites" or northern teachers;
the Union army; and cotton agents eager to get their hands on the fine
Sea Island long fiber cotton. The more conservative National Freedman's Relief Association formed in New York in 1862 was determined
that freedpeople of Port Royal become self-supporting as soon as possible. Secretary Chase sent superintendent Pierce to oversee the transition
from slavery to freedom, given his experience at Fortress Monroe. Pierce
declared that the black man "had vindicated beyond all future question,

for himself, his wife, and their issue, a title to American citizenship, and become heir to all the immunities of the Magna Carta, the Declaration of Independence, and the Constitution of the United States." It would be in Beaufort that the returned local hero Robert Smalls would recruit for the Union army. There the legendary Harriet Tubman acted as a Union scout under Colonel James Montgomery in the Combahee River Raid, which liberated nearly eight hundred slaves. (More than a century later, radical black feminists in Boston named their group the Combahee River Collective.) Eventually, the New England Freedman's Aid Society (NEFAS) hired Tubman to teach freedpeople for a "small salary." Clara Barton, the "founder" of the American Red Cross, nursed soldiers at Port Royal.

Freedom, to most ex-slaves and their antislavery allies, meant citizenship, education, land, and the ability to control one's labor—not the freedom to starve. A conflict arose between them and the corrupt cotton agents, who Pierce charged were cheating former slaves. One even assaulted him. The freedpeople carried the day. Laura Towne, a teacher, noted that freedpeople would rather grow corn than cotton. One old slave complained to her, "The Yankees preach nothing but cotton, cotton." Newly freed people knew from "past experience" that they would never get the "proceeds." Those who would force the freedpeople to grow cotton, Towne wrote, had only "changed the mode of compulsion." Despite her racial paternalism, Towne left a record of freedpeople undaunted in their fight to claim their rights. She wrote, "Lands are to be set apart for the people so that they cannot be oppressed, or driven to work for speculators, or ejected from their homesteads."

Abolitionists, including Garrison and organizations such as the NEFAS, headed by Governor Andrew, asked for land redistribution from the start. The NEFAS reported that freedpeople "desire to be proprietors themselves, for the sake of independence . . . the last thing that the friends of the Freedmen should wish is that they should be *satisfied* with the peasant condition." They complained that the chairman of the Tax Commissioners sent by the government "seems to be strongly attached to the large-plantation-and-peasantry system" and was willing to give freedpeople only two acres of land each "to grow necessaries, that they may be able to work regularly on the plantations." Many freedpeople, abolitionists reported, "in anticipation of the official assignment of the lands, had begun cultivation of corn, and had become accustomed to the idea that they were landed proprietors." Yet land had instead been sold to "white persons, for large prices." Northern capitalists were more interested in the reconstruction of the cotton plantation economy than in upholding freedpeople's rights.

A thousand miles away, in the Mississippi valley, the system of leasing plantations and making freedpeople work drew criticism. Yeatman of the Western Sanitary Commission reported, "the system of labor under which negroes worked the last year was one of the greatest impolicy and injustice" and that the "majority of the lessees were only adventurers, destitute of principle." Black lessees, General Thomas noted, seemed to do much better than white lessees. The NEFAS instructed, "when the rights of the original inhabitants of the soil and those of the adventurers from the North come into collision, the weak and the poor should be protected." When the various freedmen's aid societies came together in 1864 to form "The United States Commission for the Relief of National Freedmen," they resolved at their very first meeting to communicate to Lincoln "their earnest desire that measures be adopted to give to the slaves made free by the power of the Government a legal and quiet possession of adequate land for their residence and support, as rapidly and as early the responsibilities of the Government shall render possible."

Even though abolitionists shared important goals with freedpeople, many of the former, especially the utopian socialists and Unitarians, failed to comprehend their fervent religiosity (including the Gullah culture of the Sea Islands). Quaker women championed plain dress and misunderstood black women's demand for finery to mark their status as free women. The evangelical AMA questioned the African-inflected styles of worship of freedpeople, even though they admired their faith. Austa Malinda French, wife of a minister, exclaimed, "WE! CHRISTIANIZE THESE COLORED PEOPLE! We rather learn the true, full spirit of Christianity from them." A few, such as Rev. Charles Hall, who ministered to freedpeople, and abolitionist James McKim's daughter Lucy, who published a collection of slave songs, bridged the cultural divide. The words of "Roll, Jordan, Roll" and "Many Thousands Gone" survived in wartime compilations of spirituals, which revealed to white Americans the enslaved's deep longing for freedom and opened a window into their worldview. One woman, who had lost all but one of her children to slavery, told Lucy that the songs could not be sung "widout a *full heart and a troubled sperrit.*" Thomas Wentworth Higginson transcribed many such "negro spirituals" in his army memoir.

Freedpeople's thirst for education was not an abolitionist invention, as some critics claimed. Nor were they passive recipients of the gift of literacy. On the Sea Islands, freedpeople repaid their teachers with fresh eggs, a traditional currency in their informal internal economy. Former slaves wanted to be "an educated people"—this was one of the central ways in which they defined freedom. Like Union officers, northern teachers ranged from those who wanted to "play mistress" to committed abolitionists. Some, like Harriet Buss, returned to the South to work with black teachers and contributed to the founding of Shaw University in North Carolina. In the best cases, teachers became students of their students—acting not just as proponents of northern culture but also as emissaries of "incipient southern black politics to the North." As the NEFAS reported, "How much has been learned, how many errors and prejudices have been renounced, how many delusions dissipated!"[28]

Wartime reconstruction on the Sea Islands was a "Rehearsal for Reconstruction." No single source is more revealing of the process than the diary of Charlotte Forten. A member of the black abolitionist Forten-Purvis family of Philadelphia, Forten worked as a teacher for nearly two years in Towne's school. She was at first taken aback at the "motley assemblage" of soldiers and slaves in Port Royal but took to freedpeople's songs of the lowcountry. Soon she was teaching her students "John Brown's Body" and the history of Toussaint Louverture. In her diary, Forten wrote about enslaved people who described the tortures they had endured and rejoiced when their enslavers fled the "gun shoot." She noted that the "spirit of resistance to the Secesh" was especially strong among slaves turned soldiers and recorded encounters with Colonel Robert Gould Shaw of the Fifty-Fourth Massachusetts. She was heartbroken at news of his death at Fort Wagner. The highly educated Forten struggled to overcome the social distance between herself and the community she served, but she viewed the "long abused race" as her own people. In 1864, she returned to Boston to work at the Freedmen's Union Commission, but by 1871, she was back teaching at a school on the Sea Islands named after Shaw.[29]

The foundations of black education were laid during wartime reconstruction, starting first on Fortress Monroe and the Sea Islands and then across the Union-occupied areas of the South. The abolitionist feminist Frances Gage, who was superintendent of Parris Island, wrote that the government must prepare for the demand for schools and teachers to become overwhelming. Already by war's end, the freedmen's aid societies had sent over a thousand teachers to the South and over 200,000 freedpeople were enrolled in schools across the region. Before the war, African Americans had run their own schools in secret— and in violation of slave laws—in Alexandria, Savannah, and New Orleans. During Reconstruction, they became champions of universal, free, public education for all. Freedpeople led an "education movement" that identified literacy with citizenship and created education associations to raise funds for schools. After the Gideonites returned to the North, black schools and churches manned by black teachers and ministers flourished in the postwar South. In southern cities like Richmond and Mobile, black people fought for and maintained viable public-school systems. Freedpeople's commitment to state-funded education as a pillar of democracy, rather than as an instrument of social control, replicated the origins of public schools in New England.[30]

Black relief associations and churches raised substantial donations for freedmen's aid. In Chicago, the Colored Ladies Freedmen's Aid Society hired the abolitionist feminist Mary Ann Shadd Cary, who moved back to the United States from Canada during the war, to fund-raise. In Washington, black women formed the backbone of the city's wartime reconstruction. Elizabeth Keckley, who bought her own and her son's freedom and became Mary Todd Lincoln's dressmaker and confidante, founded the Contraband Relief Association in 1862. Its forty members, all from the Fifteenth Street Presbyterian Church, assisted thousands of refugees who had made their way to the nation's capital. Even as she mocked freedpeople's "exaggerated ideas of liberty," Keckley tapped into abolitionist networks in Boston and New York, receiving large donations from the Lincolns, Douglass, and Phillips, as well as from freedmen's aid societies in Britain. Twice elected president, she noted that the Boston branch of the society, led by Christiana Bannister and Mrs. Leonard Grimes, alone sent over eighty boxes of goods. In 1865, Congress incorporated the National Association for the Relief of Destitute Colored Women and Children. A testimony to black women's activism, it survived into the twentieth century.

Black women in the North not only sent money south, but many also volunteered, like Charlotte Forten, to teach at freedmen's schools. Northern black teachers like Rebecca Primus and Ellen Garrison Jackson, most of whom had been active in the abolition movement, acted as intermediaries between freedpeople and freedmen's aid organizations. Most did so through the AMA; around 174 black teachers out of a total of 467 AMA missionaries worked for it. Clara Duncan, a young black woman who had graduated from Oberlin College, taught at Norfolk, as did her friend Edmonia Highgate. Sara G. Stanley, another black abolitionist who had studied at Oberlin, taught at many AMA schools. Though she could pass for white, Stanley insisted on identifying as black. Black teachers had to deal with some racist colleagues, including people who refused to live with them in the AMA houses. They also found themselves posted to more dangerous and isolated rural areas. Highgate wrote, "We need *Anti-Slavery* teachers who will show that it is safe to do right." The Oberlin-educated Emma Brown first viewed herself as "colored" and her pupils as "negro," but the distinction fell away when she married an ex-slave Union veteran. She recounted hearing officials refer to "N.Ts" or "n—— teachers."

Two black women, Harriet Jacobs and her daughter Louisa Jacobs, founded a school and hospital in the contraband camps in Alexandria. In her iconic slave narrative, *Incidents in the Life of a Slave Girl* (1861), Jacobs had written from personal experience about the plight of enslaved women who suffered from sexual abuse. In the spring of 1862, Jacobs brought clothes, shoes, and blankets for the freedpeople in Washington, writing,

"Each day brings its fresh additions of the hungry, naked and sick." In Alexandria, she and Julia Wilbur of the Rochester Ladies Anti-Slavery Society were devastated when they first witnessed the conditions in the camp, where disease raged unchecked, and at the callous and abusive attitudes of military doctors and the racist Baptist minister who was superintendent of the camp. Despite tensions between them, the two women used their extensive network of abolitionist societies and churches to finance their efforts and to dismiss the minister, who had badly underestimated them. Jacobs established the Jacobs School for freedpeople, where she, Louisa, and another black teacher taught and named their hospital after Louverture. The school became a common stop for abolitionists. The NEFAS supported the Jacobs school, circulating a photograph of its pupils and abolitionist teachers to tout its success. It also denounced "Colorphobia in Washington," where African Americans were denied entrance to schools and faced segregation in public transportation.[31]

The black abolitionist feminist Sojourner Truth worked in the Freedmen's Village in Washington and in the Freedmen's Hospital, which is now Howard University Hospital. Even though she could be patronizing toward freedpeople, Truth and abolitionist Josephine Griffing labored

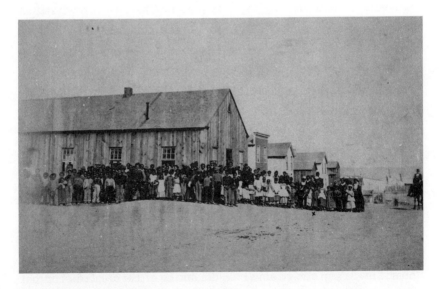

Harriet Jacobs School. *Stuart A. Rose Library at Emory University*

alongside one another to draw attention to their dismal situation, demanding the creation of a new government agency to address the scale of the problem. Truth met with Lincoln himself. She challenged racial segregation in Washington streetcars, and in 1865 she sued a conductor who injured her while trying to force her off a car she was riding with another abolitionist, Laura Haviland. Truth joked that she smoked in self-defense, having been compelled to ride the cars reserved for smokers and blacks so often.

Truth's campaign was part of a larger one that accelerated during the war years to desegregate the North. It was mainly a woman's fight, and it complemented black soldiers' struggle for equality in the Union army. From San Francisco to Philadelphia, black women challenged segregated public transportation, enduring abuse and worse from train conductors, policemen, and the railroad companies that enabled their brutality. In the 1850s, Elizabeth Jennings sued a police officer who had dragged her off a streetcar, and effectively desegregated New York City's transit system after years of struggle by black abolitionists. During the war, black women in Soldiers' Aid societies, the Colored Sanitary Commission, and the Freedmen's Aid society in Philadelphia took railroad companies and conductors to court and won, too. Charles Sumner, a champion of black civil rights, took note of Charlotte Brown's 1863 case in San Francisco, another victory. A year later Judge C. C. Pratt of the Twelfth District Court abolished segregation in the city as a "relic of barbarism." In 1866, Mary Ellen Pleasant and Emma Turner were awarded substantial damages in their desegregation suits, though the decisions were reversed by the state supreme court. Sumner's fight for civil rights seemed quixotic even to Republicans, but it manifestly reflected the grassroots activism of African Americans.

Black men, too, played key roles in these battles. The formation of the National Equal Rights League by the Syracuse national black convention in 1864 organized wartime struggles into an enduring association fighting for equal access to education and the franchise. It developed state and local chapters all over the country. In Philadelphia, war hero Robert Smalls's ejection from a Philadelphia streetcar created an uproar and mass demonstrations. Black Philadelphians led by Octavius Catto and his rival William Still, known for his work in the Underground Railroad, lodged a protest with the railroad companies. Still noted that black people were not treated in such a "vulgar" manner in any public space as in the streetcars.[32]

Southern black women founded new organizations, too. In New Bern, North Carolina, as in Port Royal, abolitionists and officials set up schools and recruited freedmen for the Union army. Most of them stayed at Mary Ann Starkey's boardinghouse. A remarkable woman, who had a child still in slavery, Starkey became free when the Union army occupied the area. Before the war, she had led a reading and Bible school out of her home. After the arrival of the Union army, she hosted officers, including General Ambrose Burnside. Starkey formed the Colored Ladies Relief Association, which collected supplies for slave refugees and black soldiers.

Wives of black Union soldiers were "company women" who tracked their own "martial route to freedom." Unlike Starkey, Susie King Taylor left behind a memoir of her wartime experience. The literate Taylor, whose family trekked to Fort Pulaski in Georgia to escape slavery, taught school on Union-occupied St. Simon's Island. She married a soldier from the First South Carolina Regiment and worked as a laundress. Taylor not only taught black soldiers but also cleaned their weapons and worked in hospitals treating wounded soldiers. Barton introduced her to nursing. For Taylor, soldiering was not a purely male affair; she participated in the war effort however she could. Her memoir was, in effect, her own version of the regimental history of the USCT in South Carolina. After the war, Taylor taught in Georgia before moving to Boston, where she met her second husband and formed the Women's Relief Corps, an auxiliary to the Grand Army of the Republic, the veterans' organization of the Union army. She wrote that people should never forget the blood of black and white comrades shed during the war.[33]

Powering wartime reconstruction were freedpeople's attempts to define the meaning of freedom, whether as education or land ownership, or on other terms. In areas such as Davis Bend in Mississippi, they conducted their own experiments in land and labor. Ironically, the enslaved of Davis

Bend belonged to Joseph Davis, brother of Confederate president Jefferson Davis, who owned an adjoining plantation. Joseph Davis was influenced by the utopian socialist ideas of Robert Owen and before the war gave his slaves considerable leeway to manage their own labor. The person responsible for the success of his plantation was a literate enslaved man, Benjamin Montgomery. During the war, most of the slaves at the Davis Bend plantations fled to the Union army. In 1863, Grant designated the entire area for black settlement, anointing it a "negro paradise." Montgomery continued running the plantation, but now as a cooperative black community, and turned a large profit from cotton production. The community established its own courts and voting system. The Davis Bend experiment began before and outlasted Reconstruction.[34]

Freedpeople found abolitionists to be staunch supporters of their postemancipation ambitions. The conventional historical wisdom, which prevailed until only recently, was that abolitionists had no practical program for emancipation. In fact, their mobilization in support of freedpeople's emancipatory aims was unprecedented. Their work would not be over until "human rights shall no longer be gauged by the color of the skin," argued Samuel Shipley, the president of the Friends' Association of Philadelphia and its Vicinity for the Relief of Colored Freedmen. For Garrison, the slave's cause had become "the cause of the freedmen." Members of the National Freedmen's Relief Association reflected that their work seemed "small as measured by the labor" before them. Often characterized as individual works of charity and benevolence, abolitionists' contributions to wartime reconstruction were, in reality, a more sophisticated and broad-based enterprise involving extensive fundraising and volunteer work that tapped into prewar networks. In 1865, the many aid societies coalesced into the American Freedmen's Union Commission. Male-dominated and led by the antiabolitionist Lyman Abbott, it sidelined women who had contributed to wartime freedmen's aid.[35]

Abolitionists also lectured and wrote for freedpeople's rights. Women abolitionists infused their writings with the emancipatory politics of the war. Abolitionist Lydia Maria Child, a famous author, was one of the first woman editors of the *National Anti Slavery Standard*. She spent the war writing anonymous essays for emancipation and aiding in contraband relief. Child compiled *The Freedmen's Book* in 1865 as a primer for freedpeople's schools; it was dedicated to Robert Smalls. Emphasizing the self-liberating actions of the enslaved, Child wrote entries on and reproduced the words of poet Phillis Wheatley as well as Toussaint Louverture, Frederick Douglass, and the abolitionist writer Frances Ellen Watkins Harper. The book functioned as both black history and political advocacy. The American Tract Society published a competing book, *The Freedmen's Third Reader,* which emphasized piety and benevolence, though it too included portraits of black ministers and the rebels of the *Amistad* shipboard rebellion of 1839. The AMA adopted it in its numerous schools, even though teachers in the field reported that freedpeople preferred Child's book and black abolitionist Henry Highland Garnet's *Freedom's Torchlight.* Harper, the "bronze muse" of abolition, penned wartime essays in abolitionist and black newspapers in which she advocated for emancipation and citizenship. In an 1862 essay, she trenchantly criticized Lincoln's "dabbling with colonization."[36]

During the war, freedpeople and their allies played a foundational role in the attempt to create an antislavery state. As W. E. B. DuBois noted, abolitionist societies came "to the aid of the government, and even before the government took definite organized hold" in the South. Abolitionists publicized the success of freedmen's schools, but also publicly shamed those military authorities and camp superintendents who mistreated freedpeople. Their complaints forced the War Department and Union army commanders to regulate the treatment of former slaves, even if they could not completely eliminate abuse and callous behavior. Frances Gage alone gave seventy-five lectures on the Port Royal experiment all over the North. A black minister, William Roscoe Davis, launched a lecture tour in the North with the assistance of the AMA to draw attention to conditions at Fortress Monroe, made worse by withheld wages. His and Gage's efforts paid off: a commission reported on the systematic abuse of freedpeople and established a new system of wages to be paid directly to them. The report was accepted by the Lincoln administration as the basis for the treatment of all slave refugees in Union lines.

Wartime reconstruction was a two-way street. Freedpeople introduced abolitionists to a grassroots politics of survival and a sense of the scale of the problems they confronted. Abolitionists realized that their own efforts and those of the enslaved were, however determined, also insufficient, and demanded the expansion of the responsibilities of the federal government. The numerous wartime relief and aid societies revealed the limits of private philanthropy but did become the basis of the first federal agency established in the South at the end of the war, the Freedmen's Bureau. Josephine Griffing, acting as an agent of the National Freedmen's Relief Association in Washington, reported that aged, disabled, and destitute freedpeople were desperately in need of assistance and urged Congress to address the situation. Other abolitionist feminists, including Julia Wilbur, Sojourner Truth, and Harriet Jacobs, demanded government intervention to alleviate the condition of freedpeople. More controversially, they sent freedpeople to work as domestics in the North. In its report, the NEFAS acknowledged the work of freedmen's aid societies but argued that "the creation of a Bureau under one of the departments of the government for the administration and superintendence of Freedmen's Affairs is a crying necessity." Such a bureau, the AMA agreed, was "an institution demanded by the wants of the Freedmen and the best interests of the country." Besides demanding government intervention, freedpeople and their abolitionist allies also demanded land reform as compensation for generations of servitude, starting a debate over reparations for slavery that is still with us today.[37]

Only the federal government, as freedpeople and their allies recognized, had the administrative capacities to realize their expansive vision of freedom. Wartime reconstruction is the forgotten origin point of social democracy in the United States—forgotten in part because Reconstruction would be brought to a violent end and many of its achievements dismantled. However, wartime reconstruction inaugurated a new and incipient conception of the federal government as the guardian of all its citizens' welfare.

CHAPTER TWO

Presidential Reconstruction

O Captain! My Captain! our fearful trip is done,
The ship has weather'd every rack,
the prize we sought is won,
The port is near, the bells I hear, the people all exulting,
While follow eyes the steady keel,
the vessel grim and daring;
But O heart! heart! heart!
O the bleeding drops of red,
Where on the deck my Captain lies,
Fallen cold and dead.

—WALT WHITMAN, 1865

"Abraham Lincoln, Sixteenth
President of the United States," by
Alexander Gardner. *Library of Congress*

A t the end of the Civil War, Abraham Lincoln was felled by an assassin's bullet, a parting shot of the vanquished. The war had formally ended on April 9, 1865, when Robert E. Lee surrendered to Ulysses S. Grant at Appomattox courthouse in Virginia, though a few battles and skirmishes followed. Six days after Appomattox, John Wilkes Booth, an actor and Confederate sympathizer from Maryland, murdered Lincoln. The Union had won the war not merely on the strength of its superiority in manpower and wealth, but because of its superior cause—emancipation—the superior generalship of its officers such as Grant, and its superior political leaders, Lincoln above all.

Booth killed Lincoln not for defeating the Confederacy but for his "preference" that the "very intelligent" and black Union soldiers be given the vote, which he heard the president propose in his last speech on Reconstruction from the balcony of the White House on April 11. Booth's words were variously recorded as "That means n––– citizenship. Now, by God! I will put him through," or "That is the last speech he will make."[1] If emancipation defined the war itself, the struggle over African American citizenship lay at the center of the reconstruction of American democracy. All other issues—federalism, or the division of powers between the federal government and states; the separation of powers between the president and Congress; the reunification of a nation torn apart by war; and the terms on which ex-Confederate states would reenter the Union—revolved around black citizenship.

Today, historians of Reconstruction tend to use the term "Presidential Reconstruction" to describe the plans of Lincoln and of his inept successor, Andrew Johnson. Yet this creates the false impression that Johnson was simply continuing Lincoln's policies for reconstructing the Union (an idea that Johnson assiduously promoted). It is important to distinguish Reconstruction under Lincoln—policies that his administration used to win the war and secure emancipation—and the restoration of white supremacy under Andrew Johnson, whose policies were an unmitigated failure. The account of Presidential Reconstruction that follows is thus focused solely on the policies of the Lincoln administration. If wartime reconstruction was largely driven by the enslaved and their allies, Presidential Reconstruction was a simultaneous process driven by Lincoln and his cabinet, though often inspired if not directed by appeals, demands, and activism from below.

Despite the expedient nature of Lincoln's reconstruction plans, they prefigured the Reconstruction eventually implemented by Congress in defiance of Johnson's attempt to restore the status quo antebellum (without outright slavery). The two signal achievements of Presidential Reconstruction were the creation of the Freedmen's Bureau and the passage of the Thirteenth Amendment, which abolished slavery. Another notable policy, Lincoln's Ten Per Cent Plan—which would admit any former Confederate state back into the Union as long as 10 percent of its population swore an oath of loyalty to the Union—is often viewed alongside these other policies, but in reality it was a wartime measure rather than a blueprint for Reconstruction after the war.[2]

Under pressure from radicals and the demands of New Orleans's activist free blacks, Lincoln acknowledged black citizenship as a component of Reconstruction, an idea that was anathema to Johnson—who, in addition to being incompetent, was an incorrigible racist. In contrast to Lincoln, Johnson not only failed miserably in the office of the presidency but remained hidebound in his commitment to outdated states' rights ideas. Johnson's appeasement of Confederates threatened the hard-fought Union victory and undermined emancipation.[3] With Lincoln's assassination, an opportunity to create an interracial democracy was seemingly lost, as defeated southerners began to re-create a postwar South based on racial subjugation, with the confidence that the man occupying the highest office in the land was now on their side. But their arrogance and brutality would force Republicans to respond.

Presidential Reconstruction started in the border slave states, which Lincoln pressured to accept emancipation from the very start of the war. In 1861–1862, unionist, predominantly nonslaveholding counties in western Virginia seceded from Virginia after the latter seceded from the Union. The new state of West Virginia was recognized by President Lincoln's proclamation in June 1863. It adopted gradual emancipation in its state constitution as a price for its admission to the Union despite the existence of proslavery sentiment. In both Maryland and Missouri, unconditional unionists and radicals gained the upper hand by 1864–1865, with conservative unionists refusing to even consider Lincoln's plans for gradual, compensated (to slaveholders) emancipation. The radicals adopted immediate, uncompensated emancipation with Lincoln's blessings.

In Delaware and Kentucky, where conservative, proslavery unionists dominated state politics, slave flight to the Union army, and the active recruitment of enslaved people, became avenues for enslaved men to gain their and their family's freedom. Emancipation in both states would come only with the passage of the Thirteenth Amendment. None of the border slave states, even those that accepted emancipation, granted former slaves civil and political rights, and some even adopted laws that were racially proscriptive. Put another way: left to themselves, even those slave states that remained in the Union resisted the idea of black rights, doing so under the guise of states' rights. None proved more obdurate than Kentucky, where racist opposition to emancipation rivaled that in the former Confederacy.

As for those states that had left the Union, Lincoln made it clear that emancipation must be the precondition for readmitting them. To give up on that aim would be "a cruel and astounding breach of faith." In his annual message to Congress in 1863—at the time, it was delivered in written form, not as a speech—Lincoln included a draft of his Proclamation of Amnesty and Reconstruction, which would allow any state in the Confederacy to reenter the Union if 10 percent of its voting population also took an oath of loyalty to the Union. Clearly designed to offer "a rallying point" for southern unionists and thereby hasten the end of the war, it was neither Lincoln's permanent plan for Reconstruction nor his final word on the issue.

In Union–occupied parts of the Confederacy, meanwhile, Lincoln used military rule to enact emancipation. The Union-directed "Restored Government of Virginia," which did not even represent 10 percent of Virginia's white voters, voted for emancipation. In Arkansas, after it was taken by the Union army, a constitutional convention adopted a state constitution abolishing slavery, which was ratified by only 20 per cent of the state's voters. In Tennessee, Johnson, at the time serving as the state's military governor, was instructed to push through emancipation, even though he had proposed a resolution objecting to emancipation as a US senator.

By 1862, Union forces under General Ambrose Burnside had occupied parts of eastern North Carolina, and Lincoln appointed Edward Stanley, an old-line Whig—the party replaced by the antislavery Republican Party in the 1850s as the main political opponent of the Democratic Party—to be military governor. Stanley proved to be a poor choice, opposing emancipation and the establishment of black schools, moving instead to restore "the old order." He resigned in January 1863 after Lincoln issued the Emancipation Proclamation; the president was glad to see him go. Conservative unionists such as Stanley caused considerable consternation among freedpeople, radicals, and abolitionists. Unapologetic racists, they would be precisely the people Johnson would put in charge after Lincoln's death.

The next year, the "colored citizens of Beaufort," North Carolina passed resolutions thanking the radicals and stating that slavery had denied them education and all rights of citizenship. Lincoln received a delegation of black North Carolinians led by Abraham Galloway, a fugitive slave, abolitionist, and Union army spy. In addition to Galloway, the delegation consisted of former slaves and free blacks—a baker, barber, carpenter, farmer, brick mason, and minister. Lincoln's gracious reception of these men constituted, as one historian has written, one of the war's "redemptive little moments." They thanked him for the Emancipation Proclamation, reminded him that in North Carolina free blacks had had the right to vote until 1835, and asked him "to finish the noble work you have begun, and grant unto your petitioners that greatest of privileges, when the State is reconstructed, to exercise the right of suffrage, which will greatly extend our usefulness, redound to your honor, and cause posterity, to the latest generation, to acknowledge their deep sense of gratitude." Lincoln assured them of "his sympathy and earnest cooperation."[4]

In Union-occupied Louisiana, Lincoln appointed General Nathaniel

P. Banks in August 1863 to form a civilian government under his Ten Per Cent Plan. The president's instructions to Banks were to establish "a practical system by which the two races could live themselves out of the old relation to each other, and both come out better prepared for the new. Education for young blacks should be included in this plan." Lincoln envisioned a "probationary period" and called for a simple, flexible labor system. Under Banks, the capital of the state was moved from Baton Rouge to New Orleans.

The city's creole *gens de couleur*—"gentlemen of color," of French descent—asked for the right to vote. In February 1864, the Lincoln administration sent an emissary to them asking about their demands. In response, the city's free black population sent two representatives, Jean Baptiste Roudanez and Arnold Bertonneau, to Washington. Both reported that Lincoln expressed regret "that you are not able to secure all your rights and that circumstances will not permit the government to confer them upon you." The two were feted by abolitionists and their visit must have made some impression on the president. Lincoln soon after sent a letter to Louisiana governor Michael Hahn, elected in 1864, urging him to give the vote to black men, "the very intelligent, and especially those who have fought gallantly in our ranks. They would probably help, in some trying time to come, to help keep the jewel of liberty within the family of freedom."

The cosmopolitan gentlemen of color of New Orleans assumed leadership of the black struggle for citizenship. In 1862, Dr. Louis C. Roudanez, Jean Baptiste's brother, along with others, had launched the French-language weekly *L'Union*, which was committed to the French republican ideals of liberty, equality, and fraternity. In July of that year, Dr. Roudanez, who had studied in Paris and at Dartmouth, started publishing the bilingual *New Orleans Tribune* as an "organ of the oppressed class." He invited the Belgian-born Jean-Charles Houzeau, who had written for the *L'Union,* to edit the paper in 1863. A radical antislavery man, Houzeau transformed it into the premier voice in the South for black rights. He had spent the early years of the war helping to spirit fugitive slaves from Confederate Texas to Mexico, and now, under him, the *Tribune* united the creole Catholic free blacks with the predominantly Protestant freed-people of the countryside to demand rights for all. The first black daily newspaper published in the United States, the *Tribune* also forged links to northern abolitionists and Radical Republicans, publishing their speeches and articles. Houzeau connected the cause of freedpeople to those of other groups around the world: the American Civil War was "only one chapter in the great universal fight of the oppressed of all colors and nations. Whether the victim is called serf in Russia, peasant in Austria, Jew in Prussia, proletarian in France, pariah in India, Negro in the United States, at heart it is the same denial of justice."

New Orleans Tribune inaugural edition. *Mark Charles Roudané and the Roudanez Family Collection*

In September 1864, Louisiana ratified a state constitution that left the decision on black male suffrage to the legislature—the first in the former slave states to do so—and made provisions for black education. One of the achievements of the short-lived Banks-Hahn government was the establishment of a Bureau of Education in Louisiana, which oversaw sixty schools with eight thousand students and one hundred teachers. Banks, though, was a political chameleon who had migrated from the Democratic Party to the nativist Know Nothings and then to the Republicans. He removed black officers from the USCT in the Department of the Gulf and instituted a labor system for freedpeople that was halfway between slavery and freedom. Freedpeople were required to work on plantations for wages, shelter, and medical care, to sign one-year contracts, and to obtain passes to leave plantations where they worked. Banks defended his "experiment" by comparing the condition of their situation favorably to that of laborers throughout the world. But Houzeau pointed out that "the wage scale was set excessively low" and criticized the restrictions on free movement.[5]

As Louisiana demonstrated, Presidential Reconstruction was significantly less transformative than wartime reconstruction. Freedpeople and abolitionists—whether they criticized the president or defended him—found themselves demanding more extensive and forceful actions than Lincoln's wartime measures. They found allies in Congress, where Radicals Benjamin F. Wade of Ohio and Henry Winter Davis of Maryland proposed a law that would allow a state to reenter the Union only when 50 percent of its voting population swore an ironclad oath of loyalty to the Union that they had never supported the Confederacy. The Wade-Davis bill, passed by Congress in July 1864, established a more stringent standard for southern unionism than Lincoln's plan and included civil protections for freedpeople. Lincoln, who objected to the bill on the grounds that it would endanger state governments already reconstructed under his Ten Per Cent Plan, pocket vetoed the bill—that is, he allowed it to expire without having to explicitly veto it. That action suggested that he sympathized with its goals. He had no objection, he said, to states still in rebellion being reconstructed according to the principles laid down in the Wade-Davis bill. Wade and

Davis's manifesto of August 5, 1864, issued in response to Lincoln's pocket veto, argued that he underestimated the "reckless ferocity" of their opponents.

Most Radicals, such as Thaddeus Stevens, followed a policy of "condemn privately but applaud publicly" when it came to Lincoln. In June 1862, Charles Sumner, in his "Stand By the Administration" letter, had asked all abolitionists and radicals to have faith in Lincoln, whom he knew personally. Though Sumner would filibuster the seating of Louisiana's delegation in Congress in 1864, he remained close to Lincoln. In the Senate, he introduced a resolution "against any premature restoration of Rebel States, without proper guaranties and safeguards against Slavery and for the Protection of Freedmen." Installing those guarantees and safeguards, he claimed, was the "solemn duty of Congress." The Wade-Davis bill revealed that a majority of Republicans contemplated some protections for freedpeople. The president moved closer to their position after his reelection. He appointed Salmon Chase, a political rival, to the Supreme Court after the latter resigned as Treasury secretary; Lincoln also accepted the resignation of two conservatives in his cabinet, Edward Bates and the race-baiting Montgomery Blair, and appointed radicals in their stead.

Even the Wade-Davis bill did not contain a provision for black suffrage, which was the central postemancipation goal of abolitionists. In a speech before the American Anti Slavery Society (AASS), Frederick Douglass demanded the "immediate enfranchisement of the slaves of the South." Representative Josiah Grinnell of Iowa and Senator Sumner tried to add black suffrage to the Wade Davis bill, but both were voted down. William Lloyd Garrison saw Lincoln's Ten Per Cent Plan as the first steps toward Reconstruction, but Wendell Phillips criticized it. In his Proclamation of Amnesty and Reconstruction of 1863, the basis of Louisiana's reconstruction, Lincoln clearly stated that the power to seat congressional representatives from any former Confederate state readmitted to the Union under his plan remained with Congress—he clearly did not think of Reconstruction as an exclusively presidential prerogative. Lincoln also became the first American president to endorse black suffrage and citizenship. In his final public speech in April 1865, he had said: "It is also unsatisfactory to some that the elective franchise is not given to the colored man. I would myself prefer that it were now conferred to the very intelligent, and on those who serve our cause as soldiers." [6]

Lincoln's approach to Reconstruction rested on securing abolition. He spent the last year of his life lobbying for a constitutional amendment to abolish slavery, to forever embed emancipation in the Constitution. Border state slaveholders, whom Lincoln had cajoled throughout the war to accept compensated emancipation and colonization, but to no avail, and most northern Democrats, opposed an emancipation amendment. Their objections rested on a hodgepodge of states' rights, strict constructionism, and crude racism, first concocted before the war by the South Carolinian planter-politician John C. Calhoun in defense of slavery. Opponents of Reconstruction and Andrew Johnson would make that argument their own.

Abolitionists and radicals demanded not just emancipation but a broader remaking of the Constitution. While they had long debated whether the Constitution was proslavery or antislavery, after the Civil War all abolitionists agreed that the Constitution had to be refashioned to secure black rights. Representative James M. Ashley of Ohio, an antislavery radical, introduced the first bill for an emancipation amendment in Congress in 1863, envisioning a far-reaching emancipation for all working people, both enslaved and free labor. Abolitionists deluged Congress with petitions demanding an emancipation amendment, and the AASS passed a resolution in 1864 formally asking for a Thirteenth Amendment that would have that purpose.

Sumner proposed an expansive version of an emancipation amendment. Modeled after the French revolutionary Declaration of the Rights of Man and of the Citizen of 1789, it said that "all persons are equal before the law." His language was amended by Senator Lyman Trumbull to read: "Neither slavery nor involuntary servitude, except as punishment for crime whereof the party shall be duly convicted, shall exist within the United States, or any place subject to their jurisdiction."

Sumner's bestowal of rights to all persons could have included women, who were legally powerless after marriage, but Trumbull's wording was an injunction against slavery and servitude only.

Trumbull had lifted the language from the Northwest Ordinance of 1787, a revolutionary-era federal enactment that had abolished slavery in territories north and west of the Ohio River. Senator Jacob M. Howard of Michigan was happy that "good old Anglo-Saxon language" had replaced Sumner's "French" constitutionalism. In his speech introducing the amendment, Trumbull argued that the founding fathers had been wrong in thinking that slavery would disappear with time, and that the nation needed a "second founding" to rid itself of slavery completely. The criminal exception in the Northwest Ordinance and, now, the Thirteenth Amendment was pro forma. Yet it would have disastrous consequences. The antislavery Republicans who formulated the amendment were not part of any nefarious conspiracy to undermine black freedom, but the exception became a loophole that southern states would exploit, enacting laws criminalizing black freedom to get around constitutionally mandated emancipation. Only the ever-vigilant Sumner foresaw this eventuality and warned against it. The second clause of the amendment gave Congress broad authority to enforce emancipation by "appropriate legislation," constitutionally tying emancipation to federal power and considerably expanding the purview of the federal government in the former slave states.[7]

The Thirteenth Amendment was a sleeping giant: it gave the federal government vast powers to protect the rights of citizens against abuse from state and private entities, which civil rights activists in the twentieth century would invoke. In April 1864, the Senate decisively passed the amendment, but it fell short of the required two-thirds majority in the House two months later. The most memorable Senate speech on the amendment came from Sumner, who was, as Douglass put it, "the best embodiment of the Antislavery idea now in the councils of the nation." Sumner proclaimed that *"Nothing against Slavery can be unconstitutional"* as there could be "no property in man." Any compensation for emancipation "must belong, every dollar, to the slave."

The final push for the amendment came with Lincoln's reelection in

November. Many, including Lincoln himself, feared that he would lose the election, after the Democrats waged a virulently racist campaign against emancipation. Two Democratic New York editors coined the word "miscegenation," for racial intermixture, and, posing as a fictitious abolitionist, recommended the practice in an anonymous pamphlet. It advocated the "superiority of mixed races" that would result from emancipation. An appendix proposed "Native Indian blood mingling with the white" as well as that of the Chinese. The racist scaremongering didn't stop Lincoln's reelection. Democratic race baiting—calling the president "Abraham Africanus I" and "a general agent for the Negroes"—only endeared him to African Americans. On the other side of the political spectrum, an "ill timed" effort led by Wendell Phillips to replace Lincoln with John C. Fremont or Salmon Chase failed to gain traction even among abolitionists. As Garrison put it, "the re-election of Abraham Lincoln to the Presidency of the United States would be the safest and wisest course." He had laid "death dealing blows" on slavery and was "detested and feared by all the southern traitors and their northern sympathizers."

Garrison, who had condemned any engagement with American politics as long as the government was dominated by slaveholders, became an ardent defender of "Our 'Partisanship' of Mr. Lincoln" against northern "copperhead" criticisms. Garrison attended the Republican Convention in 1864, a first for him. As the black abolitionist minister James W. C. Pennington observed, Lincoln was "the only American President who had ever given any attention to colored men as citizens." His reelection was the "best security" for black freedom. Most abolitionists and radicals would "Stand By the President." Douglass, who flirted with the Fremont movement, wrote to Garrison that his criticism of Lincoln should not be construed as opposition to his reelection. An overwhelming majority of Union army soldiers in the field voted for their commander-in-chief by mail—an exercise in electoral democracy that the proslavery, antidemocratic Confederacy conspicuously avoided.[8]

Lincoln's resounding victory over his proslavery Democratic challenger, ex-Union general George B. McClellan—whom Lincoln had relieved of his duties in 1862—signaled the triumph of his emancipation policy. In his annual message to Congress in December, the president called for the ratification of the Thirteenth Amendment and threw the weight of his office behind it. The "voice of the people" and the "will of the majority" had spoken, he said. In the House, Ashley helped corral votes from border state unionists and lame duck northern Democratic representatives, who were won over with promises of patronage.

On January 31, 1865, with African Americans, women, and abolitionists in the galleries, the House passed the Thirteenth Amendment by well over the required two-thirds majority. Soon enough, the states in the Union all passed the amendment. For most of the former Confederate states, ratification became a condition for reentry into the Union, though only Virginia, South Carolina, Alabama, North Carolina, and Georgia ratified it by the time the amendment was certified by Secretary of State William Seward. Twenty-seven of the thirty-six states ratified the amendment, the required three-fourths for a constitutional amendment, by the end of the year. The most extreme laggards were Kentucky, which ratified the Thirteenth Amendment only in 1976, and Mississippi, which did so, even more incredibly, in 1995.

The Declaration, Garrison declared, had been "CONSTITU-TIONALIZED—made THE SUPREME LAW OF THE LAND." He set the type for the amendment himself and by the end of 1865 ceased publishing *The Liberator*, having achieved its central aim. However, when he wanted to dissolve the AASS, of which he was president, Phillips and Douglass insisted that until black male suffrage was established the work of abolitionists was not finished. They won the day, and the AASS elected Phillips its new president. In his valedictory address, Garrison agreed that in the matter of "giving the ballot to those who have long been disfranchised" there is "no difference among Abolitionists," even though he was against the continuance of the AASS. *The Liberator* kept up the drumbeat for black suffrage until the very end.[9]

The aspirations of the enslaved were foundational to the emancipation amendment and the broader revision of the Constitution that began in 1865. Henry Highland Garnet, who became, on Lincoln's fifty-sixth birthday, the first black man to address Congress, asked the "rulers of this great nation" to emancipate, educate, and enfranchise. Various proposals to amend the Constitution and enact black citizenship had been put forward by some of the foremost legal thinkers of the day, including Francis Leiber. With the Thirteenth Amendment, Lincoln and antislavery Republicans had unleashed the forces of progressive constitutionalism—one of the central and most enduring accomplishments of Presidential Reconstruction under Lincoln.[10]

The contest over Reconstruction during Lincoln's presidency centered on not only questions of black suffrage but also freedpeople's access to land and control over their labor. Freedpeople's hunger for the very land they had cultivated for generations without compensation was manifest in their interactions with federal authorities. They tilled abandoned plantations during the war and pooled resources to buy land. They made clear their preference for cultivating food crops over cash crops such as cotton that they associated with enslavement. In Hampton, Virginia, the site of the first slave refugee camp, they formed Lincoln's Land Association and purchased hundreds of acres. Abolitionists, including the AMA's Charles Wilder, viewed wages as a means for freedpeople to "buy a spot of land."

General Rufus Saxton tried to facilitate black landholding in the Department of the South, which covered Florida, Georgia, and South Carolina. One abolitionist recommended "self-help" banks to assist freedpeople in buying land: "let the land go into the hands of actual laborers," because there can be no "complete and perfect freedom for the working men, so long as they remain the tools of capital, and are deprived of the legitimate product of the sweat of their brow." Thomas J. Durant, a radical white lawyer who helped found the New Orleans Freedmen's Aid Association in 1865, was a utopian socialist. This association, alongside the Louisiana Homestead Association, helped ex-slaves purchase farms and tools. The Kansas Homestead Association was established by freedpeople to find and buy land in that state.

Lincoln was convinced by the abolitionist solicitor for the War Department, William Whiting, that Congress could confiscate land owned by Confederates as punishment for treason. He argued that freedpeople should have "an interest in the soil." As the enslaved and freedpeople fought for land of their own, the federal government took action, acquiring plantations and farms abandoned by slaveholders or seized for nonpayment of taxes. Lincoln limited the confiscation of rebel lands, mandated by the Second Confiscation Act of 1862, to rebel planters' lifetime, but he allowed the preemption of forty-acre plots for freedpeople in the South Carolina Sea Islands auctioned by the government for nonpayment of taxes. In December 1863, he issued an order allowing single adult men to occupy twenty acres, and families and wives of black soldiers forty acres. "Thus from the president's pen, and not from an officer in the field came the first mention of forty acres," notes one historian.

On January 16, 1865, General William T. Sherman issued his famous Field Order No. 15. Thousands of runaway slaves trailed his army during its famous March to the Sea from Atlanta to Savannah at the end of 1864. A few days before the order, on January 12, Sherman and Secretary of War Edwin M. Stanton met with twenty members of Savannah's black community, some of whom were freeborn, others of whom had purchased their freedom or were freed by the Union army. Most were church leaders. The Baptist minister Garrison Frazier, who had purchased his freedom before the war from his enslaver and renamed himself after the famous abolitionist, was chosen to speak for the group. He informed Sherman and Stanton that freedpeople desired land and "to reap the fruit of our own labor." Sherman soon issued his order, which set aside land in the Sea Islands and the rice coast for the settlement of black families and those who followed his army, later providing each family with a mule from the army. Nearly forty thousand families were settled on over four hundred thousand acres of land. The slogan "forty acres and a mule" spread like wildfire among freedpeople.[11]

But it would be the labor regime established by the Union army, rather than the economic autonomy offered to freedpeople on the Sea Islands, that became the dominant system. The army put former slaves to work on sugar plantations it controlled in southern Louisiana and on cotton plantations in the Mississippi River valley. The transition from slavery to free labor in these areas was an uneven process. In the Mississippi valley, General Lorenzo Thomas established wage work on plantations leased by northerners. Northern lessors were quick to defraud their workers; these men brought capital into the destroyed southern economy even as they perpetuated the plantation system. The Treasury Department under Salmon Chase assumed control of the valley briefly, increasing wages and making plans to lease lands directly to freedpeople. In some areas of the upper South—Union-occupied Virginia, North Carolina, and Washington—freedpeople worked directly on government-owned land. The army's system of annual contracts, which provided subsistence and paltry wages but limited workers' mobility and choice, prevailed in much of the postwar South. Its coercive elements made it even worse than the northern system of wage work.

Freedpeople had their own vision of free labor. Jourdan Anderson's letter to his enslaver in Tennessee, who invited him back to work for him, illustrated their notions of the dignity of labor versus the degradation of slavery. Anderson, who had escaped to Ohio, wrote, "I want to know particularly what the good chance is you propose to give me. I am doing tolerably well here. I get $25 a month, with victuals and clothing; have a comfortable home for Mandy (the folks call her Mrs. Anderson), and the children, Milly, Jane, and Grundy, go to school and are learning well." He asked for stolen wages for the thirty-two years he had "faithfully served" his ex-master at the rate of $25 a month, which would have amounted to $11,680. Anderson clarified that he would allow him to deduct expenses incurred for past doctor's visits and a dentist visit to have one of his wife's teeth pulled out. Writing that "Surely there will be a day of reckoning for those who defraud the laborer of his hire," Anderson reminded his former enslaver that his daughters were now safe from sexual assault, and asked him if there were good schools established that he could send them to if they returned, given that "The great desire of my life now is to give my children an education, and have them form virtuous habits." As a parting shot, Anderson asked him to say "howdy" to one George Carter, who had taken his former enslaver's pistol when he shot at the escaping Anderson during the war. Long before historians "discovered" Anderson's letter, abolitionist newspapers published it. Lydia Maria Child included it in *The Freedmen's Book*.[12]

The biggest champions of freedpeople's desire for economic autonomy were abolitionists. From the early days of the war, *The Liberator* published articles demanding the confiscation and redistribution of land. One writer observed that "The conflict between capital and labor is as old as the world; but in this case the contest could never be more unequal." Elizur Wright published a pamphlet demanding an "agrarian law" that would tax the South's landed aristocracy and give "not only liberty to the loyal but SOIL TO THE TILLER." Abolitionists and radicals were hardly intent on exporting the North's exploitative wage labor system to the South; their understanding of free labor was far more capacious.

The momentum for land redistribution at the end of the war was greater than most historians today acknowledge. In Congress, Radical Republicans took the lead, hoping to destroy the plantation system as well as provide freedpeople with a modicum of economic independence. Sumner proposed, in 1863, giving ten acres of land to every black Union soldier, and George Julian put forward a homestead law that would "parcel out the plantations of rebels" into "small farms" for freedpeople. In 1864, Julian proposed to extend the Homestead Act of 1862 to the South, thereby giving forty to eighty acres of land to freedpeople, loyal southern whites, and Union soldiers. Both houses of Congress voted three times to revoke the 1862 resolution limiting confiscation of property to the lifetime of the affected rebels but failed to pass a joint resolution. As Julian argued, "The dismemberment of the great rebel estates, and their distribution among the poor, was obviously the true policy of Reconstruction."[13]

Freedpeople's hopes for economic autonomy clashed with attempts to rehabilitate a large-scale plantation system geared toward generating profits. In Haiti and the British West Indies, profitable slave labor–based plantations had collapsed in the wake of emancipation largely because freedpeople unsurprisingly preferred self-sufficient farms to the gang labor of slavery. But in the West Indies, an apprenticeship system emerged after British abolition took effect on August 1, 1834, that put freedpeople in an "intermediate condition," as Sumner put it, between slavery and freedom. That experiment in a "half-way system" had failed and eventually was done away with in 1838. Former slaves dreamed of being as far removed from unpaid coerced menial labor as possible. The Morant Bay rebellion of 1865 in Jamaica was fueled by freedpeople's demands for access to land and an end to poll taxes that disfranchised them. It was brutally put down by the British governor John Eyre, who turned to executions, floggings, imprisonment, and a scorched earth policy in which homes of freedpeople were burned, causing an outcry among abolitionists.

The question of land ownership helped shape the Freedmen's Bureau bill passed by Congress on March 3, 1865. The law provided forty acres of abandoned and confiscated land to freedmen for rent, with the opportunity to purchase the land from the government after three years. While not the outright redistribution demanded by freedpeople, abolitionists, and radicals, it was still welcomed by most. But Andrew Johnson's reversal of these initial steps would curtail the momentum for land reform. The eventual overthrow of Reconstruction ensured the death of the land question. Only 25 percent of freedpeople—still an achievement in the worst of circumstances—owned land by the end of the century.[14]

The creation of the Freedmen's Bureau was Presidential Reconstruction's greatest legacy and, not incidentally, a source of continual frustration to Johnson. From the start, the wartime expansion of the American state and the expansion of its responsibility for the welfare of freedpeople came at the behest of former slaves and their abolitionist allies. They demanded that the government play an activist role in securing black freedom, rights, livelihood, and land. Many understood this could be best accomplished through a new bureau of the federal government. In the very first year of the war, abolitionist William J. Potter argued, "let there be a new Executive bureau established. . . . to care for, and protect, and educate these four million of newborn freemen." In 1862, Garrison's Emancipation League began to advocate for an "Emancipation Bureau" to respond to the needs of slave refugees. The freedmen's aid societies, under abolitionist James McKim's initiative, sent a delegation to lobby Lincoln, and the president endorsed the idea of a federal bureau and forwarded their memorial to Congress. Abolitionist feminist Josephine Griffing, who had worked in the Freedmen's Village in Washington, lobbied Lincoln, congressmen, and federal officials for a government agency to oversee emancipation.

In 1863, the War Department created the American Freedmen's Inquiry Commission. Its three commissioners—Robert Dale Owen, Dr. Samuel Gridley Howe, and James McKaye—were antislavery men who supported emancipation but displayed a varying commitment to racial equality. The commissioners traveled to freedmen's camps, Port Royal, Union-occupied New Orleans, and even fugitive slave communities in Canada to gather information. Howe, a medical doctor, subscribed to the pseudoscience of race, and his report from Canada drew connections between climate, race, disease, and death, including speculations on black people's mental inferiority. McKaye, though the least-known member of the commission, was a radical and also the most astute of the three. As he understood, "The difficulty is not with the emancipated slave; but with the old master, still enthralled by his old infatuation." Presiding over a "monstrous system of organized barbarism," ex-enslavers had a perverted sense of reality and should be destroyed as a class, in the manner of the ancien régime of France. The work of Reconstruction, McKaye concluded, was not to uplift freedpeople but "the deliverance of the master population also, wholly and forever, from their mastership, and from the fatal delusions and depravations that are inherent in it." He recommended the breaking up of landed estates to create an independent yeomanry of blacks and whites. McKaye represented the abolitionist view.

The commission's preliminary report, rife with both racialist assumptions as well as evidence of freedpeople founding schools and churches—and thereby proving their independence—recommended government oversight of the transition of "enforced slave labor" to "free compensated labor." Its detailed plan for a government agency with superintendents, hospitals, and schools would lead to the creation of the Bureau of Refugees, Freedmen, and Abandoned Lands—the Freedmen's Bureau, as it quickly became more commonly known. The final report of the commission recommended assisting destitute whites as well as blacks and proposed a temporary bureau that would prevent the reemergence of slavery and "ill treatment" of freedpeople. Much of the final report, written by Owen, an ex-Democratic congressman from Indiana, was informed by his utopian socialist and racialist views.

Despite staunch Democratic opposition, in February 1865 the House passed a bill authored by Representative Thomas Eliot of Massachusetts that created the Freedmen's Bureau, under the War Department. It was to be in existence for a year. In the Senate, Sumner's bill would have made the Bureau a permanent entity under the Treasury Department and invested it with the power to facilitate land redistribution. In the end, it was the House bill—"An Act to establish a Bureau for the Relief of Freedmen and Refugees"—that became law. The Bureau would mediate labor contracts, manage abandoned and confiscated lands, and establish public schools. It would also provide food, clothing, and medical services (imbued with the racial science of the day) for freedpeople as well as poor white southerners. General Oliver O. Howard was appointed to lead the Bureau, while abolitionist John W. Alvord was appointed its superintendent of schools.

With the establishment of the Freedmen's Bureau, the federal government formalized its commitment to oversee the transition from slavery to freedom in the postwar South. It was taking responsibility for the well-being of destitute white southerners, too, a fact that racist critics of the Bureau elided in criticizing the Bureau for making freedpeople, in their view, "wards" of the state. As Sumner argued, only the federal government could "supply the adequate machinery, and extend the proper network of assistance, with the proper unity of operation." It was its duty to build that "bridge from slavery to freedom." To those who opposed the creation of a federal agency as some sort of special favor to freedpeople, he responded, "Emancipation is not enough. You must see to it that it is not nullified or evaded; and you must see to it especially that the new-made freedmen are protected in the rights now assured to them, and that they are saved from prevailing caste, which menaces Slavery in some new form."[15]

The roots of the modern liberal state in the United States lie in Reconstruction. Well before the creation of the Freedmen's Bureau, the Civil

War Congress passed, with Lincoln's backing, legislation that greatly expanded the authority of the federal government. As with emancipation, these measures were possible only because their inveterate opponents, southern slaveholders, were mostly no longer in the Union. The Internal Revenue Act of 1862 established a progressive income tax for the first time in US history. Under Chase, the Treasury Department levied excise taxes on luxury goods, issued war bonds, raised tariffs, and took out loans to finance the war effort. Also in 1862, the Homestead Act gave farmers 160 acres to each head of household, and the Morill Land-Grant College Act, named after Vermont Representative Justin Morill, established the nation's first public universities as agricultural colleges. Both laws, like the republic itself, were predicated on Indian dispossession. That same year, the Department of Agriculture was founded by Lincoln, increasing the administrative capacities of the government. The National Banking Act of 1863 established federal banks and a uniform currency, "greenbacks," or dollars that had been issued as early as 1861 to increase the supply of money and finance the war. Lincoln and congressional Republicans exhibited a progressive, meliorist mentality.

The two signal achievements of Presidential Reconstruction—the Thirteenth Amendment to the Constitution abolishing slavery and the creation of the Freedmen's Bureau—were animated by the same spirit. In his many evocative wartime speeches, Lincoln had tied emancipation to a transcendent nationalism, the survival of the American republic, and its experiment with representative government. The Lincoln administration's progressive constitutionalism, creation of an activist federal government, and reliance on the Union army as a means to implement political changes in the postwar South, would shape Radical Reconstruction.[16]

In his Second Inaugural Address on March 4, 1865, Lincoln had memorably linked the destruction of slavery to the meaning of the Civil War. Employing abolitionist tropes, he said, "Fondly do we hope—fervently do we pray—that this mighty scourge of war may speedily pass away. Yet, if God wills that it continue, until all the wealth piled by the bond-man's two hundred and fifty years of unrequited toil shall be sunk, and until every drop of blood drawn with the lash, shall be paid by another drawn with the sword, as was said three thousand years ago, so still it must be said 'the judgments of the Lord, are true and righteous altogether.'" Douglass, who was at first barred from the inaugural ball and whom Lincoln personally invited in, judged his speech "a sacred effort." Garrison wrote that it inspired "fresh confidence" in the president's "integrity and firmness." Lydia Maria Child advised abolitionists to measure progress by reading Lincoln's First Inaugural Address and then his second.

A month later, Lee surrendered to Grant at Appomattox. George Washington Williams wrote, "So, when the news of Lee's disaster reached the Confederate capital, it fell like a thunderbolt out of a cloudless sky. Amid the confusion and consternation, the disorder and disaster, the panic and pillage, the rapine and flames, the Negro population stood still to see the salvation of the Lord.... The whites were silent and sullen; it was not their day, although it was manifestly the funeral of their cause; the year of jubilee had come to the long-benighted bondman, however." DuBois too wrote of the enslaved's understanding of emancipation as jubilee: "God was real. They knew Him. They had met him personally in many a wild orgy of religious frenzy, or in the black stillness of the night."

Black soldiers entered the fallen capital of the Confederacy, which had been "looted and burned by its own citizens." Walt Whitman recorded one soldier saying that "the desolated, ruined south; nearly the whole generation of young men between seventeen and thirty destroyed or maim'd ... and the name of southerner blacken'd with every shame—all that is Calhoun's real monument." The enslaved would make their feelings clear. They greeted Garrison triumphantly when he journeyed to South Carolina, the heart of secession, to see the US flag hoisted over Fort Sumter. At Zion church in Charleston, they reduced him to tears. As the boat carrying the captured president of the Confederacy wound its way down the Carolina coast, freedpeople lined up and sang "We'll hang Jeff Davis on a sour apple tree." The "thunderous sound" of their song could not have left Davis ignorant of their "amiable intention," noted one sardonic observer. In Florida, too, former slaves proved to be "deficient in love for their old masters," and struck up the same ditty.[17]

But revolutions can go backwards, and the president who would be killed shortly after the war was not the traitor to the republic but its defender. Booth assassinated Lincoln on Good Friday, April 14, 1865, at Ford's Theater, where the actor was performing in "Our American Cousin." He managed to escape, but not before shouting melodramatically, "Sic semper tyrannis, the South is avenged." Earlier that day, Lincoln supported Chase's suggestion, at a cabinet meeting, to reconstruct the South by enfranchising all loyal citizens regardless of race. As the president lay dying at the Petersen boarding house across the street from the theater to which he had been carried, Sumner held vigil at his bed. Booth's action was part of a coordinated plan that saw an ill William Seward attacked with a knife by an ex-Confederate. The secretary of state survived. Andrew Johnson was another target, though his drunk assassin failed to attack, as was Grant, who was not in Washington at the time. Booth had met with Confederate agents in Canada. Whether defeated Confederates were involved or not is debatable, but the plan was to decapitate the US government.

Lincoln's legacy was bound to grow, Whitman wrote, while "history lives, and love of country lasts." Or as Secretary of War Edwin Stanton, who would oversee the hunt for the assassins and conspirators, famously put it, he now "belonged to the ages." African Americans, in particular, mourned the president. In his eulogy delivered at New York's Cooper Union in June 1865, Douglass claimed that Lincoln "was emphatically the black man's President: the first to show any respect to their rights as men." He contrasted Lincoln's attitudes with the petty prejudice of those white New Yorkers who tried to exclude black people from his funeral procession. On July 4, Washington's black community, led by abolitionists Henry Highland Garnet, Stephen Smith, William J. Wilson, and John F. Cook, formed the Colored People's Educational Monument Association to raise a monument to the memory of Lincoln. In its annual meeting, the National Equal Rights League bemoaned Lincoln's death by "the dastard assassin, who though furious and infatuated by the maddening sprit of a pro-slavery demon, but stole secretly behind his back and sent forth the fatal messenger of death."

If some black Americans blamed the foul spirit of slavery for Lincoln's murder, ex-Confederates (and copperheads in the North) reacted with barely disguised glee at the death of a man they had lampooned as an Orangutan and "Black Republican." Douglass compared how the South had applauded the assault on Sumner—he was referring to Congressman Preston Brooks's vicious attack on the senator in 1856—before the war with how it now applauded Lincoln's assassination.[18]

The Confederacy had snatched an assassin's victory at the moment of its greatest defeat, which resulted in the ascension of Andrew Johnson to the presidency. It is an irony of history that some of the greatest American presidents have been followed by some of the worst. Despite his early adherence to colonization, Lincoln had evolved on the issue of black rights during the war. Johnson's trajectory was just the opposite. Once a defender of the Union, he became putty in the hands of ex-Confederates, with whom he shared a strident commitment to white supremacy. Lincoln's personal interactions with African Americans, whether in private or public, left them impressed by his lack of condescension. Douglass had met with Lincoln three times, and wrote that he was the first "great man" who did not remind him "of the difference between himself and myself, of the difference of color." Johnson, on the other hand, could barely disguise his visceral racism. At Lincoln's second inauguration, Douglass recalled an unguarded look of "bitter contempt and aversion" from Johnson. He concluded, "whatever Andrew Johnson is, he is no friend of our race."

Most scholars today repeat the contention that abolitionists and radicals were initially Johnson supporters and thought he would be sympathetic to them. In fact, on hearing of Johnson's selection as Lincoln's running mate in 1864, Thaddeus Stevens remarked, "Can't you find a candidate for Vice President in the United States without going down to one of those damned rebel provinces to pick one up?" After Johnson's drunken "wandering and maudlin" inaugural vice presidential address, Sumner suggested that he resign his office. As early as May 1865, when Johnson issued a presidential proclamation for the reconstruction of North Carolina, Stevens warned that Johnson would "pursue his wrong course" and "usurp 'reconstruction.'" To Johnson himself he wrote that none of the leading northern unionists approved of his "Restoration" policies, which "will greatly injure the country." Sumner, who spent the summer trying to convince Johnson of his folly, wrote to Stevens in July that he had never seen such "unanimity" among abolitionists and anti-slavery Republicans in opposition to Johnson. Only his cabinet, which Johnson turned into a "company of courtiers," stuck by him.

A few abolitionists, such as George L. Stearns, gave Johnson the benefit of the doubt, though he quickly came to oppose the new president, too. By August 1865, when the results of Johnson's appeasement of the South started becoming clear, Wendell Phillips delivered a lecture, "The South Victorious," in which he goaded Republicans to act. The whole North had to be "roused" against Johnson's restoration plans. Black clergyman Rev. William H. Robinson expressed the misgivings of abolitionists over not merely Johnson's policies but his character: "Lincoln had an adequate idea of what ought to be done, but I fear Johnson has still less. Lincoln was, at least, master of himself, and master of the situation: Johnson *may* be the tool of anybody and everybody."[19]

Both Johnson and Lincoln were men of humble origins; the former was literally born in a log cabin. But while Lincoln represented the self-educated, independent ideal of northern free labor ideology, Johnson grew up as a poor white man in slave society. He began his working life as a tailor and was illiterate until the age of seventeen. He eventually found a calling in politics and began buying slaves, becoming far wealthier than Lincoln. Johnson was hardly a typical "poor white," even though he may have started out as one. Unlike Lincoln, he had no facility with the written word, even after learning to read and write. A former Democrat, Johnson had opposed attempts to restrict the expansion of slavery and had argued that the natural equality described in the Declaration of Independence did not apply to African Americans, precisely the opposite of Lincoln's positions in the 1850s.

But unlike most southern Democrats, Johnson refused to support Tennessee when it seceded from the Union, becoming the only senator from a Confederate state who stayed in Congress. In 1862, Lincoln appointed him military governor of Union-occupied Tennessee, and two years later, Johnson was nominated as Lincoln's running mate on

a National Union platform, a unity ticket meant to appeal to all unionists. The National Union Party, though, was effectively the Republican
Party, and replacing Lincoln's first vice president, Hannibal Hamlin of
Maine, also a former Democrat, with Johnson was the biggest mistake
made by the Republican Convention of 1864. Johnson's unionism and
his positions on various notable issues—he had supported homestead
laws, for example—deceived them.[20]

"Andrew Johnson's Reconstruction and How It Works," by Thomas Nast,
Harper's Weekly, September 1, 1866. *Library of Congress*

After ascending to the presidency, Johnson quickly tried to bring the former Confederate states back into the Union without any regard for freedpeople. He issued two proclamations on May 29, while Congress was in recess. The first granted pardons and amnesty to almost all Confederates, restoring their property rights, except to slaves, if they took an oath of loyalty to the Union. The proclamation did exclude fourteen groups, including those who had been US officials before secession, southerners who owned more than $20,000 in property, and men who held high office in the Confederacy. People in these categories would have to apply to the president for individual pardons. Johnson's second proclamation appointed William Holden—a unionist who had gone along with his home state, North Carolina, when it seceded, but who led a peace movement during the war—to be provisional governor of that state and authorized him to call a state constitutional convention. Johnson would appoint governors with the same mandate for six other former Confederate states—Mississippi, Georgia, Alabama, Florida, South Carolina, and Texas—in subsequent proclamations.

Most of the provisional governors had been unionists before the war but had supported the Confederacy when the war began. South Carolina's governor, Benjamin F. Perry, a proslavery unionist, persuaded his upcountry yeoman constituency to support secession and openly rejoiced at Lincoln's death. He argued that "this is a white men's government, intended for white men only" and declared that he still backed the *Dred Scott* decision. Hahn's replacement in Louisiana, James Madison Wells, who had opposed the Confederacy but was a rich sugar planter who owned nearly a hundred slaves, fired all of former General Nathaniel Banks's appointees. Wells appointed in their stead Confederate veterans who wanted to overturn the state constitution put into place under Lincoln's Ten Per Cent Plan. As Whitelaw Reid, a northern journalist who toured the South immediately after the war with a "pass" written by Johnson, observed, "Clearly enough, few Union men in the South, who have political aspirations, can be safely expected to advocate justice, much less generosity, to the negro, or severity to the Rebels."

Two provisional governors appointed by Johnson, Alexander Jackson

Hamilton of Texas, who had been Lincoln's choice, and Holden, surpassed such low expectations, coming to support Reconstruction and earning Johnson's ire. Lincoln had appointed William G. Brownlow, a staunch unionist, to replace Johnson as wartime governor of Tennessee. Now Brownlow, who wanted Jefferson Davis and Confederate leaders to suffer the highest penalties of the law, became an opponent of Johnson as well.

By the fall of 1865, Johnson's actions, which included quickly restoring the lands of Confederate rebels, revealed that the Republican Party was being horribly misled by him. He had wanted to be a "Moses" to black people, a boast that Lincoln had never made. One freedman noted, "things was hurt by Mr. Lincoln gettin' kilt." In his Circular 13 issued in July 1865, General Howard provided for the distribution of forty-acre plots to all loyal refugees and freedmen from the nearly one million acres of abandoned land in the South controlled by the Freedmen's Bureau, in accordance with orders issued by the Lincoln administration. Johnson ordered Howard to return all confiscated and abandoned lands to their former owners and the Bureau's Circular 15, issued in August, implemented his order. The colored convention of Virginia held the same month warned that Johnson's policies had "left us entirely at the mercy of these subjugated but unconverted rebels." In fact, "Johnson's restoration policy had effectively aborted the Bureau's land-allotment program" and a "landed emancipation" was not to be.

According to Reid, Johnson's revocation of lands distributed to freedmen caused "general confusion and uncertainty" among freedpeople and the Bureau's superintendents. Black people in the Sea Islands greeted the announcement, conveyed to them by Howard at a large meeting in an Edisto Island church, with despair. As Sidney George Andrews, who observed the meeting, put it, "To say that the negroes were overwhelmed with sorrow and dissatisfaction is to state a fact in sober phrase." The Edisto Island Committee of freedpeople expostulated with Johnson, writing: "Have we forfeited our rights of property in land?" Johnson had reversed the first tentative steps on land redistribution under Lincoln, "our Late and beloved President," returning property to those who had rebelled from those to whom it had been rightfully granted, "we who are freedman and have always been true to the Union." Johnson was deaf to their appeals. Nobody but God knew how they suffered, said one freedwoman named Sarah.

Johnson's exclusion of the Confederate elite from a general amnesty was worthless, as he began extending noblesse oblige to wealthy ex-slaveholders who now appealed to him for individual pardons. In September, he ordered all black Union soldiers removed from the South after listening to ex-Confederates complain about their presence. As Reid reported, "Negro troops are their especial detestation; and for the monstrosity of attempting to teach negroes how to read and write, they could find no words to express their scorn." By October, only 216,000 federal troops remained in the South, most of them stationed at the Mexican border. Carl Schurz, the German-American Republican and Union general, was sent by Johnson to tour the Deep South states in the summer of 1865. According to the resulting report, published in December by Congress, in many of these states the old rebels were back in power while unionists faced ostracism. Johnson was forced to forward Schurz's report to Congress, which he did without comment.

Johnson's restoration encouraged former Confederates to establish unreconstructed southern state governments that sought to reinstitute black servitude in all but name. Johnson backed the civilian authority of his restored governments, even when they started forming white state militias comprised of Confederate veterans, over that of the Union army and federal officials. Union officers and Freedmen's Bureau agents, however, continued to intervene at their own initiative in cases involving flagrant miscarriages of justice for freedpeople, at times incurring Johnson's wrath. Reid wrote, "wherever the flag is floating, it is a good place for friendless negroes to go." By December 1865, all former Confederate states, except Texas, were summarily declared restored by Johnson, and their newly elected legislatures grudgingly ratified the Thirteenth Amendment. But many of these states did not even meet the minimal requirements of Johnson's restoration: to nullify secession, repudiate debt incurred by the Confederate government, and endorse emancipation. They accepted emancipation only as a consequence of war. Mississippi and South Carolina did not repudiate Confederate debt, and simply repealed their ordinances of secession rather than disavowing them.[21]

Johnson himself called his policy "the work of restoration" rather than Reconstruction. With the president giving them a free hand, southern leaders unsurprisingly failed at what one historian has called "self-reconstruction"—indeed, failure was the point. A member of Alabama's constitutional convention under Johnson's restoration declaimed that slavery had been abolished by "the act of another, and not our act." Most fair-weather unionists who had joined the Confederacy were proslavery and served in the Confederate army. The die-hard southern unionists who had opposed secession and the Confederacy, a majority of them from the predominantly non-slaveholding areas in the southern states, were left by the wayside. Confederates and vigilante groups had persecuted them during the war, and they continued to do so after it. In Texas, German unionists had been hanged in the hundreds. "Lincoln's Loyalists," the thousands of white southerners who had fought for the Union, were shunned and derided as "scalawags," or traitors to the South. In a speech, the Black abolitionist feminist Frances Ellen Watkins Harper differentiated between "the scum of society"—Confederate leaders—and the "dregs of society"— poor whites and colored people in the South. She argued that the poor black man and the poor white man had common class interests, but that Johnson seemed unaware of that fundamental reality.[22]

Johnson has often been viewed as acting in the interests of poor whites, but in fact he acted as a former slaveowner upholding elite domination. With a sympathetic president, southern politicians did what they had always done before the war: they overreached. As military governor of Tennessee, Johnson had endorsed one of the first Black Codes, which put the newly free under the control of their former enslavers. Now, with the war over, freedpeople refused to work for ex-enslavers "without a contract for wages" or some other form of compensation for their labor, such as a share of the crop. In response, all the restored ex-Confederate states passed Black Codes in 1865 and 1866, a set of laws to vitiate black freedom and control black labor. The Black Codes included new vagrancy laws that criminalized black mobility and self-employment. Vagrancy laws in Anglo-American jurisprudence had always been directed against the poor, but in the postwar South they became a means to commandeer the labor of freedpeople and keep them confined to plantations like slaves.

According to a Mississippi law ridiculously titled "An Act to Confer Civil Rights on Freedmen, and for other purposes," freedpeople could not rent land in urban areas. According to the South Carolina code, if freedpeople were not involved in servile or agricultural labor, they had to pay a special tax. "South Carolina Re-establishing Slavery" read the headline of an article on the state's Black Code in the *New York Tribune*. South Carolina's code even allowed for whipping, a ubiquitous practice in and symbol of slavery. Laws against "enticing" black labor with better wages and penalizing black people for changing employment made a mockery of free labor. Even the most exploited northern wageworker did not face the racist and legal coercion directed at freedpeople.

The Black Codes were reminiscent of poor laws and slave codes, particularly laws restricting the rights of free blacks, who were often treated the same as slaves in the South. Arkansas's slave codes continued to operate until it passed its Black Code in 1867. The Black Codes prohibited interracial marriage, prevented black men from voting and serving on juries, and forbade black children from attending school with white children (or from attending public school at all). Misdemeanors and trumped-up charges were punished with fines and jail time, and if the convicted could not pay their fines, their labor went to any person who could. The convict lease labor system, which had already appeared on a small scale in slave states such as Kentucky before the war, became common in the South and would expand after the overthrow of Reconstruction. Under this system, prisoners could be coerced to work; many black people found themselves thrown into prison, leased to those who paid their fines, and forced to labor without pay in dismal conditions on plantations and in mines. Other laws declared that black people could be arrested for "loitering," that is, not working for whites; for preaching the Gospel without a license; or for any minor infraction such as "impudence." Some Black Codes restricted black ownership of guns and buying of liquor, and prescribed capital punishment for theft.

Apprenticeship laws, historically intended to provide education in the trades for children, were transformed by the Black Codes to allow planters to kidnap black children, remove them from their parents and families, and put them to work in the fields. In Maryland and North Carolina, thousands of black children and even adults were "apprenticed" without their or their parents' consent. Some Black Codes forced entire families, including women—who were accused of "absenteeism" for their refusal to work in the fields—and children to labor for planters. Others levied poll taxes on blacks and then forced them to labor for those who paid them. States such as Mississippi, Texas, and Florida introduced laws mandating racial segregation. In addition to the state-level Black Codes, many towns and parishes in restored states passed their own set of discriminatory ordinances, which could be even more oppressive.

With Union generals intervening to stop some of the most egregious laws in Mississippi and South Carolina, the latter being forced to repeal some laws, the next generation of Black Codes were less racially explicit but no less effective. They constituted a systematic attempt to criminalize black freedom, and their legacies endure. A law criminalizing not just vagrancy but also "disobedience" to former masters was amended, with the racial language removed, but then applied to everyone working in agriculture, lumbering, and milling, which pretty much encompassed most freedpeople. The Florida state assembly, "the most bigoted and short-sighted" of all the Johnson restoration state legislatures, passed a harsh Black Code in 1866 that allowed for the death penalty, whipping, and the medieval pillory, even after the earlier codes had come in for criticism. In Georgia, rape was punishable by death only when it involved a black man and a white woman.

While Johnson's restoration governments tried to re-create the slave past in state law, they were modernizers when it came to the economy, spending large sums on railroad subsidies and banking. Resentful of the presence of the federal government, southern whites condemned northern supporters of Reconstruction as "carpetbag-gers." But they welcomed northern capital with open arms, hoping to revive the region's economy. In many respects, Johnsonian restoration was a dress rehearsal for the "New South" economic policies of the late nineteenth and early twentieth centuries, which combined racial sub-jugation with economic modernization. Eager to revive the plantation economy, southern planters sought to keep freedpeople in a state of "semi peonage," Sumner pointed out.[23] The Black Codes were geared to restoring the plantation economy and designed to establish the subor-dination of black labor in law, so that the South might continue supply-ing the world market with cash crops like cotton and sugar previously grown by enslaved labor.

The South's failure at self-reconstruction indicated how much its elites clung to slavery even after emancipation. During the war, the enslaved reported that they were worked harder, provided with less food, and "trusted less, and watched more." The fact that so many ran away to Union lines and fought for their freedom aggravated south-ern fears, and many were swept up in the "insurrection scare of 1865." Northern teachers and Bureau agents remained puzzled at the notion of black people revolting *after* emancipation. Johnson's policies, Carl Schurz reported, only "stimulated the most dangerous reactionary ten-dencies to more reckless and baneful activity."

Most ex-slaveholders were unable to emancipate themselves from the habits of mastery even as former slaves sought to define and give meaning to their new freedom. As the *New Orleans Tribune* warned, the "rebels" were as "bitter and violent as ever" and could be dealt with only by "force." They must be "overawed and overpowered." Many southern-ers, such as the slavery apologist and scientific racist Dr. Josiah Nott of Alabama, believed that educating black people was a waste of money, though as planters told Schurz, the real reason for opposing black edu-cation was that it would spoil freedpeople for hard agricultural labor. Most planters correctly believed that African Americans would not work like slaves without some form of coercion. A Georgia planter com-plained that his former slave had shown himself unworthy of being a free worker because he refused to submit to a whipping! Schurz arrived at the obvious conclusion that black people were perfectly willing to work for themselves if they were treated well and paid reasonably.[24]

For any reconstruction to be successful, the defeated must accept the consequences of their loss. Ex-Confederates instead proved to be obdurate, especially after Johnson emboldened them through his restoration. Northern visitors to the South in 1865–1866 reported on the complete lack of contrition in the former Confederacy, and on southern determination to institute a reign of legal and extrajudicial terror over black people. Few of these visitors were abolitionists; Schurz, for example, was a moderate, antislavery Republican. Their reports were suffused with racialist and at times racist observations, but even they were shocked at the extent of what Sidney George Andrews called southern "barbarism" against freedpeople. In December 1865, Johnson's message to the Senate accompanying Schurz's report claimed that conditions in the former Confederacy were "more promising" than could be expected, despite "occasional disorders," and that "sectional animosity is surely and rapidly merging itself into a spirit of nationality." He included a short report from Ulysses Grant, general in chief of the Union army, who painted a more positive picture of the South, to counteract Schurz's.

Nearly all former rebels, Schurz noted, had not altered their view of slavery and opposed emancipation. According to his report, hatred of the Union army and northerners was not uncommon, but more disturbing were the violent reprisals against freedpeople and Freedmen's Bureau agents. Directly contradicting Johnson, Schurz wrote that the generosity shown by the federal government was not reciprocated by most southerners, who displayed *"an utter absence of national feeling* [emphasis in original]." The South was governed by "lawless characters under a system of terrorism," even with some US troops remaining in the region, because the civilian authority of Johnson's governments superseded them. Their withdrawal should not, in Schurz's view, be contemplated.[25]

Military occupation was the only means to reconstruct the slave South, as some have recently argued. But racial terror spread unabated, spurred on by Johnson's restoration. General James Deering Fessenden reported from South Carolina, "A spirit of bitterness and persecution manifests itself towards the negroes. They are shot and abused outside the immediate protection of our forces by men who announce their determination to take the law into their own hands, in defiance of our authority. To protect the negro and punish these still rebellious individuals it will be necessary to have this country pretty thickly settled with soldiers."

In Alabama, a Freedmen's Bureau commissioner documented the murder of hundreds of freedpeople as they were attempting to leave plantations. They were apprehended by patrols, whipped, killed on roads, dragged off boats, and forcefully drowned. Schurz recorded "reports of bloody outrages inflicted on colored people." He saw black men and women in hospitals whose ears had been cut off, who had been whipped, bludgeoned, and shot. He also saw dead bodies lying by the roadside and hanging from trees. Freedpeople, he wrote, were "in a panic of fright," and southern whites were "in a state of almost insane irritation against them." Schurz maintained that "wholesale massacres" would be perpetrated without the presence of federal troops. Even with US troops still stationed in the South, black people were murdered with impunity by "gentlemen of standing" as well as by what Schurz called the "rabble." In Texas, five hundred white men were indicted for murdering black people in 1865, but not one was convicted. While the situation was clearly untenable, black resilience in the face of racist terror nevertheless impressed northerners. Reid told the story of a freedman named Sandie, from Florida. Before the war, Sandie had cut his ankle and hip, and mutilated his left hand, rather than be sold, and had beaten the men attempting to sell him. After the war, he became one of the most prosperous men in Key West and even met Salmon Chase.[26]

The entire political and legal machinery of the restored Johnsonian state governments was geared to commandeering black labor,

criminalizing black freedom, and upholding white supremacy. Northern Democrats, conservatives, and economic elites applauded Johnson's politics of appeasement, seeking a quick reunion and revival of the
South's lucrative plantation economy. Radicals and abolitionists, however, became increasingly outraged at reports of the abuse and killing
of freedpeople, of the draconian Black Codes, and the failure to move
toward black citizenship. At no point, Garrison wrote, had abolitionists
deluded themselves that "the abolition of slavery against the wishes and
efforts of its supporters" would immediately secure justice for freedpeople or "remove every barrier of complexional caste." But even he
was surprised at the extent of former slaveholders' viciousness and was
convinced that the North heard only a small portion of the "enormities"
being committed against ex-slaves. One of his correspondents warned
of a system of "African peonage" being set up in the South, and Garrison
revived "The Barbarism of Slavery" column that he had written before
the war to highlight southern atrocities.

Lincoln was dead; his Presidential Reconstruction had been replaced
by Johnson's restoration. Sumner wrote that only Congress now
remained "as guardian, under the Constitution, of national safety . . . its
duty to see that every pretended government organized by recent Rebels is treated as a present nullity." It was difficult, he observed, to "measure the mischief" caused by Johnson: "looking at the distress it has
caused among loyal people by the revival of the Rebel spirit, it is heart-
rending." Douglass argued that the North was on the verge of being
"surrendered" by the "treachery and imbecility" of Johnson.

The radicals would win over much of the Republican Party, most
moderates, and a majority of northerners due to the "terrible failure"
of Johnson's restoration. They were soon demanding the overthrow of
Johnson's "White Reconstruction." In November 1866, the black abolitionist Sarah Parker Remond was on her way to Italy from England
and wrote in a public letter that she would never return to the United
States, given the tremendous damage done by Johnson to black rights
and American democracy. The "difficulties of Reconstruction," she felt,
were "immense." Thanks to Johnson, "a most glorious opportunity had
been lost, sacrificed to hatred of race and injustice." They now knew

"This Is a White Man's Government," by Thomas Nast, *Harper's Weekly*, September 5, 1868. (This image traffics in anti-Irish sentiment. Confederates, Irish immigrants, and rich men like August Belmont are portrayed as mainstays of the Democratic Party and Johnson's Restoration.)
Library of Congress

their "enemy," and must be "prepared for the worst." The president must be held in check, as must the "sources of his power"—southerners and northern copperheads. They endangered not just the freedpeople, but the liberty of all. Remond feared that the history of the injustice to colored people by the "dominant race" would never be written. She asked all the "friends of freedom" to battle anew for black rights.[27]

The seeds of Reconstruction were planted in reaction to Johnsonian restoration. Just as Lincoln had used his war powers to enact emancipation, Republicans in Congress would have to disband Johnson's restored state governments and resort to military intervention to uphold the rule of law and secure black rights in the South. The result would be a brief, shining historical moment when abolition democracy triumphed in much of the South and across the rest of the nation.

CHAPTER THREE

Abolition Democracy

It means, as understood by honest Republicans, just this much and no more: every man, no matter what his race or color, every earthly being who has an immortal soul, has an equal right to justice, honesty, and fair play with every other man; and the law should secure him those rights.

—THADDEUS STEVENS, 1868

Thaddeus Stevens, G. E. Perine & Co., New York.
Library Company of Philadelphia

In his history of Reconstruction published in 1935, *Black Reconstruction*, W. E. B. DuBois proposed a different term for the attempt to establish black citizenship after the Civil War: "abolition democracy." As he saw, the demand for black citizenship had its roots in the abolition movement. Abolitionists did not simply work toward an end to slavery, but also for black equality. Henry Wilson, in his three-volume

History of the Rise and Fall of the Slave Power in America, likewise traced the origins of Reconstruction to the abolitionists. Their project was realized by Radical Republicans such as Charles Sumner and Thaddeus Stevens, whom DuBois anointed the seers of American democracy.[1] They were at the vanguard of the effort to thoroughly reconstruct southern slave societies and establish an antislavery state. Sumner, Stevens, and their colleagues did not always control the policies of the federal government, but their abolitionist vision informed Reconstruction.

The alliance between abolitionists and antislavery politicians, forged in part through the push to elect Lincoln twice, would hold during Reconstruction. Two simultaneous processes defined it: an unprecedented constitutional crisis at the national level caused by the showdown between President Andrew Johnson and the Republican Congress; and the push by African Americans for Reconstruction laws and constitutional amendments. Abolition democracy meant the inauguration of a progressive, interracial democracy, securing political and civil rights for freedpeople and putting access to land and education on the nation's agenda. It was not the apotheosis of the republic created by the founders in the late eighteenth century, but a bold reimagining of it. Abolition democracy defined the Second American Republic.

After attempting to work with Johnson and in reaction to atrocities committed by unrepentant Confederates, the Republican Party's moderate and radical wings united to launch the era traditionally defined as Reconstruction. Opposed every step of the way by Democrats, conservatives (some of whom fled to the Democratic Party), southern planters, ex-Confederates, and the president, congressional Republicans laid the legal foundations of abolition democracy. Congress was now the "guardian of national safety," according to Sumner. The historic Thirty–Ninth Congress (1865–1867) was more than equal to the challenge. As its contemporary historian put it, "It depended upon the decisions of Congress whether the expected results of our victories should be realized or lost."

When the Thirty-Ninth Congress convened in December 1865, the egregious Black Codes were in the news. Johnson had issued pardons indiscriminately to former Confederates and wealthy planters. Republicans in Congress soon made black citizenship the condition for the reentry of rebel states into the Union, with Representative James Ashley arguing that all Johnson had to do was endorse "loyal suffrage" of black and white southern unionists. Sumner offered ten resolutions on Reconstruction, reminding the Senate of its constitutional duty to "guarantee to every State a republican form of government" and to enforce black freedom, as stipulated in the Thirteenth Amendment. In the house, Stevens's resolutions on Reconstruction required that freedpeople "liberated by the operations of the war and the Constitutional Amendment" be treated equally before the law and given homesteads. Sumner leapt ahead of Stevens when it came to black male suffrage, Stevens ahead of Sumner on land reform.

An imposing figure at six feet four inches, Sumner embodied the abolitionist movement in politics. DuBois wrote, "Charles Sumner was at that time thirty-five years of age, handsome, but heavy of carriage, a scholar and gentleman, no leader of men but a leader of thought, and one of the finest examples of New England culture and American courage." His speeches laid down the "Magna Carta of American democracy," equality before the law for all. A tireless advocate of black rights, big and small, Sumner introduced, at the very start of the Thirty-Ninth Congress, a memorial from the American Freedmen's Aid Commission asking for the continuance of the Freedmen's Bureau as well as a bill to reinstate the Sherman land grants to ex-slaves, which had been revoked by Johnson. He was especially critical of Johnson's attempt to "whitewash" the "sickening and heart-rending outrages" that saw the "Human Rights" of freedpeople violated by "Rebel barbarism." Sumner had received the severed finger of a black man enclosed in a letter: "You old son of a bitch, I send you a piece of one of your friends, and if that bill of yours passes I will have a piece of you."

On December 4, 1865, Senator Benjamin Wade of Ohio, a champion of "impartial suffrage" for blacks and women, introduced a bill to give black men in the District of Columbia the right to vote. Opponents organized a referendum on black male suffrage in which voters in Washington, DC rejected the proposition overwhelmingly, over 6,000 against and only 35 votes for it. Undeterred, Sumner presented a memorial for black enfranchisement, observing, "Squatters who for generations have squatted on the rights of others do not quietly give up their claim." Abolitionists had long targeted the nation's capital because it was completely under federal jurisdiction, and the Lincoln administration had first instituted emancipation in the city. Unsurprisingly, it became a testing ground for Reconstruction.

The congressional committee on the District of Columbia was stacked with radicals: Sumner, Wade, Lot Morrill of Maine, and Richard Yates of Illinois. As another radical, Representative George W. Julian, put it, "I demand the ballot for the colored men of the District on the broad ground of absolute right." The debate saw Republicans invoking African American achievements and the principles of republican government, while Democrats retorted with crude, racist slurs. Henry Wilson—who was not only Reconstruction's first chronicler, but a Republican senator—rebuked the "brutality and vulgarity" of their language. In January 1866, the House passed a bill enfranchising black men in DC, but it failed to get a hearing in the Senate. In May, the House prohibited federal territories from denying citizens the right to vote "because of race or color," and again, the Senate did not act on the House bill. A year later, a Republican-dominated Congress would enfranchise black men in Washington over Johnson's veto.[2]

While the momentum for black male suffrage built slowly, Republicans in Congress moved to ensure that the southern states were forced to respect Black people's other civil rights. The showdown began when delegations from ex-Confederate states sought to present their credentials to the Thirty-Ninth Congress in December 1865. They found their most determined opponent in Thaddeus Stevens. At seventy-three, Stevens remained a master parliamentary tactician and was "not attended with any perceptible abatement of the intellectual vivacity or fire of youth." He had supported black rights when it was an even less popular position. Stevens's commitment to black equality might have stemmed from a physical disability—he was club-footed—that led him to empathize with victims of oppression. Some have speculated that this lifelong bachelor may have had a relationship with his black housekeeper,

Mrs. Lydia Hamilton Smith, though his egalitarian views long predated her presence in his life.

Even before Congress reconvened, Stevens had floated the idea of returning "the rebel states into a territorial condition" in preparation for a thoroughgoing Reconstruction. As he wrote to Johnson in the summer of 1865, "Among all the leading Union men of the North with whom I have had intercourse I do not find one who approves of your policy. They believe that 'Restoration' as announced by you will destroy our party (which is of but little consequence) and will greatly injure the country." In a speech to his constituents, Stevens suggested confiscating "the estate of every rebel belligerent" valued at over $10,000 or exceeding two hundred acres. Freedpeople and unionists would receive farms. There can be, he said, "no 'mutilated' restoration. That would be the work of Congress alone and would be 'Reconstruction.'"

Abolitionists concurred. As early as July 1865, Wendell Phillips urged Congress to "refuse credentials of these rebel members." No rebel state, wrote William Lloyd Garrison, should be admitted without a "longer probation," and he undertook a lecture tour to criticize Johnson's elevation of "quasi rebels" in the South. Stevens asserted that only Congress had the constitutional authority to admit new states and guarantee that they had a republican form of government. He proposed constitutional amendments to eliminate the three-fifths clause and to grant voting rights to black men—and thereby ensure that they were represented in Congress. Republicans must "rebuke," he maintained, the "fashionable" doctrine that "this is a white man's government." That was "political blasphemy" against the Declaration of Independence, an "atrocious" idea that had sent Chief Justice Taney to "everlasting fame; and, I fear, to everlasting fire." In *The Liberator*'s last issue, Garrison reprinted Stevens's speech in its entirety. Abolitionist Theodore Tilton congratulated the congressman for "throw[ing] down the gauntlet." Stevens was inundated with letters from southern unionists praising him.

Following a resolution by Stevens, the Thirty-Ninth Congress created a Joint Committee on Reconstruction with nine members from the House and six from the Senate on December 13, 1865. Stevens had outmaneuvered Democratic roadblocks in the House, and his resolution had passed the Senate despite opposition from conservative Republican allies of Johnson and Democrats. Stevens and a moderate, Senator William Pitt Fessenden of Maine, would cochair the committee. Reverdy Johnson and two other Democrats secured seats. Wilson sized them up well when he remarked on the "spaniel-like fidelity" of Democrats to the South. When Congress reconvened in the New Year, it passed Stevens's majority resolution from the committee that rejected the reentry of the eleven rebel states and declared them to still be in a state of insurrection. Their delegations returned to the South, after the House clerk on Stevens's behest refused to seat them.[3]

Simultaneously, African Americans and abolitionists demanded that the Freedmen's Bureau, set to expire in 1866, be extended beyond its original one-year lifespan. The 1865 colored convention in Boston chaired by the black abolitionist Charles Remond called "upon the Congress of the United States, either by general law or through the agency of the Freedmen's Bureau, to throw around the loyal blacks such protection as shall secure them from hatred of their former owners." Senator Lyman Trumbull, chairman of the Judiciary Committee, announced in December his intention to introduce a bill to make the Bureau permanent and to create a mechanism for judicial redress for freedpeople facing abuse by state courts and ex-Confederates. He was heeding Henry Wilson's call to "continue the Freedmen's Bureau, clothe it with additional powers, and if necessary back it up with military force, to see that the rights of men made free by the first clause of the constitutional amendment are protected."

Democrats and conservatives strenuously opposed Trumbull's new Freedmen's Bureau bill, complaining about its cost and expanding the powers of the federal government, though simple racism was behind both critiques. Senator Willard Saulsbury of Delaware objected that "the great mass of the people have been taxed to support in idleness a class who are too lazy or too worthless to support themselves." The bill, according to Senator Garrett Davis of Kentucky, would establish "a great system of poor houses for the support of lazy negroes all over the southern States." Saulsbury, Davis, and their allies could not fathom why freedpeople needed protection. Senator James McDougall of California delivered vicious speeches against both "Africans" and "Indians," rhet-oric typical of racists in the American West, to oppose the bill.

Notwithstanding these racist harangues, the Republican- and northern-dominated Thirty-Ninth Congress passed Trumbull's Freed-men's Bureau bill on February 6, 1866, along party lines. Trumbull's bill not only extended the life of the Bureau; it also restored, for a period of three years, the Sherman land grants revoked by Johnson, and set aside other abandoned and confiscated lands for freedpeople. As Trumbull put it, "I believe that a homestead is worth more to these people than almost anything else; that if you will make the negro an independent man he must have a home; that as long as the relation of employer and employee exists between blacks and whites, you will necessarily have a dependent population." In the House, Stevens offered an amendment to make the land grants permanent, but it was defeated. Trumbull's bill was sent to Johnson for signing.

Even after months of Johnson's acting to placate the South, most Republicans did not anticipate the depth of his opposition to the Bureau. After all, in his annual message to Congress in December 1865, Johnson had voiced his support for the protection of freedmen's secu-rity and "just return for their labor." But on February 19, 1866, John-son peremptorily vetoed the Freedmen's Bureau Bill. He argued that the bill was unconstitutional because it extended the military jurisdic-tion of the Bureau—he was explicitly repudiating the extension of war powers. Johnson disputed the idea that the federal government had a duty to protect freedpeople. Ignoring racist violence and the Black Codes, Johnson recommended that the protection of freedpeople be left to the very southern governments that were violating their rights. Only "secessionists and copperheads," noted Garrison, sustained the "recreant President."

Johnson made matters worse with an unhinged attack against radi-cals and abolitionists on February 22, Washington's birthday, in which the president identified Stevens, Sumner, and Phillips as his mortal "ene-mies" and "traitors." Even a friend of the president wondered whether Johnson was drunk; he also managed to alienate moderate Republi-cans, including Trumbull and Fessenden. Eight northern legislatures passed resolutions censuring him. In June, Johnson did sign the Southern Homestead Act of 1866, an attempt to extend homestead legislation to loyal southerners. The initiative began with freedpeople, who, soon after the war ended, had formed homestead associations to acquire land. Though some southern black people acquired land under the new law, most met with staunch opposition from corrupt local officials and were generally given inferior land. Stevens asked Johnson to account for all the pardons he had given ex-Confederates and the confiscated property restored to them, as well as the freedpeople displaced from lands allotted to them by the Freedmen's Bureau and Union army.

Though Congress failed to override Johnson's veto of Trumbull's bill in July, the House passed a more moderate Freedmen's Bureau bill authored by Representative Thomas Eliot. Like his Senate counterparts, Eliot believed that "we owe something to these freedmen," though he incorporated some objections from the bill's critics. Eliot's bill extended the life of the Bureau by only two years and reduced its staffing and funding. Instead of restoring the Sherman land grants and setting land aside for establishing homesteads for freedmen, it recognized the sale of land confiscated from former rebels for nonpayment of taxes to freedpeople and made land available for purchase to them and unionists in twenty-acre lots. The land provision was put in at Stevens's initiative. The law also enjoined the Bureau to cooperate with freedmen's aid societies to provide education for freedpeople. Radicals in the Senate failed to win a two-thirds majority needed to add an amendment that would have provided for a more robust land redistribution. Wilson at least managed to secure an amendment allowing freedpeople to stay on the Sherman land grants until their crop was harvested. It also required planters to reimburse them for improvements on the land.

Yet Johnson vetoed Eliot's bill, too, calling it "class legislation" for freedpeople. This time both houses of Congress quickly overrode his veto by a two-thirds majority in each. Saulsbury bloviated, "You suppose the people of this country are so absolutely demented that for mere love of the idle, worthless negro race, they are going to submit to all this burden of taxation, and that this false philanthropy, the parent of idleness and vagabondism as far as that race is concerned, is going to waft you again into the seats of power." Though the Freedmen's Bureau had been established on somewhat firmer ground, the obstructionism of Johnson and conservatives had effectively stopped land reform.[4]

In addition to renewing the Freedmen's Bureau, the Thirty-Ninth Congress also passed the first federal civil rights law which is still invoked in legal cases involving racial discrimination today. The day Congress reconvened in January 1866 after its holiday recess, Sumner presented a memorial from Alabama's black convention that detailed church burnings, daily "violence at the hands of whites," imprisonment and hard labor, and extortion that freedpeople suffered. A committee of colored citizens from Mississippi lamented that they could not even hold a convention given the violent opposition of locals. Sumner presented petitions from African Americans and letters from officials documenting attempts to sell freedpeople into slavery in Cuba and Brazil. He became a conduit for black concerns in Congress.

African Americans and radicals demanded civic equality; moderates like Trumbull provided the legal mechanism. Trumbull contended that the Civil Rights Act of 1866, which passed Congress in March, was the most important congressional act since the Thirteenth Amendment, in that it "secured freedom in fact and equality in civil rights to all persons in the United States." Anticipating Democrats' objections on the grounds of states' rights, Trumbull clarified that the act "will have no operation in any State where the laws are equal, where all persons have the same civil rights without regard to color and race." Democrat Garrett Davis argued that the government was a closed corporation of white men that only Europeans could join. Stevens noted of congressional Democrats, "for so small a number, they have made a most venomous fight."

The law established national civic equality without regard to race, color, or "previous condition of slavery or involuntary servitude" for all Americans, except "Indians not taxed," who belonged to their own sovereign nations. It was clearly designed to invalidate Black Codes in bestowing the right to make contracts, hold property, sue, and testify, though not the right to vote. It made the federal government, the courts, the Freedmen's Bureau, the president, and the army responsible for the enforcement of these rights and for the punishment of anyone who would violate them. Ironically, Trumbull, a student of legal precedent, borrowed some enforcement mechanisms from the Fugitive Slave Act of 1850, but the Civil Rights Act went well beyond it. It bestowed the Freedmen's Bureau and the army with legal power, further expanding the administrative capacities of the federal government.

Put simply, the law made it the duty of the federal government to protect the civil rights of all its citizens. The Thirteenth Amendment, Trumbull pointed out, rendered "null and void" all the discriminatory "laws relating to freedmen" passed in the "insurrectionary States." The Black Codes did not quite reenslave the black man, "yet they deprive him of all the rights of a freeman." Laws that did not allow black people to travel, preach, or own property made it difficult, he said, to demarcate where "freedom ceases and slavery begins." Such rights would now be bestowed not just on freedpeople, but also on other "races," including Chinese immigrants arriving along the Pacific Coast; the law "perhaps involves a future immigration to this country of which we have no conception." Edgar Cowan, a Republican and a Johnson ally who would soon defect to the Democrats, argued that the Chinese and "Hottentots"—or the "barbarian races of Asia or of Africa"—should not be treated like European immigrants. Where is the line to be drawn, he asked—would it apply to his children, his apprentices, as well as the "quasi servitude which the wife to some extent owes her husband?" Westerners joined in, asking whether "digger Indians," a derogatory term for indigenous nations who supposedly dug roots for food, and Indians who had adopted "the white man's" ways, were eligible for citizenship. Trumbull replied that the law only excluded Indians "who do not recognize the Government of the United States at all, who are not subject to our laws."

As opponents of the Civil Rights Act grasped, the fight for black rights did not exclude other groups, but rather expanded rights for all. Congressional Republicans were proposing a fundamentally new conception of the federal government and citizenship. The Americas, Senator Lot Morrill argued, were "an asylum for the oppressed of all nations and of all races." In the House, Representative John Thayer concurred, and remarked that it is the "universal law" of nations that all "born upon the soil" were citizens. Yet in one respect, the bill was not progressive enough. Every argument made in protection of freedpeople's civil rights, Sumner pointed out, could be applied to their political rights— namely, the right to vote, which had been left out of it.

Except that Johnson would have none of it. In February, Frederick Douglass and George T. Downing had led a delegation of the National Equal Rights League to ask Johnson to support black male suffrage. In response, Johnson claimed that, in his former life as a slaveholder, he had been "their slave instead of their being mine," and that slaves had united with their masters to oppress poor whites. Johnson quarreled with the delegation incessantly, arguing that black male suffrage would lead to a race war—ignoring their argument that they needed the ballot for self-protection—and recommending colonization. Douglass answered the president: "You enfranchise your enemies and disfranchise your friends." When the delegation left, Johnson revealed his true feelings, as recorded by his secretary: "Those damned sons of bitches thought they had me in a trap! I know that damned Douglass; he's just like any n——, & he would sooner cut a white man's throat than not!"

Though the Civil Rights Act did not include a provision for black voting, Johnson still vetoed it. In his veto message, Johnson dropped all pretense of concern for freedpeople. He argued that those newly emerged from slavery cannot be said to have all the "requisite qualifications" for citizenship and complained that the law would make citizens of all blacks, Chinese, taxed Indians, and "gypsies." He even claimed that it discriminated against white foreigners by making all African Americans born in the country citizens. In declaring "the perfect equality of the white and colored races" in federal law, it infringed on the rights of the states to discriminate based on race, for instance by upending laws against interracial marriage. Endorsing the Black Codes, Johnson charged that the Civil Rights Act interfered with the judicial authority of the states to punish their citizens and was thus unconstitutional. In providing for a federal remedy in cases of discrimination, it operated "in favor of the colored and against the white race." Pioneering an argument that is still used by racists today, Johnson claimed that in giving rights to black people, the government necessarily took them away from whites, as if rights were a finite resource. He also rejected the law because it "centralized" power, by linking black equality to the federal government.

Johnson's veto message mixed racism with states' rights rhetoric, anti–big government views, and strict constructionism, a messy pottage inherited from the proslavery argument of the antebellum era. Responding to Johnson, Trumbull thought it "preposterous" that states should have the right to discriminate and invoked the second clause of the Thirteenth Amendment that enjoined Congress to make laws to enforce emancipation. If the government could not secure even the basic civil rights of freedpeople, "then the constitutional amendment proclaiming freedom to all the inhabitants of the land was a cheat and a delusion." In April, both houses quickly overrode Johnson's veto, the first such override for a major piece of legislation in US history. As shown above, Congress would override him again when Eliot's Freedmen's Bureau bill was sent to his desk months later. In the words of one observer, "The defection of the President from the principles of the party which had elected him, so far from dividing and destroying that party, had rather given it strength and consolidation."[5]

Just as the framers of the US Constitution had not anticipated secession and Civil War, neither had they anticipated the reconstruction of rebel states into the Union. Democrat Andrew Ward of Kentucky admitted that the "Constitution does not provide for its own destruction," and that there were no historical precedents "to control our action; the situation is new." While Johnson voiced old states' rights claims, Republicans brought abolitionist jurisprudence to life. Political abolitionists had long argued that the federal government should immediately abolish slavery to secure the constitutional guarantee of republican government in the slave states and that the Bill of Rights included black people, arguments that Republicans invoked during Reconstruction.

Henry Wilson pointed out that freedpeople were denied the protections of the fifth amendment in Johnson's restored southern states. The idea that freedpeople should be guaranteed basic civil rights became commonplace among Republicans, and Radicals, abolitionists, and African Americans pushed for black male suffrage. After earlier failures, Stevens introduced, in July 1866, a bill that would grant the right to vote to all men regardless of race. In an echo of the Three Fifths clause of the Constitution, the restored southern states uniformly barred African Americans from voting but now counted them fully, at five-fifths, toward congressional representation.

Republicans rooted their authority to implement Reconstruction in various constitutional theories. To radicals such as Sumner, the southern states had committed "state suicide" in seceding. Stevens had argued that they should be treated as "conquered territories," and be readmitted to the Union only if they accepted emancipation and black rights. The "dead carcasses" of slave states, a term employed by Stevens that the copperhead Democratic senator from Indiana, Daniel Voorhees, objected to, should be replaced with republican, free states. Republican congressman William Newell of New Jersey would not go as far as to accept "the dogma of state suicide," but rejected all talk of states' rights as a ruse designed to create an "oligarchy to deprive the people of their liberties."

By the time the Thirty-Ninth Congress convened at the end of 1865, some moderate Republicans agreed with the radicals. Senator Jacob Howard of Michigan maintained that states "hostile to the authority of the United States" should be treated as "conquered communities." Representative Halbert Paine of Wisconsin stated that the rebel states were "politically dead" and that he would never vote to admit a state back into the Union that gave the ballot to "white traitors" rather than "black patriots." Sumner introduced a flurry of bills to guarantee republican government in the South. Representative Samuel Shellabarger of Ohio argued that the rebel states had "forfeited" their rights by leaving the Union. Conservative Republicans such as *The New York Times* editor Henry J. Raymond—a Johnson ally who wanted "friendly relations" with the South—and Senator James Doolittle of Wisconsin insisted that the rebel states had not lost their original character even after waging war on the republic.

While not all Republicans were willing to go as far as the Radicals, most agreed that the federal government should continue to exercise its war powers to make sure that slavery was not reestablished and black freedom was secured. Richard Henry Dana Jr., an antislavery lawyer and well-known writer, expressed this view in his "grasp of war" theory, according to which the victors could and should demand certain conditions from the losers. As he argued, "We have a right to hold the rebels in the grasp of war until we have obtained whatever the public safety and the public faith require." Moreover, "we have the right to require" that freedmen should be able to own land, to testify in courts, to bear arms, and to have an "impartial ballot." Individual states can have their own governments and constitutions but must adhere to "democratic principles."[6]

The desire to ground Reconstruction in the Constitution led to the passage of the most important amendment to the Constitution, to that point or since, and the single most significant act of the Thirty-Ninth Congress: the Fourteenth Amendment. With slavery dead, Congress debated a new basis for congressional representation. Under the three-fifths clause, enslaved people's mere existence had added to the political power of their enslavers. Why should the southern states now gain extra congressional representation for their entire free black population "upon no better basis than the unvoting and therefore unrepresented colored people of the South?" Republican representative Burton Cook called such a notion taxation without representation on "a grand scale." After entertaining seventy proposals, the Joint Committee on Reconstruction proposed an amendment in January 1866 that would penalize any state that denied any male citizen the right to vote by a proportionate loss of congressional representation. It passed the House but not the Senate. Not just Democrats but radicals like Sumner opposed it because, as he put it, he had hoped that "the day of compromise with wrong had passed forever. . . . A moral principle cannot be compromised." Northern states with small black populations could deny them suffrage without undergoing much loss of representation, he noted.

In an erudite speech, Sumner made his case, perhaps the only senator until then to quote the German philosopher Immanuel Kant on the floor. A month later, he reiterated his guiding principles: "Political Equality without Distinction of Color" and "No Compromise of Human Rights." Abolitionists likewise balked at the amendment, which could effectively allow racial exclusion with loss of representation in Congress, even if such policies would now come at a political cost. They also took note that some Republican moderates, such as Fessenden, were arguing that freedmen were "ignorant" and "uneducated" and so should not be given the right to vote outright. Senator George Williams of Oregon, an ex-Democrat, said that it was not clear who was more ignorant, freedpeople or "the poor whites of the South who delight in shooting"—and who "gratify" their "savage tastes by burning"—black people. Not only did he ignore the role of elites in fomenting racist terror, but he conceded that states could deprive people of the right to vote.

Sumner presented a petition from Downing, Douglass, and others criticizing the amendment, and another from abolitionists, including Gerrit Smith, demanding black male suffrage. Garrison deemed his speech "eloquent and unanswerable," saying that it was based on "absolute justice and eternal right." The *New Orleans Tribune* also praised Sumner's unyielding devotion to the idea of equal political rights for African Americans. Henry Highland Garnet wrote Sumner directly, expressing the "gratitude of my entire race for your fearless and radical advocacy of the rights of all men." Sumner's opposition initially defeated the amendment in the Senate, where, Representative Stevens complained, "self-righteous Republicans" had united with "unrighteous copperheads," one of the few times the two men diverged. Stevens supported the amendment, even though it did not directly bestow the right to vote to black men: "It falls far short of my wishes, but it fulfills my hopes." He lived "among men and not among angels." Wilson, too, supported the amendment, believing it would lead to black male suffrage.

At the end of April, the joint committee proposed a new amendment that nationalized the first eight amendments to the Constitution and gave constitutional sanctity to the idea of national citizenship introduced by the new Civil Rights Act. Representative John Bingham of Ohio, who had prosecuted Lincoln's assassins and would prosecute Johnson during his impeachment trial, was behind the first move. For years, abolitionists had argued that the Bill of Rights, as Bingham anointed the amendments, was applicable to free and enslaved African Americans. The *National Anti Slavery Standard* printed a "proposed amendment" in every issue starting on July 22, 1865. Its text read, in part: "No state shall make any distinctions in civil rights and privileges among the naturalized citizens of the United States residing within its limits, or among persons born on its soil, of parents permanently resident there, on account of race, color or descent."

The first section of what became the Fourteenth Amendment, formulated by Bingham, encapsulated this guarantee of equality before the law and of national citizenship to all persons born or naturalized in the United States. It said that no state could make laws that abridged the "privileges or immunities" of citizens, divest them of life, liberty, and property without "the due process of law," or deny them "equal protection of laws." Unlike the representation clause that introduced the word "male" into the Constitution, Bingham's language referred to "persons." The purposefully broad, egalitarian language of the Fourteenth Amendment would later be used by disfranchised groups, including women and gay people, to claim equality before the law. The promise of national birthright citizenship, meanwhile, included children of immigrants from across the globe, much to the perennial ire of conservatives.

The second section did away with the Three Fifths clause, stating that all persons would be counted for purposes of representation except "Indians not taxed." It also penalized states with loss of representation in proportion to the number of adult male citizens denied the vote. Senator Charles Buckalew of Pennsylvania, a Democrat, warned that any state in "which persons of an inferior race or color may be found, whether Asiatics or Africans," would be subject to this "constitutional pressure"; he was trying to appeal to anti-Chinese sentiment in the Pacific states. Representative William Higby of California, another Democrat, went further, stating that "the Chinese are nothing but a pagan race" who cannot make "good citizens." Meanwhile, James Doolittle's attempt to exclude Indians living on reservations—those "subject to the jurisdiction of the United States who ought not to be the citizens of the United States," as he put it—failed by a vote of thirty to ten. His racist depictions of "Digger Indians" in California and the "wild Indians" of the West left no doubt of his views. Native Americans in his state, Wisconsin, he claimed, were "subjects" or "wards." For all its promise, the amendment's second section has never been implemented. Even when southern states disfranchised black men after the overthrow of Reconstruction, they suffered no loss of congressional representation.

The third section barred those politicians who had joined the Confederacy after holding office in the United States and taking an oath of allegiance to the Constitution, from ever holding office again, though Congress could remove the restriction on an individual by a two-thirds vote. A more punitive measure, denying such people the right to vote, appeared in the earlier iteration of the amendment and was done away with. Never have traitors felt the hand of law so lightly. The fourth section upheld the payment of the nation's public debt but repudiated the Confederate debt. (Current political threats not to raise the nation's debt ceiling are in violation of the Constitution.) The fifth section gave Congress the power to enforce the amendment with appropriate legislation. On June 13, 1866, both houses passed the amendment, with even Sumner voting for it.

Secretary of State William Seward had the amendment sent to the states as required by the Constitution, even though Johnson noted churlishly in his annual message to Congress in December 1866 that it did not meet his approval because the Confederate states were not in the Union when it passed Congress. Despite Johnson's opposition, the first southern state to ratify the amendment was his home state of Tennessee, whose staunchly unionist Governor Brownlow called the legislature to consider it on July 4th. Accordingly, Tennessee was readmitted into the Union by congressional resolution in 1866 despite the attempts of radicals, including Sumner and Representative George S. Boutwell of Massachusetts, to make black male voting a condition of readmission. Brownlow agreed with the radicals, however, and Tennessee would enact black male suffrage the next year.[7] Decades later, Tennessee would be the last state to narrowly ratify the Nineteenth Amendment, giving women the right to vote.

The actions of the Thirty-Ninth Congress played out during a moment of increasing violence in the South. The former rebel states, emboldened by Johnson, proved to be infertile ground for an interracial democracy. As the *New Orleans Tribune* editorialized, "No reconciliation, no repentance, no common sense can be expected." It was clear that "Pro-slavery men, used to despotism in their very home, and debased by the traffic in human flesh, have very strange ideas about human rights and human duties." As if trying to prove their critics correct, southern authorities orchestrated two race riots—essentially pogroms—in the summer of 1866 that drew national attention. The first started in Memphis on May 1. The local police, known for their brutality against black residents, disrupted a gathering of black Union soldiers who were hailing Lincoln, with one officer saying, "Your old father, Abe Lincoln, is dead and damned." The Irish-dominated police force was joined by firemen and ex-Confederates. Incited by the city recorder, the mob indiscriminately attacked Memphis's black community, whose numbers had swollen with the migration of freedpeople from the countryside seeking the protection of the Bureau and education for their children in its many schools. The massacre lasted for four days. The Union army did not intervene to restore order until the mob had mostly spent itself, with General George Stoneman finally declaring martial law. He was investigated for dereliction of duty but would be exonerated.

African Americans in Memphis—as even Stoneman, a Democrat, admitted to the House committee investigating the massacre —did nothing "except to be killed and abused." Forty-eight people, all but two black, and including children, had been murdered, five black women were raped, and black homes were looted. "Scanty" though they might have been, the homes "contained the hard earnings of many hours of labor," reported the Freedmen's Bureau. Black churches and schools,

"Scenes in Memphis, Tennessee, During the Riot," *Harper's Weekly*, May 26, 1866. *Library of Congress*

including one called the Lincoln Chapel that had been set up by the AMA, were burned to the ground, and black soldiers robbed of hundreds of dollars of their pay. Despite warning that details of the rapes were of "too shocking and disgusting a character" to be included in its report, the House committee described the multiple acts of sexual violence, including one of a crippled woman, by gangs of men. Another freedwoman, Mandy Wilburn, testified that the mob "abused me very badly," robbed her husband, and set fire to their home. The Bureau collected many such testimonies from victims.

The committee collected nearly four hundred pages' worth of evidence. One northern newspaper remarked on the "demoniac spirit of the southern whites toward freedmen" and how it thoroughly discredited Johnson's policy of appeasement. A minority Democratic report by George S. Shanklin of Kentucky, commending the restoration of state governments and recommending the disbandment of the Freedmen's Bureau as a "manufacturer of paupers and vagabonds," went nowhere. The racist mob, though, had succeeded in its purpose, terrorizing thousands of black people as well as northern teachers and ministers into permanently fleeing the city. As Elihu Washburn, who chaired the committee, wrote to Stevens, "The rebel spirit here is rampant, defiant, intolerant. . . . Instead of rebels being reconstructed as Union men, I find some of our late Union men re-constructed as very good rebels."[8]

The Thirty-Ninth Congress went into recess on July 28, 1866. Two days later, another massacre in New Orleans signaled both the triumph and the death of Johnsonian restoration. Even Louisiana's conservative unionist governor, James Madison Wells, became alarmed at the growing power of ex-Confederates and reconvened the state's constitutional convention, which had first met in 1864, to consider black male suffrage. Around two hundred black people marching down the city streets in support of suffrage greeted twenty-five white members of the convention, who were sympathetic to their cause. But the local police, composed largely of ex-Confederates and aligned with the city's ex-Confederate mayor, went on a rampage in response to this demonstration of interracial solidarity, resulting in the murder of forty-four African Americans, most of them Union veterans, and three white Republicans, with over a hundred other black people, many of them merely bystanders, wounded. The attackers killed, tortured, and shot indiscriminately into the convention building. As Jean-Charles Houzeau, who was attending the convention, wrote, it was a "frightful massacre." The planters hoped to stop all talk of black rights through this "bloodbath." Wendell Phillips called it "The President's Riot."

The *Tribune* publicized the details of the massacre, leading to the creation of another congressional committee to investigate it. Yet the message southern rebels were sending to Washington was perfectly clear: Any attempt to secure black rights would meet political terror and violence. Houzeau wrote that "isolated killings" continued after the massacre, and that "white liberals" left the city fearing for their lives. General Philip H. Sheridan, military commander for Louisiana and Texas, reported to General Grant that the mob attacked the convention "with fire-arms, clubs, and knives in a manner so unnecessary and atrocious as to compel me to say that it was murder." Sheridan recommended martial law, concluding that it was no riot but "an absolute massacre," an instance of "la terreur blanche," or white terrorism. Besides the massacres in Memphis and New Orleans, the Union army reported numerous atrocities elsewhere, such as a black man being burned alive on a stake outside Macon, Georgia. In May 1866 a terror group had burned a black settlement in Pine Bluff, Arkansas, and murdered twenty-four African American men, women, and children.[9]

Abolitionists sounded the alarm by not just reporting on brutality and mass murder in the South, but also through their coverage of the Morant Bay Rebellion by freedpeople in Jamaica, which resulted in the massacre of hundreds by soldiers called out by the British governor Edward J. Eyre. Abolitionist Samuel J. May wrote that if the United States were not careful it would end up like Jamaica, with blacks reduced to semi-servitude and political subjection. Black abolitionist William Wells Brown emphasized the transnational lessons of emancipation. The French, he pointed out, were still trying to reenslave Haiti, while the planters in Jamaica, thirty years after emancipation, still harbored ill will for "colored people."[10]

Andrew Johnson seemed to revel in the riots. As he wrote in an 1866 letter, "This is a country for white men, and by God, as long as I am President, it shall be a government for white men." The president's words, said Sumner, were like "dragon teeth" that had sprung "armed men. Witness Memphis, Witness New Orleans. Who can doubt that the President is the author of these tragedies?" Three members of Johnson's cabinet resigned in protest. In an attempt to subvert Congress, Johnson and a handful of conservative Republicans and Democrats called for a National Union convention in Philadelphia, to form a new party and marginalize moderate and radical Republicans. The convention took place in August, and in his address to the attendees, Johnson charged that the "National Congress" was enslaving southerners. Republicans stayed away, with conservative members of the party deciding they were unable to tolerate the presence of the former radical William Seward—who now supported Johnson. Ex-Confederates dominated. Even the notorious copperhead Clement Vallandigham, whom Lincoln had deported to the Confederacy, withdrew from the convention. In an act of poetic justice, a Philadelphia pickpocket robbed David Wardlaw, author of South Carolina's Black Code.

After the convention, Johnson undertook a "swing around the circle" campaign through major northern cities to make his case against Reconstruction. While received well by business interests in New York and Philadelphia, he was heckled elsewhere, particularly toward the end of his tour. Johnson was widely seen as demeaning the office of the presidency. When people shouted at him to hang Jeff Davis, he called for the hanging of Stevens and Phillips. A contemporary irreverently anointed him a "Presidential Ass." In Springfield, Johnson visited Lincoln's grave, much to Mary Todd Lincoln's chagrin, and blamed the radicals for the New Orleans massacre. Johnson's continued embarrassments, combined with reports of unending violence from the South, only helped Republicans, who won a thumping majority in both houses of Congress in the midterm elections of 1866. It was a rare exception to the political rule that the party in power usually loses in the midterms, though it was also an unusual instance where a president and his nominal party were at odds.[11] A majority of northern voters, who voted for the nonextension of slavery in 1860 and emancipation in 1864, voted for securing black civil rights in 1866.

It had become apparent to all except Johnson and northern Democrats that ex-Confederates continued to commit war crimes in a time of supposed peace. As Stevens described the situation, for two years "the loyal people of those ten states have endured all the horrors of the worst anarchy of any country." The war, he said, in an address to the Union's "citizen soldiers," was not over. It was Congress's "imperative duty to bring great criminals to justice." Francis Leiber, who wrote Lincoln's War Code that justified wartime emancipation, had been the first to make the argument that military occupation was necessary to secure Reconstruction. What followed proved to be an exception to the maxim that martial law is antithetical to civilian representative government, constitutionalism, and local democracy. Military oversight was the only means to check domestic terror and establish the rule of law in the former slave states. Martial law could usher in representative government, as Leiber and his son, Norman Leiber, argued in an unpublished treatise. Stevens, the primary architect of Reconstruction, made it clear that a so-called "stockade state" in the South would proceed under the civilian legislative authority of Congress.[12]

As the idea of military intervention gained more adherents in Congress, the Fourteenth Amendment emerged as the central point of contention. Southern unionists, mainly from the upper South states, met at their own convention in Philadelphia in September and endorsed the amendment. They also met with Stevens, apprising him of the latest crimes against freedpeople and unionists. Douglass, who had been discouraged from attending by moderates, strode in arm in arm with the abolitionist Theodore Tilton at the convention, and gave several speeches. Before Congress reconvened, Georgia, Texas, and Florida refused to ratify the Fourteenth Amendment. By the start of 1867, all ex-Confederate states, except Tennessee, had rejected it.

Johnson, politically humiliated and declared persona non grata by the Republican Party, continued to oppose the amendment and Reconstruction more generally. News of the murder and abuse of southern blacks and unionists kept making its way north. In one particularly egregious case, six white South Carolinians received a hero's welcome after being charged for the murder of black Union soldiers in their state. In another, Johnson intervened to release a white Virginian who had shot and killed a black man. His annual message of 1866 recommending the immediate readmission of southern states was ignored by Republicans in Congress, as was his constant ranting against black rights. Even the president's allies, such as Henry Raymond, under whom *The New York Times* nearly went bankrupt, acknowledged that freedpeople needed some protection.

The second, and shorter, session of the now lame-duck Thirty-Ninth

Congress, which convened at the end of 1866, formally inaugurated Reconstruction in order to establish the rule of law and an interracial democracy in rebel states. With a secure electoral mandate, Republicans moved to establish black citizenship. To "build up and accept" treasonous governments in "the Southern territories is a crime," Phillips proclaimed. In January 1867, after the Christmas recess, both Stevens and Ashley proposed Reconstruction bills that were referred to the Joint Committee on Reconstruction. In the end, the committee adopted a bill put forward by Representative George Julian and reported back to the House by Stevens to establish military rule in the former Confederate states, except the readmitted Tennessee, to create new state governments based on adult manhood suffrage regardless of race.

The bill was modeled on a draft written by Stevens as early as May 1866. Another draft, by Robert Dale Owen, would have delayed black male suffrage for ten years. Stevens's bill made it the central pillar of Reconstruction. His bill would have also disfranchised all persons who had held civil or military office under the Confederacy or sworn allegiance to it for five years, or until they swore allegiance to the United States; their applications would be reviewed by courts that "naturalize foreigners." The initial Stevens bill, passed by the House, provided for military rule in the South; the Senate bill, proposed by a moderate senator, John Sherman of Ohio, provided for the readmission of the rebel states after they ratified the Fourteenth Amendment.

The final Reconstruction Act, a combination of the two bills, was a decisive moment and a capstone of Thaddeus Stevens's career. No one articulated its rationale better than he, and he made sure that it passed. Dubbed the "Robespierre" of the "second American revolution" by Georges Clemenceau, a young French reporter who would become the prime minister of France, Stevens unleashed no reign of terror, but rather sought to combat one. Named after the antislavery Polish general Tadeusz Kosciuszko, who had served in the Revolutionary War, and who had left a bequest for black education and land ownership, Stevens was true to his namesake. He argued for a Reconstruction based on "moderate confiscation" and "impartial suffrage." The choice for the nation was stark, as he saw it: support southern unionism or be the "perpetual vassals" of the "irritated, revengeful South." Stevens likened his attempt to guard "the rights of the downtrodden and poor" to the never-ending labor of Sisyphus. He warned that if Congress did not act to protect unionists as well as "the colored people in the country," it would be subject to the "just censure" of the world. For Stevens, the vote on the bill was historic. His colleagues would be remembered by posterity for their "courage" or for their "meanness."

Julian maintained that Reconstruction was not "bayonet rule," as Democrats alleged, but a necessary action to make ex-Confederates respect republican government. After a long debate, enlivened by Stevens's wit, Congress passed the Reconstruction Act—and on March 2, 1867, mere days before the end of the Thirty-Ninth Congress, it overrode Johnson's veto. The South's refusal to accept the results of the war, its brazen violation of black freedom and rights in the Black Codes, its racist terror, and ultimately, its opposition to the Fourteenth Amendment, had invited federal intervention. The act divided the former Confederacy, except Tennessee, into five military districts, each to be commanded by a Union general charged with protecting the life and liberty of all citizens, and with punishing acts of violence and disorder. Under Johnson's restoration, the US Army and the Freedmen's Bureau had to defer to local and state authorities attempting to restore white supremacy in the South; now they would oversee the transition to an interracial democracy. All southern civilian authority was subject to the authority of the US Army; offenders could be brought before military tribunals. The act stipulated that the military must avoid "cruel and unusual punishment" and that no death sentence be handed down without the approval of the president, a caveat included despite Johnson's proclivities. Even in its most punitive aspects, Reconstruction would be benign if southerners only respected the rights of the formerly enslaved. Black male suffrage not military rule was the cornerstone of the Reconstruction Act. That same year, Parliament passed the Second Great Reform Act of 1867 that liberalized voting for adult men in Britain, a demand of the working-class Chartist movement, but also influenced by democratic republicanism in France and the United States.

Johnson's attorney general, Henry Stanbery, futilely argued that his restored state governments superseded federal military authority. But the Reconstruction Act provided for the election of new state constitutional conventions and governments. Black men were enfranchised: delegates to the conventions would be "elected by the male citizens of said State, twenty-one years old and upward, of whatever race, color, or previous condition." Buckalew protested that there were no protections against voter "fraud"— the very idea of black men voting was fraudulent to him. He called it "degraded suffrage." The issue of fraud kept appearing in congressional debates over Reconstruction. Senator Sherman proposed a registry of voters to allay objections, which were really just attempts to derail black voting.

The Reconstruction Act, even as it established black male suffrage, restricted voting for those accused of actively participating in the rebellion. Insurrectionists excluded from officeholding in the Fourteenth Amendment could not be elected to the conventions or new state governments. In order to reenter the Union, the ex-Confederate states had to ratify the Fourteenth Amendment and establish state governments based on universal male suffrage. The Habeas Corpus Act, passed a month earlier, extended the jurisdiction of the federal courts to issue writs for persons detained and deprived of their liberty by state authorities.

The Fortieth Congress, with its even larger Republican majority, passed a supplemental Reconstruction Act on March 23 that allowed federal military authorities to register voters and oversee elections to state constitutional conventions. In July, when Congress met in an abbreviated session, it passed another Reconstruction Act, on Stevens's initiative, which reinforced the authority of the Union army. The new Act disfranchised Confederate officeholders and imposed a $5,000 fine and one year imprisonment on anyone obstructing Reconstruction. Johnson vetoed the bill, but Congress overrode him easily.

The supplemental, clarifying Reconstruction laws were passed because of Johnson's and ex-Confederates' continuing obstructionism. Radicals again asked for the confiscation of rebel land. Most Republicans, such as Senator (and former Governor) Oliver Morton of Indiana agreed to support freedpeople's education, but not the redistribution

of land. Sumner's demands also included prohibition of racial segregation in schools and public transportation, which became law only after
his death. In March 1868, Congress passed its final Reconstruction Act,
which required the new state constitutions to be approved by a majority
of voters, rather than a majority of registered voters, as many irrecon-
cilables boycotted elections to overthrow Reconstruction. The law sped
up the process for establishing civilian governments, one in which black
men would be represented. Fessenden admitted that many southerners
had put themselves "if not in an attitude of rebellion, in an attitude of
hostility." If they refused to vote, Sherman pointed out, it was not the
fault of Congress.

Democrats harped on racial divisions in the South, as though they
had not created them, and conveniently ignored the presence of southern unionists and northerners in the region. Garrett Davis, as usual,
argued that the United States was a government of white men and if
Sumner and other "advocates of negro government" wanted the American people to decide the issue, "let them bring out their Fred. Douglass as their next candidate for the Presidency." He later harrumphed
that the new state governments would enslave whites. The "curly haired
African" was incapable of "self-government," but also, in his confused
estimation, quite capable of enslaving the "superior race." Senator
Saulsbury refused to accept that ex-Confederate states had forfeited
any rights. He compared the situation to the interregnum during the
English Civil War, which ended when the monarchy was reinstated—his
royalist defense of antidemocratic ideas was quite apt. Senator Doolittle
contended that southern whites were being "terribly punished." Republicans, he argued, were "Africanizing" the South and "Mexicanizing"
the nation by creating a "mongrel" unstable republic.

In fact, Confederates elites, who had started the war of rebellion, got
off lightly. In June 1866, the House had passed a nonbinding resolution
to try Jefferson Davis for treason. Yet Davis, though he spent a year in
prison, never went to trial. Northern antislavery men like Gerrit Smith,
Horace Greeley—who would betray Reconstruction—and the magnate
Cornelius Vanderbilt posted his bail. Stevens contrasted Davis's being
set free with the execution of deposed Emperor Maximilian, the French

puppet of Napoleon III. Mexico dealt with usurpers better than the United States, he implied.[13]

The Reconstruction Acts, in large part a product of Stevens's parliamentary acumen, lay at the center of abolition democracy. And if Stevens was one of the primary forces behind abolition democracy, Johnson was its most powerful opponent. While Johnson succeeded in halting land redistribution, he was less successful in his attempt to upend black citizenship. Indeed, his meddling invited a direct response from Congress, culminating in his impeachment—the first of a president in US history.

Johnson's vetoes set the stage. He vetoed all three of the 1867 Reconstruction Acts and refused to sign the fourth passed in 1868, setting a record for the most presidential vetoes. He vetoed statehood bills for Colorado and Nebraska, specifically because they required black male

Managers of the House of Representatives of the Impeachment of Andrew Johnson. *National Portrait Gallery, Smithsonian Institution*

suffrage. (Nebraska became the only state to be admitted over a president's veto, while Colorado would be admitted later.) Johnson reiterated that giving rights to African Americans meant taking rights away from whites. The Union army under Reconstruction, he claimed, was "commanded to superintend the process of clothing the negro race with the political privileges torn from white men."

Significantly, the earliest call for Johnson's impeachment came from freedpeople, who immediately recognized him as a foe. As early as 1865, "colored freedmen" of Savannah, Georgia sent a petition to the House of Representatives. They accused Johnson of delegating his powers "to enemies, Rebels and Outlaws against the Government Constitution and laws of the United States," and stated that "we therefore pray your Honorable body to enquire into the Truth of the facts herein charge [*sic*] against his Excellency the President of the United States." Specifically, they charged Johnson with abetting racist terror: "We Complain of our Chief Executive, of causing by his agents, and Indulgence to Outlaws, of the Outrages and Murders that have been commited [*sic*] on Loyal subjects and citizens of the Union in Ten Rebel States Since May 29th 1865."

Abolitionists, who had criticized Johnson's complicity in southern attempts to undermine black freedom, also called for the impeachment of the "Rebel in the White House." As Phillips urged, "impeach the President and while he is on trial sequester him." Antislavery societies passed impeachment resolutions. Garrison argued that unless Johnson was deposed, unionists and freedmen would not possess any rights "that rebels would be bound to respect," an intentional echo of Roger Taney's *Dred Scott* opinion. In 1867, with the threat of impeachment imminent, Johnson would try to lure leading black figures into supporting him by successively offering the top post in the Freedmen's Bureau to Douglass, John Mercer Langston of Ohio, and Robert Purvis of Philadelphia. All three turned him down.

The momentum for impeachment only grew. Mainstream Republican newspapers such as the *Chicago Tribune* started calling for it. Congress tried to curtail Johnson's powers to interfere with Reconstruction. It stipulated that Johnson could issue military orders only through General Ulysses Grant, a measure added by George Boutwell to an annual military appropriations bill. In December 1866, the first iteration of the Tenure of Office Act, which sought to rein in Johnson's powers to appoint and dismiss officers of the federal government, passed the Senate. The law was a reaction to Johnson's misuse of his patronage powers to undermine southern Republicans. It would protect members of his cabinet who had been appointed by Lincoln, particularly Secretary of War Edwin Stanton, who oversaw the Freedman's Bureau and the Union commanders implementing Reconstruction. Stevens noted that the law was constitutional because the president needed the advice and consent of the Senate to make appointments.

Early in 1867, Congress passed the Tenure of Office Act. On March 2, 1867, Johnson vetoed it as well as the first Reconstruction Act. Congress overrode both his vetoes before the end of the day. In his veto message, Johnson piously positioned himself on the side of the separation of powers, ignoring his own history of interference with congressional legislation. Five days later, the House asked the Judiciary Committee to investigate impeaching the president. In the Senate, Sumner and Wade supported the House initiative, which was led by Ashley. To Sumner, Johnson had shown himself to be "the enemy of his country." With the House Judiciary Committee moving forward, popular support for impeachment in the North grew over the course of 1867.

Instead of moderating his stance in response to the threat of impeachment, Johnson became more embittered and erratic. That summer, he issued orders to subvert the intent of the Reconstruction Acts. In August, Johnson tried to remove Stanton, the biggest supporter of Reconstruction in the cabinet, and replace him with a reluctant Grant, who pointed out that the move would be in violation of the new Tenure of Office Act. On Grant's advice, Johnson suspended Stanton and elevated Grant, awaiting Senate approval to make the move permanent. For good measure, Johnson also removed Union commanders General Philip Sheridan, in charge of the Fifth Military district of Texas and Louisiana, and General Daniel Sickles, whose district included North and South Carolina. Grant protested both decisions. Out of "simple cussedness," according to one historian, Johnson appointed a Democratic general who was against Reconstruction to take Sheridan's place.

In September, Johnson issued a general pardon to all Confederates, with a few exceptions, who had "directly or indirectly" participated in the rebellion. In his annual message in December, the president lectured Congress on the unconstitutional nature of the Reconstruction laws. That month he dismissed yet another military commander, General John Pope, who was overseeing Florida, Alabama, and Georgia, because local whites protested that he was installing "Negro Government." General Edward Ord, of the Arkansas and Mississippi district, chose on his own to step down, and was reassigned. Ex-Confederates rejoiced at Johnson's "beheadings" of Union generals.

Abolitionists petitioned Congress for impeachment more forcefully. As Phillips argued, "Impeachment and removal is the only remedy." In November, the House Judiciary Committee voted to impeach Johnson, but Republicans suffered losses in northern elections in 1867, even though, buoyed by the black vote, they formed a majority in every southern state constitutional convention. Moderate Republicans, nervous about another backlash, voted with Democrats against impeachment resolutions in the House. In January 1868, following Senator Jacob Howard's report from the Military Committee, the Senate voted against Stanton's suspension, and Grant promptly resigned. Stanton barricaded himself in his old office. Even the conservative William Tecumseh Sherman rejected Johnson's offer to make him secretary of war and then commander-in-chief. Johnson dismissed Stanton and replaced him with General Lorenzo Thomas, who drank himself into a stupor at the news. Johnson's public spat with Grant confirmed the latter's opinion of him as "a national disgrace."

By this point, Johnson's bungling viciousness had become too much for most congressional Republicans, whatever fears they had of political consequences. On February 24, 1868, a near-death Stevens had his old ally, the clerk of the House, Edward McPherson, read out a speech recommending impeachment. Stevens charged Johnson with being "guilty of as atrocious attempts to usurp the liberty and destroy the happiness of this nation as were ever perpetrated by the most detestable tyrant who ever oppressed his fellow-men." He had usurped the powers of other branches of the government, violated the law, and obstructed the execution of the law. How

Congress would deal with the "first great political malefactor" would determine the future of American democracy. The same day the House voted to impeach Johnson by a vote of 126 to 47, with 17 abstentions.[14]

Republicans impeached Johnson for his obstruction of Reconstruction, though the first nine (of eleven) articles of impeachment focused on his violation of the Tenure of Office Act in firing Stanton without Senate approval. For Radicals, it was Johnson's acute racism that made him particularly unfit for the presidency. Sumner explained, "He has all the narrowness and ignorance of a certain class of whites who have always looked upon the colored race as out of the pale of humanity." In an earlier speech, Julian indicted Johnson for his "career of maladministration and crime," "capacity for evil," "depravity," and "hoarded malignity." Even Johnson's secretary, Col. William G. Moore, recalled that he "exhibited a morbid distress and feeling against the negroes."

Abolitionists were untiring advocates of impeachment. The abolitionist feminist Frances Ellen Watkins Harper put it best: "He fails to catch the watchword of the hour, and throws himself, the incarnation of meanness, across the pathway of the nation. My objection to Andrew Johnson is not that he has been a poor white man; my objection is that he keeps 'poor whits' [wits] all the way through." In her January 1867 speech on "National Salvation," Harper had compared freedpeople with "little strange Andrew Johnson," who was not fit to "touch the hems of their garments." She advised, "impeach him . . . bring him before the bar of the nation." Douglass argued that Johnson was the "vilest embodiment of ingratitude and baseness."

Johnson's trial in the Senate began on March 30, 1868. Johnson was "the chief architect" of his own impeachment, in the view of Republicans. As one of the House managers for impeachment, Stevens charged Johnson with acting "against the laws and interests of his country" in obstructing Reconstruction. These were not ordinary crimes, but political offenses of the highest order. Too feeble to finish his speech, Stevens had Benjamin Butler read the rest of it. Johnson's defense team consisted of legal conservatives like Henry Stanbery, who resigned as attorney general to represent Johnson, and Supreme Court justice Benjamin Curtis, who had dissented in *Dred Scott* but questioned the constitutionality of emancipation.

Salmon Chase, as chief justice of the Supreme Court, presided over the trial. Much like Seward, Chase became a compromised figure during the last years of his life. Consumed by his ambition to be president, he was quixotically seeking the Democratic Party nomination on a platform of black suffrage. He was against both Andrew Johnson's impeachment and Jefferson Davis's trial for treason. Sumner had hoped for a speedy trial, but it dragged on for months. In May, a Senate majority voted to convict Johnson but fell short by a single vote of the constitutionally required two-thirds majority.

Seven Republicans, including prominent moderates Trumbull, Fessenden, and James Grimes, all members of the Joint Committee on Reconstruction, voted for acquittal when assured by Johnson's allies that he would no longer obstruct Reconstruction. Republican senators representing border states that had Democratic majorities also voted for acquittal. Conservatives and moderates also feared that Benjamin Wade, a supporter of not just racial equality but also women's suffrage and workingmen's rights, would become president if Johnson were removed; Wade, as Speaker of the House, was next in the line of succession. Some in the Senate balked at his radicalism and chose instead to abandon freedpeople. Douglass noted, "At the very mention of impeachment, Wall Street turns pale." Johnson's supporters raised thousands of dollars in his defense. Senator Edmund Ross of Kansas was bribed into changing his vote from a yes to no on conviction. After his trial, Johnson appointed General John Schofield, the only remaining Reconstruction military commander of the original five, secretary of war, a move recommended by Grant and approved by the Senate.

The May vote effectively ended the attempt to remove Johnson. Stevens, despite his ill health, tried to introduce further articles of impeachment in the House, detailing Johnson's other actions to undermine Reconstruction, especially his return of confiscated land to the planters. But there was no stomach for additional proceedings, and the House managers voted to be discharged from considering more allegations of corruption and the new articles. Stevens concluded that the failure to convict Johnson showed how difficult it is to remove a renegade president by "peaceful means," if he "retains the money and patronage of the Government."

An emboldened Johnson returned the favor by characterizing Reconstruction as the "attempt to place the white population of the South under the domination of persons of color in the South." Despite his mid-trial assurances to Republican moderates and conservatives, he never stopped opposing Reconstruction, vetoing a bill in the summer of 1868 that allowed for the entry of newly reconstructed southern states, revealing that his supposedly principled constitutional opposition to military rule in favor of civilian authority was merely a guise for his racism. Both Democrats and Republicans rejected Johnson as their candidate in the presidential elections of 1868. As a lame duck president late that year, after Grant's election on the Republican ticket, Johnson excoriated Reconstruction in his last annual message to Congress. He issued a blanket pardon for all remaining Confederates, including Jefferson Davis. In 1875, Johnson was elected to the Senate by Tennessee's legislature. From that office, he railed against President Grant and Reconstruction. He died that year.[15]

The impeachment of Johnson was no folly, as its opponents at the time and many historians have since claimed. Moderates such as James Blaine and John Sherman, who voted for impeachment but abandoned Reconstruction by the late 1870s, perpetuated the idea that it had been a mistake. Yet Johnson's impeachment was an integral part of the attempt to establish abolition democracy, even if the failure to convict him marked the waning of Radicals' power. [16]

Despite the failure to remove Johnson, Reconstruction proceeded along the path Congress had laid out and the president had opposed. Reconstruction laws and amendments, though born of compromise— the result of Radicals' navigating the opposition of enemies and the moderation of allies—laid the groundwork for an unprecedented experiment in interracial democracy.

During the 1868 presidential campaign, abolitionists demanded a constitutional amendment that would establish suffrage as a national right, and dispense with state level restrictions, as part of the Republican platform. Black men, they argued, should not be deprived of the right to vote under the pretext of "state sovereignty." One D. D. Butler wrote from New Jersey, arguing that its 7,000 black male citizens could not vote—and that once that problem was solved, women's suffrage ought to be the "next question." Border states and some northern states, abolitionists pointed out, continued to disfranchise black men even though Congress readmitted reconstructed southern states with black male suffrage.

A compromise resolution in the Republican Party platform endorsed black male suffrage but left the decision to the states. Wendell Phillips saw the value in the plank nonetheless: "Many years ago I ventured to say that the negro elected Mr. Lincoln. I think he did. It was the negro again that placed suffrage in the Republican platform."

Senator Henry Wilson predicted that a suffrage amendment would be passed by Congress and supported by the future Grant administration, while Garrison warned that a Democratic victory meant black disfranchisement. In November, Grant's win— made possible in part by black votes from the South—as well as the referendum victories for black male suffrage in Iowa and Minnesota by large majorities, paved the way for the new amendment.

The Fifteenth Amendment represented the near conclusion of the abolitionist program. In January 1869, a delegation from the National Colored Convention visited President-elect Grant to demand equal suffrage, and the House passed a resolution proposed by Representative George Boutwell for black male suffrage, whose wording would be eventually adopted in the amendment. Representatives John Bingham and Samuel Shellabarger had proposed amendments that would have established a national standard for suffrage, and Shellabarger's would have also disfranchised those who had rebelled against the government. Democratic representative Charles Eldridge of Wisconsin raised states' rights and outright racist objections to the suffrage amendment, furious that Republicans wanted to give the vote to "the ignorant, uneducated and servile negro." In the Senate, Sumner argued, "Whatever you enact for human rights is constitutional," and called for a federal suffrage law, which would be easier to pass, rather than an amendment. He proposed a bill that included a judicial mechanism to enforce voting rights and punish those who attempted to hinder citizens' right to vote, much like the Voting Rights Act of 1965, but only Radicals voted for it.

Acting on a black petition, Senator William Morris Stewart of Nevada, author of the final version of the Fifteenth Amendment, wanted to include in the amendment a ban on discrimination in officeholding as well. Black abolitionists like Reverend J. W. C. Pennington protested "the color bar" in juries. The Senate passed a version of the Fifteenth Amendment proposed by Henry Wilson that would have prohibited discrimination by property holding, education, nativity, and "religious creed" for voting, but it ran afoul of anti-immigrant sentiment, particularly anti-Chinese prejudice in the West. The House voted it down. Phillips, though he was the quintessential abolitionist radical, scolded the Senate for being too principled, and urged Republicans to resolve the deadlock with the House. On February 26, 1869, both houses of Congress agreed to the amendment proposed by Stewart, without the officeholding provision, by the constitutionally required two-thirds majority. It passed along a mostly party line vote, with a few Johnson Republicans joining the Democrats. The prescient Sumner abstained because of the loophole allowing states to pass seemingly nonracial restrictions on voting, knowing the South would exploit it.

The Fifteenth Amendment prohibited states from denying or abridging the right to vote on account of race, color, or previous condition of servitude. As in the Thirteenth Amendment, its second section empowered Congress to enforce the amendment with "appropriate legislation." The constitutional mandate for the federal government to enforce voting rights remains a crucial political principle to this day. It enabled the passage of the Voting Rights Act of 1965 as well as the Twenty-Fourth Amendment to the Constitution (1964), which prohibited poll taxes used by southern states to disfranchise African Americans. Yet the amendment had limits: it enshrined black male suffrage in the Constitution through a negative injunction, rather than through the establishment of a national standard of the kind favored by Sumner and the abolitionists. It left a huge loophole for states to use other means to disfranchise citizens, such as literacy tests and poll taxes.

In March, a resolution to clarify the amendment by Democratic representative James Augustus Johnson of California, who was born in South Carolina and grew up in Arkansas, stated that the House "never intended that Chinese or Mongolians should become voters," but this was defeated decisively. Phillips noted that the Fifteenth Amendment enfranchised all male citizens born in the United States or naturalized, regardless of race or ethnicity, and excluded only foreigners (he did not mention that it also excluded women). In 1868, George Julian had presented a suffrage amendment that would have included women. But the Fifteenth Amendment left out sex, angering suffragists, who deluged Congress with suffrage petitions. The Philadelphia Female Anti-Slavery Society, the oldest women's abolition society, nonetheless supported it as a step in the right direction.

Partisan, sectional, and ideological differences determined the response to the amendment. Democrats and conservatives used racist arguments against it, including that giving black men the right to vote would lead to racial intermarriage. Most Republicans saw it as the completion of their antislavery mission. In his inaugural address on March 4, 1869, President Grant endorsed the amendment. On March 30, 1870, it was certified after more than three-fourths of the states, thirty in all, voted for ratification. Six reconstructed southern states were among those that ratified the amendment. Four states that had not been readmitted—Virginia, Georgia, Texas, and Mississippi—were required to ratify it to reenter the Union. Tennessee rejected the amendment and was the last to ratify it—in 1997. The border ex-slave states of Kentucky, Maryland, and Delaware also ratified it in the twentieth century. New York, under a Democratic state government, unsuccessfully tried to rescind its initial ratification.

In a departure from presidential norms, Grant sent a congratulatory special message to Congress on the ratification of an amendment that made black men—who before the war had been declared by the "highest tribunal" in the land not to have any rights that a white man was "bound to respect"—voters. It was a measure, he said, of "grander importance than any other act of the kind from the foundation of our free government to the present day." Phillips had high praise for Grant's remarks: if emancipation made Lincoln "the slave's President," Grant's words made him "the Negro's President." An antislavery newspaper pronounced it "The Negro's Victory."

African Americans celebrated the passage of the amendment in parades in New York City, Baltimore, and many other cities. The American Anti Slavery Society called it the "capstone and completion of our movement." Phillips and Douglass now said that the society could be dissolved, given that the twin aims of abolition had been achieved. As Douglass argued, the work of abolition would be done when "black men" were "admitted to the body politic of America." Yet despite the shuttering of the AASS in 1870, most abolitionists, including Phillips, felt that their fight would not be over until all discriminations against black people were removed and they would be equal "in fact," not just in law. Some abolitionists like Stephen Foster wanted to continue the AASS until some form of land redistribution was achieved, while Aaron Powell, editor of the *National Anti Slavery Standard,* led the movement to convert the AASS into a National Reform League to fight against racial discrimination, but that plan petered out.[17]

Thaddeus Stevens did not live to see the ratification of the Fifteenth Amendment. The great egalitarian died on August 11, 1868, and was buried, according to his wishes, in an integrated cemetery. As his body lay in state and guarded by black soldiers, white and black mourners participated in his funeral procession, the largest since Lincoln's. His epitaph read: "I have chosen this that I might illustrate in my death The Principles which I advocated through a long life; EQUALITY OF MAN BEFORE HIS CREATOR." Phillips mourned the death of "Our 'GREAT COMMONER,'" writing, "No single mind has done more to shape this era."

Stevens had convinced the Republican majority to back black voting but had not succeeded in winning wide support for land redistribution.

Before his death, he warned that a new "system of peonage" could effectively reenslave southern blacks. In one of his last appeals, Stevens
advocated confiscation as "punishment of belligerent traitors" and a
way to compensate "loyal men who have been robbed by the rebels, and
to increase pension of our wounded soldiers." He wanted to devote "the
small remnant of my life" to that cause. He proposed yet another Reconstruction bill that would benefit the lower classes across racial lines,
but in particular the "four millions of injured, oppressed, and helpless men" whose "ancestors" had toiled for "two centuries," and who
were now left "destitute, helpless, and exposed to want and starvation
under the deliberate cruelty of their former masters." Yet as he saw it, a
new bill shouldn't truly be needed: all of Johnson's pardons and restoration of estates to former rebels could simply be revoked by the existing confiscation laws, particularly the Second Confiscation Act of 1862.
After Reconstruction, Douglass lamented that the nation could not be
"induced to listen to those stalwart Republicans, Thaddeus Stevens and
Charles Sumner." The black man "would not today be on his knees, as he
is, supplicating the old master class to give him leave to toil."[18]

Others would continue Stevens's fight for land reform. The abolitionist "theory of reconstruction," Phillips had said in 1867, was that a
black man should have "40 acres under his feet, a school-house behind
him, a ballot in his right hand, the sceptre of the Federal Government
over his head, and no State Government to interfere with him." While
the Freedmen's Bureau and the Fifteenth Amendment had supposedly
secured the latter two, land reform remained an important goal, if not
the main ambition, of freedpeople and abolitionists. Phillips believed
that the duty of abolitionists was now to buy land and give it to ex-slaves.
He asked abolitionists to rally around Representative Julian's bill to
redistribute land, which he had first proposed in 1864 as chairman of
the Committee on Public Lands and which, Phillips said, was the next
logical step after the Fifteenth Amendment. Abolitionist petitions for
land reform garnered thousands of signatures not just in the North, but
also from freedpeople in the South. The *National Anti Slavery Standard*
published numerous letters advocating for land redistribution and articles against "land monopoly" in the South. A Miss M. L. Kellog wrote

from Richmond to bear personal testimony that "some land apportion-ment is the one great need for the solution of the remaining difficulties of freedmen." The nation, Phillips maintained, had not been forced to make any true recompense to enslaved people. Each black family could "justly claim" forty acres in land, one year's support, a furnished cot-tage, farm tools and a mule, and free schools.

Freedpeople continued to petition Congress for land, while aboli-tionists, heeding Phillips, launched private schemes for land reform. At the end of the war, Governor John Andrew of Massachusetts and the abolitionist George Stearns had founded the American Land Company to sell farms to freedpeople, but after Stearns's death in 1867, the com-pany went bankrupt. Rev. John G. Fee, the founder of Berea College, purchased 150 acres of land to resell to freedpeople and urged the AMA to do the same. The AMA went on to buy plantations and resold small plots of land to freedpeople.[19]

There were other attempts, too, some relatively successful, but pri-vate philanthropy was no substitute for the state-sponsored land reform Stevens had envisioned. The achievements of DuBois's "aboli-tion democracy"—black citizenship and political representation—did make it easier for freedpeople to negotiate crop shares and wages, and they received a modicum of legal protection for their labor rights. It was only after the fall of Reconstruction that economic servitude and debt peonage came to define the limits of freedom for most ex-slaves.

PART TWO

GRASSROOTS RECONSTRUCTION, 1865–1872

"Fifteenth Amendment, Celebrated May 19th, 1870," Harry T. Peters
"America on Stone" Lithograph Collection.

National Museum of American History, Smithsonian Institution

CHAPTER FOUR

Freedpeople and the Freedmen's Bureau

The passing of a great human institution before its work is done, like the untimely passing of a single soul, but leaves a legacy of striving for other men. The legacy of the Freedmen's Bureau is the heavy heritage of this generation. To-day, what new and vaster problems are destined to strain every fibre of the national mind and soul, would it not be well to count this legacy honestly and carefully?

—W. E. B. DUBOIS, *The Souls of Black Folk*, 1903

"The Freedmen's Bureau," by Alfred R. Waud,
Harper's Weekly, July 25, 1868. *Library of Congress*

During Reconstruction, the term used to describe the epidemic of racist violence against freedpeople in the South was "outrages." The Freedmen's Bureau in North Carolina, as in other southern states, kept a record of "Outrages by Whites against Blacks," including the case of a nine-year-old boy who was kidnapped and whipped by three white men into confessing to a theft, and the case of a freedwoman, Vina Covington, who was assaulted by two white men with clubs and sticks. In Rocky Mount, a freedwoman was horse-whipped and a freedman subjected to a "cruel and inhuman beating with a rail." If former Confederates and enslavers unleashed a war of racist terror against the newly emancipated to control their lives and labor, freedpeople resisted to sustain their hard-fought freedom, enlisting the Freedmen's Bureau in their battles.

This part introduces the concept of "grassroots reconstruction" to capture the significance of a range of actions by disfranchised groups on the ground to expand the boundaries of national citizenship and belonging, often attempting to have the federal government intervene on their behalf. Indeed, it was because freedpeople pushed the Bureau to document the atrocities against them, often at great risk to themselves, that congressional Republicans could overthrow Johnson's restoration and inaugurate Reconstruction. Senator Henry Wilson, who would go on to write the first history of the era, kept a carefully compiled record of all the murders and outrages committed in the South. Freedpeople's grassroots politics of protest created "a new knowledge regime."[1]

Alongside Republicans in Congress as well as abolitionists, the four million freedpeople whose struggles shaped the course of Reconstruction were founders of the Second American Republic. As the postwar Congress, largely controlled by radical and moderate Republicans, moved to subdue the still-rebellious South and to protect black rights, freedpeople across the region fought their own battles for human rights, political recognition, and social justice. Their fight remains, remarkably, one of the most significant and underappreciated stories of the Reconstruction era, even though their actions resounded well beyond the South, connecting local concerns with national debates. Grassroots reconstruction is essentially the story of their activism.

Freedpeople made distinct claims to national belonging, citizenship, dignity, and recognition. Local organizing was based on a long history of surviving and resisting enslavement. Grassroots reconstruction also built on wartime reconstruction, when enslaved people fled to Union lines or upended the operation of plantations and slave society. After the war, freedpeople surpassed Congress itself, forming the most effective resistance to the coup d'état attempted by southern elites with Andrew Johnson's blessings. They mobilized through their own institutions: the black family, church, schools, and fraternal organizations. Most important was their use of the Freedmen's Bureau, the one alternative source of political authority in the postwar South, for their freedom claims. However limited and attenuated the Bureau's jurisdiction was—and however much Bureau agents, commissioners, superintendents, teachers, and doctors were themselves limited by their own assumptions and biases—black southerners managed to use it as a counterweight to former slaveholders and Confederates.[2] And in seeking to give meaning and protections to their emancipation, freedpeople laid the foundations of the Second American Republic, and of a more enduring political project: social democracy.

The alliance between enslaved Americans, antislavery Republicans, and the federal government inaugurated by wartime emancipation would reach its apogee during Reconstruction. And the most concrete expression of that alliance was the relationship forged between former slaves and the still-new Freedmen's Bureau, which was reviled by southern elites. It was to the Bureau that African Americans turned with testimony of violent terror, labor abuse, and other violations of their political and civil rights. The Bureau, as its critics then and now claim, did not have to invent black demands and aspirations.[3] By keeping up a drumbeat of complaints that made their way into the reports and correspondence of the Bureau's assistant commissioners, sub-assistant commissioners, superintendents, and agents in all the ex-slave states and the District of Columbia, freedpeople left a vast historical record of southern cruelty and violence. At the same time, the everyday claims filed with the Bureau built momentum for the creation of functional democratic governments in the ex-Confederate states. Petitioning, reporting, and demanding justice were political acts in themselves and helped make black citizenship the centerpiece of Reconstruction.

As we've seen, the Bureau of Refugees, Freedmen, and Abandoned Lands was established in 1865 by a Republican Congress, over the fierce objections of southern Democrats and northern conservatives, and the fight over its extension was one of the first that defined the all-important Thirty-Ninth Congress. The Bureau, as its official name suggests, performed a myriad of functions, providing food and clothing for destitute southern whites and freedpeople, establishing hospitals and schools, adjudicating labor disputes and contracts, and, near the end of its existence, supervising salary and pension claims of black Union soldiers and their families. But it was freedpeople's demands for personal security and their freedom claims that had the greatest, and most immediate, effects.

The many cases of abuse that freedpeople brought to Bureau agents indicated a complete breakdown of the rule of law in the postwar South. Each case revealed the price paid by African Americans in blood to reconstruct democracy, and the ongoing casualties in a war thought to be long over. Naturally, the Bureau documented only those cases made known to it, and thus its records capture only a portion of the atrocities committed against freedpeople, most of which are likely hidden forever from historians. Still, the cases that were recorded, and that survived, are evidence enough. Any single example can almost stand in for all of them. In Virginia, Captain Sidney Smith, charged with investigating the shooting of a young black boy named Robert Holman by Landon T. Lovett and two "accomplices," reported that the three white men had "served in the rebel army." For no good reason, Lovett, according to the deposition of Holman's employer, John F. Smith, had slapped the boy and punched him in the ribs, demanding that he stand still. Holman ran into Smith's house and locked the door behind him. When Lovett threatened to break the door down, Smith's wife opened it. Lovett shot Holman in the back. He attacked "without any provocation whatever"; the sixteen-year-old Holman testified that he had never spoken to Lovett before. Captain Smith ended his report somberly: "The boy may recover, but there is no certainty."

In another case, Captain Smith reported that "a colored man John Taylor was murdered near Mount Gilead, Loudon County" in his own house in the presence of his family. He recorded that local authorities "refuse to take cognizance of the matter although it has been reported to a justice of the peace." Taylor's murderers—"these demons were white men disguised" as black—had robbed Taylor and his wife before killing him. The perpetrator was one Bush Underwood, Smith affirmed, but "the civil authorities are not disposed to protect freedmen bringing to justice those who have and continue to commit outrages against them." The Bureau was also regularly forced to intervene in many instances of wrongful imprisonment. In 1867, Lt. Col. James Johnson, a sub-assistant commissioner in Fredericksburg, ordered the release of a freedman, "Wm. E. Crockett," in Bowling Green: "His imprisonment is through malice—rather than [to] promote the ends of justice."

Bureau agents in upper South states filed long lists of attacks on freedpeople. In North Carolina, an assistant superintendent reported four cases of assault to civil authorities, stating that if they did not act, he would. Captain Hillebrandt, reporting the murder of a black Union soldier and assaults on freedwomen, wrote that freedpeople could find no redress in state courts, which "in contrary encourages others to commit outrages on them." In Tennessee, the "Provost Marshal of Freedom" at the Bureau fined locals for "assault and battery" committed against freedpeople. A white man accused of shooting a freedman was fined $50. In one case brought before the Bureau, a freedman was given "a hundred licks" by his employer. Many southern men were fined for attacking freedpeople; records of even children brutalized, raped, and murdered dot the state Bureau's register of "outrages."

Despite the fact that Kentucky had remained in the Union, the Freedmen's Bureau reported hundreds of instances of vicious assaults on freedpeople in that state. Freedmen and women were attacked with wooden planks, sticks, clubs, and knives. As in Tennessee (and elsewhere), children were not spared: a young girl was whipped until her dress came off her in shreds, a young boy was hit with an "iron poker" and another with an "iron pitcher." Rampaging groups of southerners invaded freedpeople's homes and robbed and mercilessly beat entire families. The Bureau office in Washington, DC reported cases of assault, including one of a black schoolteacher, who was knocked down senseless by a white man, as well as "unjust imprisonment" of freedpeople, many from neighboring Maryland.[4]

The horrific abuse of black women, which had been partially hidden under the opaque veil of slavery, came to light in the voluminous records of the Bureau, evidence against endless tales of southern chivalry. Southern white women, for their part, showed no compunction in participating in brutalizing black women. In Amite City, Louisiana in August 1865, the assistant superintendent and sub-assistant commissioner reported that a black man, George Kindricks, told him that a "Mr. Pitkins beat my daughter (a young woman, about 20 years of age, has one child and is heavily pregnant) with a heavy hickory stick bout three feet in length. After he got through his daughter Ann fell on her with a hoe handle and after she was through his son Lewis, 27 years of age, beat her 35 blows with a buggy trace." The next month, James Frewell's wife was thrown on the floor, "injuring her badly (she being in the family way)," by a planter, Jack Sharkey, and the local policeman, Marshal Amica. In his report to General Canby of the Department of the Gulf, Assistant Commissioner Thomas Conway wrote, "The injustice inflicted upon the freedmen at the hands of the New Orleans police, can hardly find its equal in the history of any city of Christendom."

Southern men believed it was their prerogative to abuse freedwomen. A woman named Martha Kemp complained that a Mr. Clements "wanted me to go lay with him until morning. I told him I was a woman of the church and did not do such things." She told him to go "to a white woman's and not to trouble colored women." Eliza Kemp and Manerva Moore each testified against a group of men who "tried to run their hands under my clothes." Another woman, Cicilia, said that the same men got into her bed and "began to jab and punch me." The superintendent decided that "the evidence is conclusive of insult to females of color" and "the circumstance would warrant a heavy punishment." The offenders pleaded that they were "intoxicated" and were "good and respectable men," and merely paid a fine of $15 each.

While the evidential bar for black women accusing white men was impossibly high and the punishments were meager, these particular men had at least been forced to answer for their actions, probably for the first time in their lives, due to the existence of the Bureau. In general, though, poor black men faced the brunt of military justice in gender-related crimes. When black men were accused of rape, they could be summarily hanged by local authorities, at times with the approval of the Bureau and Union army.

Freedwomen also felt empowered to haul their husbands before the Bureau, a sign of the gendered dimensions of emancipatory politics and grassroots reconstruction. In Louisiana, the federal provost marshal and sub-assistant commissioners recorded several instances of assault and beating of freedwomen by white men or by their own husbands. In Austin, Texas, a woman named Martha accused her husband, Denmark Walton, of beating her when she remonstrated with him about flirting with another woman. Denmark confessed his guilt; he was confined in a military camp with a diet of bread and water as punishment. In Goldsboro, North Carolina, Louisa Pace complained that her husband David "continually maltreats and abuses her in a brute like manner," for which he was arrested. In Kentucky, a mother reported the extreme case of a daughter who was beaten and killed by her husband.

Freedwomen demanded that the Bureau, which recorded freedpeople's marriages in extensive "Registers of Marriages," and which also granted marriage certificates, adjudicate marital disputes that did not involve violence. In rarer cases, freedmen went to the Bureau about their wives not performing their household duties. Freedpeople, such as Lydia and Daniel Jordan in North Carolina, even sued for divorce under the auspices of the Bureau, or for custody of their children, as in the case of *Siller v. Steven Thomasson* in Georgia. The South Carolina Bureau issued an elaborate set of "Marriage Rules," authorizing certificates for marriage and their dissolution.[5] While debate raged in the North over women's suffrage, freedwomen across the South claimed rights and exerted a measure of power, using the Bureau as their primary tool.

Some of the worst instances of the abuse of black women and children anywhere in the South appear in the records of the Texas Freedmen's Bureau. Hundreds of complaints of assaults of young black girls ended up in the Bureau's "Register of Complaints." The Ellingtons, a white family, had "a young colored girl whom he has ... shamefully beaten ... the neighbors all talk about the way she is used." Sixteen-year-old Emma Morris complained that Mr. Gill Robert "struck her with a stone on the left ear cutting it badly." Phillis Peebles recorded that the Milners "whips her little boy and girl" and "cut her throat and hit her in the head with a whip handle making a large scar on her head and cut her finger with a milk pitcher." The agent overseeing the case wrote to the local judge, asking why he had not held Dr. Milner accountable. The sub-assistant commissioner in Bowie County, Texas, catalogued eight atrocities committed by one man, Warren Hooks Esq., and his family, including the murder of two black men and Hooks's hitting of "a col'd woman named Penny Lewis with a grub and his fist." He also "whipped her son Spencer 13 years of age" as well as "the sons of Judy Roberts, a colored woman." In Brazos County, during the bloody summer of 1866, a Mr. Plez Watson and F. Faulkner beat a woman for not being able to work in the field after giving birth. After Thomas Glasgow reported to the Bureau that a man named Busby had whipped his child, Busby coolly shot him. In one case of torture in April 1867 reminiscent of waterboarding, Oliver Gardner held two young black boys to the ground and poured water down their nostrils.

The Texas files reveal a deeply violent world. There were cases of black parents who were forced by white people to whip their own children. Racist terror in the borderlands extended to the abuse and dispossession of Native and Mexican Americans. Tejanos (Texans of Mexican descent) and German immigrants, who tended to be unionists, were targeted as well. Attacks on southern unionists recalled, for many, the massacre of around thirty-seven Hill Country German unionists at the Nueces in August, and the mass hangings and lynching of over forty German unionists in Gainesville, Texas by Confederates in October 1862.

Southern unionists, particularly those in mountainous, nonplantation counties, achieved a modicum of political power during Reconstruction, and were subjected to violence for it. This was nothing new. In Shelton Laurel, North Carolina, thirteen unionists, one as young as thirteen, were shot to death in cold blood during the Civil War. The *National Anti Slavery Standard* reported a "reign of terror" against unionists in Tennessee after the war. The Confederate practice of wartime reprisals against unionists continued unchecked throughout the South after the war. In responding to acts of political terror, the Bureau helped cobble together the Reconstruction alliance between freedpeople and southern unionists.[6]

The state that would pioneer the violent overthrow of Reconstruction, Mississippi, competed with Texas in its sheer number of reported atrocities. On the eve of the war, Mississippi's population was 55 percent black, and nearly 50 percent of its white households were slaveholding—so it was little surprise that the state had been rabidly proslavery and secessionist. During Reconstruction, the establishment of black citizenship upended planter rule, and many Mississippians embarked on an orgy of racist violence in response. The Mississippi Freedmen's Bureau Field Office recorded hundreds of cases of freedmen "brutally assaulted" and "life threatened." In Corinth, the subassistant commissioner reported an instance of a child hit on the head with a brick and "likely to die," and another of a group of white men who

"The Union As It Was," by Thomas Nast, *Harper's Weekly*, October 24, 1874.
Library of Congress

had gang-raped a black girl. In Columbus, the Bureau received word of three particularly brutal instances of abuse of freedwomen, one who had "head wounds," another who was assaulted with a brick and murdered, and a sick woman from whom food was withheld. In Friars Point, Greenville, and Grenada, sub-assistant commissioners and agents were presented with testimony that freedwomen had been assaulted with chairs and sticks while pregnant, and brutally whipped. In Amite County—not to be confused with Amite city, Louisiana—white men in blackface flogged freedpeople with no fear of the law.

Images of what Ann Mae Duane calls "suffering childhood" proliferate in the Bureau records. African American children, especially those who were enslaved, were typically denied any semblance of a childhood as well as the basic right to an education before the war. The writings of relatively privileged creole schoolchildren in New Orleans revealed that they imagined their future in another country, Haiti or Mexico. Black children were especially vulnerable to the traumas of war, disease, death, and abuse. The Bureau's burial records in Virginia reveal that nearly half of the wartime deaths among freedpeople were children. During Reconstruction, control over children's labor as well as their kinship claims to family often resulted in struggles between former enslavers and the formerly enslaved. Black children were subject to kidnapping and abusive apprenticeships. Like black adults, they had hope for what might follow emancipation, including access to public education, but children did not become rights-bearing citizens, and were subject to the same violent repression that all black people in the South faced.[7]

The Freedmen's Bureau became the first recourse for African Americans trying to prevent the kidnapping and abuse of their children, especially in response to the forcible apprenticeship laws of the Black Codes. On June 21, 1866, a freedman in Florida complained of a white man who had taken and "maltreated" his child from a former marriage. As late as 1869, in another case in Florida, the Bureau recorded that a "freedman's children are still being held in slavery." Freedwomen, in particular, brought hundreds of cases of the unlawful enslavement of black children. In North Carolina, Lucy Smith lodged a complaint with the Bureau against Mr. John D. Walker, who "retains possession of her five children." Freedpeople often complained of whites who "bound" their children to labor and then abused them. Delsey McCullough reported that her granddaughter, bound to a Mr. Williams, was "ill treated" and was not being "taught how to read and write," an agreed-on condition of the apprenticeship.

In the border states of Maryland and Delaware, the Bureau often intervened on behalf of black parents seeking to regain custody of children who had been kidnapped or "apprenticed" unlawfully by whites. In October 1866, Amanda Dorsey told Bureau officers that three white men and a white woman separately held each of her four children—three sons and one daughter—against their will. In yet another case, Hammeton Barkeley reported that two men, armed with pistols and clubs, had simply carried his wife and three children away. Colonel Weagle wrote that the case was resolved and "wife and children returned to complainant." Jinney Shield sought to reclaim her daughter, who was bound to a "Wm. E. Liden" by an Orphan Court "without her consent" in 1864. She finally recovered her daughter four years later.

Southern judges indiscriminately bound black children designated as "orphans" to planters. Thomas Woolf Jr., a probate judge in Linden, Alabama, was forced to explain himself to Maj. C. W. Pierce of the Bureau, who accused him of violating the Civil Rights Act and ruling in a discriminatory manner against black children. The judge replied by arguing that it was his "duty" to bind orphans without visible means of support under state law, and that for whatever reason no case involving white orphans had come before him. Woolf then went on to claim that he had been a "kind and indulgent" master, and that he was very "popular" and a "favorite" among freedpeople. Professing to be a guardian of all orphans and minors, he revealed himself: "I think I understand the race thoroughly, with all their Habits & Characteristics, with their wants and peculiar defects of character & disposition, I wish them all success in mental &moral improvement, I am sure they need it."

In Georgia, the sub-assistant commissioner in Cuthbert, Randolph County recorded the case of seventeen-year-old Tom Holly, who had been denied his wages and kept bound by John B. Holly. The agent ascertained that Tom had been kidnapped and more than $100 had been stolen from him. The "abuse" of laws allowing for binding children "has already brought back into Slavery numbers of young men," he concluded. In North Carolina, the Bureau cancelled many indentures of children, an overwhelming majority of them black.[8] Children and adolescents were abused in large part because they were especially powerless.

Successful black people were targeted simply because they existed. The case of Amaziah Peyton in Abbeville, South Carolina is revealing. Described as a "respectable, worthy man" who had come home to settle some business, he was "shot by a pistol ball" by Reuben L. Golding. Sub-Assistant Commissioner William Stone described the murder as "causeless and brutal." In another case recorded by Stone, three men, including one who had previously shot a freedman, assaulted a freedwoman, Sarah Wright, with "a heavy stick." Commissioner Stone was the son of an abolitionist and would serve as attorney general in reconstructed South Carolina. As one of the more conscientious and sympathetic Bureau agents, he presided over the Bureau's Provost Court, one of many ad hoc courts set up as federal tribunals by the Bureau for freedpeople, who could not even give testimony against whites in local and state courts before the Civil Rights Act of 1866. The Provost Court was determined to dispense equal justice to freedpeople. Stone recorded numerous other instances of assault and murder of freedpeople, with none of the perpetrators arrested.

Despite lacking structure and spread in a patchwork fashion, the Bureau courts persisted because southern courts systematically denied freedpeople equal justice even when perfunctorily giving them the due process of law. As one scholar writes, "the Bureau began the erosion of these customs to grant freedpeople legal rights." At times, freedpeople fought back. In Pickens district, four black men, known to be "loyal" and who had helped Union prisoners of war escape, tried to arrest Thomas Miller, who was wanted for "many crimes . . . committed by him against soldiers and freed people." They shot Miller dead when he drew his gun on them and appealed to the Bureau as "they do not think they can receive a fair trial before the Civil Court" for what they considered "justifiable homicide."[9]

Freedmen's Bureau records offer a glimpse into how freedpeople tried to deploy it in defense of themselves, their homes, families, and communities, even when confronted with racist or unsympathetic agents. In Georgia, hundreds of freedmen swore affidavits before Bureau officials reporting numerous instances of being shot at by local whites, who seemed to have a monopoly on the possession of guns and used it to intimidate, threaten, and at times kill freedpeople. The records from the state also reveal that southerners understood they were attacking the Bureau's jurisdiction when they assaulted freedpeople. In Campbell County, W. Nelson King "willfully and maliciously" assaulted E. S. Jackson, pounding his face with his fists and thereby "causing a fracture of his cheek bone and a certain portion of the upper jaw," all while telling him that he would "knock the damned old Bureau" out of his "carcass." Similarly, a freedman in Milton, Florida was beaten for being a "Yankee spy." As the historian Kidada Williams writes, we must pull "from historical limbo the uncounted women, men and children who lived through this violence, but whose stories have been unheard or underexamined."

The cases of "murder and outrage" recorded by the Freedmen's Bureau and Union commanders had no easy resolutions. At times perpetrators of horrific violence got off lightly or scot-free; others were prosecuted, fined, and imprisoned. In many cases, we have no evidence of any outcome. Yet in a profoundly political act of making claims on the state, freedpeople left an official archive of the continued barbarities of their oppressors, just as fugitive slave abolitionists had left narratives, before the war, that belied enslavers' attempt to portray slavery as a benevolent, paternalistic institution. And freedpeople did so after the immense trauma and lingering suffering caused by what the *National Anti Slavery Standard* called "rebel terrorism."[10] Their combined testimonies left a permanent historical record of southern violence, and also made clear the obligation of the state to redress historical and immediate wrongs.

The challenges freedpeople faced went beyond whippings, sexual assaults, murders, and other acts of violence. They also turned to the Freedmen's Bureau to settle disputes over reneged payments, attempts to defraud them of their earnings, and attacks on their property by farmers and planters. These cases themselves often entailed violence or were the prompt for it. But the effect of freedpeople's property claims and labor rights was to transform the Bureau, which had been conceived of initially as a means to distribute abandoned and confiscated lands, into an agency that settled labor and contract disputes. It became, in effect, a ministate of its own, and freedpeople's claims would expand its purview in other ways, too.

The lists of such complaints were never-ending, and as long as the Bureau existed, at least some freedpeople were able to recover stolen wages. As Commissioner Thomas Conway reported from Louisiana, "Men who were strong rebels against the Government, are, almost invariably strong opponents of free labor." The North Carolina Bureau processed the largest number of complaints of withheld wages and of workers being discharged without pay. On top of the systematic cheating of freedpeople of their wages, planters relied on intimidation. In one instance, when a freedwoman named Ann tried to quit her job, her employer threatened to "cut her throat" and kept her belongings. The Bureau intervened to allow her to retrieve her possessions. In Tennessee, Mollie Cole secured, through the intervention of the Bureau, $7.50 in wages withheld from her by her employer.

In Texas, Bureau records teem with examples of freedpeople forcing the Bureau to intervene to claim their wages, with the exact amount due and recovered duly noted. In Kentucky's voluminous "register of complaints," freedpeople reported being regularly assaulted when they tried to collect their wages. One freedwoman and her daughter were beaten for trying to leave the employ of a white man, the daughter with a stick and the mother stripped naked, tied to a tree and whipped. The sub-assistant commissioner of Athens, Georgia, John J. Knox, wrote that his agents reported that "the conduct of the freed people" was "exceedingly good," but that their treatment by southerners was "gradually growing worse."

The emergence of sharecropping, in which freedpeople cultivated parts of plantations for a share of the crop, was a compromise between the freedpeople's desire for independent farms and planters' attempt to retain gang labor from the days of slavery. While the Bureau's mandate to redistribute abandoned and confiscated land among freedpeople was peremptorily reversed by Johnson, it tried to implement the Southern Homestead Act of 1866 by settling freedpeople on public lands in states like Florida and South Carolina. Freedpeople's hunger for land was evident from the "register of Applications of Freedmen for Land" kept by the Louisiana Bureau, which recorded hundreds of such applications. More commonly, the Bureau oversaw labor contracts between freedpeople and planters that stipulated wages, provisions, and hours of labor; contracts were central to the Bureau's work to supplant slavery with a wage labor system. For the most part, payment was in the form of a share of the crop—usually one-third—in the cotton states, and wages on the sugar plantations. The Bureau adjudicated many instances of the "unjust division of crop" and tried to establish just and reasonable wages for workers and rents for tenants. In a contract dispute in Augusta, Georgia, James Dosier complained to the Bureau that his former master had agreed to feed and clothe him, and to pay him one-third of the share of the crop he cultivated. Not only did his ex-enslaver renege on providing food and clothing to James, but he drove him out of his house and stole all the corn he had raised.

The Bureau's significant role in adjudicating contracts can be best grasped by considering what happened after the fall of Reconstruction. Without the Bureau to ensure a minimum level of fairness in planter-sharecropper and tenant contracts and to oversee other violations and abuse, sharecropping and tenancy deteriorated into an oppressive system of semi-servitude that saw sharecroppers and tenants kept permanently indebted and cheated of their fair share of crops. Planters and furnishing merchants would charge exorbitant prices for and interest on tools, seeds, and rent, helping give rise to debt peonage, which made a travesty of the free labor that the Bureau had sought to establish. Debt peonage was one of the more dire predictions of Radical Republicans and abolitionists, including Thaddeus Stevens and Wendell Phillips.[11]

Before the war, enslaved African Americans in the slave states had sued for their freedom and petitioned for limited rights, but in the Bureau they found a source of local power independent of their oppressors, despite the fact that agents ranged from deeply committed to indifferent and antagonistic. Perhaps typical was Agent S. G. Spawn of Newberne, Alabama, who wrote in 1867 of his understanding of his duties to "establish permanently a equitable System of Labor in the Country—secure even justice to all parties and restore perfect confidence between the two Races; which I suppose to be the grand object of the Bureau." It was a tall order. Instead of creating harmony between former enslavers and enslaved, the agents dealt with the inevitable conflict between the two groups. For the most part, according to one historian, the sub-assistant commissioners were "well intentioned" and "honest" men, though burdened with racially paternalistic and sexist attitudes. A majority of these men were northern-born officers of the Union army, and they had great latitude in deciding cases brought before them. Even those described as "conservative" intervened on behalf of freedpeople in the worst cases of abuse, while others deemed liberal at times sided with planters and meted out harsh punishment for breach of contract. Southern agents recruited by the Bureau were particularly cavalier when it came to the rights of freedpeople.

Nonetheless, freedpeople welcomed the Bureau, regardless of the attitudes of individual agents. Some agents were even attacked and killed by southerners, such as Lt. J. B. Blanding, who was murdered in cold blood on the streets of Grenada, Mississippi. There were very few black agents, though their small number included abolitionist Martin Delany, who was a major in the Union army and was appointed assistant sub-assistant commissioner for the Freedmen's Bureau in Hilton Head, South Carolina by General Rufus Saxton. Like other agents,

Delany kept a scrupulous record of the rations and medicine he disbursed, and of the disputes that he adjudicated among freedpeople and between freedpeople and their employers. He instituted a passbook system to record purchases so that planters could not cheat their workers by charging exorbitant prices, requested the appointment of an inspector to divide crops equitably, and established a short-lived Freedmen's Cotton Agency to procure better prices for their crop. Another black agent of the Bureau, Stephen Swails, was a veteran of the Fifty-Fourth Massachusetts and would go on to serve in the South Carolina senate. In that state, white sub-assistant commissioners included the principled Captain Stone as well as the pro-southern John William de Forest, whose memoir captured local color more vividly than the records of the Bureau. His racism toward black people—"ignorant and simple and childish"—was overt and he penned one of the first "reunion romances" between a southern belle and a northern officer.

The Bureau lacked a set of uniform rules and bureaucratic procedures, and its decisions were often ad hoc. Its commitment to free labor, the safeguarding of freedpeople's civil rights, and education was personified by its paternalistic, pious commissioner, Maj. Gen. Oliver Otis Howard, known as "the Christian General," who directed operations from Washington. Gen. William T. Sherman warned Howard that he had to accomplish "Hercules' task," or, as Howard put it, the Bureau had "to make bricks without straw." Appointed by Secretary of War Stanton, Howard organized the Bureau into divisions, each headed by an assistant commissioner drawn from the Union army. The assistant commissioner supervised sub-assistant commissioners and agents. The Bureau's initial funding came from taxes and rents pooled in a "Freedmen's fund," but with the passage of the Reconstruction Act of 1867, it received a much-needed infusion of nearly $7 million through congressional appropriation.

In delineating his "principles of action," Howard made clear that the Bureau's task was not to support freedpeople in "idleness" and that its work was "temporary." It also distributed aid and supplies to all destitute southern refugees, but it became primarily associated with freedpeople, giving birth to the pernicious American myth that associates the welfare state with African Americans, casting them as "dependent" and as "wards of the state." As William Lloyd Garrison pointed out, "millions of dollars expended for the starving rebel population at the South," as well as schools established not just for freedpeople but "illiterate whites," were ignored.

The Bureau attempted to institute a free labor system that would employ and pay freedpeople, and it worked with the freedmen's aid and benevolent societies to establish freedmen's schools for their education and "moral" improvement. Its attempt to allow freedmen to keep titles of lands given to them during the war, and to reap the rewards of the crops they had raised on those lands, fell victim to President Johnson's policies. Howard began arguing that workers ought to be paid wages and allowed to choose their employers— "compulsory unpaid labor" and "acts of cruelty and oppression" were prohibited. The "old system of overseers" was to be abolished. Yet as Howard admitted, it was easy for him to issue directives, but "hard to carry such orders into execution." Howard tried to fix a minimum wage for freedpeople but noted that planters would rarely pay more than that amount. He did not position himself as an enemy of the planters, though. To those who complained of freedpeople's "idleness," he recommended the use of vagrancy laws, which were applicable to whites, too, but he advised avoiding "the whipping post," a remnant of slavery. The use of vagrancy laws by some agents and superintendents to force freedpeople to work violated the Bureau's own free labor ideology. Howard's attempt to mediate between freedpeople and unreconstructed planters and farmers, a majority of whom refused assent to the implications of emancipation, was doomed to failure. But as a clearing house for freedpeople's concerns and needs, the Bureau was still remarkably successful, given the hostile circumstances in the postwar South.

Yet it was freedpeople themselves who shaped the Bureau more than any other individual or group, and whose role in its history has not been fully recovered. The Bureau was not just the product of northern free labor ideology, but also of freedpeople's grassroots politics of survival and citizenship claims. Freedpeople brought so many grievances to the Bureau's superintendents and officers that they at times overwhelmed its apparatus. In Alabama, Major Weiner, a superintendent with the Bureau, wrote in 1866, "Outrages are committed & injustices done in this, Sumter & Green counties, almost daily. In this county (Marenge) I can manage these matters very well, but in Green & Sumter I cannot get the civil authorities to act with the promptness and impartiality necessary to secure justice to the Freedmen." It was a huge undertaking for any organization, but particularly for the understaffed Bureau. Agents in Florida repeatedly asked for Union army detachments to be posted in the state to restore the rule of law.

The biggest problems confronting the Bureau were local southern courts, which refused to accept black testimony. More generally, southern courts made no pretense of treating freedpeople fairly or impartially. In Alabama, Gen. Wager Swayne managed to force local courts to accept black testimony even as he deferred to them. In Mississippi, local courts still refused to do so. In Louisiana, the Bureau was able to prosecute successful cases on behalf of freedpeople in local courts. In South Carolina and Georgia, Gen. George Meade, in charge of the Department of the South, insisted that all cases involving freedpeople come to his provost courts. The Bureau did the same in other southern states. Howard wrote, "In some counties after their withdrawal the Bureau courts had to be reestablished to prevent open revolt by the negroes against evident legal persecution by the State courts." The work of the Bureau was especially important during Johnsonian restoration, even though Johnson fired its officers, staffed it with conservative southern sympathizers, and simply tried to destroy it. Later on, after the election of new Reconstruction state governments, freedpeople sent numerous petitions to Congress asking for the Bureau to remain.[12]

Despite their opposition to the Bureau, planters were known to call upon its agents, particularly those who were racist, local southerners, or Johnson appointees, to "discipline" their workers. A pompous ex-slaveholder in South Carolina, John A. Partlow, wrote to the Bureau that he was "glad that the negroes are freed, although it seemed at first losing all that I was worth, but it has relieve [sic] of me very great trouble and tax." He had treated them, he claimed, "with the same care as I did my children," though it is doubtful that he had whipped or sold his children or made them work in the fields. Partlow admonished "that there has been so many vagabonds turned loose in the country, who will not work but must steal or dye [sic] makes everything discouraging for the honest laborer, to work so hard to support such a class of people, but the government must look after that." Planters, though, did not solicit the help of the Bureau with the same frequency of freedpeople, and when they did, often found themselves on the wrong side of the agency's attempt to establish a free labor system. But Bureau agents acting on behalf of planters and employers could be abusive and callous toward freedpeople, enforcing contracts and curtailing their mobility to move from one workplace to another before the termination of annual contracts.

Ironically, Bureau agents also encouraged freedpeople to migrate north, turning to abolitionist feminists such as Sojourner Truth, Josephine Griffing, and Julia Wilbur as employment agents. Others, like Laura Haviland, led their own migrations of freedpeople to the North. Andrew Johnson called the resulting migrations a "traffic in negroes," and northern Democrats ginned up racist fears of black people taking "white jobs." Howard, for his part, was eager to get rid of refugees dependent on the Bureau. Most of the "female agents" tried to place black women and children in northern homes, where they often ended up in domestic service. Truth and Griffing were responsible for the relocation of thousands of freedpeople, but some abolitionists, including Anne Earle of Worcester, criticized their efforts, especially when they resulted in the separation of families. In the end, the Bureau's northern migration policy failed. Truth admitted, "this was not the best mode of procedure, as it cost a great amount of labor, time, and money." During the war and its aftermath, thousands of freedpeople made their way into the upper Midwest, bringing the fight for citizenship and equality to their new towns and cities. It was a small preview of the Great Migration in the early twentieth century.[13]

Overextended as the Bureau was, it evolved into a sort of proxy state for African Americans. As DuBois wrote, "the Freedmen's Bureau became a full-fledged government of men." Reconstruction did not entail the creation of a welfare state of the scope that many freedpeople and abolitionists called for, but the Freedmen's Bureau was the first government social welfare agency in US history. The Louisiana and Virginia Freedmen's Bureau kept extensive lists of "indigent and destitute" black people as well as southern whites who applied "for relief." Johnson complained in his veto of the Freedmen's Bureau Bill, "A system for the support of indigent persons in the United States was never contemplated by the authors of the United States Constitution."

The Bureau operated over sixty hospitals that proved woefully inadequate to the medical needs of freedpeople, but that were better than absolutely no health care at all. Its hospitals were overwhelmed by the huge medical emergency generated by the Civil War in the form of disease, starvation, and wartime wounds and injuries. Freedpeople suffered enormously during the war, and aside from their own medical traditions and know-how, and the surgeons and doctors of the Bureau, they had nowhere else to turn. As Lt. Col. Charles J. Kipp, the surgeon in chief of the Medical Department of the Bureau in the military district of Alabama, reported in 1867, eight assistant surgeons ran the hospitals throughout the state but also attended "to many thousand destitute Freedmen at their homes." The Bureau employed local physicians, attendants, and stewards, but they were few in number. State and local authorities made "no provision" for the destitute; as Kipp put it, "they must perish unless the Bureau continues to provide for them." He noted, "The laboring Freed people do all in their power to assist their sick bretheren [sic] and do a great deal of good in this respect; but unfortunately they have as yet, not the means to provide for them all." In Kentucky, the Bureau maintained monthly and weekly accounts of "the sick and the wounded."

While most medical personnel subscribed to the pseudoscience of race pioneered by proslavery theorists and the "medical racism" of their profession, Bureau hospitals and asylums were also shaped by freedpeople's needs. Historian Gretchen Long has argued that African Americans were not just victimized by death and disease but were active participants in medical care: "the clinic, the hospital, and the dispensary were important arenas of African Americans' postemancipation political action." The Medical Division of the Freedmen's Bureau "illustrates that freed slaves were the first advocates of federal health care." At least eight black doctors worked in Bureau hospitals, the most famous of whom was Alberta Thomas Augusta, who had trained in Canada and was the highest-ranking black officer in the Union army, reaching a brevet rank of lieutenant colonel. He headed the Freedmen's Hospital in Washington and later the Lincoln Hospital, a Bureau hospital for freedpeople in Savannah, Georgia, all while combatting discrimination within the army. Mainly due to the Bureau's efforts, the disparity in mortality rates between black people and whites decreased substantially in the South, despite the smallpox and cholera epidemics that tore through the region during and after the Civil War.

The Bureau's hospitals and the many orphan asylums it ran in cooperation with benevolent and freedmen's aid societies were sometimes housed in rebel buildings that had been confiscated by the federal government. In Washington, President Johnson not only pardoned a former Confederate Mr. R. S. Cox, but returned his home, in which the "National Association for the Relief of Destitute Colored Women and Children" operated an asylum. The association purchased new land, and the Bureau erected a new building for the asylum; it soon housed hundreds of orphans. Cox sued them for $10,000 for having used his home and lost. In New Orleans, the Bureau operated three orphan asylums with the National Freedmen's Relief Association. Two had been founded by the city's black population and were "partially maintained by the colored people." As Howard acknowledged, "the colored people themselves" took care of most of their orphans and "generously saved the Government much expense."[14]

Freedpeople's everyday claims instilled life and purpose into the Bureau, the first experiment in federal public policy, health care, and social welfare. They envisioned a social state whose duty it would be to provide a safety net for its most vulnerable citizens, while their conservative opponents in the South and across the nation remained mired in Victorian notions of dependence, individual self-help, and the unworthy poor. These ideas were shared by some agents, not to mention

Commissioner Howard. The more immediate problem was that southern elites had grown used to commandeering black labor and bodies
for their own benefit and resisted every attempt to redress centuries
of oppression and stolen labor. Yet however much the Bureau fell short
of its aims, and however much it was itself tainted by the racialist attitudes of the time, it should be remembered as an important early step in
reconfiguring the American state and governance.

The Bureau did not always protect freedpeople or help them when
they were sick or injured. But it had more obvious success in another
area: education. For it was in this sphere that its aims overlapped most
completely with those of freedpeople and built on the wartime work of
freedmen's aid societies and the AMA. The general superintendent of
education for the Freedmen's Bureau, J. W. Alvord, was an abolitionist who had taught in a black school in Cincinnati. Alvord noted the
two ingredients for the Bureau's strides in education: "first, a surprising thirst for knowledge among the negroes; second, teachers in large
numbers volunteering to teach them." The Bureau was aided, Howard
wrote, by "the extraordinary ardor of the pupils and the enthusiasm
of the teachers." Howard directed that the Bureau's educational work
not "supercede" the efforts of voluntary societies, but rather, "system-
atize and facilitate them." A good example of the cooperation between
the Bureau and abolitionist efforts was Captain Stone's success in
establishing a freedmen's school with the help of two Quaker teachers,
Martha Schofield and Mary Taylor, the latter whom he married. The
Schofield Industrial and Normal School continued long after its founders returned north, and it is part of the public school system in Aiken,
South Carolina today. The success of the Greenville colored school was
largely due to a black teacher, Charles Hopkins, and the aid it received
from the freedmen's relief associations.

The Bureau financed freedmen's schools and teachers because the
ex-Confederacy, unlike the North, for the most part lacked a public
school system, except for "common schools" in a few southern cities and

"Carte-de-visite of a Freedmen's School with Students and Teachers," by
John D. Heywood, ca. 1868. *National Museum of African American History and Culture,
Smithsonian Institution*

some counties of North Carolina. In 1865, the Freedmen's Bureau ran
740 schools with 90,589 students and 1,314 teachers, and the numbers
grew slightly the following year. This was a "drop in the bucket," though,
as the Bureau received hundreds of applications for new schools from
freedpeople. It built schools, transported teachers from the North, provided supplies, and paid salaries. It established night schools in Washington. In Tennessee, white children attended its schools. Hewing to
Victorian gender norms, girls, who comprised half the student population in these schools, were often taught sewing and housekeeping
in addition to basic reading and writing. For "female education," the
Bureau instructed cultivating "womanly virtues," on which slavery
had had a "frightful effect." Howard's Victorian class and gender biases
were a contrast to freedpeople's expansive vision of the state to redress
entrenched inequalities.

The most well-developed school system was in Louisiana. It was
financed through a state tax, put in place during Lincoln's wartime
reconstruction. In 1866, authorities in New Orleans, emboldened by

Johnsonian Restoration, purged the city's schools of unionist teachers and discontinued the singing of the "Star-Spangled Banner." When the state revoked the school tax, freedpeople sent hundreds of petitions demanding to be taxed to maintain the schools—surely one of the only pro-tax revolts in southern, and indeed American, history.

In addition to the work of freedmen's aid societies, Quakers maintained freedmen's schools in Maryland and South Carolina. Letters from students in the schools run by the Friends Association for the Relief of the Freedmen offer a rare look into the worldview of freed children. One child, Matilda Beckett, wrote, "The rebels want us to stay and work for nothing but we know better than that." They were "ugly to us, do us bad as they can," and paid freedpeople "half wages, and sometimes nothing." Another student, Ellen Beshears, agreed; the rebels, she wrote, "do bad to us." She added that "I love to come to school and learn." The choice, for most freed children, was between school and field labor. Thirteen-year-old Billy wanted to both study and support his widowed mother. All expressed their gratitude to their teachers, but a note of thanks from Daniel Holland, a budding poet, stood out: "My pen is poor, my ink is pale, my love for you will never fail."

As a result of congressional appropriations during Reconstruction, the Bureau schools were put on a firmer footing. But the biggest driver of the educational success of the Bureau remained freedpeople themselves. By 1867, "colored pupils" were paying school tuition and freedpeople contributed considerably to the upkeep of freedmen's schools. In Georgia, freedpeople maintained over a hundred schools, compared to just over forty funded by the Bureau and around eighty by northern benevolent societies. At the same time, poverty and lack of basic necessities, including even clothing, shaped the experience of students. Early on, Howard undertook a lecture tour of the North to solicit funds for freedmen's schools, receiving the support of abolitionists like Lewis Tappan, founder of the AMA, as well as many black leaders. John Andrew Jackson, "a colored teacher who has labored some months under the auspices of the Freedmen's Bureau, in the work of education among the blacks of the South," also undertook northern lecture tours to raise funds. (Jackson had escaped slavery in South Carolina and settled in Canada before the war.) He made regular northern tours to collect food, clothes, and farm equipment for freedpeople. In 1868, a new Freedmen's Bureau bill allowed all "unexpended balances" to be used for education.

Freedpeople's desire for education transcended age; many adults started "self-teaching." Freedpeople established their own schools in "cellars, sheds, or the corner of a negro meeting house," while black Union soldiers who had acquired literacy through their service taught others. The always-paternalistic Howard observed, "This earnestness of ignorant men on behalf of their children's education was indeed remarkable and full of promise." Howard might not have known that before the war, enslaved people had been taught, at times, by whites but more often in secret by free and literate black people. As a freedman in Richmond testified, he learned how to read and write from a free black woman, "Miss Judah," who had taught him "at peril to her life." By 1867, freedpeople fully or partly owned over six hundred schools across the South—clearly, they understood the democratic and equalizing benefits of the public school system. Like slaveholders who had starved their region of public education because they themselves could access private schools, southern elites complained about taxes that would finance public schools during Reconstruction.

Education superintendents in the Bureau generally preferred African Americans or northern whites as teachers because among "Southern white teachers, male and female . . . faith in negro education was too small, and their ignorance of practical teaching too great, to admit of any reasonable degree of success." Southern white teachers made up a greater percentage of teachers than most historians acknowledge, but black teachers from the South and the North came to dominate the schools after the demise of the Bureau and Reconstruction. The white southerners the Bureau employed were mostly unionists who were willing to bear the "ostracism" of other whites. Women formed a large proportion of teachers overall, some even ascending to the ranks of superintendents of asylums and schools, challenging the gendered hierarchy of the Bureau, which was otherwise dominated by Union officers. Some teachers, especially those who were not abolitionists, were racist or at best racially paternalistic in their attitudes. Abolitionist teachers like Sallie Holley and Caroline Putnam founded schools and continued to teach even after the fall of Reconstruction.

Whatever their politics, teachers in freedmen's schools faced overt harassment from locals. White southerners complained that abolitionist teachers taught "social equality" between blacks and whites, had students sing "John Brown's Body" and the national anthem, and celebrated the Fourth of July (apparently an intolerable affront to Confederates). They called the AMA the "American Miscegenation Society" because its schools were initially integrated. Schools became targets of racist attacks and arson. According to a recent estimate, at least 631 schools throughout the South were burned down during Reconstruction. Black people rebuilt most of them. Cases of arson against black schools and churches would continue unabated well after the overthrow of Reconstruction.

In Texas, only "loyal Germans" agreed to board northern teachers. In North Carolina, an AMA teacher was lashed a hundred times by a racist mob. In 1868, a northern teacher described the treatment she had received in Lexington, Virginia, particularly from the white male students in Washington College, whose president was the ex-Confederate general Robert E. Lee. The students had targeted her in the streets, and when she complained to Lee, she learned that "to expect protection from that quarter would be in vain." Not once did she venture out without being met "with some form of rudeness." She was called "damned Yankee bitch of a n—— teacher." It sickened her to see previously antislavery men such as Henry Ward Beecher and Horace Greeley fawn over Lee. Other teachers, particularly black women, fared worse. Some were assaulted, raped, and even killed.

However, well after Reconstruction southerners could not completely roll back black education, even as they disfranchised black men and established new systems of economic and penal servitude for all African Americans. The gains made during Reconstruction were too quick and became too entrenched. After his 1870 tour of the South, General Superintendent Alvord noted "schools of all kinds improve rapidly." He wrote that "The experiment of educating the freedmen proves to be successful, and the ignorant whites may be greatly benefitted." Gen. R. K. Scott, the Bureau representative in South Carolina, reported that while "a class of men within his jurisdiction . . . took the greatest pleasure in persecuting freedmen, and considered the murder of a colored man a practical joke," nearly twenty thousand black students attended freedmen's and private schools. As Alvord recorded, the "colored schools are the only public schools in the Capital of South Carolina." He also commented positively on the schools in Georgia—he was impressed with Atlanta University—and remarked on the moral, educational, and industrial "improvement" of freedmen.

Alvord learned much else on his tour. Most of the schools in Louisiana were "sustained by the freedmen themselves," with the planters from the southern and western parts of the state "openly against the education of freedmen." The same was true in Virginia, where Gen. S. C. Armstrong, a son of Hawaiian missionaries who disparaged the abolitionist demand for racial equality, concentrated mainly on the development of industrial education at the Hampton Normal and Agricultural Institute, later Hampton University. His favorite student, Booker T. Washington, became an ardent proponent of industrial education in the post-Reconstruction South. In Tennessee, which rivaled Mississippi in the number of attacks on freedpeople, "the status of schools was better than justice" overall. Alvord was disappointed in schools in Chattanooga and Nashville, but "leading colored men" told him they would feel "wholly unprotected" if the Bureau left. Alvord reported on three institutions of higher learning flourishing in Tennessee, especially Fisk University, which were maintained by northern funds.

In Kentucky, which "kept abreast of Tennessee" in domestic terrorism, "white citizens manifested a bitter opposition to the education of colored children" that tended to "dishearten" freedpeople and thwart the efforts of the Bureau. The eventual "disbandment" of freedmen's schools in Tennessee and the very few schools for black children in Kentucky foretold the end of Reconstruction. Other border states, such as West Virginia and Missouri, established superior school systems. The superintendent of schools for Maryland and Delaware, Lt. C. McDougall, reported that while "the prospect in the State of Delaware for future success is very flattering," Maryland suffered from a severe shortage of teachers, with "whole counties without a single school." To the south, in Texas, where "robberies, murders, and other outrageous crimes were matters of daily occurrence," military occupation under Gen. Charles Griffin allowed for the creation of a functioning school system. In Arkansas, Alvord noticed that freedpeople would not move to and labor in new towns unless their children would also be educated in them.

By 1870, nearly 3,500 black and white teachers taught around 150,000 students, including adults and a few white children, at freedmen's schools. Education superintendents documented that black children performed well in examinations, mastering complex arithmetic. Violent opposition from mobs that burned down schools and drove away and attacked students and teachers convinced Howard that "military protection alone could save our schools. Without it they would be before long utterly broken up and new ones could not be put into operation." Alvord wrote that the racist "cant" that freedpeople were "too stupid to learn" was as untrue as another proslavery claim, that they "were too ferocious to be free." He concluded that "the surprising efforts of our colored population to obtain education are not spasmodic. They are growing to a habit, crystallizing into a system, and each succeeding school term shows their organization more and more complete. If knowledge elevates, then these people are destined to rise."

Long after the fall of Reconstruction and the departure of the Bureau, black educators and activists continued their fight in state-funded southern urban public schools. An 1867 conference bringing together all the freedmen's aid societies and commissions involved in freedmen's education resolved that their efforts would succeed only if the southern states established a permanent public school system, modeled after those in the North. Southern whites would come to realize that black people were not just laborers, but "enlightened" citizens. The challenge, Alvord pointed out, was that most southerners resented being taxed for schools and thought "inferior schools" were sufficient for their "colored population." Even "poor whites" had "imbibed" the idea that free public schools were a sign of "poverty," and avoided attending them, according to the education superintendent in Tennessee. "Yet the ruling classes among southern whites was [sic] deeply offended," Howard noted, at the idea of educating blacks as a step toward citizenship and economic mobility. The "old leaders" of the South, Wendell Phillips wrote, "must be utterly crushed out and banished before any great progress can be made in civil reconstruction." In his final report, Alvord lamented that even though the Bureau had enrolled over 200,000 children throughout its existence, it had not reached millions in the countryside, schools had been shut down, and southern opposition to black education was unrelenting. Still, black illiteracy rates in the South fell from 80 percent in 1865 to 44 per cent by the end of the nineteenth century, an unsung achievement of Reconstruction.[15]

When Frederick Douglass, Henry Highland Garnet, John Mercer Langston, and J. Sella Martin, all prominent black abolitionists, interviewed Howard in 1869 about his support for universal manhood suffrage, he responded that his main goal was freedmen's education, but that he supported "eventual suffrage for the negroes" limited by "educational qualification." Abolitionists took a more expansive view of things. As Garnet declared in a rousing resolution at a public meeting in Baltimore: "Aiming to complete the establishment of our rights and liberties; and that our weapons are the spelling book, the Bible, the press, and the implements of industry; and our impregnable fortifications are schoolhouses and the Church of Christ; and our watchwords are UNCONDITIONAL LOYALTY TO GOD AND COUNTRY." The fugitive slave abolitionist Mattie Jackson felt it "a duty to improve the mind and have ever had a thirst for education to fill that vacuum for which the soul has ever yearned since my earliest remembrance." Black abolitionists described the government as well as black churches and schools as the administrative apparatus necessary to achieve full emancipation.

The fight for equal school rights, and educational activism in general, had deep abolitionist roots. Abolitionists such as Frances J. LeMoyne, Gerrit Smith, and Edna Dow Cheney left large bequests and endowments for black schools and colleges. They gave more money to southern black education in this period than some of the more famous names, such as Peabody, Slater, Carnegie, and Rosenwald, did later on. Some abolitionists, such as Calvin and Alida Clark, who founded Southland College and Normal Institute in Arkansas, worked in southern schools for the rest of their lives. Kentucky's Berea College had been founded by the abolitionist Rev. John G. Fee. The Bureau helped rebuild the college, which had been shut down by an antiabolitionist mob. By the 1890s, Berea, like many of the AMA schools, was forced to abide by southern segregation laws. Black churches and denominations would found their own schools and colleges. Many of these schools survived despite deteriorating conditions for African Americans after Reconstruction.

The Freedmen's Bureau's most lasting legacy in education was the founding of the first historically black universities and colleges (HBCUs) starting in 1867, and the first presidents of new black colleges—which included Fisk, Claflin University, and Bennett College—were abolitionists. (Before the war, mainly abolitionist schools and colleges, including Oneida Institute, Oberlin, Central, and Knox had been open to African Americans.) A whole new generation of civil rights leaders, including Walter White and Mary McLeod Bethune, graduated from these institutions. Commissioner Howard, who called himself a proponent of "higher education" for African Americans, lent his name and became president of another new school, Howard University in Washington. The AMA founded Atlanta University and Avery Institute in South Carolina. In 1869, Tougaloo University in Mississippi and Talladega College in Alabama were founded. Booker T. Washington founded what became the Tuskegee Institute in Alabama, which was geared more toward vocational training. Most of the HBCUs, however, stressed academic training and became staging grounds for the emergence of a professional black middle class, including the lawyers who fought cases against Jim Crow, as well as the student activists who led sit-ins and freedom rides during the civil rights movement later on. The first female vice president, Kamala Harris, graduated from Howard. The emancipatory power of black education lives on in our times.

Reconstruction state governments—propelled by and building on

"Glimpses of the Freedmen—The Freedmen's Union Industrial School, Richmond, VA," by James E. Taylor, *Frank Leslie's Illustrated Newspaper*, September 22, 1866. *Library of Congress*

the efforts of freedpeople, abolitionists, and the Freedmen's Bureau—established the first extensive public school systems in the South. In these same years, Charles Sumner, among others in Congress, called for a federal department of education. Republicans established one in 1867, but it was soon downgraded to a bureau under the Department of Interior. Abolitionists protested that the limited resources of an education bureau could not support southern schools and demanded the reinstitution of "a branch of the federal government" that would be responsible for education. Howard, too, recommended a federal Bureau of Education to oversee black education.

Republican senator Henry Blair's bill would have provided federal funding for public schools. It passed in the Senate but was defeated in the House thrice in the 1880s. Its final defeat in 1890 by southern Democrats and conservative Republicans allied with big business was the end of what the historian Hilary Green calls "Educational Reconstruction," and what James Anderson sees as the start of educating African Americans for "second class," rather than equal, citizenship. The Blair bill was an early precursor to the Elementary and Secondary Education Act of 1965 that established federal funding of public schools to address educational and economic inequality. The federal Department of Education was finally refounded in 1979, nearly a hundred years after the first attempt. But even today, educational inequalities persist because of state and local controls; the abolitionist dream of a "national system of education" is yet to be realized. After Reconstruction, education remained a site of contestation in the black struggle for equality. School systems developed along segregated lines with black children condemned to substandard, poorly funded schools, an issue that would spur the NAACP's legal battle for school integration, including but not ending with the *Brown v. Board of Education* case in 1954.[16]

It was through the Freedmen's Bureau that freedpeople articulated political demands and enlisted the federal government in their politics of survival—to gain land, fair wages, protection, and subsistence—and their freedom claims. The Bureau established and supported black schools; offered a modicum of justice to freedpeople treated abusively by employers, local courts, police, and state officials; and provided medical services through its overburdened hospitals and asylums, as well as what Howard called "famine relief." Besides its officers, the Bureau employed and subsidized an army of teachers, surgeons, and doctors. It was the only instance of large-scale government activism for the welfare of its citizens before the Progressive Era and the New Deal. Regarded as a "temporary necessity" even by its friends and supporters, the Bureau had to deal with the bitter opposition of southern whites, "who had not even believed in emancipation," and of "the conservatives of the north," whose sympathy "always stopped with the white population." DuBois lamented the shuttering of the Bureau in 1872: "Had political exigencies been less pressing, the opposition to government guardianship of Negroes less bitter, and the attachment to the slave system less strong, the social seer can well imagine a far better policy—a permanent Freedmen's Bureau, with a national system of Negro schools; a carefully supervised employment and labor office; a system of impartial protection before regular courts; and such institutions for social betterment as savings-banks, land and building associations, and social settlements."

Black educational institutions created a new generation of African American leaders, some who would retreat into a narrow middle-class conservatism, while others—"race men and women"—deployed the politics of respectability and uplift in the fight for black equality. DuBois's assessment of abolitionists and Bureau schools and colleges still holds: "in a single generation they put thirty thousand black teachers in the South" and "wiped out the illiteracy of the majority of the black people of the land." One in every six northern teachers the Bureau employed was black, a fact that challenges the conventional narrative focused on benevolent white teachers.[17]

The Freedmen's Bureau was an inapt name for the agency, given the centrality of women and children to its duties. But looking beyond that gendered narrowness, the name was unintentionally accurate: though it was intended to refer to the people it served, it in fact named the people who made it what it was. The Bureau was an unprecedented experiment in government action, but it was driven primarily by grassroots black activism. It reveals the centrality of freedpeople themselves to the conception and progress of Reconstruction. And despite missteps, numerous limitations, racial paternalism, and its temporary nature, it embodied the concept of a modern social state. It was foundational to the Second American Republic, as well as to two ideas that outlived it: that the government is responsible for the welfare of its neediest citizens and that, in particular, it owes a debt to the formerly enslaved. The Bureau's work in the South resulted in the expansion of two distinct political traditions in the United States: a modern liberal tradition identified with African Americans and progressives that looks to the federal government to correct local injustices and inequalities and provide for all citizens, and a conservative, predominantly southern, tradition that critiques all government intervention in the economy and society as illegitimate. The latter persists in the rhetoric against "big government" and in favor of "states' rights."[18] Reconstruction and its legacies continue to shape the contours of our democracy in ways little understood by most Americans today.

CHAPTER FIVE

Black Reconstruction

We are not here as slaves, but we are here now as
free American citizens, and representatives of a
people who have honored us with their votes.

—WILLIS HODGES, 1868

"The First Vote," by Alfred R. Waud, *Harper's Weekly*,
November 16, 1867. *Library of Congress*

However significant the Freedman's Bureau was—as a conduit
for freedpeople's claims on the state and as an origin point for
social democracy in America—it was only one tool with which
black people shaped governance in the South. Alongside southern
unionists and northern allies, they inaugurated a radical experiment
to install an interracial democracy on the ruins of a slave society.[1] The
unprecedented political mobilization of African Americans created

new state governments with a vision of the postwar South diametrically opposed to that of the state governments of Johnsonian restoration, whose Black Codes commandeered freedpeople's labor and deprived them of all rights. Freedpeople organized in Union Leagues, Republican Party Clubs, and black conventions—the last often overlooked in histories of this period.

The South's discredited elites, who had plunged the region into war and destruction, worked to undermine this emerging, fragile democracy. But for a brief period, the ex-Confederate states did enjoy the constitutional guarantee of republican state governments. The result was the establishment of the most democratic local and state governments the region saw between the American Revolution and the civil rights movement, a span of almost two hundred years.

W. E. B. DuBois titled his history of Reconstruction *Black Reconstruction* because he saw the struggles of freedpeople as central to its origins and progress. The communist historian James Allen described the activism of southern black people in a similar light but viewed bourgeois black politicians as the leading actors. I use the term "Black Reconstruction" to refer to grassroots black political mobilization as well as officeholding during Reconstruction. There wasn't a big class divide between black political leaders and their voters. The former were closely allied with the black masses, and some would die in poverty and obscurity once Reconstruction was overthrown. Many of the thousands of local and state officials emerged from the ranks of freedpeople themselves. DuBois may have exaggerated when he called Reconstruction a triumph of the black proletariat, but he was not that far from the truth.

An explosion of southern black politics at the local level combined with the efforts of Republicans in Congress made Reconstruction a potent endeavor. A genuine, if contested, democracy took hold because of it. Former slaves, rather than their former masters, had the upper hand for the first time—it was a world turned upside down. Imperfect and uneven as it was, Reconstruction was a departure from politics as usual. The wonder is that it was even attempted. But as I argue, it was always challenged and hence inherently unstable, even at the moment of its greatest triumph. The Reconstruction governments of the South represented what one scholar has called "untimely democracy," not a linear march to a progressive end but "a path to democratic promises that have been perpetually denied."[2]

Republicans in Congress looked to freedpeople themselves to implement Reconstruction, not only as soldiers and teachers, but as activists and politicians. Soon enough, African American voters would help elect the first black representatives, senators, governors, lieutenant governors, state legislators, and a host of local officials in numbers that have been matched only recently. They established democratically elected local governments, and the policies they initiated included a tax-funded public school system, protections for the rights of labor, property rights and the right to divorce for women, and civil rights laws. Black legislators also launched programs for land redistribution, though these came to less. State and local politics became arenas in which to realize the promise of black citizenship. And the self-mobilization of southern blacks at the grassroots was what made that possible.

Abolitionists argued that Reconstruction meant that those who had been confined to the bottom rung of slave society would become equal partners in postwar government. Wendell Phillips claimed that based on the principle of "self-government," working-class black people should be represented just as much as working-class whites. Rather than the enslaved, it was those southern "tyrants," who "imbruted" by their "crimes," were unsuited to representative government. Frances Harper said that in a true republic, "the humblest and poorest man has as much right and justice" as the children of presidents and governors. Harper undertook a southern lecture tour after the war, speaking to gatherings of freedpeople. In one speech, she explained how the exclusion of African Americans from political power had degraded them. "Why, it was asked, has the colored race been at the bottom of the social scale? The Jew, the German, the Irishman, were speedily merged in the body politic and became part and parcel of the nation, while the colored people were social pariahs and political outcasts."

Freedpeople were the backbone of two critical political organizations that fought for citizenship: the Republican Party, and the Union Leagues composed of southern unionists. These organizations, like the reconstructed state governments, were interracial, each a coalition of blacks, southern unionists, and northerners. As the *New Era,* a black newspaper founded by Frederick Douglass and Rev. J. Sella Martin, put it, "The Republican party, leavened with the little leaven of the despised abolitionists, has been bread to the negro in his hunger." Black people found a natural political home in the party of Lincoln, emancipation, and black rights, an allegiance that would endure until the New Deal.

Republican newspapers and the Freedmen's Bureau published state and local laws and ordinances for the political education of freedpeople. They maintained lists of African Americans running for office. The Union Leagues and Republican Party clubs became a means to gain political literacy and functioned as community associations. The clubs, in which the "intelligent colored men would talk with more ignorant ones," reached all black people. They were institutions through which freedpeople could inject their concerns into mainstream politics.

Unlike the Union Leagues and Clubs in the North that were formed by elites, the Union Leagues of the South were plebeian organizations dominated by ex-slaves and nonslaveholding unionists. Freedpeople made the leagues their own, arming themselves in self-defense to resist political terror and establishing militias. League councils, the governing committees of Union Leagues, fanned out across the rural South, even intervening in labor contract and land disputes. In the plantation regions of the South, the leagues were predominantly black; in the nonslaveholding, hilly areas, such as western North Carolina, they were composed of mostly white unionists. While membership in the leagues was restricted to adult men, that rule did not preclude black women from participating. The same was true of local Republican meetings, where women threw themselves into debates over rights, labor, and land.

The Republican clubs and Union League councils not only provided political lessons in leadership, organization, and debate, but in the process helped cement freedpeople's allegiance to the Republican Party and to the Union. Many black league officers, such as James T. Rapier of Alabama, Richard Cain and Robert Elliot of South Carolina, Henry

McNeal Turner of Georgia, Jonathan C. Gibbs of Florida, and Abraham Galloway of North Carolina, became prominent state politicians. In the Deep South, thousands of black men joined the leagues, attempting to reorder political and economic relationships in the countryside, to the ire of planters. The leagues and Republican clubs built black political networks, mobilizing them for elections to the new Reconstruction southern constitutional conventions and governments that took place from 1867 to 1869. At the same time, political participation and especially leadership entailed real risks for southern Republicans, making them easier targets of vigilante violence.[3]

While the Union Leagues and Republican clubs were interracial organizations, freedpeople also created their own autonomous political organizations: the black conventions. The colored convention movement began in the pre–Civil War North. The conventions were state and national meetings of African Americans, predominantly men, who came together to demand equal rights of citizenship. Convention delegates were either self-selected or voted in by their local institutions.

During Reconstruction, the conventions spread to the South. Whether in the North or the South, they usually issued public "addresses," with a list of their demands, to the people of the United States and to state legislatures. They were large political meetings, almost like the conventions put on by political parties, though not as regular and not focused on choosing candidates. (The Black conventions are not to be confused with the state constitutional conventions taking place as part of Reconstruction.) As literary historian P. Gabrielle Foreman argues, the conventions birthed a distinct black political practice, a *"parallel politics"* to combat exclusion from the body politic. During the Civil War, the National Black Convention of 1864, which had established the National Equal Rights League, and a smattering of state conventions which formed state equal rights leagues, were the first to raise the issue of voting rights for black men. The colored conventions held in the South in 1865 demanded the vote but also land ownership. The Colored People's Convention of South Carolina asked "that we be permitted to acquire homesteads for ourselves and children." It met in Charleston's historic Zion church in November to protest the Black Codes.

The conventions became significant venues of black protest against Andrew Johnson's restoration. The Virginia convention of freedpeople in August 1865 argued that his pardons had "left us entirely at the mercy of these subjugated but unconverted rebels." In September 1866, the *New Orleans Tribune* published a letter by a "J.W.M." calling for a "COLORED NATIONAL CONVENTION" in Cincinnati, Ohio. The author noted, "Past victories in the great work of human emancipation do not apologize or excuse the barbarity of the daily outrages that are perpetrated on our brethren in different parts of the country." The convention would advocate for "human rights," "human liberty," and equality. J.W.M. wrote, "We want the benefits of true republicanism—not the proscription of a rebellized oligarchy."

A national convention did not come together that year, but black state conventions did convene across the South, making a broad-based argument for black citizenship. At the Georgia convention in Atlanta, officials from the Freedmen's Bureau such as Capt. J. E. Bryant and its "president"—every convention elected a presiding officer—gave speeches. The convention's address to Georgia's legislature stated that "We need the power to represent our interest in every department bearing upon our condition as a people." It asked for "at least conditional suffrage"— presumably for the literate and propertied. Black conventions across the South demanded "legal protection" and "equal justice": the right to testify at trials and sit on juries, and to have fair enforcement of contracts, protection of their persons and property, and "some form of representation."

Southern state conventions spurred further black political organization. In October 1865, a freedmen's convention of 115 delegates representing 60 counties in North Carolina met in Raleigh. It established "The Educational Association of the Colored People of North Carolina." The conservative governor of the state, Jonathan Worth, a Johnson man, gave a speech exhorting freedpeople to industry. The delegates listened politely, but unlike the speech of the former unionist Governor William Holden, which was reproduced in its entirety in the convention's published proceedings, Worth's speech was merely mentioned. The convention resolved to form self-defense auxiliary leagues, which would report the "killing, shooting and robbing of unprotected people." It commended Congress for passing the Freedmen's Bureau Bill, Civil Rights Act, and Fourteenth Amendment. It tendered a special "vote of thanks" to radicals such as Sumner, Stevens, and Wade, and black leaders including Douglass and Garnet. As "colored citizens," the delegates demanded political representation and created the North Carolina Equal Rights League.

In a speech, one delegate asked for more determined action from the Bureau to prevent "injustice towards the (colored) laborer" and the binding out of children. In its formal address to the citizens of North Carolina, the convention drew attention to the outrages committed against freedpeople and their "disfranchisement." It quoted the Declaration of Independence and asked for the "right to suffrage." The Tennessee state convention in Nashville, which also took place that month, likewise commended Congress, Sumner, and Stevens and spoke on behalf of 300,000 "oppressed" and "disfranchised" citizens of the state, demanding the republican form of government guaranteed in the Constitution to all the states.

Black conventions were at the forefront of the push for black political rights in the North as well. That same month, fifty-six delegates to the Illinois state convention met in Galesburg. The convention's address to the people of the state made it clear that their fight was of a piece with that of freedpeople. It challenged the "unjust and unchristian discrimination" against African Americans in a free state that deprived them of access to public schools for which they paid taxes, of the right to sit on juries, and of the "elective franchise." As the report of the convention's committee on suffrage put it, black loyalty to the Union during the war entitled them to "all rights, privileges, and immunities in common with American citizens."

Black abolitionists such as John Jones and Charles Langston led the state conventions in Illinois and Kansas, respectively. The convention of colored citizens in Lawrence, Kansas demanded complete equality before the law, decrying segregation in public spaces and transportation as well as exclusion from the jury and ballot boxes. The convention in Albany, New York, attended by suffragist Susan B. Anthony, drew attention to "Reconstructed Terrorism" against "the loyal citizens of the Southern States." A nationwide convention of black Union soldiers and sailors met in Philadelphia in 1867, led by abolitionists such as Garnet, John M. Langston, J. W. Loguen, and William Howard Day as well as John Brown's white compatriot, Col. Richard J. Hinton. Its address argued that to deny African Americans the ballot was "false in morals and treason to the Constitution."

Black conventions cast the African American struggle for political equality as part of a global fight for democracy. The address of the Illinois convention to "the American people" framed the struggle for black rights as a transnational quest. Even though the United States was "born of resistance to tyranny" and "the great democratic idea of the natural equality of rights," it had compromised its foundations through acceptance of slavery. The address reminded the nation of "the aboriginal man of America, once the undisputed possessor of this continent" who was *"by coercion"* displaced by "civilization," and noted that "the memory of America's children of the forest, long linger in the land that was his." It referred to the uncertain fate of democracy in Europe, warning "cis-Atlantic lovers of their country and of constitutional liberty" of a reactionary "coup d'état," such as that carried out by Louis Bonaparte against the Second French Republic in 1851. Black abolitionist Martin Delany pointed out that in France political rights went hand in hand with citizenship. The lesser example was that of the English, who were content with mere "equality before the law."[4]

Black conventions met throughout Reconstruction, a sustained pressure campaign for African American rights. The conventions identified openly with the Republican Party and the Union Leagues. The Alabama convention that met in Mobile in 1867 resolved that it had no desire to start a colored man's party, given that it was part of the Republican Party. Kentucky's first black convention met in Lexington that year, with 111 delegates from 51 counties. Abolitionist John G. Fee of Berea Institute gave a speech, and the convention petitioned the legislature for basic civil and political rights, the right to testify in courts, and the right to vote. It also thanked the Republican newspapers for their support. In Delaware, leading Republicans attended an "equal rights convention" in 1867. The Iowa black convention announced its support for the "Republican Congress of the United States" and the "Republican party of Iowa," as well as its "fidelity to the Union and the Republican Party and its principles."

Black conventions also convened in states in what was then the American Northwest—states that had discriminated against African Americans with "Black Laws" that restricted their migration and denied them equal civil and political rights. The Iowa convention's address to the people of the state asked for the "privilege of the ballot-box" and for the striking of the word "white" from the state constitution. The Iowa general assembly and Governor Samuel Merrill, following the convention's demands, proposed an amendment to modify the state constitution to give black men the vote, which was approved by voters in 1868. The Equal Rights League of Ohio likewise asked that state's legislature for the abolition of "all proscriptive laws and usages."

For the first time after the Civil War, a National Black Convention convened in Washington in January 1869. As J. W. C. Pennington pointed out, "it was a blunder to give up our regular conventions years ago." Though led by prominent northern black abolitionists including Douglass, who was elected its president, Garnet said that the convention was "an assembling of the disfranchised and newly emancipated citizens of the United States." The abolitionist editor Aaron Powell gave a speech, emphasizing the importance of land and education as well as voting for freedpeople, as did Radical Republican congressman George Julian, who proposed a homestead law to redistribute land to freedpeople. The address of the convention to the people of the United States specifically named Garrison, Gerrit Smith, Lincoln, and the recently deceased Stevens as allies in the struggle for black citizenship.

While acknowledging "the original abolition movement" that had led the fight for the "immediate abolition of slavery" and for "political, educational and religious rights," the convention declared its allegiance to the Republican Party, "through which the rights legally secured to the colored American in his country" were possible. It resolved that "no other party need hope to alienate us therefrom, unless by outstripping it in consistency, and in an honest advocacy of genuine democratic principles." The convention formed a national executive committee with representatives from each state of the Union. It condemned the state government of Georgia for expelling all black members from its legislature and Kentucky for violating the rights of freedpeople with impunity.

The 1869 national convention's commitment to a broad definition of democracy was highlighted by the admission of a woman delegate, a "Miss Johnson," after some debate. A Mr. Brown from Pennsylvania pointed out that "50 ladies of Philadelphia" had voted for him as a delegate while another delegate, Isaiah C. Weir, called himself "an advocate of woman's suffrage." The reasoning usually adopted by conventions to exclude women smacked too much, in his opinion, of the rationale used to exclude "the colored race for two hundred years." J. Sella Martin settled the question by arguing that when the Bible referred to men, it meant both men and women. The resolution to seat women carried the convention.

The national convention that year represented the high point of the political influence of the black convention movement. The convention's national executive committee became a direct conduit to convey black concerns about Reconstruction to the federal government. The committee addressed the House Judiciary Committee, reminding the federal government of its duty to protect the right of suffrage, which should not be restricted by literacy or color. The executive committee also met with President-elect Ulysses Grant and delivered a clear message to him. While offering congratulations and proclaiming their confidence that he would uphold the laws and the rights of the "humblest" citizens, the committee underscored that his "duties"—"removing the rubbish, the accretions of the now dead slaveholding oligarchy"—would be especially "arduous and trying." It reminded him of "seven hundred thousand electors of African descent," who had "braved threats, who defied intimidation, whose numbers have been reduced by assassination and murder in their efforts" to vote for him. The committee petitioned the

Senate to pass George Julian's bill that would open lands in the Deep South, previously given to the railroads, for homesteading.

Land and labor rights were central to the proceedings of the first convention of the Colored National Labor Union. The event was organized by Isaac Myers, a pioneering black trade unionist, and also took place in 1869. Black politicians such as James T. Rapier, Joseph Rainey, Jefferson Long, and James Harris traveled to Baltimore to attend. Delany gave a conservative speech urging workers to industriousness in the face of racist violence, but he was an outlier. The convention's resolutions affirmed that labor was prior to capital, as well as its faith in republican government, temperance, and education, all tenets of the early labor movement. At the same time, the convention was attuned to the fact that freedpeople were primarily "agricultural laborers," and its address indicted "northern capitalists," who would have them growing cotton and sugar according to their prescriptions while paying little heed to the experiences of the workers themselves. The convention envisioned an interracial working-class coalition: "We would have 'the poor white man' of the South born to a heritage of poverty and degradation like his black compeer in social life, feel that labor in our organization seeks the elevation of all its sons and daughters." It resolved to make no distinction based on nationality, sex, or color and recommended that blacks confront proscriptions by employers and white trade unions by forming their own cooperatives and workshops. The colored national union's ideas were similar to those of the Knights of Labor, then the dominant organization of the labor movement, and to those of the national farmers' alliance that would give rise to the Populist movement. Its delegation met with President Grant to thank him for protecting "the loyal laboring classes" in Georgia by reinstating military rule in that state.

State labor conventions were held in South Carolina, Georgia, Texas, Maryland, and Virginia in 1869, and in Alabama in 1871 and 1873. They proposed laws to regulate wages and rents, and to secure the nine-hour day. The South Carolina convention recommended structured mediation in labor and contract disputes. These appeals and proposals were significant achievements, as they addressed the concerns of the black masses, even if they did not lead to new laws being passed. The

Reconstruction legislature of South Carolina was the only such body in the South to consider bills for the protection of labor, though it failed to enact the robust protections demanded by the convention. Black Republican politicians dominated the southern labor conventions, but that did not prevent the conventions from championing the interests of the black working class.[5] However, the question of land ownership was not central to the southern state labor conventions, after the failure of Congress to redistribute land to freedpeople.

Even after the establishment of Reconstruction state governments, black conventions, especially in the South, continued to meet and voice concerns arising from the grassroots. In 1871, a regional convention of southern states met in Columbia, South Carolina, inspired mainly by Henry McNeal Turner, who had served in the Freedmen's Bureau and the Georgia legislature, and by the black labor leader Isaac Myers. The Georgia colored convention issued the call, but all the southern states sent delegations, which were headed by Republican officeholders. Douglass represented Washington, although there is no evidence that he attended.

South Carolina's Lieutenant Governor Alonzo J. Ransier was elected president and, in his opening speech, he justified the meeting of a separate black organization. The convention endorsed Grant for reelection and parted with their long-time ally Charles Sumner in supporting the annexation of San Domingo (the Dominican Republic). Nonetheless, Turner read a letter from Sumner supporting his supplementary civil rights bill, which would outlaw segregation in public places. Speakers reiterated support for the Republicans but proposed a separate National Civil Rights Association (anticipating the formation of the NAACP in 1909) as well as a National Protective Union to protect black civil and political rights in the face of Ku Klux Klan "outrages." A resolution inviting the women in the galleries to be seated in the convention was tabled, however.

While backsliding on the "woman question," the Southern States Convention put issues of political economy front and center. Arguing that southern wealth depended on black labor, it recommended the formation of "Mechanics Unions" (workers were often called "mechanics" in the nineteenth century) and resolved "That every legitimate means be taken by the laboring masses to overthrow this cruel barrier to our progress—the monstrous land monopoly of the South." Its address to the people of the nation asked for no "special favors," but rather for material assistance in developing schools and access to skilled industrial work that excluded blacks. The delegates asked for these "benefits" not for themselves alone but also "for the white portion of the laboring class in our States, whose need is as great as ours." The convention's committee on emigration recommended freedpeople take advantage of the Homestead Act to acquire land, ignoring indigenous dispossession. The committee on labor recommended the formation of a National Labor Union and a federal Bureau of Labor "to advance the condition of the laboring classes," a common demand of workers throughout the era that led eventually to the establishment of the Department of Labor in the Progressive era.

The most effective speech of the convention was made by John F. Quarles of Georgia, who argued that the convention should endorse the principles of republicanism rather than the Republican Party. It was reproduced in its entirety in an appendix to the convention's proceedings. Quarles claimed that the "revolution" of emancipation and black rights was part of the larger battle between liberty and progress on the one hand, and despotism and caste on the other. It was a fight for democracy; the South had created a "complexional oligarchy" and a "landed aristocracy." But the problem of the age was the labor question and its proper "remuneration." Just as workingmen's associations and trades unions were being formed in Europe, Britain, and the North, in the South free labor and an "untrammelled ballot" must replace oligarchy, aristocracy, and caste. The "equality of rights," the "diffusion of education," and the "supremacy" of the rule of law would uplift not just freedpeople but the entire region.[6]

The momentum of the black convention movement had moved south. Indeed, nearly all the state conventions across the nation in the 1870s were held in the region, even as Reconstruction started unraveling. The

1871 Tennessee convention touted a plan for the federal government to buy land for freedpeople, selling it to them over a period of many years on easy terms. It also heard reports from counties across the state, and from its own committees, about black churches and schools being burned down, teachers assaulted and murdered, and employers reneging on wages. Its "committee on outrages," like the defunct Freedmen's Bureau, asked federal courts to take jurisdiction of all such crimes (much like the federal government can intervene and charge offenders with "hate crimes" today), especially since black people continued to be excluded from juries. The convention's memorial to Congress and the president noted, "The cry of the masses from every quarter is Protection! Protection!! Protection!!!" ever since former Confederates had come back to power in the state government. It warned of "another condition of slavery," as more and more black people were sent to the penitentiary for misdemeanors—misdemeanors for which whites were discharged—giving rise to the South's notorious convict lease labor system.[7]

A major national convention was held in Nashville in 1879. Among its leading organizers were two black Republicans, P. B. S. Pinchback, former governor of Louisiana, and Congressman John Lynch of Mississippi. Many delegates and local societies in attendance, such as the Charleston Colored Western Emigration Society, called for emigration out of the South to what they still referred to, using antebellum language, as the free states and territories. Delegates critiqued northern black leaders, like Douglass, who opposed emigration, arguing that they did not understand the plight of poor southern blacks. Congressman Joseph Rainey of South Carolina reluctantly endorsed emigration: "We have stood too much now, and I would not blame any colored man who would advise his people to flee from the oppressors to the land of freedom." Hundreds of resolutions for emigration tipped the scale in favor of it, despite opposition from a few northerners.

The convention supported the Kansas Emigration Aid Society, which coordinated what was then the largest exodus of black people out of the South. These "Exodusters," as they were known, were led by the fugitive slave abolitionist Benjamin "Pap" Singleton, who had returned to Tennessee during Reconstruction, and by Henry Adams of Louisiana, a former Union soldier and local Republican leader. The report of the committee on migration forthrightly stated, "This migration movement is based on a determined and irrepressible desire, on the part of the colored people of the South, to go anywhere where they can escape the cruel treatment and continued threats of the dominant race in the South." If the "colored voter" was denied his rights, he had the right "to seek some other place within the United States where he can exercise them without fear and hindrance." The convention resolved to create the American Protective Society to Prevent Injustice to Colored People, another in a series of attempts to form a national civil rights organization.[8]

In the 1880s, even after the overthrow of Reconstruction, black people in southern states continued to hold conventions. The 1883 Texas convention invited the Democratic governor, John Ireland, an ardent proslavery secessionist, who admonished the delegates not to get into "politics" or fight against segregation. The report of the committee on "Grievances" made clear that most white southerners opposed black citizenship because "of the great prejudice against them as a race," a consequence of slavery. Their opposition to any form of racial equality stemmed from the absence of the "mutual regard which is supposed to possess citizens of a common country." This had led to "infringements" on black rights, such as laws against racial intermarriage, less funding for black schools, the unequal treatment of black people in the criminal justice system, exclusion from juries, abuse and murder in convict labor camps, and segregation in all public conveyances. The convention's conciliatory address to the people of Texas stressed that African Americans were taxed to support railroads and schools where they were subject to inferior accommodations and treatment. Like most others, the Texas convention excluded women, even though women had been active in Republican politics and labor strikes. Three more state conventions were held in the state, one as late as 1895, in Houston.

For black Republican politicians ousted from power after Reconstruction, the conventions became a venue to keep black politics alive. In 1896, the platform of the Florida convention, led by ex-congressman Josiah T. Walls, asked forthrightly for "restoring the right to suffrage," given that many black men had been deliberately disfranchised for petty crimes. (Only in 2018 did Florida voters end this practice and allow ex-prisoners to vote. Yet the state government undermined the decision through the imposition of fees that ex-felons need to pay before regaining the right to vote.) The petition of the 1885 Kentucky convention to the state legislature explained that not protesting infringements on black rights, even in the worst of conditions, would be an act of political cowardice:

> When a free people, living in a bodypolitie [sic], feel that the laws are unjustly administered to them; that discriminations are openly made; that various subterfuges and legal technicalities are constantly used to deprive them of the enjoyment of those rights and immunities belonging to the humblest citizen; when the courts become no refuge for the outraged, and when a sentiment is not found sufficient to do them justice; it becomes their bounden duty to protest against such a state of affairs.

In the 1890s, as the convention movement finally petered out due to increasingly oppressive conditions, two southern state conventions still protested the systematic evisceration of black citizenship. At the national convention held in Washington in 1890, delegates formed the American Citizens' Equal Rights Association, an organization much like the old Equal Rights Leagues that would attempt to secure black rights. Pinchback chaired the executive committee. Its address noted that with the fall of Reconstruction, "Votes of colored American citizens in said states [of the South] are suppressed by violence and neutralized by fraud." Southern elections were "farcical formalities." Black people were subject to inferior public accommodations and were lynched and murdered "without a hearing" or "semblance of a trial." Black workers rarely received a fair share of the fruits of their labor. That year, black leaders founded the National Afro-American League, yet another early civil rights organization. In 1893, McNeal Turner, now a staunch emigrationist, called a national convention in Cincinnati. There, he issued a

"The National Colored Convention in Session at Washington, D.C.," by
Theodore Davis, *Harper's Weekly*, February 6, 1869. *Library of Congress*

trenchant indictment of lynching and called for freedpeople to be compensated for enslavement.[9]

Though historians have long focused on the Republican Party and the
Union Leagues to understand black political mobilization in Reconstruction, the conventions were similarly important engines of southern black
politics. They continued to represent black southerners after Reconstruction, allowing freedpeople to vindicate their right to assembly and share
ideas and present forceful resolutions and appeals to the nation. The
conventions demonstrated the activism of freedpeople at the grassroots.
Denied so long any rights, political or otherwise, they took quickly to a
practice that northern black abolitionists pioneered and formed associations that laid the foundation for the civil rights revolution in the twentieth
century. The conventions are the missing link between black abolitionism
and early civil rights organizations in the history of black protest.

A more familiar, though no less significant, development in the making
of Black Reconstruction was the mass voting of African American men

and the election of black politicians at the local, state, and national levels. Black electoral participation, driven by grassroots activism in ways similar to the convention movement, would change the face of American democracy for a brief period. Reconstruction, historian Eric Foner noted, inspired millennial hopes among freedpeople that centuries of oppression could be obliterated. And black men holding political office were the most prominent expression of those hopes. The process of registering heretofore disfranchised men to vote was aided by Union and Loyal leagues, Republican clubs, the Freedmen's Bureau, and the Union army. The Union Republican Congressional Committee disseminated hundreds of political pamphlets in the South. Freedpeople, abolitionist Charles Stearns wrote, "were keen-eyed in their political vision, fully justifying the buoyant expectations of those who had conferred on them political privileges."[10]

For the first time in US history, black men voted in large numbers and were elected to public office. The disfranchisement of prominent Confederates and the refusal of many southern men to participate in the elections to the state constitutional conventions of 1867–1869 resulted in large Republican majorities. Alabama, the first ex-Confederate state to elect a constitutional convention in October 1867, had eighteen black delegates, and out of a total of one hundred delegates, ninety-six were Republican. The Alabama convention wrote a progressive state constitution establishing a public school system and an agricultural college (which became Auburn University), property rights for married women, and voting rights for black men. The convention also passed a resolution that freedpeople could "collect a fair equivalent for their services" from former owners who had kept them enslaved from January 1, 1863, the date of the Emancipation Proclamation, to May 1865, weeks after Robert E. Lee's surrender at Appomattox. Maryland, a border slave state that had convened a constitutional convention earlier in 1867, clarified that former slaveholders were not to be compensated for loss of their human property. The Reconstruction constitutional conventions in the South, derisively designated "black and tan" by their enemies for their black and mixed-race members, were, as the New York diarist George Templeton Strong wrote, "a tremendous and searching social revolution."

The story of the constitutional conventions was not one of "negro domination," as their opponents accused. Even as Republicans in the Thirty-Ninth Congress dismantled Johnsonian restoration and passed numerous Reconstructions Acts, southern whites still dominated seven of the ten constitutional conventions, because they comprised a majority of the population. In many instances, black majority districts elected northern whites to represent them. Across the conventions, most southern white delegates were opposed to integration in schools and public spaces, while most northern whites advocated resolutions regarding economic modernization and civil rights. Almost all the black delegates, who still made up a minority of all delegates, fought for economic and political democracy. Freedpeople elected a majority of black delegates in states where a majority of the overall population was black, like South Carolina, or where free blacks had led the fight for equal rights, as in Louisiana. Black delegates formed 40 percent of the Florida convention but were underrepresented in Alabama, Mississippi, Georgia, and Virginia. They made up only 10 percent of the delegates in Texas, Arkansas, and North Carolina. Reconstruction constitutional conventions were, as Strong put it, "pepper and salt conventions."

White Republicans were divided between radicals and moderates, and more specifically, between the more radical northerners and mostly moderate (if not deeply conservative) southerners. The small numbers of radical southern white Republicans generally came from the mountainous, predominantly nonslaveholding, poor regions of their states. In Florida, divisions between moderates and radicals resulted initially in two separate conventions. At the Georgia convention, proposed ordinances that would have prohibited those who could not read the Bible or Constitution from voting, prevented all African Americans from officeholding, and criminalized interracial marriage by imprisonment from ten to twenty years or banishment to "Africa or Liberia," were deemed out of order. In the North Carolina convention, a Mr. Durham proposed resolutions protesting Reconstruction, arguing that to "degrade the white race to the level of the black race, are crimes against the civilization of the age and against God." He wanted to prohibit black men from officeholding and racial intermarriage; the former resolution was voted down and the latter tabled. He also cosigned a minority report that protested black male suffrage.

The Arkansas constitutional convention, with only eight black delegates, wasted an inordinate amount of time discussing racial intermarriage and passed a resolution discouraging it. The "ladies" of the state were invited to witness this debate even as William H. Grey, a leader in the AME Church, pointed out that historically, it was white men who had abused black women. William Hicks, whose wife was related to Confederate general Stonewall Jackson, insisted that only *"the Caucasian race"* was capable of republican government. Southern conservatives in Alabama and Mississippi, most of whom were not Republican, withdrew from their conventions and criticized the new constitutions that those conventions produced.

Of the over one thousand delegates to the Reconstruction constitutional conventions across the South, only 268 were black, even though 40–50 percent of the overall population of some southern states was black, and even though black men made up a large percentage of the eligible voters. Unsurprisingly, black convention delegates were generally poorer and less likely to be professionals than their white counterparts. A majority of them were ministers, illustrating the importance of the church to black politics, while many others were skilled artisans. A large portion of the black delegates at the South Carolina convention were AMA and Freedmen's Bureau teachers. Free black northerners, most of them abolitionists before the war, and Union army soldiers also served as delegates. In South Carolina and Louisiana, a substantial number of black delegates were drawn from the "brown" (mixed-race) urban elite that had been free before the war. The class divide among black delegates in both states, though, was smaller than that between whites and blacks.

Despite their varying composition, all the Reconstruction constitutional conventions secured universal male suffrage regardless of race and previous condition of servitude as required by the first Reconstruction Act of 1867. The Mississippi convention passed an ordinance that punished, by fines and disfranchisement, any party seeking to

disfranchise voters through labor contracts or dismissal from employment. After some debate, the South Carolina convention allowed Governor James L. Orr, a proslavery unionist who went along with his state
when it seceded, to address it. Orr tellingly called black male suffrage "a
novel" experiment and asked for ex-Confederates to be allowed to vote
and participate in government.

Education and land reform were extensively debated at the conventions. The Virginia convention sought to release white abolitionist John
A. Blevins, who had been jailed for fourteen years for teaching African Americans before the Civil War, and others like him, noting that
Blevins had been in prison longer than Jefferson Davis, who had been
charged with "high treason." It also passed a resolution supporting the
impeachment of Andrew Johnson, which was conveyed to Congress. A
similar resolution at the Louisiana convention was deemed out of order;
a substitute for it called "for the wheels of government to be relieved
from the clogs of treason." The convention closed with a prayer to "Bless
the President of the United States. Enable him to pause in his career of
vice and folly. May he cease from doing evil, and learn to do right." In
Mississippi, the Johnsonian Governor Benjamin Humphreys, a former
Confederate general, issued a proclamation warning of an insurrection
to seize lands and "admonishing the black race" that any such attempt
would result in "the destruction of your cherished hopes and the ruin of
your race." The state's convention issued a report, in response, that the
governor's proclamation was "utterly without foundation." He would
eventually be removed from office.

Noting the refusal of planters to sell or lease their lands to freedpeople, one Louisiana delegate suggested that uncultivated lands be taxed
at double the rate of cultivated lands, to allow government to confiscate and redistribute them. But with its free brown creole elite that
was culturally distinct and wealthier than most black communities in
the South—a few of its members had even been slaveholding planters—
the issue of land reform was not debated extensively. The most serious
debate over land redistribution took place at the majority-black convention of South Carolina. The free born Francis L. Cardozo—who, as South
Carolina's secretary of state, would become the first black man elected

to state office in American history —argued against debt relief for plant-ers, on the grounds that it would prevent the breakup of plantations. Now "that slavery is destroyed, let the plantation system go with it." He was against outright confiscation but maintained that land impounded for debt should be sold to poor black and white people. Northern-born William Whipper countered that debt relief would benefit the poor, and that if plantations were resold they would be bought up by capitalists, speculators, and "land monopolists."

Rev. Richard H. Cain, who pastored the AME Church in Charles-ton, proposed an ambitious plan for the federal government to give the Freedmen's Bureau a million dollars to buy land and sell it to freedpeo-ple, and to appropriate additional money to provide them with tools and animals. The freeborn Robert DeLarge, who would serve in the state's land commission, legislature, and Congress, supported Cain's proposal. Despite opposition from Whipper, Cain proclaimed his confidence in the Bureau to manage land redistribution. Nearly all the conventions asked for the Bureau's continuation. Even the Louisiana convention, which complained that Bureau agents had often bound freedpeople to labor for their ex-masters, expressed its support.

The state constitutions produced by these conventions were liberal in the modern sense of supporting an active government. They created tax-funded public school systems on a wide scale for the first time in the South, with South Carolina (after much debate) and Texas making attendance mandatory. Reconstruction constitutions established prop-erty taxes—long a feature of governance in the northern states but not in the slaveholder-dominated southern states—to finance not only schools but asylums and public works. They did away with undemocratic laws that penalized the poor, imprisonment for debt, as well as capital and "cruel and unusual" punishment for minor crimes. Most also protected laborers and sharecroppers by giving them the first share, or lien, on the crops they produced. The Georgia constitution allowed workers to put liens on employers' property for nonpayment of wages. South Carolina founded a commission to purchase and sell lands on long-term credit. None of the new state governments created by the Reconstruction con-stitutions put into place a comprehensive program of land reform, but most did protect labor rights and provide debt relief with homestead exemptions, or exempted homes from forfeiture. Their progressive taxation policies drew significant resistance from southern elites. After Reconstruction, the first lien would go to planters and merchants, who would also charge exorbitant interest on provisions furnished to cultivators, leading to debt peonage among sharecroppers and tenants.

Notions of individual rights and an incipient welfare state, each foreign to slave societies, found expression in the Reconstruction constitutions. The 1868 constitutions of Mississippi and South Carolina, the most rabidly proslavery and secessionist states before the war, were the most progressive, owing to their majority-black populations. The first article of the Mississippi constitution contained a comprehensive bill of rights that went beyond those enumerated in the US Constitution and declared all residents citizens of the state and of the United States. It also asserted "the right of citizens to travel upon all public conveyances." The legislature was allowed to levy a poll tax of no more than $2, and only to fund schools. Corporate property was subject to taxation, while county boards were empowered "to provide farms as an Asylum" for those who through age or infirmity, or for other reasons, "may have claims upon the sympathy and aid of society." Some of the most progressive features of these constitutions, however, were stripped away during the ratification process, due to conservative opposition.

The Louisiana constitution opened with a bill of rights that made up its first fourteen articles, while the South Carolina constitution's bill of rights ran to forty-one sections. The first contained a "Declaration of Rights" that began by quoting the Declaration of Independence: "All men are born free and equal." It stated that "Distinction on account of race or color, in any case whatever, shall be prohibited, and all classes of citizens shall enjoy equally all common, public, legal and political privileges." All property would be taxed "in proportion to its value" and all navigable waters were declared "public highways" free to all citizens. The general assembly in South Carolina was instructed to exempt from taxation public schools, colleges, asylums, public libraries, and churches, but not private associations. It was also required to establish a "liberal and uniform system of free public schools throughout the

State," under a state superintendent of education and a State Board of Education of county commissioners, all to be elected positions. Schools and colleges maintained by public funds were to be "open to all the children and youths of the State, without regard to race or color." The Louisiana constitution also mandated integrated public schools.

Far from "negro domination," the constitutional conventions and the constitutions they drafted mostly aimed to create a fundamentally interracial and egalitarian society. Texas, which was riven by violence and factionalism among Republicans, was one of the last states to be reconstructed. Because its convention, which met for over a year from 1868 to 1869, failed to produce a constitution, its resolutions were put together and ratified by voters in the summer of 1869. The resulting constitution had many progressive features. All "freemen" were bestowed with equal rights, all "persons" were granted equality before the law regardless of race, color, or previous condition of servitude, and all adult male citizens received the right to vote, unless disqualified by the US Constitution and excepting those confined in asylums and prisons. The constitution established a "system of free public schools" to be financed by state revenues and a poll tax of $1 on each man between the ages of twenty-one and sixty. It also prohibited government giveaways to private corporations and railroads. The remarkable section VIII of the Texas constitution, regarding public lands controlled by the state, donated 160 acres to every head of the family who did not have a homestead and 80 acres to single adult men, though the transfers came at the expense of indigenous nations, not the planter elite. Given the short duration of Reconstruction in Texas, it is not clear that freedmen benefitted from this clause at all.[11]

Once the Reconstruction constitutions were drafted, they were put in front of voters for ratification. Counting on a unified black vote for ratification, Republicans worked to persuade southern whites in states where the black electorate would not provide a majority on its own. Republicans faced defeat in some states, such as Alabama, where most white voters boycotted the elections, and Mississippi, where the new constitution was initially rejected because black voters were deterred by widespread racist violence. In Georgia and Florida, Republicans appealed to white voters by reneging on black rights during the drafting process, moving to exclude black men from officeholding and sitting on juries, and to allow for the enactment of educational qualifications for voting. In South Carolina and Louisiana, which had large black populations, and in states with strong nonslaveholding white unionist areas such as North Carolina, the constitutions passed easily. Notwithstanding many hurdles, new state governments were elected under these constitutions with an overwhelming majority of the black vote going to Republican candidates.

Despite Republican attempts to secure a measure of southern white support through compromise and patronage, African Americans formed the base of the party in the South. In nearly all the Reconstruction governments, whites dominated officeholding at first, but soon black people became more assertive in running for office. For the first time in American history, African Americans were elected to the

"The First Colored Senators and Representatives in the 41st and 42nd Congress of the United States," by Currier & Ives. *Library of Congress*

US Congress, with the victories in 1870 of Senator Hiram Revels from Mississippi and Congressman Joseph P. Rainey from South Carolina in 1869. P. B. S. Pinchback, who served in the Louisiana constitutional convention and was elected to the state senate, became lieutenant governor, and served briefly as the first black governor of any state when the sitting governor was impeached (Oscar Dunn was acting governor earlier when the governor was incapacitated). Blanche K. Bruce became the second black senator from Mississippi. By the 1870s, African Americans increased their share of state and local offices, and by 1901, twenty-two had served in Congress.

Many of the new black politicians were elected in majority-black plantation areas, the site of the political power of slaveholding planters before the war, a stark illustration of the political revolution wrought by Reconstruction. Across the South, over the course of Reconstruction, more than six hundred African Americans were elected to state legislatures and thousands more to local offices such as county supervisor, postmaster, tax collector, justice of the peace, county clerk, recorder of deeds, and sheriff. The *National Anti-Slavery Standard* proudly announced the appointment of the first black postmaster in South Carolina, H. J. Maxwell of Bennettsville. William Lloyd Garrison marveled at the transformation in the ex-slave states: "Colored men, jurors, sheriffs, magistrates, postmasters—filling, in a word, numerous offices of trust and emolument under the United States and various state governments." Black politicians helped create activist Reconstruction governments, expanding services and the taxation to fund them.

Generally, black officeholders had already been leaders of their local communities, as preachers, Union soldiers, and skilled artisans, while others were northern and freeborn. An overwhelming majority were literate, and a few had attended colleges in the North, such as Oberlin College, a hotbed of abolition, or were publishers of local black newspapers. Some of them were cosmopolitan, having lived and studied in Europe and Africa. South Carolina's state treasurer, Frances L. Cardozo, had attended the University of Glasgow, and some Louisiana officeholders had studied in France. Many, though, such as Robert Smalls of South Carolina and John Lynch of Mississippi, were former slaves. Pinchback became wealthy while in office, but far more common was for black officeholders to suffer for their service, as the KKK and other terror groups began targeting Republicans.

In their efforts to discredit Reconstruction, opponents leveled exaggerated charges of corruption against black politicians. They also devised anti–big government and antitaxation critiques, colored by racism, that became a permanent part of the lexicon of American political conservatism. Southern elites convened "tax-payers conventions" in the 1870s, essentially foils to the southern black conventions, where they brewed the toxic concoction. The implication of their arguments was that poor, black, and working-class people could not be allowed access to citizenship or government. This antidemocratic and antigovernment mindset found many adherents among conservatives in both the South and the North and was evident in the first popular books written to decry Reconstruction.

In *The Prostrate State* (1874), James Pike described the South Carolina legislature as "the slave rioting in the halls of the master" and "ignorant democracy." It disturbed him that the "servant" was now the "master." A disaffected Republican, he called on "the whites of South Carolina" to prevent the "Africanization" of their state, cataloguing a long list of "frauds" and corruption. Pike invented stories of voter and electoral fraud, with apparently even black women and children voting while white votes were mysteriously destroyed (many of his fabrications sound familiar today). It appalled him to see African American officeholders, some of whom had, in his estimation, a "visage" that was "as black" as those found "in the Congo," adopting the racist language of European imperialists. Tellingly, black legislators' central crime, according to the apoplectic Pike, was to vote against a railroad subsidy, the biggest source of Gilded Age corruption. Much of the testimony collected by Pike came from southerners, including ex-Confederate generals.

The political careers of the two thousand or so black officeholders in this era offer the best riposte to Pike's vitriolic racism. To Wendell Phillips, these men were "the Fifteenth Amendment in flesh and blood." They remained a minority of officeholders, even as their numbers increased during the tail end of Reconstruction. As noted by John Lynch, a black officeholder who wrote one of the first histories of Reconstruction, racist outrage over supposed "Negro Domination" was a response to the mere fact that black men could now vote. The Mississippi legislature selected its two black senators, Revels and Bruce, for an office once held by Jefferson Davis. Revels had been born free in North Carolina and educated in a Quaker seminary and then the abolitionist Knox College in Illinois. He became an AME minister and was arrested in Missouri for preaching the gospel to the enslaved. During the war, he recruited black soldiers for the Union and served as an army chaplain, and after the war, he served in the Freedmen's Bureau. After Revels joined the Senate, Garrison, not given to rhapsody, enthused at his "modest yet self-reliant and dignified deportment." Garrison hoped to live long enough to see a black president. Revels, known for his conciliatory manner—surely one reason he had advanced so far—nevertheless spoke out against the expulsion of black legislators in Georgia and segregation in Washington, DC schools. He later served as Mississippi's secretary of state and president of Alcorn University, but controversially, supported conservative Democrats at the end of Reconstruction.

Mississippi's second black senator, Blanche K. Bruce, established a national reputation for himself as a "race leader." He had escaped slavery during the war and returned to the South during Reconstruction. He was appointed to a variety of local and state offices before winning election to the position of sheriff and tax collector in the majority-black Bolivar County in 1871, where he established his political base and acquired land. Bruce was elected to the Senate in 1875 mainly due to his ability to navigate between moderate and radical Republicans. He was generally circumspect, like Revels, but spoke out against racist terror and the failure of the national party to protect southern blacks. He also spoke on behalf of Pinchback, whose election to the Senate was contested by conservatives from both parties in Louisiana. In 1876, Democrats in the US Senate joined with five Republicans to refuse to seat him. During the waning days of Reconstruction, Bruce gave passionate speeches for human rights, on behalf of freedpeople, Chinese immigrants, and Native Americans. He died in 1898, respected by both

Republicans and his Democratic opponents, but with a disfranchised black constituency.

Bruce, along with two other black leaders from Mississippi, Lynch and James Hill, both also born enslaved, controlled the Republican Party in the state well into the 1890s. Hill served as sergeant at arms and secretary of state, and was elected to the statehouse. He ran unsuccessfully for Congress and was often at loggerheads with Lynch but amassed a small fortune as a land agent and tax collector. For his part, Lynch was appointed a justice of the peace, and was later elected to the statehouse, soon enough becoming the first black man from Mississippi and, in 1872, the youngest black man (at twenty-six) elected to the House of Representatives. Lynch would serve three terms before being cheated of reelection through fraud and intimidation. In 1882, he won his seat back after he contested the results of another election he allegedly lost. Like some other black politicians, Lynch continued to serve in the federal government after Reconstruction, becoming the first black man to address the national Republican convention. He eventually acquired a law degree and settled in Chicago, where he advised the first northern black congressman elected after Reconstruction, Oscar De Priest.[12]

In the two other nearly majority-black states, free brown elites, who made common cause with freedpeople during Reconstruction, dominated officeholding. In Louisiana, New Orleans's *gens de couleur* led the movement for universal male suffrage. But it was an outsider who became the state's highest-ranking black officeholder. Born in Georgia and raised in the North by his mother, the light-skinned P. B. S. Pinchback moved to New Orleans in 1862. He became an officer in the Louisiana Native Guards and recruited for the Union. Pinchback served in the Reconstruction constitutional convention and the state senate before succeeding his rival, Oscar J. Dunn, the first black lieutenant governor in the country. It was in 1873, when the governor, Henry Warmoth, was impeached, that Pinchback became the first black governor in the United States. After Reconstruction, Pinchback held various local offices, until he moved to Washington and was appointed US marshal. One of his grandchildren, Jean Toomer, became a famous writer.

The fact that men like Bruce and Pinchback became wealthy in large part through their political careers, revealed emerging class divisions among freedpeople.

South Carolina did not produce a black governor or senator. But more often than in any other southern state, talented black men attained office at the local, state, and national level. The state elected the largest black delegation to Congress. The most famous of them was the formerly enslaved war hero Robert Smalls, who had served in the Union navy during the war and captained the *Planter,* the Confederate steamer he had almost single-handedly commandeered for the Union. With his share of the prize money, he bought land, a building in which to establish a black school, and his former enslaver's home. Smalls also founded the Beaufort Republican Club. He served in the constitutional convention and in both houses of the state legislature. Smalls was elected to Congress in 1868 and went on to serve five terms from his secure majority-black, low-country district. After the wholesale disfranchisement of black voters, he was appointed collector of customs for the port of Beaufort, a post he held for virtually the rest of his life.

Another notable figure in the Carolinian congressional delegation was the highly educated Robert Elliot, who moved to the state from Boston in 1867. Elliot was a leading organizer of the Republican Party in South Carolina and held numerous state and local offices. He served in the constitutional convention and the statehouse, where he became Speaker, and served two terms in Congress. At the end of his life, he received some minor positions in Charleston and New Orleans. But he could not make a living as a lawyer in the post-Reconstruction South and he died in poverty. Joseph Rainey, an enslaved man, who escaped to Bermuda during the war, served in the state land commission and militia before being elected to Congress in 1870. Congressman Alonso Ransier, who also served as lieutenant governor and hoped to make the Republican Party into a "progressive poor man's party," died as a day laborer in Charleston. Richard Cain, the AME minister who championed land redistribution at the constitutional convention, was elected to Congress in 1873. Of Afro-Cherokee descent, he had been educated at the abolitionist Wilberforce University in Ohio.[13]

Black politicians during Reconstruction were farsighted in imagining the creation of a modern welfare state. The freeborn Alabama congressman James T. Rapier, who was educated in Canada, fought for land redistribution and a national system of education with federally mandated textbooks, and was an advocate for tenant farmers and labor unions. After the fall of Reconstruction, he supported freedpeople's emigration to Kansas and spent his considerable fortune on black institutions. Alabama's other congressmen, Benjamin Turner and Jeremiah Haralson, had been born enslaved. Like Rapier, Turner was an advocate of land redistribution, and also like him, would die poor. After a checkered political career, Haralson moved west in 1912 even though he had opposed Kansas emigration. Georgia elected just one black congressman, Jefferson Long, also born a slave, who served very briefly in the House of Representatives in 1870–1871, when Reconstruction was

"The Shackle Broken—by the Genius of Freedom," by E. Sachse & Co., *Library of Congress*

overthrown in his state. Long had presided over Georgia's labor convention and founded a "Negro Labor Union."

Florida also elected only one black congressman, Josiah Walls, who was born a slave in Virginia and became a Union soldier. He served in the legislature and for two terms in Congress. Walls later became director of the college farm at Florida's A&M University but died in obscurity. North Carolina's sole black Reconstruction-era congressman, John A. Hyman, had been sold to Alabama as a slave but returned to his home state after the war. Elected to Congress in 1874 for one term, he died in Washington in 1891, when he was working in the Department of Agriculture. Around two decades later, another North Carolinian and a graduate of Howard University, George Henry White, was elected to the House of Representatives—the last black congressman from the South until the aftermath of the civil rights movement.[14]

A large proportion of northern blacks who held office during Reconstruction were abolitionists. They had long fought against slavery and for equality, and Reconstruction gave them an opportunity to realize their vision. The most outstanding of them was John Mercer Langston, who, along with his brother, Charles Langston, was a prominent abolitionist. (Langston Hughes was a descendant.) A graduate of Oberlin and one of the first black lawyers in the country, John had been elected to local office in Ohio before the war. He emerged as a national leader with his election as president of the National Equal Rights League in 1864. He worked for the Freedmen's Bureau and taught at Howard University. John Langston advocated land reform, education, and universal male suffrage in speeches he gave throughout the South. He later served as the American minister to Haiti, a position typically reserved by Republican administrations for African Americans. In 1888, Langston was elected to Congress in the state of his birth, Virginia. His election was contested, and he ended up serving only a few months, but in that time he proposed laws for federal supervision of elections to counter the disfranchisement of black men.

Two other black abolitionists, Tunis G. Campbell and Aaron A.

Bradley, took part in the contested reconstruction of Georgia, where conservative Republicans and Democrats united to dash freedpeople's hopes for political rights as well as economic democracy. Born in New Jersey, Campbell was employed by the Freedmen's Bureau in the Georgia Sea Islands, where he helped redistribute land and led an independent black community, until he was dismissed in early 1866 by the Johnson administration. Campbell moved inland and served in the constitutional convention and state senate. All the black members of the state legislature were expelled in 1868, only to be reinstated by Congress in 1870. Establishing a political base in the majority-black Liberty and McIntosh Counties, Campbell made sure that freedpeople's rights and interests were respected in labor disputes, eliciting the anger of planters.

In a memoir of his persecution in Georgia, Campbell described the situation of freedpeople as shaped not merely by race, but by class and economic power. They were, he wrote, "ignored and trampled by the moneyed aristocrats of this nation." The threat from those aristocrats was only increasing: "How long will it be before you will have no rights that the capitalists or property-holder is bound to respect?" Campbell, who was arrested by state authorities on trumped-up charges and who would die in Boston in 1891, left behind a legacy of organizing; his district elected black legislators until the end of the nineteenth century.

Just as radical was Bradley, a fugitive slave who escaped to Boston in the 1830s and returned to Georgia after the war. Known for his confrontational tactics, he tried to prevent the restoration of the Sherman land grants to planters, supported striking workers, and advocated land confiscation. He was banished from Georgia for a year, elected to the constitutional convention, expelled, and then elected to the state senate, from which he was expelled, too, even before the wholesale expulsion of black legislators. After the fall of Reconstruction, he left for St. Louis, where he would die in 1882. Campbell and Bradley identified early on the criminalization of black freedom in the postemancipation South. Bradley protested the Savannah metropolitan police's mistreatment of freedpeople. Campbell shed light on the emerging convict lease labor system that he personally experienced. "It is impossible to describe the way in which prisoners were worked," wrote Campbell. They were forced to labor "as soon as they could see," and "kept to work as long as it was light." They were "beaten most unmercifully"; they had to "keep up or die."

In contrast to Bradley and Campbell, Rev. Henry McNeal Turner had a long political career. Turner, who was born in South Carolina and moved to Baltimore, was a minister in the AME Church. He served as a chaplain in the Union army and a Freedmen's Bureau agent. Besides leading the AME's southern mission, his indefatigable political organizing of freedpeople led him to claim that he had created the Republican Party in Georgia. When his conciliatory gestures to white Georgians came to nothing, he charged them with desiring a "monopoly of power." While in the legislature, he introduced a bill for women's suffrage, in addition to many bills to protect freedpeople's rights. After Reconstruction, he became an advocate of emigration—guided by a black Christian vision of Exodus from a land of racial oppression—and vice president of the American Colonization Society, which had founded the nation of Liberia in 1822 on the west coast of Africa as a colony of freed slaves and free blacks. His "Back to Africa" plan proved controversial among the black Republican establishment. Turner lectured all over the world for emigration, dying of a heart attack in Canada in 1915.[15]

Another, more famous emigrationist, Major Martin Delany, had a distinguished career in the Union army, as one of only a handful of black officers, and later the Freedmen's Bureau in South Carolina. But he became conservative in his politics during Reconstruction. Freedpeople were vocal in their dissent during one of his speeches, and he was never elected to office. Known as "the father of black nationalism" for his support of emigration, Delany ended his Reconstruction career ignominiously by supporting ex-Confederate general Wade Hampton's takeover of South Carolina.

The career of one black abolitionist turned politician suggested that, for many African Americans after Reconstruction, accommodation was the the only alternative to exile. Mifflin Gibbs was a son of the abolitionist minister Jonathan C. Gibbs of Philadelphia (Mifflin's brother, Jonathan, would become the only black man to hold statewide office in

Florida during Reconstruction). A prominent abolitionist, Mifflin Gibbs had lived in California and was elected to the Victoria City Council in Canada. After studying law at Oberlin, he moved to Arkansas, where he became a leading advocate of civil rights. The most important black Republican in the state, he held a number of local offices, before being appointed US consul to Madagascar in 1897. Unlike many black Republicans, Gibbs maintained a high profile after Reconstruction by cultivating good relations with Little Rock's business and political elite. Gibbs's accommodation to the local power structure foretold the accommodationist approach to Jim Crow of Booker T. Washington, who wrote the introduction to Gibbs's autobiography.

The political careers of black abolitionists tracked the fate of Reconstruction. George T. Ruby was an antislavery journalist, teacher, and agent for the AMA and the Freedmen's Bureau in New Orleans and Texas. He was also active in the Haitian emigration movement. Ruby became prominent in Texas politics, where he organized Union leagues, Republican clubs, and black labor unions. Ruby had to navigate between radical, conservative, and "middle of the road" factions of the Republican Party, but his political base was among the freedpeople in Galveston, who elected him to the legislature and on behalf of whom he advocated for education and legal protection from violence. With the demise of Reconstruction, Ruby resigned his seat, replaced by a white Republican. He moved back to New Orleans, where he edited newspapers until his death in 1882.[16]

That Ruby went back to journalism after his political career was ended was not unusual. Reconstruction created a vibrant black print culture in the South, with new newspapers being founded (often as part of political machines) to articulate freedpeople's concerns and to confront a uniformly hostile southern press. The new newspapers were central to the legacy of the Second American Republic. In Washington, Frederick Douglass, who had edited black newspapers before the war, and the abolitionist Rev. J. Sella Martin renamed their paper the *New National Era,*

"A Colored American National Journal," in 1871. They purposefully chose to revive the name of a prewar, antislavery newspaper that had also been published in the capital. In its opening editorial, the *New Era* made clear that it would seek to represent the distinct opinions of "the races to which the Editors belong" and announced itself as a Republican paper. Local black southern papers also appeared, such as *The Colored American* in Washington, evoking the prominent black abolitionist antebellum newspaper; the *Loyal Georgian* in Augusta; *The Colored Tennessean*; and *The True Communicator* in Baltimore. Richard Cain founded *The Charleston Leader*, Robert Smalls published the Beaufort *Standard*, P. B. S. Pinchback co-owned the New Orleans *Louisianan*, and Stephen Swails, who served in the South Carolina convention and senate, edited the Williamsburg *Republican*.

As journalist I. Garland Penn put it, the Reconstruction-era black press was needed not only "as the defender of our rights" but also as a "popular educator of the masses." Penn's own *The Lynchburg Laborer*, the St. Louis *Freeman's Journal*, the *People's Journal* in Jackson, Mississippi, *Colored Citizen* of Topeka, Kansas, the *People's Advocate* of Portsmouth, Virginia, and the *People's Journal* of New Orleans constituted a vibrant mainly southern black press during Reconstruction. Yet almost all were short-lived; as with black politicians, their fate was linked to that of Reconstruction. Penn wrote of the black newspapers that "No requiem, save the night wind, has been sung over their dead bodies; no memorial service to bemoan their sad and horrible fate . . . like many a brave Union soldier their bodies lie in an unknown and unhonored spot." With the fall of Reconstruction, the energy behind black print culture moved back north. *The Detroit Plaindealer* was founded by Robert Pelham Jr., who was born in Virginia. T. Thomas Fortune, born enslaved and whose father was involved in Reconstruction politics in Florida, founded *The New York Age*, and William Monroe Trotter, whose father was born a slave in Mississippi and who served in the Fifty-Fifth Massachusetts, founded the *Boston Guardian*. The most successful of the post-Reconstruction newspapers was the *Chicago Defender*, founded by Robert S. Abbott, who had been born free in Georgia. The *Defender* played a crucial role in encouraging southern black migration to northern cities.[17]

Gains in the South influenced northern black politics throughout Reconstruction. A handful of African Americans were appointed to local and state office in the North before the war, but now black office-holding emerged as a real trend. In 1866, Edwin Garrison Walker, son of the black abolitionist David Walker, and Charles Lewis Mitchell, who had worked for *The Liberator,* became the first black men elected to the Massachusetts assembly. In 1870, George L. Ruffin, the first black graduate of Harvard Law School, was elected to the legislature. He later served in the Boston Common Council, as a judge in municipal court, and as American consul to the Dominican Republic. It was not until 1928, however, that Oscar De Priest of Chicago, the son of Alabama exo-dusters to Kansas, became the first northern black elected to Congress.

Opposition to black officeholding was universal but more vicious in the South. Black politicians dealt with unreconstructed Democrats as well as Republican allies who were willing to sacrifice them in vain attempts to attract more white southerners to the party. Many faced not just vituperative racist slander but violent threats to their lives. Abram Colby, a Georgia legislator, was stripped and beaten for three hours by Klansmen. Florida's Secretary of State Jonathan Gibbs slept with guns in his attic because he received so many threats. Some were murdered outright. Ten percent of all the black delegates to the 1867–1868 con-stitutional conventions were assaulted, and six were killed. Whatever perks black officeholders enjoyed were clearly outweighed by the risks involved. Many were driven from their homes and lost their livelihoods. This was true not just of the prominent leaders, but also the thousands of those elected and appointed to state and local office. In 1898, one of the few remaining black officeholders, Frazier Baker, the postmaster of Lake City, South Carolina, was shot by a marauding mob. He and an infant daughter died in their home, which was burned to the ground. His injured wife and other five children barely survived the attack. Baker's family moved to Boston, where his lynching became a cause célèbre. Though not confronted with endemic violence, northern black politicians (and black people in general) still encountered informal segregation and intimidation at the polls. In the Midwest, newly arrived freedpeople faced vigilante violence, though not at the same levels as in the South.[18]

Black Republican officeholders were not paragons of virtue—some were self-serving and opportunistic, like any politician—but all fought, with varying force, for freedpeople's rights. And while they could be divided among themselves, and from their constituents, by class, color, birth status, and region, they represented the full flowering of black activism. Black Reconstruction was the apex—rather than the tempering of—a radical political tradition born in the struggle against slavery and for equal rights. Hundreds of black officeholders were a mere step removed from slavery and were propelled into office by black voters and political activism at the grassroots. All black politicians were committed to equal political and civil rights, and many supported some form of land reform, ranging from outright confiscation to homestead legislation. In South Carolina, Richard Cain created what he called "Lincolnville" with land he bought. He began to sell it to freedpeople on easy terms in ten-acre lots. Separately, the state land commission, created at his initiative, managed to settle fifty black families in fifty-to-hundred-acre farms in what came to be known as "Promised Land," a community that lasted well into the twenty-first century.

While Reconstruction did not fundamentally change the plantation economy, new access to political rights and government did allow the South's laboring poor, black and white, to protect themselves from the worst excesses of planters and employers, from nonpayment of wages and exploitation to physical abuse. Workers went on strike more frequently for better wages and conditions. In 1873, black stevedores went on strike in Mobile, Pensacola, and Washington, and black workers in sawmills in Jacksonville, Florida walked out in their fight for a shorter workday and higher wages. The workers argued that the relations "between capital and labor" were "unequally and unjustly balanced." The following year, sugar workers in Terrebonne Parish went on strike to resist attempts by planters to reduce their wages from between

$15 and $18 a month to $13—the episode became known as the "war in Terrebonne."

In 1876, black rice workers at the Combahee River in South Carolina successfully struck when their wages were reduced. Robert Smalls reported that many refused to be paid in post-dated checks, and that their violence was directed only against strike breakers. The next year, black men and women in Galveston, Texas struck for higher wages. The abolitionist feminist Mary Ann Shadd Cary, who also taught in freedmen's schools, advocated for the formation of cooperatives as a solution to low wages. Southern elites blamed Reconstruction for the growing militancy of black labor, which, they claimed, would inaugurate a Communist revolution "with its sea of blood and its ocean of fire."[19]

Reconstruction failed not because its proponents sacrificed economic rights for political rights, as some historians have argued, but because it was overthrown. When political power was taken away, violently, from freedpeople, they became far more vulnerable to economic coercion, racist terror, and legal oppression. In the post-Reconstruction South, small-time white farmers, too, would lose their farms and become ensnared in a web of indebtedness and poverty. As the plight of much of the world's peasantry today illustrates, marginal land ownership is no substitute for access to political power and economic resources that often flow from it. Still, it was no surprise that freedpeople clung to the dream of land ownership, not just to establish economic autonomy but as recompense for centuries of stolen labor. There is no telling what might have happened if freedpeople's grassroots political activism that defined the Second American Republic had succeeded. The issues of social democracy and economic rights might very well have advanced if Black Reconstruction had not been upended.

CHAPTER SIX

The Reconstruction of Women's Rights

You white women here speak of rights. I speak of wrongs.

—FRANCES ELLEN WATKINS HARPER, 1866

Frances Ellen Watkins Harper. *Library of Congress*

The Second American Republic entailed not just a reordering of relations of race and class, but also of gender. The struggle for women's rights was a part of grassroots Reconstruction in the United States. Though black women were denied the same rights as black men even under many of the plans for Reconstruction, their activism unleashed emancipatory possibilities. As freedwomen labored for their communities and black rights in the South, the women's suffrage movement, led by and largely composed of white and black women in the North, intervened in the debates over the Constitution that Reconstruction inaugurated. Suffragists challenged women's political exclusion from the new constitutional amendments and federal laws. They found allies in Radical Republicans in Congress and in the Reconstruction southern governments, who helped introduce women's suffrage into national and state political debates. As the story usually goes, Reconstruction witnessed the failure not just of interracial democracy, but of the battle for women's rights, because female suffrage did not become part of the Fifteenth Amendment and was not passed into law by Congress. But in fact, the advances during this era opened new avenues in the fight for equal citizenship regardless of sex, including the idea of a constitutional amendment to enfranchise women. It was the overthrow of Reconstruction, rather than its fruition, that set back the movement for women's right to vote by decades.

The emergence of feminism from the abolition movement before the Civil War yoked women's rights to black rights. Many abolitionists, especially Garrisonians, became feminists, and most feminists were abolitionists. During the war, feminists campaigned for emancipation. Indeed, the war unleashed northern women's activism on behalf of the Union. By its end, women were claimants before the government, having mobilized to serve the nation-state in its greatest political emergency. The antebellum women's movement had put forward a broad platform for female emancipation: legal personhood that was denied by laws of coverture, economic autonomy, personal liberation from patriarchal families, and political citizenship. But if early feminism demonstrated how abolition could bring together every fight for democracy, the suffrage movement that emerged after the war shed its dependence on abolition and fractured between those who fought for women's *and* black rights, and those who fought for the former at the expense of the latter.[1]

During Reconstruction, the abandonment of principle by some suffragists proved disastrous; it alienated their natural allies. Opportunistically allying themselves with Democratic, racist opponents of Reconstruction, the wing of suffrage represented by Elizabeth Cady

Stanton and Susan B. Anthony became independent of their antislavery fellow travelers, and for paltry returns. The costs were tremendous: their abandonment of abolitionist feminists' dual commitment to racial and gender quality would have lasting consequences for the American women's movement.

Would the nation and its citizens enjoy more or less democracy? That question animated every political battle of the Second American Republic. And it is only by looking at each of the mass movements in comparison to others—and in seeing how they were all connected at every level of American politics, from the grassroots to Congress—that one can understand the truly revolutionary promise of the period and see how activists across a range of causes came close to achieving a permanent reordering of American democracy and life.

The 1848 Seneca Falls convention is seen as the origin point for the women's rights movement in the United States, but demands and petitions for women's equality, property, and voting rights predated it. In 1840, the abolition movement split over politics and religion as well as women's rights, with the Garrisonians supporting women's rights and other abolitionists forming their own organizations that excluded women from leadership positions and segregated them. Two years before Seneca Falls, Mary Miles, a black schoolteacher from Boston who married the fugitive slave Henry Bibb and moved to Canada, wrote, "The colored woman who would elevate herself must contend not only with prejudice against poverty [and] prejudice against color but prejudice against her sex. Which of these is most cruel I am not prepared to say. But that all three combined are enough to crush a lion I am prepared to testify."[2] She best articulated the intersectional nature of abolitionist feminism.

It found expression before the war in women's conventions, which were modeled on abolitionist and black conventions. Fellow travelers included abolitionist men, many of whom attended the women's conventions: Frederick Douglass, William Lloyd Garrison, Wendell Phillips, William Henry Channing, Thomas Wentworth Higginson, and

Parker Pillsbury, among others. Women activists built on abolitionist networks, ideology, and organizing principles. When the editor Jane Grey Swisshelm objected to introducing "the question of color" at the first national women's convention in Worcester, Massachusetts, in 1850, Pillsbury replied: "That ANY woman have rights, will scarcely be believed; but that colored women have rights, would never have been thought of, without a specific declaration." Phillips asked delegates to remember "the trampled womanhood of the plantation," the "million and a half slave women." Besides property rights, female education, and suffrage, other issues emerged at the women's conventions, including equality in marriage and divorce, wage parity, and access to professions. At a time when public opinion and the church were arrayed against women's equality, the conventions became sites to demand rights and debate opponents. The first state-level conventions took place in states whose soil had been fertilized by abolitionism—New York, Ohio, and Massachusetts—and then spread to other northern states.[3]

The organizing force behind the conventions was an abolitionist feminist from Massachusetts, Lucy Stone. Born into a farming family and braving the opposition of her father, Stone worked hard to acquire an education. She attended Mt. Holyoke Female Seminary, where she challenged school authorities through her commitment to abolition. At Oberlin, an anonymous black woman offered her home to Stone and to Antoinette Brown—her future sister-in-law and the first woman to be ordained a Christian minister—to hold a public discussion on women's rights when they were barred from doing so at the college. Stone made her first speech for gender equality at her brother's church in 1847 and was soon celebrated as an orator. She wrote later that "I think we ought to puncture the bubble that the Seneca Falls meeting was the *first* public demand for suffrage." She retained her maiden name when she married, and other women who did the same came to be called "Lucy Stoners." Stone was criticized by other abolitionists for devoting too much of her speeches to women's rights. She decided to lecture for abolition, as a paid agent, on the weekends, and for women's rights during the week.[4]

Unlike Stone, Anthony and Stanton came to abolition late and left it early. Anthony, a Quaker schoolteacher from Rochester, began her

Lucy Stone. *Library of Congress*

career as a temperance advocate and attended her first women's rights convention in Syracuse in 1852. She became a lecturing agent for the American Anti Slavery Society (AASS) four years later. The single Anthony, who berated Stanton, Stone, and Brown for expending their energies and valuable time on their marriages and children, came to personify the suffrage movement. Stanton, married and beset by child-bearing and rearing, usually sent letters of encouragement to the conventions rather than involving herself in the details of organizing. She remembered the sting of knowing her father had wished she was a boy, and outlearned most men, becoming the philosopher of the nascent women's movement and the principal author of the Declaration of Sentiments at Seneca Falls. She was not an abolitionist, though her husband, Henry Stanton, and a cousin, Gerrit Smith, were. Her beau ideal was the Quaker abolitionist feminist Lucretia Mott, present at the founding of the AASS in 1833 and at Seneca Falls in 1848.[5]

In the decade before the war, women's rights overlapped not only with abolition but also with temperance and dress reform, the latter the attempt to replace restricting corsets and dresses with pantaloons called "bloomers" after the woman who popularized them, Amelia

Bloomer, though they were invented by Gerrit Smith's daughter, Elizabeth Smith Miller. Abolitionist feminists such as Sojourner Truth, who attended and spoke at women's rights conventions, often dressed soberly to defy popular caricatures that associated women's activists with the "free love" movement, which sought to get rid of the sexual double standard and Victorian notions about women's purity and subordination within marriage. The conservative male-dominated temperance movement, however, barred and segregated African Americans and attempted to silence abolitionist feminists. Other women in the antebellum temperance movement were purveyors of the politics of domesticity rather than women's rights.[6] Abolition, rather than temperance, served as the organizational and ideological inspiration for the women's rights movement.

Black abolitionist feminists were prominent champions of women's rights. Douglass and Truth, "representing the enslaved African race," attended the Worcester convention. Truth did not utter the slogan, "Ar'n't I a Woman?"—the story is apocryphal—though she did lecture under a banner inscribed with the words, "Am I not a Woman and a Sister?" She challenged the hypocrisy of the prevailing gender conventions of true womanhood, domesticity, and separate spheres for men and women at a time when enslaved women were forced to perform hard physical labor and watch their children sold away from them, experiences she knew intimately. As a former preacher, Truth gave the best answer to orthodox ministers who cited the Bible to uphold female subordination. God and woman created Jesus, she said: "man had nothing to do" with it. She concluded pithily, "I am a Woman's Rights."

At the 1853 "mob convention" in New York City, where hecklers shouted down the speakers, Truth likened the crowd to hissing snakes and geese. She demanded the right to speak as a "good citizen" of, as well as a former slave from, the state of New York. The crowd was exercised, she said, "to see a colored woman get up" and speak about women's rights. Another black abolitionist, Nancy Prince, who had written narratives based on her travels to Russia and the West Indies, spoke at the fifth national women's convention in Philadelphia in 1854. The Forten sisters, Harriet and Margaretta, from the storied black abolitionist family, helped organize it. Prince anticipated Frances Ellen Watkins Harper in 1866 in claiming that she "understood woman's wrongs better than women's rights." Harriet Tubman was a suffragist and attended the 1859 New England Women's Rights Convention in Boston.[7]

Harper and another black abolitionist feminist, Mary Ann Shadd Cary, became involved with the women's movement after the Civil War. The niece of pioneering black abolitionist William Watkins, the orphaned Harper was educated by him and worked as a teacher, seamstress, and domestic servant. She published poetry and became known for her evocative speeches for abolition. As a lecturing agent for the Maine Anti-Slavery Society and an active member of the Underground Railroad in Philadelphia, she emerged as an astute political commentator during the Civil War and Reconstruction. Cary was the eldest daughter of Abraham Shadd, one of the originators of the black convention movement. She was an advocate of black emigration to Canada. As the first female black editor of the *Provincial Freeman* in Canada, she reported on the progress of abolition and antislavery politics. Cary faced criticism of her role as "editress," but as she proudly noted, "To colored women, we have a word——we have 'broken the Editorial ice' for your class in America." After the war, Cary returned to the United States and graduated from Howard Law School. An ardent suffragist, she headed the Committee on Female Suffrage for the Colored National Labor Union.[8]

The overlap between abolition and women's rights peaked on the eve of the Civil War. In 1860, Stanton was invited by Garrison to address the annual meeting of the AASS. There, she insisted that women's rights were part of abolition, which included "the whole human family, irrespective of nation, color, caste or sex." In "settling the question of the negro's rights," she continued—in words that would come back to haunt her—"we find the exact limits of our own, for rights never clash or interfere." Stanton observed that abolition was the "only organization" where "the humanity of woman is recognized." She called her speech to the Judiciary Committee of the New York legislature, on enlarging women's property rights, "A Slave's Appeal," likening the plight of white women to that of slaves, a common trope at the time. A surprising

"Ye May Session of Ye Woman's Rights Convention," *Harper's Weekly*, June 11, 1859. *Library of Congress*

disagreement between Stanton and Phillips over marriage and divorce at the tenth women's convention in New York the same year was a portent of the split to come. While Stanton advocated for marriage as a legal contract and easier access to divorce for women, her opponents were eager not to associate abolition with "free love."[9]

The war presented an opening for many northern women to shake off the fetters of domesticity which saw women confined to a private, almost housebound life as wives and mothers. Of course, the reality was already very different for vast numbers of black, immigrant, and working-class women, many of whom worked in factories and other people's homes. Northern women, excluded from citizenship and military service, mobilized in an unprecedented fashion on the home front. The Civil War has been portrayed as a "crisis in gender," given the sudden absence of male heads of household. Crisis or not, northern women seized the opportunity to reconstruct gender relations in service to the Union. In their history of woman suffrage cowritten with Matilda

Gage, Stanton and Anthony claimed that the war "created a revolution in woman herself, as important in its results as the changed condition of the former slaves, and this silent influence is still busy."[10]

Women became foot soldiers in the civilian arm of the federal government, continuing an antebellum tradition of social reform. They were eager to prove their patriotism. Besides ladies' and soldiers' aid societies, thousands of women were organized, under the auspices of the United States Sanitary Commission (USSC), into women's auxiliaries to render aid and comfort to Union soldiers as nurses and as collectors of vast amounts of blankets, clothes, food, and medical supplies that they shipped to the front with military-like efficiency. The first national social services agency in American history, and a forerunner of sorts to the Freedmen's Bureau, the USSC was created by Lincoln—despite his initial skepticism—through an executive order on June 18, 1861. Josephine Shaw Lowell began her storied career as a social reformer by sending packages to the USSC. The impulse for its formation came from activist women like Dr. Elizabeth Blackwell, one of the first women doctors and sister-in-law to the feminists Lucy Stone and Antoinette Brown Blackwell. Her Women's Central Association of Relief in New York dispatched medicine and nurses to field hospitals and became the New York branch of the USSC.

Headed by three men—Unitarian minister Henry Bellows, the antislavery conservationist Frederick Law Olmsted, and the conservative unionist George Templeton Strong—the USSC deployed a vast network of paid and volunteer northern women, who managed depots, disbursed goods, and inspected army camps and hospitals. As Bellows put it, "Hundreds of women evinced talents there, which, in other spheres and in the other sex, would have made them merchant-princes, or great administrators of public affairs." Like the American Freedmen's Union Commission that co-opted abolitionist aid societies, the USSC's male leadership depended on the drive and grassroots work of women.

Northern women's civilian mobilization, across class lines, in the Sanitary Commission paralleled men's mobilization in the Union army. (A few women did manage to disguise themselves as men and serve as soldiers.) Jane Hoge of the Northwestern Auxiliary, in her tribute to

Union soldiers, took special note of "the self-denying liberality, labor and zeal of thousands of our countrywomen" as well. She provided a detailed look at their labors, which, as she put it, were "calculated to stimulate and encourage women in all time to come." By the end of the war, over a thousand women's auxiliaries of the overall twelve thousand relief organizations operated under the umbrella of the USSC. Abby W. May, "Chair" of the New England Women's Auxiliary Association, known for her "over-commanding" manner, organized an administrative system of assistant managers to coordinate the work of hundreds of local societies, a model that was soon adopted by other auxiliaries. The New England Auxiliary also formed a Ladies Industrial Aid Association that employed nearly a thousand poor and widowed women. This was the recollection of Mary Livermore of the Northwestern USSC auxiliary:

> Here were packed and shipped to the hospitals or battle-field 77,660 packages of sanitary supplies, whose cash value was $1,056,192.16. Here were written and mailed letters by the ten thousand, circulars by the hundred thousand, monthly bulletins and reports. Here were planned visits to the aid societies, trips to the army, methods of raising money and supplies, systems of relief for soldiers' families and white refugees, Homes and Rests for destitute and enfeebled soldiers, and the details of mammoth sanitary fairs.

Livermore tapped into the abolition tradition of women's fund-raising fairs, organizing the successful Northwestern Soldiers and Sanitary Fairs in Chicago alongside Hoge, and raising enormous sums. In 1863, the soldiers' fair raised over $80,000, far more than the projected $25,000. Two years later, another fair at Chicago managed by Livermore and others raised nearly $400,000. Paid attendance at Philadelphia's Great Sanitary Fair of 1864, which netted more than a million dollars, was 250,000 and included the Lincolns. The president donated signed copies of the Emancipation Proclamation to sell at the fair. The Sanitary Commission reported Superintendent of Nurses Jane Stuart Woolsey, a founding member of Women's Central Relief Association, "always promptly and generously" filled requisitions at their hospital in Fairfax, Virginia, sending their own wagons laden with supplies. "Barrels of flannel shirts," gallons of the finest wine, and casks of homemade pickles were welcome gifts.[11] Northerners donated their best and choicest possessions, rather than the cast-offs and secondhand goods that they sent to freedmen's aid societies.

African American women organized their own soldiers' relief societies, many connected to black churches. In Brooklyn, Elizabeth Gloucester, wife of Rev. James Gloucester of the Siloam Presbyterian Church, had raised money for John Brown's raid on Harpers Ferry. During the war, she raised funds for Union soldiers, freedpeople, and the Colored Orphans' Asylum, which was destroyed in the 1863 draft riots in New York City. Abolitionist entrepreneur Mary Ellen Pleasant also

"The Great Sanitary Fair," by A. Watson, 1864. *Library of Congress*

reportedly donated vast sums to Brown and soldiers' relief. Pleasant not only fought to desegregate public transportation in San Francisco, but also founded the Franchise League in the city to advocate for black and women's voting rights. In Virginia, ex-slaves, including Annetta M. Lane of Norfolk and Harriet M. Taylor of Hampton, founded one of the first organizations for freedwomen, the United Order of Tents. In Philadelphia, the Ladies Sanitary Association at St. Thomas' Church and the Colored Women's Sanitary Commission were affiliated with the USSC. Even in small towns such as Worcester, Massachusetts, black women like Martha Brown sent donations to the Ladies Sanitary Fund. In 1864, black women formed an independent Ladies Union Association (LUA) geared specifically to meet the needs of wounded and sick black soldiers. After the war, the LUA became involved in freedpeople's relief, collecting clothes and food to send south. Some of its members taught in freedmen's schools.[12]

Northern women's wartime relief work exemplified gendered notions of feminine benevolence and care, even as it signaled a transition to professionalization. As many women (and men) understood, there would be no turning back. Relief work had immediate effects but also vast implications. Hoge, for instance, was a pioneering social worker who had opened a homeless shelter in Chicago before the war, and she and other women identified their social work with the expansion of the government's reach and power. Abolitionist feminists, in particular, demanded that the government intervene actively on behalf of freedpeople. The USSC would disband in 1870, but by that point it had launched a tradition of national social work that would flower in the Progressive era among settlement house workers such as Jane Addams, and would become central to the emergence of the modern liberal state.[13]

The Civil War also accelerated women's entry into nursing, and they shaped its emergence as a profession. According to Bellows, women nurses "were really heroines," the female counterpart to heroic soldiers. The work of the legendary Florence Nightingale and the British Sanitary Commission in the Crimean War were well known in the United

States. At the start of the Civil War, Dorothea L. Dix, already famous for her work in asylum and prison reform, was appointed superintendent of army nurses. She entertained peculiar notions, insisting that all nurses be middle-aged, plain-looking, and simply dressed. Though responsible for recruiting many nurses, the conservative Dix, who opposed abolition and women's suffrage, was against pensions for them. She was eased out of her position by the War Department in 1863. Like their British precursors, the USSC doctors were also riddled with medical racism toward freedpeople, which treated them as inherently inferior, and an imperialist mindset that propped up the pseudoscience of race.

Many doctors resented female nurses and initially resisted working with them. Civil War nurses such as Mary Ann "Mother" Bickerdyke, Georgeanna Woolsey, and the more famous Clara Barton were responsible for the evolution of nursing as a profession. Bickerdyke went on lecture tours to fund-raise for the Sanitary Commission, while Woolsey founded the Connecticut Training School for Nurses after the war. They too were not immune from racial condescension. We know more about white, middle-class nurses, some of whom left wartime memoirs, than we do of the many black and working-class women who worked at army hospitals in various capacities. Susie King Taylor, a black woman who did leave behind her reminiscences, learned nursing in the Sea Islands from none other than Barton herself. In 1879, Mary Eliza Mahoney became the first black woman to graduate from a nursing school operated by the New England Hospital for Women and Children. Mahoney founded a black women's nursing association and was an ardent suffragist.[14]

Many northern women, following Barton, who began her career as a clerk in the US Patents Office, made the transition to professional nursing and relief work during the war. But the war also saw the movement of thousands of northern women into jobs vacated by enlisted men in industry and government, forgotten predecessors of the "Rosie the Riveters" of the Second World War. Douglass's second wife, Helen Pitts, worked with him as a clerk in the US Marshal's Office before marrying him. As Stanton, Anthony, and Matilda Gage wrote, "The social and political condition of woman was largely changed by our civil war.

Through the withdrawal of so many men from their accustomed work, new channels of industry were opened to them, the value and control of money learned, thought upon political questions compelled, and a desire for their own personal, individual liberty intensified." This was true not just for white middle-class women. In New York, seamstresses formed the Working Women's Union to demand better pay, just as freed-women laundresses went on strike in Galveston.[15]

A few women broke into the male bastion of professional medicine, a field that emerged in the heyday of slavery and colonialism and was deeply shaped by pseudoscientific notions about race. The women's rights advocate Harriot Kezia Hunt, who attended the first national women's convention in Worcester, was repeatedly denied admission to Harvard Medical School. But she practiced medicine nevertheless and received an honorary medical degree from the Female Medical College in Philadelphia. The most famous woman doctor in the war was the feminist Mary Edwards Walker, known for donning pants and for her work as an accomplished surgeon. She refused to be commissioned as a nurse, and in 1864 finally secured the rank of an assistant surgeon in the Union army. Also a Union spy, she was captured and imprisoned by the Confederacy, and released through a prisoner of war exchange. Lincoln, who had balked at appointing Walker to the medical corps at the start of the war, sought to meet her on her release. Walker became the first and only American woman to ever receive a Medal of Honor. She was a suffragist and wrote essays on women's rights, from dress reform and divorce to labor and "woman's franchise."

Black women also managed to win jobs that their skills would obviously have suited them for, had they been men. The abolitionist feminist Sarah Mapps Douglass, who gave lectures on female physiology, attended the Female Medical College in Philadelphia. In 1864, Dr. Rebecca Lee Crumpler, a graduate of the New England Medical College, became the first black female doctor in the country. (The black abolitionist Sarah Remond became a doctor after being educated in Florence, Italy, where she settled.) Crumpler worked with male doctors in contraband camps and for the Freedmen's Bureau. She returned to Boston after Reconstruction, where she practiced medicine for women and children. In 1883, she authored a medical treatise, the first by an African American, titled *Book of Medical Discourses,* which she dedicated to nurses. She noted the prejudice against female medical knowledge: "That woman should study the mechanism of the human structure to better enable her to protect life, before assuming the office of nurse, few will agree." A nineteenth-century version of *Our Bodies, Ourselves,* it focused on maternity and natal care. The Hyde Park black community mourned her death in 1895 with that of abolitionist Theodore Weld, who died the same year and was its "moral lodestar."[16]

Before the Civil War, the novelist Nathaniel Hawthorne, a conservative on the question of slavery, had ridiculed "the damn'd mob of women scribblers." He was referring to the outpouring of words, written by women, for abolition. During the war, northern women's writing continued to serve as essential political work, whether to advocate for emancipation and black rights, vindicate their own interventions in the public sphere, or foster support for the Union war effort. Southern elite women, for the most part, remained unreconstructed, bemoaning the war and the destruction of slavery. Northern women lent their pens to the Union cause and emancipation. The war, wrote Elizabeth Stuart Phelps, had made her give up "old ideas of womanhood."

Nurses such as the author Louisa May Alcott, and Sanitary Commission workers like Livermore, recorded their experiences of working in field hospitals and on the home front. From the anonymous *Notes on Hospital Life,* which was published in 1864, to reminiscences published much later in the 1900s, nurses left significant accounts "of the marrow of the tragedy concentrated in those Army Hospitals." Most of these books were dedicated to their patients, the soldiers. Descriptions of the toll that disease and war wounds took reveal that these nurse writers shared Walt Whitman's fear that "the real war would never get in the books," and his observation that, "The hospital part of the drama from '61 to '65, deserves indeed to be recorded." Some women, such as Hannah Ropes, were themselves martyred. Ropes died while working in a hospital but left behind her letters and diaries. She had mentored

Alcott, the most famous woman writer to emerge from the war. Alcott herself cheated death after she contracted typhoid during her time as a nurse.[17]

Alcott's account of her nursing experience, which she first published in the Boston *Commonwealth*, combined a documentary portrait of war's consequences with her abolitionist convictions. In a memoir disguised as a novella, *Hospital Sketches* (1863), she likened her time as a nurse to reporting for military duty, and her work as akin to that of the soldier. As she wrote, "I long to be a man but as I can't fight, I will content myself for working for those who can." She called the rooms in the field hospital in Washington her "duty room" and her "headquarters," and her time away from nursing "off duty." Whitman described this sensibility in the snippet "Burial of a Lady Nurse," in *Specimen Days*: "It was her request that she should be buried among the soldiers, and after the military method. This request was fully carried out. Her coffin was carried to the grave by soldiers, with the usual escort, buried, and a salute fired over the grave."

Alcott was also one of the few who acknowledged the labor of "colored sisters" in military hospitals; black women are still mostly overlooked in accounts of Civil War nursing. She could be paternalistic to enslaved people but viewed the war as a "great struggle for the liberty of both races," for black people from slavery and for whites from their own racism. Alcott, who wanted to go to Port Royal as a teacher, hoped to be a nurse for the newly mustered "colored regiments" in 1863, but her nursing career was cut short by her illness. Jane Woolsey began her nursing career only with the recruitment of black soldiers. Nurses, she reported, like the wounded soldiers they tended to, were deeply invested in the politics of war and emancipation. The nurses in her hospital sang "Glory Hallelujah" when the Thirteenth Amendment passed Congress in 1865.[18]

Women's abolitionist fiction, like their political advocacy, envisioned an interracial democracy. Lydia Maria Child's first novel, *Hobomok* (1824), was an interracial romance between a white woman and an indigenous man. Her last novel, *A Romance of the Republic* (1867), was a labyrinthine story of two enslaved, mixed-race sisters. It questioned rigid notions of race while portraying the brutalities of slavery and claimed that the United States was already an interracial country. Alcott based her short story of interracial romance, "M.L." (1863), on the true romance of Professor William Allen and his student, Mary King, who were forced to leave the country. After Reconstruction, the romance of reunion between North and South would supplant such iconoclastic, abolitionist novels. Frances Harper's *Iola Leroy* (1892) broke the mold. Its mixed-race heroine rejects a white suitor to marry a black doctor and work among freedpeople.[19]

Unsurprisingly, abolitionist women also became orators for emancipation. The Quaker Anna Dickinson did much to push northern public opinion toward black rights. The "young lady has statesmanship much beyond our twaddling politicians," reported one admirer. Dickinson was the first woman to address Congress, invited by Republicans for her contribution to their success in the 1864 elections. After the war, she became a suffragist. Sarah Parker Remond, from a prominent black abolitionist family in Salem, Massachusetts, won international renown for her eloquence. Thousands attended her speeches denouncing the partiality of the British press for the Confederacy. Remond joined the London Emancipation and Freedmen's Aid Society, and British abolitionists presented her with an inscribed watch in recognition of her success. Another Black woman, Oneda DeBois, had escaped slavery in Alabama and settled in Haiti, where she ran a school for girls. She took to the abolitionist lecture circuit in the United States during the Civil War, arguing for emancipation and vindicating the Haitian revolution. Frances Harper, who was introduced as "You have your Anna Dickinsons; and we have ours," undertook a lecture tour of the postwar South, where she mainly addressed freedpeople, especially women. As in her novel *Iola Leroy*, Harper argued that black women must work for "the welfare of the race."[20]

For Stanton and Anthony, the war presented an opportunity to enter the debate over emancipation in order to demand female citizenship. In 1863, they founded the Woman's National Loyal League (WNLL).

Abolitionist women in northern towns and cities formed Loyal Leagues, counterparts to the male-dominated Union Leagues and Clubs. The war gave rise to a "national feminist abolitionist network" that built on the work of female antislavery societies and the women's conventions. In her appeal "To the Women of the Republic," Stanton called for a national movement for abolition, equality, and "pure democracy." The members of the WNLL included abolitionist feminists such as Stone and the temperance suffragist Frances Willard. The league explicitly rejected jingoism—"Our Country Right or Wrong"—for true patriotism: "Freedom and Our Country." Angelina Grimke Weld's address to the League made clear that abolitionist women saw themselves as foot soldiers of "our Second Revolution." Black abolitionists joined the League; Harriet Jacobs was on its Executive Council and Sojourner Truth was a member.

While northern women's work in the Sanitary Commission and in nursing could be viewed as expanding traditional notions of women's moral authority into the public sphere—though many, such as Livermore, chafed at the gendered hierarchy they encountered in these organizations and became suffragists—the WNLL embraced the decidedly unconventional approach of agitation. The AASS passed a resolution in 1863 demanding a constitutional amendment to end slavery, reviving a demand that first appeared in the black abolitionist newspaper *Freedom's Journal* in 1827. On Garrison's prompting—Stanton initially asked for an emancipation law—the WNLL sent a massive petition, with 100,000 signatures, to Senator Charles Sumner in 1864, asking for an amendment to end slavery. Two black men carried the rolls of the women's petition to Sumner, who then gave a speech endorsing their demand, the "Prayer of One Hundred Thousand." By the end of the war, the WNLL had 5,000 members and had sent 20,000 petitions to Congress. According to Sumner, the women's petitions had a catalytic effect on the passage of the Thirteenth Amendment. Anthony recruited women, including Olympia Brown, the first woman to be ordained in the Unitarian Universalist Church and a suffragist, to circulate petitions at the grassroots among teachers and clergymen and form local auxiliary leagues to the WNLL.

A fracture in the WNLL leadership over the presidential elections of 1864 presaged future divisions. Stanton and Anthony (like Phillips and Douglass) flirted with John C. Fremont's candidacy, but Stone and Mott (like Garrison) viewed any move to undermine Lincoln's renomination as a copperhead plot to destroy the antislavery political coalition. As Mott noted, "we must admit that Lincoln has done well. . . . Doubtful if one *could* have been elected, who wd. have done more." Stone warned Anthony against any "union with peace Democrats," who would rejoice over a split in Republican ranks. Writing about the faction of peace Democrats, she said that "Its love of country is less than its hate of Lincoln. Pray don't work for that party Susan! You will be sure to be sorry for it. Radical antislavery is our work,—its weapons are ours."[21] Like most abolitionists, Stanton and Anthony came around to support Lincoln, and the abolitionist feminist alliance held firm, at least through the end of the war.

Like abolition, the struggle for women's rights was a transnational one in the nineteenth century. That fight dated to feminists Mary Wollstonecraft and Olympe de Gouges in the eighteenth century, but the idea of women's citizenship was now debated in mainstream politics, galvanizing thousands who supported it and many who opposed it. In 1866, the British philosopher of liberal democracy, John Stuart Mill, presented a petition for women's suffrage and property rights in Parliament at the behest of his stepdaughter, Harriet Taylor. A year later, British women formed the National Society for Women's Suffrage after women were excluded from the second reform bill that expanded voting rights for men. The Society started publishing *Women's Suffrage Journal* in 1870, the inaugural year for Stone's similarly named newspaper. American suffragists hailed the publication of Mill's *The Subjection of Women* (1869) and the passage of a married women's property act in Parliament, which gave them the right to hold property independently from their husbands. Mill's book was a joint production that included the ideas of his late wife, Harriet Taylor Mill, who was inspired by the 1850 women's national convention in Worcester, and by her daughter.

Mill laid out the goals of his book as establishing that "the legal subordination of one sex to the other" was "wrong in itself" and that "a principle of perfect equality" should guide relations between the sexes.

Women's subjection was a custom so old that it seemed like nature, but women's equality was essential for the "general good" of society, Mill wrote. Like slavery, female subjection flowed from the principle of tyranny or "political absolutism." Slavery had likewise been defended as a natural good by slaveholders. Those who argued for women's subordination as a necessary precondition for family, marriage, and childbearing were similar to slaveholders in South Carolina and Louisiana, who insisted that slavery was necessary for growing cotton and sugar. Mill likened St. Paul's admonition to wives to obey their husbands to his admonition to servants to obey their masters. Women, Mill insisted, had the political ability not only to vote but also to hold office. Not surprisingly, Mill's ideas elicited the interest of American feminists. He was one of Harper's favorite authors.[22]

The Subjection of Women was still a few years off when American feminists relaunched the women's conventions after the Civil War. Mott argued that women ought not to be ignored in any true Reconstruction, as that omission would represent a "come down." After a wartime hiatus, the National Women's Rights Convention reconvened in 1866 to hitch women's rights to black citizenship. The call put out by Anthony and Stanton stated that the convention's aim was "to reconstruct a government on the one enduring basis that has never been tried—'EQUAL RIGHTS TO ALL.'" Their strategy was to petition legislatures for "the right to suffrage to every citizen, without distinction of race, color, or sex." Letters of support from Garrison, Douglass, Higginson, and Child were included in the convention record.

Phillips gave an eloquent speech at the convention, arguing that it was not just a woman's right, but her duty, to vote. Just a year earlier, as the newly elected president of the AASS, Phillips had declared it the "negro's hour," and rejected Stanton's demand to remake the AASS into an equal rights organization. Now, in her speech to the convention, Stanton called for broad equality between the sexes and appealed to antislavery editors and abolitionist ministers for their support. It was politicians in Congress, she implied, who failed to recognize that this was also the "woman's hour." Mott agreed with Phillips that it was "emphatically the negro's hour," but she also supported Stanton and Anthony's efforts to let "the woman slip in."

While the convention invoked the broad, intersectional goal of abolitionist feminism—citizenship for all—Stanton and Anthony would soon make clear that their primary allegiance was to women's rights. Earlier on, they had petitioned Congress to prohibit any state from disfranchising its citizens "on the ground of sex." Stanton and Anthony made the aim of the convention "the right and duty of woman to claim and use the ballot," which was as a "crowning right of citizenship." Anthony introduced resolutions that condemned the Fourteenth Amendment for introducing the word "male" into the Constitution. Abolitionists also complained that the Fourteenth Amendment had not directly enfranchised black men, but only punished states that denied black men the vote with a loss of congressional representation. Yet most still followed Thaddeus Stevens, who noted that "It falls far short of my wishes, but it fulfills my hopes," in supporting it. Stanton and Anthony, though, were willing to delay black male suffrage for women's suffrage. Once the word "male" got into the Constitution, Stanton predicted, it would take a century to get it out. Only in hindsight would the duo recognize the egalitarian potential of the Fourteenth Amendment.

At the convention, Anthony moved to create the American Equal Rights Association (AERA), which would fight for universal suffrage, for black people and for women. The association would have not just a "Woman's Rights platform," but "a Human Rights platform," advocated first by Angelina Grimke in 1837. The preamble of the AERA constitution, written by Stanton, claimed that the Civil War had "resolved society into its original elements" and that in the coming "second revolution," the reconstruction of government must be based on equal rights for all. Stanton became the first president of the AERA, but abolitionist men like Robert Purvis, Douglass, Pillsbury, Stephen Foster, and Henry Blackwell, Stone's husband, held offices in the organization. It would send a petition to Congress, demanding universal suffrage and asking that as Congress considered "safeguards" for freedpeople, it should also consider women's suffrage, given that women were "the only remaining class of disfranchised citizens." The AERA developed state chapters, including one in Washington, DC, and would launch a state-by-state campaign to remove the words "white male" from state constitutions.

The speech that defined the convention, however, came from Frances Harper, who insisted that the delegates pay more attention to racism. Left penniless and with four children to care for by her late indebted husband, Harper argued that she had certainly come to appreciate, through personal experience, the necessity of demanding women's equality before the law. She famously said, "You white women here speak of rights. I speak of wrongs." Black women, herself included, had been thrown out of Jim Crow streetcars in Philadelphia. Even Tubman, "who has received the name 'Moses,' not by lying about it"—a swipe at Andrew Johnson, who had claimed to be the Moses of black people— "but by acting it out," had been left with swollen hands after a confrontation with a conductor. Yet while white women could certainly make the ballot box their fight, African Americans had to deal with racism, or "this brutal element in society," daily. Moreover, to refuse black men citizenship rights after they had fought and died for the Union would be the "depth of infamy." For Harper, the fight against racism and for black male suffrage were integral parts of the women's movement, a claim that Stanton and Anthony failed to appreciate. But she impressed the grand dame of abolitionist feminism, Lucretia Mott, who called for the younger generation, "the Harpers," to "come forward to fill our places."[23]

The first annual meeting of the AERA took place in New York on May 9–10, 1867, and it focused on suffrage for black men and all women. As Robert Purvis put it, the simple demand of the convention was for "that primal element of republican freedom—the ballot." In her address to the delegates, Anthony reported on efforts for universal suffrage in all the states, as well as Mill's speeches in Parliament for enfranchising women. The main struggle took place in Kansas, where Lucy Stone and Henry Blackwell were campaigning for enfranchising blacks and women on behalf of the AERA. As Stone argued, "The law puts its foot alike on the colored man and the woman. Why should they not make common cause?" Stanton claimed that black men and all women be "buried in the citizen," and that if freedom was the "key-note" of victory in the war, universal suffrage was the keynote of Reconstruction. But much of her speech was a vindication of women's rights and a rebuke of abolitionists who, as she believed, only said a "passing word" for women's equality. It rankled Stanton that ignorant men had the vote, but learned women like herself did not—a glimpse of the elitism that would evolve into outright racism during the Kansas campaign. Anthony proposed resolutions against the equal manhood suffrage endorsed by Republicans and the AASS, on the grounds that such laws were examples of class or caste legislation for leaving women out. Stone argued for simultaneously getting rid of racial and gender distinctions in voting.

In his speech, Samuel J. May, alluding to a sermon he had given for women's rights delivered twenty-two years prior, did not necessarily disagree with Stanton's diagnosis. During Reconstruction, most abolitionists prioritized the rights of black men. May said that his "first conviction" for the "well-being of the country" was the "treatment of colored men," and his "second conviction" was for the equality of women in education and politics. Sojourner Truth countered that she spoke "for the rights of colored women," and that if "colored men" got their rights and black women did not, "it will be just as bad as before." Truth's argument had more to do with the right of black women to control their wages than with the vote. Frances Gage, speaking for the "slave woman," seconded Truth, recalling her work with freedpeople. For Pillsbury, the very idea of giving blacks and women the vote was blasphemy, because in a democracy all possessed the right, and it was not the singular power of white men, he said, to grant others their rights. Women's rights activist Ernestine Rose disputed that argument, saying that even though their rights were "as old as humanity itself," in practical terms they were obliged to ask men for their rights. Like Stanton, she accused Republicans of hypocrisy in giving black men the suffrage but ignoring women. Mott, who was elected the new president of the AERA (Stanton's one-year term having expired), claimed that women "had a right to be a little jealous," as the "colored man" could oppose "woman's enfranchisement."

The tension among abolitionist feminists became evident in the course of AERA state campaigns, starting in New York in 1867. Charles Remond asked the New York Constitutional Convention to remove all discriminations related to race and sex when it came to voting. His speech, though, referred mainly to the disfranchisement of black men. Olympia Brown complained that during the New York AERA campaign, Remond had stressed "the injustice done to the negro as so much greater than the wrongs of women" and had "no patience with the presentation of our claims." Truth and Louisa Jacobs, daughter of Harriet Jacobs, lectured for women's suffrage in New York, but white suffragists, as a general matter, used the symbolism of black women yet rarely acknowledged them. White suffragists employed a condescending tone when they compared women's "humanitarian labors" during the war with the "negro's rough services in camp and battle." It was a long way from Harper's intersectional reasoning: "We are all bound up together in one great bundle of humanity, and society cannot trample on the weakest and feeblest of its members without receiving the curse in its own soul."[24]

Not willing to risk constitutional amendments and laws protecting freedpeople by extending them to protect women, Republicans and abolitionists downplayed women's suffrage, infuriating Stanton and Anthony. Some conservative Republicans and racist Democrats, for their part, became sudden converts to women's rights to derail Reconstruction. In 1865, Senator Edgar Cowan of Pennsylvania, a Johnson man, tried to tack woman suffrage onto a bill giving black men the right to vote in the District of Columbia, to defeat it. Senators Sumner and Justin Morrill opposed the maneuver. Sumner, who supported universal suffrage, noted when he introduced petitions for women's suffrage that it was not the "proper time" to consider it. The only senators to advocate, on principle, for immediate woman suffrage were not Democrats, but Republicans like Benjamin Wade and Gratz Brown of Missouri. Stanton and Anthony would cite congressional debates in their history of women's suffrage as justification for their decision to form an alliance with Democrats. The veneer of unity barely held at the annual meeting of the AERA in 1868. In vain, Douglass tried to convince Stanton and Anthony that there was no conflict between black men's and women's rights and that the Republicans and Democrats, the latter of whom "desired a white man's government," were substantially different.

Stone, not Stanton or Anthony, was the tribune of abolitionist feminism. As one observer wrote of her at the time, "the claims of woman to political rights should be urged, but she was always glad to maintain the rights of the negro." Before the war, Douglass mistakenly accused her of lecturing before segregated audiences, and Stone, a staunch Garrisonian, parted with him over the insult. Douglass was personally closer to Anthony—they both lived in Rochester—but now, during Reconstruction, it was Stone who shared common ground with him. In 1867, Stone and Blackwell launched an AERA campaign for women's suffrage in New Jersey, where they lived. In her address to the state judiciary committee, Stone reminded them of the brief period when New Jersey allowed women and black people to vote, between 1776 and 1807. Disfranchisement deprived women of economic equality, personal autonomy, and access to higher education. Her speech was a masterpiece of the intersectional, transnational, and radical logic of abolitionist feminism. She compared denying blacks and women the right to vote to the disfranchised status of the British working class, each an affront to democracy comparable to Louis Napoleon's antidemocratic coup d'état against the French republic. Two years later, Stone addressed the Massachusetts judiciary committee on women's suffrage. In both cases, she won over the committees, but not the state legislatures.

In their appeals, Stone and Blackwell also made conventional arguments about the purity and superiority of American women, and political ones about ensuring the victory of the Republican Party. In a pamphlet, Blackwell urged southern states to accept black suffrage but to also give women the vote—so that whites would still form a majority of the voting population. Of course, unreconstructed southerners refused to tolerate either blacks' or women's suffrage. Asking southern states to accept black suffrage but counterbalance it with women's suffrage was not the start of the suffragists' so-called southern strategy, as some historians today claim, but a quixotic attempt to persuade the South to accept the

AERA platform. The "southern strategy" deployed by suffragists later on entailed an appeal to southern women at the cost of black people's rights, who were largely excluded from suffrage conventions.

It was during the ongoing equal rights campaigns in New York and Kansas that the women's movement split over whether to stick with old allies or form new alliances with former enemies. At New York's constitutional convention of 1867, Republican George William Curtis led the fight for women's suffrage, with most Democrats opposed. Horace Greeley's suffrage committee recommended doing away with property-holding qualifications for black men, but not extending the vote to women. Stanton, who had addressed the legislature, smartly sent a petition for women's suffrage to his committee that was signed first by Greeley's wife. The proposed constitution with black male suffrage was defeated at the polls. Greeley would soon oppose Reconstruction, heading the breakaway Liberal Republican and Democratic presidential ticket in 1872 against President Grant. Greeley's conservatism hardly makes him an example of radicals abandoning women, a claim made at the time and since.

In Kansas, the break was more bitter. The referendums for black men's and women's suffrage were both defeated amid charges and countercharges fueled by Democrats and conservatives who opposed both causes. Stone and Blackwell campaigned for women's and black suffrage—or, in the new umbrella term, "impartial suffrage"—in the state. Stone criticized a black clergyman for opposing women's suffrage but would not countenance racism. Blackwell thought that impartial suffrage had a chance of passing in Kansas, despite "some Republican politicians and papers" that were willing to drop women's suffrage. Anthony and Stanton joined the campaign in Kansas late and ended up blaming Wendell Phillips for not allowing them to use the abolitionist Charles Hovey's bequest for their campaign. They resented monies being diverted to aid freedpeople. Henry Blackwell, for his part, felt that Anthony and Stanton had squandered the funds they did have access to.

The split between Stanton and Anthony and abolitionist feminists was not over funds, though. It stemmed from an ideological divide between fundamentally different visions of feminism. Stanton and

Anthony blamed Republicans and abolitionists for not supporting them sufficiently in Kansas. They horrified their critics and supporters alike by campaigning with a flamboyant, racist Democrat, George Francis Train. Train, who quipped that "when blacks and 'Rads' unite to enslave the whites, 'Tis time the Democrats championed woman's rights," would bankroll their short-lived newspaper, *The Revolution*. Most abolitionist feminists, including Stone, Mott, Phillips, and Garrison, naturally recoiled at using racist arguments for women's suffrage, and from the idea that white women should be enfranchised before black men to safeguard white supremacy.

Stone, who suggested a sixteenth amendment to enfranchise women, could not stomach Train's racism. The AERA promptly disowned Stanton and Anthony's tactics. As even the modern historian most sympathetic to them, Ellen DuBois, has observed, allying with Train "violated the historical traditions and political principles" of abolition. Long after this episode, and on the eve of reconciliation between the two factions of suffragists, Train endured as a point of contention. He was the main reason Stone refused to collaborate with Anthony and Stanton in writing the history of women's suffrage.[25]

Abolitionists disgusted with Stanton and Anthony's expedient tactics, as well as suffragists like Olympia Brown and Parker Pillsbury who still supported them, together founded the New England Woman Suffrage Association (NEWSA) in November 1868, the first organization in American history devoted solely to women's suffrage. It demanded women's suffrage in Washington and the federal territories, and it supported the Fifteenth Amendment that enfranchised black men but also called for a sixteenth amendment for women's enfranchisement. It also lobbied the Massachusetts legislature every year for suffrage in the state, as a precursor to an amendment.

Stanton and Anthony opposed the Fifteenth Amendment, using increasingly elitist arguments to oppose giving black and immigrant men the right to vote before women. As Stanton put it, she could not accept "Patrick and Sambo and Hans and Yung Tung" making laws for her, an educated daughter of the republic. The bankruptcy of Stanton and Anthony's tactics was amply illustrated by the fact that the only congressmen willing to introduce a sixteenth amendment and raise the issue of women's suffrage were their reviled Republican allies: Representative George Julian, Senator Henry Wilson, Senator Samuel Pomeroy of Kansas, Representative Benjamin Butler, and, later, Senators George F. Hoar and Oliver Morton. Senator Benjamin Wade was particularly forthright in his support for "female suffrage." Men and women, he argued, were equally affected by the laws passed by Congress. Why then "should not the females have the right to participate in their construction as well as the male part of the community?"

The staunchest opponents of women's suffrage in Congress were conservative, states' rights, racist Democrats. According to Senator Garrett Davis of Kentucky, God "never intended that woman should take part in national government among any people, or that the negro, the lowest, should ever have equal and coordinate power with the highest, the white race, in any government, national or domestic." Senator Willard Saulsbury Jr. of Delaware would oppose the Nineteenth Amendment, which finally extended the vote to women in 1920, as doggedly as his father Senator Willard Saulsbury Sr. opposed the Reconstruction amendments in the 1860s. Democratic representative James Brooks tried to add the word "sex" to the Fifteenth Amendment in Congress in 1869 with the express purpose of defeating it.

Though Republicans were willing to set aside women's suffrage to enact black male suffrage, many of them still supported the former. By contrast, Democratic senators who opposed both made speeches about domesticity and women's "proper domain," which, as they saw it, ought not to be defiled by "party politics." Senator James Bayard of Delaware, whose brother was married to Stanton's sister, likened suffragists—as Democrats had done abolitionists before the war—to communists and socialists, calling them "unsexed fanatics." Democrats' misogyny was equal to their racism, but Stanton and Anthony nevertheless allied themselves with the Democratic opponents of Reconstruction in 1868, in the hopes that it would benefit their cause. Anthony attended the Democratic National Convention that year, throwing her support behind its presidential candidate, Horatio Seymour. Stanton, writing in the *Revolution*, endorsed its vice presidential candidate Frank Blair, a virulent racist. According to Stone and Blackwell, Blair's rabid followers stood for "Death to the Negro."

In 1872, Stanton and Anthony recanted, issuing an endorsement of the Ulysses Grant–Henry Wilson Republican presidential ticket and repudiating the Liberal Republican/Democratic ticket of Greeley and their former supporter Gratz Brown, who reneged on Reconstruction and women's rights. This was the "New Departure" in their tactics, a term used by Democrats who acquiesced to Reconstruction. The Republican National Convention that year, due to Blackwell's efforts, passed a resolution for women's suffrage. He reported that Anthony was now in "a very reasonable mood." Stanton, stumping in California, was glad to have Republicans' "big tents" and "able arguments" for women's rights. Congressman John Bingham, she wrote, gave a "great speech" on the Reconstruction amendments in which "every principle he laid down literally enfranchised the women of the nation." But still, he refused to advocate woman suffrage because of "practical politics," she noted.

Many suffragists attempted to cast ballots for Grant in the 1872 presidential elections, including Anthony, Truth, and a group of women from a utopian socialist community in New Jersey. A year earlier, Mary Ann Shadd Cary had attempted to register to vote in Washington. It was not the first time that suffragists had tried to vote as a political tactic, but it was the most concerted attempt yet. Anthony was arrested, imprisoned, and fined when she refused to post bail. Her case made news across the country, and at her hearing she subjected the unsympathetic Supreme Court justice Ward Hunt to a good suffragist lecture. She recommended that propertied women refuse to pay taxes because they lacked political representation.

Reconstruction's progressive constitutionalism gave suffragists a powerful rationale for the enfranchisement of women. Radicals in Congress like Benjamin Butler and suffragists such as Isabella Beecher Hooker, the youngest member of the famous Beecher family, invoked abolitionist jurisprudence from the eighteenth century as well as the expansive language of equality in the Fourteenth Amendment and even the Fifteenth Amendment, to make their case. Frances Gage praised "the nationalization of liberty" that had occurred during Reconstruction and rejected the doctrine of states' rights, which protected local tyranny. Suffragists referred often to the late Thaddeus Stevens, who had said that the right to vote was an inalienable natural right of all American citizens, as well as to Sumner's many speeches on equality before the law, which he sent to Anthony for her to use against gender discrimination. Anthony even evoked Phillips's argument that freedom without enfranchisement is incomplete. She undercut her position, however, when she insisted that oligarchies of wealth and race were more bearable than those of sex.

Some of the comparisons suffragists made were overblown. When the Illinois High Court (and later the Supreme Court in 1873) denied Myra Bradwell the right to practice law, some likened it to the Dred Scott decision. At times, the arguments for women's rights resorted to racialist logic. In Missouri, Virginia Minor attempted to register to vote on the basis that she was "a native-born free white citizen." Her case, *Minor v. Happersett,* went all the way to the Supreme Court in 1875, which ruled that the equal protection clause of the Fourteenth Amendment did not bestow the right to vote on all citizens. The Supreme Court's conservatism on suffrage was part of its general retreat from Reconstruction, which saw the court vitiate or overthrow amendments and laws designed to protect freedpeople's rights.

The few successes for suffragists occurred in western territories that were trying to expedite statehood by increasing their voting population. In 1869, Wyoming territory became the first territory or state to give women the right to vote, when a Democrat introduced a women's suffrage bill as a check on black, native, and Chinese men voting. (Twenty years later, it became the first state to grant women suffrage.) However, Anthony observed that most of the women of Wyoming voted solidly Republican and continued to do so when an attempted repeal of the law was vetoed by the Republican governor. The next year, Utah territory gave women the right to vote to allay charges of female subordination leveled over the Mormon practice of polygamy. When Utah joined the Union as a state in 1896, it did so with a state

constitution that enfranchised women. Other western states would follow suit, giving women the right to vote well before the passage of the
Nineteenth Amendment.[26]

The formal break within the abolitionist feminist movement occurred
before Stanton and Anthony's return to supporting the Republicans and
during the last meeting of the AERA in May 1869. And even after their
"New Departure" tactics, it never healed. Abolitionist feminists such
as Harper and Stone had refused to be drawn into a zero-sum game.
Harper opposed the notion of *white women's rights*, not *women's rights,*
she reportedly said: "When it was a question of race, she let the lesser
question of sex go. But the white women go all for sex, letting race occupy
a minor position." If the nation was capable of handling only one question at a time, she would not let black women "put a single straw in the
way" of the enfranchisement of black men. The point was not to repudiate feminism, but to stay true to abolitionist feminism. While Anthony
claimed that white women were more intelligent than "the negro,"
Douglass pointed out that black men and women were being lynched
and tortured in the South. As for Stone, it was Stanton, of all people, who
captured her feminism best: "Mrs. Stone felt the slaves' wrongs more
deeply than her own—my philosophy was more egotistical."

The 1869 convention took place amid state-level and national debates
over the Fifteenth Amendment. The convention arrived at a compromise
resolution on the question, "heartily" approving of the amendment and
expressing "profound regret" that Congress had not passed a "parallel
amendment" for women's suffrage. But it could not bridge the two factions, with Stanton and Anthony opposing the Fifteenth Amendment.
They founded the National Woman Suffrage Association (NWSA) at the
Woman's Bureau in New York mere days after the convention ended.
Though it was devoted to woman's suffrage, it also began campaigning
against the Fifteenth Amendment. Stanton and Anthony decided that
only women should occupy positions of authority in the new organization. Abolitionist men such as Pillsbury and Purvis, however, joined it.

Stone repudiated Stanton and Anthony's "crazy opposition" to the

Fifteenth Amendment. The leaders of NEWSA called for the formation of the American Woman Suffrage Association (AWSA), which met for the first time in Cleveland that November. Unlike Stanton and Anthony, who left Stone out when they formed NWSA, Stone invited all suffragists to attend its founding meeting, and Anthony did so. One of its resolutions commended the National Labor Congress for admitting men and women, blacks and whites. Unlike NWSA, AWSA allowed men to hold office, and elected the "respectable" Rev. Henry Ward Beecher its first president. Beecher was a figurehead; much of the work in AWSA was done by Julia Ward Howe, author of the "Battle Hymn of the Republic" and president of NEWSA, and Stone, AWSA's next president.

In May 1870, a rump executive committee of the AERA met in Theodore Tilton's home in Brooklyn and decided not to hold any more annual conventions. Stone argued that the rump group did not have the authority to dissolve the AERA, though it was clear that the organization was in its death throes. Black male suffrage had been established with the ratification of the Fifteenth Amendment only a few months before, and now all energies should be concentrated, Henry Blackwell wrote, on women's suffrage. He acknowledged that the AERA had "done good service in its day." But it was clear that NWSA and AWSA had taken its place. Both organizations would hold their first anniversary convention in the same spot as the AERA, but Tilton's efforts to unite them into a "Union Woman Suffrage Association" failed. Despite their opposition to Stanton and Anthony's tactics, Mott, Truth, and Douglass attended and spoke at NWSA meetings. Black suffragists split between the two organizations, with a majority, including Harper, sympathizing with AWSA, and a few, such as Cary, joining NWSA. Unlike Stanton and Anthony, Truth, Cary, and other black suffragists who joined NWSA, which was considered the more radical of the two suffrage organizations, never opposed the Fifteenth Amendment.[27]

Within AWSA, a debate emerged over whether to pursue suffrage through state and local societies or to pursue the long dreamed of constitutional amendment. Antoinette Brown Blackwell recommended a combined strategy: "Congress must give us the sixteenth amendment;

but the State Legislatures will be called on to ratify that amendment; and the great American populace must stand behind all legislation, as the only ultimate impelling power." Stone, a proponent of a sixteenth amendment, also called for the simultaneous petitioning of state and federal governments. In short, AWSA did not simply follow a "states only" strategy, as is often claimed to distinguish it from NWSA.

In 1875, NWSA, which had started meeting annually in Washington a year earlier, took a "new position," endorsing a sixteenth amendment. Stanton wrote its text, closely following the wording of the Fifteenth Amendment that she and Anthony had so vehemently opposed: "The right of citizens of the United States to vote shall not be denied or abridged by the United States or by any State on account of sex." Unlike George Julian's proposed sixteenth amendment, from 1868, which made citizenship and suffrage a federal responsibility, Stanton's amendment, like the Fifteenth, would allow southern states to maneuver around it with restrictions on voting such as literacy tests and poll taxes. In 1878, Republican senator A. A. Sargent of California introduced Stanton's sixteenth amendment. Stanton, Matilda Josyln Gage, Olympia Brown, Belva Lockwood, and Phoebe Couzins of NWSA addressed Congress in support of it, and Stanton also appealed to Sumner's nationalist reading of the Constitution. The allegedly "liberal" former vice president of the Confederacy, Alexander Stephens, now representing Georgia as a Democrat in Congress, charmed the suffragists. But the amendment went nowhere because of the opposition of Democrats who controlled the Senate.

The difference between AWSA and NWSA was not one of strategy—state action versus a constitutional amendment—or even of radicalism, in a sense. It was, rather, the old ideological division between intersectional abolitionist feminism and feminism "pure and simple." That phrase comes from labor history; the American Federation of Labor (AFL) formally advocated unionism "pure and simple," in contrast to the Knights of Labor and, later, the Congress of Industrial Organizations (CIO), which did not eschew politics or exclude unskilled workers. AWSA posited an expansive abolitionist vision of equality: equal rights before the law. At its Tenth Annual Convention in Cincinnati in 1879, the banner adorning AWSA's platform read "Equal Work" and "Equal Wages." Like Stone, Anthony was also interested in aligning with working-class women. However, the conservatism of the early labor movement on gender stymied them and their allies.

Perhaps the greatest tragedy of Stanton and Anthony's brand of feminism was that their deployment of racist logic for women's rights would find new adherents later on, especially after the overthrow of Reconstruction in the late nineteenth century. The foremost thinker and strategist of early American feminism—which Stanton and Anthony surely were, respectively—had an effect that long outlasted them. Stanton and Anthony explicitly laid out their "southern strategy," which was premised on "educated women" who understood "the genius" of republican government. Enfranchising southern women would "mitigate the hostility they would naturally feel" in seeing their former slaves made their "political superiors." Women's suffrage would check the "incoming tide of ignorant voters from the Southern plantations and from the nations of the Old World." Stanton even subscribed to the racist lie that enfranchised black men would rape southern white women, the frequently invoked canard that served as justification for the epidemic of lynching in the post-Reconstruction South. Later, when black suffragists such as Ida B. Wells insisted that the women's movement address the issue of racial violence and lynching, they were told that these were not women's issues and of no concern to white women. As Lydia Maria Child had warned, enfranchising southern "rebel" women at the cost of black people resurrected the very forces that abolitionist feminists had fought against.

Stanton and Anthony conceptualized women's suffrage in lily white and nativist terms. They acknowledged "newly-freed women" and accomplished black feminists, but their logic was as parochial as that of those whom they critiqued for advocating only manhood suffrage. Stanton complained that northern men could see oppression on a southern plantation, but not in their own homes. She even argued that it was in "bad taste" to blame the South for slavery and "throw any stigma on Jefferson Davis" when opposing an NWSA resolution against "amnesty for former rebels." As if to mitigate the effect of their choices on their own legacies, Stanton and Anthony (and their coauthor, Matilda Gage) briefly acknowledged, in the *History of Woman Suffrage*, "the struggle of black men and women" during Reconstruction and "women of that oppressed race."

The suffrage movement did not achieve independence from other movements when Stanton and Anthony repudiated abolitionist feminism during Reconstruction. It only became politically independent when suffragists recognized that the Democratic Party had nearly died trying to "sustain slavery" and continued to uphold racial and gender hierarchies, and that the Republican Party was repudiating its antislavery past after the fall of Reconstruction, "in fostering land, railroad and money monopolies . . . building up a commercial feudalism dangerous to the liberty of the people."[28]

That realization came after the overthrow of Reconstruction and the transformation of the Republican Party from the party of antislavery to the party of big business. Reconstruction, however, bequeathed a legacy of political activism and progressive constitutionalism to the suffrage movement. Legislatures throughout the country considered amendments and laws for women's suffrage during this time. Suffragists won the right to vote in municipal and school board elections in some states. Women's suffrage also appeared in some of the Reconstruction constitutional conventions that took place in the South from 1867 to 1869. Reconstruction state constitutions recognized married women's property rights, and in South Carolina women won the right to divorce in courts, which had previously only been possible by an act of the legislature.

In South Carolina, the black Rollin sisters—Charlotte, Louisa, and Frances—led the fight for women's rights. Louisa addressed the house of representatives for women's suffrage in 1869. In 1870, freedwomen, encouraged by local officials, attempted to vote, two years prior to the big push by northern suffragists. In 1872 and 1874, black legislators such as Charlotte's husband, William J. Whipper, as well as Beverly Nash and

Alonso Ransier, proposed amendments and spoke out in favor of women's suffrage. Charlotte Rollin was active in the all-black South Carolina Woman's Rights Association; wives of Republican politicians were members, and the organization was affiliated with AWSA. She argued, "We ask suffrage not as a favor, not as a privilege, but as a right based on the ground that we are human beings, and as such entitled to all human rights."

Black women, in particular, inherited the intersectional vision of abolitionist feminism. As Harper put it in her 1873 speech at the AWSA convention, "much as white women need the ballot, colored women need it more." She was invited by South Carolina's secretary of state Francis Cardozo to address the legislature. The state with the largest number of black officeholders and voters during Reconstruction gave women's suffrage another respectful hearing, even though it did not enact it. "There is not a state in the Union I prefer to Carolina," Harper wrote. Stone, in her newspaper, *The Woman's Journal,* published articles on "Suffrage for Freedwomen." Referring to Judge Hunt's decision in Anthony's case—when she had voted illegally—that the Reconstruction amendments applied only to race, color, and previous condition of servitude, one contributor to *The Woman's Journal* argued that freedwomen should demand suffrage on those grounds. Another remarked on how freedwomen had asserted their rights after emancipation, leaving marriages they no longer wanted and eagerly seeking education in freedmen's schools.

Historians have largely missed southern Reconstruction debates over women's suffrage. At the Louisiana constitutional convention, an attempt to drop the word "male" from the state constitution died in committee. At the Texas convention, T. H. Mundine's resolution to allow citizens to vote "without distinction of sex" garnered a favorable majority report from the committee of state affairs. The convention, though, upheld the dissenting minority report by a vote of 52 to 13. Martha Goodwin Tunstall, an antislavery unionist from the Austin Friends of Female Suffrage, confessed that her own husband, a delegate, opposed women's suffrage.

One of the most extensive debates over women's suffrage in the South took place in the Arkansas constitutional convention in 1868. Miles Ledford Langley from Clark County, an abolitionist who had been incarcerated for his beliefs before the war, wished to amend the state constitution to give all citizens above the age of twenty-one the right to vote and "equal political rights and privileges." He argued that all literate adult citizens should get "the elective franchise" and be "entitled to equal political rights and privileges." One Mr. Gantt facetiously proposed to refer his motion to "Mrs. Lucy Stone." Langley objected to maneuvers to shut him up, claiming freedom of speech. He affirmed that women were "endowed with equal rights, social, political, and legal, with man." He proceeded to make an eloquent argument for women's equality, maintaining that many women were better qualified to vote and hold office than those who opposed "female suffrage." He insisted that the government be reconstructed on the basis of "radical principles" and "scientific truth," including universal suffrage. Langley gave the longest speech in favor of female suffrage of any at the Reconstruction conventions, despite hooting by conservatives.

Mr. Dale, a black delegate, supported Langley's motion and identified opposition to it with Confederates, rebellion, and racism. Black Arkansans, he argued, were for "universal suffrage, universal freedom, and universal responsibility." The men who opposed it were those who had "lived off the sweat and blood of their fellow-man." Langley's motion did not succeed, but not one conservative Democrat refuted Dale's argument. They agreed with him that women's suffrage and black citizenship were linked—though, in their view, both were to be feared and opposed.[29] Arkansas would be one of the few southern states to ratify the Nineteenth Amendment in 1920.

During Reconstruction, freedwomen mobilized politically and participated in electioneering even though they did not have the right to vote themselves. At the grassroots in South Carolina, Alabama, Mississippi, and Virginia, they emerged as vehement Republican partisans and participants in Reconstruction politics. Almost single-handedly, Harper in her southern lecture tours tried to connect the largely northern women's rights movement with the grassroots struggles of freedwomen during Reconstruction that she captured in her book of poems, *Sketches of Southern Life* (1872). In ignoring their efforts and in allying themselves with their Democratic opponents, the Stanton and Anthony wing of suffragists lost an ideal opportunity to establish a truly radical interracial movement. It would be decades before another presented itself.

PART THREE

AMERICAN THERMIDOR, 1870–1890

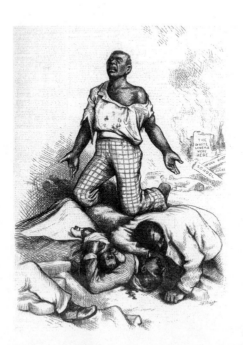

"Is This a Republican Form of Government?" by Thomas Nast,
Harper's Weekly, September 2, 1876. *Library of Congress*

CHAPTER SEVEN

The Waning of Reconstruction

But pray tell me who is the barbarian here, the murderer or the victim?

—CONGRESSMAN ROBERT B. ELLIOT, 1871

"Colfax Massacre," *Harper's Weekly*, May 19, 1873.

American Antiquarian Society

It is a measure of Reconstruction's initial success that it drew such
a vicious response. The toppling of Reconstruction was a process almost as complex and multifaceted as that by which it was
constituted in the first place. At the center of the war against Reconstruction were domestic terrorists, whose brutal, ongoing campaign
saw them outlast the federal government and the national Republican

Party. Ex-Confederates and the violence they perpetrated led to a "crisis of legitimacy" for Reconstruction state governments.[1] While the Grant administration initially reacted vigorously to stop domestic terror, the president was handicapped by a series of economic crises and political scandals in his second term that set the stage for the retreat from Reconstruction.

Unreconstructed southerners called the overthrow of Reconstruction "redemption," for how they "redeemed" the region for white supremacy. It was a fundamentalist religious idiom that had long informed proslavery ideology and extended to biblical arguments to defend slavery. They also adopted the term "Home Rule," borrowing from Irish and Indian nationalists fighting British imperialism, and thereby falsely likening their condition to that of nations that had been colonized; generations of southern historians would embrace the idea. Some radical Irish nationalists disdained the comparison; one Fenian called it "a parallel between light and darkness—Heaven and Hell." Another wrote that "The South drew the sword for the maintenance of the vilest kind of slavery; Ireland draws the sword for Liberty." Instead, many Irish nationalists compared their struggle against colonialism to the black struggle for equality. Frederick Douglass argued that while Home Rule was a term "dear to the Irish heart," in the American South it was a cloak for treason, outrage, and murder.

Southern conservatives claimed that they fought against "Negro domination" and "Negro supremacy," when in truth their fight was against black equality. A more accurate descriptor than "redeemers" was "Bourbons," which evoked the ancien régime of the French monarchy overthrown in the late eighteenth century. Black congressman Robert Elliott used the term in an 1871 speech to describe conservatives opposed to Reconstruction, and it was employed most often in Louisiana, given the state's French heritage. Historians today use "Bourbons" more commonly to describe the one-party rule of conservative Democrats in the "Solid South" *after* the fall of Reconstruction. Perhaps the best term to describe southern conservatives in this period was a simpler one chosen by Alrutheus Ambush Taylor, a pioneering black historian of Reconstruction working in the 1920s: "reactionaries."[2]

Whatever they were called then or are best called now, white conservative elites led the charge in the overthrow of Reconstruction, launching a yearslong guerilla campaign to disrupt elections and governance—and the very notion of interracial democracy. In the process, they helped make possible other antidemocratic policies and forces, from the conquest of the Plains Indians to the establishment of American empire to the crushing of the first mass labor and farmer movements in US history. I have called the third part of this book "American Thermidor," a reference to the unwinding of the French Revolution and a term intended to encompass developments that are not normally seen as part of the history of Reconstruction's unmaking.

The first state to overthrow Reconstruction was Tennessee, the home state of both Andrew Johnson and the Ku Klux Klan. Under the leadership of Republican governor William G. "Parson" Brownlow, a staunch political enemy of Johnson, Tennessee had become the only ex-Confederate state to abolish slavery and inaugurate black suffrage on its own. It was also the first southern state to be readmitted to the Union and to ratify the Fourteenth Amendment. Brownlow's strong reaction to Klan atrocities in 1868—he declared martial law in nine counties—earned him the support of freedpeople. The Klan, he noted, had armed itself "with an eye to the overthrow of the State government, and ultimately, to carrying the state in the Presidential election." The next year, though, when Brownlow left for the Senate, his chosen successor, De Witt Senter, allied with Democrats and pardoned ex-Confederates who were flocking to the Klan. Most black Tennesseans had supported Senter's radical opponent, William B. Stokes, who promised to counter the terror group, which he referred to as a "hellish organization."

Newly empowered, Democrats and conservative Republicans united to undo laws favoring workers and black education, and repealed a state law against the Klan. By 1870, a Democratic-dominated state convention rewrote Tennessee's Reconstruction constitution. The new constitution included a poll tax for voting, beginning the process of disfranchising black men and, at times, poor whites. Senter's lenient policies unsurprisingly did little to stop violence by the Klan and ex-Confederates. He belatedly pled for federal intervention. The fall of Reconstructed Tennessee provided a template to other southern states—a combination of racist terror, exploitation of Republican factionalism between radicals and conservatives, and voter suppression—to overthrow Reconstruction.

In addition to Tennessee, border slave states such as Kentucky and Delaware introduced racial segregation and opposed black education. In much of the upper South, Democrats embraced a "new departure"—taken up differently, as we have seen, by Elizabeth Cady Stanton and Susan B. Anthony—superficially accepting Reconstruction but creating new coalitions with conservative Republicans to undo its gains. In Missouri, Democrats allied with disaffected Liberal Republicans—a breakaway group of laissez-faire Republicans friendly to business and opposed to Reconstruction—and in West Virginia, they openly argued for the restoration of the "white man's government." Increasingly, southern Democrats portrayed themselves as natural leaders of the "New South," as propertied landowners, boosters of railroads and manufacturing, and "taxpayers." Their "Taxpayers' Conventions" questioned progressive taxation for schools and government services and sought to reinstall a propertied oligarchy. Democrats also concocted charges of "voter fraud," and exaggerated instances of Republican corruption (from which conservatives themselves were hardly immune) to question black male suffrage and officeholding.

Once in power, conservatives passed laws that adversely affected all poor and working people, including fence laws that cordoned off common grazing lands and laws restricting hunting and fishing. They also rescinded lien laws that protected sharecroppers and wage workers. Virginia, which practically forewent Reconstruction when conservative Republicans allied with Democrats and railroad boosters to elect a government that shut out African Americans in 1869, even authorized whipping for petty theft. As the black state senator George Teamoh protested, "We ask in the name of republican civilization, that law inflicting stripes as punishments for crimes be repealed." Georgia, where Klan activity spiked with the galvanizing assassination of a white Republican politician George W. Ashburn—and which unlike most other reconstructed states did not go for Grant in the 1868 presidential elections—became the first Deep South state to fall to white supremacy. Democrats won both houses of the legislature and the governorship in 1871. The Klan and another terror group, the Knights of the White Camellia, decimated the Republican vote in Georgia and Louisiana through violent intimidation. The *National Anti-Slavery Standard* editorialized, "The masses of Southern whites today are aliens in spirit, more inimical to republican government than the bulk of foreign emigrants who seek homes within our national domain."[3]

The terrorism carried out against black people and their political allies indicated that the violence of slave society endured, though it had been transformed. Besides the Klan, founded in Fort Pulaski, Tennessee, in the summer of 1866, assorted armed racist groups composed of ex-Confederates such as the Knights of White Camellia, White Brotherhood, "white liners" and White Leagues, and the "palefaces," proliferated throughout the postwar South after 1868. They targeted black and white Republican politicians, teachers in black schools, and everyday freedpeople. In much of the South, racist terror organizations were dominant. In Georgia, Alabama, and Tennessee, the Klan destabilized Reconstruction state governments and eventually overthrew them through a combination of voter intimidation and political assassinations.

Though sometimes still called "vigilante violence," these acts were not directed toward suspected criminals, but against innocent people, prominent and not. African Americans, and successful black people, in particular, were the special targets of Klansmen, though they attacked white Republicans and southern unionists too. Historian Elaine Frantz writes, "From 1866 through 1871, men calling themselves 'Ku-Klux' killed hundreds of black southerners and their white supporters, sexually molested hundreds of black women and men, drove thousands of black families from their homes and thousands of black men and women from their employment, and appropriated land, crops, guns, livestock, and food from black southerners on a massive scale."

White terror was designed to discipline black labor, discourage black men from voting, remove Republican officeholders, and otherwise undermine the region's incipient democracy. The mask of chivalry worn by elite southerners, many of whom led the Klan as its Grand Dragons, Titans, Cyclops, and other ridiculous titles, was easy to see through. Some of them were directly involved in the violence, while others maintained a complicit silence as common whites did their dirty work. The first Klan sported outlandish costumes, including horns and ghostly white sheets to impersonate the Confederate dead. The northern press documented the Klan's atrocities but helped spread its legend to many racist readers at the same time. Southern reaction made its peace with northern capital, with the railroads lining the postwar South serving as symbols of that entente cordiale. Some of the most prominent Klan leaders became railroad and insurance magnates, faces of the new and old South simultaneously. One contemporary observed that "the capitalists and speculators of the North" who wanted to revive the cotton kingdom were sympathetic to the Klan.

Yet the first Klan—in contrast to its reincarnated version in the early twentieth century as a national antiblack, anti-Semitic, anti-Catholic organization—was a decidedly southern phenomenon. And its deadly serious political purpose far outweighed its carnivalesque performative aspects and sensational presence in the national press. While it resembled, in some respects, earlier racist organizations like the nativist Know Nothings and the Knights of the Golden Circle that hoped to establish a proslavery empire through filibustering—the term for illegal invasions of Latin American countries—in the antebellum era, its deployment of political terror was unmatched. The Klan specialized in rituals of violent humiliation, such as whippings and the rape of black women, that could evoke slavery, as well as gruesome forms of torture that would come to define the Jim Crow South. It actively recruited former Confederate generals like Nathan Bedford Forrest, who led it in 1867 as the "Grand Wizard of the Empire," George W. Gordon, John

C. Brown, and John B. Gordon of Georgia, who was a Grand Dragon. The Klan's bizarre, secretive initiation ceremonies were revealing of its grisly purpose. As its members allegedly intoned: "Whoever dares our cause reveal, Shall test the edge of glitt'ring steel; And if the torture proves too dull, We'll scrape the brains out from under his skull." Only "true southrons" willing to continue the war were allowed to join.

The Klan aimed to dismantle black citizenship and destroy its political vehicle, the Republican Party in the South. In Alabama, it systematically targeted the Union League, the cornerstone of black political organization in the state. While the KKK may have been less organized than both its opponents and supporters claimed, it inspired similar groups as well as individual acts of political terror throughout the South. In this sense, the Klan's lawless violence bred southern terrorism on a massive scale. Southern terrorists avoided areas with decisive majority black populations, like lowcountry South Carolina, and used "cowardly" tactics, including attacking African Americans in the dark as "night riders," or assaulting them when they were otherwise alone and vulnerable. Their patron saint was apparently John Wilkes Booth, Lincoln's assassin. Southern terror revived the "slave patrols" of the antebellum era, but in doing so wrote a new chapter in homegrown domestic terrorism: their purpose was not to apprehend and return fugitive slaves, but to attack and murder black citizens and their white allies.

As an early critic noted, "The constitutions, oaths, proceedings of the Ku-Klux Klan, are a sufficient indication of the blood-thirstiness of Southern sentiment at the moment; and they are positively indicative of the real state of feeling among the Southern leaders." Writing in 1877, this critic counted nearly 400,000 southern men and women in the Klan—in fact, the figure was closer to 550,000, with 40,000 in Tennessee alone—and predicted a rapid increase in the membership of terrorist groups. Southern women were avid supporters of the KKK. The South Carolina Klan kept a register of names of women who sympathized with them; these women were led by the supercilious Mrs. John B. Adger, wife of a famous proslavery clergyman. Many other prominent white ministers in the state (and elsewhere) provided succor to arrested Klansmen. Southern barbarism was the other side of southern piety.

African Americans were not merely victims of Klan violence. Many defended themselves, or retaliated by burning down Klan barns and storehouses. And those who survived racist violence left behind testimonies of horrific torture at tremendous personal cost. Congressman Robert Elliot pointed out that it "was the custom of the south" to stigmatize black people as semi-barbarians. Those targeted in the first place were often leaders of their communities—officeholders, ministers, teachers, or successful farmers and shopkeepers. As historian Kidada Williams argues, "These victims' and witnesses' subsequent refusal to endure violence silently constitutes an underappreciated form of resistance to white supremacy." At the same time, the "orchestrated, premeditated, and spectacular violence produced an overwhelming and more traumatic effect," upending individual lives, families, and communities.[4]

Racist violence increased with the establishment of Reconstruction state governments and as the KKK spread to other southern states from its initial bases in Tennessee and Alabama. The new level of violence also coincided with a decreased federal military presence, the winding down of the Freedmen's Bureau, and state and national elections, when the Klan operated as the armed wing of the Democrats. The brutality of Klan attacks increased alongside their number. Holofernes Snow, "a respectable colored man" in Vicksburg, Mississippi, refused to be warned off by the Klan to abandon his "small cabin." The next day, he was found lynched, his body riddled with fifty-six bullets, the "fingers and toes shot," "all the bones of the legs and arms" broken, and his head no longer resembling a "human head-piece." In Montgomery, Alabama, a report was more succinct: a "colored register" was "outraged in an infamous manner." The Klan often castrated their male victims instead of killing them, though they frequently ended their tortures with murder. In Maury County, Tennessee, a black man was hanged with his "privates cut off and shoved in his mouth."

Black and white women, especially teachers, were not spared; nor were black children. Phoebe Blanchfield, a twenty-two-year-old white woman from New England, was gang-raped and mutilated with knives, and had her ears and breasts cut off; she died shortly thereafter. In an awful case in North Carolina, a freedman, Joseph Harvey, was given 150 lashes and his baby was clubbed to death. Klansmen shoved a burning firebrand into the mouth of a black woman who screamed when her husband was murdered, and they forced a black man to rape a young girl, as her father watched. In Georgia, Perry Jeffers and his four sons hid from the Klan, who were trying to punish him for voting for Grant. He left a crippled son and his wife in their home. The Klan shot and burned his son, hanged his wife, and later killed the rest of the family, except for one son, who managed to escape. The Klan's "diabolical crimes," wrote one of its earliest chroniclers, would leave "the devil aghast."

In Tennessee, where the Klan first perfected its terrorist methods, white unionists were targeted throughout Reconstruction. In Chattanooga, the unionist David Greene was hanged and shot. Another unionist, Pat Haney, was kicked and beaten, had his hair and beard plucked out, and his body left for his wife and children to find. Black men in Giles County, the site of many "outrages," had to arm themselves to protect their schoolhouse. The Klan nonetheless shot up the school, murdered a Mr. M. Burkle, and warned the black teacher, George F. Bowles, to leave town.

Tennessee Klansmen went after black Union soldiers, such as Pink Harris, who was stripped and whipped. In Bedford County, they whipped a schoolteacher from Ohio, John Dunlap, who had been sent by the Western Freedmen's Aid Commission, and two black men, James Franklin and William Scott. In Maury County, the Klan gave eighteen-year-old Charles Belefont two hundred lashes because he "was a damned n——" and a "Yankee soldier." They also ran off another soldier, Wesley Alexander, who lost his crop and farm. T. J. Gaskins of Obion County, a Union soldier who had been elected constable, fled his home to escape being murdered. In Marshall County, the Klan terrorized black families if the men were suspected of belonging to the Union League. Because some black men would fight back, it also started disarming them systematically.

The political nature of Klan terror was manifest. Klansmen in Tennessee cheered for Andrew Johnson and Jefferson Davis, and damned Governor Brownlow, "n—— teachers," and preachers during their depredations. They threatened Republican newspaper editors, officeholders, and anyone who voted the radical ticket. In the town of Pulaski, only 664 black men out of a total of 2,100 voted in 1868, due to Klan violence.

Alabama matched Tennessee in Klan terror. In Crenshaw County, Mrs. E. A. Clancy, a northern teacher paid by the black community, testified that her schoolhouse was burned down because black men had voted for Grant. Col. Perry Harrison reported that the Klan terrorized his county so frequently that out of 175 eligible voters, only 2 voted in the 1868 presidential elections. One black man was whipped for voting, and another, named Rueben, was found on the roadside with his head split open. In Mobile, T. J. Burns, a justice of the peace, was assaulted and driven away from the polls on election day. Later that night, these men came to his house and beat him, "gashing him terribly." One woman alleged that her husband was hanged in front of her and their small son. Anthony Jones testified about how Klansmen dragged him out of his cabin and whipped him, while others raped his wife.

In Alabama, Tennessee, and elsewhere in the South, not all the violence was conducted under cover of night or against the most vulnerable. Samuel Gardner, who was elected judge probate in Greenville, Alabama, was assaulted by the Klan, which was aligned with local sheriff Isaac Long, and his office was ransacked. In Huntsville, the Klan opened fire at a Republican meeting, killing a local judge, while state Senator J. D. Sibley was told that his throat would be slit if he did not leave Alabama. The Huntsville police made no arrests. Not surprisingly, the campaign of violent intimidation resulted in a Democratic takeover of the state legislature in 1870. A similar dynamic played out across the South, with Democrats seizing power in all but three ex-Confederate states by 1876.[5]

The complicity of local law enforcement and inability of state authorities to curb Klan atrocities led to calls for federal intervention. Southern Republicans deluged the federal government and northern Republicans with pleas for action. A northern minister in Andersonville, Georgia compiled a list of statements by freedpeople describing Klan outrages— though some, he wrote, were "entirely too gross for me to repeat"—and published them in a public letter to Senator Charles Sumner. A black

"President U.S. Grant," by Matthew
Brady. *Library of Congress*

delegation from Washington, DC which included Lewis Douglass, Frederick Douglass's son, met with Secretary of the Interior Columbus Delano to demand government protection.

Congress and the Grant administration responded to the breakdown of the rule of law in the South by creating the Department of Justice on July 1, 1870, significantly expanding the investigative and law enforcement capacities of the federal government. Under the first attorney general, Amos Akerman, a Georgia unionist who had migrated from New Hampshire before the war, the DOJ began vigorously prosecuting the Klan and other southern terror groups. The first solicitor general, Benjamin Bristow, a Kentucky unionist, became known for his prosecution of crimes against freedpeople. Local Freedmen's Bureau agents as well as detectives sent South by the federal government helped assemble a long list of atrocities triggered by the complaints they received. The Justice Department would appoint special prosecutors and send instructions to federal officials in the South that they must bring the Klan to heel. James Melville Beard, who wrote a history of the Klan in 1877, noted that "the K. K. K. cabal, for the first time in its history, was receiving that attention from the government authorities which its importance demanded."

Congressional Republicans also passed three Enforcement Acts in 1870 and 1871 that were, in a sense, the first federal hate crime laws. The first, passed in May 1870, enforced the Fifteenth Amendment by guaranteeing the right to vote regardless of race, color, or previous condition of servitude. It outlawed discrimination by state officials as well as voter intimidation and suppression by individuals, punishable with a $500 fine or imprisonment for up to a year. Conspiracies—if people banded together to prevent voting—were punishable by a $5,000 fine and a prison sentence of up to ten years; all conspirators would be permanently barred from officeholding.

The act gave federal courts jurisdiction over cases of voter interference and enjoined federal marshals and district attorneys to enforce the law by calling out the militia or a posse comitatus of armed men. It also authorized the president to use the military to enforce the decisions of federal courts. Former Confederates barred from office under section 3 of the Fourteenth Amendment could be prosecuted if they were elected, as could those who were elected as a result of voter suppression.

The second enforcement act, passed in February 1871, allowed for federal supervision of elections in towns with more than 20,000 inhabitants. It was primarily directed against corrupt urban political machines in the North but could also be implemented in the South. The third and final Enforcement Act, a law to enforce the Fourteenth Amendment known popularly as the Ku Klux Klan Act, was drafted by Representatives Benjamin Butler and Samuel Shellabarger and passed in April 1871, after Grant specifically requested congressional authorization to put the Klan down with the US military. It expanded on section 6 of the first enforcement act, concerning conspiracies and the authority of the military to stop them. It made crimes committed by terrorist conspiracies such as those by the Klan into federal crimes that could trigger military rule. For violating "the equal protection of the laws" and "obstruction of justice," offenders "shall be deemed guilty of high crime," tried in federal district or circuit courts, and punished starting with fines of up to $5,000 and imprisonment for up to five years. More severe crimes could be punished with fines up to $10,000 and imprisonment up to twenty years, with execution for the worst crimes.

If state and local authorities were unable to handle these "numerous and powerful" combinations and conspiracies like the Klan, and if the conspirators did not disperse as commanded by presidential proclamation, the president was empowered to declare the areas in question to be in rebellion, suspend habeas corpus protections for rebels (as had been done during the Civil War), and use the army to restore the rule of law. The act also disallowed men involved in conspiracies from serving on juries for such cases and penalized those who may have knowledge of terror attacks by making them liable to the victims. The Ku Klux Klan act remains the most comprehensive federal law to combat domestic terror, and its usefulness is being discovered anew today, over 150 years after it was passed, amid calls to enforce it against the January 6th insurrectionists of 2021.

On March 10, 1871, a Senate select committee had reported on "crimes and outrages of a political character" in North Carolina, and on March 23, President Grant had sent a message to Congress to pass legislation to restore the rule of law in the South. The War Department and Congress had launched investigations into southern terrorism as early as 1869 and 1870. Even before the passage of the KKK act, the Republican-controlled Congress had formed a Joint Select Committee on the "Condition of Affairs in the Late Insurrectionary States." Senator John Scott, who headed the Senate investigative committee on Klan violence in North Carolina, was appointed to lead it, and the committee heard witnesses testify on terrorist violence. Subcommittees of congressmen traveled to most southern states to collect evidence (some Reconstruction state governments had already created their own committees to investigate insurgencies). In the resulting multivolume report, African Americans and their allies bore witness to widespread political violence. Many Democrats argued that the testimonies were shaped and tailored by Republican interlocutors, and a few historians have followed suit.

In fact, black southerners traveled to give testimony at grave risk to themselves and their families, with some having already lost everything they had worked for since emancipation: land, personal property, and social mobility because of violent harassment. Many were attacked by the KKK for giving testimony to Congress and the subcommittees. The testimony by black southerners belies sensationalist stories of African Americans being scared out of their wits by racist terror; their sobering accounts gauged its political purpose well. Some black people, such as a group from Frankfort, Kentucky, petitioned Congress for federal intervention, having themselves documented over a hundred acts of violence by "regulators." Further evidence of black resistance and courage can be found in a case from 1870, in which the Klan lynched a Canadian teacher, William Luke, and four black men in Cross Plains, Alabama. Luke wrote, in his last letter to his wife, "I have only sought to educate the negro." At the trial of his murderers, "the court was besieged by blacks offering to testify against the Klan."[6]

Even with the federal government empowered to deal with terrorism, success in controlling it still depended, to a degree, on local authorities. In Texas, a version of the Klan, Knights of the Rising Sun, systematically targeted Republican politicians. They lynched Captain George Smith, a Union officer from New York and a leading radical who had been jailed for his own protection in the town of Jefferson, as well as two black men incarcerated there; two others with them managed to escape. In response, the army arrested fifty-nine men, and military authorities convicted twenty-nine of them. As one observer judged, the result was "almost breathtaking by comparison with that of the civil courts." The election of a Republican state government in 1870 and the arrest of over four thousand white men, nearly a thousand of them for murder, further deterred racist violence. In Georgia, by contrast, the Klan operated with impunity, as military authorities refused to take strong action against them. The KKK shot and beat Sheriff John C. Norris of Warren County and murdered state senator Joseph Adkins. When Abram Colby, a black legislator, refused to be bribed into resigning his office, the KKK beat him for three hours with sticks and belts, leaving him crippled and, they thought, dead. Georgia was quickly restored to white supremacy due to unchecked Klan terror that prevented black voting. Florida's local authorities—in this case the governor—also did little to combat Klan violence, with disastrous results for freedpeople.

In Arkansas, by contrast, Governor Powell Clayton, a northern Republican, reacted forcefully against Klan terrorism even before Grant took office (Clayton received little help from Andrew Johnson). Confederate colonel Robert G. Shaver led the Klan in the state that he described as a guerilla military operation. Clayton armed and strengthened the state militia, which included black men, and declared martial law in the most lawless counties. He kept a catalog of crimes and murders perpetrated against freedpeople and unionists. A Dr. A. M. Johnson wrote to Clayton that freedpeople and their families lived in the woods to escape Klan terror. Johnson's heartbroken wife soon found him lying on the road, dying, having been attacked for his testimony. She heard "the frantic cries of my distracted children." Klansmen set their eyes on local officials, lynching Deputy Sheriff William Dollar and a black man named Fred Reeves. They attempted to kill state senator Stephen Wheeler, and murdered a black political leader, Bill (also called Ban) Humphries as well as Captain Simpson Mason of the state militia. Albert H. Parker, sent as a detective by Clayton to ferret out Klan members, was killed, and his skinned, bloated body was discovered later. The Klan assassinated Arkansas congressman James M. Hinds, the highest officeholder ever murdered by the terror group, while he was campaigning for Grant in 1868.

Clayton's militia campaign, modeled after Brownlow's in Tennessee, was the most successful of any carried out by southern Reconstruction governors. As he put it, "The majesty of the law should be vindicated. The assassin should be visited with a just retribution for his crime." Still, he encountered resistance among white Arkansans sympathetic to the Klan. Watching local juries set murderers free, he confessed that "the great mistake I made was in entrusting the trial of these murderers to the civil law." But of the thirteen counties where Clayton had declared martial law, he judged his campaign in stamping out the Klan a success in eleven. The counties of Crittenden (close to the Tennessee border) and Conway continued to witness Klan atrocities. In 1871, Clayton beat back an impeachment attempt by Arkansas Democrats. Despite his successes, the need for federal intervention was clear to him.

The federal response came when it did in large part due to the atrocities and assassinations in another state: North Carolina. In his 1870 message to Congress, President Grant sent a long list of horrific crimes, mainly in North Carolina, as requested by the Senate, whose committee to investigate conditions in the state compiled extensive testimony. The Klan and its local iterations, such as the White Brotherhood, went unchecked, targeting white unionists along with freedpeople. The state's closely contested elections gave terrorists—encouraged by "respectable" conservatives—additional incentive to intimidate Republican voters. A disabled northern teacher, Alonzo Corliss, who was whipped by the Klan (they shaved half his head and painted it black), had four of his assailants arrested, but they were released by local authorities. The Klan lynched Wyatt Outlaw, a Black Union soldier, the president of the Union League, the organizer of a black school and church, and the town commissioner in Graham, Alamance County; they slashed his mouth and hanged him. In May 1870, a state senator, a poor unionist named John W. Stephens, was murdered by the Klan in Caswell County. Constantly threatened because he had introduced a law for the suspension of habeas corpus and for the formation of a militia to contain the Klan, state senator T. M. Shoffner moved to Indiana. Wilson Carey, a black legislator, also fled North Carolina.

Republican governor William Holden, who had repeatedly issued proclamations to deter terrorism in the state, eventually acted on the Shoffner militia law passed by the Republican majority legislature and declared Alamance and Caswell Counties to be in a state of insurrection. Under George W. Kirk, a southern Union officer, the state militia arrested hundreds of Klansmen in the so-called Holden-Kirk war, even though most were released by state courts. Holden's suspension of habeas corpus was deemed unconstitutional for violating the due process rights of Klansmen under the Fourteenth Amendment by the US District Court, inaugurating the judicial counterrevolution against Reconstruction. While Holden managed to weaken the Klan in Alamance and Caswell, KKK terrorism flipped ten of fifteen counties from Republican to Democratic in the 1870 state elections. The newly empowered Democrats, controlling both houses of the legislature, impeached the governor in 1871 and repealed the Shoffner law a year later. The leading impeachers were members of the Klan themselves, and they specifically impeached Holden for his suppression of the Klan, as they could not pin fake charges of corruption on the scrupulously honest Holden. Holden became the first governor in American history to be impeached and removed from office. In 2011, the North Carolina legislature belatedly pardoned him.

Defending Holden, seventeen black legislators issued an address "To the Colored People of North Carolina": "The only offence of Gov. Holden, and that which has brought down the wrath of the dominant party upon him is that he thwarted the designs of a band of Assassins, who had prepared to saturate this State in the blood of the poor people on the night before the last election on account of their political sentiments, and to prevent them from voting." Because "he dispersed this murderous host," conservatives wanted "to destroy him." They "are mad because their slave property is lost. They are mad because the Reconstruction measures have triumphed, and we are permitted to represent you in this body. They are mad because we refuse to bow the knee to them." The black legislators pointed out that conservatives had gotten control of the assembly "by deception, fraud, and intimidation," passed laws for "a system of disfranchisement," and repealed the Shoffner law designed to check terrorism. They asked black people to pray for Holden and "avert the evils hanging over our heads."

KKK terrorism in North Carolina, especially in counties adjacent to the Klan-infested South Carolina upcountry, continued until federal authorities stepped in. Klansmen attacked a railroad construction camp, whipping black men and women who worked there, and sexually assaulting an eighteen-year-old girl. A black church built on land donated by a local unionist was burned to the ground. The KKK even whipped an old white unionist and veteran of the War of 1812, John Nodine. White women who were unionists or from the North did not escape the Klan's chivalry. A farmer named Aaron Biggerstaff, known for his unionist sympathies during the war and active in the Loyal

League, was Ku Kluxed, or attacked by the Klan, twice and his married daughter whipped. Commissioner Webster Shaffer reported on "horrible outrages" committed on black and white girls, including the Klan's genital mutilation of a "colored woman."

Eventually several such cases were tried in the federal circuit court in Raleigh, the first mass trials under the Ku Klux Klan Act of 1871. Seven hundred sixty-three defendants were indicted, twenty-four were convicted, twenty-three pleaded guilty, thirteen were acquitted, and nine were not prosecuted. The local jail, joked Republicans, was a "Democratic hotel," and prominent conservatives defended the Klansmen. The trials "tended to the greater security of life, person, and property" in the state. Federal authorities, aided by the army, continued to arrest Klansmen in the state. Judge Albion Tourgee, a northern Republican, would make a name for himself by prosecuting the Klan and its crimes in Reconstruction North Carolina. He would later pen a fictional memoir of his experiences, *A Fool's Errand* (1879), a classic of Reconstruction literature, and the novel *Bricks without Straw* (1880), telling the story of the Klan's terrorism and the federal government's eventual abandonment of freedpeople.

In neighboring South Carolina, the "Knights of the Invisible Empire" went on a rampage in the piedmont, targeting black leaders. One of the most memorable testimonies given in person in front of the congressional joint select committee was that of Elias Hill, "a remarkable character" who impressed its Republican members. Born a slave—his father purchased his mother's freedom—he had been left disabled from a disease that might have been polio. His master was happy to be rid of him, given that he could not work or take care of himself. The self-taught Hill became a Baptist preacher. One day in May 1871, six Klansmen came looking for him and attacked his brother's wife. Hill would testify that "I heard them have her in the yard. She was crying, and the Ku-Klux were whipping her to make her tell where I lived."

The Klansmen found Hill's cabin and dragged him out, accusing him of all kinds of crimes. But they soon revealed the real reason for their interest in him, asking him whether he had held a meeting of the Union League and who its president was. Hill informed them that he was the president, but that he had held no meeting since the prior fall. They accused him of preaching "political sermons" and of writing to congressmen, and forced him to read the names of students from a book that Hill kept—he was also a teacher. The six white men proceeded to horsewhip Hill and announced that they would kill him unless he swore not to subscribe to Republican newspapers, to "quit preaching," and to publicly renounce Republicanism. And then, oddly, they forced him to pray for them and ask God to forgive, bless, and save the Klan! After recounting the horrifying, strange episode, Hill announced his intention to migrate to Liberia and intimated that most of his neighbors wanted to accompany him. He said, "we do not believe it possible, from the past history and present aspect of affairs, for our people to live in this country peaceably, and educate and elevate their children to that degree which they desire." Those who planned to stay on in America, he informed the committee, hoped that the government would punish the Klan so that "they can live in peace."

The Joint Committee had a majority of Republican members, but the members of the Democratic minority, one of whom was an ex-Confederate, tried to trip up witnesses and defend the Klan. Democratic senator Philadelph Van Trump of Ohio attempted to force Hill to admit that he was in fact guilty of preaching "political sermons," as the Klan had charged—the twisted implication being that Hill had invited the violence visited upon him. Hill stood his ground, answering at various points that he taught the Gospel, "love universal," and faith in "republicanism" (he meant representative government). The Democrats called witnesses of their own—including prominent members of the Klan, such as Forrest, who outright denied his participation, while others bragged about it—to testify to alleged black crimes. The minority report of the committee submitted by Frank Blair, the 1868 Democratic vice presidential candidate known for his racist screeds, defended southern terror by characterizing Reconstruction as a set of "atrocious measures by which millions of white people have been put at the mercy of the semi-barbarous negroes of the South, and the vilest of the white people, both from the North and the South." The Democratic members described voter fraud in which black women allegedly dressed as men to vote. Like southern Democratic newspaper editors, they argued that the Union Leagues, rather than the Klan, were terrorist organizations. Georgia secessionist Henry L. Benning, for instance, tried to discredit the Republican politician George W. Ashburn, who had been assassinated by the Klan.

The majority report, in stark contrast, correctly concluded that Ku Kluxism was a violent attempt to overthrow black citizenship, on the pretexts of crime, rebellion, and corruption. As the report put it, Klansmen were "cowardly midnight prowlers and assassins who scourge and kill the poor and defenseless." The report was realistic but still forceful in its view of the broader situation in the South: "while we invoke this forbearance and conciliation, fully recognizing that from the largest part of the southern people a reluctant obedience is all that can be hoped for, let it be understood that less than obedience the Government cannot accept." The majority report ran to over ten thousand pages, spanning twelve volumes, with testimony from over five hundred witnesses, of which a majority were white, including Klansmen and conservatives. It remains the single most valuable historical source for Reconstruction-era political and everyday violence by southern terror groups.[7]

One of the worst atrocities the report documented was the Meridian massacre in Mississippi in 1871, when the Klan lynched seven black men and a white man, and burned down a black church and the home of state legislator Aaron Moore. They forced the Republican mayor to resign and then viciously massacred thirty more African Americans, leaving their bodies mutilated. As a Republican judge noted, the Klan "committed & applauded outrages which History must hand down as only equaled by the most uncivilized of the Human Race." US Attorney G. Wiley Wells secured 678 indictments against the Klan, and 262 people were convicted. Most pleaded guilty and received only minor sentences and fines, however, and only one went to trial.

The majority report also documented how spurious claims of black men raping white women were the excuse, or impetus, for many if not most lynchings. In Mississippi, Allen Bird was lynched even though his alleged victim, a white woman, did not recognize him initially; she only did so after he was made to change his clothes. In another case, the Klan brutally tortured a black man and white woman living together in Jackson County. In Georgia, Henry Lowther, accused of "illicit commerce" with the woman he worked for, was castrated. Charles Clarke, accused of rape, was found not guilty by a jury but still taken from jail and lynched. The congressional committee also heard testimony about sexual violence against black women. Freedman Edward Carter testified to how Klansmen raped his daughter and threatened to rape and kill his wife. In Florida, the Klan used not just murder and mayhem but also rape to divest black people of their land. They terrorized the Tutson family, raping Hannah Tutson. The Tutsons had to pawn their property because they, rather than their tormentors, were jailed by the local sheriff.

While state and federal officials acted against the Klan, with mixed results, federal military intervention sounded its death knell in upcountry South Carolina. The KKK had become entrenched there, especially in lower piedmont counties with slight black majorities, where violent intimidation could flip elections easily. But even in upper piedmont counties with clear white majorities, the Klan was notably active. Reports of domestic terror from South Carolina exploded around the 1868 elections, after Republican victories led to the creation of a mostly black state militia by Republican governor Robert K. Scott, a former Union officer. Two years later, he won a decisive reelection in the majority-black state.

Undeterred, the Klan and similar groups harnessed the region's history of violent vigilantism. In Laurens County, armed whites not only tried to interfere with elections, but led a manhunt against freedpeople and Republicans, killing a dozen men after the black militia was disarmed by a federal commander, who ironically wanted to prevent race warfare—a misjudgment that would be replicated by other officials in the state. Wade Perrin, a black legislator, and a white Republican elected probate judge, were assassinated. Conservatives formed a "Council of Safety," with local councils across the state, precursors to the White Citizens Councils of the civil rights era. James Chesnut, South

Carolinian planter politician and ex-Confederate, aired his grievances against Reconstruction and, as chairman of the Taxpayers' Convention, entered its proceedings into the records of the Congressional Joint Committee. He justified KKK violence by claiming that black people were inclined to disorder.

Major Lewis Merrill of the Seventh Cavalry, who was sent to restore order in the countryside, was aghast at the venomous nature of racist violence in the state. Merrill compiled an extensive list of nearly six hundred whippings, assaults, and other incidents of violence. In his opinion, local civilian authorities, who were dealing with dishonest or intimidated juries and perjured testimony, were incapable of stemming Klan atrocities. Governor Scott concurred, pleading with Washington for federal troops. The three-man congressional subcommittee in South Carolina, headed by Senator Scott—it would leave the largest body of affidavits by black people concerning Klan terrorism in any southern state, in three large volumes—held hearings in Columbia, the state capital, as well as in Union, Spartanburg, and Yorkville. Attorney General Akerman himself traveled to Yorkville to investigate Klan atrocities.

Grant followed Scott's and Akerman's recommendations to activate the Ku Klux Klan Act. He suspended habeas corpus and declared martial law in the nine piedmont counties where the KKK was most active. (Initially, Union County was misidentified as Marion, but that was quickly corrected.) More soldiers were sent to South Carolina, and mass arrests of Klansmen soon followed, but prominent Klan leaders and thousands of rank-and-file Klansmen managed to flee the state. Dr. J. Rufus Bratton, who led fifty Klansmen in the lynching of Jim Williams, a black militia captain, and the ex-Confederate Klan leader and wealthy merchant James Avery, who was also implicated in the Williams lynching, escaped to Canada. The Canadian government refused to extradite them, calling them "political refugees." US government agents sent to hunt down Avery returned instead with Bratton, who was released on $12,000 bail and promptly made his way back to Canada. Hundreds of other suspects voluntarily surrendered, while many others stayed in the state but evaded arrest. Klansmen soon swelled the prisons and the federal courts' docket, leading Akerman to instruct US Attorney

David T. Corbin, a former Union officer and Freedmen's Bureau agent, to prosecute only the worst offenders. Corbin was assisted by the state's attorney general, Daniel H. Chamberlain, and by Merrill. Conservatives hired their best legal minds for the defense, Reverdy Johnson and Henry Stanbery—Andrew Johnson's lawyers during his impeachment— who argued that the Enforcement Acts were unconstitutional.

The prosecution won a victory when federal circuit judge Hugh Lennox Bond, a staunch Maryland unionist who had also presided over Klan cases in North Carolina, empaneled interracial juries whose white members were not involved with the Klan, as required by the law. Bond also made sure that African Americans had a chance to testify on Klan violence, and accounts of sadistic rapes and murders were entered into court documents for posterity. Akerman arranged for a court stenographer to fully record the proceedings of the KKK trials in South Carolina. Unlike Bond, the local Charleston District judge George S. Bryan, who had been appointed by Johnson, was sympathetic to the Klan. Bond doled out harsher punishment for Klan leaders than for the "ignorant" who seemed to have merely followed their social betters. A few prominent Klansmen, including John W. Mitchell and Thomas B. Whitesides, were convicted, and the journalist Randolph Abbott Shotwell was sentenced to prison in Albany, New York. Klan leader Dr. Edward T. Avery (no relation of James Avery) absconded to Canada in the middle of his trial, forfeiting his $3,000 bail. Some Klansmen received one-year sentences and light fines, but two were jailed for ten years and fined $10,000. Even though most Klansmen were not punished for their crimes, the prosecutions and enforcement effectively disbanded the KKK in South Carolina. Over one thousand cases against the Klan remained pending when the trials came to an end.

Like Reconstruction itself, victory against the Klan was shortlived. When Democrat Wade Hampton was elected governor in 1876 and restored South Carolina to white supremacy, he arranged for the return of Bratton from Canada. Akerman, who had resigned his office in 1871 after being pushed out by Grant and his conservative cabinet and due to flagging political support for prosecuting racist terror, put it best: "Though rejoiced at the suppression of Ku Kluxery, even in one neighborhood, I feel greatly saddened by this business. It has revealed a perversion of moral sentiment, among Southern whites, which bodes ill to that part of the country for a generation. Without a thorough moral renovation, society there will for many years be—I can hardly bring myself to say savage, but certainly far from Christian." One northerner suggested that veterans and workers should be sent south as settlers to fight Klan terror. The vicious southern opposition to black citizenship, however, would long outlast all northern intervention. As Akerman noted, "the real difficulty is that very many of the Northern Republicans shrink from any further special legislation in regard to the South. Even such atrocities as Ku Kluxery do not hold their attention. . . . The Northern mind, being full of what is called progress runs away from the past." Akerman's successor, George H. Williams, adopted a policy of clemency after the Klan prosecutions ran their course. By 1873, Grant too pardoned most ex-Confederates and some convicted Klansmen. Major Lewis Merrill warned that "the blind unreasoning, bigoted hostility to the results of the war is only smothered not appeased or destroyed."[8]

The presidential elections of 1872 were relatively free of violence, but only because unreconstructed southerners were fearful of federal retribution. Yet new cracks in the Republican Party, signaled by the candidacy of Horace Greeley, the Liberal Republican and Democratic candidate who opposed Grant, boded ill for the federal enforcement of Reconstruction laws. In Congress, for the first time, prominent moderate Republicans such as Carl Schurz and Lyman Trumbull opposed the Ku Klux Klan Act on allegedly constitutional grounds, discovering a newfound respect for states' rights. Frederick Douglass grieved the "apostasy" of Schurz, who was a "queer sort of Republican," denouncing the Klan but unable to bring himself to vote against it. Trumbull, Douglass noted, had been a lost cause ever since he voted to acquit Johnson.

Liberal Republicans—not to be confused with modern liberals in the United States—championed reform of the patronage system and laissez-faire or free markets and trade, and their opposition to government "corruption" echoed conservatives' campaign against Reconstruction.

In Missouri, Liberal Republicans, benefitting from Democratic votes, had unseated the Republican governor, a "dress rehearsal" for the presidential campaign they mounted in 1872 against Grant. As Douglass wrote, Schurz, who had engineered the Missouri win alongside Gratz Brown, had delivered the state into the hands of "rebel Democrats."

The leading Liberals were precursors of the "best men" of the Gilded Age—intellectuals whose commitment to free markets and small government condoned rapacious unregulated capitalism and the abandonment of Reconstruction, even as they fashioned themselves as classical republicans upholding political virtue. Others who joined the liberal movement, such as Charles Francis Adams Jr. and E. L. Godkin, editor of *The Nation,* were elitists opposed to black equality and sympathetic to the whining of the South's allegedly "natural leaders" against Reconstruction. They not only championed civil service reform and free trade but were also explicitly opposed to federal intervention in southern affairs. William Lloyd Garrison referred to Adams as the "degenerate grandson of the revered John Quincy Adams." Abolitionists recalled that his father Charles Francis Adams Sr., also a Liberal Republican, had been willing to compromise with the South during the secession crisis of 1860–1861.

The Liberals' platform called for ending Reconstruction and for reconciliation with the South. Greeley, the former Republican editor of the *New York Tribune,* had never been an abolitionist. In the 1840s, he had gotten into a debate with Garrison, claiming that northern workers were more oppressed than the enslaved. Other Republicans, including Frederick Law Olmsted, Cassius Clay, and William Cullen Bryant joined the Liberal bandwagon. They quixotically linked black male suffrage with universal amnesty for ex-Confederates, just as the latter unleashed a murderous onslaught on African Americans. Spurious charges of voter fraud and "electoral corruption" coalesced into a systematic attack on black male suffrage and the southern Reconstruction governments under the guise of reform. The Liberals also condemned the use of the army to check domestic terror, caricaturing Grant as a military tyrant.

Congressional Republicans, nervous about being voted out of office, partially adopted Greeley's platform of sectional reconciliation by passing a general amnesty law in May 1872, well before the election. It was a bill they had rejected earlier and that encouraged a conservative counterrevolution in the South by allowing high-ranking Confederates to hold office. The lone abolitionist who supported the amnesty program was Gerrit Smith, who had helped pay Jefferson Davis's bail, even though he remained putatively committed to black rights. Garrison excoriated the new amnesty law, pointing out that Confederates were not disfranchised unfairly but had been justly denied office for their "treason." They had, in fact, been dealt with "leniently," and allowing them to hold office would reinaugurate a reign of terror and stoke "insurrections" in the South.[9]

Most surprising of all was Charles Sumner's support for Greeley's candidacy. One of the ideological architects of Reconstruction, Sumner backed Greeley after a bitter falling out with the Grant administration. As chairman of the Senate Foreign Affairs Committee, Sumner strongly opposed Grant's scheme to annex the Dominican Republic, which Sumner believed presented a threat to the neighboring black republic of Haiti. The Haitian minister had visited him "full of emotion" in 1870 after Grant's message recommending annexation on May 31. It would, as the minister said, entail "trampling his country underfoot." Sumner did not conjure the threat to Haiti out of nothing, as most of Grant's biographers still argue; he was specifically asked by the Haitian government to oppose this threat to its independence.

Nor was this champion of interracial democracy motivated by racist reasoning, as some antiannexationist Liberal Republicans were. To this day, Haiti's capital, Port au Prince, has an avenue named after Sumner in gratitude for his opposition to Dominican annexation. The Republic of Haiti also awarded him a medal for "defending our independence in two solemn occasions"—the first being when Sumner had urged the Lincoln administration in 1862 to recognize Haiti as a sovereign nation. Sumner responded to the medal by reiterating the importance of black "self-government" that the Haitian commendation mentioned. He added that, in the eyes of international law, all nations are equal—an indictment of imperialism and a prescient warning against the rise of American empire.

The annexation issue divided the Republican Party and made for strange political bedfellows. Liberal Republicans like Schurz and God-kin opposed the annexation of "Santo Domingo" on racist grounds, with the former believing that republican government could not survive in "tropical" climates and the latter criticizing the idea of the incorporation of "semi-barbarous races" into the United States. Copperhead Democrats, such as Clement Vallandigham, strongly supported annexation, repurposing the southern dream of a proslavery empire in the Caribbean and Central America, which had animated so many expansionist Democrats before the war. Many Democrats saw the acquisition of the Dominican Republic as the first step toward the acquisition of Cuba, which was in rebellion against Spain, and which they viewed as a greater prize. While some Democrats deployed the same racist rationale adopted by Liberals to oppose annexation, conservative Republicans and most Democrats supported it in the hope that they could exile freedpeople to the Dominican Republic, a revival of the old racist fantasy of colonization that also beguiled Grant.

Grant not only proposed to send freedpeople to the Dominican Republic to form their own state but wanted to establish a US naval base at Samana Bay in that country. In his 1870 message to the Senate recommending annexation, he invoked the Monroe Doctrine, a long-standing principle of American foreign policy that warned off European powers from the Americas, which the United States claimed as its sphere of influence. Emulating British imperialists, Grant also argued that the annexation of the Dominican Republic would promote emancipation in Cuba, "Porto Rico," and Brazil, the remaining slave societies in the Western Hemisphere. Most abolitionists, however, strongly opposed Grant's imperial and colonizationist aims. The National Reform League, composed mainly of former abolitionists, endorsed not only women's right to vote, workingmen's rights, and military suppression of the Klan, but also Sumner's opposition to annexation. An exception was Henry Blackwell, Lucy Stone's husband, who giddily promoted annexation after visiting Santo Domingo. In 1871, Grant appointed Douglass to his commission to explore annexation.

Garrison penned the most thoughtful critiques of Grant's annexation plans. Condemning "Territorial Greediness," he linked annexation to proslavery imperialism. In his review of Sumner's eloquent speech against annexation titled "Naboth's Vineyard," Garrison questioned the Grant administration's claim that the Dominican people were yearning to join the United States. The country's head of state, President Buenaventura Baez, who had offered the Dominican Republic for sale to Grant, was a corrupt despot clearly willing to sell out his own people. The fact that Haiti opposed annexation should alone prevent American meddling. Garrison prophesized, "Our national decadence will be accelerated in proportion as we grasp at foreign colonial possessions." He called Grant's message for annexation a "humiliating spectacle" when the southern states were in "quasi rebellion" against the federal government. The administration should concentrate on preserving the lives and liberties of freedpeople from the "all abounding Ku-Klux atrocities and terror." The United States had no right to interfere in other nations, even to supposedly extend "free institutions," when its own "loyal population especially the colored people" were denied all protection because of the "timidity and imbecility of the government."

Henry C. Bowen, Republican editor of the *Independent,* mounted a revealing defense of Grant's imperialism. He claimed that the United States needed to expand "energetic Anglo-Saxon influence" in the Caribbean, as it had already done in the cases of Louisiana, Florida, Texas, and California before the Civil War, linking western expansion to the case for an overseas American empire. As for Haitians, they should "swim or sink" on their own, like black people in the South. In a bitingly brilliant response titled "American Swagger and Manifest Destiny," Garrison argued that this "is simply the despotic principle in republican guise," adding that it was a "lawless principle." Americans had shown no "special love" for black people or their interests at home, and they would not do so abroad, either. As he saw it, annexation was an echo of southerners' dream to create a "vast slaveholding empire."

Imperialism had no place in an antislavery platform. Sumner also likened Grant's annexation schemes to proslavery imperialism before the war and criticized the capitalist logic behind any imperialist action. Soon the United States would be threatening Cuba, the West Indies, Mexico, and the South American republics because of its desire for their plantation cash crops such as sugar, tobacco, and coffee, Sumner argued. Indeed, having seen how quickly proponents of "the gospel of prosperity" had revived cotton plantations in the South at the expense of freedpeople's demands for land, abolitionists and radicals like Sumner saw the interconnection between the revival of the southern plantation economy and the expanding imperial dreams to profit off products of plantation economies throughout the Americas.

Sumner's principled opposition to American imperialism earned him the vindictive enmity of Grant's conservative and racist secretary of state, Hamilton Fish. Grant himself had misunderstood Sumner's promise to study the annexation treaty as a sign of support. When Sumner virtually single-handedly stopped the annexation treaty in the Senate in 1870, Grant, who was not the best judge of character—the corruption scandals of those he associated with, in public and private life, would plague his presidency, hobble Reconstruction, and eventually ruin him financially—followed Fish in disparaging the senator. Fish engineered Sumner's removal as chair of the Senate Foreign Affairs Committee on the spurious pretext that he had held up State Department work. It was an unprecedented rebuke of one of the founders of the Republican Party, and of the man who was its abolitionist conscience in the Senate. As Garrison put it, Sumner's "costly testimonial" had resulted in this "mean political act." He condemned Grant's "undignified flings" at Sumner at the instigation of Fish. Sumner, he concluded, was "an American Senator in honor above reproach, wounded, and outraged in the house of his friends."

Sumner's subsequent opposition to Grant's reelection did not mean he had converted to Liberal Republicanism, but it was nevertheless a political mistake. In the Senate, he had eloquently championed the passage of the KKK Act, an administration measure. Torn between the Liberals, whom he abhorred for their opposition to Reconstruction, and the imperialist Grant, Sumner belatedly and halfheartedly said he would support Greeley. He was in Europe during the campaign, recuperating from a bout of poor health. It is doubtful if he even voted in the election. While Sumner was right in opposing annexation, Douglass, Garrison, and other abolitionists were correct in backing Grant's reelection.

Grant's defeat would have been disastrous, nearly all abolitionists understood, as the Liberal agenda spelled "the doom of Reconstruction." While Douglass could not bring himself to criticize his beloved Sumner, he published others who did. They had differed on Dominican annexation and Grant's reelection. Garrison expressed "profound astonishment and heartfelt sorrow" at Sumner's refusal to support Grant.

Most Republicans stayed true to their party, and the Liberal Republican movement fizzled out, especially after the Democratic Party decided to support Greeley. Douglass, who had predicted such an outcome, called Liberals "catspaw" in the hands of the Democratic Party, "a party of murder, robbery, treason, dishonesty, and fraud." Mainstream Republicans, with Grant as their standard bearer, portrayed their party as "the party of reform," workingmen's rights, and women's rights. Grant, "the Galena Tanner," and his vice president, Henry Wilson, "the Natick shoemaker," represented the northern masses, while the Liberals and Democrats were the party of southern treason. Greeley only won a handful of southern states where Reconstruction had been overthrown, such as Tennessee, as well as border states like Kentucky and Maryland. He won Texas, too, and a majority of the electoral votes in Missouri and Georgia. Election irregularities in Arkansas and Louisiana prevented their electoral votes from being counted, but even if they had been counted against Grant, he would still have won easily. Greeley died soon after the election, even before the electoral college met. In the 1890s, Trumbull would join the Populist movement and Schurz would write in defense of black rights. But they had helped dig the grave of Reconstruction in their support for the Liberal platform of 1872, which, despite its failure, discredited Reconstruction in the eyes of many and associated it with political corruption and economic malfeasance.[10]

Even in victory, the Grant administration and the Republican Party adopted the Liberals' ambivalent attitude toward Reconstruction, as well as their emphasis on civil service reform and economic retrenchment. In 1873, the country faced a financial panic—one of the periodic depressions in the boom-and-bust cycle of early capitalism—brought on by overspeculation in railroad bonds that resulted in the collapse of Jay Cooke & Co., an investment bank. (Cooke was known as the financier of the Civil War.) The stock market crashed, but the government's fiscal conservatism made matters worse. Republicans rushed toward the gold standard, which entailed a contraction of the supply of greenbacks, paper currency, that had been issued to finance the war. Currency linked to the gold standard favored creditors, usually bankers, and greenbacks favored debtors and producers: workers, farmers, and even manufacturers who sought easy credit that they could use to invest and grow. Grant's hard money stance earned him the plaudits of the Liberals who rejoined the Republican Party after the election, but it cost him mass support, especially in the Midwest. A new divide—this one sectional—between mostly hard money northeasterners and soft money midwesterners now threatened the unity of the Republican Party. The Grant administration's effective renunciation of greenbacks was also a repudiation of the Lincoln administration's war economy.

The new realignment, which anticipated Gilded Age politics, began to eclipse the North-South conflict that had defined slavery, the war, and Reconstruction. Economic collapse also hastened the withdrawal of the federal government from Reconstruction. A new party, the Greenback Party, which favored increasing the money supply and government action to alleviate indebtedness and poverty, emerged with the support of farmers and workers. Radicals sought the end of "the reign of gold," but the Republican Party, which rallied around the gold standard through successive depressions, was slowly transforming from the party of Lincoln and antislavery into the party of big business and fiscal conservatism. In the government-regulated wartime economy, conservative businessmen had been junior partners, but the collapse of Reconstruction made subsequent Republican administrations a handmaiden of corporations. Industrial capitalism had arrived.

The most tragic casualty of the financial Panic of 1873 and the long depression that followed was the Freedmen's Saving and Trust, or the Freedmen's Bank, which was founded in 1865 by John Alvord of the Freedmen's Bureau. It had over thirty branches across the country and 700,000 depositors, mostly newly free black citizens who had

"The Great Financial Panic of 1873—Closing of the Door of the Stock Exchange on Its Members, September 20th," *Frank Leslie's Illustrated Newspaper*, October 4, 1873. *Library of Congress*

deposited their hard-earned savings since emancipation; its collapse in July 1874 was a calamity for them. Recent research reveals how deposits increased in times of peace and federal prosecution of southern terrorists, but dropped sharply in moments of unchecked racist terror. Racial violence in the postwar South was an attack not only on the political citizenship of African Americans, but also on their economic well-being.

Douglass had argued that the Freedmen's Bank "conspicuously and pre-eminently represents the idea of progress, and elevation of a people who are just now emerging from the ignorance, degradation, and destitution entailed upon them by more than two centuries of slavery." He was called to lead it, just prior to its collapse. By that point, hundreds of thousands of ex-slaves had already lost their life savings. The bank's finance officer, Henry Cooke, like his brother Jay Cooke, speculated in railroad stocks, jeopardizing its financial stability. Just as racist violence in the South targeted local black community leaders, the failure of the bank affected the same group, because they stuck it out till the end, and lost the most as a result. The few white depositors withdrew their savings or recouped their loss. Less than half of black depositors recovered any of their savings, and most who did could not recover their full value. They received, on average, just 60 cents for every dollar deposited. While the failure of the Freedmen's Bank generated a congressional investigation, its promise for black mobility in the South went unfulfilled. The bank, instead of building black wealth, had depleted it.[11]

If southern terrorists and other Democrats were primarily responsible for the overthrow of Reconstruction, blame must also be assigned to the Liberal Republicans and northern corporate interests. Unregulated northern capitalism and unchecked southern reaction revived the unholy prewar alliance between the lords of the loom and the lords of lash, northern textile factory owners and slaveholding cotton planters, and more broadly northern finance and business and southern slavery. The result was a successful reconstruction of *capitalism* throughout the nation, including the rise of the "New South" that combined economic development with racist hierarchy. Put another way, sectional reconciliation signaled not just the defeat of interracial democracy, but the triumph of capital. Grant's imperialist ambitions, which anticipated the rise of American empire, played a role as well, in dividing the Republicans and pushing the Republican Party from its antislavery moorings toward rapacious capitalism and imperialism.

The efforts of the federal government, including the new Department of Justice, to protect freedpeople came to an end. Freedpeople still found ways to defend themselves, but without federal intervention they would be defeated by the violent counterrevolution of the vengeful South.

CHAPTER EIGHT

The Counterrevolution of 1876

A reaction has taken place. The old regime is reinstated,
and everything, save legal chattelhood, is to be restored.
Race distinctions, class legislations, the dogmas that this
is a white man's government, that the negro belongs to an
inferior race, that capital should control if it does not own,
labor, are now in the ascendant, and CASTE, if slavery may
not be, is to be the "corner-stone" of Southern civilization.

—HENRY WILSON, *History of the Rise and Fall of the
Slave Power in America,* VOL. 3, 1877

"National Republican Chart 1876,"
by H. H. Lloyd & Co. *Library of Congress*

The fall of the Second American Republic was a historical tragedy of global proportions, and its roots lay in President Ulysses S. Grant's second term. Grant's reelection in 1872 should have signaled, as most African Americans and radicals hoped, that the federal government's commitment to Reconstruction would remain in place, or at least would not collapse. Yet his second term was marred not only by an increase in racist terrorism in the South, a crippling depression, and corruption scandals, but also by the fall of Reconstruction state governments. As the enthusiasm and political will necessary to buttress black citizenship waned, white conservatives in the South retook control in one state after another. The federal retreat from Reconstruction would also be epitomized by a series of Supreme Court decisions that vitiated Reconstruction laws and constitutional amendments.

If Reconstruction was a revolution, the campaign against it was a counterrevolution. Though terrorist violence predated it, the period between the so-called Mississippi Plan of 1875 and the overthrow of the last Reconstruction state governments in Louisiana, Florida, and South Carolina after the presidential elections of 1876, was the crucible moment. It was in this twenty-four-month span that the incipient interracial democracy in the South itself was murdered. If the presidential election of 1860 inaugurated the rise of the Second American Republic, that of 1876 signaled its demise.

Three Deep South, black-majority states—Louisiana, Mississippi, and South Carolina—led the counterrevolution. Louisiana was an epicenter of racist terror. In 1868, the violent campaigns of the Knights of the White Camellia and other Klan-like groups had handed the recently reconstructed state to the Democratic presidential candidate, Horatio Seymour. Republicans were murdered in cold blood and massacres of freedpeople became common. In Natchitoches, for example, Klansmen assassinated the black Republican Alfred Hazen and came close to lynching a white Republican officeholder and freedmen's teacher, Richard Faulkner. They murdered Hal Frazier, who ran a mill and housed a freedmen's school on his land, as well as his hired hand. In 1871, they assassinated Delso White, an ex-Freedmen's Bureau agent and Republican who was determined to bring them to justice for Frazier's murder. Even as terrorism surged in the state, federal troop levels dropped precipitously, from around two thousand in 1868 to just over four hundred in 1872.

Reconstruction in Louisiana had led to the election of Republican governor Henry Clay Warmoth. He established the Metropolitan Police force in New Orleans and an interracial state militia, under the command of ex-Confederate general James Longstreet, a convert to Reconstruction, to contain domestic terrorism. An opportunist, Warmoth tried to empower himself by changing the state constitution, which limited the governor to one term, and established a regulatory commission, to be appointed by the governor, to verify election results. He also vetoed a black civil rights bill and adopted an almost whites-only patronage policy, antagonizing African Americans, including his own lieutenant governor, Oscar J. Dunn.

In 1872, Warmoth, now a Liberal Republican, joined with conservatives to support the fusion gubernatorial candidate, Democrat John McEnery, and oppose the regular Republican, or radical, candidate, William Pitt Kellogg. Warmoth was impeached by members of his own party and was opposed by the so-called Custom House clique in New Orleans. When the impeachment proceedings started, Warmoth was forced to resign, as required by state law. Lieutenant Governor P. B. S. Pinchback, who had replaced Dunn on his death, briefly occupied the governor's chair, becoming the only black Reconstruction governor. (Dunn had served as interim governor briefly when Warmoth was incapacitated.) The 1872 elections resulted in competing state governments in Louisiana and two presidential electoral slates from the state. Backed by a federal judge and the Grant administration, Kellogg assumed the governorship and had the electoral victory of Republicans certified. McEnery's attempt to violently overthrow the Kellogg government in New Orleans on March 5, 1873—what became known as the Battle of Cabildo—backfired. Longstreet's forces stopped the putsch and arrested fifty-three men in McEnery's armed militia, while Grant dispatched federal troops to the state, including the Seventh Cavalry, which had quelled Klan terror in upcountry South Carolina.

The armed McEnery insurgents roamed the countryside, however, attempting to capture local county governments. In the newly created Grant Parish, with its seat at Colfax—named after the president and his former vice president, respectively—bands of paramilitary groups led by a McEnery-appointed "sheriff," Christopher Columbus Nash, as well as Klansmen, began killing African Americans indiscriminately. One victim was Jessie McKinney, whose only crime was that he owned his farm. Republicans, led by black militia captain and state representative William Ward, fortified the Colfax courthouse in preparation for an attack, while other black people fled their homes. On April 13, Easter Sunday, armed white men with guns and cannons perpetrated one of the worst mass murders of Reconstruction, soon called the Colfax massacre of 1873. Between sixty and a hundred people—though with some claiming one hundred fifty—were murdered, burned alive in the courthouse, or shot as they escaped. The thirty to forty more men taken prisoner were assassinated in cold blood later that night. Almost all the victims were black. Three of the perpetrators were killed, including ex-Confederate and Klan leader James Hadnot.

Governor Kellogg and the Grant administration sent marshals and troops to Colfax, and they reported horrific accounts of butchered and mutilated bodies lying around the courthouse. The US attorney in New Orleans, the New York–born James R. Beckwith, brought indictments against a hundred men, of whom only five were prosecuted and a mere three convicted. But Supreme Court justice Joseph Bradley, riding circuit in Louisiana, voided even these meager convictions, despite the dissent of the local judge, arguing that the crimes committed were state, not federal, crimes, and casting doubt on the constitutionality of the Enforcement Acts. Decades later, the town of Colfax would erect a monument to the three white men "who fell in the Colfax riot fighting for white supremacy." Nash lived long enough to see his heinous crimes commemorated. The victims, whose bleached bones lay exposed into the twentieth century, were forgotten. In 2021, the marker was finally removed thanks to the dogged efforts of history graduate students from Louisiana State University.

The Colfax coup d'état would soon be replicated at the state level. In 1874, the White League, a paramilitary group, operated openly in Louisiana and neighboring states. Its stated aim was to eliminate black men from electoral politics and establish "the superiority of the Caucasian over the African." League members included prominent planters, politicians, editors (one published a newspaper in Alexandria called the *Caucasian*), and former Klansmen. The White League was a significant presence in half of the state's parishes, numbering fourteen thousand men in total. It became the armed wing of the state Democratic Party. In Natchitoches, it forced the resignation of Republican officials in a bloodless coup. Then it targeted Coushatta, which the Vermont-born Marshall Twitchell, who had led USCT troops and was a former Freedmen's Bureau agent, had transformed into a Republican stronghold, with members of his extended family settling in the newly created Red River Parish. A prosperous mill town, with a freedmen's school and homes, it was known as a place where freedpeople were treated decently and paid well, and it attracted African Americans from neighboring towns. Along with local unionists, black residents elected Twitchell to the state senate. Twitchell married into a leading planter family, but that did not protect him or his supporters from the violence to come.

In late August, armed white men killed two black men near Coushatta; one attacker died when the victims fired back in self-defense. The League then descended on the town, where they murdered three black Republicans—they tortured one of them first by breaking his limbs and roasting him over a fire—and "escorted" six white Republicans, including members of Twitchell's family, to Texas. On the way, one "Captain Jack" and his gang robbed, killed, and mutilated the prisoners—the largest mass murder of white Republicans during Reconstruction. Nash was purportedly involved in the massacre as well. The primary target of the Coushatta attack was Twitchell, but he was away in New Orleans at the time. In a similar manner, the White League overthrew eight Republican parish governments. US Attorney Beckwith appealed to Grant, who issued a proclamation asking the armed men to disperse as required by the Enforcement Act. Federal marshals arrested fifteen

men in connection with the Coushatta massacre. The massacre, however, only emboldened the League.

On September 14, 1874, a well-armed White League in New Orleans led
by ex-Confederate general Frederick Ogden launched another attempt
to overthrow the Kellogg government. This time the violent coup was
successful; the White League commandeered weapons, occupied state
buildings, and sent Kellogg into hiding. Even white schoolboys became
"regulators," throwing black students, including Pinchback's sons, out
of integrated schools. Nearly all of the ex-Confederates in the state militia, including Longstreet's friends and comrades, defected to the paramilitary groups, and he resigned the following year. The destruction of
Longstreet's militia in the so-called Battle of Canal Street left the state
government vulnerable.

The White League's campaign of terror in the countryside resulted
in a conservative majority in the state house, while Pinchback's election
to the US Senate was put in limbo; he would be denied the seat due to the
machinations of Warmoth. African Americans in Louisiana petitioned
Grant: "It is impossible Mr. President for we colored people to live in the
condition we stand in. We look to you and you alone. To give us aid in
this cause." Grant finally intervened by sending federal troops to reinstate Kellogg. But Lieutenant Merrill of the Seventh Cavalry testified
before Congress that there was no government or rule of law in Louisiana. "The White League is the only power in the state." A congressional
committee sent to investigate the violence around the 1874 state elections issued a compromise report. Conservatives retained the statehouse and Kellogg remained governor. At the end of his term, Kellogg
returned to Vermont. Warmoth, who switched back to the Republican
Party, settled in Louisiana and wrote a self-serving memoir.

In 1875, Grant ordered General Philip Sheridan, who had inaugu-
rated Reconstruction in Louisiana, to investigate lawlessness in the
state. Sheridan telegraphed back, "I THINK THAT THE TERRORISM
NOW EXISTING IN LOUISIANA, MISSISSIPPI, AND ARKANSAS
COULD BE ENTIRELY REMOVED AND CONFIDENCE AND FAIR
DEALING ESTABLISHED BY THE ARREST AND TRIAL OF THE

RINGLEADERS OF THE ARMED WHITE LEAGUES." But Sheridan was overly optimistic. Facing criticism from Liberal Republicans and Democrats—as well as resistance from his own commander-in-chief, General William Tecumseh Sherman (who was unsympathetic to Reconstruction), and conservative judges who refused to hold southern terrorists accountable—Grant protested in his annual message to Congress: "everyone of the Colfax miscreants goes unwhipped of justice, and no way can be found in this boasted land of civilization and Christianity to punish the perpetrators of this bloody and monstrous crime."

Liberals and mainstream northern newspapers blamed black people themselves for the terror visited on them, and for "bayonet rule"—the sight of federal troops in legislatures. Many roundly criticized Sheridan's suggestion of mass arrests. Frederick Douglass noted, "The civilized part of Louisiana leads its white people to attempt by murder and outrage to drive the colored people out of the state." Abolitionist John G. Whittier lamented that the South should have been remanded to territorial status under the federal government, until a republican form of government could be established there. The political turmoil in Louisiana continued until the presidential elections of 1876, when disputed election results led to the overthrow of Reconstruction. That year, the League finally got to Twitchell. Shot at numerous times, he had both arms amputated due to his wounds. While he survived, he left Louisiana, giving conservatives a majority in the state senate. The campaign of terror had won.[1]

The Grant administration, on the defensive, did not take the decisive action recommended by Sheridan, and southern terrorists' efforts to violently acquire political power—or, as one abolitionist put it, "the politics of murder" and "the politics of slaughter"—were predictably successful, not just in Louisiana but across the region. Douglass, seething from the "treachery" of a few Republicans who voted successively in 1872, 1873, and 1874 against Sumner's new civil rights bill that outlawed racial segregation, argued that protecting suffrage was the most important duty of Republicans and the federal government. He cried out, "Where is the President? Where are our great Generals?" as new "blood-chilling horrors" were being perpetrated on southern "colored voters." William Lloyd Garrison joined him in decrying the new reign of terror in the South, demanding that the "general government" protect loyal black and white citizens from the "dominating band of assassins." The South, with its "obnoxious rebel spirit," had not transformed its "heart."

But abolitionist and radical opinion was in the minority, even within the Republican Party. In March 1874, Douglass was forced to stop publishing the *New National Era* due to financial difficulties. And Reconstruction ended in Washington that year when the city declared bankruptcy, another victim of the 1873 Panic. Black male suffrage had been instituted in the capital in 1867, and the city's activist black community had elected a white radical, Sayles J. Bowen, mayor the following year. In 1871, Washington became a federal territory by congressional legislation. The territorial governorship and legislature, however, were abolished and replaced by three commissioners appointed by the president in 1874. The commissioners lashed out at the capital's emancipated black community—at its educated professional middle class by thinning the rolls of officeholders, and at the mass of unskilled black labor by slashing their wages from $1.50 a day to $1. Four years later, Congress passed a law that put DC under federal control. To this day, DC statehood remains an unfulfilled promise of Reconstruction.

In 1873 and 1874, as freedpeople and their white allies in Louisiana endured the terror of the White League, four other southern states—Virginia, Arkansas, Texas, and Alabama—were restored to white supremacy. In Texas and Virginia, conservatives retook the legislature and governorship in 1873. Even though Republican political culture was "integrated" in the South, factionalism within the party still provided conservatives with an opening. Allying with moderate Republicans, conservatives won the elections that year in both states through fraud and violent intimidation. In the Coke-Davis war, Texas' unionist governor, Edmund Davis, appealed to Grant after the state supreme court invalidated Democrat Richard Coke's election. Grant refused to intervene and Reconstruction fell in Texas.

In 1874, terrorism also curbed black voting in Alabama. According to federal officials, in no other state were the Klan and White Leaguers "more active, more cruel, or more hellish." They assassinated black voters and Republican officeholders and threatened Congressman James T. Rapier. In the most spectacular instance of terror in the state, and one of the worst of the counterrevolution against Reconstruction, hundreds of black voters were shot at by the White League in Eufaula on election day. Captain A. S. Daggett, the local army officer, refused to intervene, and around eighty mostly black men were wounded; at least ten died. In Spring Hills, north of Eufaula, armed terrorists murdered the sixteen-year-old son of a prominent southern Republican, Elias Keils, while local authorities imprisoned a black man for perjury when he identified a White Leaguer involved in the Eufaula massacre. A three-month congressional investigation into Alabama's elections concluded that conservatives had won the state through terrorism, but by then it was already restored to white supremacy. In 1876, only ten black men from Eufaula, where over a thousand black men had voted before 1874, would cast their ballot.

In Arkansas, the Republican Party self-destructed in the "Baxter-Brooks war," an election battle that divided even African Americans. Elisha Baxter was the regular Republican candidate and Joseph Brooks had the support of Liberal Republicans, but both sides sought conservative Democratic support, confusing the choice. Baxter won and Brooks's armed supporters forcibly removed him from office, but Grant recognized Baxter and had him reinstated. After years of Republican infighting, conservatives managed to retake the state in 1874, electing a Democratic legislature and governor. That year, the Democratic Party took back the US House of Representatives for the first time since the war, with Republicans losing over ninety—nearly half—of the seats they held, in a broad, public reaction to the economic depression triggered by the Panic of 1873.[2]

The success of terrorism in Louisiana inspired similar acts in neighboring Mississippi. The state's conservative Democrats had resolved, at the very start of Reconstruction in 1868, "that the government of the United States, under the Constitution, is a government of *white men;*

that the negro, has, rightfully, no lot or part therein, except the right of protection of person and property." KKK terror ensured that even those minimal protections were denied to black citizens. Long before the myth of the "Lost Cause" rewrote the history of the Civil War and Reconstruction in popular culture and academia, terrorists deployed it in Mississippi. As one Klansman said: "Then with the skulls and bones of the 'Lost Cause' before us, we will swear that, 'This is a White Man's Government.'" In 1871, Klansmen had lynched northern Republican Allen P. Huggins in Aberdeen, assassinated a white Republican judge, and killed about thirty African Americans in the Meridian massacre. The Mississippi outrages had provided part of the rationale for the passage of the Ku Klux Klan act. But as one antislavery newspaper noted, "the law does not count for much in most of the southern states."

White Republicans in Mississippi, as elsewhere, were divided between northern radicals and southern moderates, with freedpeople generally supporting the former. Adelbert Ames, a Union general married to Blanche Butler, the daughter of radical congressman Benjamin Butler, was appointed provisional governor and then elected to the Senate in 1870. Blanche's mother warned her that she "should be a little careful in Mississippi. Some of the people are very brutal. No one can tell what they might think to do." Adelbert and Blanche were serenaded in the governor's mansion by "colored well-wishers," and Blanche laughed off the social ostracism and insults of Mississippi's provincial elites. Radicalized by his experience in the postwar South, Ames was opposed by moderates led by the former governor, James Alcorn, a planter who had done little to stop Klan terrorism. In 1873, Ames, the Republican candidate, defeated Alcorn, who was the fusion conservative candidate, for the governorship on the strength of an overwhelming majority of black votes. Almost immediately, his own election contested, Ames had to deal with the White Liners, a terror group inspired by Louisiana's White League.

The next year, White Liners attacked the courthouse and overthrew the government in Vicksburg, Warren County. Ames allowed the black sheriff, Peter Crosby, to gather a posse to retake the sheriff's office. When Crosby and his men marched back to Vicksburg, they were met

Portrait of Gen. Adelbert Ames.
Library of Congress

by well-armed White Liners and 160 White Leaguers from Louisiana. Crosby was imprisoned and agreed to retreat, but his men were treacherously attacked on their way out of the city, resulting in the death of sixty to eighty freedmen. Large planters who belonged to the Grange, a cooperative agrarian movement that in the South doubled as a white supremacist organization, also contributed to the violence. The Vicksburg massacre, at the site of Grant's famous victory, decimated the black Republican vote, with most freedpeople terrified of going to the polls. Ames wrote to Blanche, "Of arming and intimidation by these white liners reports come from all sides. They will do anything to carry the state."

White Liners also longed to get rid of Albert T. Morgan, an Oberlin-educated Quaker abolitionist and Union veteran from Wisconsin. Morgan had married a black schoolteacher from New York, Carolyn Highgate, sister of Edmonia Highgate, in 1870, after he had Mississippi's law against racial intermarriage repealed in the legislature. Morgan's letters to Ames reveal his deep commitment to freedpeople. He wrote that they were "being subjected to all manner of insults + injuries. To suppose they do not feel these things is to suppose they are <u>not</u> human."

The only solution, he felt, was "to give land to these people" and "removing the terrorism + oppression of the whites." He objected in particular to the abuse of freedwomen: "Every day women are being taken out, outraged + whipped, because they will respect themselves and their husbands." Before being elected to the state constitutional convention and legislature, Morgan rented a plantation and ran a sawmill in Yazoo County. He refashioned the local "negro jail" into a schoolhouse. A ditty, "If you belong to the Ku Klux Klan," targeted him:

> Old Morgan thought he would get bigger,
> By running a saw-mill with a n——.
> The crop it failed and the saw-mill busted,
> And the n—— got very badly wusted.

When Morgan was elected sheriff of Yazoo City in 1873, his predecessor tried to forcibly stay in office, resulting in a shootout in which he was killed. Morgan was cleared of all wrongdoing by a jury that did not indict him, and by a judge in Jackson.

Undeterred, White Liners launched a campaign in the fall of 1875 to eliminate all Republican officeholders, starting with Morgan, who escaped to Jackson, never to return to Yazoo City. In Clinton, White Liners opened fire at a Republican barbecue, killing men, women, and children. Some black men, Ames reported, though "unarmed and unprepared," fought back "bravely and killed four of the ring-leaders." Led by ex-Confederates, White Liners spread terror in Hinds County, lynching a black Republican named Square Hodge, targeting the state senator, Charles Caldwell, and killing between thirty and fifty men in total. They murdered a local unionist and teacher, William Haffa. Nearly five hundred African Americans fled to Jackson, where they reported the attacks to Ames. In Macon, White Liners also assassinated a nominee for treasurer, Richard Gray. The motto of Mississippi conservatives was, "CARRY THE ELECTION, PEACEABLY IF WE CAN, FORCIBLY IF WE MUST." The *Yazoo Democrat* added, "Try the rope." Ames mustered the state militia to combat the spreading terrorism, issuing a proclamation demanding that the White Liners disperse.

Unlike its response to the situation in Louisiana, the Grant administration did not quickly come to the assistance of Mississippi's state government. Ames telegraphed Grant, appealing for federal troops to put down the insurrection. But Grant's conservative cabinet members, Secretary of State Hamilton Fish and Attorney General Edward Pierrepont, a Democrat, were against intervention. Even Grant complained, "The whole public are tired out with these annual, autumnal outbreaks in the south." Pierrepont sent George K. Chase from the Department of Justice to broker a compromise between Ames and the White Liners, who were represented by ex-Confederate general James George. When the negotiations finished, the state militia was disbanded and conservatives pledged not to interfere in the elections—as if one could take the word of assassins in good faith. Just after the sham peace conference, White Liners commanded by Alcorn and ex-Confederate general James Chalmers deposed Sheriff John Brown, a schoolteacher from Oberlin elected by black voters, and murdered numerous African Americans in Coahoma County. Chase admitted that without federal troops, it was impossible to hold a fair election in Mississippi.

By the time the federal government did decide to forcibly intervene, it was too late. Before Election Day on November 2, 1875, Ames wrote, "The reports which come to me almost hourly are truly sickening. Violence, threats of murder, and consequent intimidation are co-extensive with the limits of the state." The emboldened White Liners even fired shots into the governor's mansion and discussed among themselves whether they should assassinate him. The terror won conservatives the legislature in a majority black state. In Yazoo County, Republican votes fell from nearly three thousand during the height of Reconstruction to seven, or only two by another count, in 1875. Unsatisfied with their vicious victory, White Liners assassinated Caldwell and his brother a few days before Christmas. So called "bulldozers" continued to intimidate majority black counties, murdering African Americans with impunity. Grant later confessed to Congressman John R. Lynch that he avoided intervening in Mississippi in order to retain Ohio, where the idea of enforcing Reconstruction was supposedly unpopular, in the elections that year. He reportedly called his inaction a "grave mistake."

In control of the legislature, conservatives impeached the black lieutenant governor, Alexander K. Davis, so that when they next impeached
Ames, a black man would not ascend to the governorship. They proceeded to investigate and impeach most black state officeholders and
drew up articles of impeachment against Ames on spurious charges.
Ames resigned in return for having charges against him dropped, making the conservative president of the state senate the governor. Mississippi was restored to white supremacy. As Ames wrote, "Yes, a *revolution*
has taken place—by force of arms—and a race are disfranchised—they
are to be returned to a condition of serfdom—an era of second slavery.... The political death of the Negro will forever release the nation
from the weariness from such 'political outbreaks.'" Abolitionist journalist James Redpath published an article on the 1875 terrorist Mississippi campaign after interviewing Ames, Morgan, and Chase. But the
northern response, judging by mainstream newspapers, was not one of
outrage, but of indifference and, among Democrats, explicit support for
murderous racists. Morgan acknowledged, "We had 'failed,' that was
certain. We could feel it in our bones." Lynch recalled, "The administration of Governor Ames was one of the best the state had ever had."
Ames himself defended Reconstruction until his death.[3]

Radical and "stalwart" Republicans—those still committed to Reconstruction—in Congress tried to check the campaign of terror unfolding
across the South. Two new proposed laws attempted to shore up Reconstruction. The first, a new enforcement act put forward by Benjamin
Butler to counter terrorism, failed due to the opposition of conservative
Democrats and Liberal Republicans. The second was Charles Sumner's
Supplementary Civil Rights bill, which he had first introduced in 1870, and
which would outlaw segregation in public accommodations and schools.

The demand for desegregation had come from freedpeople themselves, who still viewed Sumner as their preeminent advocate in Congress. Sumner received numerous complaints from African Americans
across the nation, recounting their mistreatment in streetcars, trains,
schools, theaters, and public spaces. Black Republican congressmen,

who were his closest political allies, regaled Sumner with their stories of mistreatment in public conveyances and hotels, even after being elected to high office. Black conventions passed resolutions against public racial proscriptions. In the South, black Republicans led the effort to pass similar civil rights state laws, facing opposition from conservatives and moderate Republicans. Thousands of "colored citizens" from all over the country, including northern states, sent petitions to Congress in support of Sumner's bill, in a coordinated campaign that reprised an old abolitionist tactic.

In defending his bill, Sumner famously laid down two principles that would be revived by civil rights activists in the twentieth century: "equality before the law," and "equality not found in equivalents." The latter was a critique of the "separate but equal" illusion of the Jim Crow South. Sumner undertook a global survey of discrimination: he invoked the Indian caste system, the unreasonable prejudice against Chinese immigrants in the United States, and the European conquest of Africa to make his point to the Senate, most of which could barely grasp his wide-ranging explication of universal human rights. It was like casting pearls before swine. When the Senate passed a severely hollowed-out version of the Civil Rights bill in his absence in 1872 (it failed in the House), Sumner castigated Republicans for their backsliding.

Sumner's bill was reintroduced in December 1873, and in his message to Congress, Grant magnanimously supported it. Sumner, for his part, argued that it was "an urgent necessity," given the "daily outrages" African Americans were subject to and their exclusion from public schools in the South. "There ought to be no delay." Sumner again emphasized "how justice to the African race was contrasted with generosity to those who struck at the life of the Republic." He gave his last speech in support of the bill in January 1874. Momentum in its favor picked up after his death from a heart attack on March 11 of that year; his last words, whispered to Douglass and Representative George Frisbie Hoar of Massachusetts, as he lay in his sick bed, were to not let his Civil Rights bill fail in Congress. If Thaddeus Stevens's death in 1868 marked the start of Reconstruction, Sumner's demise came at its unwinding.

The most eloquent supporters of the Civil Rights Act, surpassing even

Sumner himself, were newly elected black Republican congressmen from the reconstructed states. Their speeches were widely reprinted, representing the last hurrah of Reconstruction on the eve of its fall. Representative Alonzo Ransier of South Carolina described the plight of African Americans and the need for the law: "Five millions of people, citizens of our country, who bode you no evil, suffer today the most humiliating discriminations, in the matter of the most ordinary privileges attaching to them as human beings, because of their color and previous condition of imposed servitude." All they asked for was equal rights and "equality of opportunity," not the "bugbear" of imposed social intimacy, as opponents fantasized. The law, as Robert Brown Elliot, Ransier's colleague from South Carolina, clarified "simply asserts equal rights and equal public privileges for all classes of American citizens." Recalling black service in the Revolutionary, 1812, and Civil Wars, Elliot was responding to Alexander Stephens, the ex-Confederate vice president, who was now representing Georgia thanks to an amnesty law passed in 1872 (to which Sumner had tried to append his Civil Rights bill, at the time).

Stephens made the same arguments that he and so many others had used to defend slavery, namely that the proposed law was "unconstitutional" and violated states' rights. Elliot responded by saying that "The constitution of a free government ought always to be construed in favor of human rights," and reminded Stephens of the passage of the Thirteenth, Fourteenth, and Fifteenth Amendments that had abolished slavery and established national citizenship. Was Stephens's judgment "warped by the ghost of the dead doctrines of States-rights? Has he been altogether free from prejudices engendered by long training in that school of politics that well-nigh destroyed this Government?" Elliot observed, trenchantly: "I do not shrink from saying that it is not from him that the American House of Representatives should take lessons in matters touching human rights or the joint relations of the States and national governments." It was a "poor return," he argued, for the "magnanimous treatment" accorded to Stephens—who could now hold office even after committing treason—that he "throws himself" against "the full enfranchisement of my race." Millions of black people prayed for the success of the government at a time when, Elliott said, in reference to Stephens, "the gentleman was seeking to break up the Union of these States and to blot the American Union from the galaxy of nations." Loud applause greeted Elliot's eloquent rebuttal of Stephens, who had published a tedious two-volume tome justifying secession, *A Constitutional View of the Late War Between the States*. In this founding text of Lost Cause apologia, Stephens, who himself had argued differently at the founding of the Confederacy in his notorious "cornerstone" speech, contended that federal infringement on states' rights, not slavery, was the cause of the war.

Representative John R. Lynch of Mississippi noted that "absolute State sovereignty as understood by the Calhoun school of politicians...has been a continuous source of political agitation for a number of years." Representative Richard Cain of South Carolina excoriated conservative representatives for their open advocacy of white supremacy, calling it un-American, especially their argument that "this idea of all men being created equal is a fallacy, announced some years ago by Thomas Jefferson, that old fool-hardy man." It was his "foolish ideas," Cain went on in this sarcastic vein, "that have made the nation strong, great and powerful." Representative James Rapier of Alabama recounted how black congressmen were refused the most common accommodations while traveling to perform their duties. There is not an inn, he said, that would house him in the thousand miles between Montgomery and Washington. Black people were denied the "basic right of locomotion without hindrance," even though they had long fought for their right to travel unhindered.

Radical Republicans and abolitionists strongly supported the bill. As a lame duck congressman who had lost his reelection bid, Benjamin Butler observed, "The colored men are either American citizens or not." He noted, archly, that there were "many white men and white women whom I would prefer not to associate with," but who enjoyed the same right to travel in railroad cars and stay in hotels. The true originators of the idea of equality were abolitionists like John Brown, Butler went on, causing a stir in the House. As he argued, the reason the Republican Party had been repudiated in the polls was not that it supported black rights, but because it had become a "do-nothing" party, unable to stop the terrorism of the Klan, the White League, and similar groups. The father-in-law of Adelbert Ames knew exactly of what he spoke. Butler tried to couple Sumner's bill with new enforcement and army appropriations bills, but while the former succeeded, the latter failed.

A radical, Butler would eventually become involved in the labor movement. Most white southerners had detested him since the Union occupation of New Orleans during the war, and he was forever associated with the contraband policy that paved the way for emancipation. During Reconstruction, white southerners contended that radicals like Butler were forever waving "the bloody shirt" to subjugate the South for starting a deadly war. It was not just a metaphor; Butler was accused of actually waving the bloodied shirt of Allen P. Huggins, who had been lynched in Aberdeen, Mississippi, on the floor of Congress during the debates over the Enforcement (Ku Klux Klan) Act in 1871. He had not, in fact, waved a shirt, but he had described in some detail the atrocities visited on Huggins and others. "Waving the bloody shirt" became a part of the

"Charles Sumner's Death," by Matt Morgan, *Frank Leslie's Illustrated Newspaper*, March 28, 1874. *Library of Congress*

conservative critique of Reconstruction, as though talking about horrific crimes was in some way oppressive to those who had committed them.

The Civil Rights Act of 1875 passed a little less than a year after Sumner's death, on March 1 after Grant signed it, mainly as a tribute to the late senator who had devoted his life to the creation of inter-racial democracy. He died exhorting, "Don't let the Civil Rights bill fail." Bearing the official title, "An Act to Protect All Citizens in Their Civil and Legal Rights," it went further than previous Reconstruc-tion amendments and laws. It guaranteed "full and equal enjoyment of the accommodations, advantages, facilities and privileges of inns, public conveyances on land or water, theaters, and other places of pub-lic amusements." But it did not include Sumner's provision for school desegregation, a cause dear to his heart ever since he had fought for it in Massachusetts before the war. (In 1954, when the Supreme Court outlawed school segregation in *Brown v. Board of Topeka, Kansas,* the plaintiffs' lawyer, the NAACP's Thurgood Marshall, consulted Sumner's brief from the 1849 Boston school desegregation case.) Nor did it include the provisions for the desegregation of churches and cemeteries that appeared in earlier versions.

The law did contain Sumner's enforcement mechanisms: "the person aggrieved thereby" could sue for personal damages of up to $500, and if convicted, culprits could be fined for $500 to $1,000 or imprisoned for between thirty days and a year. These would be civil suits, prosecuted in federal district and circuit courts by US marshals and attorneys. Contrary to conventional historical wisdom that it was rarely enforced, southern black people, especially women, used the law to challenge seg-regation in public transportation in federal courts. In 1876, Rev. Fields Cook, a Baptist minister from Virginia, sued a Philadelphia innkeeper for refusing him accommodations under the new law. The innkeeper was fined $500.

Abolitionists had agitated for desegregation for decades and had sup-ported Sumner's bill since he first introduced it. They were bitterly dis-appointed that its provision for desegregating schools had been done away with. Elizur Wright argued that by denying black people "equal school education," the law "can bring no satisfaction to a thoughtful and logical mind." Even in its attenuated form, however, the law illustrated, as one legal scholar has argued, that "the vision of Sumner and the abolitionists was a hundred years ahead of its time."[4] Indeed, though it was declared unconstitutional by the Supreme Court in 1883, Sumner's bill effectively outlawed Jim Crow before it was instituted, and anticipated the Civil Rights Act of 1964 that would finally end Jim Crow.

The passage of the Civil Rights Act of 1875 did not stop the violent counterrevolution in the South, especially given the flagging federal commitment to enforce the rule of law. Like Louisiana and Mississippi, the experience of South Carolina, another majority-black state, reveals how domestic terrorism defeated Reconstruction. As one Mississippian advised a South Carolinian, "A dead Radical is very harmless."

In 1872, the conservatives in South Carolina were in such disarray due to Grant's actions against the Klan that two Republicans faced off against each other for the governorship. Franklin J. Moses was a southerner, while Rueben Tomlinson was a northern Quaker and former Freedmen's Bureau agent. Moses won, but his term was marred by corruption scandals, and in 1874, D. H. Chamberlain, a former Union officer from Massachusetts, won the gubernatorial elections on a reform platform. His lieutenant governor, R. H. Gleaves, was black. An independent ticket headed by southerner John T. Green, with Martin Delany as his lieutenant governor, had openly courted the conservative vote. Delany was bitterly attacked by most black South Carolinians, who voted overwhelmingly for the radical ticket, as well as by abolitionists. Delany blamed freedpeople for being rude and "demoralized," repeating racist caricatures. He cast aspersions on "mulatto" political leaders and their northern allies. Douglass responded, "Were you not M. R. Delany, I should say that the man who wrote thus of the manners of colored people of South Carolina has taken his place with the old planters." Douglass said he did not prefer the "lash-inspired manners of the past."

Electoral failure led many conservatives to turn to terrorism again, even as Chamberlain sought to appease them. Illegal rifle clubs led by the planter elite started proliferating across the state. The flashpoint was Edgefield County, which had been a hotbed of secessionism before the war. Adelbert Ames, who had been stationed there, wrote of the local whites that "They think about as much of taking the life of a Freedman as I would that of a dog." The terrorism in the county was animated by four men, principally: ex-Confederate general Martin Witherspoon Gary, a hot-headed planter who had refused to surrender at Appomattox; another ex-Confederate general, Mathew C. Butler, who now rode with the Klan; and the volatile Tillman brothers, Benjamin and George. Benjamin, an advocate of lynching, would become the state's premier racist demagogue in Congress. The four men headed local rifle clubs; their plan was "to provoke a riot and teach the negros a lesson." Benjamin Tillman recalled, "nothing but bloodshed and a good deal of it could answer the purpose of redeeming the state." In 1874, only the intervention of federal soldiers stationed nearby had prevented a bloodbath when around eighty state militia men were surrounded by hundreds of armed men from rifle clubs. Many black people had already been murdered by the latter.

The rifle clubs soon got their wish with the Hamburg massacre of 1876. Early in Reconstruction, African Americans congregated in the desolate Edgefield County town of Hamburg, setting up schools, churches, and stores, and buying homes. They elected as trial justice (magistrate) and then intendant (mayor) the remarkable Prince Rivers. An enslaved coachman, Rivers had made his way to the Union army at Port Royal during the war and joined the First South Carolina Volunteers. His abolitionist commanding officer, Thomas Wentworth Higginson, called him a "King amongst men," and a "natural leader." After the war, Rivers served in the state's constitutional convention and legislature. More than just about any other single development in the county, his political rise upset white elites. He "is so black that charcoal would make a snowy mark on his august phiz" wrote the local newspaper. Southerners were obsessed with skin color, even after living among enslaved black people for generations. Former slaves, especially "pure blacks," exercising any measure of political rights appeared to drive them insane.

The pretext for attacking the black officials of Hamburg came when two young white men deliberately drove their buggy into a parading black militia during a Fourth of July celebration. (The Fourth of July in the postwar South was preeminently a holiday celebrated by freed-people and their radical allies, with most ex-Confederates sitting it out sullenly.) The militia captain let them through, after exchanging a few words. The next day the white men lodged a formal complaint against the captain in Rivers's court, causing more heated words. The captain countersued. Rivers postponed the hearing to the eighth of July to allow everyone to cool off. The day of the hearing, Mathew Butler, the lawyer who represented the two whites, appeared at the court with hundreds of armed men. The militia officers, certain that they would be assassinated, refused to appear. They barricaded themselves in a building when Butler asked them to hand over their arms to him. The militia captain replied that the arms belonged to the state. Rivers suggested a compromise, asking the men to surrender their arms and to have them boxed up and sent to the governor in Columbia, the state capital.

Butler refused, and brought up more armed men from Augusta, Georgia. Supplemented by Benjamin Tillman's rifle club as well, the mob started shooting at the building. The thirty-eight militia men inside shot back in self-defense, killing one of their attackers. The terrorists then brought forward a cannon and used it to blow holes in the building. They moved forward to tear it down with axes, and to chase down the retreating militiamen. They killed the town marshal, Jim Cook, and cut off his tongue, placing it in his hand. They proceeded to murder in the most gruesome manner six of the militiamen who surrendered, mutilating their bodies. Butler was "the instigator and ringleader of the butchery," according to eyewitnesses. In a night of terror, armed whites killed more black men, ransacked houses, including Rivers's home, and warehouses. They also went after a local Jewish man, Louis Shiller, who printed a Republican newspaper in his home. He barely escaped, fleeing to Columbia. An antislavery newspaper noted, "These are the kind of outrages all over the south that have intimidated the blacks, and given the white rebels such a supremacy."

Black South Carolinians met in Columbia shortly after the Hamburg massacre in a Convention of Colored People in July 1876, and issued "An

Address to the People of the United States," probably composed by Congressman Robert Elliot. It was signed by sixty black leaders. It asked the nation's citizens to condemn "this wanton and inhuman butchery," the governor to maintain "the supremacy of the law," and the president to enforce the Constitution and protect American citizens. When news of the Hamburg massacre spread, Butler claimed that his was "a class of people who do not commit outrages of that sort." He preposterously blamed instead "the system of insulting and outraging of white people which the negroes had adopted there." Rivers held an inquest to gather testimony, and issued an arrest warrant for eighty-seven men, including Butler and Tillman. Their attorney, Martin Witherspoon Gary, had most of them bailed out, and fabricated affidavits of an alleged plot by local black people to kill all whites—a common pretext to justify southern massacres. US Attorney D. T. Corbin reported that many witnesses were intimidated, and he delayed prosecuting the case until after the elections in the fall. New outrages followed in Ellenton, where armed groups massacred around a hundred black people, according to one count, including Simon Coker, a state representative from Barnwell. Chamberlain ordered the illegal rifle clubs to disband and pleaded for federal intervention. Just before the 1876 elections, Grant issued a proclamation to suppress the insurrection and sent more than a thousand troops to South Carolina, but they were barely enough to counter the militarized terrorists armed with weapons stolen from the state.

The rifle clubs, numbering around 290 in total, renamed themselves "baseball," "sewing" clubs, and the like, and continued their campaign of terror; as unionist J. G. Winnsmith wrote to Grant, "It is in every sense a military campaign." During the 1876 elections, Edgefield, a county that was 60 percent black, voted like a majority-conservative county. Due to violent voter suppression and fraud, the total vote count exceeded the number of voters by 2,000, and the conservative count exceeded the number of white voters by 3,000. Tillman, Gary, and Butler paraded with hundreds of armed Red Shirts, a name that played on the "bloody shirt" trope—and that, perhaps unintentionally, evoked their aims. The Red Shirts were an antecedent to Mussolini's Black Shirts and Hitler's Brown Shirts, fascist paramilitary organizations that brought terror and violence to cities in Italy and Germany in the twentieth century. They disrupted a Republican rally, demanding equal speaking time and drowning out the governor's speech with rebel yells. Ruder epithets were hurled at Congressman Elliot. The Red Shirts followed Chamberlain to all his campaign stops. Their "military campaign" engulfed the piedmont; the lowcountry, where 90 percent of residents were black, remained relatively safe.

Ex-Confederate general Wade Hampton, the conservative gubernatorial candidate in 1876, played the patrician while riding at the head of the Red Shirts. He promised not to overturn black male suffrage, even as he allied himself with the more rabid racists. His own rebel cry was "The South now, the South Forever." Delany, who had completely defected to the conservative side, supported him. Where black men could vote freely, they continued to vote solidly for the radical ticket. On claiming the governor's office after a disputed election, Hampton fired Rivers,

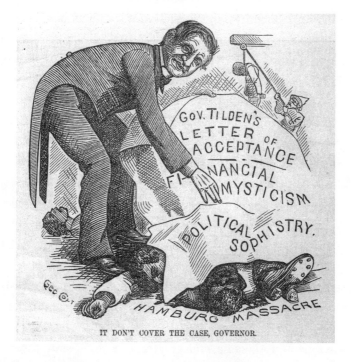

IT DON'T COVER THE CASE, GOVERNOR.

"It Don't Cover the Case, Governor," *Harper's Weekly*, September 2, 1876.
American Antiquarian Society

who died driving a coach, the same job he had performed as an enslaved man. The slaveholding secessionist and ex-Confederate colonel William Dunlap Simpson replaced Lieutenant Governor R. H. Gleaves. In an 1879 essay for *The Atlantic,* Chamberlain defended Reconstruction, perceptively noting that northern advocates of business and empire had grown tired of the so-called race issue in the South. Unlike Ames, however, Chamberlain recanted his commitment to black citizenship. He became a convert to states' rights and the reigning ideas of Gilded Age America: laissez-faire and social Darwinism. He opposed the 1884 Blair bill for a national education system and the 1890 Lodge bill to enforce election laws in the South, viewing both as unwarranted federal intervention. By that point, Chamberlain had become a welcome guest of his former opponents in South Carolina.[5]

The 1876 presidential elections demonstrated how thoroughly political terror had undermined the Second American Republic. In majority-black Mississippi, now restored to minority rule, a combination of violent intimidation and economic coercion of vulnerable sharecroppers and laborers handed the state to the Democratic presidential nominee, Samuel Tilden. Mississippi also elected a conservative congressional delegation. The decline in Republican votes in black belt counties was dramatic. Reconstruction in North Carolina ended with the election to the governorship of the man who had served as Confederate governor of the state during the war, Zebulon Vance, on a platform of white supremacy. In states that had overturned Reconstruction, electoral fraud was brazen. In Texas, Klan terror saw numerous black women raped and German unionists attacked. Those arrested for the crimes were let off by conservative juries. Rev. James Gilliard, a graduate of Oberlin, was arrested and murdered for being a "horse thief"—merely for riding his own horse. When his black congregation tried to defend him, they were driven away by armed thugs.

In Georgia and Alabama, conservative control of state government handed the elections to Democrats. White paramilitaries from both states often crossed borders to attack black people and their allies in Mississippi and South Carolina. Electoral violence during the elections of 1876 in Alabama and Mississippi were "fit subjects of investigation," wrote one abolitionist. A Senate committee headed by George Boutwell produced a report on the violence during the 1875 Mississippi elections; it recommended the passage of more federal laws to protect voters, to deny congressional representation to states controlled by lawless armed bands as stipulated in the Fourteenth Amendment, and, if violence persisted, to remand the state back to a territorial stage. It concluded: "The nation cannot witness with indifference the dominion of lawlessness and anarchy in a State with their incident evils and a knowledge of the inevitable consequences." None of its recommendations was followed. Investigating electoral violence in 1876, Senator John Sherman reported on similar events in Louisiana: "It seems more like the history of hell than of civilized and Christian communities." "The Southern Elections," the antislavery *The Commonwealth* editorialized, "was an absolute farce." In the South, "a negro massacre has come to be a very small matter indeed." The shirt is "bloody—*very* bloody—*dripping* with blood!" If the president was elected through wholesale murder, intimidation, and "damnable outlawry," it would be "the last throb of popular liberty" in the republic.

The extent of voter suppression and terror in the South could be seen in the large majorities for Democrats in states with substantial black populations. *The Commonwealth* noted that "Terrorism has added its horrors; and to-day, seven States in the South that, under a peaceful order of things, were likely to vote for the national Republican candidates, may all be placed either in the Democratic column or in the list of doubtful." Tilden won a majority in the national popular vote, an illusion resulting from the violent suppression of black votes in southern states. With a "fair and un-trammeled election," most of the Deep South states would have been as Republican as those in the Northeast. The Democratic nominee had won 184 electoral college votes, though some states had not yet been decided. Tilden needed just one more electoral vote from "bribery in Oregon, usurpation in South Carolina, forgery in Florida, and slaughtering in Louisiana," to win the presidency. The Republican nominee, Rutherford B. Hayes, needed nineteen electoral college votes from the states of Louisiana, South Carolina, and Florida, which still had Reconstruction governments, to win. If the Republicans had acted with firmness against racist terror, the whole country would have been behind them, *The Commonwealth* concluded, but "Timidity has invited aggressions."

It became clear that disputed returns from Laurens and Edgefield Counties, where the Red Shirts were particularly active, would decide the gubernatorial and presidential elections in South Carolina. "Imported" Red Shirts from Georgia voted fraudulently in both counties, while Federal army officers reported that hundreds of black men were prevented from voting at all. The state Board of Canvassers threw out the returns from the two counties and declared Chamberlain and the Republicans victors, but the state Supreme Court awarded the elections to Hampton and the Democrats. In Louisiana, as in South Carolina, conservatives had nominated a former Confederate general, Francis Nicholls, for governor, a supposedly moderate cover for the White League's violent political campaign. But it was open season on black people and Republicans in the countryside, with "bulldozers" hanging two black women, one of whom was pregnant, in East Feliciana Parish, and assaulting a German Republican in West Feliciana Parish. In Ouachita Parish, they lynched African Americans—in one case killing a black man, assaulting his wife, and slitting the throat of their baby—and assassinated the tax collector. Like Hampton, Nicholls quickly set up a shadow state government before the official winner was declared. Florida, with a 40 percent black population, gave a painfully narrow majority to the conservative gubernatorial candidate, George F. Drew, that was upheld by the state courts.

Republican-controlled state election boards in all three states, however, certified Hayes as victor. Their Democratic challengers responded by sending in competing returns in favor of Tilden, creating an impasse in Washington. In January 1877, Congress created an Electoral Commission, composed of congressmen from both parties and four Supreme Court justices, to decide the victors in the three disputed states. In March, the Commission, with a one-man Republican majority, gave

Hayes the electoral votes of all three states and averted a Democratic filibuster in the Senate. One observer, unable to predict January 6, 2021, wrote that "No Congress will again want to go through another session of such disorder, anxiety and threatenings." Hayes took office that same month, and after a suitable delay, as advised by Carl Schurz, ordered federal troops stationed at statehouses in Louisiana and South Carolina back to camp, effectively handing over the state governments to conservatives and their armed paramilitary forces. The federal troops in Florida had already been withdrawn in January. Just over 3,000 federal officers and soldiers were now stationed in the South, a steep drop from the over 60,000 in 1866. Most of the withdrawn soldiers were reassigned to the West to fight against indigenous nations.

The standing down of federal troops in Louisiana and South Carolina at Hayes's direction formally ended Reconstruction. The dark irony of the situation was not lost on observers. As Chamberlain summarized the developments to South Carolinian Republicans: "Today—April 10, 1877—by order of the President whom your votes alone rescued from overwhelming defeat, the Government of the United States abandons you, deliberately withdraws from you its support . . . and by the withdrawal of troops now protecting the State from domestic violence, abandons the lawful Government of the State to a struggle with insurrectionary forces too powerful to resist." The next day Chamberlain handed over the seal of his office to Hampton. A black South Carolinian remarked, "To think that Hayes would go back on us when we had to wade through blood to help place him where he is now." On April 25, black Louisianans were dealt the same fate. Hayes's associates had probably struck an informal deal: he would get the presidency in exchange for conservative rule in the three disputed states. The unholy bargain was supposedly struck at Wormley's Hotel in Washington, which was owned by a prominent black entrepreneur, James Wormley. Wormley had been an agent of Garrison's *The Liberator* and a Sumner confidant. His family was involved in black education, the black convention movement, and contraband relief. His son had served in the Union army. Lynch, who lost his seat in Congress, was apoplectic: "To such a bargain I did not care to be even an innocent party."

Historians have speculated on the exact terms of the unwritten Wormley Bargain, better known as the Compromise of 1877, or whether it even occurred. For instance, did it involve railroad interests, or did it simply concern the election of a Republican president in exchange for restoration of white supremacy in the South? The southern historian C. Vann Woodward believed the railroads had had their say. While such specific claims have been disputed, northern business interests certainly favored the end of Reconstruction. Abolitionists at the time understood that clearly. Wendell Phillips claimed that the "treacherous bargain" included a provision to "charter the Southern Pacific Railway, giving away millions of national acres and millions of national bonds (let workingmen take notice)." Hayes, as even his supporters conceded, took advice "from the ruling classes in business and financial circles." Indeed, the Republican Party soon proved to be more assiduous in protecting business than freedpeople. By the end of the century, it had transformed from the party of antislavery and black rights into the party of big business.

A small contingent of federal troops remained in the South, and sporadic efforts to combat voter suppression continued in the 1880s. But Reconstruction as a national policy came to an end in 1877 even though some Republicans continued to champion black rights and attempted to halt the slide in the 1880s. In 1878, the Posse Comitatus Act severely limited the use of federal troops to restore the rule of law in states. Nine years later the Electoral Count Act of 1887 tried to prevent the submission of rival electoral votes from states, which has never happened since 1876. In 2022, however, attempts to overthrow the results of the presidential election led to the passage of election reform in Congress that would prevent such illegal maneuvers. Reconstruction would be completely overthrown only with the formal rise of Jim Crow and legal disfranchisement of black men in the South in the 1890s. The counterrevolution of 1876 did not completely end Reconstruction, even if it was an important steppingstone in its unwinding.

Perhaps fittingly for a nation that sanctioned slavery at its inception, 1876 was also the centennial of the birth of the republic. The Centennial Exhibition in Philadelphia, with displays from countries across the globe, signaled the dawn of a new age of political reaction and industrial revolution. Its wonders were colossal machines, such as steam engines and a hydrocarbon engine, an early version of the internal combustion engine, impressing foreign visitors like the emperor of Brazil. African Americans, who commissioned a statue of Richard Allen, the founder of the AME Church, which was completed only a few days before the exhibition closed, were virtually invisible. They were mostly refused entry; even Douglass was barred when he appeared at the exhibition grounds. In a physical representation of the beliefs powering Western imperialism, which replicated domestic racial hierarchy, the United States and European countries were given prime spots, and the rest of the world was consigned to the margins. Nonetheless, Benjamin Montgomery of the Davis Bend experiment in Mississippi won the prize for the finest cotton, competing with varieties from all over the world, and the black sculptor Edmonia Lewis's *Death of Cleopatra* drew wide admiration.

Racist terrorism was forgotten by most white Americans amid "the centennial gush." A South Carolina Klansman expressed his

Philadelphia Centennial bandanna. *Library Company of Philadelphia*

"Centennial Sentiments," amazed that the self-regarding festivities "seemed to have opened the Northern mind to a new light, and to have inspired their breasts with a charity equally new"—by which he meant charity for former enslavers, rather than freedpeople, for whom, apparently, it was all spent. Even in Boston, ex-Confederate general Fitzhugh Lee was cheered in the shadow of Bunker Hill. As one writer observed, "And there was a remarkable degree of good-will, a forgetfulness of party divisions, and even an oblivion of all disagreements growing out of the late war." The poem, "The Story of Hamburg," written by an anti-slavery poet, struck a discordant note amid the celebrations:

> Let others tell of the nation's glory—....
> I chant the lay of the nation's wrong
> I strike no chords of mirth and gladness;
> I tell the tale of the nation's shame

The triumph of racist reaction was imminent.

President Hayes made clear from the start of his presidency that he would retreat from Reconstruction and appease southern conservatives. Not only did he reassure southerners of noninterference in return for an empty assurance that they would not upend black rights, but he also nominated men to his cabinet known for their opposition to Reconstruction. Schurz was made secretary of the interior and could exult that the Liberals' agenda had finally triumphed. Hayes's secretary of state was one of Andrew Johnson's defense lawyers in his impeachment, William Evarts. Besides the moderate John Sherman, who was made secretary of the treasury, most stalwart Republicans found themselves shut out of the executive branch and federal patronage. Hayes even nominated an ex-Confederate from Tennessee as his postmaster general, rather than James Alcorn, perhaps the most pro-conservative southern Republican, who coveted the post. In the South, Hayes's patronage policy was focused on conservatives, instead of southern Republicans, who were being impeached or violently intimidated. Southerners boasted that the moment "federal arms" retreated, "the superior vigor of the white race will drive the colored voter into obscurity," and that they were determined to regain political power even if "they exterminate every black in the south."

Abolitionists, at least those who were still living, were outraged by Hayes's appointment of Charles Devens of Massachusetts as attorney general. As a US marshal, Devens had been involved in the infamous rendition of the fugitive slave Thomas Sims from Boston in 1851. Just before the war, Devens tried to make amends by putting up money to buy Sims back from his enslaver, but Sims became free only after escaping to the Union army. Devens's attempted "poor atonement" did not make up for the fact that Sims had been whipped mercilessly on recapture and suffered eleven more years of slavery. Phillips spoke of "the slave hound cabinet" of Evarts, Devens, and others. Abolitionists were a bit mollified by Douglass's appointment as the first black marshal of Washington. Douglass was representative of "all the enfranchised black men in the country" as "the lord-chamberlain of the social and legal world, the attendant of magistrates, diplomatic corps, senate-house, and all, an emancipated slave," one abolitionist proclaimed. Significantly, though, Douglass was shorn of the marshal's ceremonial role of standing next to the president to introduce dignitaries visiting the White House. Patronage appointments also went to Samuel Packard, the Republican gubernatorial candidate in Louisiana, and to Republican members of the election board in the state, as small consolations.

While some Republicans professed to take some comfort in the fact that Wade Hampton and Francis Nicholls had publicly promised to respect black rights, radicals, abolitionists, and African Americans scoffed at such self-deception. Nicholls was "as profuse of promises for good conduct as was Hampton," but unlike Hayes, they were not fooled. Phillips heard "the crack of the old slaveholding whip" every time Hampton spoke. He pointed out that the federal government had tried appeasing ex-Confederates under Johnson and failed: "To trust a southern promise would be fair evidence of insanity. The white South stands today perjured before the world, her cartel of honor broken and forfeited." During his presidency, Hayes vetoed bills sent to his desk by Congress that would have weakened federal enforcement laws, but to little effect: nonenforcement was already his policy. Both Hampton and Nicholls showed their true colors immediately after Hayes ordered federal troops back to their barracks, removing Republican and black officeholders and turning a blind eye to racist terrorism that reduced black male voting to almost zero.

In September 1877, Hayes undertook a victory lap in the form of a southern tour. In his speech in Nashville, which was cheered by local elites, he naively claimed, "I think the colored people are safer tonight with their rights in Tennessee, with no federal bayonets undertaking to protect them, than when there were armies here trying to protect them." Hayes was "under the impression" that his reconciliation policy was working. In a 1909 speech to the Holden Farmers and Mechanics club in Massachusetts, northern Republican Henry Warren, who had participated in Reconstruction in Mississippi, starkly described the betrayal of black citizens, saying that "the colored Republicans of the State felt that they had been abandoned to the tender mercies of their former masters."[6]

The radical wing of the Republican Party, the one most committed to Reconstruction and black rights, was no longer the vanguard of the party. Stevens and Sumner were dead. The failure to pass a new enforcement law against political terror was further evidence that it was a new era. Benjamin Wade bemoaned the fact that he had done so much to get Hayes elected, while George Julian defected to the Democratic Party. Some old abolitionists had lived to see their vision realized, only to see it then destroyed.

They would not live to see it made real again. The "year 1874 had been marked by an unusual mortality in anti-slavery ranks," a writer for *The Commonwealth* noted. Garrison would die in 1879 and Phillips five years later. Garrison spent the last years of his life attending funerals for and writing eulogies to dead abolitionists—an extended elegy for abolition democracy—and criticizing Republicans for abandoning Reconstruction. He had told a black correspondent before the 1876 election that African Americans had no choice but to vote for Hayes. The old abolitionist now wrote, "The millennial state, if it ever come on earth, is yet in the far distant future." Even as Phillips moved into the labor movement, Garrison argued that as long as freedpeople were "ruthlessly deprived of their rights as American citizens, and no protection is extended to them by the Federal Government, on the ground of impotency, the old anti-slavery issue is still (and must be persistently insisted as constituting) the paramount issue before the country."

Only a few abolitionists disagreed. Parker Pillsbury—who had already broken with Garrison and Douglass in supporting Stanton and Anthony's alliance with the racist George Frances Train during the AERA Kansas campaign—was one of them. He wrote that both old abolitionists "seem still bent on the bloody shirt," and supported Hayes's policy of promoting "cooperation" between southern planters and "colored laborers."

Before his death in 1875, the former senator and Grant's vice president, Henry Wilson, voiced his regret that the Confederate states had not been remanded to a territorial stage, as Stevens and Sumner had proposed. Wilson left to posterity his three-volume *History of the Rise and Fall of the Slave Power in America*. The last volume, published two years after his death, was completed by other writers. Its dismal conclusion, quoted in the epigraph to this chapter, was a fitting epitaph for Reconstruction. At a rapid clip, the southern states that restored white supremacy undid the laws and progress of Reconstruction. They abolished progressive taxation and symbols of Reconstruction state activism, including the central boards of education and aid to the poor and disabled. As Wilson noted, with the "Democratic ascendancy" in the South, many northern states, and the House (Republicans still controlled the Senate after 1876), "the wonder ceases that education languishes, that the number of scholars diminishes, school laws are repealed or rendered useless." The former Republican governor of Arkansas Powell Clayton, who wrote a vindication of Reconstruction, agreed. When the Democrats came into power, "they, as quickly as possible, undid everything that the Republicans had accomplished. True to their desire to keep the masses ignorant, the free school system was their starting point."

The Reconstruction amendments were a dead letter, especially in the

Deep South. White supremacist southern regimes dismantled local governments, gerrymandered electoral districts, and invented a variety of new mechanisms for voter suppression. They repealed state civil rights laws while terror groups continued to intimidate black voters. In 1883, a white mob lynched William H. Foote, the black tax collector of Yazoo City, Mississippi. In 1889, John M. Clayton, the Republican nominee in a congressional election and Governor Clayton's brother, was assassinated. Conservatives enacted new laws to control labor—some, including vagrancy laws, represented a reprise of the Black Codes—as well as new anti-enticement and sunset laws that made it a criminal offense to offer employment to contract labor and prevented farmers, tenants, and sharecroppers from selling their products at night. New lien laws gave landlords the first right on a crop over the sharecroppers and tenants, who steadily drifted into debt peonage, permanently indebted to local planter merchants for seed, tools, and livestock. The criminalization of blackness accelerated, as new laws prescribed draconian punishment for minor and nonexistent crimes, giving rise to the notorious convict lease labor system, which provided cheap, expendable prison labor— "slavery by another name"—to the plantations and factories of the "New South." Countless black men and women were trapped in a system that was "worse than slavery" in some respects.

Southern elites did not rule the nation, as they had before the war, but they had regained almost total power over their region. Some of these men were old slaveholding planters, others a rapacious new planter mercantile class. Democracy died, but cotton plantations survived, and—alongside new railroads and extractive and heavy industries— they represented the reconstruction of capitalism in the South. High-ranking Confederates such as Alexander Stephens and Lucius Quintus Lamar, who was seated after the congressional inquiry into Mississippi's 1875 pogrom, represented their states in Congress as if they had not waged a bloody war against the United States just a few years earlier and had not encouraged terrorism ever since. Abolitionists were particularly appalled by the election of the disgraced Andrew Johnson as a senator from Tennessee in 1874. In a notable contrast, the British government refused to seat Irish nationalist John Mitchel, the proslavery "hypocritical shrieker for freedom" who had fought for the Confederacy after his election to the House of Commons. Out of the 107 southern congressmen elected in 1874, 80 had served in the Confederate army, and 35 were former generals. These men now chaired 21 of the 34 House committees. In national politics, southern Democrats, segregationist "Dixiecrats," would be a profoundly reactionary bloc, stymieing any legislation that would expand democracy by securing labor's demands, women's suffrage, and civil rights until the mid-twentieth century. The South, Phillips argued, "clings to her ideas with all the energy of angry defeat." The "Solid South" is "the old slave power with a new name."

As Powell Clayton wrote about the decimation of the Republican Party in the South, "It is plain that the basic principle of good government, which depends on two parties, the 'outs' watching the 'ins,' is completely destroyed." Despite the railroad and new factories, the New South's economy remained predominantly agrarian, with northern and foreign capital invested in mainly extractive industries that were shaped by the white supremacy and antilabor policies of local ruling elites. Phillips predicted, "blood and starvation will rule the south." In the 1930s, President Franklin Delano Roosevelt would declare the South to be the nation's number one economic problem. White supremacists bestowed a legacy of not only racism, violence, and exclusion, but also poverty and underdevelopment. They achieved their goal in two crucial respects: in their restoration of the plantation economy, especially cotton cultivation, dependent on severely exploited labor; and their destruction of the black wealth and mobility promised by emancipation. African American land ownership, literacy rates, and representation in the professions increased even in the worst of circumstances, but the fundamental wealth and income gap left by slavery and its long-after lives have yet to be rectified. The New South was hardly a colony of global capitalism; it set the pace for the exploitation of the working poor, especially black people. Its reactionary political elites were willing to bargain regional development for private profits and racial apartheid.[7]

The counterrevolution against Reconstruction took another form, too, in addition to violent disfranchisement at the local and state levels and retrenchment at the national. A parallel reaction unfolded in the US Supreme Court. The court did not just mostly fail to implement the Reconstruction laws and amendments; it eviscerated and repurposed them for the age of capital. It dismantled the legal edifice of Reconstruction. While the court would occasionally strike down unconstitutional voter suppression laws such as poll taxes and "grandfather clauses"—which said you could vote only if your grandfather had—on the whole it turned a blind eye to and legitimized the inhuman and brazenly unconstitutional system of racial segregation and disfranchisement in the South. Civil Rights activists in the twentieth century who fought the South's entrenched racial apartheid claimed that the Constitution was on their side, pointing to the remaking of the Constitution during Reconstruction. It was a simple and obvious claim that somehow escaped earlier generations of the nation's allegedly best legal minds.

The first indication of the court's hostility to "the national civil rights enforcement administration" of Reconstruction came with the *Slaughter-House Cases* in 1873. *Slaughterhouse* did not involve the rights of freedpeople, but rather those of the butchers of New Orleans, who sued the state of Louisiana under the Fourteenth Amendment for infringing on their right to property and to make a living. For public health reasons, the state government had given one company a monopoly on slaughtering animals, because in general the practice was carried out in an unsanitary and unregulated fashion by the butchers. The conservative Supreme Court Justice Joseph Bradley had decided that the state law was unconstitutional while riding circuit in a lower federal court by uncharacteristically (for him) taking a broad view of the Fourteenth Amendment. In a narrow five-to-four decision, however, the Supreme Court dismissed the butchers' suit, arguing that the amendment was supposed to narrowly protect freedpeople's citizenship rights and upholding the power of the state government to regulate the slaughter of animals. The decision was a vindication of public health rules and the police powers of the state, and three years later, in *Munn v. Illinois,* the court upheld the power of states to regulate the economy. Yet by the early twentieth century, the Supreme Court would reverse this trend, declaring most attempts by states to pass labor laws and regulate corporations unconstitutional.

Slaughterhouse thus did not create a long-lasting judicial precedent in those areas of law, but it did become a precedent for justifying narrow readings of Reconstruction laws and amendments—readings that would, in the hands of unsympathetic justices, undermine their clear purpose. In an obiter dictum (an opinion not part of the legal decision) worthy of Roger Taney in *Dred Scott,* Justice Samuel F. Miller, who had written for the majority in *Slaughterhouse,* challenged the Fourteenth Amendment's establishment of national citizenship. Miller claimed that all the rights nationalized by the amendment—what Republican senator John Bingham had called "the nationalization" of the Bill of Rights in 1866—were still granted only by states. The only national rights that the federal government could enforce were limited to access to ports and waterways, travel to the capital, the right to run for federal office, and protection abroad and on the high seas. By this stunning logic, the federal government could ostensibly protect the rights of black citizens abroad but not where they lived, whether in the South or other parts of the nation. The discredited states' rights argument seemed to have triumphed over the Constitution itself.

The judicial retreat from Reconstruction occurred alongside the unraveling of a national political commitment to uphold it. But the Supreme Court was not merely reacting to political developments or public sentiment; it played an active role in destroying the rule of law. As early as 1872, in *Bylew v. United States,* the court overthrew the conviction of two white men for the brutal ax murder of a black family in Kentucky. The accused had been prosecuted under the Civil Rights Act of 1866, but the court ruled that states had exclusive police powers to punish crime. (At the time, Kentucky did not even allow black people to testify against whites.) A majority of federal judges at lower levels ruled in accordance with the Reconstruction amendments; the Supreme Court was the outlier.

That became apparent once again in the court's decision in *United*

States v. Cruikshank in 1876. The case stemmed from the prosecution of nine men charged with leading the 1873 Colfax massacre in Louisiana. Federal authorities had indicted ninety-eight men for the massacre under the Enforcement Act of 1870 but brought only nine of them to trial. The first resulted in a mistrial, and in the second, only four were convicted for violating the civil rights of African Americans. These four, including a William B. Cruikshank, whose name will forever grace a legal travesty, appealed their conviction at the US Circuit Court of Appeals. Their appeal was heard by the original trial judge and by Justice Bradley of the Supreme Court, who was riding circuit, as was customary in that era. While the trial judge upheld the conviction, Bradley opined that the men could not be convicted because the authority to punish crimes lay with the states, blithely undermining the Enforcement Acts that tasked the federal government to protect black citizens. Due to the divided decision, the case went up to the Supreme Court, which this time supported Bradley.

The Supreme Court's intruding into the legislative sphere and upending Congress's law-making powers went beyond the customary scope of the judicial review of the constitutionality of laws. It simply ignored the plain meaning of the Fourteenth and Fifteenth Amendments. Writing the majority opinion in *Cruikshank*, Chief Justice Morrison R. Waite, a legal mediocrity appointed by Grant, cited the *Slaughter-House Cases*, revealing how the court built judicial precedent from one bad decision to another. "The Fourteenth Amendment prohibits a State from depriving any person of life, liberty, or property, without due process of law; but this adds /nothing to the rights of one citizen against the other," he opined. According to this "state action" understanding of the amendment, the law would not hold southern terrorists accountable for murder because they were private citizens.

The Supreme Court effectively declared open season on African Americans. Racist terrorists could now act with impunity, knowing they would never be punished for their crimes, especially after the former Confederate states were restored to white supremacy. Even under Reconstruction, state courts and southern juries had proven unequal to the task of protecting black life and rights. That reality was precisely what had necessitated federal laws and constitutional amendments that the Supreme Court now scuttled. The perpetrators of the Colfax massacre were never brought to justice, but the effects were more far-reaching than that. US Attorney James Beckwith, who prosecuted the Colfax cases, observed that because of Bradley's reasoning, "the armed White League organizations of the South" sprang into life.

In donning the mantle of states' rights, the court paralyzed Reconstruction's progressive constitutionalism. If *Cruikshank* rendered meaningless the equal protection and due process clause of the Fourteenth Amendment, *United States v. Reese et al.*, decided during the same term, ended the voting guarantee of the Fifteenth Amendment. The Kentucky case arose when William Garner, a black man, was turned away from the polls by two election inspectors, Hiram Reese and Matthew Foushee, in violation of the Enforcement Act of 1870, which sought to protect black men's right to vote from intimidation. Kentucky officials had refused to let black men pay poll taxes, and then denied them the right to vote based on nonpayment of poll taxes. Reese and Foushee were indicted in federal court, but a divided opinion by the two judges hearing the case sent it to the Supreme Court. In the majority decision authored by Waite, the court declared unconstitutional the parts of the Enforcement Act that mandated punishment of state election officials for voter suppression.

In another obiter dictum, Waite argued that the Fifteenth Amendment had not, in fact, given the right to vote to anyone; rather, it merely prevented the states from discriminating against voters on the basis of race, color, or previous condition of servitude. According to this argument, states could use devices like the poll tax, which was supposedly race-neutral, to specifically target black men. The year before, in *Minor v. Happersett*, Waite had argued, in denying women the right to vote, that suffrage was not an essential component of citizenship. Conservatives heard Waite clearly; states soon began to employ a slew of requirements for voting that ostensibly did not target black voters. The court's decisions had a chilling effect on attempts to uphold black rights and to prosecute southern terrorists. Time and time again, the court's majority followed Democratic critics of Reconstruction laws and amendments, rather than their Republican authors. At the turn of the century, an ex-Confederate and White Leaguer from Louisiana, Edward D. White, became not only a Supreme Court justice, but chief justice.[8]

The violent and legal counterrevolution against Reconstruction inaugurated in the 1870s would accelerate in the last few decades of the nineteenth century, when racial subjugation rather than racial equality became the watchword of the nation. Democratic decay coincided with the triumph of industrial capitalism, as the government and the courts moved to protect the privileges of capital rather than the rights of citizens. It also coincided with and was connected to, as we shall see, the colonial subjugation of western Indian nations.

CHAPTER NINE

The Conquest of the West

And over it all, with a burning pen,
Erasing the record of Sheridan
Moke-ta-va-ta, who dared to die
Rather than utter a base lie;
Whose pleading women and children were slain
In the light of morn, on the crimson'd plain
By a mounted host of merciless men

—"SHERIDAN'S LAST RIDE," 1869

The strikingly handsome Kintpaush "Captain
Jack." *Reprinted with permission of the Modoc Tribal
Nation. Autry Museum of the American West*

In 1893, the historian Frederick Jackson Turner proposed a famous thesis of the western frontier, describing it as a crucible for the making of American democracy and individualism. Defining the West as "the meeting point between savagery and civilization," he argued that the region, with its seemingly limitless land and no history except the disappearance of the "primitive Indian," shaped the distinct American character. The "Indian frontier" was a "consolidating agent"; it kept alive a "spirit of resistance" in the "rugged" frontiersman. The story of the frontier was a story of "pioneer farmers," immigrants attracted by "cheap," "unexhausted," and "easily tilled" land—an area of "wilderness freedom" where Europeans became Americans. It was not the controversy over slavery, Turner contended, that created American democracy and a national government. It was the West.[1]

A more accurate account would see the late nineteenth-century West as a site of dispossession, enslavement, and colonialism—as a springboard for larger imperial aspirations, whose roots can also be traced to earlier periods, and as a graveyard of not just indigenous sovereignty but also for the Second American Republic. The only contemporaries who subscribed to this view were a handful of remaining abolitionists and radicals, who protested the fall of Reconstruction as well as the dispossession of western Indians. In the same years that Reconstruction was being dismantled, the US Army would wage relentless war against Indian nations in the western half of the continent. The rise of the Jim Crow South and the conquest of the West, often told as separate stories, were parallel events connected at a fundamental level. The waning of Reconstruction set the stage for the final campaign in the brutal subjugation of the indigenous nations. It fully diverted the energies of the nation-state from emancipation to empire.

The so-called Indian wars in the West predated the Civil War and Reconstruction, leading historians to develop the idea of a "Greater Reconstruction" of the West, spanning from the Mexican War (1846–1848) to the end of Reconstruction in 1877. But during and after the Mexican War, indigenous nations remained powerful entities. The reconstruction of the West also did not end in the 1870s; it accelerated and became more brutal when the federal government's attention fully shifted from freedpeople to western Indian nations. Its proper end point was the 1890 Wounded Knee massacre of the Lakota Sioux, a Plains native power whose influence had rivaled American hegemony. Indeed, the sale of "public lands" in the Trans-Mississippi West after 1890 increased to levels never seen, a direct result of the military defeat of western indigenous nations.[2] Just as the unraveling of southern Reconstruction was an extended process that took until the end of the nineteenth century, so was the reconstruction of the West.

The conquest of the West was also a dress rehearsal for an overseas American empire. After dispossessing indigenous nations, the United States joined the European rush for empire. The American republic would no longer be merely a settler colonial society asserting its hemispheric dominance and its "manifest destiny" to overspread the continent, but an imperial power on the world stage. The roots of American imperialism can, of course, be traced far back to the early American republic, but the acquisition of large foreign colonies marked an accelerated phase in the history of US empire. The treatment of black southerners and Indians was, in this sense, a precursor for the colonization of native populations in the Pacific and the Caribbean. By the turn of the century, Reconstruction was dead and the United States was both a global empire and the leading industrial power in the world. The overthrow of Reconstruction was not just a southern story, but a transregional and transnational one.[3] Without such a broad view, the full historical significance of the demise of the Second American Republic is impossible to grasp.

To understand US history from indigenous perspectives is to engage with a very long history of American colonialism, defined by violent dispossession and the destruction of lives, nations, and cultures, which some historians deem genocidal. That history begins before the founding of the American republic, with the European settlement of the Americas in the sixteenth and seventeenth centuries. By the mid-nineteenth century, disease, warfare, exploitation, servitude, and land grabs had severely diminished the numbers of indigenous peoples. Many of the survivors were confined on reservations or in "Indian territory" after successive, forced expulsions. Americans like Turner justified dispossession through claims about "the disappearing Indian" and "Indian savagery" in the face of allegedly inexorable forces. Native Americans, however, continued to resist attempts to erase them. North America was an "Indigenous Continent" for much of its history, and it would remain so, to a degree and in different ways, even after the fall of the Second American Republic.[4]

When recalling his time in an Illinois militia in the Black Hawk war of 1832, Abraham Lincoln, whose settler grandfather had been killed by Indians, joked that the only thing he had killed were mosquitoes. The so-called Black Hawk war, named after a Sauk chief, was a merciless slaughter of Sauks and Foxes (Mesquakies), who had returned to their lands after being forcibly exiled by the US Army. Like other settlers who served in the militia, Lincoln received a land grant for his service, further dispossessing the Sauks.

During the Civil War, preoccupied with defeating the Confederacy, President Lincoln—who, compared to many Americans, was not a die-hard Indian hater—did not give much thought to the Indian wars. In 1862, 303 Dakota warriors were condemned to execution in a summary military trial after the Dakota-US conflict led by Little Crow in Minnesota, after years of reneged treaties, land grabs, and mistreatment that had reduced the Dakota Sioux to starvation and desperation. Lincoln pored over the trial records and commuted the sentences of all except thirty-nine accused of particularly egregious actions. In the end, thirty-eight were hanged—the largest mass hanging in American history and a blot on Lincoln's presidency. And like most US presidents, Lincoln signed off on laws dispossessing Indians. Besides indigenous people themselves, only abolitionists like the Indian advocate John Beeson protested. As he put it, the Dakota were a "sovereign people" and "their hostile acts in Minnesota... [were] one of war, and not rebellion; and for what the most civilized nations would deem sufficient occasion for war." The Dakota Sioux and some Ho-Chunks (Winnebagos), who had not taken part in the uprising, were expelled from their homes and consigned to reservations.

The Civil War brought devastation to Native America. Even as army regulars stationed in the West were summoned east, volunteers under generals such as James Carleton continued to wage war on the Indian frontier. The gruesome Sand Creek Massacre in Colorado Territory in 1864 saw volunteers of the Third Colorado Cavalry murder nearly four hundred Arapaho and Cheyenne, mainly women and children. Captain Silas Soule, an abolitionist, blew the whistle on his commanding officer, Col. John Chivington, a Methodist minister, who ordered the massacre. At a court-martial led by Samuel F. Tappan of the abolitionist Tappan family, another officer, Major Patrick Wynkoop, testified that the Indian women had been tortured and "profaned" in a manner that was truly "sickening."

The report of the Congressional Joint Committee on the Conduct of the War, written by radical Benjamin F. Wade, strongly condemned Chivington's actions and the victims were given forty thousand dollars. Congress passed a joint resolution suspending all pay and allowances to Chivington's regiment. Charles Sumner called it an "exceptional crime," the "most atrocious in the history of any country." Despite congressional inquiries, Chivington went mostly unpunished. A month after the Sand Creek massacre, a Colorado cavalry regiment killed Lean Bear, a Cheyenne chief and one of the peace chiefs who had met with Lincoln in 1863 to protest settler encroachments. He was still wearing the peace medal Lincoln had given to him when he was murdered.[5]

Indigenous nations in "Indian territory," what is now the state of Oklahoma,—the so-called five civilized nations that had been expelled from their homelands in the 1830s—signed treaties with the Confederacy and fought on its behalf. Yet substantial numbers of people in these nations, especially among the Creeks and the Seminoles, many of whom had intermarried with former slaves, sided with the Union. Such indigenous unionists formed the first Indian regiments of the Civil War, in Kansas. Stand Watie, like many of the "mixed blood" slaveholding elites of the Cherokee nation, supported the Confederacy and rose to the rank of a brigadier general in the Confederate army. His rival, John Ross, the "principal chief" of the Cherokees, whom abolitionists had lauded before the war, had initially advocated neutrality and supported the Union. The Cherokees eventually surrendered to Union forces, and

Ross met with Lincoln in 1862, trying to preserve the sovereignty of his nation. In a subsequent letter, Ross assured Lincoln that his nation had signed a treaty with the Confederacy out of necessity and that the true loyalty of Cherokees lay with the United States. At the end of the war, the fact that many of these nations were slaveholding—a mark of "civilization" in the South—left them vulnerable when they signed treaties with the United States in 1866 that abolished slavery and recognized the equality of Indian freedpeople. (The status of Afro-Indians as full-fledged members of Indian nations continues to be disputed.) In the late nineteenth century, the federal government gave Indian freedpeople and black settlers land in Indian territory, even as the abolitionist dream of land reform in the South withered.

The pitting of freedpeople's rights against tribal sovereignty was the tragedy of formal Reconstruction in Indian territory. The southern Creeks, Chickasaws, and Choctaws abused freedpeople in much the same way as southern ex-slaveholders, reported agents of the Freedmen's Bureau. The remarkable northern Creek chief, Oktarsars Harjo, posited an alternative and, unfortunately, a minority vision: native sovereignty that *included* freedpeople. As he put it, "we were all one nation." Black settlers, fleeing southern terrorism, also cannot simply be viewed as equal participants in American colonialism in the West. The 1866 treaties between the US government and the five "civilized" southern Indian nations resulted, C. N. Vann of the Cherokee nation argued, in land being taken from them and given to railroad corporations or designated as public domain. He was outraged "that the Government shall rob its wards and cover itself with ignominy, in order that these corporations may pile up mountainous fortunes." Indian territory would be opened to white settlement in 1889, paving the way for further dispossession and Oklahoma statehood. The loss of sovereignty suffered by indigenous nations in the West was compounded by wartime laws that were predicated on their dispossession: the Homestead Acts, which gave homesteads to settlers, citizens as well as immigrants, on "public" lands, and the Pacific Railroad Act, which allowed for the construction of a transcontinental railroad through Native America.[6]

The subjugation of indigenous nations, through imperialist warfare, dispossession, and attempted cultural annihilation, was an essential aspect of the reconstruction of the West. The American West had been a battlefield of empires and nations, native and European, dating back to the precolonial era. The balance of power shifted during the course of the nineteenth century. The growth of the war powers of the president, and the expansion of the US Army itself, was intimately connected to native dispossession. On the eve of the Civil War, 80 percent of the troops in the regular army—around 12,000 men—were posted on the frontier. Many of its southern, West Point–trained officers would defect to the Confederacy. Their vision of a proslavery empire was not only based on the servitude of black people, but also the defeat of Indians.

The Civil War in the West was a "three-cornered" contest among the Union, the Confederacy, and indigenous nations. Union generals Edward R. Canby, James Carleton, and the Kentucky-born "Kit" Carson managed to beat back a Confederate invasion of New Mexico territory. They then attacked and defeated the Apache and Navajo with the help of Hispano settlers as well as the Ute and Pueblo nations, confining the Apache and Navajo on reservations and putting an end to a borderlands political economy of raiding and captivity. Thousands of Apache and Navajo were sent to the barren Bosque Redondo, where many died or were enslaved. (In 1868, the Navajo signed a peace treaty with the United States that allowed them to leave for their old homelands.) Like Carleton, another Californian officer, Patrick E. Connor, marched his volunteers into the West, waging ruthless warfare against Indians in Utah, Nevada, and Idaho. Most of the western volunteers were veterans of genocidal warfare against indigenous people in California and Oregon in the 1850s. Connor's forces razed a Shoshoni village of men, women, and children, in what became known as the Bear River massacre in 1863. The number killed is estimated to be well over two hundred, comparable to later massacres at Sand Creek in 1864 and Wounded Knee in 1890. Treaties negotiated after the war led to the dispossession of all indigenous nations. Those deemed enemies of the United States, like the Apache, and those considered its allies, such as the Ute, lost lands.

The correct comparison for the Indian wars is not the Civil War, but

European wars for empire of the same era. The savagery of the American wars in the West, reaching their apogee in the late nineteenth century, lay outside the bounds of "civilized" warfare and international law embodied in Lincoln's Code of War. In American history as it is usually told, individual wars are often named for indigenous chiefs, nations, and places, implicitly justifying conquest. Americans excused the atrocities they committed with claims about the alleged barbarism of native nations. A similar explanation was often offered for the brutality of European imperial wars in Africa and Asia. Like colonized peoples elsewhere, Indian nations put up effective military resistance against settler incursions, forcing the United States to make vast expenditures in blood and money. Some indigenous people allied with the United States to settle old scores, even though in the end it gained them no extra protection, as all natives, "friendly" or "hostile," were dispossessed. An 1867 Senate Committee on Indian Affairs report acknowledged, "Most Indian hostilities, the evidence showed, could be traced to white encroachment or white provocation."[7]

With the end of the Civil War, the US Army was steadily redeployed

Sioux and Arrapahoe Indian Delegation. Left to right, seated: Red Cloud, Big Road, Yellow Bear, Young Man Afraid of his Horses, Iron Crow; left to right, standing: Little Bigman, Little Wound, Three Bears, He Dog. *Brady-Handy Photograph Collection. Library of Congress*

from the South to the West. The primary function of the military transitioned from securing emancipation and black rights to "winning the West." According to one observer, the Indian wars "saved" the military from complete demobilization after the Civil War. A nation reconciled to white supremacy and an army of reunited Union and Confederate veterans would eventually conquer the region. Warfare in the western plains was not the "total war" of the Civil War, which prefigured the trench warfare and the strategy of attrition that would characterize the First World War. It was, instead, an exterminationist campaign spurred on by gold rushes, expansion of settlements, and railroad construction, and it was more like wars of empire. The Fort Laramie Treaty of 1851 with western Indian nations permitted safe passage to settlers in exchange for recognition of territorial rights and annuities, yearly payments of cash, food, and supplies, paid by the government for fifteen years. But its provisions were violated in the following years.

The most formidable resistance to American encroachment was offered by the Lakota, composed of different Sioux tribes, in the Northwest and by the Apache and the Comanches in the Southwest. In 1866, in the so-called Red Cloud's war, named after the Oglala Lakota leader, the Sioux, in alliance with northern Cheyenne and Arapahos, sought to put an end to the steady stream of settlers and miners along the Bozeman trail in Montana. The Crow, who previously held sway in the area and had been defeated by the Lakota, allied with the United States. Besides raiding settler caravans and the military forts that dotted the frontier, Red Cloud's and Crazy Horse's soldiers decisively defeated a contingent of over eighty US soldiers led by Captain William Fetterman, every one of whom was killed in the engagement. On hearing of the Fetterman debacle, William Tecumseh Sherman—whose middle name was a "trophy name" taken from the great Shawnee chief, and who now headed the Military Division of Missouri that oversaw the vast western territory—coldly resolved, "We must act with vindictive earnestness against the Sioux even to the extermination of men, women, and children." Sherman sent an army commission to England to study British colonial campaigns so that the US Army could deploy similar tactics against Indians. By the 1870s, abolitionists had soured so much on Sherman that they attributed his success in the Civil War to Grant's overall strategy, arguing that the latter was the far superior general.

In 1867, the Indian Peace Commission, composed of advocates of indigenous rights like Samuel Tappan as well as Indian haters like Sherman (who did not participate in the negotiations, however), forged treaties with western Indian nations. In the second Treaty of Fort Laramie, signed in 1868 after Fetterman's rout, Red Cloud secured from the United States the Great Sioux Reservation, which included much of present-day South Dakota, including the sacred Black Hills (Paha Sapa), as well as recognition of Sioux hunting rights in unceded territory. The following year, Red Cloud and Spotted Tail of the Brules met in Washington, DC with President Grant and his Indian commissioner and former aide-de-camp, Col. Ely S. Parker, a Seneca and grand sachem of the Iroquois confederacy, who was educated as an engineer and lawyer. Red Cloud then traveled north to New York City, where he gave a memorable speech at Cooper Institute, indicting the United States for its bad faith and for reneging on treaty obligations. The Medicine Lodge Treaty, which included three separate treaties signed over the course of 1867 with the Kiowas, Comanches, Apache, southern Arapahos, and Cheyenne, was ratified by the Senate along with the Fort Laramie Treaty. The treaties restricted these nations to reservations and called for a cessation of all hostilities but promised annuities and allowed for off-reservation hunting south of the Arkansas River. The Indian Peace Commission also issued a report in which it held the US government and settlers culpable for broken treaties and subsequent hostilities.

Even as the treaties were negotiated and signed, the wars continued. General Winfield Scott Hancock torched an abandoned village in April 1867 during his unprovoked campaign against the Cheyenne, and soldiers murdered Cheyenne chief Black Kettle the following year. Black Kettle (Moke-ta-ve-to), who had escaped the Sand Creek massacre with his severely wounded wife, had tried to negotiate peace between his nation and the United States. His small band and hundreds of their horses were killed in cold blood by Lt. Col. George Armstrong Custer (his brevet rank was major general, earned during the Civil War) and his troops in Washita, Oklahoma territory. In a bloody campaign against the southern Cheyenne and Arapaho in 1868–1869, Lt. Gen. Philip Sheridan, who had also fought in the Indian wars of the 1850s and, more recently, succeeded Sherman as the head of the Missouri military division, "cleared" Kansas and Nebraska of "hostile Indians," as he put it, using the language of ethnic cleansing. It was during this time that Sheridan supposedly coined the insidious maxim (he denied having said this), "The only good Indian is a dead Indian," which took on a life of its own.[8]

Congress also dealt another blow to indigenous sovereignty. The Indian Appropriations Act in 1871 appropriated monies for annuities to be given to Indian nations. The first such act had been passed in 1851 after the first Fort Laramie Treaty and the development of Indian reservations in the West. But the new act also declared that no Indian nation or tribe within the United States would be recognized as a sovereign, treaty-making power, putting an end to the so-called treaty regime and a hundred-year diplomatic tradition that dated to the founding of the republic. Cherokee leader C. N. Vann saw the law as a rebuke of the professed ideals of the US government. "Is it possible they are of no importance? Is morality, then, a myth?—the teachings of Christianity unreal as a dream, or binding only on the weak? Are national and personal honor and good faith things of the past, to be disregarded without remorse and without shame? Or is all of this true only when the rights of Indians are concerned?"

The 1871 law marked the culmination of the idea that, as Chief Justice John Marshall had put it many decades before, that Indians were "domestic dependent nations." Native Americans, as an editorial in *The Independent* pointed out, had been excluded from the Fourteenth Amendment because they "form political communities by themselves." The distinct nationalities of Indians were a "positive" thing. But they would be "wards" of the government, as Marshall had decided in the Cherokee Nation cases of 1831–1832, which, as the editorial explained, presupposed the political death of Indian nations and probably did not even reflect the reality of the situation in the West. The writer concluded that Indians should not be forced to trade sovereignty for citizenship: "Those who are talking so flippantly about denationalizing the Indian tribes, and by the law of force remitting them to the condition of mere inhabitants, irrespective of their own choice, are simply proposing that the US should become the killer of Indian nations and the robber of the territory which belongs to them, and that too, in the face of four hundred treaties which have explicitly recognized their nationality."

The roots of the 1871 law lay in Chief Justice Roger Taney's "plenary power" doctrine in *United States v. Rogers* (1846), a *Dred Scott* for indigenous people, which exempted Congress from respecting any constitutional limit when exercising authority over Indians. They would no longer have sovereign nations of their own, but neither would they be American citizens. This "constitutional anti-canon" subjected indigenous people to extermination, expulsion, detention, kidnapping of children, forcible religious conversions, and cultural indoctrination, a blueprint for the kinds of atrocities that accompanied European imperialism in Asia and Africa. As legal scholar Maggie Blackhawk concludes, studying federal Indian laws should lead one to the "view that not only is colonialism a moral abomination, it is also inconsistent with our constitutional democracy and an anachronistic artifact of empire." For some Indians, citizenship became a way to claim rights, land, and autonomy in straitened circumstances, especially after Reconstruction laws and amendments challenged racially restrictive definitions of American citizenship. But the Indian fight for maintaining indigenous sovereignty continued and was vindicated by the 1930s. Tribal sovereignty is alive and well today thanks to a long Indian tradition of survival and resistance.[9]

While western Indian nations debated whether to go to war again or to negotiate (again) for peace—and whether to unite to oppose settler incursions or ally with the United States against native enemies and competitors—the federal government gave them little choice. President Grant continued with the "peace policy," also called his "Quaker policy," toward indigenous nations as it was shaped by Quakers and other religious reformers. Christian missionaries were appointed Indian agents and superintendents to replace corrupt agents who regularly stole annuities. Besides the Office of Indian Affairs founded in 1824, a Board of Indian Commissioners was created in 1869 by Congress, to advise the federal government. Its secretary was the Quaker reformer Vincent Colyer, who was a founding member of the United States Christian Commission and had worked with freedpeople in New Bern, North Carolina. The reformers' "peace policy" promoted Christianization and "civilization" on reservations and was as much a colonial policy as any military campaign. It, too, was premised on indigenous dispossession, and while Indian wars literally killed native people, the peace policy sought to assimilate them through cultural death. Racist agents, the government's reneging on rations and annuities, and dismal conditions on reservations also meant actual death for thousands of Indians under the "peace policy."

In 1871, Ely Parker, who was Grant's commissioner of Indian affairs and the first Native American to occupy the post, resigned when he was wrongly accused of corruption, though he was cleared of all charges. He was also forced out by the evangelical William Welsh of the Board of Indian Commissioners. Parker, who had famously written the terms

Col. Ely S. Parker.
National Archives

of Lee's surrender at Appomattox for Grant, had informally advised him on Indian affairs since the 1860s. Parker viewed settlers rather than the army as the main threat to Indian nations. He advocated the return of the Office of Indian Affairs to the War Department from the corrupt Interior Department, where it was susceptible to the influence of railroads, settlers, and mining companies. His views promoted indigenous sovereignty and had influenced the Indian Peace Commission in 1867–1868. The western reconstruction visualized by Parker bore similarities to southern Reconstruction: the federal government and the army would protect Indian land rights and sovereignty while also providing pathways for education and "inclusion." His ideas found support among Radical Republicans like Henry Wilson, Grant's second vice president. During his brief tenure as commissioner from 1869 to 1871, Parker sought to represent Indian perspectives and balance them with demands for assimilation. His vision for western Reconstruction was never implemented, and instead, the military conquest of the West and forcible cultural assimilation became the order of the day.

Abolitionist views of the Indian wars and reservations were shaped by the struggle for black citizenship. They did not see the expansion of the nation-state into the South and West as complementary processes; on the contrary, they saw those actions as essentially opposed to one another, and understood that the federal government had reneged on its commitments to freedpeople and, simultaneously, its treaty obligations to indigenous nations. Though criticized by many other Americans, as they had been before the war for their "sickly sentimentality," abolitionists condemned the horrific Indian massacres in the West perpetrated by the military, local authorities, and settlers.

In 1870, the Second US Cavalry, led by a drunk Maj. Eugene Baker, massacred women, children, the old, and diseased in a Piegan village already ravaged by smallpox on the Marias River in Montana territory. (Only recently was a mountain in Yellowstone National Park named after one of the perpetrators of the Marias massacre, Gustavus Doane, renamed, fittingly, First Peoples Mountain.) The public outrage, especially among abolitionists, bolstered those who advocated peace with western Indians. Wendell Phillips thundered, "I only know the names of three savages upon the Plains, Colonel Baker, General Custer, and at the head of all General Sheridan." The *National Anti-Slavery Standard* editorialized, "We hoped that we had heard the last of such warfare, such inhuman and indiscriminate butchery of old men, women and children among the Indians, under the authority and sanction of the government of the United States. But it would appear that the limit of national degradation had not yet been reached."

Perhaps no one displayed a more acute understanding of the government's actions than William Lloyd Garrison, who was nearing the end of his life. He penned an article, "Massacre of the Piegans," in which he invoked the Marias massacre to critique the government's Indian policy overall. Garrison excoriated Baker, Sheridan, and Sherman, and Republican politicians and newspapers such as the *Chicago Tribune* for justifying the massacre. History will testify, he wrote, that next to "our dehumanizing oppression" of black people was the American treatment of indigenous people. He denounced the entire settler population for their "atrocious lies" and for their "hellish tortures" and "extremities" for the "slightest retaliation" to their incursions and abuse. He saved his full wrath for Sheridan and Sherman. The Indian massacres, he argued, were worse than the Fort Pillow massacre of black Union soldiers, and he compared the two Union generals to Confederate war criminals, including the detested Nathan Bedford Forrest. For Sheridan to vindicate his "butcherly policy" toward natives by referring to the Civil War was outrageous: "There is no analogy between the two cases." Sherman, too, could "claim no exemption" for his "wholesale slaughter" of Indians from any "military service" he had performed for the Union.

Garrison understood that the Indian wars represented a betrayal of the emancipatory aims of the Civil War: "the same contempt is generally felt at the west for the Indians as was felt at the south for the negroes," he lamented. The Indian problem was the creation of the "brutal acts of the whites" and the "perfidious manner in which treaty stipulations have been dealt with by the Government." The US massacres of western Indians were not an extension of the Civil War, but rather called to mind "the blowing into fragments transfixed at the mouths of the British cannons, of the rebel sepoys in India for the gratification of British vengeance." The Indian wars, Garrison grasped, were wars of imperialism. He attacked the "territorial greediness" of the United States, which was also behind the Grant administration's scheme to annex the Dominican Republic, and traced it back to William Seward's purchase of Alaska from Russia in 1867, which brought thirty thousand indigenous Alaskans under the US government. Owing to treaty stipulations and the lack of settler interest in frigid Alaska, native Alaskans would not suffer the fate of western indigenous nations. But in time, dispossession and loss of sovereignty would afflict them too.

Garrison wrote that the notion that it was the "Manifest Destiny" of the American republic to expand over the entire continent, first propounded by Democrats like the newspaper editor John O'Sullivan (who coined the term) before the Civil War, was really "American Swagger." It was not a positive term. Rather, it was "simply the despotic principle in republican guise." He predicted that the United States would soon apply the same principle to Cuba, the West Indies, and Mexico, and also threaten the South American republics, in its search for marketable products like tobacco, sugar, cotton, and coffee. American imperialism, as he saw it, was born in the plantation economy of the slave South.

Despite condemnation from some quarters, the army and settlers continued to perpetrate massacres with sickening frequency. On April 30, 1871, around 150 Apache women and children near Camp Grant in Arizona were massacred by Americans, Mexicans, and Tohono O'odham Indians in retaliation for Apache raids. Most of the victims were sleeping when they were attacked. An enraged President Grant called for the punishment of the killers, but a jury acquitted all of them. The Camp Grant massacre revealed that even when living under government protection, Indians could be targets of mass murder. It also demonstrated that the "peace policy," already in place since 1867, was failing.

Indigenous nations confronted an impossible choice between assimilation and extermination. Assistant Secretary of the Interior Benjamin R. Cowen argued that the "savage nature" of Indians had given Europeans and Americans an excuse to seize their lands under the guise of civilization and religion. Republican editor Henry C. Bowen of *The Independent* lauded Grant's "extensive missionary effort" to educate and civilize Indians who were, as he put it, "utterly besotted by igno-rance and barbarism." Rev. Samuel T. Spear argued that Indians should be placed on reservations as "rapidly as possible" to isolate them from settlers, and to educate and "civilize" them. He recommended consol-idating Indian reservations to give those who lived in a "nomadic sav-age state" a "permanent home." If they are a "dying race," they must be made citizens and protected by American laws. According to Spear, Indians apparently had more territory than they could use, and were simply in the way of settlers. The president, he said, should use military force to suppress "Indian outrages"; the "law of force" must be blended with "kindness" to remove Indians from their homes. Another writer recommended that all natives be confined to Indian territory, give up their "tribal existence," alienate their "land titles," and adopt the man-ners and customs of whites.

Efforts to confine native nations to reservations also caused blood-shed, including the Modoc War of 1872–1873, when "Captain Jack" (Kintpuash) tried to lead some of his people back to their ancestral lands. The conflict dated to an unjust treaty in 1864 that forced the Modoc to cede all their territory and sent them to an inhospitable, cold, and barren reservation in Oregon. The choice was between slow death on the reserva-tion, or an escape at the risk of war. After fleeing, the Modocs entrenched themselves in California's lava beds, and were put under siege by a much larger US force, numbering one thousand troops at its peak, in one of the costliest Indian wars for the government. A parley went awry when the Modocs killed General Canby and Rev. Eleazer Thomas. Alfred B. Mea-cham, a former Indian superintendent, who was scalped and almost died, nevertheless became a staunch advocate of indigenous rights.

Many Modocs, including Captain Jack, were hunted down, tried, and beheaded, while others were sent to a miserable reservation in Indian territory. Captain Jack, before his execution, declared, "You people can shoot any Indians any time you want whether we are in war or in peace. I charge the white people with wholesale murder." Even the son of the slain Reverend Thomas argued that it was "the wickedness of white men that caused my father's death." A writer who condemned the Modocs' "horrid crime" still acknowledged, "But that the sad fact may not be forgotten that it is the white man's injustice which drove these two hundred and fifty men to desperation." Even *The Independent* argued that the real culprits were the members of the "ruffian" settler army that had massacred a group of Modocs in 1852. Comparing the killing of the Modocs with massacres of freedpeople in the South, it asked: "When the nation in its official capacity can enact such heartless butchery it is altogether to be expected that Southern whites will not mince over the matter of the killing of a few 'n——.' " In 1873, the Supreme Court ruled that the Modocs were not "lawful combatants" and could be summarily executed or punished.

Violent encounters in the Southwest further eroded Grant's peace policy. In the Red River War of 1874–1875, the army launched an encircling campaign devised by Sheridan against the Kiowas, Comanche, southern Cheyenne, and Arapahos to force them into reservations. The excuse for the military action was an attack on buffalo hunters by the Quahadi Comanches under Isa-Tai, a "medicine man" or religious leader, and Quanah Parker, the "mixed-blood" son of a Comanche chief, and a captive but incorporated American, Cynthia Parker. After the Medicine Lodge Treaty, the southwestern Indian nations had been driven to desperation by inadequate, tainted provisions and the systematic destruction of the buffalo by settlers encroaching on lands promised to the Indians as hunting grounds. The Red River war ended in a victory for the US Army and the natives' final dispossession, with their warriors and chiefs imprisoned very far from home, in Fort Marion, Florida. After his surrender, Quanah Parker led his people to Fort Sill reservation in Oklahoma, where the Apache bands also ended up, and was recognized by the authorities as the head of all Comanches. Parker negotiated between settler and native cultures and went on to acquire considerable property as a cattle rancher.[10]

On the northern plains, indigenous nations continued to hold their ground. By the mid-1870s, Red Cloud's Oglalas, along with some northern Cheyenne and Arapahos, were living in the Red Cloud Agency, a reservation. But nonagency Lakota—("nonreservation" or "nonagency" referred to those who had not signed treaties)—led by the famous Hunk-papa chief Sitting Bull (Tatanka Iyotanka) and his allies, successfully resisted the government's attempt to confine them on reservations through guerilla warfare in the unceded lands. Their strategy was simi-lar, in broad respects, to the one American patriots, learning from Indi-ans, had used against British redcoats during the Revolutionary War. In the summer of 1874, Custer led a military expedition to the Black Hills in the Great Sioux reservation, ostensibly to build a military fort, but in reality to protect those miners illegally prospecting for gold. He returned with overstated accounts of gold in the region, setting off a settler stam-pede to the hills, a massive violation of the 1868 Fort Laramie Treaty.

Reservation and nonreservation Lakota emphatically rejected American attempts to purchase the sacred Black Hills, or Paha Sapa, holding the government to its treaty commitment. Just as the Grant administration was giving up on fighting racist terror in the South, it also gradually abandoned its checkered peace policy toward Indians. It issued all nontreaty Lakota an ultimatum—report to the agencies by the end of January 1876—even though the government knew that mov-ing in the winter months would be difficult. The army was given free rein to subjugate "hostile" Indians led by Sitting Bull and the charis-matic Oglala leader, Crazy Horse, if they did not abide by the ultima-tum. The bombastic Custer, a Democratic opponent of Reconstruction, nearly lost his command when he testified in Washington, DC against the Grant administration's Indian agents, who were being investigated for corruption in the Indian Ring scandal of 1876, which also implicated the Secretary of War William Belknap and his family.

During the Civil War, Custer had been George McClellan's protégé. After it, he accompanied Andrew Johnson in his "Swing Around the Circle" fiasco of a public tour in 1866. Like other Democrats and their Liberal Republican allies, all opponents of Reconstruction, Custer deliberately whitewashed the violence against those who were non-white and deemed uncivilized. The famous 1872 John Gast painting showing "American Progress" and the empire of liberty, with settler wagons flowing west as Indians fled before them, epitomized the Lib-eral Republican view of "settling" the West, like the Democrats' earlier slogan of the "Manifest Destiny" of the United States to expand into a continental power. It was an expression of a "civilizationist" colonial ideology, with the fittest leaving those designated unworthy, freedpeople and Native Americans, in the dust. Democrats like Custer made no pretense of civilizing others and subscribed to an even more brutal exterminationist philosophy. As Emerson Etheridge, a Tennessean who followed Johnson in bitterly opposing Reconstruction, put it, "The Indian stuck to his wigwam would not affiliate with the white race; let the Negro stick to his Loyal League, and his fate will be the same." This vision was the antithesis of that for Reconstruction.

Custer led the ill-fated Seventh Cavalry in what became the Battle of the Little Big Horn, named after the river in Montana territory, in the summer of 1876. (He detested Maj. Lewis Merrill, who had tenaciously fought against racist terrorism in the South and did not accompany him.) Surrounded, divided, and outnumbered, the overconfident Custer, two hundred fifty-eight of his troops, and three Crow scouts were destroyed by Lakota and Cheyenne warriors, led by Crazy Horse and Sitting Bull. The victory showcased the power of the Lakota, who were still a formidable presence in the West. One of the biggest military debacles in US history, Custer's "Last Stand" came to rival the neo-Confederate Lost Cause in the mythos of the American West. It became the Lost Cause of the West. Both military disasters were soon dressed up in the garb of martyrdom. Custer was seen by his apologists as a latter-day Maj. Gen. George Pickett, who had led the inept Confederate frontal attack ordered by Robert E. Lee during the Battle of Gettysburg. Like the United Daughters of the Confederacy, who assiduously promoted the alleged prowess of Confederate generals such as Lee, Custer's wife Elizabeth "Libbie" Custer almost single-handedly sanctified her husband's death. She proved as adept as Sallie Pickett was in mythologizing *her* husband's humiliating defeat. For Indians, the destruction of Custer and his men became literal and symbolic retribution for centuries of land robbery and broken treaties, similar to how African Americans and even Lincoln viewed the Civil War as divine retribution for the slave South and a guilty nation.

Abolitionists made that connection explicit when the country heard sensational news of the Custer debacle, which to most Americans was merely "the latest Indian atrocity." *The Commonwealth* editorialized, "The Indians of our national domain have once more asserted their purpose not to be deprived of their rights, solemnly guaranteed to them by treaty, without resistance even to blood." It was not an incident of native perfidy or savagery: "we are the aggressors, and the Indians stung to madness by our treachery, and our duplicity, feeling doubtless that it is a fight for existence, have turned upon our soldiers, and with cunning and hardihood combined, have dared everything in an unequal contest." (The discovery of gold had led settlers to "swarm" the Black Hills in violation of prevailing treaties.) *The Commonwealth* castigated the federal government for simultaneously trying to pressure the Lakota into selling the hills while warning intruders away. In the end, though, "it seems to us that the whole American people, who have been indifferent to the injustices towards Indians, are morally responsible."

Tragically, "Custer's Last Stand" turned out to be the last stand of the Lakota to preserve their hard-won lands. While Grant, at least, recognized Custer's military blunder, most Americans were baying for revenge. The federal government forced agency Lakota to sign over claims to most of the Great Sioux Reservation, including the sacred Black Hills, under the threat of withholding rations. Within a year, the army's operations starved nonagency Cheyenne and Lakota into surrender. Crazy Horse was murdered after he had surrendered, due to misunderstandings with army officers and the treachery of Red Cloud's men. Sitting Bull escaped to Canada with what was left of his people, but the dearth of game, as well as the specter of a diplomatic conflict between the United States and Canada, forced him to surrender in 1881. Even though he was promised refuge at the Standing Rock Agency, he was arrested as a prisoner of war. He was finally returned to the reservation two years later. In a bizarre turn of events, he toured the country with Annie Oakley and Buffalo Bill Cody's Wild West show, a sort of Indian minstrel performance. For their part, the Crow, who had scouted for the United States in the war against the Sioux, also found their lands and buffalo herds diminished. In 1884, they were relocated from Yellowstone—which had been converted from indigenous hunting grounds into a national park by the 1872 Yellowstone National Park Protection Act—to the Crow agency on the Little Big Horn River.[11]

The destruction of indigenous sovereignty in the West, through sustained military campaigns, settler incursions, and the construction of transcontinental railroads, culminated in the Nez Perce war of 1877, the last major conflict of the era. The war with the Nez Perce (Nimiipuu)—the French name given to them for their pierced noses—began in familiar fashion. The Nez Perce had coexisted with European settlers and missionaries for nearly one hundred years, even befriending Meriwether Lewis and William Clark when their expedition reached the Pacific Northwest in 1805. By midcentury, some Nez Perce chiefs had signed a treaty, ratified in 1855, that gave away large portions of their lands to the United States. An 1863 treaty that confined them to a tiny area was especially egregious, nothing short of theft, with many "non-treaty" Nez Perce bands refusing to sign on to it. Confusion over borders, and mass migration fueled by yet another prospective gold rush, stoked violence between the Nez Perce and settlers. Many Nez Perce, calling themselves "Dreamers," sought comfort from a new, prophetic Indian religion, and were looked upon with suspicion by local authorities. Then, in June 1877, a settler murdered a Nez Perce, and the crime went unpunished. The act and the lack of consequences led to violent retaliation by some young Nez Perce men, officially launching the war.

Most Americans adopted a narrative of "inverted conquest," to borrow a term from the historian Richard White, describing how the victims were represented as the perpetrators. Nontreaty Nez Perce like "Chief Joseph" (Heinmot Tooyalakekt) resisted being sent to reservations into which the army was ordered to literally herd the "hostile" Indians. The man in charge of the operation was Gen. O. O. Howard of the Freedmen's Bureau; no longer working to uplift freedpeople in the South, he was now overseeing a program to "civilize" indigenous people. The "Christian General" had no doubts about the morality of his mission and the need to bring "civilization" and Christianity to Indians, as his tone-deaf attempts to force the nontreaty Nez Perce into compliance

revealed. For months, the Nez Perce, even though they were outnumbered and outgunned, eluded capture, leading Howard into Montana
territory and defeating detachments of the army. They barely missed
Sherman, who was visiting Yellowstone.

The Nez Perce had been forced to abandon their homeland, and their
prior strategy of peaceful coexistence with settlers had definitively
failed. In Montana, they encountered Col. Nelson Miles, who was determined to prevent their escape to Canada and a prospective alliance with
Sitting Bull. With Howard and his troops closing in, too, Chief Joseph
finally surrendered, saying, "From where the sun now stands, I will
fight no more." In return, he secured a promise to be returned to his
Idaho home. At least one-third of the Nez Perce did manage to escape
to Canada, but with no means to sustain themselves, some returned.
Joseph and his followers were exiled to what was, for them, the terribly hot Indian territory in Oklahoma, far from the natural beauty and
cooler weather of their home. More Nez Perce, especially the most vulnerable, including babies and children, died in captivity in the Southwest. Joseph, though, became something of an American celebrity for
his fortitude. He would use his newfound fame to eventually lead some
of his people back to the Northwest, to the Colville reservation in Washington. In 2021, the scattered Nez Perce bought 148 acres in their ancestral home and rode back into it in traditional regalia.

The Civil War has been called an "irrepressible conflict," and the
American wars against indigenous nations are often viewed in the same
terms. The conquest of the West after the war, though, was not inevitable. Nor did it represent the mindless expansion of a newly empowered nation-state and proto-empire. As even the most adept proponent
of the modern thesis that the reconstruction of the West was a part
of the Reconstruction of the South admits, "the two missions grated
against each other." (Of course, Reconstruction was hardly a "mission"
launched by the North; its essential protagonists were freedpeople.)
While many Republicans, especially breakaway Liberal Republicans,
supported the Indian wars, the main military actions took place as
Reconstruction started to wind down—as southern Republicans were
forced out of office, including through intimidation and terrorism. It is

the counterrevolution against Reconstruction, rather than Reconstruction itself, that mirrors the wars against the Indians. That said, the very same US Army, as the military careers of men like Sheridan and Howard illustrate, used by the federal government to protect freedpeople's rights, was deployed to violently dispossess Native American nations in the West. Ely Parker's Reconstruction vision of the US Army protecting freedpeople's rights in the South and Indian land rights in the West never came to pass; both were overthrown.

The conquest of the West coincided with the long unwinding of Reconstruction in the South, with the army steadily reduced in size and withdrawn from one theater and sent to the other. White supremacy and racist terror triumphed in the South and West simultaneously. We can go further: the revanchist South won the nation and the West and blazed the path to empire. Some prominent army officers, such as Nelson Miles, who earned their spurs in the Indian wars, would fight in the wars of American imperialism. A few outliers would become champions of indigenous claims, having witnessed firsthand the injustice of American aims and actions in the West. Abolitionists remained among the small minority of Americans who could not help but compare the massacres of freedpeople in the South with the Indian massacres in the West by settlers and the army.[12] Indians, whether they fought against or alongside the United States, like freedpeople engaged in a much longer struggle to retain their rights and cultural identity even after dispossession, one that continues to this day and will continue into the future.

Indigenous nations in the West were defeated and forced onto reservations by the end of the century. The Apache and the Sioux—perhaps the two most formidable military powers among the western Indians then—put up a strong resistance. The 1871 surrender of the Chiricahua Apache leader Cochise unraveled when the government tried to put his people on a reservation in New Mexico. The next year, they agreed to live on a reservation in Arizona. But warfare erupted again after the Chiricahua Apache were moved to San Carlos reservation, which had a record of abuse and substandard rations, at around the same time as the war against the Nez Perce, 1876–1877. Their last battles saw Geronimo, a Chiricahua Apache medicine man, commanding a little more than thirty warriors against the US Army during a ten-year period. He had long fought Mexicans, who had killed his family, and Americans. In his last years of resistance, Geronimo, who refused to be confined to a reservation, was joined by the generally pacific Naiche, Cochise's son, who turned away from the US government due to its bad faith. In 1886, Geronimo surrendered to Nelson Miles, now a general. Along with twenty-seven of his followers, Geronimo was exiled by Grover Cleveland, the first Democratic president after the Civil War, to Florida. Only 540 Chiricahua survived, their numbers thinned by nearly 60 percent. Geronimo was imprisoned and eventually sent to Fort Sill in Oklahoma. He never saw his homeland again. But with President Theodore Roosevelt's blessing—even though Roosevelt was an imperialist and no friend to indigenous people—he got the last word, dictating a memoir that can still be read today.

The fall of the Lakota followed the loss of Apacheria. And the man responsible was, again, General Miles (Indians called him Bear Coat), who led thousands of troops to stamp out the Ghost Dance, a new

"Geronimo,"
by A. F. Randall
Wilcox, A.T.
Library of Congress

religion and social movement spreading among the Lakota. In 1889, Congress had carved the Great Sioux reservation into five separate agencies, appropriating nearly eleven million acres from the Lakota. That same year, Wovoka, a Paiute medicine man in Nevada, also known as Jack Wilson, had a vision of an indigenous, Jesus-like messiah that spread among the Plains Indians. A syncretic mix of Christianity and Indian religion, the Ghost Dance was performed to hasten an apocalyptic event when whites would disappear and the native dead would be resurrected. The religion was adopted among those living in the Lakota agencies, who made it their own after sending emissaries to Wovoka, alarming American agents and settlers. (Just a few years earlier an agent had suppressed the practice of the Sun Dance at the Pine Ridge agency by threatening to withhold rations, and worse.)

For the Sioux confined to reservations and at the mercy of mostly corrupt and incompetent agents, the Ghost Dance provided succor. The Lakota Ghost Dancers wore Ghost shirts and dresses, which they believed would protect them, as they danced to bring the onset of the millennium. (Their belief was comparable to that of the rebels in the 1900 Boxer Rebellion in China, who believed they would be immune to foreign weapons.) Miles surrounded the reservations with his troops, planning to arrest the Ghost Dance leaders, including Sitting Bull. When the agent at Standing Rock, James McLaughlin, who had married a woman of mixed Indian heritage, sent Indian Police to arrest Sitting Bull, the Hunkpapa chief was shot in a melee, distressing all the Lakota bands across the different agencies. McLaughlin fashioned himself a friend of indigenous people and dedicated his memoir thus: "To My Friend the Indian whose good parts survive as a monument over the graves of a vanishing race." In "displacing" Indians, he claimed settlers had carried out "the immutable law of the survival of the fittest."

But the worst was yet to come. Fleeing Hunkpapa Lakota had joined the Minneconjou Lakota led by the severely ill Big Foot, who were on their way to the Pine Ridge agency to broker peace. Miles, though, was convinced that they were poised to launch an attack. Big Foot's band was intercepted by an army detachment commanded by Maj. Samuel Whitside of the Seventh Cavalry, who ordered them to Wounded Knee Creek, where they set up camp. Whitside asked for reinforcements from Pine Ridge to guard the camp. Col. James W. Forsyth of the Second Battalion of the Seventh Cavalry, who styled themselves "Custer's Avengers," took over from Whitside, and on December 29, 1890, confiscated rifles from the Minneconjou, most of which were old and worthless. The forcible search and disarming led to a confused shoot-out after a deaf Lakota man, Black Coyote, refused to hand over his gun. The army trained their recently invented Hotchkiss machine guns at the Lakota, firing indiscriminately, and hunting down and mercilessly killing those trying to escape. Around three hundred Lakota, a majority fleeing women and children, were massacred or injured at Wounded Knee. Big Foot would die with his people, his body frozen like theirs after a blizzard. Twenty-five American soldiers were killed, some from friendly fire, and over thirty wounded. If a few Lakota men had not fought back and fired at their attackers, the carnage would have been worse. Most of the dead were dumped and buried in a mass grave days later, in early January. The remaining Lakota chiefs met with the commissioner of Indian Affairs in February 1891 in Washington, DC and squarely blamed the military for the massacre. As American Horse put it, having been "so loyal" to the government, his "disappointment was very strong," and he had "come to Washington with a very great blame in my heart." He would be almost "grateful" if only the men had been killed, but women and children, especially "young boys and girls who are to go to make up the future strength of the Indian people is the saddest part of the whole affair and we feel it very sorely."

The Ghost Dance movement persisted, retaliatory raids by the Sioux increased in the immediate aftermath of the massacre, and Miles was forced to broker peace with the Lakota. There had been no Lakota uprising, as he had feared; instead, many of them were murdered in an unprovoked attack. Twenty of the perpetrators of the massacre received Medals of Honor. While a military commission investigated Forsyth's actions at Miles's urging, the former was absolved of any wrongdoing and went on to become a general. The ambitious Miles ascended to the position of commander-in-chief of the US Army. The Wounded Knee massacre did not signal the end of the Lakota—far from it—but it did mark the end of their predominance. Their rise on the western plains had paralleled that of the American republic. In 1973, the American Indian Movement occupied Wounded Knee, using its potent moral symbolism to demand native sovereignty and rights. The Lakota persist as a people today. Since 1990, the centennial of the Wounded Knee massacre, they have reenacted Big Foot's tragic last journey in an annual memorial ride.

In the early twentieth century, the Mount Rushmore monument, bearing the gigantic faces of George Washington, Thomas Jefferson, Abraham Lincoln, and Theodore Roosevelt, was carved into the sacred Paha Sapa (Black Hills). Initially, the massive sculptures were meant to include Red Cloud, Sacagawea, and Crazy Horse as well. But the sculptor commissioned to carve Mount Rushmore, Gutzon Borglum, conceived of it as a tribute to American democracy and as epitomizing the triumph over the Lakota. Borglum was also hired for the initial work on the Stone Monument memorial to Confederate leaders in Georgia, which was funded, in part, by the Ku Klux Klan, and completed only in the 1970s. Together, the two monuments memorialize the simultaneous conquest of the West and the overthrow of Reconstruction. In 1980, the Supreme Court ordered the government to compensate the Sioux nations for its use of Paha Sapa, taken illegally and in violation of the Fort Laramie Treaty. The original amount, $100 million, has now grown to over $1 billion—yet it lies unclaimed because the Sioux refuse to relinquish their claim to the sacred hills.[13] The colonial legacies of the subjugation of indigenous nations live on in our times.

The conquest of the West must be viewed not only in relation to the Civil War or Reconstruction but also as a central episode in the larger global history of Western imperialism in the late nineteenth century. In the American West, US soldiers gained experience in putting down native peoples abroad—experience they would rely on in colonial actions beyond North America. The "Buffalo Soldiers," the name Native Americans gave black soldiers serving in the army, are a particularly complex example. They were involved in the Indian wars and, later, wars of empire in Cuba and the Philippines. For all their excellence, they were constantly reminded of their subordinate position, were given inferior provisions and harder assignments than their white counterparts, and faced harsher punitive discipline by military authorities. Despite gaining some redress for systemic inequalities in pay and rank during the Civil War, African American soldiers continued to face discrimination within the armed forces.

Like colonial powers all over the world, the US government exercised its authority over indigenous nations and reservations with native collaboration. The Bureau of Indian Affairs developed new techniques for controlling indigenous people, short of war. They turned to native troops and the dreaded Indian police on reservations.[14] The strategies of fostering native collaboration and developing policing regimes were deployed by European imperial powers at around the same time. In these ways, the United States was as much a colonial power as any Western European country when it came to indigenous people on reservations. From wars of conquest to peacetime strategies to "pacify" native populations, US imperialism shared common tactics and goals with European colonial regimes in Africa and Asia.

For indigenous peoples, "peace" did not mean an end to the onslaught against their religions and cultures, or an end to dependence and poverty on reservations. Under Grant's policies, the missionaries and Quakers who were appointed to positions previously held by corrupt officials moved to convert and educate Indians, a supposedly benevolent program to "civilize" and remake them into Christians. After the collapse of the peace policy, things got worse. The BIA bureaucracy came to reflect the civil service reform championed by Liberal Republicans like Secretary of the Interior Carl Schurz. The new Indian service "reformers" continued the campaign to stamp out native spiritual practices such as the Sun Dance and the Ghost Dance movements. Any traditional customs deemed "heathen" or "savage" were disallowed on pain of starvation, deprivation, and withheld annuities.

Missionary schools on reservations, the first of which were established in the early nineteenth century, gave way to a system of boarding and day schools that acted as "reeducation centers" for indigenous children, who were forcibly taken or cajoled from their parents. At the Indian schools, they were renamed, had their hair cut, were forced to wear western clothing or uniforms, made to speak only English, subjected to corporal punishment, made to labor for their alleged benefactors, and required to adhere to a strict, military-like daily routine. Some were rescued by their parents, a few tried to flee, and many died in the schools. Settler women were often involved in these colonial projects, as they "mothered" native children and gained authority at the cost of indigenous women and families. These schools had counterparts in other settler colonial societies, Canada and Australia. The recent discoveries of mass graves at the sites of some of these schools is testimony to the history of cultural, sexual, and physical abuse and deprivation borne by indigenous children kidnapped from their homes and communities.

The model for these schools was the original Indian military-style boarding school, founded by Capt. Richard Henry Pratt in Carlisle, Pennsylvania in 1879. Pratt practiced his "educational" techniques, appropriately enough, as jailor at Fort Marion, Florida before he converted the military barracks at Carlisle into his Indian industrial school. His main goal was, speaking of Indians, "any course towards them which tends to their civilization." Pratt sent his first students to Hampton Institute but soon came to the conclusion that it was not good "to unite the two race problems" and that Indians needed "fellowship with the whites, and not with the negro" for their "civilization."

Pratt won over Secretary of the Interior Schurz, Congress, and General Sherman, who at first dismissed his school as "old woman's work" but came to endorse the idea of "educating" Indian boys and girls. Journeying to the Sioux reservations at Rosebud, Pine Ridge and elsewhere, Pratt convinced indigenous leaders into sending their children to his school. He told Spotted Tail that he would not have been deceived when signing a treaty had he been literate. (Eventually Spotted Tail rescued his children from Carlisle, one of whom had been subjected to harsh corporal punishment for an infraction.) Pratt believed individual allotment of lands and education to Indians should lead to "tribal disintegration and individuality" and assimilation. One of Pratt's primary supporters was Massachusetts senator Henry Dawes, chairman of the Indian Senate Committee.

Pratt dismissed reports of abuse at his school as the "stories of its alleged graduates, which were false in every particular, the names, locations and acts being without any foundation in fact." But he was forced to admit that many students sought to escape and had to be "brought back" or "sent back." He started placing students outside the school as child laborers, using the euphemism of "the outing" and calling the program a "great success." In his brutal system, Indian students were allowed to go home only once every three years, and later, only once in five years. Pratt smarted from the criticisms of "missionaries" and "ethnologists" who disapproved of his single-minded determination to stamp out indigenous culture, and who argued that "separation of children from parents was cruel." But he remained defiant: "Do not feed America to the Indian, which is a tribalizing and not an Americanizing process, but feed the Indian to America, and America will do the assimilating and annihilate the problem."

The militarized Indian schools were far removed from the still relatively new freedmen's schools in the South, and, for that matter, from the public school system established in early America to create an educated citizenry. They were centers of cultural terror, resembling more than anything else colonial education projects in countries such as British India. Pratt's British counterpart was the staunch imperialist Thomas Babington Macaulay, who claimed that a bookshelf of Western learning was worth more than thousands of years of education in the "orient." Pratt's aphorism, "kill the Indian, save the man," echoed Macaulay's recommendation to create "a class of persons, Indian in blood and colour, but English in taste, in opinions, in morals, and in intellect."[15]

American courts also played a role in the "pacification" that followed the military defeat of indigenous nations. The courts' stance on Indian sovereignty was contradictory. In *Standing Bear v. Crook* (1879), the US District Court in Omaha, Nebraska ordered the release of a Ponca chief named Standing Bear—who had been arrested by Gen. George Crook, on Schurz's orders, for returning to his home to bury his son after the forced expulsion of the Poncas to Indian territory—on a writ of habeas corpus. The district court ruled that Standing Bear was entitled to all the protections of the law and the Constitution. But the Supreme Court ruled in *Ex Parte Crow Dog* (1883) that the government did not have the power to prosecute crime on Indian reservations when Crow Dog, a Brule Sioux involved with the Ghost Dance, was prosecuted for the murder of Spotted Tail, the Lakota chief who accommodated his people to American rule to preserve them.

Such was the legal flexibility of imperialism. In 1885, Congress passed the Major Crimes Act, which brought serious crimes in Indian country under federal jurisdiction. More consequential was Senator Dawes's severalty, or allotment, act, which President Grover Cleveland signed into law in 1887. It gave the president plenary power to dispose of and divide Indian land into individual allotments and leave the rest open to settlement. It furthered the coercive assimilationist program by making Indians into individual property holders, farmers, and ranchers, while stealing most of their lands for settlers as well as mining and railroad corporations.

The Dawes Act paved the way for dispossession even in Indian territory, which was inhabited by "assimilated" and "civilized" native nations. Between 1885 and 1889, settlers were allowed to buy "unassigned" lands or lands not assigned to any nation in Indian territory, even though land grabs in this area had begun earlier. In 1889, Congress formally opened the "unassigned lands" to non-Indian settlement according to the provisions of the Homestead Act of 1862, setting off a land run. The next year these lands became incorporated as Oklahoma territory. The Dawes Commission and the 1898 Curtis Act divided the rest of Indian territory among individual Indian households, terminating tribal sovereignty among the "five civilized tribes," which had long before adopted individual property ownership as well as English education, Western government, and Christianity. By the turn of the century, most indigenous nations, including those sent to the increasingly crowded Indian territory, had lost two-thirds of their lands to settlement, and even those that had received individual allotments were easily defrauded of their deeds by unscrupulous settlers. In 1907, Oklahoma entered the Union as a state. After decades of dispossession and loss of sovereignty, Native Americans received the "reward" of US citizenship in 1924, having been mostly excluded from the civil and political rights of citizenship during Reconstruction as "Indians not taxed."

It would not be until the Indian Reorganization Act, or "the Indians' New Deal," in 1934 and the Indian Self-Determination and Education Assistance Act of 1975 that native nations began to regain some of their lost sovereignty. However uneven, the decolonization of Indian country, spurred in modern times by the American Indian Movement, paralleled similar processes in Asia and Africa after the Second World War.

Like their counterparts in other colonized places, indigenous people nevertheless managed to resist *within* colonial institutions. Many graduates of the Indian schools joined the Indian civil service, gaining access to employment and helping to negotiate the chasm between native needs and the government's goals. Often agents and officials in the Indian service, especially women, were paid less than whites and posted far from their homes, but many nevertheless became champions of the people they served. The practice of native officeholders mediating indigenous interests and cultures is common in colonial societies. The bureaucratic and institutional structures of the government allow not only for systemic administrative control, but also for colonized people to use it for their own ends. Like colonized people in Asia and Africa, and African Americans in the United States, Native Americans have also served in the armed forces in greater percentages than their numbers in the American population. In 2021, Deb Haaland became the first Native American to serve as US secretary of the interior.[16]

While freedpeople fought to become equal citizens, indigenous nations sought to retain their sovereignty. Even the "friends of Indians" spoke from a colonial viewpoint, seeking to incorporate people that did not wish to be a part of the nation-state. Some abolitionists, outraged as they were by the treatment of Indians, came up with "solutions" that involved Native Americans' loss of sovereignty and their being encompassed into the vision of national citizenship and interracial democracy. One writer in the *National Anti-Slavery Standard* recommended in 1870, "The time has come to recognize in the Indian not an outlaw and an alien, but a human being with human rights in common with other people in this country; to make him a citizen, and give him protection due to citizenship, and in turn require of him the same obedience that is extracted from others." In an editorial response to a letter from A. J. Grover, a western settler, who had advocated a "military" solution to the "Indian Problem," the newspaper asserted: "For the sake of the white race, as well as the Indian, we oppose the policy of extermination. We trust the time will come when the whites can live amicably with negroes, Indians and the Chinese." In 1880, Senator Blanche Bruce of Mississippi, who also opposed Chinese exclusion, called for a reversal of federal Indian policy, "not to exterminate them but perpetuate them in this continent." Yet he envisioned their recognition as equal citizens, deeming their mistreatment an affront to Reconstruction's progressive constitutionalism.

Before the Civil War, abolitionists protested the expulsion of the five Indian nations in the Southeast along the trail of tears and the Seminole wars as a dual assault on Indians and fugitive slaves (many of whom were Seminoles). Some indigenous leaders such as William Apess and John Ross, even though the latter problematically was a large slaveholder, tried to make common cause with abolitionists. A number of Afro-native and Native abolitionists have also been misidentified or designated as simply "black." In the 1850s, John Beeson exposed settler atrocities and the cruelties of Indian wars in Oregon and California in his self-published *A Plea for the Indians*, converting many abolitionists to the "Indian's cause." The Native American, he wrote, "from the very moment the White Man set his foot upon our shores, has been constantly the subject of monopoly and wrong, in every shape in which the over-bearing and all-engrossing spirit of our people could suggest." Seeing indigenous people reduced to starvation and beggary, he argued that at the very least, the government owed them the necessities to sustain themselves: "surely it would be but a poor return for the lands which we have deprived them." He described the warfare against Indians in the West as "deliberate massacre" and "murder in its most aggravating and revolting form." Since everything that Indians did in "self-defense" was publicized as "savage barbarism," he took it upon himself to "state a few things that have been done against them by those who claim to be superiors." As he explained: in California and Oregon, the same settlers who think government was made only for "white male American citizens" and who tried to "keep down the 'N——'," thought nothing of exterminating indigenous people, enslaving their children, and abusing their women.

Despite his obvious sympathies, Beeson viewed Indians as a mass of victims rather than as members of distinct nations that had ruled the continent for generations and resisted their subjugation in a variety of ways. Yet he saw himself as different from those missionaries who assumed "superiority over heathens" and who were just as complicit as any other Indian haters or killers, in his estimation. While indigenous people had acted with discretion and mainly on the defensive, "professedly Christian" settlers moved with murderous intent. Such are the "White Savages of our Border Settlements," Beeson wrote. The cruel subjugation of the western Indians, he predicted, was part of global, imperialist warfare. "Every departure from the fundamental principles of Right, must influence, with more or less direct power all of human society. Central America and the Isles of the sea are made to feel it; and the massacre in Panama, and the war in Oregon, are some of its legitimate results." The American republic had become a "many-headed monster" that enacted "the petty despotism of home tyrants." He recommended, somewhat paternalistically, "Let us heed the dumb remonstrances that come to us, and avowed defenders of Human Rights, from all the oppressed Races of Mankind, and learn conciliation and justice." While not completely immune to civilizationist discourse himself, Beeson repeatedly made the case for native sovereignty, until his death in 1889.[17]

For her part, the abolitionist Lydia Maria Child had high hopes for a more "enlightened and liberal" policy toward Indians after the Civil War. She asked, in an adept reversal, whether "the Anglo-Saxon race are capable of civilization." In *An Appeal for the Indians* (1868), modeled after her abolitionist classic, *An Appeal on behalf of that Class of Americans whom we call Africans* (1833), she argued that "The white and Indian must jointly occupy the country, or one of them must abandon it. If they could have lived together, the Indian would have been civilized, and war prevented." Child recommended education and "civilization"

for Indians, even as she mounted a critique of the latter idea: "Civilization has driven him away from the home he loved; it has tortured and
killed him; but it could never make him a slave. Considering we have so
little respect for those we did enslave, we ought, for consistency's sake,
to admire this element of Indian character." The comparison to enslaved
people was based on the myth of the noble savage; she did not take into
account the centuries of enslavement and ongoing servitude suffered by
indigenous people. At the same time, Child objected to forcing Indians
to learn English and to embrace American culture. That program, she
argued, "partakes too much of our haughty Anglo-Saxon ideas of force."
(Child's first iconoclastic novel, *Hobomok* [1824], depicted an interracial
romance between an Indian man and an American woman set in colonial New England.)

Child's pamphlet was torn between recommending a paternalistic
care for Native Americans and condemning the "civilization" foisted
on them. Why couldn't they learn English voluntarily, she wonders, by
relating their "own traditionary stories" and the "honorable" history of
their own braves and chiefs, a suggestion that recalled her account of
African American history and literature in *The Freedmen's Book* (1865).
Child's contradictions were typical of abolitionists. At her best, she
could be properly scathing, and sound almost like a modern historian:
"The plain truth is, our relations with red and black members of the
human family have been one almost unvaried history of violence and
fraud." As she concluded, "But I think the time has come, without inter-
mitting our vigilant watch over the rights of black men, it is our duty to
arouse the nation to a sense of guilt concerning the red man."

The writer Helen Hunt Jackson gained greater renown than Child as
a champion of Indian rights and as a one-woman critic of the government's Indian policy. Jackson is best known for her novel *Ramona* (1884)
and the nonfiction work, *A Century of Dishonor* (1881), both devoted to
exposing the oppression of Indians. Jackson's advocacy was inspired
by Standing Bear, whom she heard speak in Boston in 1879. For years,
she deluged government officials and newspaper editors with letters
describing the plight of Native Americans and lobbying for a change in
Indian policy. Jackson was less interested in stopping assimilation than

she was in Indian land rights and the treaty obligations of the US government. While *A Century of Dishonor* did not turn out to be the *Uncle Tom's Cabin* of the Native American cause, as she had hoped, it was influential enough that historians today feel obligated to clarify that it is not accurate history, but a polemic against land robbery.[18]

Activists for Indian rights followed Beeson, Child, and especially Jackson in defending indigenous sovereignty, culture, and land. In 1885, the Quaker physician Dr. Thomas A. Bland and his wife Dr. Cora Bland founded the National Indian Defense Association that strongly opposed the Dawes Act, which they saw as a thin pretext for land appropriation. A friend of Alfred Meacham, Bland and his wife took over editing duties of his Indian advocacy journal, *Council Fire,* in which they published native leaders and writers. A true radical, Bland supported the cause of labor and farmers in industrializing America. An antimonopolist and critic of concentrated wealth, he supported the Greenback-Labor and Populist Parties and published a biography of the radical Benjamin Butler in 1879. Like Parker, Bland argued that the federal government should protect rather than despoil Indian land and sovereignty. Unlike Pratt, Bland advocated a liberal arts rather than an industrial education for Indians that would be voluntary rather than coercive. One of his allies was the abolitionist officer Samuel Tappan, who had sought to punish the perpetrators of the Sand Creek massacre of 1864. Carolina Weldon, who was determined to prevent the government from stealing more land from the Great Sioux Reservation and became personal secretary to Sitting Bull, was a member of Bland's organization. Agent James McLaughlin thought her a bad influence for encouraging him to follow the Ghost Dance movement, but she actually predicted that the government would use it as an excuse to attack the Lakota and steal more of their lands.

Bland, Weldon, Jackson, and other activists for Indians like the journalist Charles Lummis, must be distinguished from the more conservative Indian reformers and missionaries, who acted as the handmaiden of American imperialism, as such people often did in the history of European imperialism. Many so-called "Indian reformers" were responsible for some of the federal government's most disastrous assimilation policies. Some, such as Samuel C. Armstrong, the son of missionaries in Hawaii, who led black troops during the Civil War but deplored black voting and promoted industrial education at Hampton Institute, and Clinton Fisk, who had worked in the Freedmen's Bureau and endowed Fisk University, and had been appointed by Grant to the Board of Indian Commissioners, tried their hand at black education before getting involved in Indian reform. Herbert Welsh, William Welsh's nephew, of the ironically named "Indian Rights Association," argued for the severalty law, compulsory education of indigenous children, and the subjection of Native Americans to civil law. Like Armstrong, most "reformers" believed that nonwhite peoples should be kept in strict tutelage to become "civilized." Even some of the most sympathetic Indian reformers like Bishop Henry Whipple believed in acculturation.

When it came to missionaries, it wasn't only Protestants who had a history of abusive behavior toward Native Americans. Franciscan and Jesuit missions in the Southwest and California had forced conversions and abused indigenous people going back to Junipero Serra in the eighteenth century and earlier. Men and women of all Christian denominations worked hand in glove with settlers toward the broader aims: the dispossession of Indian nations and the destruction of indigenous cultural and religious life. Even some Quakers were little different. The Quaker teacher Thomas Battey wrote of the "detestable howlings" of Indian women, the "demoniac forms" of Indian dances, and their "hideous masks" and "wild orgies." He proclaimed, "they must be changed, if changed they ever are, from this savage, heathen life to that of Christian civilization." Battey's blunt racism aligned perfectly with that of settlers.[19] The regressive reformers far outnumbered the progressive ones.

The regressive reformers and the critique of Reconstruction and "big government" leveled by settlers, a line of attack tied to racist views of freedpeople and indigenous people, carried the West, and the day. Writing from Arkansas City, where he ventured for another one of his schemes, settler Daniel Grant sent his wife Caroline a poem he transcribed from a local newspaper that, as he put it, "expresses the simple truth":

I want to be an Indian
An Arapahoe or Ute
I'm tired of being a white man
An unprotected brute
I want to be an Indian
A Ward of Government
It's the biggest thing in America
Except the President
I want to be an Indian
A warrior on the Plains
I want to wield a tomahawk
And scoop out people's brains
I want to build a campfire
On a human being's breast
And watch his writhing agony
With a noble savage zest
. . . .
I want to be an Indian
An Apache or Cheyenne
I want to bid defiantly
To the laws of man
When I do a bit of arson
Murder tragedy or rape
I want to know I have a friend
At Washington—Red Tape

The well-circulated 1872 poem, whose author remains anonymous, had an interesting afterlife. It was published in various forms in several western newspapers including, for example, *The Colorado Miner* and the Arkansas newspaper that Daniel read. By the early twentieth century, it was possibly performed under the title "I Want to be an Indian," by African Americans in theaters in Baltimore and Philadelphia, where one observer noted that "the colored actors and actresses comprising the company were especially capable in impersonating the members of the Blackfoot Indian tribe."

"If I Were an Indian" personified the poisonous mixture of racism and antigovernment feeling that most settlers subscribed to, even as they of course benefitted from the federal government's actions in "clearing" land for settlement, in dividing "public lands" into homesteads, and in spending huge sums on land improvement and irrigation to make the West hospitable to ranching and farming. Settlers bemoaned the paltry annuities for Native Americans and celebrated their own success. As Daniel Grant complained to his wife, "They say it is wrong to crowd the Indian. Give him the country to roam over it is his. Let him alone they say. If this had been the policy in years gone by where would be our country now." He thanked God for sending a "pestilence" to clear Massachusetts for his forebears. The poem, Daniel wrote, woke him up to the government's Indian policy, but he could not be bothered about it too much, he concluded, as he had staked claims on two homesteads (courtesy of the federal government), one in Arkansas City, the other in Kansas. He gave voice, though, to a politics that would be honed to perfection in the South and the West, and that would come to form the foundation of modern political conservatism in the United States. That particular brand of reactionary politics, full of antigovernment and imagined racial grievances, is one legacy that southern slaveholders and western settlers left to the nation.[20]

The end of the nineteenth century was as much a nadir in Native American history as it was in African American history. Freedpeople were systematically locked out of the promise of citizenship and rights, after enjoying both briefly during Reconstruction, even as the conquest of the West was completed and native sovereignty destroyed. The fact that indigenous people persisted in these circumstances is a testimony to their endurance, survival, and resistance, rather than to the efforts of their alleged friends and enemies. Now, with its subjugated and excluded peoples of color, the United States would adopt the habits of empire at home and abroad even more readily. With the triumph of industrial capital, the end of the century also represented the nadir for all American workers.

CHAPTER TEN

The Reign of Capital

Equally out of place and absurd is the argument that
capital will pay only what it pleases, and labor must submit. This is slavery. . . . Saying to such men that "You
shall have no voice in fixing your wages, and you shall
take what is offered to you or starve," is slavery.

—WENDELL PHILLIPS, 1877

"Wendell Phillips," *The Irish World*, November 3, 1877.

American Antiquarian Society

The American thermidor started in the South but extended to the entire nation and across the continent. Starting around 1870, the Industrial Revolution took off in the United States, replicating the rise of industrial capitalism in Britain earlier. By the end of the First World War, the United States emerged as the foremost industrial power in the world, overtaking Britain. This fifty-year period also witnessed the mass emigration of southern and eastern Europeans to the United States, and the accelerated proletarianization of the American working class. By the end of the nineteenth century, nearly half of the American workforce was foreign-born. Immigrant contract labor—from Europe, Mexico, and Asia—fueled nativism in the post-Reconstruction era.

The deskilling of workers by rapid mechanization and growth of the factory system, as well as the commercialization of agriculture, which impoverished farmers, put most Americans under the control of capital: railroads, banks, and large corporations. The small producer—the backbone of a free labor economy and the antislavery Republican Party—became increasingly obsolete in the new economic order of industrial capitalism. Before the Civil War, both the slave and free states were predominantly agrarian. After it, heavy industry started dominating the national political economy even though agriculture also contributed to the nation's rapid economic ascent.[1]

As Reconstruction waned in the late nineteenth century, the reign of capital and the dominance of robber barons, a monied aristocracy, began. With industry and those who controlled it becoming more and more powerful, protests by wage workers, many of whom toiled in subhuman conditions, and those whose lives were upended by the financial Panic of 1873 and the ensuing long depression, increased in frequency and size. New movements opposed the growth of monopolistic corporations that dominated large sectors of the economy. The postbellum status quo was challenged by the Greenback Party; the Grange and the Populist Movement, which represented farmers; unions in industries powering the Industrial Revolution; and new Workingmen's and Labor Reform Parties.

Popular understandings of Reconstruction miss the fact that these events were tied to—indeed, flowed from—the counterrevolution against it.[2] The end of Reconstruction signaled the empowerment of the forces of reaction in most areas of American life, from the economy to politics. Yet the fall of the Second American Republic would be contested, just as its rise had been, and some of its legacies date from its twilight years.

During Reconstruction, Radical Republicans supported pro-labor legislation, as did a few northern Democrats who represented cities with large immigrant working-class populations. Senator George Julian sponsored a bill for an eight-hour working day (many laborers at the time worked from sunrise to sunset). Representative George F. Hoar of Massachusetts proposed a federal labor commission, modeled after state labor commissions and bureaus of labor statistics, to study wages, hours of labor, and profits. It would represent, as he saw it, a continuation of Reconstruction-era state-building and regulatory policies. Benjamin Butler, who would eventually join the Greenback Party, supported a shorter workday and other demands of labor. The high point of Radical Republicans' labor policy was the passage of an eight-hour day law in 1868 for federal workers; Julian was a sponsor.

Radical Republicans and their small number of Democratic allies on labor issues were opposed by conservative Democrats and Liberal Republicans—the same political coalition that brought about the downfall of Reconstruction—who were set against government activism, except when it came to conquering the West or protecting the interests of corporations. Liberal Republicans, whose views came to dominate the party, criticized the push for an eight-hour day on rigid laissez-faire grounds. While they did not favor vagrancy laws or anything resembling the poor laws of England that forced the poor into workhouses, they believed that workers should be subject to the rule of the free market without any government regulation, even if that meant long hours, unsafe conditions, and starvation wages. Despite executive orders issued by President Grant to implement the 1868 eight-hour day law for

federal workers, his attorney general and the courts interpreted it in a
fashion that made it unenforceable. The eight-hour day did not become
the standard until the twentieth century. Those workers who benefitted from the new laws—some states and cities passed laws modeled on
the federal law—were effectively punished, because their employers
reduced wages for the shorter hours.

In Massachusetts, the pro-labor abolitionist tradition found concrete expression in a state labor commission. The Labor Reform Party
enlisted black and white abolitionists and in 1870 ran Wendell Phillips for the governor's office—the only time he ran for any public office.
The black Republican lawyer and husband of black suffragist and clubwoman Josephine St. Pierre Ruffin, George L. Ruffin, also ran, for
state attorney general. Both made a good showing at the polls against
mainstream Republicans, with Phillips winning 14 percent of the vote,
though they did not win. At the same time, abolitionists did not hesitate
to criticize trade unions of skilled native workers that excluded immigrants, African Americans, and women. They condemned the Franklin
Typographical Society, named after Benjamin Franklin, for excluding
a black printer and introducing "the color-line in Boston." When Benjamin Butler was elected governor on the Greenback-cum-Democratic
ticket in 1883, he appointed Ruffin to a judgeship, making him the first
black judge in the country.

The overthrow of Reconstruction, however, created an opening
for conservatives to forge a national consensus on the rights of workers. Northern states emulated southern states by passing their own
vagrancy laws as well as restrictive voting laws against immigrant workers, making the retreat from the democratic promise of Reconstruction
truly national. The "reconstruction of the North" was marked by the
triumph of industrial capitalism, whose dark underside was the misery
of the working classes, made even more acute by mass unemployment
and drastic cuts in wages after the Panic of 1873.

Workers had understood the revolutionary cast of Reconstruction,
and made citizenship claims in demanding a "living wage" and the
eight-hour day, which had a more expansive meaning to them: eight
hours for work, eight hours for sleep, and eight hours for leisure and

self-improvement. After all, they argued, the health of the republic was dependent on the virtue of its independent citizen workers. With a dash of nativism, their opponents claimed that immigrant workers would spend eight hours not on self-improvement but in tippling houses. In 1866, the eight-hour movement and trade unions formed the National Labor Union (NLU), presided over by William Sylvis of the Iron Molders International Union. The NLU published *The Workingmen's Advocate*. Sylvis proposed the creation of the Labor Reform Party because "The working-people of our nation, white and black, male and female, are sinking to a condition of serfdom."

Many abolitionists still alive supported the eight-hour-day movement. William Lloyd Garrison sent a contribution to the antislavery machinist Ira Steward, another leader of the eight-hour-day movement, writing that his support stemmed from "the same principle which has led me to abhor and oppose the unequalled oppression of the black laborers of the South." Richard Hinton, an associate of the executed abolitionist John Brown, joined Karl Marx's International Workingmen's Association (IWA), which was founded in 1864 in London and supported the eight-hour-day movement. The *National Anti-Slavery Standard* endorsed the platforms of both the NLU and IWA.

When the IWA formed the Social Democratic Workingmen's Party in the United States in 1876, its newspaper adopted the name of the old abolitionist paper, *Emancipator*. Phillips, identified as the "chief among the conquerors of black slavery" and who now "reorganized his soldiery and keeps right on in battle against white slavery," lent his support to the IWA. "White slavery," like "wage slavery," became a common term among labor reformers to describe the oppressive conditions of wage workers, though it was fraught with contradictions, since it was based on the assumption that the American working class was only white.

The fight for American democracy after the fall of Reconstruction was led by mostly workers and farmers, the latter reduced to sharecropping, tenancy, and debt peonage in the South. As the historian David Montgomery pointed out, "Thaddeus Stevens's aspiration for a community, 'freed from every vestige of human oppression,' jettisoned by a nation in frantic pursuit of wealth, were left in trust to its labor movement." Labor reformers attempted to abolish the exploitative wage work of the new industrial era, in much the same way abolitionists had confronted slavery. If the early labor movement borrowed the language of abolition in its fight against "wage slavery," abolitionists also borrowed ideas from the labor movement, calling southern secession a "Rebellion of Capital against labor" and "an effort of the slave-driving capitalists to enslave the labor of the entire nation . . . *white as well as black.*" One antislavery writer noted that the newly minted "great millionaires" were "contrary to the genius of American institutions." He recommended that "a wider and more generous distribution of so large an estate would accord much better with the general sense of mankind."

The leaders of industrial capitalism and southern reaction saw otherwise. Most workers found themselves in unhealthy and unsafe sites of large-scale industrial production, such as mining and railroad construction. Increasingly, labor reformers, like freedpeople, spoke of the "rights of children" to education and against abusive child labor. Low wages, unsanitary conditions, and nonexistent safety standards rendered workers expendable cogs in an industrial machine controlled by a few railroad and manufacturing magnates and their corporations. Workers called the railroad corporations, which acquired mines and factories, "oppressive monopolies," the result of "the concentration of capital in the hands of a few monopolies."

Railroad construction spiked in the 1870s, and by 1900, the total length of track in the country had more than quadrupled from 45,000 to over 200,000 miles. The railroad corporations funneled stocks, cash, and perks to politicians from both parties and lobbied them for land and bonds, spurring corruption and hobbling representative government. The Pacific railroads alone, wrote labor advocate E. T. Peters, received over 124 million acres in the West from the government. The "unoccupied public domain," he argued, was the "common heritage" of humans and not of "land monopolists." In his view, American society would soon resemble aristocratic societies in Europe. But this intrepid critic of the great land grab by railroads did not say a word about indigenous dispossession.

"Frauds in railroad management" were particularly rife and became worse after the financial collapse of 1873 and the depression that followed. Even a writer sympathetic to the railroads noted that, "The condition of business for the last three or four years has severely taxed the resources of our best railroad companies, while those which have suffered from bad management are resorting to various methods of throwing their burdens upon the public." Why should the American people pay for the losses of railroads—losses that represented the people's money in the first place, transferred to the railroads through federal subsidies? The "railroad men" believed they could force the public to "pay for their follies" to satisfy "their creditors and stockholders."[3] The railroad men, unfortunately, usually got their way.

The hegemony of corporations led by ultra-wealthy industrialists helped bring European-style violent class conflict to America. The bloated railroads that had helped cause economic collapse would soon lead the way in suppressing labor opposition. Strikes demanding better wages and conditions had long been American workers' prime tool for redress. But by the 1870s, business and the "respectable" upper classes also grew fearful that activist workers would adopt socialism and communism—similar to how slaveholders had linked abolition to "red republicanism" and socialism. American elites reacted to news of the Paris Commune of 1871, when workers took over the city of Paris and were brutally suppressed by the French government, with a horror reminiscent of southern reactions to slave rebellions, especially the Haitian Revolution. "Dr. Karl Marx," identified as the preeminent "socialist" in the world by American newspapers, remarked on the "persistent calumny hurled against the heroic effort of the Paris Commune to make possible a genuine republic in France. The American press has lent itself with wicked, indecent haste, and an ignorance of the facts so glaring as to offer no excuse for the willful misrepresentation of which it has been guilty, to the bloody designs of the old order."

The Commune would become a lodestar in the battles between labor and capital in America. Marx condemned its brutal suppression: "The civilization and justice of bourgeois order comes out in its lurid light whenever the slaves and drudges of that order rise against their masters. Then this civilization and justice stand forth as undisguised savagery and lawless revenge." Marx's defense of the Commune spelled out its world-historical lessons for British and American workers. The Commune, according to him, was "essentially a working-class government, the produce of the struggle of the producing against the appropriating classes"—it represented nothing less than the emancipation of labor. Marx clarified that the Commune wished to get rid of "class-property that makes the labor of the many the wealth of the few." It hoped to replace capitalist production with "co-operative production" or a "national production upon a common plan" to end "wages-slavery." The workers of Paris, he wrote, had revolted because they had no "alternative." He compared the retaliatory executions of communards to the massive violence of imperialism in the Americas, China, and India and the militaristic nationalism of warmongering European governments. The ruling elites of Europe, rather than the workers' commune, would be subject to the "eternal pillory" of history, he wrote, decades before they made the whole world their killing field.

The abolitionist press, which was connected to the IWA, was sympathetic to the Paris Commune. Frederick Douglass at first condemned it, but soon wrote that his sympathies had been "reversed" by "the savage cruelty with which the government is wreaking revenge on those deluded, ill-starred men." The communards, abolitionists argued, were like slave rebels, who fought in self-defense. By contrast, the Republican Party press condemned the Commune as a spasm of anarchy. Editor Henry C. Bowen argued that France must not return to Bonapartism, but that a constitutional republic was better than one formed by the "worst parts" of society. *The Independent* huffily wondered whether France was "capable of self-government," pointing somewhat prematurely to the success of Reconstruction in the South.

While many workers and radicals saw socialism as an extension of the promise of democratic republicanism, employers and other conservatives viewed socialists as dangerous revolutionaries who had to be stamped out with violence, if necessary. Many German Forty-Eighters— men and women who had participated in the republican European revolutions of 1848, and some of whom were Marx's compatriots—had joined

the abolition movement and the Union army after emigrating to the
United States. Marx himself had sent a congratulatory letter to President Lincoln on behalf of the IWA and had praised abolitionists like
Garrison and Phillips, one of whose speeches he had reproduced ver-
batim in an article. Marx's *The Communist Manifesto* (1848) was translated into English by the abolitionist and communitarian—the term for
those involved in utopian communities—Stephen Pearl Andrews, and
published for the first time in the United States in feminist Victoria
Woodhull's *Woodhull and Claflin's Weekly* in 1871, as the manifesto of
the German Communist Party.

Though some American social reformers deplored the *Communist*

"The Samson of the World," *The Irish World,* August 11, 1877. (Despite its
anti-capitalist and anti-imperialist illustrations, *The Irish World* frequently
trafficked in anti-Semitic imagery.) *American Antiquarian Society*

Manifesto for its "bitter" tone, they still agreed that workers faced the kind of oppression Marx had described in it. After the suppression of the Paris Commune, Marx's IWA, also known as the First International, developed many sections in the United States composed of both native and immigrant workers; it reportedly had "several million members" around the world in the 1870s. American reformers and German Marxists found enough common ground to unite under IWA auspices. Briefly headquartered in New York, the US section attracted abolitionists, labor reformers, and feminists like Woodhull. William West, whom Garrison had debated in *The Liberator,* joined the IWA and contributed regularly to Woodhull's newspaper, where he addressed "the radical difficulties arising out of the subsisting relations between capital and labor, arrayed against each other, as they undoubtedly are." Woodhull published communitarians and utopian socialists such as Josiah Warren, Albert Brisbane, and Robert Dale Owen. But Marx would expel Woodhull's Section 12 for her dabbling in spiritualism, "free love," and her founding of a Wall Street brokerage firm with help from the millionaire Cornelius Vanderbilt. Eventually divisions between Marxists and other radicals led to the demise of the American IWA in 1876, which held its last conference in Philadelphia. A rump group founded the Socialist Labor Party.[4]

Liberal Republicans joined in the fight against the labor movement, giving rise to the "first red scare." Some Republican papers differentiated between trade unions and communists, but all warned against the "seduction" of Phillips's pro-labor, socialist rhetoric. *The Independent,* alarmed at the growth of the IWA in Cincinnati and Chicago, editorialized that "The theory of these radical and crazy communists must be met at once by the stern rebuke of public sentiment, and if necessary by the sterner appliances of law and force."

Employers moved to suppress trade unions while claiming to be fighting communism. In 1868, miners in Pennsylvania's anthracite region formed a union, the Workingmen's Benevolent Association. It included Irish, English, and Welsh miners and was praised not just for representing workers' interests, but also for bringing order to labor relations.

Franklin Gowen, the owner of the Philadelphia and Reading Railway, and later the Reading Iron and Coal Company, instigated a showdown with the union when he, in collusion with other mine operators,
announced a 20 percent pay cut in December 1874, leading the union
to go on strike in 1875. Gowen managed to break the strike and union
when workers were reduced to near-starvation. The mine bosses' newspaper crowed, "The struggle is over. The war between Capital and Labor
is ended, and Labor is not victor. It is not even the drawn battle signified
by compromise: it is an unconditional surrender, a capitulation of all the
army, and relinquishment of all the claim for which it fought." Workers
noted that they felt "the lash" now "wielded by a gigantic Corporation,
which runs the Commonwealth and ruins the nation."

The destruction of the union was linked to the Molly Maguires, an
Irish organization associated with violent resistance to landlords in Ireland and against mine operators in Pennsylvania in the 1870s. The Molly
Maguires were known to fight policemen deployed by bosses. Gowen
and his allies had purposefully conflated the peaceful tactics of the
Workingmen's Benevolent Association, which explicitly repudiated the
Maguires, with the violent tactics of the latter. He hired the Pinkerton
detective agency to supplement the police forces already arrayed against
the union. Allan Pinkerton had spied for the Union during the Civil War
and infiltrated terror groups in the South. As a young man in Scotland,
he supported the British Chartist workers' movement, but he now presented his agency as a tool for employers to infiltrate and undermine
unions. Even a Pinkerton spy sent to observe the union, James McParlan, deplored the vigilante beatings and murders of suspected Maguires
(including one woman) as the kind of "lynch law" that armed racist
groups used against black southerners. More than the Maguires, though,
freedpeople shared a hunger for land with the Irish Land League, which
advocated land reform in Ireland and was supported by Irish Americans.

In the late 1870s, fifty Irish workers associated with the Ancient
Order of the Hibernians were indicted as Maguires, even though they
apparently had no connections to the group. They were convicted
mainly by the testimony of informers of questionable knowledge and
motivation, and by that of McParlan, who may have acted as an agent

provocateur. Gowen—who had been elected district attorney on a Democratic ticket—joined the prosecution. After exhausting all appeals, ten of the suspected Maguires were publicly executed by hanging on a single day, June 21, 1877, "Black Thursday," in Pottsville, Pennsylvania.[5]

The crackdown on the Maguires, while extreme, was nevertheless representative. In the post-Reconstruction era, employers across the country hired the Pinkertons (as Pinkerton's agents were known), private armies, and militias, and like southern reactionaries also enlisted the courts, in their heavy-handed suppression of unions. In the summer of 1877, workers across the country rose to protest drastic wage cuts and the complete loss of control over their working conditions, in what came to be called the Great Railroad Strike. Strikes that began with railroad workers spread to ancillary industries and expanded into the first national uprising of American labor. The railroads, the "circulatory system" of the new industrial economy, were capitalized at $5 billion, employed two hundred thousand workers, and had a total of seventy-nine thousand miles of track. They were too big to fail. The strike led to federal troops, once deployed to secure freedpeople's rights, being used on a wide scale to put down striking workers.

It was not a result of the growth of the state during the Civil War and Reconstruction, but rather signaled continuity with the antebellum era when the federal government mostly acted at the behest of the "Slave Power." Like southern slaveholders before the war, who invoked states' rights but demanded a federal slave code and punitive measures against abolitionists and fugitive slaves, railroad and manufacturing corporations decried any effort to regulate working hours, conditions, and safety even as they demanded that the armed might of the federal government be used against unions. Declining wages were a result of "inexorable laws of supply and demand," proponents of laissez-faire argued, even as they applauded state repression of strikers.

The Great Railroad Strike started spontaneously at the Camden, West Virginia junction of the Baltimore & Ohio line in June 1877 and spread to Martinsburg the next month, when the railroad company cut wages three times that year. Just as the economy was improving in the long aftermath of the Panic of 1873, railroad magnates announced a 10 percent (or even deeper) cut in workers' wages. Tom Scott, the owner of Pennsylvania Railroad, who some suspected was behind the corrupt bargain of 1876 that made Rutherford Hayes president, and other railroad owners remained deaf to appeals by their workers and unions to rescind the cuts. As one of the workers in Camden wrote, "We eat our hard bread and tainted meat two days on the sooty cars up the road, and when we come home, find our children gnawing bones and our wives complaining that they cannot even buy hominy." The strike spread like wildfire along the railroad tracks to other states, prompting Governor Henry Mathews of West Virginia to telegraph President Hayes, asking for federal troops to suppress it. With the help of obliging mayors and police forces, the owners called for the arrest of strike leaders and brought in strikebreakers. But many people in local communities took the side of the striking workers, whose wages had been reduced to "starvation point." In Baltimore, the state militia was brought in, and one worker died in an exchange of gunfire. Soon canal workers and miners joined the striking railroad workers, and local townspeople made their sympathy for them clear.

As was typical of most strikes in this era, corporations, with the help of private and state armed forces, killed and injured striking workers and their allies, while workers retaliated by destroying property. President Hayes labeled the strike an "insurrection" and sent federal troops to disperse the strikers, after refusing to use the army to uphold Reconstruction in southern states. Hayes's cabinet was dominated by Liberal Republicans as well as southern sympathizers; only later would the president bemoan a government of the corporations, by the corporations, and for the corporations that he had helped create. Governor John Carroll of Maryland not only called out the state militia, but also requested federal assistance from the obliging Hayes. By the start of July, over a thousand troops and Gatling guns were deployed in the streets of Baltimore and at Camden to quell the strike, after workers

"Sixth Maryland Regiment Firing on the Rioters in Baltimore, 1877," from
James Dabney McCabe, *The History of the Great Riots*, 1877. *American Antiquarian
Society*

uncoupled railroad cars and thousands of angry citizens set fire to the
B&O office and a telegraph office near it. One writer said of the "railroad
troubles" that "it is evident that the discontent of the workingmen is to
form a new feature of our political relations."

The "great labor uprising of 1877," as it was known by contemporaries, saw workers across the country draw inspiration from each other. In
Pittsburgh, railroad workers on Scott's Pennsylvania Railroad, as well
as miners and the unemployed, went on strike to halt all freight trains,
while allowing passenger and mail trains to continue unhindered. The
railroad companies in the city had cut wages and increased the work-
load of their workers. The strike, which began with Pennsylvania Railroad, spread to other lines. The city's businessmen pleaded with the
railroad companies to reach a settlement with the strikers, and much
of the local population sympathized with the workers' grievances. The
railroads brought in the state National Guard from Philadelphia, which
indiscriminately attacked the crowds who refused to disperse, killing twenty people, including a woman and three children, with bullets

and bayonets. Twenty-nine more were injured. A grand jury called the Pittsburgh strike "The Lexington of the Labor Conflict."

Angry workers armed themselves, forcing the Pennsylvania guards to retreat, and proceeded to set railroad cars ablaze and smash the windows of the building where the state guards had regrouped. The fire destroyed thirty-nine buildings and hundreds of cars and engines belonging to the Pennsylvania Railroad. Even though they were forced out of the city, the guardsmen killed twenty more people as they pulled back. The strike expanded to other cities and towns in the state, including Reading, where Franklin Gowen called in federal troops and state militia after local militia refused to shoot on workers. The new arrivals fired into a crowd of strikers, killing ten and wounding forty. Among the wounded were bystanders, including women and children, and even five police officers.

The strikes spread to the West, South, and Northeast. In Terre Haute, Indiana, the Brotherhood of Locomotive Firemen went on strike when the owner of the Vandalia line, Riley McKeen, refused to negotiate with them. Eugene V. Debs, the future socialist leader and founder of the American Railway Union, which included all railroad workers, was a member of the Brotherhood. The union, more cautious than railroad workers elsewhere, foreswore the support of the unemployed and any destruction of property, earning the approval of Terre Haute's mayor, but it still billed the strike as "our resistance to the encroachments of capital on unprotected labor." Federal troops helped break the strike and several strikers were imprisoned.

Workers on the Erie line in Hornellsville, New York were more successful, even though Governor Lucius Robinson, egged on by the *New York Times* (known as a conservative outlet at the time), sent militia to suppress their strike. By literally soaping the railroad tracks running uphill to their town, the strikers prevented both the regular trains and those carrying the militia from arriving. Local townspeople and businesses supported them. The arrogant Hugh Jewett, president of the Erie Railroad, who threatened strike leaders with arrest and worse, was forced to rescind the wage cuts he had implemented. One of the major transcontinental railroads, the Union Pacific, followed suit. Meanwhile, workers on the Michigan Central railroad line, joined by factory, packinghouse, and lumberyard laborers, successfully avoided violence by dispersing at the appearance of police and reconvening elsewhere. The press bemoaned the allegedly bad precedent set by Erie when workers won without either side resorting to violence. *The Nation,* then an organ of Liberal Republicans, smugly argued that "it would be a national calamity" for "concession as to wages or the retention of persons engaged in the strike." Employers and corporations often blacklisted striking workers to discourage labor activism.

In most places, however, "the respectable classes" and armies of small businessmen took it upon themselves to aid corporations in forcibly suppressing strikes. In Scranton, Pennsylvania, armed local businessmen shot and killed six miners from the Lackawanna Iron & Coal Company. Railroad workers of the Delaware, Lackawanna & Western Railroad, whose wages had fallen by 35 percent in one year, went on strike. When federal troops and the militia arrived to provide the company with more firepower, they were called "the firing squad" by the workers.

In Chicago, a strike by railroad switchmen quickly became a general strike of workers in 1877—and thirty-five were killed and two hundred wounded in the violence that followed. The police broke up Workingmen's Party meetings, clubbing people on their heads and shooting at them. In one instance, policemen attacked workers inside the German Turner Hall, forcing many to leap out of the building's windows. The Chicago police's actions led to warfare in the city's streets, when workers retaliated. The city's elite called for "law and order," and some recommended the application of the southern remedy of lynching. The governor of Illinois requested federal troops and sent in the National Guard, while workers and their allies condemned the city's violation of their rights to assembly and speech. The military proved decisive in defeating the Chicago labor uprising. As Hayes wrote in the fall of 1877, "The strikers have been put down by *force.*" The federal government was becoming reactionary.

The Great Railroad Strike of 1877 spread to the South, too, even though the region's labor movement was small, and in many places nonexistent—another legacy of slavery. Where workers did strike, they often did so across racial lines. In Kentucky, black and white rail workers went on strike when the Louisville & Nashville and the Louisville, Cincinnati & Lexington Railroads announced a 10 percent cut to their already paltry wages. Workers in other industries in Louisville also struck against wage cuts. The mayor of Louisville raised a citizens' army against the strikers, an army that included Louis Brandeis, the future progressive Supreme Court justice. The mayor called for federal troops, even though the striking workers were dispersed when fired on by the police. In Missouri, a strike starting with railroad workers in East St. Louis (Illinois), represented by the Brotherhood of Locomotive Firemen, spread to other workers, white and black. Huge rallies organized by the Workingmen's Party demanded laws to end child labor, install an eight-hour day, and revert wages to pre-depression levels. Committed to nonviolence, the executive committee of the local party virtually took over St. Louis. In response, Mayor Overstoltz assembled an armed private militia with the help of local businessmen and the city's gun club.

The owner of St. Louis & Southeastern Railroad appealed to Secretary of the Interrior Carl Schurz, a native of the city and Liberal Republican, who in turn activated army regiments led by the appropriately named Col. Jefferson C. Davis—who was known mainly for being suspended from his command for abandoning escaped slaves to vengeful Confederates during the Civil War, and for butchering Modocs in 1872–1873. Missouri governor John S. Phelps contributed arms and ammunition. Armed troops and police arrested workers in St. Louis and in East St. Louis, and the strike ended because the workers, who never budged from their nonviolent stance, never fought back. The "St. Louis commune" collapsed without a single casualty except for its interracialism, when some white workers embraced the race baiting of their critics and disavowed the participation of black workers. To commemorate their victory, city leaders celebrated the end of the St. Louis general strike by parading in white, Klan-like hoods and robes the next year. It became an annual event, known as the Veiled Prophet Ball, that continues to this day. The strike was still "the era's most compelling example of interracial radicalism—a final flash lit image of the fading promise of abolition democracy," as one historian put it recently.[6]

The use of the US Army to put down the strikes of 1877 and the conquest of the West in the same period have led some scholars to draw facile conclusions about the rise of the American nation-state during the Civil War and Reconstruction. These historians argue that the growth of the federal government across the period ultimately had negative effects, because its increasing power was deployed to dispossess Indians and to suppress striking workers. For workers and other subaltern groups, however, the state could act as a counterweight to the power of private corporations and plutocrats. The expansion of the government during the war was a necessary development, to defeat the South, emancipate the enslaved population, and abolish slavery. The alternative was the persistence of the Confederacy, and surely its expansion into an imperial, hemispheric slaving power. The progressive constitutionalism of Reconstruction, meanwhile, is the foundation of our modern nation—even if it took many more decades for it to be realized, given the reactionary, one-party South and US Supreme Court. That some of the new powers of the federal government were turned on its own citizens and on indigenous nations is indisputable. Yet the enlarged central state was and remains the only counterweight to reaction, the only force powerful enough to secure the very things the Civil War was waged over and that Reconstruction attempted to realize. For that reason, planter politicians before the war and southern elites and monopolists after the war opposed the institutional development of the state, even as they used its repressive powers to further their own interests.

Liberal Republicans like Schurz asked for the expansion of the army specifically to police American cities and workers, while decrying the growth of the federal government during Reconstruction. Still, most labor leaders, antimonopolist reformers, and radicals (with the exception of anarchists), followed freedpeople and abolitionists in looking to the government, state and federal, to address their grievances. As one labor newspaper put it, "These men are citizens. Many of them carried the banners of Grant and Sherman over the battle-fields of the slave-holders' rebellion. Their labor aids wealth in the nation. They are the support of its institutions, they obey the laws of society, its taxation." [7]

The threat that the rise of industrial capitalism posed to the American experiment in republican government preoccupied workers, labor reformers, and later, progressive intellectuals. One "striker" wrote, "unless a reduction in the hours of labor shall be adopted I see nothing left for unemployed labor but to underbid the employed, and go on repeating that process until the degradation point is reached." He suggested that "capital will find it better to take less and give labor more than to degrade and starve labor, and then pay a soldier to keep him in subjection." That should be the "conclusion of those who look upon human beings as something above machines and animals."

Intense debates over the problems of "the industrial age" played out in the pages of antislavery newspapers. In *The Commonwealth,* W. G. H. Smart, who described himself as a "simple mechanic," touted the benefits of "social democracy." Social democrats like Smart believed that government must alleviate the condition of workers and the poor, and were especially critical of those who argued that growing inequality and poverty were a matter of personal choice and of differences in individuals' skills and talents. The working poor, social democrats pointed out, were given a choice between bad working conditions and pauperism, suffered through no fault of their own. Instead of blaming workers, the "extension of democracy to the domain of wealth" would solve the glaring problem of a very small class of wealthy and a very large class of working poor. Extreme social inequality would eventually destroy American republicanism, according to Smart. Instead of investing in society, "*unproductive* capital" used capital to make more money—he was ahead of his time in describing finance capitalism—and did not even pay "sufficient taxes," while workers faced starvation and declining wages.

Even a monarchy like Germany's, Smart pointed out, had adopted the principles of social democracy, providing workers with health care and insurance against industrial accidents—protections that would represent nothing, he argued, but an extension of the Declaration of Independence's promise of life, liberty, and the pursuit of happiness for all citizens. (Smart did not mention that Otto von Bismarck, the chancellor of Germany, had co-opted socialist ideas in part to suppress them.) All critical resources ought to be controlled by the nation, rather than by the wealthy, and all industry should be organized on a "cooperative" basis, Smart proposed. Abolitionists had often shamed the slaveholding republic before the Civil War by raising the fact that Britain, another constitutional monarchy, had abolished slavery before the United States. And now, the Industrial Revolution, Smart noted, created new challenges for American democracy, just as slavery had: "Large incorporated companies have been founded in every important branch of industry, with millions of dollars of capital under the control of a few, and sometimes only one man." Yet when Smart wrote to William Lloyd Garrison for assistance in the cause of "industrial reform" to prevent a "bloody struggle," the old abolitionist demurred. Garrison responded that unlike the enslaved, workers could rely on "their own collective will and unquestionable strength" to establish "new safeguards for their freedom, safety and happiness." By the 1880s, Smart was writing for an anarchist magazine, having given up on inaugurating a social democracy in the United States.

Garrison's response to Smart was perhaps expected because even though he always supported labor, he viewed racism as the more pressing issue. While abolitionists were pro-labor, they balked at the violence of the 1877 strikes. Instead of revolution, they advocated for the creation of a modern welfare state that would tame and regulate rapacious capitalism. Phillips, unfairly tarred as just another middle-class reformer, argued that labor's wrongs did not justify a violent uprising. He thought the government had to pass laws to protect labor, because businessmen were "too blind or too wicked" to do the right thing—and that if workers continued to be oppressed, the American republic would cease to exist. He dismissed "the babble and chaff of 'supply and demand,'" the "false political economy" of the laissez-faire economists and Liberal Republicans that justified starvation wages and mass unemployment. Abolitionist Stephen Pearl Andrews went further, arguing that the American worker will "GET NO JUSTICE on the present plan of conducting business; and he has discovered that fact and means to right things, at all hazards." Since laboring people were in the majority, "the theory of shooting them down" would not work in a republic. To avoid violence, he argued, all railroads and essential industries should be transferred to the control of the government, which would pay "fixed and equitable wages" to government employees.[8] Many of these ideas—though not Andrew's socialist proposal to nationalize industry—would be realized in the twentieth century.

A new generation of postbellum reformers leveled more fully developed critiques of industrial capitalism. Henry George was one of the first radical economic thinkers to grasp in full the conflict between capitalism and democracy. An impoverished journalist, George became famous when he published *Progress and Poverty* in 1879, a seminal study of the problem, as its subtitle put it, of "increase of want with increase of wealth." Just as freedpeople demanded land to assert their economic independence from planters, George saw land as a solution to growing inequality. He argued that overvalued land, as a result of railroad construction, monopolies, and speculation, was the root cause of all economic problems. As he wrote, "private property in land" leads to "the enslavement of the laboring class." But while communists called for the abolition of private property, George advocated for its equal distribution. He wanted to unite the ideas of Adam Smith and David Ricardo with the contemporary radicalisms of Pierre-Joseph Proudhon (an anarchist) and Ferdinand Lassalle—or, put more simply, to show how classical political economy could lead to "the noble dreams of socialism." He appears not to have read Marx, but like him maintained that the laws of political economy by themselves could not explain the persistence of poverty amid "advancing wealth." Also like Marx, he accepted Smith's labor theory of value, the notion that wages did not come from capital but were the "produce of labor."

The widely traveled George rejected the idea that overpopulation, as Thomas Malthus had argued earlier in the century, was the cause of poverty and famines in India, China, and Ireland. Instead, George blamed the land monopoly created by imperialist rule: "India is now like a great estate owned by an absentee and alien landlord." For George, rents did not represent the intrinsic value of land, but "the price of monopoly" arising from private ownership of it. It was the "speculative advance of rent" compared to depressed wages that caused cyclical depressions. The reason why wages "tend to a minimum which will give but a bare living" despite increases in production was that rents increased at a much faster rate. As land increases in value, "poverty deepens and pauperism appears."

Examining all the proposed remedies for declining wages and poverty, from conservative self-help ideas to trade unions and socialism, George concluded that the only solution was to *"make land common property."* As long as monopoly in land existed, he wrote, workers would be enslaved and the Declaration of Independence and the emancipation of the slaves would be "in vain." In practical terms, government could solve the problem of poverty by appropriating the rental income of individual landowners through taxation. Unlike earlier land reformers such as George Henry Evans, who had clarified that no Native Americans would be dispossessed in making workers landowners, Henry George did not say a word about indigenous inhabitants of the land Americans claimed as their own.

Progressive taxation of land to meet the needs of the state and society had been a cornerstone of Reconstruction and had aroused the ire of southern elites. George proposed a higher rate of taxation than the Reconstruction state governments had. Later, he advocated for municipal ownership of public utilities and goods. In his deceptively simple and popular scheme, rents caused inequality, while taxes promoted equality. George was in fact expounding the basic tenets of modern liberalism, even though his emphasis on rents is outdated. His socialist critic, Laurence Gronlund, instead advocated a "cooperative commonwealth" and popularized Marx's critique of capitalism in the US. Most socialists supported George's run to become the mayor of New York City in 1886. With the growth of inequality, especially in cities, which George described as centers of wealthy decadence as well as great poverty, the rich could buy and pervert elections. Like the abolitionists, George ended his appeal with "the central truth" of the Declaration of

Independence, the equality of man, now threatened by gross economic inequality. But unlike them he was a Sinophobe and stoked racist fears of a "yellow peril"—another major failing alongside his disregard for Native America.[9]

Well before Henry George published his magnum opus, antimonopolist parties and movements—the Grange, the Labor Reform and Workingmen's Parties, the Greenback Party, and others—had been calling for the regulation of the economy by the government as the democratic representative of ordinary citizens. These groups saw themselves arrayed against Democrats and Republicans alike. The *National Labor Tribune,* the official organ of the Amalgamated Association of Iron and Steel Workers of the United States, which was published from the heart of anthracite country in Pittsburgh, explained:

> Labor has begged for many years and begged in vain, for some legislation in its interest. We asked for bread and they gave us a stone. Each time we have sworn vengeance against them, but when election day comes we go to the polls and vote again, not as workingmen, but as Republicans and Democrats. How long will this last; will workingmen always be the dupe of politicians? Or shall they awake to their true interests and vote for men who know what they need, and are pledged by all that men hold sacred, to vote and work in the interest of labor? Men, whose hands are hard with honest toil, and who know the wants of the laborer from stern experience, the best of teachers.

After the strikes of 1877, some of these antimonopolist forces and labor organizations coalesced into a third party, the Greenback-Labor Party. Besides paper currency, it supported an eight-hour day, progressive taxation, and women's suffrage. But the rise of postwar, antimonopoly egalitarian movements took place in the shadow of the defeat of Reconstruction, and most of these movements also embraced racial exclusion, not seeing (or caring) that it set back their cause. The southern Grange represented mainly large planters and was white supremacist. Radicals such as Woodhull subscribed to the southern understanding of the overthrow of Reconstruction; she decried "carpetbag rule." The National Labor Union's founder and president William Sylvis, a Democrat, argued, implausibly, that "Even now a slavery exists in our land worse than ever existed under the old slave system." In a trip to the South, Sylvis claimed that he conversed with black and white southerners and that they had revealed there was no such organization as the KKK. Southern whites were "orderly and well disposed," in his estimation.

Little wonder that black workers, under the leadership of Isaac Myers, held a national convention and founded a separate organization, the Colored National Labor Union (CNLU), in 1869. It continued to support the Republican Party even though *The Workingmen's Advocate* asked it to eschew partisan politics, a request that made little sense during Reconstruction. Sylvis's successor as NLU president, Richard Trevellick, attended the first CNLU convention in 1869, but while he asked the CNLU to support the Labor Reform Party, the NLU rarely disciplined white workers for excluding African Americans from their unions. And black people and immigrants were in fact excluded from most trade unions, which allowed corporations to use them often as strike breakers. In this way, racism and nativism within the labor movement cost it dearly, as employers perfected a divide-and-rule strategy to control their labor force.

Nevertheless, some black and white workers did perceive that the only true protection afforded them would result from organizing into "co-operative Trades Unions" and land associations. The CNLU sent delegates to the NLU in an attempt to unite black and white workers. But it broke off all ties with the NLU when it refused to seat John M. Langston, the black lawyer and politician, in 1870. The leadership of the CNLU included abolitionists such as George Downing, J. Sella Martin, and Frederick Douglass's son Lewis Douglass, the last of whom had been barred from an all-white typographical union. Sumner sent his felicitations to the first convention, and Congressman Robert Elliott addressed it. Black and white abolitionists—Douglass, Hinton, Robert Purvis, Aaron Powell, Edward M. Davis, John M. Langston, Giles Stebbins, and Susan B. Anthony—participated in subsequent conventions. The CNLU endorsed abolitionist and radical plans to redistribute land to freedpeople, and Douglass squelched all talk of supporting the Labor Reform Party, instead of Republicans.

During Reconstruction, when southern black workers organized and struck for better wages and conditions, they often became targets of racist violence. In 1878, in refusing to support the third party bid of Benjamin Butler for the governorship of Massachusetts on the Greenback Labor ticket, Garrison wrote to Phillips, "While the freedmen at the South are, on 'the Mississippi Plan' and 'by the shotgun policy,' ruthlessly deprived of their rights as American citizens, and no protection is extended them by the Federal Government on the ground of impotency, the old anti-slavery issue is still (and must be persistently insisted [on] as constituting) the paramount issue before the country." Before he died in 1879, Garrison set up a fund-raiser for the Exodusters, the freedpeople fleeing from Mississippi and Louisiana to Kansas. Their plight, he wrote, was that of the "millions of colored people" in the South, "now under ban and virtually disfranchised." For Garrison, the racist oppression of freedpeople still trumped the labor question—just as slavery, he had insisted to labor leaders before the war, was the most pressing issue, even though he sympathized with wage workers.

At least in principle, if not always in practice, the NLU, the IWA, and the Workingmen's and Labor Reform Parties supported racial equality. Woodhull's sister, Tennie Claflin, commanded an all-black militia called the Skidmore guards in New York, named after Thomas Skidmore, an early labor leader and land reformer. Woodhull herself, despite her conservative views of Reconstruction, touted "Colored Communism" in lowcountry South Carolina, where black farmers pooled their resources to buy farms for joint ownership. Perhaps the most important African American leader to join the Workingmen's Party was Peter Humphries Clark, a fugitive slave, abolitionist, and schoolteacher from Ohio. Clark was influenced by German socialists in Cincinnati and became a supporter of the Workingmen's Party in 1876. In a speech to striking railroad workers in 1877, Clark said, "The blood of those men murdered at Baltimore cries from the ground against these men who by their greed have forced their men to the desperate measure of a strike, and then invoked the strong arm of the government to slaughter them in their misery." He advocated government ownership of railroads and argued that "Capital must not rule, but be ruled and regulated." He repeated an article of faith for most African Americans during Reconstruction: "Government is good, it is not an evil," at least when it acted as the democratic representative of the people to stop racist terror and check capital. Clark exhorted workers to remain peaceful, and his appeal was credited with preventing violence in Cincinnati during the great strike. He joined the Socialist Labor Party but returned to the Republican Party after the former, like many third parties of the time, disintegrated. In the 1880s, he joined the Democrats, losing black support.[10]

One organization dedicated to the rights of labor surpassed all others in its attempts to transcend racial, trade, and gender lines within the working class. The Knights of Labor was founded in 1869 by Uriah Stephens of the Garment Cutters Association as a secret organization to "shield themselves from persecution and wrong." It expanded quickly in the 1880s, becoming the largest labor organization in the country. An abolitionist before the Civil War, Stephens emphasized worker solidarity over all other loyalties. Like many other labor reformers at the time, he proposed to replace capitalism with a cooperative system that would benefit all. The man most responsible for the transformation of the Knights from a craft union into "the first mass labor organization" that cut across trades, however, was Terence Powderly, who became its grand master workman in 1879. A year earlier, Powderly had been elected mayor of Scranton, Pennsylvania on the Workingmen's Party ticket. After the suppression of the great strike in 1877, Powderly had become wary of strikes, and as the head of the Knights, he now opened membership to all "producers"—allowing for the organization's exponential growth—and sought to restore harmony between capital and labor. His views were reminiscent of the free labor ideology of the early Republican Party. As he put it, "I not only did not favor the ordering of strikes, but opposed entering upon them until the depths of the last harbor of peaceful adjustment had been sounded."

Instead of unions, the Knights formed district and state level assemblies that met annually in a national general assembly, much like prewar abolitionist societies. The assemblies, unlike the trade unions, admitted workers regardless of skill, and its slogan, "An Injury to One is the Concern of All," became a galvanizing recruitment tool. Besides trade assemblies of mainly workers in a particular industry, it also operated "mixed" assemblies that included members outside the working class. In 1880, the Knights admitted women to their General Assembly for the first time, and six years later, 10 percent of their membership was female. Leonora Barry, an Irish American immigrant, headed the Department of Women's Work, until she resigned in 1890. Later, Barry became a suffragist and was active in the Women's Christian Temperance Union.

Despite attempts by southerners to enforce the color line, the Knights recruited thousands of black men and women in the region. Still, most of the southern assemblies were either white or black, rather than interracial. And the Knights' embrace of black workers did not go unchallenged within the organization. For instance, the election of black machinist Frank Ferrell to the New York district assembly delegation created some consternation, when the Knights general assembly held its annual meeting in Richmond in 1886. The New York delegation refused to stay in a hotel that denied Ferrell accommodations, and racist mobs marched to attack the delegation. At the assembly, Powderly had Ferrell introduce him—a show of support that curtailed much of the controversy over the fact that Ferrell would address the assembly, too. Powderly had to issue a public statement making clear that the "colored delegates" to the Knights assembly would not "intrude where they are not wanted."

Still, the Knights became the preeminent union of disfranchised black workers in the South. Powderly called for the education of black and white labor on the grounds that "southern cheap labor is more a menace to the American toiler than the Chinese." As that comment revealed, the one type of discrimination the Knights them-selves approved of was Sinophobia. Powderly excluded Chinese workers from the Knights, calling for an end to Chinese immigration altogether. In 1882, the Knights supported Congress's passage of the first Chinese Exclusion law. Powderly later argued that while an act of "inhuman-ity and butchery is inexcusable"—referring to the massacre of nearly forty Chinese workers in Wyoming in 1885—he understood "desperate" white workers who enacted "a terrible revenge on the Chinese." When the socialist-dominated New York assembly of the Knights wanted to admit assemblies of Chinese workers, their proposal was voted down.

Opposition to the Chinese, whom Powderly designated one of the "servile races," was not based merely on opposition to contract labor. It was simple racism, too. The use by railroad and mining corporations of convict and contract labor did, however, pose a serious challenge to the labor movement. The Knights' organizing philosophy was based on "the nobility of toil," or the dignity of all labor. Its opposition to convict lease labor won the support of African Americans, who were subjected to that brutal system in the South far more frequently than whites. Corpora-tions and railroads contracted European, Mexican, and Asian work-ers to labor through long-term contracts and paid their passage to the United States. The Knights' plans for the social, moral, and intellectual uplift of wage workers, with an emphasis on education and temperance, echoed the Freedmen's Bureau programs for freedpeople. The long sub-title of Powderly's book about the Knights, published in 1889, read: "The sword may strike the shackles from the limb of the slave. But it is educa-tion and organization that makes him a freeman."

Like other contemporary labor organizations, the Knights firmly believed in "an inevitable and irresistible conflict between the wage-system of labor and republican system of government." They drew on the antislavery political tradition, which posited an irresistible conflict between northern freedom and southern slavery. In towns and cities across the country, the Knights fielded candidates on the Workingmen's and Union Labor Party tickets, posing a grassroots challenge to white supremacist rule in the South and the national political hegemony of industrial capitalists. The Knights also continued the NLU's fight for a National Labor Bureau, which was finally established in 1884, and became the Department of Labor four years later. The state, Powderly argued, must protect labor from millionaires who "curse the nation with their baneful presence." One Knights' song articulated its anti-monopoly, producerist ideology: "Still robbed by sly and subtle wrong, Monopoly defiant, strong, By trick of law, usurping right—At last I'll conquer by the might, Of right divine; I ask for mine!" But the "cooperative commonwealth" and the "republic of producers" visualized by the Knights was undermined by the violent response of the robber barons of the Gilded Age to workers' organizations and unions.

Despite Powderly's strategic conservatism, the Knights took on Jay Gould, the financial speculator and railroad magnate, initiating a walk-out to protest wage cuts on his Wabash Railroad line in February 1885. It soon spread, along the Missouri Pacific line, to Missouri, Arkansas, Texas, and Kansas. The Knights not only forced Gould to negotiate with them, but extracted concessions, including a pledge not to discriminate against its members or blacklist them. A year earlier, a mass walkout on the Union Pacific by the Knights had forced the railroad's new president, Charles Francis Adams Jr.— of the Adams political dynasty but far more conservative than prior generations—to accede to all their demands. Already the largest labor organization in the country, the Knights saw their membership jump from 80,000 to 700,000 in 1886, the surge coming not just from railroad workers but iron and steel workers, firemen, local sympathizers in mixed assemblies, shop workers, streetcar and gashouse workers, plumbers, brick masons, and carpenters—in short, a broad swath of the American working class and their allies.

In 1886, black and white workers in Gould's railroad empire in Missouri, Texas, Arkansas, and Kansas initiated another walkout when his managers refused to honor the prior year's agreement against black-listing or to address other grievances: low wages, long hours, and lack of compensation for industrial accidents. The immediate trigger was the firing of C. A. Hall, a carpenter, who had attended a Knights' meeting with his foreman's permission. Eventually the strike was killed by a combination of court injunctions against strikers, divisions between skilled and unskilled workers, strikebreakers, Gould's use of police and armed guards, and the governors of the affected states' declaration that the strike was against the public interest. The Knights lost many of the gains they had made just a year prior. They also lost some community support, after some workers turned to sabotage and the supply of goods to local towns came to a halt. When Powderly interceded with Gould to find a compromise, the latter reneged on his promises after the strike was called off. Martin Irons, one of the strike's leaders, died blacklisted and in poverty.

The Knights, however, were at the margins of one of the most influential clashes between labor and capital in that same year, 1886. A depression in 1884–1885 fed into not only the Knights' strike in the Southwest, but into what became known as "the Great Upheaval" of 1886, when worker unrest expanded into protests against wage cuts and the renewal of the eight-hour-day movement. An 1883 Senate investigation into the conditions of labor revealed that workers in hazardous industries worked ten to fifteen hours a day, with women and children facing the longest hours, lowest pay, and greatest chance of workplace injury. In Chicago, the center of the American Industrial Revolution, output and profits far outpaced wages. On May 1, 1886, workers across the country took to the streets to demand an eight-hour day. The mass protest was organized not by the Knights—Powderly opposed a stockyard strike in Chicago and distanced himself from the call for enforcing an eight-hour day, even though he supported the demand—but by the Federation of Organized Trades and Labor Unions of the United States and Canada (a precursor to the American Federation of Labor, or AFL). May 1—"May Day"— is still a workers' holiday around the world today, except, ironically, in the United States, the country of its birth.

On May 4, more than a thousand workers in Chicago gathered off Haymarket Square to protest the killing of six strikers by police at the McCormick Reaper works. A bomb hurled at a column of police officers who had marched into the crowd prompted them to start shooting indiscriminately, killing eight civilians and wounding many more. Seven police officers died, from a combination of friendly fire and the bomb. Eight men identified as anarchists, including the former Confederate turned labor firebrand Albert Parsons, were arrested.

Parsons had "transformed himself from a Republican loyalist to a self-proclaimed anarchist." He had joined the International Working People's Association, otherwise known as the "Black International," which was founded in London in 1881, but he was also a member of the Knights and head of Chicago's Eight Hour League. Anarchists and their syndicalist allies—the latter believed in union or workers' collective ownership of property—preached violent resistance, but had seldom acted on their words. In August, all eight men were found guilty in a case marred by a prejudicial judge, mass hysteria whipped up by the press, and perjured testimony. The Haymarket eights' case was appealed all the way to the Supreme Court, where they were represented by the radical Benjamin Butler, another living link to the Civil War and Reconstruction, among others. The Haymarket eight became internationally famous as their case garnered the sympathy of eminent people throughout the world. Four of the men, including Parsons, were hanged on November 11, "Black Friday." Thousands attended their funeral. As for the other four, two had their sentences eventually commuted to life in prison, one was given a prison sentence of fifteen years, and another committed suicide. The actual perpetrator of the bomb-throwing was never caught. Albert's wife, Lucy Parsons, who chose to pass as Mexican, kept the memory of her husband alive and continued to agitate for workers' emancipation. American labor radicals invoked the American Revolution and abolition and compared the martyred Parsons to abolitionist John Brown.

The Haymarket bombing resulted in a backlash against immigrants, radicals, and the labor movement. Six of the eight were Germans, fueling nativism and hysteria about "imported" radicalisms; the other two were Parsons and the Methodist minister Rev. Samuel Fielden, who was speaking when the bomb exploded. Middle-class Americans, fed a steady diet of the horrors of labor radicalism by the mainstream press, championed "law and order." Employers across the country used Haymarket as a pretext to clamp down on unions. The Knights resolved in their general meeting in 1887 that while they asked for "mercy for the condemned men, we are not in sympathy with the acts of the Anarchists, nor with any attempts of individuals or associated bodies that teach or practice violent infractions of the law, believing that peaceful methods are the surest and best means to secure necessary reforms." Powderly took pains to distinguish orderly socialists from the "mire of anarchy." But while anarchists often threatened violence, far more violence was meted out against, rather than by, them and other radicals. Powderly resented the Knights being associated with Haymarket, though he admitted that many in its executive council sympathized with the falsely accused men. In his view, anarchists had grabbed "an attention which would have been undivided and centered wholly upon the aggressive, grasping monopolist and speculator" if the Knights had had their way. But for the Chicago Knights, as for much of the labor movement—whether or not they agreed on every point with anarchists—the Haymarket Martyrs became a cause célèbre. An ode to them pointed out that they were convicted for their politics, rather than the bombing itself: "In Chicago stand convicted, Seven of nature's noblest men, Jailed because they have predicted, What was truth and clear to them." In 1893, the pro-labor governor of Illinois, John Peter Altgeld, pardoned the remaining three incarcerated Haymarket men and arraigned the prejudicial trial against those executed.

Less well known today than the Haymarket bombing is the massacre of sixty black sugar workers in Thibadoux, Louisiana, a year later. During Reconstruction, cane cutters on sugar plantations had struck for better wages, and in 1887 they joined the Knights. Sugar workers were paid scant wages, labored in conditions little better than slavery, and were at times paid in scrip—money that could only be used in the planters' own overpriced plantation stores. The Louisiana Sugar Producers Association, representing the planters, refused to meet or negotiate with the workers, and the Knights coordinated a widespread strike in the sugar parishes. Planters reacted viciously, firing striking workers and bringing in strikebreakers from Mississippi. The governor of Louisiana, Samuel McEnery, sent in the state militia, armed with Gatling guns, under former Confederate general P. G. T. Beauregard, who had ordered the first shot of the Civil War at Fort Sumter in April 1861. The militia evicted striking workers from the plantations, and groups of white vigilantes intimidated them. When workers, including some Union veterans, shot back in self-defense, they were killed en masse, their bodies dumped in a landfill. Some planters themselves were involved in the massacre, and one of those who took part would be elected to Congress the following year. No one was punished for the mass murder of black workers, and the Knights' interracial organizing in the South suffered a grave setback.

By the 1890s, the once vibrant Knights of Labor were in decline. Terence Powderly became a lawyer (a profession excluded from Knights' membership), the owner of a coal company, and a government bureaucrat. The Knights' place of preeminence in the labor movement was usurped by the AFL, which avoided explicit political commitments after the Great Upheaval of 1886: it was for unionism "pure and simple," and its membership was mostly skilled, native, white, and male. The AFL, though, did seek to enlist the state to counteract the power of corporations and arbitrate between workers and employers during the Progressive era.[11] Not until the rise of the Industrial Workers of the World in 1905 and the Congress of Industrial Organizations in 1935 would the Knights' legacy of mass organizing reemerge.

Reformers continued to address the labor question and to imagine a better future. Along with Henry George, Edward Bellamy and Henry Demarest Lloyd were the most influential American radical writers of the era. Many others, including Mark Twain, who coined the term "the Gilded Age," wrote fiction and nonfiction protesting the abuses of industrial capitalism and American imperialism, but even Twain did not surpass this trinity. T. Thomas Fortune, the black journalist and activist—he was the son of a politician of Seminole heritage in Reconstruction Florida— published *Black and White: Land, Labor, and Politics in the South* (1884). He is often forgotten as a leading radical thinker. Born enslaved, Fortune, like George, argued that land monopoly was the cause of inequality and that labor should make common cause with freedpeople in the South in their fight against the oppression of capital. Unlike George, he acknowledged Indians' dispossession but viewed their alleged passing away as inevitable. And unlike Twain, he became a champion of empire. "Chattel

Edward Bellamy portrait,
copyrighted by Philpott,
1889. *Library of Congress*

slavery," he contended, was giving way to "industrial slavery." Fortune visualized an interracial labor movement that would revive the promise of Reconstruction's abolition democracy. Other reformers like Bellamy recommended statist solutions to the problem of rapacious capitalism.

In 1888, Bellamy, a Massachusetts journalist, published a best-selling novel, *Looking Backward*. Set in the future, Bellamy's novel predicted that the growth of monopolies in industry and finance would eventually lead to state ownership of all industries, or the "nationalization" of all economic and political life. Inspired by the Civil War and the Union army, Bellamy's "industrial army," modeled after the Grand Army of the Republic, which had emerged as a large Union veterans' organization by this time, would require all citizens to serve until the age of forty-five, and then they could retire to a life of prosperity. He predicted a peaceful revolution that would do away with strife, greed, corporate monopolies, and social evils like poverty and starvation, all replaced by a society based on cooperation and unselfishness, the opposite of laissez-faire economics. Bellamy turned to activism, speaking and writing on the problem of inequality. His book inspired the founding of "Nationalist Clubs" devoted to propagating his ideas all over the country. Instead of Bellamy's solution of nationalization of monopolies and trusts of businesses colluding to control entire industries, Republicans in Congress passed the Sherman Anti-Trust Act of 1890 (named after its chief sponsor Senator John Sherman) to restore competition and dismantle trusts and monopolies. Ironically, the Anti-Trust Act would be used more frequently against trade unions than corporate monopolies and trusts.

For his part, Lloyd, a journalist radicalized by the miscarriage of justice in the Haymarket trials, wrote many antimonopoly articles, making him a model for muckraker journalists during the Progressive era who exposed the awful conditions in factories. He published *Wealth Against Commonwealth* in 1894. The product of extensive research, the book was a moral indictment of John D. Rockefeller's Standard Oil Company, which controlled 95 percent of the national oil refining business. George, Bellamy, Lloyd, and Fortune self-consciously invoked the abolitionist tradition; Fortune's and Lloyd's role models, in particular, were Garrison and Phillips respectively.[12]

Yet however forceful and brilliant the radical critiques were, the 1890s still marked "the Fall of the House of Labor," due not just to worsening workplace conditions but also to spectacular confrontations between capital and labor that destroyed powerful unions. The Homestead strike of 1892 and the Pullman strike of 1894 bookended another cyclical downturn, the global financial Panic of 1893. As before, the strikes followed brutal wage cuts and a concerted attempt by management to crush unionism. At Andrew Carnegie's Homestead steel plant in Pennsylvania, Henry Clay Frick (named after the slaveholding senator and compromiser from Kentucky) was determined to break the Amalgamated Association of Iron and Steel Workers, a union of skilled workers that was part of the AFL. He gave the union a deadline to agree to the company's wage cuts, and when it refused, he locked out the workers. The workers responded with a strike and were joined by the more numerous non-unionized workers at Homestead. Their unity was expressed in the poem "The Homestead Strike": "Now boys, we are out on strike, you can help us if you like, But you need not till I tell you what it's about. They want to lower our wages, we think it is not right; So for Union's cause I want you all to shout." Frick encased the steel works with high barbed wire fences and called in three hundred Pinkerton detectives armed with Winchester rifles to act as company guards. Yet the workers drove the Pinkertons away and the strike spread to steelworkers in other towns.

By the end of 1892, though, Carnegie and Frick managed to suppress the Homestead strike, with nine workers killed and eleven wounded. After the Pinkertons had failed, management called in National Guardsmen and state militia, whose combined firepower proved too much for the workers, local citizens who supported them, and the pro-union mayor of Homestead, who was hounded out of town. Capitalism trumped democracy once again. The courts incarcerated strikers, who could not afford bail, and charged them with treason, as they had abolitionists who defied the fugitive slave law in the antebellum era. As one worker, Hugh O'Donnell, put it, they could not take on both the state of Pennsylvania and the US government. Frick survived an assassination attempt by anarchist Andrew Berkman in July 1892. Carnegie, a grandson of a Chartist and son of a worker, assuaged his guilt through philanthropic acts. Yet as one newspaper commented, "Ten thousand Carnegie Public Libraries would not compensate the country for the direct evils resulting from the Homestead lockout." If the union and workers could have made a successful international appeal, the way abolitionists had against slaveholders, they might have damaged Carnegie's reputation more among his liberal and radical friends in Britain.

Carnegie and Frick crushed the Amalgamated, a trade union of skilled workers; Pullman destroyed an early industrial union. In 1893, Eugene Debs formed the American Railway Union (ARU) to unify all railroad workers across skill lines. Unlike the Knights, the ARU was not open to black workers, but it grew spectacularly fast and gained recognition from some railroad corporations. Workers from the Pullman car company—named after its owner, George Pullman—joined the ARU, and in 1894 went on strike when Pullman cut their wages by an average of 25 percent. Pullman workers lived in a company town, in houses owned by Pullman, and the wage cuts came with no corresponding reduction in rents. Like southern planters and merchants who garnished the returns of sharecroppers and farmworkers in plantation stores, the Pullman company effectively stole from workers through rents and company stores. The company refused Debs's offer to arbitrate, and Debs called for a boycott of Pullman cars, after being pushed by others in the ARU to do so, resulting in an industry-wide strike—and a national showdown between railroad workers and owners.

George Pullman won through a familiar combination: federal troops called in over the protest of Governor Altgeld, who was sympathetic to labor, and the use of strike breakers and court injunctions against the striking workers, whose leaders were imprisoned. The troops were commanded by none other than General Nelson Miles, who had fought the Sioux in the 1870s. Miles, who had at least spoken out against the Wounded Knee massacre of 1890, was loath to fire on the workers. President Grover Cleveland, a Democrat, showed no states' rights scruples, nor did Attorney General Richard Olney, a former railroad lawyer. Enraged workers overturned railroad cars while armed guardsmen and troops killed around thirty workers and wounded many more. Debs, who advised against violence, was arrested. His imprisonment was commemorated by railworkers in "the John Brown song": "They hanged John Brown, but Chattel Slavery Passed Away. They arrested Eug. Debs, and May Kill Him, But Wage Slavery will Pass Away. Such Souls go Marching On." Debs's ARU had lost the battle, but the government's

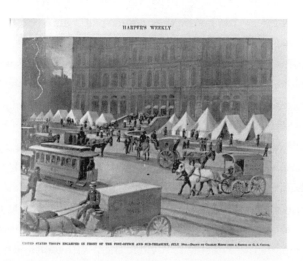

"The Great Railway Strikes—Scenes in and about Chicago," *Harper's Weekly*, 1894. *Library of Congress*

actions to back Pullman led Debs to found the Socialist Party, in order to organize American workers into a political force. The party reached a peak in the early twentieth century, but unlike European social democrats and socialists, Debs remained true to internationalism and refused to support his country's drift into WWI. He was arrested and imprisoned for two years, and political repression during the following "Red Scare" eroded support for the Socialist Party.

The same year as the Pullman strike, a reformist businessman from Massillon, Ohio, named Jacob S. Coxey, led thousands of unemployed, calling themselves the "Commonweal of Christ," on a march to the nation's capital. The depression of 1893 had created a vast "unemployed army of labor." On May 1, 1894, Coxey's army arrived in Washington to present their demands to Congress—including the construction of good roads by the government as a means of providing employment, an idea that would come to fruition in the Works Progress Administration of the New Deal. The marchers were not "tramps," as unemployed workers were often stigmatized. As the Populist leader Henry Vincent noted, "This is not an unintelligent aggregation, hoping to affect for the better the welfare of the country." The Commonwealers were dispersed by the police. Coxey and Carl Browne, a middle-aged showman who eloped with Coxey's teenaged daughter, were arrested for trampling on the grass in the capital before they could read their Good Roads bill to their followers.

The military metaphor adopted by these men and some women clearly evoked an earlier fight for justice and democracy: the Civil War. The men who marched in Coxey's army were "Union men—men who fought in Sixty-one, Who faced ev'ry danger 'neath the broiling Southern Sun." Women also joined the uprising and Coxey's Army inspired other marches. The New England–born printer "General" Charles T. Kelley led an "industrial army" from Oakland, California all the way to Washington, partly on foot and partly on trains. While the governors of Utah and Iowa prepared to call out the militia against Kelley's army, sympathetic townsmen provided them with food and other donations. Another army, led by "General" Lewis Frye, marched from the West Coast to Washington with its own constitution and "petition in boots." In Chicago, Vincent supported the commonwealers and wrote a contemporary history of the movement. Coxey's 1894 army was the first group to march on Washington in American history, a protest tradition that continues in our time. Despite the opposition of railroads and the use of militias to drive them away, the commonweal movement attracted the sympathy of other reformers and some politicians.

Even as the large strikes and demonstrations of the era failed to transform the plight of workers, labor's opponents did moderate their approach in some respects. Both Carnegie and Olney would eventually support arbitration, and "enlightened" large capitalists would form the National Civic Federation in 1900, with representation from business, unions, and the government, to mediate labor conflicts. Whether the NCF and later the New Deal—during which labor finally won the right to organize and the legal recognition of unions—represented a triumph for workers, is an ongoing debate among historians. Labor would win a seat at the table, though in the process its militancy was tempered by the state.[13]

All along, black workers fought for inclusion in unions, for unions of their own, and for their civil rights, often without help from white reformers and workers. Black railroad workers, including the well-traveled Pullman porters, pioneered a tradition of workers' civil rights that would extend to white workers as well. They often waged a two-pronged battle against their employers and coworkers who discriminated against them—with both groups frequently confining them to hard service labor. Women, too, faced a segmented labor market in which they were often confined to unskilled and low-paying jobs, a problem compounded for black women. As shown above, the so-called "titans of industry" were quite happy to employ immigrants and African Americans as strikebreakers, and the labor movement trafficked in racism—including Chinese exclusion and "hate strikes" against the employment of black workers—and in doing so weakened itself. In a few remarkable instances, interracial cooperation among workers prevailed and led to tangible victories.[14] One lesson of the history of labor, in the late nineteenth century and later, is that no progressive movement could afford to ignore the promise of interracial democracy realized during Reconstruction.

PART FOUR

FROM REPUBLIC TO EMPIRE, 1890–1920

"The Reconstruction Policy of Congress, as illustrated in California." *Library of Congress*

CHAPTER ELEVEN

American Empire

> Privately and confidentially, it is merely an outside
> cover, gay and pretty and attractive, displaying the
> special patterns of our Civilization which we reserve
> for Home Consumption, while inside the bale is the
> Actual Thing that the Customer Sitting in Darkness
> buys with his blood and tears and land and liberty.
>
> —MARK TWAIN, 1901

"Rough-Riders, Col. Theodore Roosevelt, U.S.V. Commander,"
by Kurz & Allison. *Library of Congress*

Americans took pride in what they saw as the differences between their republic and the Old World monarchies of Europe. As Thomas Paine wrote in *Common Sense* in 1776, "We have it in our power to begin the world over again." Paine and other radicals had high hopes that the new nation would be a beacon of democratic republicanism, a secular version of John Winthrop's "City on a Hill."[1] Yet the first American republic grew into an empire for slavery, and its "manifest destiny" to overspread the continent required the destruction of native nations and war against Mexico, both of which were rooted in an expansionist imperialism.[2]

The Second American Republic born during the Civil War was thus a massive course correction, resulting in the destruction of racial slavery and the enactment of national citizenship regardless of color and previous condition of servitude. Its fall, rather than success, paved the way for the triumph of a *global* US empire and revived the specifically southern dream of an imperium built on and intended to perpetuate racial subordination. As I argue in this chapter, slavery and its long afterlives in the United States—not emancipation—propelled the drive for an overseas empire, whether in the form of formal annexations and colonization or more informally through foreign interventions to serve US strategic and economic interests.[3]

A racist thermidor resulted from the unwinding of Reconstruction, which involved not just the subjugation of African Americans and western Indians but also the exclusion of Asian immigrants. The rise of Jim Crow in the South and other internal regimes of racist hierarchy fed into the logic and momentum of US imperialism. These domestic developments were, in fact, the preconditions for the rise of an overseas American empire. The 1890s proved to be a crucial decade when all these events played out, and when the Second American Republic finally crumbled with the establishment of US hegemony in the Caribbean and the Pacific.

The fight against unfree labor was not a pretext for empire, as is commonly argued. On the contrary, the persistence of unfree labor even after the abolition of slavery laid the groundwork for colonizing nonwhite nations and peoples. Well before the Civil War was won, abolitionists did not limit themselves to attacking slavery when condemning exploitative labor systems. In 1862, President Lincoln signed a law prohibiting American participation in the shipping of "coolie" labor—indentured labor from China, mainly—yet it specifically allowed for

Chinese immigration to the United States. There was no automatic linking of Chinese immigrants with "coolie" labor. Five years later, Congress abolished peonage, a form of economic servitude that trapped many indigenous people in the West, a law supported by abolitionists and put forward by Radical Republicans. The Supreme Court held that both peonage and contract labor—immigrant workers from Europe, Latin America, and Asia often had little choice but to sign long-term contracts to work in mines and railroads in exchange for transportation and pitiful wages—were prohibited by the Thirteenth Amendment. However, debt peonage, sometimes referred to as the "shadow of slavery," continued to flourish in the plantation South, ensnaring black and some white sharecroppers and tenants in a cycle of debt and poverty well into the twentieth century. In the West, peonage and other forms of unfree labor also persisted. The inheritors of the abolitionist critique of unfree labor included immigrant workers and sharecroppers who resisted oppressive conditions.

By the late nineteenth century, the global fight against the vestiges of slavery and exploitative labor regimes was led not by Western imperialists but by those who opposed them: indentured servants, "peons," and nationalists struggling against colonialism. Abolitionists as well as anticolonial movements fought for the end of mainly Indian (South Asian) indentured servitude in the British empire, continuing the battle against the enslavement and oppression of labor across the world. Soon the fight was led primarily by the colonized rather than the waning abolition movement in Britain.[4]

In the United States, the issue of contract labor became entangled with nativist hysteria over Chinese workers, particularly on the West Coast. Chinese contract workers had worked on the transcontinental railroad and in gold mines before the legalization of Chinese immigration by the Burlingame Treaty of 1868 with the Qing empire. That same year Congress, after a case involving Irish American Fenians arrested in Britain as subjects of the Crown, passed the Expatriation Act, which allowed immigrants to renounce their prior citizenship. Theoretically, this could apply to Chinese laborers, despite the racist tendency to view them as permanent aliens. It is not entirely correct, though, to claim that Reconstruction "nationalized" immigration, as some historians argue today, or that it resulted in immigration laws at the national level for the first time in US history. The federal naturalization law of 1790 had restricted naturalization to immigrants defined as "free white" persons. In 1870, when Charles Sumner tried to get "white" stricken from the law, he initially failed because of the opposition of western senators who feared that Chinese immigrants would become citizens. Sumner's amendment striking out the words "free white persons" passed after Congress allowed for the immigration and naturalization only of people of African descent. The law did not include Asian immigrants, and immigration and naturalization remained dominated by Europeans.

The mere presence of Chinese workers in the Pacific West, and the fact that they were paid lower wages than whites, stoked racism and violence. California became the center of anti-Chinese sentiment in the United States. Democrats in the state co-opted antislavery criticism of servitude to advocate the restriction, and later exclusion, of Chinese immigration. Stigmatizing all Chinese immigrants as "coolies" or prostitutes, sinophobes turned to violence, a parallel to racist terrorism in the South. The Ku Klux Klan in California and "anticoolie" associations and clubs attacked Chinese workers and neighborhoods, burning churches that welcomed them. In 1871, a mob raided Chinatown in Los Angeles and lynched eighteen Chinese men. The 1877 strikes in San Francisco also degenerated into mob attacks against the Chinese led by Denis Kearney, the founder of the Workingmen's Party of California. Their slogan, "The Chinese Must Go," encouraged racist violence. The state of California, where southerners had tried to establish slavery before the Civil War and Indian peonage was common, targeted Chinese miners through taxation. It was the only free state not to ratify the Fourteenth and Fifteenth Amendments, for fear that those amendments would bestow citizenship to the Chinese and extend voting rights to Chinese men. Sinophobia soon transcended class and party lines. The Page Act of 1875, named after the Republican senator from California, Horace Page, barred Chinese, Japanese, and "oriental" workers from migrating to the United States. It targeted Chinese women, in particular, saying that they were brought to the country for "immoral purposes."[5]

In *The Chinese in California*, G. B. Densmore, echoing "the Negro problem" discourse of critics of Reconstruction, demanded a national solution to "the Chinese problem." Edward L. Pierce, a veteran of wartime reconstruction, denounced the Republican Party platform of 1876 for including restrictions on "Mongolian" immigration. He characterized the plank as anti-Christian and believed it subverted the Declaration of Independence, whose doctrine was not "confined to the Caucasian or Aryan, to the exclusion of African, Mongolian, or Semitic races." An abolitionist editorial on the "Ostracism of Yellow Labor" condemned California Republicans for competing with Democrats to see who could abuse the Chinese more viciously. The idea of the dignity of labor should be extended, it concluded, to Chinese and black workers. One antislavery correspondent met two cosmopolitan Chinese brothers in San Francisco who spoke German, French, and English fluently and had lived in Australia. They "warmly and bitterly" condemned anti-Chinese prejudice. Another abolitionist writer clarified that "Chinese immigration" was voluntary, and that the Chinese had as much right to immigrate as Europeans. Abolitionists condemned Western imperialists for foisting missionaries and the opium trade on China, and then opposing the immigration of Chinese people fleeing oppressive conditions.

In his last public protest, in 1879, William Lloyd Garrison deemed Sinophobia a "fresh stain of caste proscription to the many that have sullied our national character" and called for "the indignant protest of every lover of his country, every friend of the whole human race." He warned the Republican Party against advocating this "utterly indefensible proscription" of Chinese immigration. Anti-Chinese sentiment, he pointedly argued, was similar to nativism against Irish immigrants—a comparison aimed at Kearney, who, like many of his followers, was Irish—and racism against "the Southern slave population." James Blaine, a Republican aspirant to the presidency, responded that he was merely opposed to "coolie" labor that reduced white workers to starvation, and that the Chinese were incapable of being converted to Christianity. Retorting, Garrison criticized Blaine's "vulgar assumption of superiority of race." He wrote that "Against this hateful spirit of caste I have earnestly protested for the last fifty years. . . . The same assertion was formerly made in disparagement of our colored population. But it was false in their case, and it is not less false now." If the Chinese wished to better their condition by emigrating to the United States, they should be received "with hospitality and kindness." They had the right to live, eat, follow their own customs, and have their own religion. He went on to school Blaine, who argued that Confucius would soon replace Christ on the Pacific coast, on the history of Chinese civilization, pointing out that Confucius came up with the Golden Rule before Christ.

Garrison was glad when President Hayes vetoed the Fifteen Passenger bill of 1879 that made it illegal to carry more than fifteen Chinese people in ships to the United States, but was disheartened by the narrow grounds of the president's opposition. Three months later, Garrison was dead. The United States negotiated a new treaty with the Chinese emperor in 1880 that allowed it to restrict immigration. In 1882, Congress, with an overwhelming Democratic majority and half of Republican votes, passed the Chinese Exclusion Act, which prohibited the immigration of Chinese workers for twenty years. The prohibition was amended by Senator Page and limited to ten years after President Chester Arthur vetoed the initial bill because he thought it violated treaties with the Chinese government. Antislavery Republicans raised principled objections. Senator George Frisbie Hoar of Massachusetts called the act "the legalization of racial discrimination," which the Jim Crow South would soon codify. The pretense of opposing "coolie" labor fell apart when all foreign contract labor—Asian, European, and Latin American—was banned by the Foran Act of 1885. Yet all Chinese immigrants were barred from North American shores by the start of the twentieth century. That same year, Canada passed the Chinese Immigration Act that placed a hefty head tax of $50 on Chinese immigrants entering the nation.

Chinese exclusion and the denial of equal protection and rights to freedpeople were two sides of the same coin; African Americans and the Chinese were both viewed as unassimilable aliens and inherently unworthy of civil rights. Despite the exclusion law, or rather because of it, the Chinese faced more violent attacks from Wyoming to Colorado as well as more scurrilous caricatures, similar to antiblack cartoons, in popular magazines like *The Wasp*. The Chinese American activist and journalist Wong Chin Foo founded the Chinese Equal Rights League, clearly modeled after the black equal rights leagues during Reconstruction, to fight exclusion and violent attacks. The Chinese government also threatened retaliation.

The Supreme Court pronounced the Exclusion Act and other discriminatory laws like the Scott Act of 1888, which prevented Chinese Americans from returning to the United States if they visited China, constitutional in *Chae Chan Ping v. United States* (1889). The court's decision relied on the plenary power of the federal government to regulate immigration without concern for the protections the US Constitution offered citizens, just as it had done to support repressive government policies regarding Native Americans. The Supreme Court did, however, uphold the Fourteenth Amendment guarantee of birthright citizenship, jus soli, for Chinese Americans who were born in the country in *United States v. Wong Kim Ark* (1898). Unlike Chae Chan Ping, Wong Kim Ark was born in the United States and had the right to return to his country. Justice John Marshall Harlan dissented, the one time the "Great Dissenter" was on the wrong side of history. Despite having his citizenship upheld by the Supreme Court, Wong Kim Ark was targeted for deportation in El Paso, Texas, a couple of years later.

Chinese exclusion marked the waning of Reconstruction's promise of an interracial democracy as well as the rise of American imperialism. William Lloyd Garrison Jr., son of the abolitionist, protested against the Geary Act of 1892, named after its principal sponsor and author, Democratic representative Thomas J. Geary of California. The act extended the Chinese Exclusion Act of 1882 for another ten years and required all Chinese Americans to carry residence permits or suffer deportation. It also deprived them of certain judicial rights, including the right to bear witness in court or to take advantage of habeas corpus. It was the "height of hypocrisy," Garrison Jr. wrote in an article published in *The Advocate of Peace*, to argue that the Chinese were "unassimilable" when a majority of white Americans held them "in contempt as an alien race." He noted, "The misrepresentations and abuse then showered upon the colored race have been transferred to the Chinese." Character traits that were regarded as virtues among European immigrant workers were viewed as sins among the Chinese. They were "disfranchised and defenseless" while their "bitter opponents" had the vote. The Chinese would eventually attain the right to vote, he hoped, "unless imperialism prevails." In a republic, he concluded,

"The Chinese Question," by Thomas Nast, *Harper's Weekly*, February 18, 1871. (Nast's anti-Irish prejudice is again evident in this portrait, in which they are blamed for the burning of the Colored Orphan's Asylum as well as attacks on Chinese immigrants.) *Library of Congress*

a "disfranchised class" is unable to protect its rights. By the 1890s, most black citizens in the South would also be formally disfranchised.

A social activist, suffragist, and anti-imperialist pacifist, Garrison Jr. chastised his friend and ally, Henry George, for his anti-Chinese prejudice, and the labor movement for its opposition to Chinese immigrant workers: "The union of labor for self-protection against the oppression of wealth cannot reasonably be decried, but when it in turn becomes aggressor upon less fortunate workers, it is time to raise a voice in protest." He also connected Sinophobia to the rise of US empire. The "exercise of Federal power to stop immigration" was a "prelude to imperialism." When a country like South Africa or the Philippines was invaded, the natives had a right to resist, but "personal dislike of foreign and strange immigrants is no excuse for maltreatment and barring out." Garrison Jr. concluded his article by quoting his father and other proponents of abolition democracy like Wendell Phillips, James Freeman Clarke, and Senator Hoar, who said that Chinese exclusion undermined "the principles on which the American republic rests," by "striking at human beings because of their race, and at laboring men because they are laborers." Chinese exclusion was an important stepping-stone not only for American empire but for a more broadly restrictive domestic immigration regime based on pseudoscientific notions of race, where all Asians were excluded from naturalization, and southern and eastern Europeans were viewed as "lesser whites."[6]

Chinese exclusion did not merely coincide and mirror other developments in the fall of the Second American Republic; it was directly connected to them. The late nineteenth century saw the legal perversion of the Reconstruction amendments to ensure the ascendancy of corporations—and that process began with the Chinese question. Lawyers representing Chinese workers and the corporations who hired them challenged California's constitution and laws that barred businesses from hiring the Chinese. The Ninth Circuit Court held the prohibition unconstitutional in *In re Tiburcio Parrott* (1880), not on the basis of the rights of Chinese workers but the right of corporations to hire

Chinese workers under the Fourteenth Amendment's equal protection clause. Rather than simply apply the equal protection clause of the Fourteenth Amendment to Chinese workers, corporate lawyers extended the amendment's purview to the alleged rights of corporations. Six years later, in the classic case *Santa Clara County v. Southern Pacific Railroad Company*, railroad lawyer and Senator Roscoe Conkling argued that the equal protection clause of the Fourteenth Amendment applied to railroads and corporations, making them immune to government regulation, even as freedpeople for whom the amendment was intended were systematically being deprived of its protections in the South.

Nothing symbolized the downfall of Reconstruction better than the use of the protections of the Fourteenth Amendment for corporations rather than freedpeople. The legal fiction of artificial personhood for corporations had been established since the early days of the republic; at the same time, unions were treated as criminal conspiracies. But the mangling of the Fourteenth Amendment and its framers' design, upheld by Chief Justice Morrison Waite, went further, giving corporations all the protections and rights bestowed on citizens during Reconstruction. It became conventional judicial wisdom. It was not an "expansive" reading of the Fourteenth Amendment, but rather a perverse one. By the early twentieth century, over half of cases involving the Fourteenth Amendment before federal courts concerned corporations, and many of the resulting opinions protected them from state regulation and labor laws. Corporations, not freedpeople, were construed by the Supreme Court as "the special favorite of the laws" in the Gilded Age.[7] Not until the second half of the twentieth century would the Fourteenth Amendment again be used for its intended purpose: the equal protection of all American citizens, prohibiting discrimination on the basis of sex and legalizing gay marriage.

The Supreme Court, in fact, played a central role in the overthrow of Reconstruction. The court signaled its adherence to outdated states' rights ideas as well as an unseemly willingness to reverse the constitutional revolution wrought by the Civil War and Reconstruction. It had already made clear its intent in the 1870s with the *Slaughterhouse* and *Cruikshank* cases discussed in chapter seven. Now, the court used "state action" doctrine, which posited that the courts could act to protect citizens' rights only from the state and not from private individuals, to eviscerate Reconstruction amendments and laws. It also turned to the doctrine of "state neglect" to trigger federal action only in certain cases. Whatever approach it took, it enforced Reconstruction laws selectively. In *Strauder v. West Virginia* (1880), the court ruled that the exclusion of African Americans from a jury violated the equal protection clause of the Fourteenth Amendment. That same year it upheld the conviction of Baltimore election officials who stuffed ballots and destroyed black votes, but overturned the conviction of a Cincinnati election official for violating the Enforcement Acts. In *Ex Parte Yarbrough* (1884), the court upheld the conviction of Jasper Yarbrough and seven others for intimidating and threatening a black man, Berry Saunders, to prevent him from voting—even though, a year earlier, in *United States v. Harris*, it had rejected the conviction of a Tennessee mob that attacked four imprisoned white Republicans, killing one. In *Harris*, the court declared parts of the Ku Klux Klan Act of 1871 unconstitutional.

The most consequential Supreme Court decision came in the *Civil Rights Cases* (1883), which pronounced unconstitutional Sumner's Civil Rights Act of 1875 that prohibited segregation in public accommodations. In 1878, the court had signaled its intent, reversing the decision of the Louisiana Supreme Court, which had awarded damages to Josephine DeCuir, a black woman denied access to a cabin in a steamship, in violation of a state civil rights law. The Louisiana law was influenced by the French conception of "public rights" that may have also inspired Sumner's attempt to ensure equal access to public accommodations when he initially proposed this law. The *Civil Rights Cases* brought together similar cases from all over the country, and the court ruled that since these were "private" acts of discrimination by corporations and businesses and not "state action," they were not, in fact, covered by the Fourteenth Amendment. Black people could not be made the "special favorite of the laws," Justice Joseph Bradley opined rather bizarrely, since equal access did not mean special treatment.

Opponents of the 1875 act argued that the court was just making a distinction between civic and social equality. The law, however, did not force whites to interact with or marry black people, but it did guarantee

African Americans public equality, an essential aspect, as Harlan stated in his dissent, of equal citizenship. Racial discrimination in public places was a "badge of servitude," he noted. If anyone was legislating on people's social relations, it was the southern states. That same year, the Supreme Court unanimously (including Harlan) upheld Alabama's "antimiscegenation" law in *Pace v. Alabama*, which punished marriage and any intimate relationship between blacks and whites by two to seven years of imprisonment, in a case involving an interracial couple. The court sanctioned southern caste laws, violating individual citizens' rights in the most personal and intimate sphere. The highest court in the land let stand the racist decision of the Alabama Supreme Court that had declared the "amalgamation of the two races" an "evil" for producing a "mongrel population and a degraded civilization."

Abolitionists viewed such rulings as grave setbacks. As Frederick Douglass noted, the outcome of the 1883 *Civil Rights Cases* "has inflicted a heavy calamity upon seven millions of the people of this country, and left them naked and defenseless against the action of a malignant, vulgar, and pitiless prejudice." It was an affront to human dignity. Following the ruling, northern and western states, effectively rejecting the Supreme Court's decision, passed laws replicating the language of the 1875 Civil Rights Act, making formal legal racial segregation, like antebellum slavery, a peculiar institution of the South. Black lawyers from the Brotherhood of Liberty, which published *Justice and Jurisprudence* in 1889, criticized the Supreme Court's reactionary decision and highlighted its origins in the DeCuir case. They set out to reveal "the transparent veils of legal fiction under cover of which the civil rights of all races are being slowly undermined" and "the unconstitutional drift of the courts and public sentiment away from the Fourteenth Amendment." Black people, women in particular, continued to challenge segregation even after the *Civil Rights Cases* decision.[8] The legal retreat from Reconstruction sanctioned by the Supreme Court not only bolstered racial apartheid in the South but also paved the way for later decisions in which the court would designate inhabitants of US colonies or territories as outside the protections of the US Constitution and citizenship. The court, in denying the protections of the Reconstruction

amendments and laws for southern black people, laid the legal groundwork for American empire.

In the 1880s, the promise of interracial democracy was not completely
dead, however. Freedpeople and their allies refused to admit defeat and
continued to fight for Reconstruction, especially in the upper South.
Some white southerners, who rejected the political fraud and violence
perpetrated by Bourbon Democrats and supported Independents, the
Greenback-Labor Party, and Populist Party, formed coalitions with
southern black Republicans. Between 1876 and 1896, Virginia, Tennessee, and North Carolina elected a number of Republican congressmen, including two African Americans, John Mercer Langston from
Virginia and George H. White from North Carolina. In Virginia, where
the Reconstruction government had fallen fast, an unlikely fusion of
black and white Republicans with disgruntled Democrats resulted in an
interracial state government from 1879 to 1883. Led, astonishingly, by a
former Confederate general, William T. Mahone, their new party—the
Readjusters—defended black voting and government activism on behalf
of education, labor, and farmer rights. The party's name came from its
advocacy of repudiation of state debt that had been incurred before the
war and threatened the financing of public education. The Readjusters, in
attempting to resurrect some of the policies of Reconstruction, pointed
to an alternative and more progressive route for southern politics.

The Republican Party in the South had become a party of mainly African Americans even as the national party moved away from black rights
to support corporate interests. Republican alliances with some southern whites were real and notable. In both 1886 and 1890, Tennesseans
elected governors from third parties allied with Republicans. In 1894,
North Carolina elected a Populist-Republican fusion legislature. Two
years later, Republican Daniel R. Russell won the governorship. Many
of the farmers in the upper South had been "mountain Republicans,"
white unionists from predominantly nonslaveholding areas. Even in
some Deep South states such as Alabama and Texas, white workers and
farmers crossed party lines to vote for third-party candidates.

The Readjusters were a local movement. It was the rise of the Farmers' Alliance and the Populist Party that posed the first serious threat to conservative Democratic rule in the South since the fall of Reconstruction. The farmers' alliances were cooperative organizations of farmers that first arose in Texas and Kansas and sought to secure better rates from railroads to transport their crops, and better farm prices by pooling their crops. In the South, the alliances opposed an exploitative lien system that kept sharecroppers and tenants indebted and in poverty. The national Farmers' Alliance promoted the so-called Subtreasury Plan to store farmers' crops in government warehouses: The state would extend credit to farmers until they sold their crops, and farmers would pay a small fee to the government for storing them. In short, they demanded government intervention in the economy to level the playing field for farmers. By 1890, the Farmers' Alliance, as well as the Colored Farmers' Alliance of black farmers and sharecroppers, together represented nearly four million members. The Farmers' Alliance incorporated many of labor's demands, including an eight-hour day and prohibition of convict labor, and forged connections with the Knights of Labor. Black southerners also joined the Agricultural Wheel, an organization of farm laborers, by the thousands.

The Farmers' Alliance, confronted by the inaction of the two main parties in the United States that both catered to corporate and planter interests, converted their movement into a third party, the Populist Party. Populists built on the legacy of prior third parties, the Greenback-Labor Party and the workingmen parties, as well as the Reconstruction legacy of government activism. In 1891, the Farmers' Alliance, the Grange, and labor representatives (mainly Knights) formed the Populist Party in Cincinnati on a platform of a progressive income tax, direct election of the president and vice president, universal suffrage, the nationalization of railroads, and an eight-hour day. With their appeal to southern white and black workers and farmers, the Populists made inroads into the solidly Democratic South, and secured significant electoral victories in the West as well. Their 1892 presidential candidate was James B. Weaver, an ex-Union general, and their vice presidential candidate was ex-Confederate officer James G. Field. But in

1896, Populists supported the Democratic candidate, William Jennings Bryan. Co-opted by Democrats, they had ceased to exist as an independent party by the end of the century.[9]

In response to Populism, Bourbon Democrats used race baiting, electoral fraud, the rewriting of state constitutions, racial segregation laws, and violence to eliminate black voting and prevent third-party challenges in the South. Just as Mississippi had pioneered the violent overthrow of Reconstruction in 1875, it launched the legal disfranchisement of black men in 1890. Its state constitutional convention met that year, and it was dominated by conservative Democrats. It passed literacy tests and poll taxes to effectively end the black vote, and in doing so disfranchised some poor whites as well. The body of a white Republican candidate was found riddled with bullets during the convention elections, while the one black Republican member of the convention, Isaiah Montgomery of Davis Bend, thought it best to accept disfranchisement. But accommodation to white supremacy would bring no peace for southern blacks, who would face the barbaric epidemic of lynching and other racist violence in the "New South."

This second "Mississippi Plan" became a model for other southern states, which started calling constitutional conventions in order to eliminate black voting by legal chicanery. By the early twentieth century, nearly all of them had done so. Southern states became profoundly antidemocratic, one-party states of Bourbon Democrats—not only the New South, but "the Solid South"—removing all black men as well as other political opponents and many poor whites from the electoral process. Some passed a "grandfather clause," creating a loophole for whites, who could bypass the literacy and poll taxes if their grandfathers had voted, and a "Constitution-understanding" clause that could be deployed selectively against African Americans. Other states, such as South Carolina, had passed complicated registration and voting laws like the "eight-box ballot," which required voters to cast ballots for eight offices in correct boxes simultaneously or their votes would be disqualified. At South Carolina's constitutional convention in 1895, Robert Smalls protested both the earlier eight-box law and the Constitution-understanding clause: "To embody such a provision in the election law would be to mean that every white man would interpret it aright and every negro would interpret it wrong."

As Mississippi moved toward legal disfranchisement, one of the last efforts to provide federal oversight of southern elections failed in Congress in 1890. Two years before, the Republican Party had gained control of the presidency and both houses of Congress for the first time in fourteen years. While radicals such as Judge Albion Tourgee demanded a uniform federal electoral system, conservative Republican representative Henry Cabot Lodge of Massachusetts and the radical Republican senator George Frisbie Hoar sought to revive the Enforcement Acts to secure black voting in the South. Lodge put forward a bill that narrowly passed the House but was filibustered in the Senate by Democrats, who dubbed it a "Force Bill." (The Knights of Labor's T. V. Powderly contradictorily opposed both the Lodge bill and black disfranchisement in the South.) Along with the Blair federal education bill, which would have funded and overseen a uniform national system of primary and secondary education, and which failed to pass Congress for the last time in 1890, the Lodge bill represented a dying gasp of the national Republican commitment to Reconstruction.

Only four years later, in 1894, a Democratic Congress repealed all federal election laws. Two years after that, the Republican Party dropped federal enforcement of voting rights in the South from its platform altogether. The Panic of 1893 had helped drive the transformation of the GOP into the party of big business and empire, its antislavery origins and commitments a thing of the past. By the time the Republicans won back the presidency in 1896 and created a self-sustaining political majority, nearly all the southern states had disfranchised black men by state laws. A few Republican politicians called for southern representation in Congress to be cut back, as stipulated by the Fourteenth Amendment as a response to voter suppression, but nothing came of it. The fall of the antislavery Republican Party and the rise of the conservative Republican Party happened simultaneously, and were rooted in the same racist views shared by a new generation of Republican politicians. Lodge, who became an avid imperialist and nativist, personally embodied these contradictions.

In 1890, the year that Mississippi disfranchised black men, Louisiana passed a racial segregation law requiring blacks and whites to use separate railway cars. In 1892, Homer Plessy, who was "seven-eighths Caucasian," refused to vacate a white car and was arrested under the new law. He sued the state and was represented by the Reconstruction-era judge Albion Tourgee. (A year later, halfway across the world, a young Indian lawyer named Mohandas Gandhi was thrown out of a first-class whites-only compartment in South Africa.) In the infamous *Plessy v. Ferguson* (1896) decision, the Supreme Court upheld segregation, arguing that the notion of "separate but equal" did not violate the equal protection clause of the Fourteenth Amendment and that state-mandated discrimination was not unconstitutional, effectively making African Americans second-class citizens. Black people were and would continue to be subject to inferior accommodations and schools in the Jim Crow South; separate was inherently unequal. In the majority decision, Justice Henry Billings Brown, educated at Yale and Harvard, cited the *Civil Rights Cases* as a precedent and even an 1849 Boston school desegregation case that black abolitionists and Charles Sumner had brought (and lost) before Massachusetts ended school segregation in 1855. Invoking the police powers of states, Brown justified segregation by arguing that it was not the place of the law to legislate racial equality—though apparently the law could legislate racial *inequality*. As he concluded, revealing

"Justice Harlan," by C. M. Bell.
Library of Congress

his ill-disguised racism, "If one race be inferior to the other socially, the Constitution of the United States cannot put them upon the same plane."

In his dissent, Harlan held that "in view of the Constitution, in the eye of the law, there is in this country no superior, dominant ruling class of citizens. There is no caste here." (He also argued that unlike black people, the Chinese in America were not subject to formal legal segregation, a discrimination that he sanctioned as the United States became a Pacific power.) Harlan predicted that *Plessy*, like the Dred Scott decision, would join the anti-canon of Supreme Court decisions, even though it took another half century for that prediction to be proven accurate, a process that started with the decision in *Brown v. Board of Education* (1954). Racial segregation went against the equality before the law established by the Constitution, Harlan argued; it was a "badge of servitude wholly inconsistent with civil freedom" and could not be "justified upon any legal grounds." In *Williams v. Mississippi* (1898), the court further held, unsurprisingly, that all the legal subterfuges used to disfranchise black men—the literacy clause, poll taxes, the grandfather clause—were constitutional because they did not explicitly mention race, even though the last of these, in particular, targeted African Americans with surgical precision. Not until 1915 would the court declare the grandfather clause unconstitutional, but by then a whole slew of voter suppression laws, the discriminatory actions of voter registrars, and all-white Democratic primaries effectively disfranchised most southern black voters.[10]

The contraction of American democracy was a national phenomenon, as northern states passed voter restriction laws tied to literacy targeting immigrants, workers, and the poor, but it was most egregious in the apartheid regime of the South. By the end of the century, national voting rates had plummeted precipitously across the nation, yet especially among disfranchised southern black men. Some historians argue that disfranchisement and racial segregation became a substitute for white mob violence, but the claim is difficult to support in view of the carnival of racist attacks that defined the turn-of-the-century South.

While the region had witnessed white terrorism for decades by this point, the death knell of the fusion politics of the upper South was sounded by a violent coup against the interracial city government of

Wilmington, North Carolina, and the subsequent massacre of its black residents, in 1898. That year, the state Democratic Party launched a racist campaign to wean white Populists off the fusion government. The Democrats managed to win state elections marred by fraud and widespread violence by terror groups such as the Red Shirts, egged on by one of its founders, the South Carolinian racist demagogue Ben Tillman, and "White Government Union" clubs. In Wilmington, the fusion local government was not up for reelection. But that didn't stop the local elites, led by ex-Confederate colonel Alfred Moore Waddell, who were determined to topple it and destroy the city's prosperous black community.

The state press helped whip up a racist frenzy, printing a speech by former Populist Rebecca Latimer Felton of Georgia that described all black men as beasts and rapists (of white women) who needed to be lynched. Alexander Manly, the black editor of Wilmington's *The Daily Record,* responded that such interracial relationships were consensual and that white men had a history of abusing black women. This was viewed as "a horrid slander," and an excuse to demand that Manly stop publishing his paper. Waddell issued a "White Declaration of Independence"—even though most of the city's officeholders, including the mayor, were white—and demanded a response from its black citizens. He promised to choke the Cape Fear River, which ran through the city, with black bodies. Black city leaders sent a conciliatory response to him, but a mob composed of men from the Wilmington Light Infantry, newly returned from the Spanish-Cuban-American War and personifying the connection between racism at home and imperialism abroad, proceeded to burn the black community center where Manly's paper was housed. They forced the entire city government to resign, elevating local Democrats in its place. Waddell replaced the white Republican mayor, Silas P. Wright. The mob then went on to randomly kill African Americans, and to exile prominent blacks on the threat of lynching. The official number of black people murdered was sixty, but in all likelihood, hundreds lost their lives. African Americans hid in nearby swamps, while hundreds fled Wilmington, which was a black majority city. Many of those who had instigated the terror and the coup attained high office and went on to have streets and parks named after them, some of which were only renamed in the aftermath of George Floyd's murder in 2020.

A year after the coup, the North Carolina legislature passed a suffrage amendment that disfranchised all black men through poll taxes, literacy tests, and the infamous grandfather clause; the amendment was approved by voters in 1900, in an election again shaped by fraud and Red Shirts violence. As elsewhere in the South, black voting virtually disappeared and even white voting rates fell. Manly had decamped to Washington to the home of the black congressman from the state, George H. White. He remained active in early civil rights organizations like the Afro-American Council, the NAACP, and the predecessor to the Urban League. For his part, White, in his 1901 farewell speech to Congress, mounted a defense of his race, citing the black literacy rates and professional success that had characterized Wilmington's black community before the massacre. And he took southern demagogues to task: "After enforced debauchery, with many kindred horrors incident to slavery, it comes with ill grace from the perpetrators of these deeds to hold up the shortcomings of some of our race to ridicule and scorn." Black achievements had come "in the face of lynching, burning at the stake, with the humiliation of Jim Crow cars, the disfranchisement of our male citizens, slander and degradation of our women," and despite factories, mines, railroads, and labor unions being closed to them. He predicted that his departure would be "the Negro's temporary fare-well to the American Congress." As the last southern black congressman after Reconstruction, his "parting words are in behalf of an outraged, heartbroken, bruised and bleeding, but God-fearing people, faithful, industrious, loyal people, rising people, full of potential force."[11]

That same year, North Carolina's most accomplished nineteenth-century black novelist, Charles W. Chesnutt, published *The Marrow of Tradition,* a novel based on the Wilmington massacre and set in the fictional town of Wellington. Chesnutt captured Waddell and his ilk perfectly in the character of Major Carteret, who says, at one point: "I merely object to being governed by an inferior and servile race." Cateret and his friends drink to "White Supremacy," the ancient southern recipe concocted by the "great John C. Calhoun." But the novel also indicted the federal government, and the nation overall, for doing nothing in the face of vicious southern violence. The federal government did not *see* the massacre, as one black character in the novel, Dr. Miller, notes: "The government can only intervene under certain conditions, of which it must be informed through designated channels. It never sees anything that is not officially called to its attention." During the actual insurrection in Wilmington, President William McKinley had claimed that his hands were tied because the governor of North Carolina had not asked for assistance.

Another black writer, David Bryan Fulton, who wrote under the pen name Jack Thorne, also endeavored to tell the story of the Wilmington massacre in a thinly fictionalized account. Fulton's *Hanover; or The Persecution of the Lowly. Story of the Wilmington Massacre*, which begins with the true story of the near lynching and banishment of city official George Z. French, recalled the subtitle of Harriet Beecher Stowe's iconic antislavery novel, *Uncle Tom's Cabin; or, Life Among the Lowly*. Describing the Wilmington coup and picking up on the anti-Chinese slogan, Fulton wrote that the city's white residents proclaimed "WHITE MEN MUST GO TOO," if they were "white Republicans" like "assertive Negroes, who are considered dangerous to the peace of the community." The book's characters include "The Editor" and "The Colonel," clearly based on Manly and Waddell, respectively. It ends with exiled black North Carolinians making a hard living in the North but preferring its limited freedom to the Jim Crow South. In fact, the exiled black "Sons and Daughters of North Carolina" protested the Wilmington massacre in Brooklyn and met in other cities like Worcester, Massachusetts to worship and congregate. Waddell himself wrote a self-serving memoir that whitewashed the massacre, designating Wilmington a "race riot" and blaming a fictitious black man for starting the violence.[12]

African American novelists and writers at the turn of the century wrote in the abolitionist tradition, confronting the betrayal of emancipation as well as the Lost Cause myths about slavery, the Civil War, and Reconstruction. Yet the dominant literary and scholarly works of this period enshrined the Confederate view. The originator of the Lost

Cause narrative was the proslavery ideologue and secessionist Edward A. Pollard, who had advocated the reopening of the African slave trade on the eve of the war in his bizarrely titled *Black Diamonds Gathered in the Darkey Homes of the South*, a response to abolitionists. After the war, Pollard wrote the first Lost Cause books, recasting the Confederacy's battle for human bondage into a noble fight for states' rights and, more honestly, "the supremacy of the white race." Following his lead, the ex-Confederate vice president and ex-President, Alexander Stephens and Jefferson Davis, spun similar tales, in which they identified the southern cause with the Constitution and the American Revolution. The decisively defeated Confederate army emerged, in such accounts, as the militarily superior and more successful side. In this upside-down world, treason became patriotism, destroying the Constitution meant upholding it, losing became winning, and the sordid defense of slavery was transformed into a defense of southern honor and heritage. Their books and stories were published by the leading publishing houses and journals and found a big audience in the North. Northern writers also contributed to "the romance of reunion," penning novels in which northern men married southern belles.

Saccharine plantation novels and stories of "faithful darkies" dominated the racist nostalgia of industrializing America and all talk of the "New South." Thomas Nelson Page's novel of Reconstruction, *Red Rock* (1898), transformed black political leaders into beasts who raped white women and deserved to be lynched by southern mobs. The more paternalistic Joel Chandler Harris reproduced African American folktales in his famous Uncle Remus books, but still posited a benign view of slavery. In the early twentieth century, Thomas Dixon Jr. of North Carolina wrote a trilogy of novels on Reconstruction along similar lines. The first novel, *The Leopard's Spot: A Romance of the White Man's Burden, 1865–1900*, tellingly deployed the motto of European imperialism to justify the overthrow of Reconstruction. The second novel, *The Clansman: A Historical Romance of the Ku Klux Klan*, portrayed the Klan as chivalric heroes and became the basis of Hollywood's first blockbuster, *The Birth of a Nation*. It was screened by his friend, Woodrow Wilson, the first southern president since the Civil War, who introduced segregation in the capital, the federal government, and the White House. Its screening in theaters was protested by the NAACP across the nation.

Sectional reconciliation was the prevailing narrative, and the Civil War was recast as a family quarrel of brother against brother, its emancipatory legacy submerged or undercut. Groups like the United Daughters of the Confederacy and Sons of Confederate Veterans littered the South with statues of Confederate generals, marking their triumph politically and ideologically. They shaped the popular memory of the war and Reconstruction as a period of "carpetbaggers" and black misrule and corruption, helping indoctrinate generations of Americans. United Daughters of the Confederacy Secretary Mildred Rutherford not only wrote history textbooks for southern schools, but also insisted that all southern children read Page's novels. Ex-Confederate generals like Jubal Early assiduosly promoted Lost Cause mythology and neo-Confederate histories of the Civil War and the South.

Down to the mid-twentieth century, when Nazism finally made racism unfashionable in academic and popular circles, Lost Cause mythology in movies such as *Gone with the Wind,* based on Margaret Mitchell's sappy, Pulitzer Prize–winning novel, pervaded popular culture. In academia, a similar "propaganda of history," as W. E. B. DuBois put it, shaped interpretations of Reconstruction. Yet an alternative memory of Reconstruction lived on among African Americans, southern dissenters, and northern radicals, forming the foundation of an accurate history of the period. Besides those who had participated in Reconstruction like John Lynch and Albion Tourgee, others such as Alrutheus Ambush Taylor and James Allen sought to write balanced histories of the period that have become dominant only in the recent past.[13]

It was no coincidence that Lost Cause mythology emerged during the heyday of scientific racism and imperialism. Abolitionists had long challenged the pseudoscience of race that proslavery "intellectuals" had developed to legitimize slavery. Now, once again, science was used to justify black subjugation in the South. Like Andrew Johnson, another allegedly poor white, Hinton Rowan Helper of North Carolina peddled racism during Reconstruction. Helper's *The Impending Crisis of the South* (1857) was an indictment of slaveholders, from the perspective of nonslaveholding whites, for ruining the South economically. Later, he identified black people as the bane of the Americas in his racist screed, *Nojuque: A Question for a Continent* (1867). A colonizationist before the war, he advocated the forcible expulsion of black people—ethnic cleansing—after it. At Harvard, Nathaniel Shaler, a student of the polygenist proslavery Swiss professor Louis Agassiz and a member of a slaveholding Kentucky family, defended both slavery and polygenesis, or the notion that each "race" had its own origins and was a distinct species.

Social Darwinism—the British scholar Herbert Spencer's belief that the idea of the "survival of the fittest" could be applied to human society—provided further intellectual justification for southern apartheid, for indigenous dispossession, for Chinese exclusion, for imperialism, and for a rapacious economic order of robber barons and a largely immigrant workforce under them. Albion Tourgee's *A Fool's Errand* (1879), a fictional memoir of his days as a Reconstruction judge in North Carolina, put it best: the nation's message to "the colored man, in the language of the pseudo-philosophers of that day," was "Root, hog, or die!" As Spencer's primary American acolyte, William Graham Sumner of Yale, wrote, the rich, the philanthropic, the religious, and the government owed nothing to the poor in the "struggle for existence." He believed "poverty is the best policy" and that it was "not wicked to be rich," ideas that made him a celebrated sage of Gilded Age conservatism. If abolitionists had spent a lifetime trying to fight for a society based on the Gospel's Golden Rule of do unto others, Spencer argued that the laws of "social science" meant that we owed each other nothing. Ironically, Spencer opposed American imperialism, even as his philosophy helped legitimize it. The use of racial science and eugenics to justify Jim Crow and empire at the turn of the century was what led DuBois to pronounce that "The problem of the twentieth century is the problem of the color-line,—the relation of the darker to the lighter races of men in Asia and Africa, in America and the islands of the sea."[14]

The 1890s saw not only justifications for an overseas American empire but the violent rise of one. Before the Civil War, proslavery imperialism had played no small part in the emergence of an antislavery Republican Party. In addition to continental expansion and the annexation of Mexican territory, the Franklin Pierce administration unilaterally acquired the so-called Guano islands in the Pacific, prized for their valuable guano fertilizer. Proslavery imperialists and northern capitalists hoped to make a windfall from guano. Their recipe for capitalist imperialism—the use of foreign labor in subhuman conditions and sponsorship of corporate interests by government, despite a commitment to laissez-faire when it came to economic regulation and the interests of labor—was born in the hunt for guano. In 1867, the United States formally annexed two of the Guano islands as well as the Midway Islands (Atoll) and bought Alaska from the Russian empire—the last deemed "Seward's folly," after the secretary of state, because it was viewed as a barren, cold piece of worthless land. Native Alaskans were not consulted in the imperial transaction. Seward valued Alaska for its strategic location. He viewed the Aleutian Islands as "the drawbridge to Asia," island steppingstones across the Pacific. This idea of islands linking the United States to Asia was why Midway, Hawaii, and eventually Guam, were valued as coaling stations to enable navy and commercial ships to operate far from North America. Seward's support for Andrew Johnson also aligned with his imperialism, and he with proslavery Democratic administrations had sponsored the acquisition of the Guano islands before the war. Democratic expansionist Robert J. Walker of Mississippi, like Seward, dreamed of US hegemony in Panama, the Caribbean, and the Pacific. Many Deep South slaveholders had long envisioned slavery's empire extending from Texas to California, from Nicaragua to Cuba.[15]

The emergence of an overseas American empire, though, was not inevitable. The abolition of slavery and the defeat of the Confederacy reverberated throughout the hemisphere. In 1861, the Mexican republic was overthrown by the French, who installed the brother of the Austrian emperor, Maximilian I, as the emperor of Mexico. That same year, Spain annexed the Dominican Republic. With American moral support, Mexicans defeated and executed France's puppet leader in 1866. Benito Juarez, who had been ousted by the French, was reinstated as president. In 1862, Lincoln hailed the end of a long conflict in the Argentinian republic, which had abolished slavery nine years prior. Lincoln's policy toward Latin American countries was a repudiation of the proslavery and Democratic expansionism of his chief political rival, Stephen A. Douglas. By the end of the Civil War, republicanism seemed ascendant in the Americas, and antislavery appeared to be prevailing across the globe, from British India and the Ottoman Empire to the Dutch and Portuguese colonies. The Dutch began the process of abolishing slavery in 1863, the same year as the Emancipation Proclamation.

As Charles Sumner predicted during Reconstruction, "Slavery will end very soon in Cuba, it cannot remain much longer in Brazil." Antislavery republicanism spread to Cuba during the Ten Years War (1868–1878) for independence from Spain, with Afro-Cuban generals and soldiers making emancipation a complementary goal. In the Reconstruction South, many freedpeople named their newborn sons Maceo, after the most famous of these generals, Antonio Maceo Grajales. The Spanish Cortes (Parliament) and the Brazilian government passed free womb laws, which freed children of the enslaved, in 1870 and 1871, respectively, the first tentative steps toward emancipation (and to forestall the rebellion of the enslaved). In these remaining slave societies, enslaved people had revolted unsuccessfully in the early 1860s, confident that Lincoln was an ally, and inspired by the Union's war against the Confederacy and Lincoln's Emancipation Proclamation. In 1873, the Cortes enacted an abolition law for Puerto Rico.

The largest slave societies in the hemisphere after the American South, Cuba and Brazil, abolished slavery by decree rather than revolution, in 1886 in Cuba, after the reimposition of Spanish rule, and in 1888 in Brazil. In both countries, enslaved people used a variety of means to gain freedom—self-purchase, military service, fugitivity, outright rebellion, and participation in abolition movements. Yet freedpeople in post-slavery Cuba, Brazil, and Puerto Rico, as in the postwar American South, soon found their dearly won freedom constrained by the political economy of plantation agriculture, which was tied to a global market, and by a lack of civic equality and economic autonomy. Southern Confederates in Brazil, and American corporations and imperialists in Cuba, warned of the disruptions to the plantation economy and the perils of interracial democracy that they had witnessed during Recon-struction. Capital's revived alliance with provincial reactionary planter-merchant elites throughout the Americas signified the lost promise of emancipation. Wary of the revolutionary precedent of Reconstruction, local elites defeated freedpeople's access to the ballot and demands for land. The proven recipe—the Mississippi Plan of 1890—was first imple-mented in Brazil in 1881 when the conservative, proslavery government disfranchised the majority of its population, including nearly all former slaves. As in the United States, the emancipatory promise of abolition and democratic reform lay defeated with the reimposition of plantation economies and the reconstruction of capitalism.[16]

The dismantling of black citizenship became the norm in post-slavery societies. The international significance of the fall of the Second Amer-ican Republic was evident in the lesson that Western imperialists drew about the supposed impossibility of interracial democracy, about the necessity of ordering "the relations between ruling and subject races" and the notion of "the unfitness of non-white races for political rights." Pronouncing Reconstruction a failure and the conquest of the West a success, the United States joined European nations in the scramble for empire. A majority of Americans, the historian Nina Silber observes, "internationalized the race problem, identifying the common, back-ward characteristics of all nonwhite peoples, as well as a common supe-riority of Anglo-Saxons, around the world."

Indeed, the alleged failure of Reconstruction became the specific grounds on which American intellectuals and politicians justified not only despotic rule at home, but an overseas empire—Jim Crow on a global scale. John W. Burgess, a southerner and Columbia University politi-cal scientist who vilified black citizenship as a "monstrous thing," com-mended the now-imperialist Republicans for taking on the white man's burden of civilizing the world and for "imposing the sovereignty of the United States upon eight millions of Asiatics" in the Philippines after the Spanish-Cuban-American War of 1898. In founding an overseas empire, the administration of William McKinley had steered the Republican Party from supposedly false notions of racial equality to an understanding of the "vast differences in political capacity between the races." (Burgess inspired his colleague William A. Dunning, who with his mostly southern students formed the Dunning school of Reconstruction historiography. The first professionally trained historians to write on Reconstruction, they perpetrated racist stereotypes and gave scholarly legitimacy to the Jim Crow South.) Similarly, Charles Francis Adams Jr. wrote about the new conception of "the race problem" in the United States, which was taking "less of a theoretical and humanitarian" approach and instead embracing the reigning shibboleths of the pseudoscience of race. Proslavery Confederates had been right all along, in this view.

Ironically, it was Republicans who finally realized slaveholders' dream of an empire in the Caribbean and Central America. Murat Halstead, the journalist known for his riveting accounts of the presidential party conventions that led to the election of Lincoln in 1860 and who became a Liberal Republican, now penned cheerleading reports of American empire in the Philippines, Hawaii, Cuba, and Puerto Rico. As he wrote rhapsodically about the Spanish-Cuban-American War and the acquisition of the Philippines by the United States: "The deed was done with a flash of lightening, [sic] and lo! We hold the golden key of a splendid Asiatic archipelago of a thousand beautiful and richly endowed islands in our grip." Halstead portrayed an overseas empire both as a new step for the nation as well as the logical end of settler colonialism: "it seems to be Divinely appointed that our paths of Empire may, with advantage to ourselves, and the world at large be more comprehensive that our fathers blazed them out." He recalled the continental expansion sponsored by Washington and Jefferson, writing that "We walk in the ways of the fathers when we go conquering and to conquer along the Eastward shores of Asia."

The Spanish-Cuban-American War, which resulted in the annexation of the Philippines and US hegemony in the Caribbean, began with the explosion on February 15, 1898, of the USS *Maine*, an American battleship in Havana, Cuba, killing over two hundred of its crew. (Cubans had revived their independence struggle against Spain in 1895, when the Cuban nationalist Jose Marti, a great admirer of Lincoln and influenced by Afro-Latino radicals, had returned home from his exile in New York City.) The American press, already reporting sensationally on Spanish atrocities against the Cubans, and Congress blamed the Spanish for the catastrophe, though the Spanish government disavowed any responsibility. The war's primary booster was McKinley's assistant naval secretary of state, Theodore Roosevelt, who aspired to embody a cult of Anglo-Saxonism and virile masculinity, personally leading the Rough Riders—the name given to the First US Volunteer Cavalry—in Cuba during the war after his many "adventures" in the West. He downplayed the role of black soldiers after the fact, though they had bailed out his supposed Rough Riders. The "splendid little war" came to a speedy conclusion by the end of 1898 with a Cuban and American victory that saw ex-Confederate and ex-Union soldiers united in the romance of empire. Black soldiers left behind to occupy Cuba were called "immunes," based on the false notion that they were immune to tropical diseases.

Rather than supporting "Cuba libre" and independent anticolonial republics, the United States inaugurated a policy of intervention and outright annexation in the Caribbean and the Pacific. With the Treaty of Paris signed on December 10, 1898, Spain ceded Puerto Rico and Guam to the United States and relinquished its claims on Cuba. The Philippines emerged as a point of contention but was eventually sold to the United States for $20 million. Native populations—Puerto Ricans, Chamorros, and Filipinos—were not consulted. Cuba was not directly annexed because the Teller amendment, passed by Congress in 1898 after the declaration of war, prohibited it. But the Platt amendment, passed in 1901 when US troops eventually left Cuba, sanctioned American intervention and severely compromised Cuban sovereignty. It was the blueprint for an informal American empire. The US government justified its interventions in the affairs of other countries to protect its strategic and economic interests.

Cuban and Filipino independence fighters could be forgiven for initially thinking that an American republic born in an anticolonial revolution would support them. The logic of imperialism, fueled by a desire to exploit the world's resources for both national glory and profits, and justified by the conviction that much of the world's racially nonwhite peoples were incapable of self-government, dictated otherwise. Halstead reported that General Emilio Aguinaldo, who led the Filipino revolt against the Spanish, was set on "Philippine independence," but he proposed an American protectorate over the former Spanish colony. Halstead sanguinely predicted that they would "walk hand in hand with us, and become the greatest of our dependencies—not states, but territories." When Aguinaldo formed an independent republican government and a congressional vote for Philippine independence was narrowly defeated, the US–Philippine War (1899–1913) began.

The brutal Indian wars in the West served as a precedent for the horrific suppression of the republic led by Aguinaldo. The US Army sent many veterans of those wars, including its commanding general in chief, Nelson Miles, who also led the annexation of Puerto Rico, to "pacify" the Philippines. General Leonard Wood, known for his diary record of the "hunt" for Geronimo, for which he received a Medal of Honor, became successively the military governor of Cuba and the governor general of the Philippines. In Congress, Filipinos were likened to Indians, in need of "civilization" and Christianization—no matter that most were Catholic. The senators who had voted for the Dawes Severalty Act of 1887 now voted to annex the Philippines, guided by the same logic of "benevolent assimilation." Filipino guerilla fighters, referred to as "n---," were treated like Native Americans—that is, as outside the bounds of "civilized warfare." War crimes on both sides abounded. The torture technique of "waterboarding" was born in this war, and the herding of civilians into "reconcentration camps"—precisely the Spanish atrocities in Cuba the American press had condemned—was reminiscent of the American reservations policy toward indigenous people. General Arthur MacArthur, who was involved in capturing Geronimo, persuaded Aguinaldo to surrender. In 1900, he was appointed military governor of the Philippines. His son Douglas MacArthur, who "liberated" the Philippines from Japanese rule during WWII, claimed to understand the "Asian mind." His mother was a Virginian, whose brothers had fought for the Confederacy. Father and son, known for defying civilian authority, illustrated the continuity of US empire in the Pacific.[17]

The launching of an overseas American empire was the final act in the fall of the Second American Republic. Imperialism, its critics noted even at the time, is the highest form of capitalism. Northeastern capitalists had rushed to make a killing, first in the West and then in the newly founded overseas empire, based on the exploitation of indigenous populations. Not only did the United States subjugate the former Spanish colonies, but it also annexed the Kingdom of Hawaii to protect American business interests. US missionaries and settlers had a long history of intervening in Hawaiian affairs, forcing a constitutional monarchy and then a republic on Hawaii. European and American sugar planters had prospered there on the strength of indigenous dispossession and immigrant labor from Portugal and Asia. These immigrant workers signed long-term contracts, the kind that freedpeople were made to sign after emancipation. Sugar production in Hawaii increased by 100 percent between 1876 and 1890.

In 1887, the planter elite forced a "Bayonet Constitution" on the Kingdom of Hawaii that introduced property-holding qualifications for voting and officeholding, disfranchising most of the native and Asian populations. These new laws were appropriately called the "Mississippi laws." In 1893, with the assistance of the US minister to Hawaii, American businessmen and planters overthrew Queen Lili'uokalani, who had attempted to reestablish Hawaiian sovereignty, and President Benjamin Harrison signed a treaty of annexation with their provisional government. The push to annex Hawaii by treaty failed when his successor, Grover Cleveland, refused to support it or recognize the Americans' provisional government. In 1894, the businessmen and planters, instead of handing power back to the queen, created the "Republic of Hawaii," which the Cleveland administration recognized. Its constitution, modeled after the Jim Crow South, completely disfranchised native Hawaiians and Asians. Democratic senator John Morgan of Alabama had the temerity to assure Hawaiians that they would enjoy the right to vote—just like black southerners.

President William McKinley, who supported annexation, backed another treaty in 1897. Thousands of Hawaiians, under the leadership of Queen Lili'uokalani, signed petitions to Congress that were introduced by Sumner's protégé, Senator George Frisbie Hoar, against annexation.

Queen Lili'uokalani in 1900. *Hawaii State Archives*

The treaty was defeated. Yet in 1898, the McKinley administration succeeded in annexing Hawaii by a joint resolution of Congress, precisely the manner in which Texas had been annexed in 1845 by proslavery and expansionist Democrats after the defeat of the Texas annexation treaty. The Queen testified,

> Perhaps there is a kind of right, depending upon the precedents of all ages, and known as the "Right of Conquest," under which robbers and marauders establish themselves in possession of whatsoever are strong enough to ravish from their fellows.... So it happens that, overawed by the power of the United States to the extent that they can neither themselves throw off the usurpers, nor obtain assistance from other friendly states, the people of the Islands have no voice in determining their future, but are virtually relegated to the condition of the aborigines of the American continent.

She drew a straight line from indigenous dispossession to American empire. The white planter oligarchy, trained in the habits of "autocracy," were anything but "ideal citizens of democracy." The annexationist party was dangerous to the health of the American republic itself, she warned.

Opposition to the annexation of overseas territories led to the formation of the Anti-Imperialist League in Boston in 1898. A conglomeration of business, labor, and political leaders, its first president was George S. Boutwell, the Radical Republican who had been one of the House's managers in Andrew Johnson's impeachment and who had served as secretary of the treasury in the Grant administration. Still a staunch defender of Reconstruction, Boutwell was joined by other antislavery men such as Oscar Garrison Villard, Garrison's grandson, Thomas Wentworth Higginson, and Moorfield Storey, who would become the founding president of the NAACP. Perhaps its most famous member was Mark Twain, whose caustic essays on American atrocities in the Philippines, his essay "The United States of Lyncherdom," and denunciation of European imperialism and Sinophobia are timeless. In addition to opposing the annexation of Hawaii, the League exposed US war crimes in the Philippines. It adopted an address in 1899 that compared Aguinaldo's government and the Philippines constitution to the Continental Congress of 1775. Attacking what it identified as a "war of subjugation," the address declared: "Any right that we assert to ownership of the Philippines must rest, therefore, either upon conquest or purchase from their Spanish oppressors, or upon both, and in any case it is, as we believe, inconsistent with the principles of this Republic, and fraught with danger to its peace and the peace of the world." The address decried imperialism, militarism, and colonialism, demanding that the United States recognize the independence of the Philippines and withdraw all its military forces from the archipelago.

According to Boutwell, McKinley had created "subject races" in violation of the Thirteenth Amendment and governed the new colonies as if "the Constitution did not exist." Tracing his own anti-imperialism to his antislavery beliefs, Boutwell accused the president of "subjecting ten million people to involuntary subserviency under his rule," questioning his claim to extend "the blessings of liberty and civilization to the inferior races of the earth." The United States was a colonial power no different than Spain, Boutwell surmised, even though "America was a republic." The League and Boutwell supported Democratic candidate William Jennings Bryan against McKinley in the 1900 presidential elections, which alienated some of its conservative, business-oriented members. Some die-hard southern racists like Benjamin Tillman also opposed the acquisition of overseas territories, nervous that nonwhite populations would become a part of the United States. (John C. Calhoun had used similar reasoning to oppose the Mexican War in the 1840s.) Though the Anti-Imperialist League lasted until 1920, it never gained sufficient traction in the age of empire. Its warnings were vindicated, however, with the onset of the Great War among global imperial powers in 1914.

The United States joined imperialist nations in carving the world among themselves. While Europeans feared the continental behemoth, "American Danger," the US rushed to participate in the scramble for empire. Alfred Thayer Mahan, the famous nineteenth-century proponent of sea power, like Seward had visualized a Pacific trading empire. The United States acquired Wake Island and American Samoa in 1899, the US Virgin Islands in 1917 (Seward had attempted to buy the islands from Denmark in 1867), and the Northern Marianas after the Second World War. While Hawaii and Alaska became states in 1959, the rest of these islands, along with Guam and Puerto Rico, remain US territories. In the Insular Cases (1901), the Supreme Court put the inhabitants of island territories outside the purview of the Constitution and the national citizenship clause of the Fourteenth Amendment. In his dissent, Justice Harlan noted that the majority's decision would "engraft upon our republican institutions a colonial system such as exists under monarchical governments."

Today, with the exception of American Samoa, most inhabitants of these territories are US citizens, but the "unincorporated territories" are still in a colonial relationship with the mainland. Their nonwhite populations came under the plenary power of the US government just as surely as indigenous nations. One American newspaper differentiated, in 1901, between the long history of settler colonialism and formal empire: "We are now following the footsteps of England, not in planting colonies as it did in Australia, but in conquering and ruling unwilling alien races as it did in India and incidentally exploiting them." American imperialism also represented "the U.S. practice of viewing foreign people through the lens of racial categories at home," a direct fallout of the demise of Reconstruction, the conquest of the West, and racial restrictions on immigration. The informal "offshore empire" of the United States in the twentieth century would come to encompass protectorates, and thereby legitimize interventions and outright occupations, in the Caribbean and Central America.[18]

By the twentieth century, the United States replaced Britain as the dominant industrial, military, and political—if not territorial— imperium. The establishment of racial apartheid in the former slave states is not often seen as an integral part of the history of American imperialism. But the two processes were, in fact, interlinked, and together reveal the world-historical significance of the fall of the Second American Republic. The long afterlives of slavery and imperialism posed a dire threat to democracy. As DuBois understood, the First World War was nothing if not a war over imperial greatness; its roots were in the "scramble for Africa" among European powers at the turn of the century.[19] And indeed, the contest between forces of civic republicanism and authoritarianism, between social democracy and the global political economy of capitalism, that characterized Reconstruction has continued down to our times.

The defeat of black citizenship occurred simultaneously with battles over labor and immigrant rights as well as with the conquest of indigenous nations in the West and the rise of an overseas empire. All of these events were linked, at the most fundamental level. In this atmosphere of political revanchism, American women would jumpstart their fight for suffrage. That fight would revive the lost promise of Reconstruction democracy, but it also entailed expedient compromises with the new racial order of American empire, at home and abroad.

CHAPTER TWELVE

The Last Reconstruction Amendment

When and where I enter, in the quiet, undisputed dignity of my womanhood, without violence, and without suing or special patronage, then and there the whole Negro race enters with me.

—ANNA JULIA COOPER, *A Voice from the South*, 1892

"Mrs. A.J. Cooper,"
by C. M. Bell. *Library of Congress*

Though it fell and was replaced by an imperialist state, the Second American Republic left legacies that had an immediate effect, well before the civil rights movement of the 1950s and 1960s—the so-called Second Reconstruction. The women's suffrage movement is not often seen as integral to the history of Reconstruction, but, in fact, its ultimate success, in the form of the Nineteenth Amendment (1920), was one of the significant results of efforts to forge an interracial democracy after the Civil War. Other struggles for women's emancipation also continued to be shaped by the legacies of Reconstruction, especially the era's emphasis on government activism and on the intersecting nature of campaigns for black and women's rights.

This is not to suggest that the women's movement left behind its own, earlier issues with racism in the drive for an amendment. The struggle for women's suffrage proved to be long and arduous—and throughout, some white women continued to acquiesce to black disfranchisement, whether out of racism or expedience, or both. As we saw in Chapter Six, the two wings of the suffrage movement, the American Woman Suffrage Association (AWSA) and the National Woman Suffrage Association (NWSA), had split in 1869 over race—over whether to fight for women's vote exclusively or to fight for women's rights and black rights simultaneously. Reunited in 1890 under the National American Woman Suffrage Association (NAWSA), suffragists found themselves on a political terrain where African American men had been disfranchised and Reconstruction overthrown. By privileging appeals to southern white women and condoning segregation in local and state organizations, the suffrage movement now sacrificed black rights at the altar of women's rights.[1] Nonetheless, Reconstruction had bequeathed to women's suffrage a political language and strategy of enfranchisement based on the use of federal and state laws to expand rights. Suffragists, black and white, persevered to reignite the battle to reconstruct democracy.

Despite the fact that women did not win the right to vote during Reconstruction, in that era women's suffrage became a permanent part of the political vocabulary of democracy not just in America but throughout the world. The French writer Victor Hugo had dubbed the nineteenth century the "woman's era." Black clubwoman and suffragist Josephine St. Pierre Ruffin adopted that term as the title of her newspaper in Boston, which she edited. The overthrow of Reconstruction ended the momentum for the first major push for a suffrage amendment, which would have been the Sixteenth Amendment. But it did not—could not—end the demand for women's emancipation, whether in the United States or abroad.[2]

In the late nineteenth century, the emergence of what was known as social feminism revived a broader movement for women's emancipation and social justice that was not just restricted to suffrage. Jane Addams, Lillian Wald, and Florence Kelley were suffragists, leaders in the Settlement House movement that focused on the urban and immigrant working poor, and champions of labor and black rights. Addams was the founder of the famous Hull House in Chicago, Wald of the Henry Street settlement in New York City. These organizations were "social settlements" that Addams modeled after utopian socialist societies and cooperatives. Wald and Addams even operated arts programs in their settlement houses. Unlike the suffrage movement, which was increasingly dominated by Susan B. Anthony and Elizabeth Cady Stanton, Addams, Wald, and Kelley did not sideline the issue of racial oppression; they would, in fact, become founding members of the NAACP. Addams welcomed black activist Ida B. Wells and her suffragist Alpha club to Hull House. The German Jewish Wald refused to tolerate racial segregation at Henry Street. Addams's racial egalitarianism stretched beyond the borders of the United States; she was a pacifist and joined the Anti-Imperialist League. (She was awarded the Nobel Peace Prize in 1931.) Wald was also active in the nineteenth-century international peace movement led by Quaker and working-class socialist groups in opposition to nationalist and imperialist warfare.

Addams and Wald never married, forming intimate relationships with female coworkers, as did Anthony and other suffragists such as Anna Howard Shaw and Frances Willard of the Women's Christian Temperance Union (WCTU), the largest women's organization in the United States. Wald, who had trained as a nurse, was also an advocate for public health. Addams's early battles with physical impairment (a curved back from tuberculosis) left her particularly empathetic to the plight of the working classes. She was a pioneering figure in the fields of social work and sociology, or what she called "socialized education," and taught at the University of Chicago. Addams and Wald, often dismissed as middle-class reformers, were, in fact, progressive advocates of the modern welfare state in an age of rapacious capitalism. Addams invoked Leo Tolstoy's Christian humanitarianism and pacifism as her main inspiration (as did Mahatama Gandhi) in the book she wrote about Hull House, titled *Twenty Years at Hull House.* In it, she also recounted her experiences with Russian anarchists, German socialists, and trade unionists. Her book summarized her social philosophy well: "The educational activities of a Settlement, as well its philanthropic, civic, and social undertakings, are but differing manifestations of the attempt to socialize democracy, as is the very existence of the Settlement itself."

Both women worked with the labor movement, with Wald going on to join the Women's Trade Union League. Addams and Wald lobbied for laws regulating the hours and work conditions of labor, a minimum wage law, and decent housing for the working poor who lived in overcrowded

Hull House. *Swarthmore Peace Collection at Swarthmore College*

urban tenements. Though they trained their efforts mainly on women and children, some of the labor reforms Addams and Wald advocated eventually encompassed the entire working class. Writing many years later, Wald explained that the "private gifts" and philanthropy that sustained the settlement houses paved the way for the government's "social responsibility" to its citizens.[3]

Florence Kelley was more radical than either of them. She was born just before the war, in 1859, the daughter of the Radical Republican congressman, Willian D. Kelley, and niece of the abolitionist feminist Sarah Pugh of the Philadelphia Female Anti-Slavery Society. She was educated at Cornell University and University of Zurich and earned a law degree from Northwestern. Kelley sought refuge in Addams's Hull House to escape her abusive husband, and from there became a prominent labor reformer. A socialist feminist, Kelley corresponded with Marx's collaborator, Friedrich Engels, and translated his 1845 book, *The Condition of the Working Class in England*, into English. She finally published it with the help of Rachel Foster, Anthony's lieutenant in NWSA, under the auspices of the Socialist Labor Party in 1887.

As Kelley wrote in a letter to Engels, clockmakers, shirtmakers, and bookbinders unions met at Hull House and were united in a "systematic endeavor to clear out the sweating dens." She founded a "Bureau of Women's Labor" at Hull House and decided to "cast my lot with Mrs. Addams." Kelley noted that she had learned more in a week at Hull House about the "actual conditions of proletarian life in America than in any other previous year." Later, when she moved to New York City, she stayed at Wald's Henry Street settlement. Rejecting bourgeois reform, Kelley fought for the abolition of "wage slavery," self-consciously tapping the abolitionist tradition, and to alleviate the condition of the working classes. She was appointed chief factory inspector in Illinois in 1893 by Governor John Peter Altgeld and, with Addams, founded the National Consumer League in 1899, which certified products not made by child or sweatshop labor. (They would be horrified by current advocates of reintroducing child labor in the United States.)

The socialist feminism of the late nineteenth century not only inspired progressive social legislation, but also laid a foundation for the

New Deal state. In a suffragist pamphlet, Kelley argued that working women, in particular, needed the vote to protect themselves and their children. Rather than revolution, Kelley, who had helped write Illinois's pioneering 1893 factory law outlawing child labor and mandating an eight-hour day for women workers, preached "ethical" legislation to tame capitalism. Working-class children had as much a right to childhood, and adult workers to leisure time, as their "sordid" employers— and only the state could intervene to correct the abuses of industrial capitalism. Protective legislation for women workers, opposed by some reformers as a sign of women's *inequality*, eventually included men. Social feminists such as Addams, Wald, and Kelley as well as women trade unionists and "labor feminists" such as Rose Schneiderman and Leonora O'Reilly, all inspired Frances Perkins, who would go on to become the first woman appointed to a cabinet-level post as secretary of labor under Franklin Delano Roosevelt. Kelley, who died in 1932, did not live to see the full fruits of her labor.[4] These women supported the rights of labor, women's suffrage (Kelley was vice president of NAWSA for several years), black rights, and the peace movement, embodying the abolitionists' overlapping commitments to multiple radical causes.

Socialists wrote some of the most influential feminist texts of the era. One of the founders of the German Social Democratic Party, August Bebel, published *Woman and Socialism* (1879), in which he advocated for women's equality in all spheres. He argued that ancient "primitive" societies had been matriarchal until women were enslaved by men. Bebel critiqued the institution of marriage, viewed prostitution as a kind of capitalist exploitation, and called for the social liberation of all women and the economic liberation of working-class women. The "woman in the future," he predicted, "is no longer subject to even a vestige of dominion and exploitation; she is free, the peer of man, mistress of her lot." Bebel pointed out that socialist parties were the only ones that included women's suffrage in their political platform. He asked the "female proletarians in particular" to join the socialist movement, in which their "redemption and emancipation are at stake." When social democrats came into power in Weimar Germany in 1918, they gave women the right to vote.

Following Bebel's book was Engels's *The Origin of the Family, Private Property and the State* (1884). It was based on the research of anthropologists such as Lewis H. Morgan, who had written on the Iroquois. (Women's officeholding among the Seneca Iroquois in upstate New York also inspired abolitionist feminists such as Amy Post.) Engels, too, claimed that families in early human history were matrilineal. As he maintained, it was only with the emergence of private property and bourgeois families that women became subordinated to men. Engels's argument that the downfall of matrilinealism, or "maternal law," was "the historic defeat of the female sex," offered a compelling feminist critique of male-dominated families. Once men "seized the reins" of the household, "women were stripped of their dignity, enslaved" and became "tools for men's lust and mere machines for the generation of children." Women's position was "clad in a milder form," but their subordination was not "obliterated." Like "slavery and private property," marriage "develops the welfare and advancement of one by the woe and submission of the other."

According to Engels, Marx was the first to note the class antagonism between the sexes as the first "division of labor," over rearing children. The formal legal equality and consent of women, he noted, masked the "economic oppression" and "domestic slavery" of women. The "emancipation of women" was dependent on their "re-introduction" from the private to the public sphere. Engels defended modern "sex love," monogamy, and gender equality—all of which he found more prevalent among the working classes than among the bourgeoisie. Only "the abolition of capitalistic production and of the property relations created by it" would create true gender equality, because all economic motives for marriage would be removed. The "supremacy of man in marriage is simply the consequence of his economic superiority and will fall with the abolition of the latter." Socialism thus held the key to women's emancipation. Florence Kelley disagreed with his romanticized notion of working-class families as more egalitarian, arguing instead that modern industrial capitalism was destructive of working-class marriages and families, and maternal health and education.[5]

Stanton, the philosophe of American feminism, also referred to Morgan's work and indigenous societies to support her contention that all human society began originally as matriarchies, or what she called "the mother-age." In her paper, the "Matriarchate," which was read in 1891 by Anthony to the National Women's Council, an umbrella group of different women's organizations such as women's clubs, NAWSA, and the WCTU, she pointed to the Tuareg people of northern Africa, the Senecas in North America, and the Nairs of southern India as lingering proof that women had been, in the beginning, rulers of their homes and society. It took men centuries to dethrone women and establish patrilineal descent. The "violent suppression" of women produced patriarchy. Stanton did not advocate for a return to matriarchy, but rather for the "untried experiment" in equality.

In 1892, Stanton, in her "Solitude of Self" speech before the House Judiciary Committee in Congress, which was considering a law to give women the right to vote in federal elections, made the case for a sixteenth amendment for women's suffrage. In an extended philosophical meditation, she drew on Protestant theology, American republicanism, and utilitarianism to demand women's "birthright to self-sovereignty." She demolished the notion that women's identity should be confined to their domestic roles as wives and mothers, ever dependent on men's capriciously protecting them and being their political representatives. Each woman, like each man, is an independent sovereign who is self-governing, in her "awful solitude." Stanton tempered her radical individualism by speaking about education and political duties that would allow women to contribute to the "general good." But, she concluded, "Who, I ask you, can take, dare take on himself the rights, duties, the responsibilities of another human soul?" She delivered the same speech as her "valedictory address" to the annual suffrage convention later that year. So moved was Lucy Stone by her speech that she published it in its entirety in *The Woman's Journal*.[6]

By the end of the century, a new generation of suffragists who admired both Anthony and Stone worked to effect a rapprochement between their respective organizations, NWSA and AWSA, though the initiative for reunion came mainly from Stone herself. Stone's health had deteriorated, and she sought to reunite the suffrage movement to push for a sixteenth amendment that would enfranchise women. Both wings of the movement left a record of their activities. Stanton, Anthony, and Matilda Gage's multivolume history of the movement echoed the manner in which abolitionists had preserved their history, in that it was a compilation of primary documents, recollections, images, and narratives. Harriot Stanton Blatch, Stanton's daughter, added a chapter on AWSA to the *History of Woman Suffrage*, to fill a gaping hole. For their part, Stone, Henry Blackwell, and their daughter Alice Stone Blackwell published the most successful newspaper for women's rights, *The Woman's Journal*, from 1870 to 1917, which continued in different iterations well into the 1930s. Carrie Chapman Catt, who would head the united suffrage movement, called it the "voice of the women's movement."

The schism in the suffrage movement, which first appeared in 1869, had endured as fundamental ideological differences proved difficult to bridge. AWSA pushed for state laws for suffrage, while NWSA adopted a federal strategy. AWSA was the larger organization of the two, with many more state auxiliaries and members, but NWSA was more adept at publicizing its actions. In 1876, Anthony, an activist almost without equal, Gage, and a few others presented what they called the Declaration of Rights of the Women of the United States at the centennial celebrations in Philadelphia, despite the organizers' official exclusion of suffragists from the day's proceedings. If AWSA was the larger body, Anthony's savvy gave NWSA the advantage. Stone and Anthony had honed their skills as abolitionist lecturers and agents. Stone matched William Lloyd Garrison's editorial tenacity, Anthony his activism. In 1878, Anthony invited Garrison and Wendell Phillips to the celebration of the thirtieth anniversary of Seneca Falls, and both sent cordial replies, eager to bury the hatchet after Anthony's and Stanton's opposition to the Fifteenth Amendment.

In 1885, Anthony and Stone had each received a large bequest from Eliza Eddy, the daughter of the abolitionist Francis Jackson, who had also left a similar bequest to abolitionist feminists in 1861. Deprived of custody over her children after her divorce, Eliza (and her father) were fervent supporters of women's rights. Anthony invested the bequest in publishing the subsequent volumes of the history of the woman suffrage movement, and Stone in *The Woman's Journal*. Stanton met William Henry Channing, a socialist abolitionist, in 1882 to thank him for his favorable review of their history and both reminisced, she wrote, "with tenderness on our divisions and disappointments." Stone thought that Stanton and Anthony had hoodwinked Channing and that their volumes on women's suffrage presented neither an "accurate" nor "adequate" account of the "*real* history of the woman suffrage movement." She wrote that "we ought to puncture the bubble" that Seneca Falls was the "*first* public demand for suffrage."

In 1887, the suffrage amendment that had languished in committee for nearly ten years was again defeated in the Senate. (It had been introduced by Republican senator Aaron Sargent of California in 1878. Sargent's wife, Ellen Clark Sargent, was a leading suffragist.) NWSA had kept alive the agitation for the Sixteenth Amendment, with its leaders speaking before Congress and writing to a succession of presidents. Stone tracked its fate and advocated for it in the pages of *The Woman's Journal*. But in another blow, Congress revoked women's suffrage in Utah territory that same year. AWSA, at its annual meeting in Philadelphia, voted to consider unification with NWSA at Stone's urging and appointed her to represent it in negotiations. In December, Anthony and Rachel Foster met Stone and Stone Blackwell in Boston. As Stone Blackwell put it, "Nothing really stood in the way [of unification] except the unpleasant feelings engendered during the long separation, and those could be overcome, and were overcome, for the good of the cause, to which both sides were sincerely devoted."

Stone was keen to exclude all three pioneers—Stanton, Anthony, and herself—from a leadership role in a new organization, to avoid old divisions, but Anthony insisted on having Stanton lead it. After two years of back-and-forth, compromise prevailed, with Anthony squelching all opposition to unification. Stone succeeded in naming the new organization National American Woman Suffrage Association, or NAWSA. She died three years after unification, in 1893, shortly after receiving news of the first country in the world to grant women the right to vote, New Zealand. Despite her and Anthony's earlier pettiness toward Stone, Stanton acknowledged that "Lucy Stone was the first person by whom the heart of the American public was deeply stirred on the woman question." Anthony confessed that she had been converted to the women's cause by reading a speech of Stone's. The unified suffrage movement may have been the result of Stone's behind-the-scenes labor, but her rivals dominated it after her death. Stanton became the first president of NAWSA but spent most of her time in England. Never an organization woman, she resigned in 1892. Anthony, who succeeded her, led NAWSA until 1900. NAWSA's membership remained far behind the WCTU's, around 13,000 to the latter's more than 200,000, but it would spearhead the demand for women's suffrage.[7]

In 1888, Stanton had proposed an International Council of Women (ICW) that would bring together all women's organizations to celebrate the fortieth anniversary of Seneca Falls. (The organization still exists today.) Representatives from nine countries attended, including Pandita Ramabai, an Indian feminist reformer who joined the WCTU. While Stone and Blackwell traced the origins of the women's movement to abolition, Stanton and Anthony continued to emphasize Seneca Falls. A subsidiary organization, the National Women's Council (usually referred to as the "Women's Council"), was also founded in 1888 in accordance with the ICW's constitution. Like its parent, it would endeavor to bring together and foster collaboration among women's organizations, though only those based in the United States. WCTU's Frances Willard, who subsequently spoke before the Congressional Suffrage Committee for the first time, was elected its president, and Anthony vice president. At the NWC's triennial conference in 1891, the WCTU and NAWSA still dominated, though the national council also included the newly formed General Federation of Women's Clubs.

The women's club movement, representing mainly professional, middle-class women excluded from a male-dominated public sphere, began with the formation of Sorosis in New York City in 1868, and soon spread throughout the country. In 1890, over sixty clubs convened to establish the General Federation. Jane Cunningham Croly, the founder of Sorosis and the moving spirit behind the General Federation, wrote its first history. As she put it, "When the history of the nineteenth century comes to be written, women will appear as organizers, and leaders of great organized movements of their own sex for the first time in the history of the world."

In her presidential address at the 1891 NWC convention, Willard pointed out that a "Valhalla" of great American women would include Lucretia Mott, Stone, Stanton, Anthony, Mary Livermore, and Julia Ward Howe. She did not mention a single black woman but concluded by quoting Wordsworth's ode to Toussaint Louverture of the Haitian Revolution: "There's not a breathing of the common wind, That will forget thee; thou hast great allies; Thy friends are exultations, agonies, And love, and man's unconquerable mind." Similarly, Kansan Mary Lease invoked the abolitionist John Brown on behalf of the "half a million" women of the Farmers' Alliance. The daughter of Irish immigrants, Lease supported African American citizenship, the cause of labor, the Populist movement, and women's suffrage. She ended her speech by describing an egalitarian vision: "no more millionaires, no more paupers, and no more waifs in our streets." Aside from some Radical Republicans during Reconstruction, only insurgent third parties, including the Greenback-Labor, Populist, Socialist, and Prohibition Parties, endorsed women's suffrage in the late nineteenth century. In 1896, when the Populist Party was incorporated into the Democratic Party, "the political rights of women were hopelessly lost," as one suffragist put it.

When it came to Native Americans and African Americans, the Woman's Council, WCTU, and NAWSA fell short. At the 1891 conference, those questions were confined to a discussion of the "Duty to Dependent Races." Alice Cunningham Fletcher, an ethnologist who worked among indigenous people, coined the phrase. She spoke on behalf of the Woman's National Indian Association. Blithely assuming that all "human progress" and "arts and sciences" had emanated from the "white race," she condemned the treatment of Indians, who were subject to wars, disease, and alcohol. The Indians had once been "independent" and "self-sufficient," yet Fletcher's prescription for them now was to educate and "civilize" them into white society. Despite the violent overthrow of Reconstruction, she upheld the "progress" of former slaves as citizens as an example of what was in store—in a positive sense—for Native Americans. Frances Ellen Watkins Harper spoke after Fletcher, and vigorously disagreed with her. She made it clear that she thought it was a "privilege" to represent African Americans not as a mere "dependent," but as a "member of the body politic" entitled to government protection and "simple justice." In a passionate speech, she condemned the federal government as "vicious" and "weak" for not being able to protect the life and liberty of black southerners. If Americans acted according to the basic precepts of Christianity of do unto others, "the drink traffic would be abolished, the Indian question answered, the negro problem solved." Ramabai, who met Harriet Tubman, also a suffragist, wrote that she identified with African American and native women more during her visit to the United States.

Suffragists' elitism, however, was evident in the language they used. They referred, for example, to the care of "vicious and dependent classes" and the opposition of "ignorant immigrant men" to women's suffrage. They also tended to set women's rights in competition with those of other groups, implicitly constructing women's rights as white. Stanton argued, "Are not women, as a factor in civilization, of more importance than Indians?" Matilda Gage contended that black men had allegedly not asked for citizenship, and that "red men" had citizenship foisted on them—and to enfranchise both was "degrading" to women. Rev. Anna Howard Shaw, who became president of NAWSA in 1904, complained that more South Dakotans were willing to give the vote to indigenous men, dressed in "blankets and moccasins," than to Anthony and other "eminent women." Carrie Chapman Catt, who both preceded and succeeded Shaw as NAWSA president, deplored granting the vote to immigrant, black, and Indian men before educated American women. Charlotte Perkins Gilman, who developed a radical feminist critique of women's economic subordination to men, advocated a system of forced labor for African Americans. She was also an anti-Semite.

The establishment of a formal American empire by the end of the nineteenth century allowed mainstream suffragists more opportunities to display their elitism. The ICW and NAWSA supported American

THE LAST RECONSTRUCTION AMENDMENT 437

imperialism as part of a project to spread Western "civilization" as well as women's suffrage. In Anthony's 1899 "Hawaiian Appeal" to Congress, NAWSA demanded that the women of Hawaii be enfranchised along with men when the United States formed a territorial government for Hawaii. Stanton and Anthony asked for the right to vote for women in US colonies like Hawaii, Puerto Rico, and the Philippines by alluding to "ignorant native men" who would form "barbaric male governments" in these islands. In her "Statement on Territorial Constitutions," Anthony further deplored "the half-savage character of the men of these countries."

In deploying imperialist logic on behalf of women's suffrage, she also made clear that the demand for suffrage did not include "the status of those in Indian Reserves or on Southern Plantations." Like British suffragettes, American suffragists made women's suffrage an integral part of "Anglo-Saxon civilization," based on the assumed "racial" inferiority of nonwhite peoples. Catt, who promoted American women's duty to "uplift" colonized peoples, also fashioned white women as saviors of Chinese sex workers in the United States.

Some suffragists promoted literacy requirements for the vote. Stanton had long supported educational qualifications for suffrage. After Stone's death, Henry Blackwell argued for "educated suffrage." He also said that Chinese and "Hindoo coolies" represented "ancient and fossilized types of civilized society." Blackwell had been a booster of Grant's scheme to annex the Dominican Republic, even though he opposed the Spanish-Cuban-American War. In 1885, writing from Alabama, Blackwell had tried to convince Stone and their daughter to come out for educational qualifications for voting, so that literate men and women might outvote "ignorant men." It could be the basis, he suggested, of uniting with Stanton and Anthony. But Stone Blackwell realized that such a position could be used as "an instrument of color prejudice." All the way back in 1868, Stanton and Anthony had called for educated suffrage regardless of color or sex in *The Revolution,* when an overwhelming majority of African Americans were freedpeople. As Stanton acknowledged in 1898, "The National association has been growing White and conservative for some time."[8]

"Elizabeth Cady Stanton and Susan B. Anthony," by Napoleon Sarony. *National Portrait Gallery, Smithsonian Institution*

The tragedy of Stanton and Anthony's stance on voting restrictions was that they were so radical on other matters, and at times too radical even for NAWSA, the organization they helped found. In 1895, Stanton and her chosen committee of women shocked the respectable world by publishing *The Woman's Bible*, a commentary on the Bible that challenged passages upholding women's inferiority and rewrote other passages. God, Stanton claimed, created both man and woman in his image—Eve was not created from Adam's rib, as the Bible had it. The next year, despite Anthony's best efforts, NAWSA passed a resolution condemning *The Woman's Bible*. Undeterred, Stanton published a second volume of *The Woman's Bible* in 1898, with an even larger committee of coauthors. Stanton got some of her ideas from Matilda Gage, who on her own had published *Woman, Church, and State* (1893), an even more radical critique of the Bible. Estranged from NAWSA, Gage died in 1898. Stanton died in 1902, obstreperous, elitist, and brilliant as ever.

Anthony would die four years later, having devoted her life to women's suffrage, leaving to the cause her conviction that "failure is impossible." Anthony was the "general" of the movement, and the Nineteenth Amendment would be called the "Anthony amendment," though she was not its originator. A coauthor of the subsequent volumes of the *History of Woman Suffrage*, Ida Husted Harper, wrote Anthony's authorized two-volume biography as, effectively, another history of the movement.[9]

The growing conservatism of the suffrage movement was reflected in its failure to address racism, and more particularly in its drive to include southern white women. NAWSA initially concentrated on winning the states rather than pushing for a constitutional amendment. That strategy was apparent in the structure of the third and fourth volumes of the *History of Woman Suffrage*, which divided chapters state by state, and, more notably, in the leeway given to southern affiliates of NAWSA to develop segregated locals. The states' rights strategy was adopted in deference to southern white women, who staunchly opposed a constitutional amendment for suffrage, connecting it to Reconstruction. Instead, they sought state laws that would enfranchise white women only.

The emergence of southern white suffragists completed "the final divorce between suffrage and abolitionism," according to one historian. While the path to the movement's southern strategy had been paved by Stanton and Anthony, who had opposed the Fourteenth and Fifteenth Amendments in the 1860s, the rise of southern white women, such as the irredeemably racist Kate Gordon of Louisiana, to positions of power within NAWSA made things far worse. Before Gordon, Kentuckian Laura Clay, daughter of the antislavery Republican politician, Cassius Marcellus Clay, had founded with her sisters the Kentucky Equal Rights Association and the Kentucky Suffrage Association. Estranged from her father, Clay, a Democrat, butted heads with Henry Blackwell, an equally staunch Republican, over party affiliation at the 1897 NAWSA convention. Both agreed on an educational qualification for suffrage, yet Blackwell, who had tried to get Mississippi's 1890 constitutional convention to enfranchise women, repudiated the idea of a "white man's government" and felt educated black women ought to be enfranchised. Clay and Gordon were the principal proponents of NAWSA's southern strategy.

Southern white women, most of them purveyors of Lost Cause mythology, brought a special racial animus to the movement. The most famous of them was Rebecca Latimer Felton, a suffragist best known for her virulent prolynching advocacy. Like her fellow Georgian, Tom Watson, Felton began her career as a Populist reformer who fought against the convict lease system but ended as a racist demagogue. While one may view her as an antirape activist, she became, preeminently, a champion of "white women's supremacy." In 1922, on Watson's death, she was briefly sworn in as the first woman US senator ever.

As southern white women joined NAWSA, black women were excluded. In 1895, NAWSA's annual convention was held for the first time in the South, in Atlanta. Jefferson Davis's cousin was greeted "with roars of enthusiasm" and Frederick Douglass, who would die that year, was asked to stay away. Many of the speakers were men, including the former Confederate general, Robert Hemphill, who lauded the southern white women attending for their beauty. After the convention, Anthony and Catt undertook a lecturing tour of southern cities because, as they put it, "this section was practically an unvisited field." The light-skinned Adella Hunt Logan, a teacher at Tuskegee Institute in Alabama, often managed to slip into NAWSA's conventions, but was sidelined by Anthony from speaking at its national convention. At the 1899 NAWSA convention, Lottie Wilson Jackson, a black suffragist from Michigan, introduced a resolution condemning segregation in railroad cars that confined black women to smoking cars. It was met with the unified opposition of southern white women, led by Clay. Anthony intervened, arguing that such matters were not pertinent to a suffrage convention, and advocating instead a "pure and simple" feminism that effectively sacrificed black rights to appease southern women. The motion was defeated.

In 1903, NAWSA met in New Orleans for its first racially segregated convention. Belle Kearney of Mississippi gave a racist diatribe of a speech, "A Slaveholder's Daughter," in which she argued that the southern way of "Anglo-Saxon" rule was the national way. Catt demurred, talking about a time when the Romans had considered Anglo-Saxons barbaric. She, Stone Blackwell, and Anthony visited a local black literary club named after Phillis Wheatley to make amends after the convention. But the damage was done. An appalled William Lloyd Garrison Jr. wrote to a mortified Stone Blackwell, "To purchase woman suffrage at the expense of the negro's rights is to pay a shameful price." Ten years later, Gordon and Clay founded the Southern States Suffrage Conference, which adopted a racist states' rights platform to argue for white women's enfranchisement and opposed NAWSA's revived push for a constitutional amendment for women's suffrage, on the grounds that it would enfranchise black women. The motto of their newspaper was "Make the Southern States White."

In the end, the southern strategy was not just morally bankrupt but tactically flawed, as the South remained hostile ground for NAWSA. Catt and Anna Howard Shaw came to understand as much, and Stone Blackwell recoiled at the crude racism of southern white women. As the historian Marjorie Spruill Wheeler trenchantly puts it, "the South has yet to astonish the world with its precocity in regard to women's rights." Still, a younger generation of southern suffragists, such as the racially liberal Sue Shelton White, who was instrumental in getting Tennessee to ratify the Nineteenth Amendment, supported the drive for a constitutional amendment. The most important was Sophonisba Breckinridge, of the famous Breckinridge family of Kentucky; her Confederate uncle was the southern Democratic presidential candidate against Lincoln in 1860. A peer of Jane Addams, Breckinridge was a pioneering social scientist and cofounder of the School of Social Service Administration at the University of Chicago, "the other Chicago school." Like Addams, she was a social feminist, pacifist, suffragist; an advocate of immigrant and labor rights, universal health care, and social welfare; and a founding member of the NAACP. Though her parents were Confederates, Breckinridge admired abolitionists and repudiated her racist heritage.

Only four southern states would eventually ratify the Nineteenth Amendment: Kentucky, Arkansas, Tennessee, and Texas. The racist demagogue Senator James Vardaman of Mississippi was prepared to accept white women's suffrage by a constitutional amendment—as long as the Fifteenth Amendment was repealed. Southern senators would try unsuccessfully to insert the word "white" into the Nineteenth Amendment. On the eve of ratification, NAWSA still refused membership to a black suffrage federation from the Northeast, fearful of alienating white southerners.[10]

Despite being shunted to the side by NAWSA, black suffragists founded their own organizations, including clubs, and worked in black institutions, most notably the Black church. As the historian Rosalyn Terborg-Penn argued, despite the "racism in the movement," the "vast majority" of black women still supported it. While many white suffragists were willing to sacrifice black rights in their quest for the vote, black women remained advocates of both. The most consequential of the postwar generation were Ida B. Wells and Mary Church Terrell, who inherited the abolitionist feminist tradition of intersectionalism. Both were daughters of slaves, and their activism was born of Reconstruction. Terrell's father had testified before Congress after the Memphis massacre of 1866, when he was shot and his saloon destroyed. He recuperated financially but was a changed man, suffering blinding headaches from a bullet lodged in his neck. Wells's father was a Republican and Union League member in Mississippi, and she was educated in black schools and colleges founded during Reconstruction. In 1884, she was among many black women who sued a segregated railroad car company.

Wells was a schoolteacher before her articles on the conditions in black schools got her fired. She became an editor and part owner of the Memphis newspaper *Free Speech and Headlight*. In 1892, her friend Thomas Moss and two other black men, all of whom worked at the People's Grocery store, were lynched by a mob egged on by a rival grocer. The local police were complicit, and the local judge compliant—no one was charged with a crime. The perpetrators claimed that the men they had murdered had raped white women. Wells's press was burned down after she called that excuse an "old threadbare lie." Wells published a long article on the lynching in T. Thomas Fortune's *New York Age*. As she wrote, "I felt that one had better die fighting against injustice than to die like a dog or a rat in a trap." She became the country's foremost campaigner against not just the lynching of black men but also the rape of black women.

Wells soon published her article as a pamphlet, *Southern Horrors*, and launched her crusade against what Douglass called "the new southern barbarism." He anointed her "Brave Woman," noting that "we are deserted by earth and Heaven, and yet we must still think, speak and work." Wells refuted the common justification for lynching—the rape of white women—and showed how the Memphis case illustrated, rather, that black success was often the real cause. "The Afro-American is not a bestial race," she wrote, questioning the sudden upsurge of reports of black men raping white women. Lynching was a tool to keep blacks subjugated; there was little difference, in her view, between the slave South and the "New South." White southerners had "cheated" the black man of his vote, deprived him of his civil rights, "robbed him of the fruits of his labor and were still murdering, burning and lynching him."

Wells pioneered the study of lynching. In 1895, she published *A Red Record*, which was more comprehensive than anything she had written to that point. During Reconstruction, "hundreds of colored men and women were mercilessly murdered," she documented. The myth of "negro domination" became the "sanguinary banner of the sunny South, and under it rode the Ku Klux Klan, the regulators, and the lawless mobs." Reconstruction's overthrow was accomplished by "fraud, violence, intimidation, and terror." Once the "white man's government" was established, southerners created a new canard, the myth of the black rapist, to stymie black progress. Where, she asked, was southern chivalry when white southerners abused northern teachers as "N--- teachers?" Protecting women was clearly a convenient excuse for the "national crime" of lynching. The real criminals were southern mobs and a guilty nation that tolerated their brutal acts.

Wells's antilynching activism helped to reactivate the abolitionist international. In Britain, anti-imperialists such as the Quaker Catherine Impey and Isabella Mayo invited Douglass to give an address in London on lynching, and he recommended that Wells go in his stead.

The charismatic Wells completed two successful lecturing tours in Britain in 1893 and 1894, shining an international spotlight on America's shame. When she was criticized by southern detractors for her lectures, Garrison's son came to her defense: "It is the power of truth simply and unreservedly spoken, for her language was inadequate to describe the horrors exposed." Wells maintained her right to "appeal to the world." During her second tour, Wells embarrassed Frances Willard for her antiblack statements in an 1890 interview, which she had published in a British newspaper *Fraternity*. Wells apparently met Willard, who admitted that she had been prone to believe white southerners but was now disabused. Perhaps in response to Wells, the WCTU passed antilynching resolutions each year between 1893 and 1899. Wells was personally closer to Anthony than she was to Willard, though she refused to accept Anthony's justification of the color line in the suffrage movement. As she wrote of Anthony, "She had endeavored to make me see that for the sake of expediency, one had to stoop to conquer on this color question."

Wells was supposedly not an organization woman, but she participated in many black associations. In 1895, she settled down in Chicago, marrying an activist lawyer, Ferdinand Barnett, and established the Anti-Lynching League. She would write more investigative pamphlets on lynching and so-called race riots, the commonly used euphemism for white mob violence against black people. "Eternal vigilance is the price of liberty," she wrote in her autobiography, repeating the revolutionary maxim. Wells was at the founding of the National Association of Colored Women (NACW), the National Afro-American League (later Council), and the NAACP. The Alpha Suffrage club she founded in Chicago was renamed for her. Wells enlisted Jane Addams to successfully prevent the segregation of the city's school system. She developed a black vision of the settlement house in founding the Negro Fellowship League, and served as a probation officer in the city's municipal court—she was a community activist before that term was coined. When white suffragists tried to stop Wells from marching with the Illinois delegation in the 1913 suffrage parade in Washington, DC, she defied their restriction. On the eve of her death in 1931, the indomitable Wells-Barnett made a run for state senate.[11]

Wells's antilynching campaign spurred black women's organizing. They came to her defense and backed her work. A meeting in St. Paul, Minnesota organized by the "Ladies Home Circle" commended her for bringing attention to this "crime against humanity." The production of her first pamphlet was paid for by funds raised by Maritcha Remond Lyons and Victoria Earle Matthews of the Women's Loyal Union of Brooklyn and New York, at a dinner hosted in Wells's honor. Lyons, along with Sarah Garnet, wife of abolitionist Henry Highland Garnet and the first black female principal in New York's school system, had founded an Equal Suffrage League in the 1880s. In 1895, Matthews attended the Congress of Colored Women in Atlanta. After investigating the condition of black women in the South, she formed the White Rose Home for Colored Working Girls and Industrial Association, known as the White Rose Mission, in New York, a settlement house for migrant young black girls. Black women also operated the Lincoln Settlement House that catered to black New Yorkers.

Black women's activism in the North spanned suffrage, community activism, and racial uplift. In Boston, Josephine St. Pierre Ruffin, a member of AWSA, founded the New Era Club in 1890. Its motto was Lucy Stone's injunction, "Make the World Better." Married to Republican legislator George Ruffin, she was a formidable activist in her own right and had worked for the Sanitary Commission during the war. Her club and her newspaper, *The Woman's Era*, spearheaded the first national organization of black women. In 1900, Ruffin was denied permission to represent her "colored" club at the General Federation of Women's Clubs; she was admitted only as a member of the Massachusetts federation. Though Ruffin was a member of the New England Women's Club, most black women were excluded from women's clubs. Ruffin pointed out that both her association and the Chicago clubs had black members, and blamed "Southern women" for introducing the "color line" into the club movement. She recommended a resolution against racial exclusion, though she saw that the executive committee of the federation was terrified of "the threat of the Southern State Federations to secede."

In 1895, James Jacks, president of the Missouri Press Association, insulted black women as thieves and prostitutes as a way to discredit their antilynching activism. It became the occasion to unite black women's associations from all over the country, what Fannie Barrier Williams of Chicago called the "organized anxiety" of black women. Ruffin issued the call, extending the invitation to women who were not members of any club or association. The resulting meeting took place in Boston in 1895, and Ruffin's address urged all "intelligent" and "progressive" women to defend their "dignity," a classic statement of the politics of respectability, invoked by black club women against racist and misogynistic attacks. As Ruffin put it, "Our woman's movement is a women's movement, in that it is led and directed by women for the good of women and men, for the benefit of all humanity, which is more than one branch or section of it." With these words, she asked black men and white people to join black women, given that her organization, the newly formed National Federation of Afro-American Women, did not draw "the color line."

With its appeals to race consciousness, domesticity, maternalism, and respectability, black women's activism was seemingly conservative in its values, though radical in its methods. In 1896, the National Federation of Afro-American Women convened in Washington, where it joined with the Colored Women's League, organized by Mary Church Terrell and Anna Julia Cooper four years prior, to form the NACW, marking, in the words of its official historian, "a new epoch in the History of Negro Womanhood." Its motto, "Lifting As We Climb," exemplified the uplift strategies embraced by the educated, professional women who led the organization. Its constitution read, in part: "We the Colored Women of America, feeling the need of united and systematic effort, and hoping to furnish evidence of the moral, mental, and material progress made by people of color through the efforts of our women, do hereby unite in a National Association of Colored Women."

The NACW paid homage to pioneering abolitionist feminists such as Harriet Tubman (after whom black women in New York City named their club), Mary Ann Shadd Cary, who died in 1893, and Frances Harper. Cary had founded a black suffragist organization, the Colored Women's Progressive Franchise Association, in 1880 in Washington. Many of the clubs were named after abolitionists, including Sojourner

Truth. Black women also organized within their churches, deploying a "feminist theology" for race work. Women formed the backbone of black churches, which were houses of worship as well as breeding grounds for black political and civic activism. Nannie Helen Burroughs, who led the Women's Convention in the Baptist Church, joined the NACW. Neither Wells nor Harper, who was made one of the vice presidents of NACW in 1896, was ever elected president. Out of the black women's club movement and black churches emerged a new activist "citizen woman" who had an immense role in shaping the larger movements for black rights and women's rights.[12]

The deceptively genteel Terrell, a graduate of Oberlin, was elected the first president of the NACW. Terrell studied in Germany and was fluent in German and French. H. G. Wells, with whom she stayed in England, wrote the preface to her autobiography. Long before scholars did so, Terrell wrote that while white women had to overcome "the handicap" of sex, as a black woman she had "two" handicaps: "both sex and race." Her parents had been favored by their enslavers, but she was overcome with "disgust" when anyone portrayed slavery as paternalistic. Beneath the veneer of respectability, Terrell was a radical feminist. A schoolteacher, she was selected to the District of Columbia Board of Education. When the NACW met in Chicago, Addams hosted Terrell and its members for tea. In 1919, Addams would introduce Terrell's resolution condemning racial discrimination in the United States at the Women's International League of Peace and Freedom. Terrell also protested Jim Crow in Washington, sarcastically dubbing the city "A Colored Paradise."

Terrell, a member of NAWSA, was one of the few black women mentioned in the *History of Woman Suffrage*. As a freshman at Oberlin in 1881, she had penned an essay asking for a sixteenth amendment enfranchising women. Much later, she fondly recalled her personal relations with Anthony and Catt, both of whom, she wrote, never exhibited any prejudice toward her. Her speech at the 1898 NAWSA convention, "The Progress of Colored Women," was reprinted in pamphlet form but not reported in the *History of Woman Suffrage*. In it, she best articulated her double burden thesis, saying, "For not only are colored women with ambition and aspiration handicapped on account of their sex, but they are everywhere baffled and mocked on account of their race." She informed the convention of the work of the NACW and black women's clubs, missions, and orphanages, and of their struggles against the convict lease labor system and Jim Crow in the South. At the 1904 NAWSA convention, she declared, "My sisters of the dominant race, stand up not only for the oppressed sex but also for the oppressed race!" In 1917, Terrell and her daughter Phyllis, named after Phillis Wheatley, picketed the White House with Alice Paul's Woman's Party in the last push toward the Nineteenth Amendment.

Traveling all over the world and widely acclaimed as one of the most influential women of her time, of any race, Terrell still repeatedly ran headlong into the color line. An article she wrote on the convict lease system was printed in Britain, as no American publisher would carry it. She wrote, "While I am grateful for the blessings that have been bestowed on me, and the opportunities which have been offered, I cannot help wondering sometimes what I might have become and have done if I lived in a country which had not circumscribed and handicapped me on account of race, but had allowed me to reach any height I was able

"Suffragists Protest Woodrow Wilson's Opposition to Woman Suffrage," by Burke & Atwell, Chicago. *Library of Congress*

to attain." Terrell and Margaret Murray Washington, wife of Booker T. Washington, dominated the NACW during its early years. Washington was her more conservative rival and produced its newsletter. By 1900, the NACW had 125 branches in 26 states, and a total of 8,000 members.

The election of Lucy Thurman of the WCTU to the NACW presidency in 1907 marked the rise of local community activists. Barrier Williams, Hallie Quinn Brown, Fannie Jackson Coppin, and Charlotte Hawkins Brown came to define the grassroots activism of the NACW. Its famous members included self-made businesswoman Madam C. J. Walker and the writer Jesse Fauset. The most outstanding NACW president was the founder of the National Council of Negro Women, Mary McLeod Bethune. Born of enslaved parents in South Carolina, Bethune founded a school for black girls in Florida that lives on as the Bethune-Cookman College. She was the last of the "race women" of the era who sought to rekindle Reconstruction's promise by appealing to the federal government to enforce black rights. An ally of Eleanor Roosevelt, she led the black political realignment into the Democratic Party during FDR's 1932 presidential campaign.[13]

In the early twentieth century, NACW was eclipsed by the NAACP as well as by partisan politics and anti-imperialist and Pan-African organizations, such as the National League of Colored Republican Women, the International Council of Women of the Darker Races, and the Marcus Garvey movement. Yet NACW nurtured a generation of black women activists after the fall of Reconstruction. They fought for suffrage and desegregation, and against the convict lease system and lynching in the Jim Crow South, laying a foundation for future black feminists. Critical to this generation of black women activists was a comprehensive statement of intersectional feminism by Anna Julia Cooper.

Like Terrell and many other black women who rose to the forefront of women's movements in this era, Cooper had been born enslaved. A classmate of Terrell's at Oberlin, she eventually received a doctorate in history from the Sorbonne, writing her dissertation on slavery and the French revolution. A cofounder of the Colored Women's League, Cooper was more of a thinker than an activist. Her 1892 treatise, *A Voice from the South*, quoted in this chapter's epigraph, is the philosophical foundation of black feminism. Like nineteenth-century maternalists, Cooper emphasized motherhood as the most "solemn and sacred trust" granted to humans by God. She argued that Christianity produced the "vitalizing, regenerating, and progressive influence of womanhood on the civilization of today."

Cooper, however, flipped the narrative of civilizationist discourse on its head. The black woman's work for the "regeneration" of her race was more "Herculean" than that of white women, owing to centuries of oppression. No effort to "elevate" the race would succeed without "an elevated and trained womanhood." Taking on social Darwinism and scientific racism, she rejected the notion of dominant and weak races and sexes. Christianity taught the opposite: "meekness, nonresistance and forgiveness." Even though accomplished women had existed since antiquity, the "feminine" side of "truth" and "civilization" had not been fully developed. Cooper confessed that "the high ground of generalities is alluring but my pen is devoted to a special cause," one she identified as "THE HIGHER EDUCATION OF COLORED WOMEN."

While praising some suffragists, Cooper criticized white American, especially southern, women. Such people, "never renowned for their reasoning powers," displayed "caste" feeling or outright racism. She indicted the Jim Crow South as the less civilized and barbaric part of the country, notably in its treatment of "the southern black woman" in segregated public transportation, recounting her own experiences with uncouth conductors. She took Anna Howard Shaw to task for her belief that Indians were a "weaker" race. The "cause of freedom" was not that of any particular race, class, sex, or "sect"; it was the "birthright of humanity." The argument for women's rights must not rest on "Indian inferiority" or "Negro depravity," as suffragists often suggested. Rather, it was "women's mission" to plead the cause of all who were treated as inferior.

Women's "wrongs," she wrote, evoking Frances Harper's 1866 national women's convention speech, were "indissolubly linked with all undefended woe, all helpless suffering, and the plenitude of her 'rights' will mean the final triumph of all right over might, the supremacy of the moral forces of reason and justice and love in the government of the nation." Embracing the radicalism of Edward Bellamy's nationalist movement and criticizing a "dollar-worshipping civilization," Cooper called on women to rescue society from the clutches of rapacious capitalism. Black women, in particular, might have something to contribute on "the relations of labor and capital." In politics, they hewed to progressive principles more reliably than even black men. Cooper paid homage to abolitionist feminists such as Harper, Truth, her friend Charlotte Forten Grimke, clubwomen like Quinn and Coppin, and black teachers as a group. America's "race problem" was a global one, and a problem of democracy—it was the attempt to create a "white man's country" by lynching black people, excluding the Chinese, deporting immigrants, and dispossessing Indians.

In her survey of American literature, Cooper revealed the inability of whites to represent African Americans fairly, holding up Albion Tourgee's works on Reconstruction as coming closest to understanding a black perspective. She noted Americans' failure to see blacks as "free American citizens" instead of the "humble slave" of *Uncle Tom's Cabin*. In a chapter in *A Voice from the South* titled "What Are We Worth?," Cooper drew attention to the racial proscriptions that African Americans were subject to: they were excluded from the professions and skilled labor and compelled forever to answer the proslavery ideologue John C. Calhoun's "sneer" that black people were only suited to slavery. Also critiquing Booker T. Washington's philosophy of vocational training and educating blacks for manual labor, she argued that a "liberal and progressive democracy" must be based on "universal suffrage" and "universal education."[14]

While its aims were much broader, the NACW consistently asked for a federal constitutional amendment for women's suffrage. The larger suffrage movement eventually adopted the progressive constitutional and statist ideas of abolitionist, social, and black feminists, though not their intersectionalism. In returning to the Reconstruction dream of a suffrage amendment that would give American women the right to vote, white suffragists finally gave up on their unsuccessful southern strategy.

At the start of the twentieth century, "the American woman was still a political pariah," wrote Harriot Stanton Blatch. Yet the failure of suffragists' southern strategy was counterbalanced by a steady stream of victories in the West. Blatch counterposed the constitution of Georgia, which stated that "Females are not entitled to the *elective* franchise; nor can they hold any civil office or perform any civil functions," to that of Wyoming, which read: "Since equality in the enjoyment of the natural and civil rights is made sure only through political equality, the laws of this state affecting the political rights and privileges of its citizens shall be without distinction of race, color or sex."

In western states, progressive, pro-labor, and socialist forces made such victories possible. In the 1890s, four states—Wyoming, Colorado, Utah, and Idaho—all gave women the right to vote. In Colorado, the insurgent Populist Party became the first major political party to endorse women's suffrage. About a decade later, the suffrage movement picked up again, when the states of Washington, California (after an intensely fought campaign), Oregon, Kansas, Arizona, Nevada, and Montana established women's suffrage. In 1912, Congress also passed a woman suffrage amendment for the territorial constitution of Alaska. Montana elected the first female congressperson in American history, suffragist and pacifist Jeannette Rankin, in 1916. Even before it gave women the right to vote, the state allowed women to hold local political office, while Kansas allowed them to vote in school elections. Western suffragists, Catt argued, should inspire women elsewhere.

The emergence of a women's international, engaged in pacifist, socialist, and suffragist activism, also spurred the movement in America. Stone Blackwell was ardently interested in the Russian Revolution and the Armenian cause, devoting as much of her time to them as she did to women's suffrage. Suffragists like Addams, Rankin, and Catt were active in the international peace movement. Black women forged their own networks of radical and anticolonial protest. In 1902, Catt convened a conference to explore the formation of an international organization of suffragists, though most of the attendees were from Europe. Two years later, a meeting in Berlin resulted in the founding of the International Woman Suffrage Alliance, "to secure the enfranchisement of the women of all nations and to unite the friends of woman suffrage throughout the world in organized cooperation and fraternal helpfulness." The speech of the convention was given by Terrell in impeccable German. In the following years, its annual conferences were held in Europe and dominated by European, American, Australian, Canadian, and New Zealand suffragists, with an occasional South African delegate. In 1913, it admitted a Chinese Woman Suffrage Society. Personally, Catt was "in touch" with suffragists from India, Persia, Turkey, Palestine, Egypt, Burma, Japan, Java (Indonesia), and the Philippines. In 1920, delegates from India and Japan attended the alliance's annual meeting for the first time.

In 1902, Anthony, in her testimony before Congress, had pit women's suffrage against the rights of colonized men, an unfortunate continuation of her Reconstruction-era strategy: "I think we are of as much importance as are the Filipinos, Port Ricans, Hawaiians, Cubans, and all of the different sorts of men that you have before you. When you get those men, you have an ignorant and unlettered people, who know nothing about our institutions." After 1920, suffragists campaigned for women's right to vote in American territories and colonies such as the Philippines and Puerto Rico. In doing so, they reinforced the legitimacy of US colonial rule in these countries. Native women, however, formed their own suffragist organizations, as in Puerto Rico, or joined anticolonial nationalist movements elsewhere in order to win rights. Many women of color, including black, Asian, and indigenous women, fought for suffrage in the United States, broadening its purview and contributing to its final success.

American suffragists closely tracked the progress of the movement across the world. In the 1890s, news such as that of women winning the vote in New Zealand and most of Australia was recounted systematically in the last volumes of the *History of Woman Suffrage*. On the eve of the passage of the Nineteenth Amendment, suffragists pointed to Britain and Canada, which had granted qualified women's suffrage, and shamed congressmen for being disloyal to American ideals of equality and democratic citizenship. Women's emancipation could not be judged, though, by only a suffrage yardstick. Economic and educational parity, equality in marriage, divorce, and family, and bodily rights remained (and remain to this day) areas of feminist contestation.[15]

The final momentum for the Nineteenth Amendment resulted from the expansion of the suffrage movement, represented by NAWSA, as well as the increasing radicalism of suffragists. NAWSA acquired two million members by the early twentieth century. It also attracted wealthy backers such as Mrs. Frank Leslie and Alva Belmont, and launched a formal congressional lobbying effort in Washington led by the politically astute Maud Wood Park. Catt's "winning strategy" drew from Reconstruction but was given fresh impetus by the social liberalism and broad-based demand for government regulation of the economy in the Progressive era. Besides enfranchisement in the West, women won a patchwork of voting rights throughout the country in school district and municipal elections as well as in presidential elections and primaries. In 1917, New York became the first eastern state to grant women suffrage, after a vigorous campaign that included working-class women and women of color. The spectacles of picketing and parades were important, too; one parade included the young Chinese American suffragist Mabel Ping-Hua Lee astride a horse. The New York campaign was a dress rehearsal for the national campaign for the Nineteenth Amendment.

Younger suffragists, inspired by transnational activism, brought new energy into the movement. Led by Blatch's Women's Political Union and Alice Paul and Lucy Burns of the National Woman's Party (NWP), younger women adopted the radical tactics of British suffragettes like the Pankhursts that would come to define popular perceptions of women's suffrage around the world. Paul and other members of the NWP picketed the White House and were arrested. They were imprisoned in a Virginia jail, where they launched hunger strikes and were force-fed by guards, as black prisoners came to their aid. Paul's radicalism, however, did not encompass them; like NAWSA, the NWP refused to take a public stance against lynching and the convict lease system. President Woodrow Wilson and the Democratic Party, coaxed by suffrage lobbyists and responding to the public embarrassment of suffragists picketing and starving in jail, endorsed women's suffrage, even as most southern Democrats remained opposed. Catt later noted that of the ten states that did not ratify the Nineteenth Amendment, nine were southern. (Delaware, a Union border slave state, she designated as northern.) Most southern states saw the Nineteenth Amendment as a reprise of the Fifteenth Amendment and as a back door to black suffrage.

The Nineteenth Amendment was not inevitable. The battle was a bitter one to the end, with antisuffragists waging a fierce campaign of their own. The antis formed their own organizations, using biologically essentialist, biblical, and politically conservative arguments to oppose suffrage. They coalesced into a National Anti Suffrage Association that denounced suffragists as radicals, socialists, and pacifists. In 1919, the amendment crossed the hurdle of a two-thirds majority of both houses of Congress, after testimony from NAWSA, the NWP, and the Anti Suffrage Association. The nail-biting finish to obtain ratification from three-fourths of the states, with Tennessee ratifying the amendment by one vote in August 1920, gives us an exciting narrative but one that obscures a historical genealogy of the amendment going back to Reconstruction.

As Ida Husted Harper announced in the fifth volume of the *History of Woman Suffrage*, "After Seventy Years Came the Victory." In 1920, white women as well as black women in the North won the right to vote. The latter would help elect the first African American congressmen since Reconstruction. In the southern states, black women attempted to vote after the ratification of the Nineteenth Amendment (as did Puerto Rican women), though they were turned away from the polls and harassed. As Terrell put it, black women should use suffrage as a "weapon of defense." Indigenous people did not get the ballot until the 1924 Citizenship Act, and even after that, western states resorted to Jim Crow tactics to prevent Indians from voting. Idaho, which gave women the right to vote before the ratification of the Nineteenth Amendment, disqualified felons, Indians, and people of Chinese descent. The racial boundaries of citizenship continued to be policed. After the passage of the amendment, NAWSA was reconfigured as the League of Women Voters to fight for women's political representation. The League, whose first president, Maud Wood Park, was supposedly sympathetic to black women, did little to assist southern black women in their ongoing efforts to secure the vote.

Under Paul, the NWP came up with the idea of the Equal Rights Amendment (ERA) in 1923, calling it the Mott amendment, after the famous abolitionist feminist Lucretia Mott. The ERA was resurrected in the 1970s by modern feminists, though it still awaits ratification. In the 1920s, some were wary that it would strike down laws that specifically protected women workers. But today, when labor laws apply equally to all, and women are equally represented in the workforce yet face systematic salary and workplace discrimination, the need for its passage is evident. At the same time, the South persisted for decades in limiting black voting. The wording of the Nineteenth Amendment, based on the Fifteenth Amendment, which gave black men the right to vote, evoked the progressive constitutionalism unleashed by Reconstruction. Yet neither amendment created a national standard or mechanism to enforce voting rights, and some states used legally deceptive methods to deny citizens the right to vote. With the passage of the Voting Rights Act of 1965, nearly fifty years after the Nineteenth Amendment and a hundred years after the Civil War, one of the central goals of Reconstruction was finally realized, at least in law if not everywhere in practice. Black citizenship, the central achievement of Reconstruction, continues to be contested down to our times.

The Nineteenth Amendment was both a legacy of and an important stepping-stone in the history of the reconstruction of American democracy. Neither the nonevent that some claim, nor the triumphant conclusion of women's quest for equal citizenship in an unequal nation and world, it remains an important political marker of women's equality, and an example of the vision of democratic American citizenship born during Reconstruction. In order to fully implement that vision, voting rights activists today still call for federal intervention to secure suffrage, especially after a conservative majority on the Supreme Court gutted the enforcement mechanisms of the Voting Rights Act of 1965 in *Shelby County v. Holder* (2013). As the suffragists claimed, "In a true democracy every citizen has a vote."[16]

The Nadir

When the moral sense of a nation begins to decline and the wheel of progress to roll backward, there is no telling how low the one will fall or where the other may stop.

—FREDERICK DOUGLASS, 1894

1. T. THOMAS FORTUNE, Journalist.   2. BOOKER T. WASHINGTON, Educator.
3. HON. FREDERICK DOUGLASS, Statesman.
4. I. GARLAND PENN, Author, Orator;   5. MISS IDA B. WELLS
Chief Commissioner, Atlanta Exposition.   Lecturer, Defender of the Race.

Black leaders at the turn of the century.

New York Public Library Digital Collections

The tragedy of Reconstruction was not that it failed but that it was destroyed and subverted, even as the fight for democracy and the resistance to oppression continued under the most dismal circumstances. On the eve of his death, Frederick Douglass would not let go of the Second American Republic, even as black leaders debated among themselves whether to accommodate or fight a new regime of racist terror. He wrote about the violent barbarism of Jim Crow existing alongside US attempts to "civilize" others: "We claim to be a Christian country and highly civilized nation, yet, I fearlessly affirm that there is nothing in the history of savages to surpass the blood chilling horrors and fiendish excesses perpetrated against the colored people by the so-called enlightened and Christian people of the South." The Deep South was an "American Congo," replicating the violence and brutal exploitation of colonized peoples.[1]

A younger generation would build on Douglass's legacy and inaugurate the long civil rights movement for black equality. Even during the nadir of Jim Crow, the black tradition of protest flourished, extending a rich strand of American democratic discourse. The year Douglass died, 1895, brokenhearted at his country's backsliding, Booker T. Washington delivered his famous Atlanta Compromise speech, urging black people to "cast down your bucket" in the South and southern whites to employ black labor. Born in slavery and educated at Hampton, Washington preached accommodation to segregation and disfranchisement and promoted "industrial education." Surreptitiously, he financed challenges to segregation and lynching. From his base at Tuskegee Institute in Alabama, Washington was the main recipient of northern philanthropy from tycoons like Andrew Carnegie, John Rockefeller, Collis Huntington, and more liberal donors such as Julius Rosenwald and Olivia Phelps Stokes. Washington became famous for his White House dinner with Teddy Roosevelt, which drew the ire of southern demagogues in Congress, like James Vardaman and Ben Tillman, who spent much of their time in elected office stoking racism and trying to repeal the Fourteenth and Fifteenth Amendments.

Some northern black leaders, such as DuBois and the Boston

journalist William Monroe Trotter, opposed the "Wizard of Tuskegee's" politics of public accommodation to Jim Crow and imperialism.
(Black people trained at Tuskegee were recruited to introduce cotton
cultivation in Germany's African colonies.) Their ideas fed into the
founding of the NAACP and the civil rights struggle that eventually
ended southern segregation and disfranchisement. Others, such as
T. Thomas Fortune, became allies of Washington, whose "Tuskegee
machine" dispensed patronage and funds until his death in 1915. By the
early twentieth century, black nationalists, most notably the Jamaican-
born Marcus Garvey, combined Washington's ideas of racial separation
and economic uplift with black pride and national self-determination.
Garvey, though, leveled a significant challenge to Western imperialism.
DuBois, who opposed both Washington and Garvey, also championed
anti-imperialist Pan-Africanism and became a Marxist, which led to
his being hounded out of the country. Born in the year Andrew Johnson
was impeached in 1868, and dying during the March on Washington in
1963, DuBois, more than any other black leader, personified the ongoing
African American struggle for freedom and equality.[2]

Over the course of his long lifetime, thousands of African Americans
were lynched, a horrific practice that white mobs also used against other
minorities, resistant workers, and political dissidents. The antiblack
"race riots" continued, becoming more virulent, including in Atlanta
in 1906, an event that DuBois witnessed. From Springfield (1908) and
East St. Louis, Illinois (1917), to Tulsa, Oklahoma (1921) and Rosewood,
Florida (1923), racist pogroms became almost commonplace. Not only
were black people murdered indiscriminately, but their communities
and businesses were razed. Often the victims were tried and convicted
for the violence visited upon them. During the "red summer" of 1919,
southern defiance of the rule of law became a national phenomenon,
from the massacre of hundreds of black sharecroppers and their union
allies in Elaine, Arkansas to the deadly "race riot" in Chicago that began
with the drowning of a young black man stoned by an irate white man.
American "race riots" early in the new century resembled colonial
massacres perpetrated by European countries, like the infamous Jal-
lianwalla Bagh massacre of 1919 by British colonial administrators, in

which nearly four hundred Indian men, women, and children died and over a thousand were injured, according to the official British report. State persecution of suspected radicals—including the Red Scare after the Bolshevik revolution in Russia—also fostered a climate of domestic terror and political repression.

Yet black people and other oppressed groups continued to resist. The founding of the NAACP in 1909, by black activists including DuBois, Ida B. Wells, and Mary Church Terrell, as well as by descendants of abolitionists and progressive and socialist reformers, was a direct response to this orgy of racist violence. It revived the fight for political and civil rights, and relied on courtroom strategies as well as agitation, to chip away at the legal edifice of Jim Crow. A new underground railroad, which combined black activism with appeals to the rule of law in northern states, sought to protect black refugees from racial apartheid in the South. Thousands of black southerners left the rural South for northern and western cities in the "Great Migration," voting with their feet as their enslaved ancestors had done before the Civil War and like the "Exodusters" of Reconstruction, permanently redistributing much of the African American population. While these cities eventually became centers of black political power, and New York City witnessed the flowering of black arts and literature in the Harlem Renaissance, black people in the region (and out West) also faced police brutality, racist mobs, dilapidated housing and neighborhoods, and informal segregation in all walks of life.[3]

Even with the many successes of the black freedom movement in the twentieth and twenty-first centuries, the betrayal of Reconstruction haunts American democracy. The nation still lives with the competing legacies of democracy and authoritarianism bequeathed by the rise and fall of the Second American Republic. The overturning of an interracial democracy and the unrestrained triumph of capitalism and imperialism in the United States created a political thermidor that ultimately affected other groups as well—indigenous people, women, immigrants, farmers, and workers—in short, all Americans and democracy itself. Until the second Reconstruction of American democracy in the 1960s, which unleashed other progressive social movements as well, the

United States during the nadir was not a democracy but a racist, authoritarian state comparable to European colonies in Asia and Africa and its lingering vestige, apartheid South Africa.

Our own era is one of renewed challenges to American democracy, including the revival of voter suppression, the overturning of women's and gay rights, unprecedented economic inequality, and a resurgent domestic and global authoritarianism that defies democratic governance. The reemergence of an authoritarian right in the United States—more reminiscent of the Jim Crow South than of European fascism, to which it is more often compared—has led many activists and scholars to call for a "third Reconstruction" of American democracy. Indeed, one wonders whether it is even accurate to speak of "legacies": The great contest that defined the Second American Republic—between democracy and what DuBois called "a system by which a little knot of masterful men would so organize capitalism as to bring under their control the natural resources, wealth and industry of a vast and rich country and through that of the world"—is ongoing. Today, unregulated capitalism threatens not only democracy but the very existence of human beings and a livable planet.[4] The lines have long been drawn. It is up to current and future generations of American citizens to decide which side they are on—whether to serve the common good or to selfishly and ignorantly doom humans of every "race."

ACKNOWLEDGMENTS

Perhaps I was destined to write a history of Reconstruction. My most challenging assignment during my first semester as a doctoral student at Columbia University was to present a report on Eric Foner's book manuscript on Reconstruction. I don't think I had ever worked that hard. The best part was when Eric said he liked the report and might use some of it for his introduction. Decades later, when I thought he had forgotten all about it, he recounted the incident to my graduate students. I never planned, though, to write a book on Reconstruction. Years of teaching a Civil War and Reconstruction lecture course and having students repeatedly ask me why Reconstruction was overthrown and what happened after that led me to expand my lectures. I want to acknowledge my numerous students, whose questions have shaped this book.

I initially conceived of this book narrowly, as a dual biography. The person who convinced me to write the bigger book on Reconstruction is my wonderful editor Dan Gerstle, who saw something in my book proposal that had eluded me. I thank Dan, who carefully edited the book, asked for clarifications at just the right spots, and curbed my tendency to overwrite. I may be biased, but he is the best in the business. I also want to thank my fabulous agent Sandra Dijsktra, who has been my biggest champion from the start. Anyone who knows Sandy, knows she is the person to have in your corner. Sandy has an uncanny sense of what makes a good book, and I am terribly grateful for her unstinting encouragement and good advice. Thanks to the entire team at Liveright and Norton, especially Zeba Arora, Rebecca Homiski, and Gary Von Euer.

Numerous fellowships allowed me to research and write this book. The John Simon Guggenheim Memorial Foundation Fellowship helped me to finish it. A Mellon-Schlesinger fellowship at the Radcliffe Institute, Harvard University, allowed me time to research and write Reconstruction's important history of women's suffrage. I want to thank my entire Radcliffe cohort for stimulating conversation and support. During the pandemic, I was one of the fortunate few who had access to the archives as the Distinguished Mellon Scholar in Residence at the American Antiquarian Society, whose unmatched pamphlet and newspaper collections allowed me to research uninterrupted for a year. I want to thank all the AAS staff, especially Ashley Cataldo, who dug up every relevant manuscript source for me. Research on this project was jumpstarted by a National Endowment for the Humanities long-term fellowship at the Massachusetts Historical Society, where I was lucky to be in residence with Kara Swanson of Northeastern and Christine Desan of Harvard.

I want to thank the University of Connecticut and the Draper Foundation for supporting my research at the Newberry Library in Chicago and for allowing me to host the Draper Conference on Reconstruction, which brought leading scholars on the subject to Storrs. In particular, I want to thank Presidents Susan Herbst and Radenka Maric and all my colleagues in History, Africana, and American Studies. I thank my Draper research assistants, Mary Mahoney and Kathryn (Katie) Angelica, whose diligence is unmatched. Thanks also to Winifred Maloney and Ashlyn Markowsky, former Master's students at UConn, and my undergraduate research partners at Harvard College, Chico Payne, Piper Winkler, and especially Selket Jewett, who did stellar work in the Schlesinger Library.

I would also like to thank all those who gave me the opportunity to present my research and helped me to conceptualize this book while I was writing it: Nina Silber for the annual Baker lecture of the History Department at Boston University; Jacqueline Jones, Daina Ramey

Berry, Peniel Joseph, and Jeremi Suri for the Littlefield lectures in the History Department and a symposium at the LBJ School for Public Affairs at the University of Texas, Austin; Jessica Marie Johnson and Francoise Furstenberg for the Harrison lecture of the History Department at Johns Hopkins University; Lloyd Benson for the annual George B. Tindall lecture of the History Department at Furman University; Liam Riordan and Mary Freeman for the Howard B. Schonberger Peace and Justice lecture of the Department of History, University of Maine; Dean Sakina Hughes for the Mandela Day lecture at the University of Southern Indiana; Noel Voltz and John Bickers for the Bi-annual Ubbelohde Endowed lecture of the History Department at Case Western University; and Joe Rezek for the Mahindra Humanities seminar at Harvard. I also want to thank Peter Wirzbicki and Matt Karp for organizing the Antislavery Conference at Princeton University and Carrie Janney for the American Civil War Museum symposium in Richmond, where I was able to present some of my ideas for this book. I thank Pepijn Brandon and George Blaustein for inviting me to present from the book at Vrije Universiteit and the University of Amsterdam. Above all, I thank Jan Stieverman, Manfred Berg, and Anja Schuler for a delightful month as the Pennington Visiting Professor in the Heidelberg Center for American Studies at the University of Heidelberg, Germany. Thanks to Mischa Honeck, Pia Wiegmink, and Heike Raphael-Hernandez, I got to test my arguments at the University of Kassel, University of Wurzburg, and the Bonn Center for Dependency and Slavery Studies at the University of Bonn.

Thanks to those who provided crucial input and support at various stages of the book: Ed Baptist, Sven Beckert, Nick Bromell, Richard Brown, Ken Burns, Heather Cox Richardson, Amy Dru Stanley, Eric Foner, P. Gabrielle Foreman, Beverly Gage, Skip Gates, Steven Hahn, Evelyn B. Higginbotham, Doris Kearns Goodwin, Robin D. G. Kelley, Jill Lepore, Jon Meacham, Tiya Miles, James Oakes, Rebecca Scott, James Sidbury, Nina Silber, John Stauffer, and John Fabian Witt. I would especially like to thank my colleagues at UConn, Nancy Shoemaker, Chris Clark, and Frank Costigliola, for generously reading chapters of the book and providing helpful suggestions.

I want to thank all my family, neighbors, and friends, especially my online Zumba, Cardio kicks, HIIT, and Barre instructors, who kept me moving when I was chained to my desk. My still sharp ninety-six-year-old mother, Premini Sinha, has taken over from my late father in encouraging me at the start of each new day of writing. My husband, Karsten Stueber, reliably came to my aid while completing his third monograph. This book is dedicated to our sons, Sheel and Shiv Stueber. Sheel's "best dog in the world," Wylie, kept me company in my sunlit home office during the pandemic. Shiv's note to me when he was six, "Did you edit your book and is that how you spell edit?," still adorns my desk. Sheel's many accomplishments at a young age, when his parents were struggling graduate students, are a source of immense joy. Shiv is off to college now; we will miss him terribly. Even in the most dismal times, their generation gives me hope for our democracy and planet.

NOTES

TC	*The Commonwealth*
TCR	*The Christian Recorder*
TFJ	*The Freedmen's Journal*
TFR	*The Freedmen's Record*
TI	*The Independent*
TIW	*The Irish World*
TL	*The Liberator*
TWJ	*The Woman's Journal*
WCW	*Woodhull and Claflin's Weekly*

INTRODUCTION: THE GREAT CONTEST

1. Amy Circuit Case, South Carolina Freedmen's Bureau Files; W.E.B. Du Bois, *Black Reconstruction in America: An Essay Toward a History of the Part Which Black Folk Played in the Attempt to Reconstruct Democracy in America, 1860–1880* (New York, 1935), 30.

2. Daniel to Caroline Grant, Arkansas City, June 4, 1872, Grant-Burr Family Papers, AAS; Michael Witgen, *Seeing Red: Indigenous Land, American Expansion and the Political Economy of Plunder in North America* (Chapel Hill, 2022).

3. James D. McCabe, *The History of the Great Riots: Being A Full and Authentic Account of the Strikes and Riots on the Various Railroads of the United States and in the Mining Regions* (Philadelphia, 1877), 370–71; Jacqueline Jones, *Goddess of Anarchy: The Life and Times of Lucy Parsons, American Radical* (New York, 2017), 60–67.

4. Koritha Mitchell, *From Slave Cabins to the White House: Homemade Citizenship in African American Culture* (Urbana, 2020): 62; Rebecca Primus to her parents and sister, April 6, June 2, 1866, Primus Family Papers, CHS; Ellen Garrison Jackson to Rev. S. Hunt, May 21, 1866, AMA Records, Amistad Research Center, Tulane University.

5. Jane Burbank and Frederick Cooper, *Empires in World History: Power and the Politics of Difference* (Princeton, 2010), chaps. 9–12; David Prior, ed., *Reconstruction and Empire* (New York, 2022), introduction.

6. Louis Hartz, *The Liberal Tradition in America* (New York, 1955); Patrice Higonnet, *Sister Republics: The Origins of French and American Republicanism* (Cambridge, MA, 1988); James T. Kloppenberg, *Toward Democracy: The Struggle for Self-Rule in European and American Thought* (New York, 2016); Andrew F. Lang, *A Contest of Civilizations: Exposing the Crisis of American Exceptionalism in the Civil War Era* (Chapel Hill, 2020); Roy P. Basler, ed., *The Collected Works of Abraham Lincoln*, vol. 5, 1861–1862 (New Brunswick, 1953), 537.

7. Jill Lepore, *These Truths: A History of the United States* (New York, 2018); Steven Hahn, *A Nation without Borders: The United States and Its World in the Age of Civil Wars, 1830–1910* (New York, 2016); David Prior, ed., *Reconstruction in a Globalizing World* (New York, 2018); Andrew Zimmerman, "Reconstruction: Transnational History," in John David Smith, ed., *Interpreting American History: Reconstruction* (Kent, 2016), 171–96.

8. Eric Foner, *Reconstruction: America's Unfinished Revolution, 1863–1877* (New York, 1988); Richard White, *The Republic for Which It Stands: The United States During Reconstruction and the Gilded Age, 1865–1896* (New York, 2017). White subsumes Reconstruction under an overarching interpretation of laissez-faire liberalism and

contract freedom that downplays the radicalism of emancipation and Reconstruction. Ironically, he replicates the old consensus view of American history.

9. Richard Franklin Bensel, *Yankee Leviathan: The Origins of Central State Authority in America, 1859–1877* (Cambridge, 1991); Richard Franklin Bensel, *The Political Economy of American Industrialization, 1877–1900* (Cambridge, 2000); Stephen Skowronek, *Building a New American State: The Expansion of National Administrative Capacities, 1877–1920* (Cambridge, 1982).

10. Jonathan Levy, *Ages of American Capitalism: A History of the United States* (New York, 2021), chap 7; Sven Beckert, *Empire of Cotton: A Global History* (New York, 2014); Ellen Meiksins Wood, *Democracy against Capitalism: Renewing Historical Materialism* (New York, 1995); Barrington Moore, Jr., *Social Origins of Dictatorship and Democracy: Lord and Peasant in the Making of the Modern World* (Boston, 1966), chap. 3; Amy Dru Stanley, *From Bondage to Contract: Wage Labor, Marriage, and the Market in the Age of Slave Emancipation* (Cambridge, 1998); Nancy Cohen, *The Reconstruction of American Liberalism, 1865–1914* (Chapel Hill, 2002); Nell Irvin Painter, *Standing at Armageddon: The United States, 1877–1919* (New York, 1987); Jackson Lears, *Rebirth of a Nation: The Making of Modern America, 1877–1920* (New York, 2009); Edward J. Blum, *Reforging the White Republic: Race, Religion, and American Nationalism, 1865–1898* (Baton Rouge, 2005); Jefferson Cowie, *Freedom's Dominion: A Saga of White Resistance to Federal Power* (New York, 2022).

11. James M. McPherson, *The Struggle for Equality: Abolitionists and the Negro in the Civil War and Reconstruction* (Princeton, 1964), 65; *TL*, October 2, 1863; Arno J. Mayer, *The Persistence of the Old Regime: Europe to the Great War* (New York, 1981).

12. I want to thank Yohanna Alimi-Levy for the following citations: Jean-Pierre Sainton, "De l'état d'esclave à l'état de citoyen. Modalités du passage de l'esclavage à la citoyenneté aux Antilles françaises sous la Seconde République (1848–1850)," *Outre-Mers. Revue d'histoire* 338–39 (2003): 47–82; Nelly Schmidt, *La France a-t-elle aboli l'esclavage? Guadeloupe-Martinique-Guyane, 1830–1935* (Paris, 2009).

13. Caitlin Fitz, *Our Sister Republics: The United States in the Age of American Revolutions* (New York, 2016); Alan Taylor, *American Republics: A Continental History of the United States, 1783–1850* (New York, 2021); Yesenia Barragan, *Freedom's Captives: Slavery and Gradual Emancipation on the Colombian Black Pacific* (Cambridge, 2022); Isadora Moura Mota, "Other Geographies of Struggle: Afro-Brazilians and the American Civil War," *Hispanic American Historical Review* 100 (2020): 35–62; Samantha Payne, "The Last Atlantic Revolution: Reconstruction and the Struggle for Democracy, 1861–1912" (PhD diss., Harvard University, 2022).

14. Benedict Anderson, *Imagined Communities: Reflections on the Origins and Spread of Nationalism* (London, 1983); Marilyn Lake and Henry Reynolds, *Drawing the Global Color Line: White Men's Countries and the International Challenge of Racial Equality* (New York, 2008); Carroll P. Kakel III, *The American West and the Nazi East: A Comparative and Interpretive Perspective* (New York, 2011); Edward B. Westermann, *Hitler's Ostkrieg and Indian Wars* (Norman, 2016); Stefan Kuhl, *The Nazi Connection: Eugenics, American Racism, and German Nazi Socialism* (New York, 1994); James Q. Whitman, *Hitler's American Model: The United States and the Making of Nazi Race Law* (Princeton, 2017); John W. Cell, *The Highest Stage of White Supremacy: The Origins of Segregation in South Africa and the American South* (Cambridge, 1982).

15. Susan Neiman, *Learning from the Germans: Race and the Memory of Evil* (New York, 2019); Gregory P. Downs, *After Appomattox: Military Occupation and the Ends of War*

(Cambridge, MA, 2015); Lisset Marie Pino and John Fabian Witt, "The Fourteenth Amendment as an Ending: Constitutional Beginnings and the Demise of the War Power," *JCWE* 10 (March 2020): 5–28; David Blight, *Race and Reunion: The Civil War in American Memory* (Cambridge, MA, 2001); Caroline E. Janney, *Remembering the Civil War: Reunion and the Limits of Reconciliation* (Chapel Hill, 2013); Heather Cox Richardson *How the South Won the Civil War: Oligarchy, Democracy, and the Continuing Fight for the Soul of America* (New York, 2020); Karen L. Cox, *No Common Ground: Confederate Monuments and the Ongoing Fight for Racial Justice* (Chapel Hill, 2021).

16. Compare Kris Manjapra, *Black Ghost of Empire: The Long Death of Slavery and the Failure of Emancipation* (New York, 2021); Roberto Saba, *American Mirror: The United States and Brazil in the Age of Emancipation* (Princeton, 2021).

17. Theda Skocpol, *Protecting Soldiers and Mothers: The Political Origins of Social Policy in the United States* (Cambridge, MA, 1992); Brandi Clay Brimmer, *Claiming Union Widowhood: Race, Respectability, and Poverty in the Post-Emancipation South* (Durham, 2020); Alison M. Parker, *Articulating Rights: Nineteenth Century American Women on Race, Reform and the State* (DeKalb, 2010); Dorothy Sue Cobble, Linda Gordon, and Astrid Henry, *Feminism Unfinished: A Short, Surprising History of American Women's Movements* (New York, 2014).

18. Charles Postel, *Equality: An American Dilemma, 1866–1896* (New York, 2019); Steven Hahn, *A Nation under Our Feet: Black Political Struggles in the Rural South from Slavery to the Great Migration* (Cambridge, MA, 2003); Elizabeth Sanders, *Roots of Reform: Farmers, Workers, and the American State, 1877–1917* (Chicago, 1999); Larry M. Bartels, *Unequal Democracy: The Political Economy of the New Gilded Age* (Princeton, 2016); Michael Thompson, *The Politics of Inequality: A Political History of the Idea of Economic Inequality in America* (New York, 2007); William J. Novak, *New Democracy: The Creation of the Modern American State* (Cambridge, MA, 2022).

19. Ted Tunnell, "Creating 'the Propaganda of History': Southern Editors and the Origins of the Carpetbagger and Scalawag," *JSH* 72 (2006): 789–822.

CHAPTER ONE: WARTIME RECONSTRUCTION

1. James G. Blaine, *Twenty Years of Congress: From Lincoln to Garfield, With a Review of the Events which led to the Political Revolution of 1860*, vol. 1 (Norwich, 1884); James M. McPherson, *Battle Cry of Freedom: The Civil War Era* (New York, 1988), chap. 7; Douglas R. Egerton, *Year of Meteors: Stephen Douglas, Abraham Lincoln, and the Election That Brought On the Civil War* (New York, 2010); Manisha Sinha, *The Counterrevolution of Slavery: Politics and Ideology in Antebellum South Carolina* (Chapel Hill, 2000); Stephanie McCurry, *Confederate Reckoning: Power and Politics in the Civil War South* (Cambridge, MA, 2010).

2. Robin D. G. Kelley, *Freedom Dreams: The Black Radical Imagination* (Boston, 2002), 9–12.

3. Franny Nudelman, *John Brown's Body: Slavery, Violence, and the Culture of War* (Chapel Hill, 2004); Drew Gilpin Faust, *This Republic of Suffering: Death and the American Civil War* (New York, 2008); Megan Kate Nelson, *Ruin Nation: Destruction and the American Civil War* (Athens, 2012); Yael A. Sternhell, "Revisionism Reinvented? The Anti-War Turn in Civil War Scholarship," *JCWE* 3 (June 2013): 239–56.

4. *The Works of Charles Sumner* (Boston, 1874), 5:345–47; Joseph P. Reidy, *Illusions of*

Emancipation: The Pursuit of Freedom and Equality in the Twilight of Slavery (Chapel Hill, 2019), chap. 3.

5. Sinha, *Counterrevolution of Slavery*, 255; *NASS*, August 1, 1863; Charles Francis Adams, Sr., The Civil War Diaries, April 12, 1861, MHS; *Works of Sumner*, 5:351; Adam I. P. Smith, *The Stormy Present: Conservatism and the Problem of Slavery in Northern Politics, 1846–1865* (Chapel Hill, 2017); Matt Karp, *This Vast Slaveholding Empire: Slaveholders at the Helm of American Foreign Policy* (Cambridge, MA, 2016).

6. Yael A. Sternhell, *Routes of War: The World of Movement in the Confederate South* (Cambridge, MA, 2012); Steven Hahn, *A Nation under Our Feet: Black Political Struggles in the Rural South from Slavery to the Great Migration* (Cambridge, MA, 2003), 13; Thavolia Glymph, *The Women's Fight: The Civil War's Battles for Home, Freedom, and Nation* (Chapel Hill, 2020), 2; Sinha, *Counterrevolution of Slavery*, 256–57; Ira Berlin et al., eds., *Freedom: A Documentary History of Emancipation, 1861–1867 Series I, Volume 1 The Destruction of Slavery* (Cambridge, 1985), 9.

7. Berlin et al., eds., *Destruction of Slavery*, 12, 14, 71; Elizabeth D. Leonard, *Benjamin Franklin Butler: A Noisy Fearless Life* (Chapel Hill, 2022), chap. 3; James Oakes, *Freedom National: The Destruction of Slavery in the United States, 1861–1865* (New York, 2013), 99, 138–44; David W. Blight, ed., *A Slave No More: Two Men Who Escaped to Freedom Including Their Own Narratives of Emancipation* (New York, 2007), 186; Silvana R. Siddali, *From Property to Person: Slavery and the Confiscation Acts, 1861–1862* (Baton Rouge, 2005), chap. 4; Glenn David Brasher, *The Peninsula Campaign and the Necessity of Emancipation: African Americans and the Flight for Freedom* (Chapel Hill, 2012); Kristopher A. Teters, *Practical Liberators: Union Officers in the Western Theater During the Civil War* (Chapel Hill, 2018); Elizabeth Varon, *Armies of Deliverance: A New History of the Civil War* (New York, 2019).

8. *Emancipation League. Declaration,* Broadside, AAS; *TL*, May 3, December 13, 1861, January 10, 24, April 11, December 5, 1862; *TCR*, June 28, 1862; David Lee Child, *Rights and Duties of the United States Relative to Slavery under the Laws of War* (Boston, 1861); *The Abolition of Slavery the Right of the Government under the War Power* (Boston, 1861); *DM*, July 1861, 493, September 1861, 514; Manisha Sinha, "Allies for Emancipation? Lincoln and Black Abolitionists," in Eric Foner, ed., *Our Lincoln: New Perspectives on Lincoln and His World* (New York, 2008), 176–80; *William Lloyd Garrison, 1805–1879: The Story of His Life Told by His Children*, vol. 4, 1861–1879 (New York, 1889), 21–32, 118; Adams, Sr., *The Civil War Diaries,* December 31, 1861; Edward L. Pierce, *Memoirs and Letters of Charles Sumner* (Boston, 1894), 4:41–47; Matthew J. Clavin, *Touissant Louverture and the American Civil War: The Promise and Peril of a Second Haitian Revolution* (Philadelphia, 2009).

9. Roy P. Basler, ed., *The Collected Works of Abraham Lincoln* (New Brunswick, 1953), 4:506, 517–18, 532; *DM*, October 1861, 535–43, November 1861, 546–47, December 1861, 563; *TCR*, July 12, 1862; Basler, ed., *The Collected Works of Abraham Lincoln* (New Brunswick, 1953), 5:49; Siddali, *From Property to Person,* chap. 5.

10. *TL*, May 23, December 12, 1862; Berlin et al., *The Destruction of Slavery*, 108–9, 124; Basler, ed., *The Collected Works of Abraham Lincoln*, 5:222–23; Edward A. Miller, Jr., *Lincoln's Abolitionist General: The Biography of David Hunter* (Columbia, 1997).

11. *TCR*, April 26, May 17, 1862; Oakes, *Freedom National*, 224–45; *Speech of Hon. Lyman Trumbull of Illinois* (Washington, 1861), 3–7; Ryan Roske, *His Own Counsel: The Life and Times of Lyman Trumbull* (Reno, 1979); *The Death of Slavery—The Life of the Nation: Speech of Hon. Henry Wilson of Massachusetts* (Washington, 1862): 2–4;

Siddali, *From Property to Person,* 227–50; *DM*, May 1862, 642; Pierce, *Memoirs and Letters of Charles Sumner,* 4:64–66; *The Works of Charles Sumner* (Boston, 1874), 6:391–93, 419–23; Adams, Sr., *The Civil War Diaries,* July 22, October 4, 1862, MHS; T. Stephen Whitman, *Antietam 1862: Gateway to Emancipation* (Santa Barbara, 2012).

12. Henry Wilson, *History of the Antislavery Measures of the Thirty-Seventh and Thirty-Eighth United-States Congresses, 1861–1865* (Boston, 1865); Basler, ed., *The Collected Works of Abraham Lincoln,* 5:370–75, 434, 519–21, 534–35; Pierce, *Memoirs and Letters of Charles Sumner,* 4:68–71, 81, 175–77; *The Works of Charles Sumner* (Boston, 1874), 6:448–85; *TCR*, September 27, October 4, 18, 1862, March 21, July 5, 1863; *TL*, August 1, 22, September 5, 29, December 12, 1862; *NASS*, March 21, June 27, 1863; Manisha Sinha, "Abraham Lincoln's Competing Political Loyalties: Union, Constitution, and Antislavery," in Nicholas Buccola, ed., *Abraham Lincoln and Liberal Democracy* (Lawrence, 2016), 164–91; Eric Foner, *The Fiery Trial: Abraham Lincoln and American Slavery* (New York, 2010), chap. 7; Jonathan W. White, ed., *To Address You as My Friend: African Americans' Letters to Abraham Lincoln* (Chapel Hill, 2021), chap. 2; compare Phillip W. Magness and Sebastian N. Page, *Colonization after Emancipation: Lincoln and the Movement for Black Resettlement* (Columbia, 2018).

13. *NASS*, January 3, 1863; *TL* January 9, 1863; Roy P. Basler, ed., *The Collected Works of Abraham Lincoln* (New Brunswick, 1953), 6:30; Louis Masur, *Lincoln's Hundred Days: The Emancipation Proclamation and the War for the Union* (Cambridge, MA, 2012): 214, 280; *William Lloyd Garrison,* 4:69–71, 86–92; *TCR*, March 14, 1863; Emilie Davis, "January 1, 1863," *Memorable Days: The Emilie Davis Diaries,* Falvey Library, Villanova University, https://davisdiaries.villanova.edu/; Sinha, "Allies for Emancipation," 182–86.

14. *DM* November 1861: 548, February 1862: 605; Pierce, *Memoirs and Letters of Charles Sumner,* 4:149–75; Adams, Sr. *The Civil War Diaries,* November 15, 1861, June 20, 1862; *TL* November 23, December 12, 1862; *William Lloyd Garrison,* 4:65–68, 71–77; Richard J.M. Blackett, *Divided Hearts: Britain and the American Civil War* (Baton Rouge, 2001); Sinha, *The Counterrevolution of Slavery,* 256; Don H. Doyle, *The Cause of All Nations: An International History of the American Civil War* (New York, 2015); Ann L. Tucker, *Newest Born of Nations: European Nationalist Movements and the Making of the Confederacy* (Charlottesville, 2020); Niels Eichhorn, *Liberty and Slavery: European Separatists, Southern Secession, and the American Civil War* (Baton Rouge, 2019); Douglas R. Egerton, "Rethinking Atlantic Historiography in a Postcolonial Era: The Civil War in a Global Perspective," *JCWE* 1 (March 2011): 79–95.

15. W.E.B. Du Bois, *Black Reconstruction in America: An Essay Toward the Part Which Black Folk Played in the Attempt to Reconstruct Democracy in America, 1860–1880* (New York, 1935), 67; Hahn, *A Nation Under Our Feet,* 7; Sinha, *The Counterrevolution of Slavery,* 257; Thomas Wentworth Higginson, *Army Life in a Black Regiment and Other Writings* (1869: reprint, New York, 1997): 17–18; *TL* November 23, 1862; Erik Mathisen, *The Loyal Republic: Traitors, Slaves, and the Remaking of Citizenship in Civil War America* (Chapel Hill, 2018).

16. Ira Berlin et al., eds., *Freedom: A Documentary History of Emancipation, 1861–1867 Series II The Black Military Experience* (Cambridge, 1982): 1, 60; *Memorable Days: The Emilie Davis Diaries,* June 29, 30, July 7, 1863; Edward L. Ayers, *The Thin Light of Freedom: The Civil War and Emancipation in the Heart of America* (New York, 2017): 87–88; Brian Taylor, *Fighting for Citizenship: Black Northerners and the Debate over Military Service in the Civil War* (Chapel Hill, 2020); *DM* May 1862: 641; Holly A. Pinheiro, Jr. *The Families' Civil War: Black Soldiers and the Fight for Racial Justice* (Athens, 2022).

17. Foner, *The Fiery Trial*, 230; Berlin et al., eds., *The Black Military Experience*, 1–16; *TL* June 27, 1862; James G. Hollandsworth, Jr. *The Louisiana Native Guards: The Black Military Experience During the Civil War* (Baton Rouge, 1995); Blight, ed., *A Slave No More*, 251; Cate Linberry, *Be Free or Die: The Amazing Story of Robert Smalls' Escape from Slavery to Union Hero* (New York, 2017).

18. *TL* May 30, 1862; Sinha, "Allies for Emancipation," 188–89; *NASS*, March 14, April 11, 1863; Foner, *The Fiery Trial*, 249; David W. Blight, *Frederick Douglass: Prophet of Freedom* (New York, 2018): 385; Douglas Egerton, *Thunder at the Gates: The Black Civil War Regiments that Redeemed America* (New York, 2016).

19. John Stauffer and Benjamin Soskis, *The Battle Hymn of the Republic: A Biography of the Song that Marches On* (New York, 2013): Appendix; Joseph T. Wilson, *The Black Phalanx: African American Soldiers in the War of Independence, the War of 1812, and the Civil War* (Hartford, 1887); Bob Luke & John David Smith, *Soldiering for Freedom: How the Union Army Recruited, Trained, and Deployed the US Colored Troops* (Baltimore, 2014): 81; *NASS*, September 5, December 5, 1863; McPherson, *Battle Cry of Freedom*, 862; Higginson, *Army Life in a Black Regiment*, 3; John T. Galvin, "The Hallowells: Fighting Quakers," *Proceedings of the Massachusetts Historical Society* 104 (1992): 42–54; Joseph T. Glathaar, *Forged in Battle: The Civil War Alliance of Black Soldiers and White Officers* (New York, 1990): 206.

20. George Washington Williams, *A History of the Negro Troops in the War of the Rebellion, 1861–1865* (New York, 1887): 41–55, 257; Richard Nelson Current, *Lincoln's Loyalists: Union Soldiers from the Confederacy* (Boston, 1992); Basler ed., *The Collected Works of Abraham Lincoln*, 5:436–37, 6:374; General N.P. Chipman, *The Horrors of Andersonville Rebel Prison* (San Francisco, 1891); *NASS*, May 7, September 3, 1864; *TCR* April 30, May 21, 1864; "Fort Pillow Massacre," *Report of the Joint Committee on the Conduct of the War*, House of Representatives, 38th Congress, 1st Session, 2, 6; John Cimprich, *Fort Pillow, A Civil War Massacre, and Public Memory* (Baton Rouge, 2005); Andrew Ward, *River Ran Red: The Fort Pillow Massacre in the American Civil War* (New York, 2005); Mark Grimsley, *The Hard Hand of War: Union Military Policies Toward Southern Civilians, 1861–1865* (Cambridge, 1995); John Fabian Witt, *Lincoln's Code: The Laws of War in American History* (New York, 2012): 70–79, 240–49; Bruce Levine, *Confederate Emancipation: Southern Plans to Free and Arm Slaves During the Civil War* (New York, 2006); Kevin M. Levin, *Searching for Black Confederates: The Civil War's Most Persistent Myth* (Chapel Hill, 2019).

21. Sinha, "Allies for Emancipation," 189–91; Berlin et al., eds., *The Black Military Experience*, 19–21; *TFJ*, March 1865, 10; Higginson, *Army Life in a Black Regiment*, 217–19; Jonathan Lande, "Trials of War: African American Deserters during the U.S. Civil War," *Journal of Social History* 49 (Spring 2016): 603–709; Virginia M. Adams, ed., *On the Altar of Freedom: A Black Soldier's Civil War Letters from the Front Corporal James Henry Gooding* (Amherst, 1991), 117–24; *TCR*, January 2, 9, 30, February 20, 27, April 2, 16, May 7, June 25, July 23, 30, August 3, 6, 20, 1864; *NASS*, April 30, 1864; *TL*, May 13, October 7, 1864; *William Lloyd Garrison*, 4:86; Pierce, *Memoirs and Letters of Charles Sumner*, 4:181–82; Donald R. Shaffer, *After the Glory: The Struggles of Black Civil War Veterans* (Lawrence, 2004); Brandi Clay Brimmer, *Claiming Union Widowhood: Race, Respectability, and Poverty in the Post-Emancipation South* (Durham, 2020) ; Elizabeth A. Regosin and Donald Shaffer, eds., *Voices of Emancipation: Understanding Slavery, the Civil War, and Reconstruction through the U.S. Pension Bureau Files* (New York, 2008).

22. William Wells Brown, *The Negro in the American Rebellion: His Heroism and His Fidelity* (Boston, 1867); Carole Emberton, "'Only Murder Makes Men': Reconsidering the Black Military Experience," *JCWE* 3 (2012): 369–93; Sinha, "Allies for Emancipation," 185, 191–92; *Opinion of Attorney General Bates on Citizenship* (Washington, 1862); Basler, ed., *The Collected Works of Abraham Lincoln*, 6:409–10; Allen Guelzo, "Defending Emancipation: Abraham Lincoln and the Conkling Letter, 1863," *CWH* 48 (2002): 313–37.

23. Leon F. Litwack, *Been in the Storm So Long: The Aftermath of Slavery* (New York, 1979); Jim Downs, *Sick from Freedom: African-American Illness and Suffering during the Civil War and Reconstruction* (New York, 2012); Amy Murrell Taylor, *Embattled Freedom: Journeys through the Civil War's Slave Refugee Camps* (Chapel Hill, 2018); Ira Berlin et al., eds., *Freedom: A Documentary History of Emancipation, 1861–1865*, series 1, vol. 3, *The Wartime Genesis of Free Labor: The Lower South* (Cambridge, 1990), introduction.

24. Hahn, *A Nation under Our Feet*, 83–89; Thavolia Glymph, *Out of the House of Bondage: The Transformation of the Plantation Household* (Cambridge, 2008), 102; "Rose's War and the Gendered Politics of a Slave Insurgency in the Civil War," *JCWE* 3 (December 2013): 501–32; Thulani Davis, *The Emancipation Circuit: Black Activism Forging a Culture of Freedom* (Durham, 2022), 29; Sharon Romeo, *Gender and Jubilee: Black Freedom and Citizenship in Civil War Missouri* (Athens, 2016), chaps. 1–2; Stephanie E. Jones-Rogers, *They Were Her Property: White Women as Slave Owners in the American South* (New Haven, 2019).

25. *TL*, February 14, 1862; *TCR*, August 9, 1862; David Silkenet, *Driven from Home: North Carolina's Civil War Refugee Crisis* (Athens, 2016), chap. 1; Ira Berlin and Leslie S. Rowland, *Families and Freedom: A Documentary History of African American Kinship in the Civil War Era* (New York, 1997), introduction; *TFJ*, March 1865, 10; "Harriet Carrington Searching for Her Son Patrick Finch," *The Daily Dispatch*, Richmond, VA, April 19, 1871, *Last Seen: Finding Family After Slavery*, https://informationwanted.org; Heather Andrea Williams, *Help Me to Find My People: The African American Search for Family Lost in Slavery* (Chapel Hill, 2012); Abigail Cooper, "'Away I Goin' to Find My Mamma': Self-Emancipation, Migration, and Kinship in Refugee Camps in the Civil War Era," *JAAH* 102 (2017): 444–67; Romeo, *Gender and Jubilee*, chap. 5; Tera W. Hunter, *Bound in Wedlock: Slave and Free Black Marriage in the Nineteenth Century* (Cambridge, MA, 2017), chap. 4.

26. Taylor, *Embattled Freedom*, 129, 193; Berlin et al., *The Destruction of Slavery*, 41–42; Leslie Schwalm, "Between Slavery and Freedom: African American Women and Occupation in the Slave South," in LeeAnn Whites and Alecia P. Long, eds., *Occupied Women: Gender, Military Occupation, and the American Civil War* (Baton Rouge, 2009); Kim Murphy, *I Had Rather Die: Rape in the Civil War* (Afton, 2014); Romeo, *Gender and Jubilee*, chap. 4; Crystal N. Feimster, "Rape and Justice in the Civil War," Opinionator, *New York Times*, April 25, 2013; Gerald Schwartz, ed., *A Woman Doctor's Civil War: Esther Hill Hawks' Diary* (Columbia, 1984), 34; Hannah Rosen, *Terror in the Heart of Freedom: Citizenship, Sexual Violence, and the Meaning of Race in the Post-Emancipation South* (Chapel Hill, 2009), 9–11.

27. *TL*, February 6, 1863; Chandra Manning, *Troubled Refuge: Struggling for Freedom in the Civil War* (New York, 2016); John Eaton, *Grant, Lincoln and the Freedmen: Reminiscences of the Civil War, with Special Reference to the Work for the Contrabands and Freedmen of the Mississippi Valley* (New York, 1907), 2, 10, 13, 24, 34–37; *Freedmen. The American Missionary Association: Its Work among Them.* (New York,

1864); *History of the American Missionary Association* (New York, 1874), 11–16, 21–
24; Augustus F. Beard, *A Crusade of Brotherhood: A History of the American Missionary Association* (Boston, 1909); Joe M. Richardson, *Christian Reconstruction:
The American Missionary Association and Southern Blacks, 1861–1890* (Tuscaloosa,
1986), chaps. 1–3; Edward L. Pierce, "The Freedmen at Fortress Monroe," *Atlantic
Monthly* 8 (November 1861): 632–36; Rev. Lewis C. Lockwood, *Mary S. Peake, The
Colored Teacher at Fortress Monroe* (Boston, 1862), 35, 53; *DM*, November 1861, 559,
February 1862, 605; *NASS*, May 16, August 29, 1863; George R. Bentley, *A History
of the Freedmen's Bureau* (Philadelphia, 1955), 26–29; Rosen, *Terror in the Heart of
Freedom,* 32.

28. Edward L. Pierce, "The Freedmen at Port Royal," *Atlantic Monthly* 12 (September
1863): 291–315; *DM*, February 1862, 599; *TL*, May 9, 1862, October 16, 1863, Sep-
tember 1, 1865; *Second Annual Report of the New England Freedmen's Aid Society
(Educational Commission)* (Boston, 1864), 8–10, 16–22, 39–44, 50; "A Plea for the
Freedmen," *Pennsylvania Freedmen's Relief Association* (n.p., 1863); *First Annual
Report of the National Freedman's Relief Association, New York, February 19th, 1863*
(n.p.), 1–3; Thomas P. Knox, *Startling Revelations from the Department of the South
Carolina and Expose of the So Called National Freedmen's Relief Association* (Boston,
1864); Rupert Sargent Holland, ed., *The Letters and Diary of Laura M. Towne Written
from the Sea Islands of South Carolina, 1862–1884* (Cambridge, 1912), 7, 20, 55, 66,
73, 85, 103, 143, 181; Glymph, *The Women's Fight,* chap. 5; Mrs. A. M. French, *Slavery in South Carolina and the Ex-Slaves, or, The Port Royal Mission* (New York, 1862),
xi, 49, 185–86, 237, 308; James E. Yeatman, *A Report on the Condition of the Freedmen of the Mississippi* (St. Louis, 1864); *TFR*, January, March, April, 1865; Willie Lee
Rose, *Rehearsal for Reconstruction: The Port Royal Experiment* (Indianapolis, 1964),
22, 95, 105–9; *Slave Songs of the United States* (New York, 1867), xxiii; Samuel Char-
ters, *Songs of Sorrow: Lucy McKim Garrison and the "Slave Songs of the United States"*
(Jackson, 2015); Higginson, *Army Life in a Black Regiment,* chap. 9; Taylor, *Embattled
Freedom,* 183, 237; Heather Andrea Williams, *Self-Taught: African American Education in Slavery and Freedom* (Chapel Hill, 2005), 6; Jonathan W. White and Lydia J.
Davis, eds., *My Work among the Freedmen: The Civil War and Reconstruction Letters
of Harriet M. Buss* (Charlottesville, 2021); Christopher Hager, *Word by Word: Emancipation and the Act of Writing* (Cambridge, MA, 2013), 225–28.

29. *TL*, December 19, 1862; Charlotte Forten, "Life on the Sea Islands," parts 1 & 2, *The
Atlantic Monthly* (May–June 1864); Brenda Stevenson, ed., *The Journals of Charlotte
Forten Grimke* (New York, 1988), 39–40, 382, 388–97, 402–7, 430–31, 439–45, 480,
490–94; *Report of the Executive Board of the Friends' Association of Philadelphia and
Its Vicinity, for the Relief of Colored Freedmen* (Philadelphia, 1864), 21–23; Kay Ann
Taylor, "Mary S. Peake and Charlotte L. Forten: Black Teachers During the Civil War
and Reconstruction," *Journal of Negro Education* 74 (Spring 2005), 124–37.

30. *TL*, July 10, 1863; *Second Annual Report of the New England Freedmen's Aid Society,*
31–34; Elizabeth Hyde Botume, *First Days among the Contrabands* (Boston, 1893),
86; *TFR*, February 1865, May 1867; James M. McPherson, *The Struggle for Equality:
Abolitionists and the Negro in the Civil War and Reconstruction* (Princeton, 1964),
172, 392–95; James D. Anderson, *The Education of Blacks in the South, 1860–1935*
(Chapel Hill, 1988), chap. 1; Robert C. Morris, *Reading, 'Riting and Reconstruction:
The Education of Freedmen in the South, 1861–1870* (Chicago, 1981); Hilary Green,
Educational Reconstruction: African American Schools in the Urban South, 1865–1890

(New York, 2016); Carl F. Kaestle, *Pillars of the Republic: Common Schools and American Society, 1780–1860* (New York, 1983).

31. *TFR*, February, March, October, November, December 1865; Elizabeth Keckley, *Behind the Scenes, or Thirty Years a Slave, and Four Years in the White House* (New York, 1868), 139–43; Jennifer Fleischner, *Mrs. Lincoln and Mrs. Keckley: The Remarkable Story of the Friendship between a First Lady and a Former Slave* (New York, 2003); *TL*, May 20, 1864; Lucy N. Coleman, *Reminiscences* (Buffalo, 1891), 60–64; David S. Cecelski, *The Fire of Freedom: Abraham Galloway and the Slaves' Civil War* (Chapel Hill, 2012), 104; Judith Weisenfeld, "'Who Is Sufficient for These Things?' Sara G. Stanley and the American Missionary Association," *Church History* 60 (December 1991): 493–507; Christina Leonore Davis, "The Collective Identities of Women Teachers in Black Schools in the Post-Bellum South" (PhD diss., University of Georgia, 2016); Jean Fagan Yellin, *Harriet Jacobs: A Life* (New York, 2004), 158–87; Glymph, *The Women's Fight,* 183–86; Carol Faulkner, *Women's Radical Reconstruction: The Freedmen's Aid Movement* (Philadelphia, 2004): 15–26, 141–47.

32. *TL*, December 23, 1864, January 27, 1865; *TFR*, February 1865; Nell Painter, *Sojourner Truth: A Life, A Symbol* (New York, 1996), 212–16; Keith E. Melder, "Angel of Mercy in Washington: Josephine Griffing and the Freedmen, 1864–1872," *Records of the Columbia Historical Society* (1963/1965), 243–72; Pierce, *Memoirs and Letters of Charles Sumner,* 4:179–81, 185–87; Tamika Y. Nunley, *At the Threshold of Liberty: Women, Slavery, & Shifting Identities in Washington, D.C.* (Chapel Hill, 2021); Lynn M. Hudson, *The Making of "Mammy Pleasant": A Black Entrepreneur in Nineteenth Century San Francisco* (Urbana, 2003), 47–55; *A Brief Narrative of the Struggle for the Rights of the Colored People of Philadelphia in the City Railway Cars; and a Defence of William Still* (Philadelphia, 1867); Daniel R. Biddle and Murray Dubin, *Tasting Freedom: Octavius Catto and the Battle for Equality in Civil War America* (Philadelphia, 2010).

33. Cecelski, *The Fire of Freedom,* 69–70, 86–88, 104; *TFR*, February 1865; Taylor, *Embattled Freedom,* 115, 127; Susie King Taylor, *Reminiscences of My Life in Camp with the 33rd U.S. Colored Troops, Late 1st South Carolina Volunteers: A Black Woman's Civil War Memoirs,* ed. Patricia W. Romero (New York, 1988), 12, 52, 89–90, 135–43; Catherine Clinton, "Susie King Taylor (1848–1916): "I Gave my Services Willingly,'" in *Georgia Women: Their Lives and Times,* ed. Anne Short Chirhat and Betty Wood (Athens, 2009), 1:130–46.

34. *TFR*, September 1865; Janet Sharp Hermann, *The Pursuit of a Dream* (New York, 1981); Janet Sharp Hermann, *Joseph E. Davis: Pioneer Patriarch* (Jackson, 1990).

35. *Report of the Executive Board of the Friends' Association,* 26–29; *TFR*, May 1865, March 1866; *The National Freedman,* March 1, May 1, 1865; *Annual Report of the New York National Freedmen's Relief Association, of New York, with a Sketch of Its Early History* (New York, 1866), 5, 8–10; *Statistics of the Operation of the Executive Board of Friends Association of Philadelphia and Its Vicinity, for the Relief of Colored Freedmen* (Philadelphia, 1864), 29–30; *The American Union Commission* (n.p., 1864, 1865); *NASS*, June 6, 13, 1863, January 18, 1864; *TL*, December 30, 1864; Linda Warfel Slaughter, *The Freedmen of the South* (Cincinnati, 1869), 177; *History of the American Missionary Association,* 18–19; Faulkner, *Women's Radical Reconstruction,* chap. 3.

36. Lydia Maria Child, *The Freedmen's Book* (Boston, 1865), 251, 265–67; *TL*, April 18, May 2, 1862, March 13, 20, April 3, May 8, October 9, 1863, April 8, 1864, February 3, November 24, 1865; Carolyn L. Karcher, *The First Woman in the Republic: A Cultural*

Biography of Lydia Maria Child (Durham, 1994), 495–510; *TCR*, September 27, 1862; McPherson, *The Struggle for Equality,* 172–74; Wendy Hamand Venet, *Neither Ballots Nor Bullets: Women Abolitionists and the Civil War* (Charlottesville, 1991); Manisha Sinha, "The Other Frances Ellen Watkins Harper," *Common-Place* (Spring 2016).

37. Du Bois, *Black Reconstruction in America,* 77–78; Taylor, *Embattled Freedom,* 42–46, 200–204; Faulkner, *Women's Radical Reconstruction,* 31–33; Glymph, *The Women's Fight,* 192–93; *Second Annual Report of the New England Freedmen's Aid Society,* 50; *First Annual Report of the National Freedmen's Relief Association of the District of Columbia* (Washington, DC, 1863); *History of the American Missionary Association,* 17; Katherine Franke, *Repair: Redeeming the Promise of Abolition* (Chicago, 2021); Ana Lucia Araujo, *Reparations for Slavery and the Slave Trade: A Transnational and Comparative History* (New York, 2017).

CHAPTER TWO: PRESIDENTIAL RECONSTRUCTION

1. James McPherson, *Tried by War: Lincoln as Commander in Chief* (New York, 2008); Ken Lawrence, "Yes, John Wilkes Booth Did Speak Those Notorious Words at Lincoln's Last Speech," *History News Network,* May, 10, 2020.

2. Brooks D. Simpson, *The Reconstruction Presidents* (Lawrence, 1998); La Wanda Cox, *Lincoln and Black Freedom: A Study in Presidential Leadership* (Columbia, 1981).

3. Eric L. McKitrick, *Andrew Johnson and Reconstruction* (Chicago, 1960); Annette Gordon Reed, *Andrew Johnson* (New York, 2011).

4. Roy P. Basler, ed., *The Collected Works of Abraham Lincoln* (New Brunswick, 1953), 6:365; *TL*, September 4, 1863; Eric Foner, *The Fiery Trial: Abraham Lincoln and American Slavery* (New York, 2010), 239, 271–84; David Silkenet, *Driven from Home: North Carolina's Civil War Refugee Crisis* (Athens, 2016), 58; Patricia C. Click, *Time Full of Trial: The Roanoke Island Freedmen's Colony, 1862–1867* (Chapel Hill, 2001); David S. Cecelski, *The Fire of Freedom: Abraham Galloway and the Slaves' Civil War* (Chapel Hill, 2012), chap. 8.

5. Roy P. Basler, ed., *The Collected Works of Abraham Lincoln* (New Brunswick, 1953), 7:49–56, 243; *NASS*, January 17, February 21, March 14, 1863, January 9, 24, 1864; *NOT*, July 24, 1864, March 28, 29, 30, 1865; Jean-Charles Houzeau, *My Passage at the New Orleans Tribune: A Memoir of the Civil War Era,* ed. David C. Rankin, trans. Gerard F. Denault (Baton Rouge, 1984), 75–83, 104–6; Caryn Cosse Bell, *Revolution, Romanticism and the Afro-Creole Protest Tradition in Louisiana, 1718–1868* (Baton Rouge, 1997); James D. Anderson, *The Education of Blacks in the South, 1860–1935* (Chapel Hill, 1988), 9; Peyton McCrary, *Abraham Lincoln and Reconstruction: The Louisiana Experiment* (Princeton, 1978); Nathaniel Prentiss Banks, *Emancipated Labor in Louisiana* (n.p., 1864), 6–11; *TL*, November 11, December 2, 1864, February 10, 24, 1865; Ted Tunnell, *Crucible of Reconstruction: War, Radicalism, and Race in Louisiana, 1862–1877* (Baton Rouge, 1984), part one; John Rodrigue, *Reconstruction in the Cane Fields: From Slavery to Free Labor in Louisiana's Sugar Parishes, 1862–1880* (Baton Rouge, 2001).

6. *TL*, January 29, February 5, August 11, September 2, October 6, November 3, 11, December 16, 1864, January 13, 1865; Basler, ed., *The Collected Works of Abraham Lincoln,* 7:433–34; *William Lloyd Garrison, 1805–1879: The Story of His Life Told by His Children,* 1861–1879 (New York, 1889), 4:95–99; Edward L. Pierce, *Memoirs and Letters of Charles Sumner,* 1860–1874 (Boston, 1893), 4:214–29; H. L. Trefousse, *Benjamin Franklin Wade: Radical Republican from Ohio* (New York, 1963), chap. 18; *The Works*

of Charles Sumner (Boston, 1974), 7:116–18; Cox, *Lincoln and Black Freedom,* chaps. 2–4; *NYT,* August 11, 1864; *Letter of Thomas J. Durant to the Hon. Henry Winter Davis* (New Orleans, 1864); *The Equality of All Men before the Law Claimed and Defended; in Speeches by Hon. William D. Kelley, Wendell Phillips, and Frederick Douglass, and Letters from Elizur Wright and Wm. Heighton* (Boston, 1865); James M. McPherson, *The Struggle for Equality: Abolitionists and the Negro in the Civil War and Reconstruction* (Princeton, 1964), 238–46; Xi Wang, *The Trial of Democracy: Black Suffrage and Northern Republicans, 1860–1910* (Athens, 1997); *The Works of Charles Sumner,* 7:75–79; Roy P. Basler, ed., *The Collected Works of Abraham Lincoln* (New Brunswick, 1953), 8:403.

7. Pierce, *Memoirs and Letters of Charles Sumner,* 4:183–85; *Speech of Hon. Reverdy Johnson, of Maryland in Support of the Resolution to Amend the Constitution so as to Abolish Slavery Delivered in the Senate of the United States, April 5, 1864* (n.p.); William C. Harris, *Two Against Lincoln: Reverdy Johnson and Horatio Seymour, Champions of the Loyal Opposition* (Lawrence, 2017), part 1; *CG,* 38th Congress, 2nd session, 138–46; Rebecca E. Zietlow, *The Forgotten Emancipator: James Mitchell Ashley and the Ideological Origins of Reconstruction* (Cambridge, 2017); Amy Dru Stanley, "Instead of Waiting for the Thirteenth Amendment: The War Power, Slave Marriage, and Inviolate Human Rights," *AHR* (June 2010): 732–65; *Speech of Hon. Lyman Trumbull of Illinois, Amending the Constitution to Prohibit Slavery. Delivered in the Senate of the United States, March 28, 1864* (n.p., n.d.), 4–6; *TL,* January 20, February 3, 1865; Alexander Tsesis, *The Thirteenth Amendment and American Freedom: A Legal History* (New York, 2004); Michael Vorenberg, *Final Freedom: The Civil War, the Abolition of Slavery and the Thirteenth Amendment* (Cambridge, 2001).

8. Risa L. Goluboff, "The Thirteenth Amendment and the Lost Origins of Civil Rights," *Duke Law Journal* 50 (April 2001): 1609–85; *The Works of Charles Sumner,* 5:351–401; *Have Faith in God and the People. Speech of Hon. Wm. D. Kelley, of Pennsylvania* (Washington, 1864), 1–2; Leonard L. Richards, *Who Freed the Slaves? The Fight over the Thirteenth Amendment* (Chicago, 2015); *Miscegenation: The Theory of the Blending of Races, Applied to the American White Man and the Negro* (New York, 1864), 9, 69–70; Forrest G. Wood, *Black Scare: The Racist Response to Emancipation and Reconstruction* (Berkeley, 1968); Manisha Sinha, "Allies for Emancipation? Lincoln and Black Abolitionists," in Eric Foner, ed., *Our Lincoln: New Perspectives on Lincoln and His World* (New York, 2008), 186–87; McPherson, *The Struggle for Equality,* chap. 12; *NASS,* April 4, 1863, February 13, April 2, November 5, 1864; *TL,* February 5, March 18, May 10, June 24, July 8, 15, 29, August 5, 26, September 23, October 7, 14, 21, 28, November 18, 1864; Henry Wilson, *History of the Rise and Fall of the Slave Power in America* (Boston, 1877), 3:546–49, 559–61; *William Lloyd Garrison,* 4:107–12.

9. *TL,* November 18, 1864, May 19, December 22, 29, 1865; Basler, ed., *The Collected Works of Abraham Lincoln,* 8:149–52; Manisha Sinha, *The Slave's Cause: A History of Abolition* (New Haven, 2017), 586–88; Beverly Wilson Palmer and Holly Byers Ochoa, eds., *The Selected Papers of Thaddeus Stevens,* vol. 1, January 1814–March 1865 (Pittsburgh, 1997), 520–24; Charles Francis Adams, Sr., "The Civil War Diaries," February 15, 1865, MHS; Michael Burlingame, *Abraham Lincoln: A Life* (Baltimore, 2008), 2:745–61; *Secretary Seward's Proclamation Declaring the Thirteenth Amendment to the United States Constitution to Have Been Adopted. Printed from the Types Set by William Lloyd Garrison with His Own Hand for the Last Number but One of The Liberator* (Boston, 1902); *William Lloyd Garrison,* 4:122–24, 129, 153–74.

10. Sinha, "Allies for Emancipation," 187; Francis Leiber, *Loyal Publication*

Society...Amendments to the Constitution, Submitted to the Consideration of the American People (New York, 1865); Sidney George Fisher, *The Trial of the Constitution* (Philadelphia, 1862); David A. J. Richards, *Conscience and the Constitution: History, Theory, and Law of the Reconstruction Amendments* (Princeton, 1993); Guyora Binder, "Did the Slaves Author the Thirteenth Amendment? An Essay in Redemptive History," *Yale Journal of Law and the Humanities* 5 (Summer 1993): 471–506; Mark E. Neely, Jr., *Lincoln and the Triumph of the Nation: Constitutional Conflict in the American Civil War* (Chapel Hill, 2011).

11. Ira Berlin et al., eds., *Freedom: A Documentary History of Emancipation, 1861–1867,* series 1, *The Wartime Genesis of Free Labor: The Lower South* (Cambridge, 1990), 3:7, 60, 331–38; *TL,* June 13, 1862, February 5, 1864, February 10, December 1, 1865; *NOT,* February 13, May 19, 20, 1865; Houzeau, *My Passage at the New Orleans Tribune,* 37, 110; Joseph J. Tregle, Jr., "Thomas J. Durant, Utopian Socialism and the Failure of Presidential Reconstruction in Louisiana," *JSH* 45 (November 1979): 485–512; Charlene Gilbert and Quinn Eli, *Homecoming: The Story of African-American Farmers* (Boston, 2000), 13–14; Douglas R. Egerton, *The Wars of Reconstruction: The Brief, Violent History of America's Most Progressive Era* (New York, 2014), 99; "Colloquy with Colored Ministers," *JNH* 16 (January 1931): 88–94; Jacqueline Jones, *Saving Savannah: The City and the Civil War* (New York, 2008), 218–20.

12. *NASS,* December 12, 1863; Louis S. Gerteis, *From Contraband to Freedman: Federal Policy Toward Southern Blacks, 1861–1865* (Westport, 1973); Berlin et al., eds., *The Wartime Genesis of Free Labor,* 38–40, 49–53; Steven Hahn et al., eds., *Freedom: A Documentary History of Emancipation, 1861–1867,* series 3, Land and Labor, 1865 (Chapel Hill, 2008), 1:27–40; Lawrence N. Powell, *New Masters: Northern Planters during the Civil War and Reconstruction* (New Haven, 1980), chaps. 1–2; *TL,* September 1, 1865 (Jourdan is identified as George).

13. *TL,* February 5, 1864; *NASS,* January 9, 1864; *The Programme of Peace. By a Democrat of the Old School* (Boston, 1862), 9–11, 15–16; McPherson, *The Struggle for Equality,* 247–57, 320–21, 407; George W. Julian, *Speeches on Political Questions* (New York, 1872), 216.

14. *NASS,* July 18, 1863; Edward Magdol, *A Right to the Land: Essays on the Freedmen's Community* (New York, 1977); Berlin et al., eds., *The Wartime Genesis of Free Labor,* 1–6, 15; Sinha, *The Slave's Cause,* 352–54; *The Works of Charles Sumner,* 8:491–92; Claude F. Oubre, *Forty Acres and a Mule: The Freedmen's Bureau and Black Land Ownership* (Baton Rouge, 1978).

15. *TL,* April 18, 1862, February 6, 1863, June 16, 1865; *NASS,* July 11, 1863; S. G. Howe, *The Refugees from Slavery in Canada West: Report to the Freedmen's Inquiry Commission* (Boston, 1864), 22–28, 59, 81–83, 98–99, 102; McPherson, *The Struggle for Equality,* 145–47; James McKaye, *The Mastership and Its Fruits: The Emancipated Face to Face with His Old Master. A Supplemental Report to Hon. Edwin M. Stanton* (New York, 1864), 21–36; *Preliminary Report Touching the Condition and Management of Emancipated Refugees Made to the Secretary of War by the American Freedmen's Inquiry Commission* (New York, 1863), 21–23, 27–33; *Final Report of the American Freedmen's Inquiry Commission to the Secretary of War* (n.p., 1864), chap. 3; Robert Dale Owen, *The Wrong of Slavery The Right of Emancipation and the Future of the African Race in the United States* (Philadelphia, 1864): 8–9; Oz Frankel, "The Predicament of Racial Knowledge: Government Studies of the Freedmen during the US Civil War," *Social Research* 70 (Spring 2003): 45–81; Pierce, *Memoirs and Letters of Charles Sumner,*

4:178–79; *The Works of Charles Sumner,* 8:475–524; William S. McFeely, *Yankee Step-father: General O. O. Howard and the Freedmen* (New Haven, 1968).

16. Heather Cox Richardson, *The Greatest Nation of the Earth: Republican Economic Policies during the Civil War* (Cambridge, MA, 1997); Ariel Ron, *Grassroots Leviathan: Agricultural Reform and the Rural North in the Slaveholding Republic* (Baltimore, 2020); Mark Wilson, *The Business of Civil War: Military Mobilization and the State, 1861–1865* (Baltimore, 2006); Fergus M. Bordewich, *Congress at War: How Republican Reformers Fought the Civil War, Defied Lincoln, Ended Slavery, and Remade America* (New York, 2020); Roger Lowenstein, *Ways and Means: Lincoln and His Cabinet and the Financing of the Civil War* (New York, 2022); Dorothy Ross, "Lincoln and the Ethics of Emancipation: Universalism, Nationalism, and Exceptionalism," *AHR* 96 (September 2009): 379–99.

17. Basler, ed., *The Collected Works of Abraham Lincoln,* 8:332–33; Ronald C. White Jr., *Lincoln's Greatest Speech: The Second Inaugural* (New York, 2002); John Stauffer, *Giants: The Parallel Lives of Frederick Douglass and Abraham Lincoln* (New York, 2008): 280, 295; *TL,* March 10, 24, April 7, 14, 28, 1865; George Washinton Williams, *History of the Negro Race in America From 1619 to 1880* (New York, 1883), 300–301; W.E.B. Du Bois, *Black Reconstruction in America: An Essay Toward a History of the Part which Black Folk Played in the Attempt to Reconstruct Democracy in America, 1860–1880* (New York, 1935), 124; Walt Whitman, "Calhoun's Real Monument," in *Complete Prose Works: Specimen Days and Collect, November Boughs and Good Bye My Fancy,* Project Gutenberg; Whitelaw Reid, *After the War, A Southern Tour: May 1, 1865 to May 1, 1866* (Cincinnati, 1866), 158–59, 162.

18. *TL,* April 21, 1865; Whitman, "Death of President Lincoln," April 16, 1865, in *Specimen Days;* Foner, *The Fiery Trial,* 332; Pierce, *Memoirs and Letters of Charles Sumner,* 4:237–39; Adams, "The Civil War Diaries," April 26, 1865; Wilson, *History of the Rise and Fall of the Slave Power in America,* 3:579–89; Sinha, "Allies for Emancipation," 195; Du Bois, *Black Reconstruction,* 165; Elizabeth D. Leonard, *Lincoln's Avengers: Justice, Revenge, and Reunion after the Civil War* (New York, 2004); Harold Holzer, ed., *President Lincoln Assassinated!! The Firsthand Story of the Murder, Manhunt, Trial, and Mourning* (New York, 2015), 308–24; *Celebration by the Colored People's Educational Monument Association in Memory of Abraham Lincoln on the Fourth of July, 1865* (Washington, 1865), 15–16, 29; Foner and Walker, eds., *The Proceedings of the Black State Conventions, 1865–1900,* 1:12, 67–68; Martha Hodes, *Mourning Lincoln* (New Haven, 2015), 70–74, 78–90, 273; Jon Meacham, *And There Was Light: Abraham Lincoln and the American Struggle* (New York, 2022), chap. 28.

19. Stauffer, *Giants,* 293–94; Sinha, "Allies for Emancipation," 181–82; Allen Thorndike Rice, ed., *Reminiscences of Abraham Lincoln by Distinguished Men of His Time* (New York, 1909), 323; Jonathan W. White, ed., *To Address You as My Friend: African Americans' Letters to Abraham Lincoln* (Chapel Hill, 2020), 238; John E. Washington, *They Knew Lincoln,* ed. Kate Masur (New York, 2018); compare Robert S. Levine, *The Failed Promise: Reconstruction, Frederick Douglass and the Impeachment of Andrew Johnson* (New York, 2021); Beverly Wilson Palmer & Holly Byers Ochoa, eds., *The Selected Papers of Thaddeus Stevens,* vol. 2, April 1865–August 1868 (Pittsburgh, 1998), 6–8, 10; Wilson, *History of the Rise and Fall of the Slave Power,* 3:578; *NASS,* July 8, 15, October 28, 1865; *TL,* October 27, 1865; McPherson, *The Struggle for Equality,* 314–15, 337–40.

20. McKitrick, *Andrew Johnson and Reconstruction,* chap. 4; LaWanda C. Fenlason Cox and John Henry Cox, *Politics, Principle, and Prejudice, 1865–1866* (New York, 1963);

Hans Trefousse, *Andrew Johnson: A Biography* (New York, 1989); Keri Leigh Merritt, *Masterless Men: Poor Whites and Slavery in the Antebellum South* (Cambridge, 2017), 1–61; Paul Bergeron, *Andrew Johnson's Civil War and Reconstruction* (Knoxville, 2011); James D. Richardson, *A Compilation of the Messages and Papers of the Presidents, 1789–1897* (Washington, 1897), 6:301–5.

21. Edward McPherson, *The Political History of the United States of America during the Period of Reconstruction* (Washington, 1871), 7–17; Richardson, *A Compilation of the Messages and Papers,* 307–38; McKitrick, *Andrew Johnson,* 7–10, 48–50; Reid, *After the War,* 45–46, 50; Pierce, *Memoirs and Letters of Charles Sumner,* 4:268; Carl Schurz, *Report on the Condition of the South, 39th Congress, 1st Session, Senate* (n.p., 1865), 10–14; Sidney George Andrews, *The South Since the War* (Boston, 1866), 46, 213; *NYDT,* August 2, 1865; *NASS,* November 25, 1865; *TL,* December 1, 1865; Du Bois, *Black Reconstruction,* 130; Hahn et al., eds., *Land and Labor 1865,* 11, 16, 50–53; Oubre, *Forty Acres and a Mule,* chap. 2; Julie Saville, *The Work of Reconstruction: From Slave to Wage Laborer in South Carolina, 1860–1870* (Cambridge, 1996), chap. 3; Michael Perman, *Reunion without Compromise: The South and Reconstruction, 1865–1868* (Cambridge, 1973), part 2; Eric Foner, *Reconstruction, 1863–1877: America's Unfinished Revolution* (New York, 1988), chap. 5; *The Reminiscences of Carl Schurz,* vol. 3, 1863–1869 (New York, 1908), 188–93, 202–9.

22. Dan T. Carter, *When the War Was Over: The Failure of Self-Reconstruction in the South, 1865–1867* (Baton Rouge, 1985); Richardson, *A Compilation of the Messages and Papers,* 358; Palmer & Ochoa, eds., *The Selected Papers of Thaddeus Stevens,* 2:28; *Reminiscences of Carl Schurz,* 3:209; Foner, *Reconstruction,* 240; James Alex Baggett, *The Scalawags: Southern Dissenters in the Civil War and Reconstruction* (Baton Rouge, 2002); *NASS,* June 24, August 19, 1865; *NYDT,* September 28, 1865.

23. Reid, *After the War,* 52, 85, 152; Wilson, *History of the Rise and Fall of the Slave Power,* 3:594; McPherson, *The Political History of the United States,* 18–44; Theodore Branter Wilson, *The Black Codes of the South* (University, AL, 1965), 75; *NASS,* July 1, October 7, 1865; *NYDT,* November 14, 1865; *TL,* December 8, 1865; Carter, *When the War Was Over,* 146; Foner, *Reconstruction,* 198–215; Andrews, *The South since the War,* 4; Schurz, *Report on the Condition of the South,* 24–27, 37, 39.

24. Reid, *After the War,* 52, 93, 114–17, 222; *NOT,* April 27, 28, 1866; Andrews, *The South Since the War,* 25–26, 100, 208, 337–38; *Reminiscences of Carl Schurz,* 3:202; Schurz, *Report on the Condition of the South,* 18, 27–29, 31–32, 35–36, 40–41.

25. Reid, *After the War,* 53, 73–79; Andrews, *The South Since the War,* chap. 43; Schurz, *Report of the Condition of the South,* 2, 6–8, 14–15; *TL,* December 15, 1865; Wilson, *The Black Codes of the South,* 86–88; Hans L. Trefousse, *Carl Schurz: A Biography* (Knoxville, 1982).

26. Gregory P. Downs, *After Appomattox: Military Occupation and the Ends of War* (Cambridge, MA, 2015); Andrew F. Lang, *In the Wake of War: Military Occupation, Emancipation, and Civil War America* (Baton Rouge, 2017); John Fabian Witt, "A Lost Theory of American Emergency Constitutionalism," *Law and History Review* 36 (August 2018): 551–91; *Reminiscences of Carl Schurz,* 3:175–76; Schurz, *Report of the Condition of the South,* 19–22; Andrews, *The South since the War,* 100, 291–301, 373; *TL,* August 25, 1865; Foner, *Reconstruction,* 203–5; Reid, *After the War,* 184–89.

27. *TL,* July 7, August 18, 25, September 15, October 13, 20, 27, November 3, 1865; *The Works of Charles Sumner* (Boston, 1874), 9:501–2; *NASS,* September 16, November 18, 25, 1865, November 3, 1866.

CHAPTER THREE: ABOLITION DEMOCRACY

1. W.E.B. Du Bois, *Black Reconstruction in America, 1860–1880* (New York, 1935), 184–87, 191–99; Henry Wilson, *History of the Rise and Fall of the Slave Power in America*, vol. 1 (Boston, 1872).

2. Edward L. Pierce, *Memoirs and Letters of Charles Sumner*, vol. 4, 1860–1874 (Boston, 1893), 85, 268; William H. Barnes, *History of the Thirty-Ninth Congress of the United States* (New York, 1868), 1, 11, chap. 4; *TL*, November 3, 10, 24, 1865; *NASS*, December 9, 30, 1865, January 6, 1866; *NYT*, December 27, 1865; *CG*, Senate, 39th Congress, 1st Session, December 4, 3, December 11, 1865, 16, December 13, 1865, 39–43, December 20, 1865, 90–96, December 21, 1865, 107; Beverly Wilson Palmer and Holly Byers Ochoa, eds., *The Selected Papers of Thaddeus Stevens*, vol. 2, April 1865–August 1868 (Pittsburgh, 1998), 37; Du Bois, *Black Reconstruction,* 193; *The Works of Charles Sumner* (Boston, 1874), 10:5–19, 45–98; James M. McPherson, *The Struggle for Equality: Abolitionists and the Negro in the Civil War and Reconstruction* (Princeton, 1964), 341; George W. Julian, *Speeches on Political Questions* (New York, 1872), 290.

3. Beverly Wilson Palmer and Holly Byers Ochoa, eds., *The Selected Papers of Thaddeus Stevens*, vol. 1, January 1814–March 1865 (Pittsburgh, 1997), xvii; Palmer & Ochoa, eds., *The Selected Papers of Thaddeus Stevens*, 2:10–27, 38, 43–56, 69–88; *NASS*, July 22, 1865; *TL*, August 18, September 22, December 29, 1865; *CG*, House of Representatives, 39th Congress, 1st Session, December 4, 1865, 3–7, in Senate, December 12, 1865, 24–30; Barnes, *History of the Thirty-Ninth Congress,* 15–20, 24, 28–30, 34–35, 94–100; *Works of Charles Sumner*, 10:3; Bruce Levine, *Thaddeus Stevens: The Making of a Revolutionary* (New York, 2021); Henry Wilson, *History of the Rise and Fall of the Slave Power in America* (Boston, 1877), 3:542; Benjamin B. Kendrick, *The Journal of the Joint Committee of Fifteen on Reconstruction* (New York, 1914), 37–39, 126–97.

4. *TL*, December 1, 1865; *NOT*, January 12, May 1, 1866; *NASS*, August 26, 1865, March 10, 1866; *CG*, 39th Congress, 1st Session, December 13, 43, December 20, 1865, 77, January 18, 299, January 19, 315–23, January 22, 340, January 23, 362, January 24, 396, February 1, 585–90, February 8, 744–45, February 19, 915–17, February 20, 941–43, May 23, 2772–79, May 24, 2809, June 26, 3409–10, July 2, 1866, 3524; Edward McPherson, *The Political History of the United States of America during the Period of Reconstruction* (Washington, 1871), 68–74; Barnes, *History of the Thirty-Ninth Congress,* 28, chaps. 6–8, 12; Palmer & Ochoa, eds., *The Selected Papers of Thaddeus Stevens*, 2:145–47; James D. Richardson, *A Compilation of the Messages and Papers of the Presidents, 1789–1897,* vol. 6 (Washington, 1897), 360, 398–405, 422–26; *William Lloyd Garrison, 1805–1879: The Story of His Life Told by His Children*, vol. 4, 1861–1879 (New York, 1889), 176–77; Corey Brooks, "The Freedmen's Bureau Act of 1866: What President Johnson Vetoed, Which Veto Congress Overrode, and Why It Matters" (unpublished paper in author's possession); Michael L. Lanza, *Agrarianism and Reconstruction Politics: The Southern Homestead Act* (Baton Rouge, 1990); Eric L. McKitrick, *Andrew Johnson and Reconstruction* (Chicago, 1960), 277–95.

5. *CG*, 39th Congress, 1st Session, in Senate, January 5, 127–28, January 9, 146, January 12, 211, January 29, 474–81, January 30, 497–502, January 31, 522–30, February 1, 570–76, March 2, 1151–54, March 3, 1162–64, March 9, 1291–96, March 27, 1679–81, April 4, 21, 1866, 1761; *Works of Charles Sumner*, 10:101–3, 271–79; Barnes, *History of the Thirty-Ninth Congress,* chaps. 9–11, 294, 419; Christian G. Samito, ed., *The Greatest and Grandest Act: The Civil Rights Act of 1866 from Reconstruction to*

Today (Carbondale, 2018); McPherson, *The Political History of the United States of America,* 52–56, 74–82; *NASS,* February 17, April 7, 1866; Wilson, *History of the Rise and Fall of the Slave Power,* 3:595–96; Richardson, *A Compilation of the Messages and Papers of the Presidents,* 405–13; McKitrick, *Andrew Johnson and Reconstruction,* 310–18, 323–24.

6. Pierce, *Memoirs and Letters of Charles Sumner,* vol. 4, 72–74; *The Works of Charles Sumner* (Boston, 1874), 4:301–5, 10:1–2, 21–37; *CG,* 39th Congress, 1st Session, December 12, 24, 29, December 18, 72–75, December 21, 122, 125–26, December 22, 1865, 120–25, January 8, 142–45, January 9, 150–57, January 31, 562–66, February 10, 781–83, February 15, 866–69, 1866; Palmer & Ochoa, eds., *The Selected Papers of Thaddeus Stevens,* 2:174–79, 196–201, 207–11; Barnes, *History of the Thirty-Ninth Congress,* chap. 13; *Speech of Richard H. Dana, Jr. at a Meeting of Citizens Held in Faneuil Hall* (Boston, 1865), 1–4; McKitrick, *Andrew Johnson and Reconstruction,* chap. 5.

7. *Report of the Joint Committee on Reconstruction* (Washington, 1866), 11–12, 17, 22; Kendrick, *The Journal of the Joint Committee of Fifteen on Reconstruction,* 43–48, 50–62, 83–93, 98, 101–6, 115–20, 292–319; *NASS,* July 22, 1865, February 3, 17, June 9, August 4, 11, 1866; *CG,* 39th Congress, 1st Session, January 27, 461–68, February 6, 673–87, February 7, 702–8, 730–33, February 10, 784–98, February 16, 878–85, February 17, 899–904, February 21, 957–64, February 27, 1056–57, February 28, 1088–91, March 7, 1224–31, March 9, 1281–82, May 30, 1866, 2890–97; Barnes, *History of the Thirty-Ninth Congress,* chaps. 17–20; *United States Statutes At Large,* vol. 14, *Public Acts of the Thirty-Ninth Congress of the United States,* 39th Congress, 1st Session, June 16, 1866, 358–59; *Works of Charles Sumner,* 10:115–269, 282–345, 490–94; Pierce, *Memoirs and Letters of Charles Sumner,* 4:276–83; Palmer and Ochoa, eds., *The Selected Papers of Thaddeus Stevens,* 2:94–95, 116–17, 122–23, 131–42, 156–59; *New Orleans Tribune,* June 6, 8, 1866; Wilson, *History of the Rise and Fall of the Slave Power,* 3:624–28; McPherson, *The Struggle for Equality,* 351–58; Eric Foner, *The Second Founding: How the Civil War and Reconstruction Remade the Constitution,* 64; Gerard N. Magliocca, *American Founding Son: John Bingham and the Invention of the Fourteenth Amendment* (New York, 2013); Akhil Reed Amar, *The Bill of Rights: Creation and Reconstruction* (New Haven, 1998); Michael Kent Curtis, *No State Shall Abridge: The Fourteenth Amendment and the Bill of Rights* (Durham, 1986); Garrett Epps, *Democracy Reborn: The Fourteenth Amendment and the Fight for Equal Rights in Post–Civil War America* (New York, 2006); Kurt T. Lash, *The Fourteenth Amendment and the Privileges and Immunities of American Citizenship* (Cambridge, 2014); Randy E. Barnett and Evan D. Bernick, *The Original Meaning of the Fourteenth Amendment: Its Letter and Spirit* (Cambridge, MA, 2021).

8. *NASS,* May 19, 1866; *NOT,* June 6, July 28, August 5, 1866; "Reports of Outrages, Riots, and Murders, January 15, 1866–August 12, 1868," *Records of the Assistant Commissioner of the State of Tennessee, Bureau of Refugees, Freedmen, and Abandoned Lands,* NARA, microfilm 34; "Memphis Riots and Massacres," *The Reports of the Committees of the House of Representatives Made during the First Session of the Thirty-Ninth Congress, 1865–66* (Washington, 1866), 1–44; Palmer and Ochoa, eds., *Selected Papers of Thaddeus Stevens,* 2:150–51; Stephen Ash, *A Massacre in Memphis: The Race Riot That Shook the Nation One Year After the Civil War* (New York, 2013).

9. *NOT,* July 11, August 3, 4, 5, 1866; Jean-Charles Houzeau, *My Passage at the New Orleans Tribune: A Memoir of the Civil War Era,* ed. David C. Rankin, trans. Gerard

F. Denault (Baton Rouge, 1984), 122–35, 155–61; Gilles Vandal, *The New Orleans Riot of 1866: Anatomy of a Tragedy* (Lafayette, 1983); James K. Hogue, *Uncivil War: Five New Orleans Street Battles and the Rise and Fall of Radical Reconstruction* (Baton Rouge, 2006), chap. 2; McKitrick, *Andrew Johnson and Reconstruction,* 426–27; Thulani Davis, *The Emancipation Circuit: Black Activism Forging a Culture of Freedom* (Chapel Hill, 2022), 304.

10. *NASS*, February 3, April 7, May 26, June 16, August 18, 1866, May 11, 18, 1867; Thomas C. Holt, *The Problem of Freedom: Race, Labor, and Politics in Jamaica and Britain, 1832–1938* (Baltimore, 1992), chap. 8; Demetrius L. Eudell, *The Political Languages of Emancipation in the British Caribbean and the U.S. South* (Chapel Hill, 2002). Gad J. Heuman, *"The Killing Time": The Morant Bay Rebellion in Jamaica* (Knoxville, 1994); Jonathan Greenland, *Uprising: Morant Bay, 1865 and Its Afterlives* (Kingston, 2015); Bernard Semmel, *Jamaican Blood and Victorian Conscience: The Governor Eyre Controversy* (New York, 1963).

11. *NASS*, April 28, May 5, August 25, September 8, 15, 1866; *NOT,* October 14, 1866; McPherson, *The Political History of the United States of America,* 127–41; Pierce, *Memoirs and Letters of Charles Sumner,* 4:300–301; Palmer and Ochoa, eds., *The Selected Papers of Thaddeus Stevens,* 2:186–87; Gordon-Reed, *Andrew Johnson,* 112; Michael Perman, *Reunion without Compromise: The South and Reconstruction, 1865–1868* (Cambridge, 1973), 198–233; McKitrick, *Andrew Johnson and Reconstruction,* 428–38.

12. Wilson, *History of the Rise and Fall of the Slave Power,* 3:608; Palmer and Ochoa, eds., *The Selected Papers of Thaddeus Stevens,* 2:152, 207–11, 268–74; McPherson, *The Political History of the United States of America,* 84–101; Mary Frances Berry, *Military Necessity and Civil Rights Policy: Black Citizenship and the Constitution, 1861–1868* (Port Washington, 1977): 98–99; Francis Leiber and G. Norman Leiber, *To Save the Country: A Lost Treatise on Martial Law,* ed. Will Smiley & John Fabian Witt (New Haven, 2019), esp. chap. 1; Gregory P. Downs and Kate Masur, eds, *The World the Civil War Made* (Chapel Hill, 2015), introduction.

13. *NASS*, August 12, 1865, September 22, October 13, December 15, 22, 1866, January 5, 12, 19, February 9, 16, May 25, June 1, 8, 22, 1867; *CG*, 39th Congress, 2nd Session, January 3, 1867, 251–53, 40th Congress, 1st Session, March 11, 49–56, March 14, 68–69, 94–105, March 15, 109–18, March 16, 137–71, July 9, 526–36, July 10, 549–58, July 11, 569–86, July 12, 610–12, July 13, 625–33, July 15, 1867, 649–55, 40th Congress, 2nd Session, December 10, 1867, 99–100, January 8, 405–6, January 23, 699–709, January 29, 823–25, February 10, 1072–76, February 25, 1412–17, February 26, 1431–36, July 10, 3905–11, July 20, 1868, 4235–36; Barnes, *History of the Thirty-Ninth Congress,* chaps. 21–22; Kendrick, *The Journal of the Joint Committee of Fifteen on Reconstruction,* 126–28, 357–86; Robert Saunders, *Democracy and the Vote in British Politics, 1848–1867: The Making of the Second Reform Act* (London, 2011); Palmer and Ochoa, eds., *The Selected Papers of Thaddeus Stevens,* 1:xvii; Palmer and Ochoa, eds., *The Selected Papers of Thaddeus Stevens,* 2:143–44, 174–79, 185, 189, 192, 196–201, 211–22, 224–33, 238–39, 241–42, 246–61, 305, 314–22; Wilson, *History of the Slave Power,* 3:616–20; Julian, *Speeches on Political Questions,* 360; Richardson, *A Compilation of the Messages and Papers of the Presidents,* 445–49, 472–83; Perman, *Reunion without Compromise,* 271–72; McKitrick, *Andrew Johnson and Reconstruction,* chap. 14; Foner, *Reconstruction,* 270–80; Cynthia Nicoletti, *Secession on Trial: The Treason Prosecution of Jefferson Davis* (Cambridge, 2017); Robert Icenhauer-Ramirez, *Treason on Trial: The United States v. Jefferson Davis* (Baton Rouge, 2019).

14. *Savannah Freedmen's Petition* 1865 (I am extremely grateful to Dan Carpenter for sending me this petition); *NASS*, March 24, October 20, November 3, 10, December 8, 1866, February 23, March 9, 16, September 21, 1867; McPherson, *The Struggle for Equality,* 367–70; McPherson, *The Political History of the United States of America,* 154–81, 335–37, 261–64; Wilson, *History of the Slave Power,* 3:622–23; *NASS,* March 16, July 20, 27, August 17, 24, September 7, 28, October 5, 12, 19, 26, November 30, December 7, 1867, January 4, 11, February 29, March 7, 14, 1868; Palmer and Ochoa, eds., *The Selected Papers of Thaddeus Stevens,* 2:235–36, 243–46, 301–2, 319–21, 352–59; Pierce, *Memoirs and Letters of Charles Sumner,* 4:307–8; Richardson, *A Compilation of the Messages and Papers of the Presidents,* 483–511, 531–35, 536–45, 547–49, 556–71, 583–94, 602–27, 672, 708–18; Perman, *Reunion without Compromise,* chap. 10; McKitrick, *Andrew Johnson and Reconstruction,* chap. 15.

15. *NASS,* January 12, 1867, March 21, April 4, May 2, 9, 16, 23, June 6, July 18, 1868; Barnes, *History of the Thirty-Ninth Congress,* 566–67, 571; McPherson, *The Political History of the United States of America,* 264–93, 384–91; Palmer and Ochoa, eds., *The Selected Papers of Thaddeus Stevens,* 2:366, 401–18, 429–31, 445–65; Julian, *Speeches on Political Questions,* 361; Pierce, *Memoirs and Letters of Charles Sumner,* 4:350–53; *Proceedings of the Eleventh National Woman's Rights Convention* (New York, 1866), 91; Eric Gardner, "Frances Ellen Watkins Harper's 'National Salvation': A Rediscovered Lecture on Reconstruction," *Common Place* 17, no. 4 (Summer 2017); J. W. Shuckers, *The Life and Public Services of Salmon Portland Chase* (New York, 1874), 535–43, 555–57, 635–62; Robert Bruce Warden, *An Account of the Private Life and Public Services of Salmon Portland Chase* (New York, 1874), 675–716, 804; Edmund G. Ross, *History of the Impeachment of Andrew Johnson* (Sante Fe, 1896); Michael Les Benedict, *The Impeachment and Trial of Andrew Johnson* (New York, 1973); David O. Stewart, *Impeached: The Trial of President Andrew Johnson and the Fight for Lincoln's Legacy* (New York, 2009), 5, 331–42; Brenda Wineapple, *The Impeachers: The Trial of Andrew Johnson and the Dream of a Just Nation* (New York, 2019), 50, 59, 85, 160, 163, 228–52, 403–4.

16. *Impeachment of the President Majority Report* (n.p., 1868], 17–25, 59; Michael Les Benedict, *A Compromise of Principle: Congressional Republicans and Reconstruction, 1863–1869* (New York, 1974); Forrest A. Nabors, *From Oligarchy to Republicanism: The Great Task of Reconstruction* (Columbia, 2017).

17. *CG,* Fortieth Congress, Third Session, January 11, 282–86, January 15, 378–79, January 23, 541–43, 554–61, January 25, 580–83, January 27, 641–45, 650–58, January 29, 668–74, 688–99, 705–13, 721–29, 899–907, February 9, 1029–44, February 23, 1470, 1492–93, February 25, 1593–94, February 26, 1623–33, February 27, 1645–47, 1869, Forty-First Congress, First Session, March 6, 27, March 22, 187–204, April 9, 653–62, 1869, Forty-First Congress, Second Session, December 17, 201–5, 1869, January 10, 325–35, January 12, 380–94, February 3, 1013–14, February 8, 1095, February 10, 1173–84, March 30, 2298, 1870; *TI,* January 13, April 7, 28, 1870; McPherson, *The Political History of the United States of America,* 399–406, 415–17, 545, 576–78, 611; Wilson, *History of the Slave Power,* 3:667–83; Pierce, *Memoirs and Letters of Charles Sumner,* 4:365–66; William Gillette, *The Right to Vote: Politics and the Passage of the Fifteenth Amendment* (Baltimore, 1965); Foner, *The Second Founding,* chap. 3; McPherson, *The Struggle for Equality,* 412–16, 422–30; Manisha Sinha, *The Slave's Cause: A History of Abolition* (New Haven, 2016), 588; Aaron M. Powell, *Personal Reminiscences of the Anti-Slavery, and Other Reforms and Reformers* (New York, 1899).

18. Palmer and Ochoa, eds., *The Selected Papers of Thaddeus Stevens*, 2:276–96; *NASS*, August 22, 1868; Julian, *Speeches on Political Questions,* 352–53; *CG*, Fortieth Congress, Third Session, December 17, 129–43, December 18, 145–51, December 19, 156–57, 1868; Eric Foner, "Thaddeus Stevens, Confiscation and Reconstruction," in *Politics and Ideology in the Age of the Civil War* (New York, 1980), 128–49; Hans L. Trefousse, *Thaddeus Stevens: Nineteenth-Century Egalitarian* (Chapel Hill, 1997), chaps. 12–16; Fawn Brodie, *Thaddeus Stevens: Scourge of the South* (New York, 1959), 366; Bruce Levine, *Thaddeus Stevens: The Making of a Revolutionary* (New York, 2021); McPherson, *The Struggle for Equality,* 408, 416.

19. *NASS*, March 2, 16, April 13, 20, 1867, May 6, June 13, 20, 27, August 1, 29, November 7, 21, December 12, 19, 1868, January 2, 9, 16, February 13, 20, March 13, 20, April 10, May 15, June 5, July 3, 10, September 25, December 11, 1869, January 22, 29, April 2, 16, 1870; *TI*, May 2, 1867; Charles Stearns, *The Black Man of the South, and the Rebels; Or, the Characteristics of the Former and the Recent Outrages of the Latter* (New York, 1872), 512–30; Carol Faulkner, *Women's Radical Reconstruction: The Freedmen's Aid Movement* (Philadelphia, 2006), chap. 6.

CHAPTER FOUR: FREEDPEOPLE AND THE FREEDMEN'S BUREAU

1. North Carolina Freedmen's Bureau Records, Fayetteville, roll 14, Report of Outrages, June 1866–November 1868, Greensboro, roll 20, Report of Outrages, June 1867–October 1868, Rocky Mount, roll 55, Report of Outrages, 1866–1868, Magnolia, roll 30, Register of Outrages, 1866–1868, Newberne, roll 38, Report of Outrages, 1865–1868; Leon F. Litwack, *Been in the Storm So Long: The Aftermath of Slavery* (New York, 1979); William A. Blair, *The Record of Murders and Outrages: Racial Violence and the Fight over Truth at the Dawn of Reconstruction* (Chapel Hill, 2021); Thulani Davis, *The Emancipation Circuit: Black Activism Forging a Culture of Freedom* (Durham, 2022), 7.

2. Jason P. McGraw, *The Work of Recognition: Caribbean Columbia and the Postemancipation Struggle for Citizenship* (Chapel Hill, 2014); Steven Hahn, *A Nation Under Our Feet: Black Political Struggle in the Rural South from Slavery to the Great Migration* (Cambridge, MA, 2003); William L. Richter, *Overstretched on All Sides: The Freedmen's Bureau Administrators in Texas, 1865–1868* (College Station, 1991); Dale Kretz, *Administering Freedom: The State of Emancipation after the Freedmen's Bureau* (Chapel Hill, 2022); Dylan C. Penningroth, *The Claims of Kinfolk: African American Property and Community in the Nineteenth-Century South* (Chapel Hill, 2003).

3. Paul A. Cimbala and Randall M. Miller, eds., *The Freedmen's Bureau and Reconstruction: Reconsiderations* (New York, 1999); Donald G. Nieman, *To Set the Law in Motion: The Freedmen's Bureau and the Legal Rights of Blacks, 1865–1868* (Millwood, 1979); Robert Harrison, "New Representations of a 'Misrepresented Bureau': Reflections on Recent Scholarship on the Freedmen's Bureau," *American Nineteenth Century History* 8 (June 2007): 205–29; Jim Downs, "Emancipating the Evidence: The Ontology of the Freedmen's Bureau Records," in David W. Blight and Jim Downs, eds., *Beyond Freedom: Disrupting the History of Emancipation* (Athens, 2017), 160–80.

4. Virginia Freedmen's Bureau Records, Alexandria, roll 43, Register of Letters Recorded, vol. 1, July 1866–March 1867, roll 48, Unregistered Letters Received, May 1866–April 1869, Bowling Green, Carolina County, roll 58, Letters Received January 1866–December 1868, roll 59, Register of Outrages Committed on Freedmen,

January–December 1868; North Carolina Freedmen's Bureau Records, Fayetteville, roll 14, Report of Outrages, June 1866–November 1868, Greensboro, roll 20, Report of Outrages, June 1867–October 1868, Rocky Mount, roll 55, Report of Outrages, 1866–1868, Magnolia, roll 30, Register of Outrages, 1866–1868, Newberne, roll 38, Report of Outrages, 1865–1868; Tennessee Freedmen's Bureau Records, Memphis, roll 54, Register of Complaints, 1865, roll 24, Complaint Book of the Freedman's Court, vol. 169, October 1865–March 1866; Kentucky Freedmen's Bureau Records, Covington, roll 91, Register of Complaints, January–August 1866, Louisville, roll 119, Affidavits and Records Relating to Complaints, 1865–1867, Paducah, roll 132, Complaints, Affidavits and Evidence Relating to Court Cases, April–December 1866, roll 132, Register of Complaints, September 1865–October 1868, Russellville, roll 133 Complaints, August–September 1866; Tennessee Freedmen's Bureau Records, roll 34, List of Outrages Perpetrated by the Whites upon the Freedmen in the State of Tennessee from April 1865 to March 1866, Register of Outrages, vol. 28, October 1865–July 1868; District of Columbia Freedmen's Bureau Records, roll 21, Miscellaneous Reports and Lists, 1865–1869.

5. Louisiana Freedmen's Bureau Records, Amite City, roll 58, Register of Complaints, July 1865–March 1866, Provost Marshal, roll 7, Complaints, vol. 1, October–December 1864, vol. 2, August–September 1865, Register of Complaints, vol. 3, March 1865–January 1866, Baton Rouge, roll 62, Register of Complaints, vol. 1, January–August 1867, Franklin, roll 77, Register of Complaints, February–June 1867, Lake Providence, roll 82, Narrative Trimonthly Report of Complaints, August–December 1867, New Roads, roll 97, Complaints, March 1866–August 1868; Thomas W. Conway, *The Freedmen of Louisiana: Final Report of the Bureau of Free Labor* (New Orleans, 1865), 6; Georgia Freedmen's Bureau Records, Savannah, Attempted Sexual Assault, 1865, Albany, roll 35, Letters Received, vols. 1–3, 1867, Thomasson Custody Dispute; Texas Freedmen's Bureau Records, Austin, roll 12, Register of Complaints, vol. 52, June 1867–December 1868; North Carolina Freedmen's Bureau Records, Goldsboro, roll 17, Complaints and Dispositions, March–August 1868, Graham, roll 18, Register of Complaints, vols. 1–2, October–December 1867, March–November 1868, Lexington, roll 27, Report of Outrages, November 1867, Wilmington, roll 75, Register of Complaints, vols. 1–2, August 1865–December 1867; Kentucky Freedmen's Bureau Records, Maysville, roll 124, Register of Complaints, May 1866-May 1867; Alabama Freedmen's Bureau Records, Demopolis, Freedmen's Complaint Against Wife, November 30, 1866; Florida Freedmen's Bureau Records, Freedmen's Marriage Certificates, 1861–1869; Missouri Freedmen's Bureau Field Office Records, 1865–1872, roll 24, Register of Marriages at Cape Girardeau, July–August 1865; Mississippi Freedmen's Bureau Records, roll 42, Register of Marriages of Freedmen, vols. 1–3, 1863–1865; Louisiana Freedmen's Bureau Records, Freedmen's Marriage Certificates, 1861–1869; South Carolina Freedmen's Bureau Records, Charleston, roll 44, Other Records, 1866; Laura F. Edwards, *Gendered Strife and Confusion: The Political Culture of Reconstruction* (Champaign-Urbana, 1997), esp. chap. 4; Tera W. Hunter, *Bound in Wedlock: Slave and Free Black Marriage in the Nineteenth Century* (Cambridge, MA, 2017).

6. Texas Freedmen's Bureau Records, Austin, roll 12, Register of Complaints, vol. 52, June 1867–December 1868, Bastrop, roll 13, Register of Complaints, vol. 62, February 1867–December 1868, Belton, roll 13, Register of Complaints, vol. 54, May 1867–February 1868, Boston, roll 13, vol. 70, July 1867–June 1868, Bryan, roll 14, Register of Complaints, vol. 58, 1866–1868, Columbus, roll 18, Register of Complaints, vol. 75, April 1867–November 1868, Jefferson, roll 23, Register of Complaints, vol.

118, August–December 1868, Marlin, roll 24, Register of Complaints, vol. 131, October 1867, Meridian, roll 24, Register of Complaints, vol. 138, February 1866–November 1867, roll 32 Registered Reports of Murders and Outrages, September 1866–July 1867; *NASS*, February 16, 1867, June 27, July 4, 1868; Barry A. Crouch, *The Freedmen's Bureau and Black Texans* (Austin, 1992); Christopher P. Bean, *Too Great a Burden to Bear: The Struggle and Failure of the Freedmen's Bureau in Texas* (New York, 2016); Robert B. McCaslin, *Tainted Breeze: The Great Hanging at Gainesville, Texas, 1862* (Baton Rouge, 1994); Phillip S. Paludan, *Victims: A True Story of the Civil War* (Knoxville, 1981); Steven E. Nash, *Reconstruction's Ragged Edge: The Politics of Postwar Life in the Southern Mountains* (Chapel Hill, 2016).

7. Mississippi Freedmen's Bureau Field Office Records, 1865–1872, Columbus, roll 12, Letters Sent Relating to Complaints, July–October 1867, roll 14, Orders Issued Relating to Complaints, December 1867–December 1868, roll 15, Register of Complaints, vols. 1–2, August 1867–May 1868, Corinth, roll 15, Register of Complaints, ca. 1867, Friars Point, roll 16, Register of Complaints, February–December 1868, Greenville, roll 17, Register of Complaints, September–December 1867, Grenada, roll 19, Register of Complaints, vols. 1–2, July 1866–January 1868, March–December 1868, Lake Station, roll 26, Register of Complaints, September 1867–September 1868, Natchez, roll 34, Court Records, 1864–1865; Anna Mae Duane, *Suffering Childhood in Early America: Violence, Race, and the Making of the Child Victim* (Athens, 2010); Mary Niall Mitchell, *Raising Freedom's Child: Black Children and Visions of the Future After Slavery* (New York, 2008); Catherine A. Jones, *Intimate Reconstructions: Children in Postemancipation Virginia* (Charlottesville, 2015).

8. Florida Freedmen's Bureau Records of Field Offices, Register of Letters Received, vol. 1, 1865–1866, Register of Letters Received, vol. 3, 1869–1870; North Carolina Freedmen's Bureau Records, Wilmington, roll 75, Register of Complaints, vols. 1–2, August 1865–December 1867, roll 35, Indentures, September 1865–August 1867, Magnolia, roll 30, Register of Complaints, March 1867–December 1868; Maryland and Delaware Freedmen's Bureau Records, Complaint Division, roll 37, Register of Complaints, vol. 17, July 1866–February 1868, Rockville, roll 42, Register of Complaints, June 1866–September 1867; Alabama Freedmen's Bureau Records, Demopolis, Thomas Woolf Probate Decision, 1866; Georgia Freedmen's Bureau Records, Albany, roll 35, Letters Received, vols. 1–3, 1867; Mississippi Freedmen's Bureau Records, roll 42, Register of Indentures of Colored Orphans, August 1865–May 1866; *NASS*, January 5, February 9, 1867; Barbara Jeanne Fields, *Slavery and Freedom in the Middle Ground: Maryland during the Nineteenth Century* (New Haven, 1984), chap. 6; Mary J. Farmer-Kaiser, *Freedwomen and the Freedmen's Bureau: Race, Gender, and Public Policy in the Age of Emancipation* (New York, 2010), esp. chap. 4.

9. Alabama Freedmen's Bureau Records, roll 23, Miscellaneous Papers, 1865–1866, Bluffton, roll 19, Fair Copies of Letters Received and Endorsements Sent, May 1868; Florida Freedmen's Bureau Records of Field Offices, Letters Sent, vol. 2, 1866–1868; South Carolina Freedmen's Bureau Records, Anderson Courthouse, roll 44, Letters Sent, March 1866–September 1867, Abbeville, Press Copies of Letters Sent, vols. 1–2, April 1867–October 1868, Aiken, roll 36, Letters Sent, August 1866–August 1868, roll 35, Reports of Murders and Outrages, 1866–1868; Suzanne Stone Johnson and Robert Allison Johnson, eds., *Bitter Freedom: William Stone's Record of Service in the Freedmen's Bureau* (Columbia, 2008); Zachary Newkirk, "A Brief Moment in the Sun: The Reconstruction-Era Courts of the Freedmen's Bureau," *Judicature* 101 (2017);

Peter Kolchin, *First Freedom: The Response of Alabama Blacks to Emancipation and Reconstruction* (Westport, 1972); Martin Abbott, *The Freedmen's Bureau in South Carolina, 1865–1872* (Chapel Hill, 1967).

10. Georgia Freedmen's Bureau Records, Albany, roll 37, Affidavits of Freedmen and Charges and Specifications Against Citizens and Military Personnel, June 1866–July 1868, roll 34, Letters Sent, February 1866–December 1868, roll 35, Letters Received, vol. 4, 1868, Atlanta, roll 45, Specifications and Charges Against Freedmen and White Citizens, 1865–1866; Florida Freedmen's Bureau Records of Field Offices, Pensacola Letters and Orders Received, 1866–1867; Paul A. Cimbala, *Under the Guardianship of the Nation: The Freedman's Bureau and the Reconstruction of Georgia, 1865–1870* (Athens, 1997); John David Smith, "'The Work it Did Not Do Because it Could Not': Georgia and the 'New' Freedmen's Bureau Historiography," *GHQ* 82 (1998): 331–49; Kidada E. Williams, "Regarding the Aftermaths of Lynching," *JAH* 101 (December 2014): 856–58; *NASS*, November 9, 23, 1867, February 15, April 4, 1868.

11. North Carolina Freedmen's Bureau Records, Charlotte, roll 9, Register of Complaints, October 1867–September 1868, Fayetteville, roll 14, Register of Complaints, August–December 1867, March–October 1868, Franklinton, roll 15, Register of Complaints, May 1866–May 1867, Goldsboro, roll 17, Complaints and Dispositions, March–August 1868, Graham, roll 18, Register of Complaints, vols. 1–2, October–December 1867, March–November 1868, Hillsboro, roll 26, Register of Complaints, May–October 1868, Lincolnton, roll 28, Registers of Complaints, July–October 1867, March–July 1868, Lumberton, roll 29, Register of Complaints, vols. 1–3, December 1865–December 1866, April 1867–December 1868, Newberne, roll 42, Register of Complaints, March–May 1866, Rockingham, roll 54, Register of Complaints, June 1867–August 1868, Wilmington, roll 75, Register of Complaints, vols. 1–2, August 1865–December 1867; Tennessee Freedmen's Bureau Records, Memphis, roll 54, Register of Complaints, July 26, 1865, Jonesboro, roll 21, Daily Journal of Complaints, 1867; Conway, *The Freedmen of Louisiana,* 12; Texas Freedmen's Bureau Records, Belton, roll 13, Register of Complaints, vol. 1, May 1867–February 1868, Columbus, roll 18, Register of Complaints, vol. 75, April 1867–February 1868, Houston, roll 22, Register of Complaints, vol. 3, December 1865–June 1867, Jefferson, roll 23, Register of Complaints, vol. 118, August–December 1868, Marlin, roll 24, Register of Complaints, vol. 131, January–October 1867, Kentucky Freedmen's Bureau Records, Bowling Green, roll 91, Register of Complaints, June 1866–February 1868, Paducah, roll 132, Complaints, Affidavits and Evidence Relating to Court Cases, April–December 1866; Georgia Freedmen's Bureau Records, Albany, roll 35, Letters Received, vols. 1–3, 1867, Letters Received, vol. 4, 1868, Athens, roll 42, Reports Sent to Assistant Commissioner, 1867–1868, Augusta, roll 48, Affidavits and Complaints, Contract Dispute, 1866; Florida Freedmen's Bureau Records of Field Offices, Register of Letters, vol. 1, 1865–1866, Register of Letters Received, vol. 2, 1866–1869, 1869–1870, Monthly Reports of Abandoned or Confiscated Lands, 1865–1868, Reports of Board of Officers Created to Establish Rental Values, 1866–1869, Unregistered Monthly Reports of Homesteads Located By Bureau Agents, 1867–1869; Louisiana Freedmen's Bureau Records, roll 34, Register of Applications of Freedmen for Land, 1865–1869; Ira Berlin et al., eds., *Freedom: A Documentary History of Emancipation, 1861–1867,* series 1, vol. 2, *The Wartime Genesis of Free Labor: The Upper South* (Cambridge, 1990), and series 1, vol. 3, *The Wartime Genesis of Free Labor: The Lower South* (Cambridge, 1993); Amy Dru Stanley, *From Bondage to Contract: Wage Labor, Marriage, and the Market in the*

Age of Slave Emancipation (Cambridge, 1998); Howard Ashley White, *The Freedmen's Bureau in Louisiana* (Baton Rouge, 1970); Claude F. Oubre, *Forty Acres and a Mule: The Freedmen's Bureau and Black Land Ownership* (Baton Rouge, 1978); Edward Magdol, *A Right to the Land: Essays on the Freedmen's Community* (Westport, 1977).

12. Alabama Freedmen's Bureau Records, Demopolis Record of Daily Injustices, October 17, 1866; Florida Freedmen's Bureau Records of Field Offices, Register of Letters Received, vol. 2, 1866–1869; Oliver Otis Howard, *Autobiography of Oliver Otis Howard* (New York, 1907), 1:, 254–55, 277–89, 296–308, 312–13; *NASS*, March 9, 1867; Gordon C. Rhea, *Stephen A. Swails: Black Freedom Fighter in the Civil War and Reconstruction* (Chapel Hill, 2021); John William De Forest, *A Union Officer in the Reconstruction*, ed. James H. Croushore and David Morris Potter (New Haven, 1948), 91; *CG*, Fortieth Congress, Third Session, January 5, 182, January 13, 347 1869; Henry Wilson, *History of the Rise and Fall of the Slave Power in America* (Boston, 1877), 3:472–73, 486–90; Steve Hahn et al., eds., *Freedom: A Documentary History of Emancipation, 1861–1867*, series 3, vol. 1, Land and Labor, 1865 (Chapel Hill, 2008), 170–82; Chad Alan Goldberg, *Citizens and Paupers: Relief, Rights, and Race from the Freedmen's Bureau to Workfare* (Chicago, 2007), chap. 2.

13. South Carolina Freedmen's Bureau Records, Abbeville, Letters Received, November 1867–October 1868; Alabama Freedmen's Bureau Records, Demopolis, 1866, Clairborn, 1868; Howard, *Autobiography of Oliver Otis Howard,* 256–57; Conway, *The Freedmen in Louisiana,* 35; James L. Roark, *Masters without Slaves: Southern Planters in the Civil War and Reconstruction* (New York, 1977); Carol Faulkner, *Women's Radical Reconstruction: The Freedmen's Aid Movement* (Philadelphia, 2006), chap. 7; Leslie A. Schwalm, *Emancipation's Diaspora: Race and Reconstruction in the Upper Midwest* (Chapel Hill, 2009).

14. W.E.B. Du Bois, *The Souls of Black Folk* (Chicago, 1903), 24; Louisiana Freedmen's Bureau Records, roll 33, Reports Relating to the Condition of Freedmen, 1868; Florida Freedmen's Bureau Records of Field Offices, Monthly Reports of Rations, Clothing and Medicine Issued, Reports 1866–1869; Alabama Freedmen's Bureau Records, Surgeon, January 7, 1867; Elizabeth Cann Kambourian, *The Freedmen's Bureau in Virginia: Names of Destitute Freedmen Dependent upon the Government in the Military Districts of Virginia* (Berwyn Heights, 2009); James D. Richardson, *A Compilation of the Messages and Papers of the Presidents, 1789–1902* (New York, 1902), 4:401; Rana Hogarth, *Medicalizing Blackness: Making Racial Difference in the Atlantic World, 1780–1840* (Chapel Hill, 2017); Leslie A. Schwalm, *Medicine, Science & Race in Civil War America* (Chapel Hill, 2023); Gretchen Long, *Doctoring Freedom: The Politics of African American Medical Care in Slavery and Emancipation* (Chapel Hill, 2012), 5; Jim Downs, *Sick from Freedom: African American Illness and Suffering during the Civil War and Reconstruction* (New York, 2012), 167; Kentucky Freedmen's Bureau Field Office Records, Chief Medical Officer, Monthly and Weekly Reports of the Sick and the Wounded, roll 81, December 1866–June 1868, roll 82, December 1866–December 1868, Weekly Reports of Sick and Wounded, Covington, Lexington, Louisville, roll 8386, 1866–1868, roll 87, Monthly Returns of Medical Officers and Reports of Attendants, June 1866–December 1868; Conway, *The Freedmen of Louisiana,* 14–15; Gerald S. Henig, "The Indomitable Dr. Augusta: The First Black Physician in the U.S. Army," *Army History* 87 (Spring 2013): 23–44; Howard, *Autobiography of Oliver Otis Howard,* 258–62.

15. *NASS*, August 17, 31, 1867, February 22, May 9, June 20, 1868, April 10, October 23, 1869; Katherine Smedley, *Martha Schofield and the Re-education of the South,*

1839–1916 (Lewiston, 1987); De Forest, *A Union Officer in the Reconstruction,* 118–20; Robert C. Morris, ed., *Freedmen's Schools and Textbooks,* vol. 1, *Semi-Annual Reports on Schools for Freedmen by John W. Alvord Numbers 1–10, January, 1866–July, 1870* (reprint, New York, 1980); Inspector's Report, January 1866, 1–6, 10, Second Semi-Annual Report on Schools and Finances of Freedmen, July 1, 1866, 2, 7–9, 12, Third Semi-Annual Report on Schools and Finances of Freedmen, January 1, 1867, 4–5, 17, 22–29, 35–37, Fourth Semi-Annual Report on Schools and Finances of Freedmen, July 1, 1867, 3, 30–34, 46, 53, Fifth Semi-Annual Report on Schools and Finances of Freedmen, January 1, 1868, 4–10, 48, Sixth Semi-Annual Report on Schools and Finances of Freedmen, July 1, 1868, 3–4, 62–64, 75–76, Seventh Semi-Annual Report on Schools and Finances of Freedmen, January 1, 1869, 55, Eighth Semi-Annual Report on Schools and Finances of Freedmen, July 1, 1869, 3–5, 20–24, 30, 61, 74–75, 80, Ninth Semi-Annual Report on Schools and Finances of Freedmen, January 1, 1870, 3–5, 57, Tenth Semi-Annual Report on Schools and Finances of Freedmen, July 1, 1870, 3–4; Howard, *Autobiography of Oliver Otis Howard,* 270–76, 292, 317, 322, 328–29, 335–49, 359–60, 390–416; *NYT,* October 14, 1866; Campbell F. Scribner, "Surveying the Destruction of African-American Schoolhouses in the South, 1864–1876," *JCWE* 10 (December 2020): 469–94; J. W. Alvord, *Letters from the South, Relating to the Condition of Freedmen, Addressed to Major General O. O. Howard* (Washington, 1870); John Andrew Jackson Broadside, n.d., AAS; John Andrew Jackson, *The Experience of a Slave in South Carolina* (London, 1862); Susanna Ashton and Jonathan D. Hepworth, "Reclaiming a Fugitive Landscape: The Escape of John Andrew Jackson in 1843," *Brewminate: A Bold Blend of News and Ideas,* July 17, 2019; Florida Freedmen's Bureau Field Office Records, 1865–1872, Monthly Statistical School Reports Sent to Bureau Headquarters, 1866–1870, Monthly School Reports from Teachers, 1867–1870, Monthly Statistical School Reports from Subordinates, 1868; Mississippi Freedmen's Bureau Field Office Records, 1865–1872, Superintendent of Education, roll 1, Letters Sent, vols. 1–2, July 1865–June 1866, Teachers' Monthly School Reports, October 1865–November 1868; Maryland & Delaware Freedmen's Bureau Records, roll 5, Narrative Reports from the Assistant Inspector General, the Superintendent of Education, and the Officer in Charge of the Complaint Division, October 1866–June 1867; *TI,* February 2, 1870.

16. *NASS,* June 26, 1869; *The Story of Mattie J. Jackson* (Lawrence, 1866), 2; Robert C. Morris, *Reading, 'Riting, and Reconstruction: The Education of Freedmen in the South, 1865–1870* (Chicago, 1976); Jeffrey A. Jenskins and Justin Peck, "The Blair Education Bill: A Lost Opportunity in American Public Education," *Studies in American Political Development* 35 (April 2021): 146–70; Hilary Green, *Educational Reconstruction: African American Schools in the Urban South, 1865–1890* (New York, 2016); James D. Anderson, *The Education of Blacks in the South, 1860–1935* (Chapel Hill, 1988), chap. 1; James M. McPherson, *The Abolitionist Legacy: From Reconstruction to the NAACP* (Princeton, 1975), part 2.

17. Howard, *Autobiography of Oliver Otis Howard,* 423–25; Du Bois, *The Souls of Black Folk,* 33–34; Kevin Gaines, *Uplifting the Race: Black Leadership, Politics and Culture in the Twentieth Century* (Chapel Hill, 1996); Michelle Mitchell, *Righteous Propagation: African Americans and the Politics of Racial Destiny after Reconstruction* (Chapel Hill, 2004); McPherson, *The Abolitionist Legacy,* 223; Ronald Butchart, *Schooling the Freed People: Teaching, Learning, and the Struggle for Black Freedom* (Chapel Hill, 2010); Faulkner, *Women's Radical Reconstruction,* 36–42; Ronald E. Butchart et al.,

The Freedmen's Teacher Project: Teachers among the Freed People in the U.S. South, 1861–1877 (2022), vol. 1, Harvard Dataverse, doi:10.7910/DVN/0HBDZD.

18. Gregory P. Downs, *Declarations of Dependence: The Long Reconstruction of Popular Politics in the South, 1861–1908* (Chapel Hill, 2011); Eric Foner, "Blacks and the US Constitution," *New Left Review* 183 (Sept./Oct. 1990): 63–74.

CHAPTER FIVE: BLACK RECONSTRUCTION

1. Justin Behrend, *Reconstructing Democracy: Grassroots Black Politics in the Deep South after the Civil War* (Athens, 2017); Eric Foner, *Reconstruction: America's Unfinished Revolution, 1863–1877* (New York, 1988), chaps. 7–8.

2. James S. Allen, *Reconstruction: The Battle for Democracy, 1865–1876*, foreword by Eric Foner (1937; reprint, New York, 2021); Nick Bromell, *The Time Is Always Now: Black Thought and the Transformation of US Democracy* (New York, 2013); Gregory Laski, *Untimely Democracy: The Politics of Progress after Slavery* (New York, 2018), 4.

3. *NASS*, July 25, 1868, January 9, June 5, June 19, 1869; *NE*, February 24, 1870; Suzanne Stone Johnson and Robert Allison Johnson, eds., *Bitter Freedom: William Stone's Record of Service in the Freedmen's Bureau* (Cambridge, MA, 2003), 58; Richard Lowe, "The Freedmen's Bureau and Local Black Leadership," *JAH* 80 (December 1993): 989–98; Steven Hahn, *A Nation under Our Feet: Black Political Struggles in the Rural South from Slavery to the Great Migration* (Cambridge, MA, 2003), 173–89; Michael W. Fitzgerald, *The Union League Movement in the Deep South: Politics and Agricultural Change during Reconstruction* (Baton Rouge, 1989); Elsa Barkley Brown, "Negotiating and Transforming the Public Sphere: African American Political Life in the Transition from Slavery to Freedom," *Public Culture* 7 (Fall 1994), 107–46. Richard H. Abbott, *The Republican Party and the South, 1855–1877: The First Southern Strategy* (Chapel Hill, 1986).

4. P. Gabrielle Foreman et al., eds., *The Colored Conventions Movement: Black Organizing in the Nineteenth Century* (Chapel Hill, 2021), 29; Selena R. Sanderfer, "The Emigration Debate and the Southern Colored Conventions Movement," in Foreman et al., eds., *The Colored Conventions Movement*, 286–87; Philip S. Foner and George E. Walker, eds., *Proceedings of the Black National and State Conventions*, vol. 1, 1865–1900 (Philadelphia, 1986), 87–88, 101, 121–22, 181, 193, 222–23, 232–36, 249–83, 289–97, 416–19; *Equal Suffrage. Address from the Colored Citizens of Norfolk, Virginia to the People of the United States* (New Bedford, 1865); Thomas Holt, *Black over White: Negro Political Leadership in South Carolina during Reconstruction* (Urbana, 1977), chap.1; "Minutes of the Freedmen's Convention Held in the City of Raleigh, on the 2nd, 3rd, 4th and 5th of October, 1866," "The Colored State Convention at Nashville," "Proceedings of a Convention of Colored Citizens: Held in the City of Lawrence, October 17, 1866," "New York State Convention of Colored Men, Albany, October 16, 1866," *Colored Conventions Project Digital Records*, https://omeka .coloredconventions.org; *NASS*, May 15, October 9, 16, 1869; *TI*, January 27, 1870.

5. *NE*, January 13, February 24, 1870; Foner and Walker, eds., *Proceedings of the Black National and State Conventions*, 1: 300–317, 320–24, 326–405, 412–14; *Address of the Colored Men's Border State Convention [Baltimore, 1868]* (n.p., n.d.); "Report on the Ohio State Equal Rights League Convention, Cincinnati, January 16, 1867," "Report on the National Equal Rights League Convention held in Washington, D.C., January 28, 1867," *Colored Conventions Project Digital Records*, https://omeka

.coloredconventions.org; *NASS*, September 14, 1867, June 20, October 24, 1868, January 30, February 20, 1869; Kate Masur, *Until Justice Be Done: America's First Civil Rights Movement from the Revolution to Reconstruction* (New York, 2021); Philip S. Foner and Ronald L. Lewis, *The Black Worker: A Documentary History from Colonial Times to the Present* (Philadelphia, 1978), 2:2–138.

6. "Proceedings of the Southern States Convention of Colored Men, held in Columbia, S.C., Commencing October 18, Ending October 25, 1871," *Colored Conventions Project Digital Records,* https://omeka.coloredconventions.org.

7. "Civil Rights: Memorial of National Convention of Colored Persons, Praying to be Protected in Their Civil Rights [1873]," "Convention of Colored Citizens in Texas [1873]," "State Colored Men's Convention [New Orleans, 1873]," "Proceedings of the Convention of Colored People Held in Dover, Del., January 9, 1873," "Proceedings of the State Colored Educational Convention Held at Frankfort, Kentucky, August 22, 1877," "Proceedings of the Colored People's Educational Convention Held in Jefferson City, Missouri, January, 1870," "Proceedings of the State Convention of the Colored Citizens of Tennessee, Held in Nashville, Feb. 22d, 23d, 24th & 25th, 1871," *Colored Conventions Project Digital Records,* https://omeka.coloredconventions.org.

8. "Proceedings of the National Conference of Colored Men of the United States, Held in the State Capitol at Nashville, Tennessee, May 6, 7, 8 and 9, 1879," *Colored Conventions Project Digital Records,* https://omeka.coloredconventions.org; Hahn, *A Nation Under Our Feet,* chap. 7; Nell Irvin Painter, *Exodusters: Black Migration to Kansas after Reconstruction* (New York, 1976).

9. "Proceedings of the State Convention of Colored Men of Texas, Held at the City of Austin, July 10–12, 1883," "Proceedings of the State Conference of the Colored Men of Florida, Held at Gainesville, February 5, 1884," "Proceedings of the Colored State Convention Assembled in St. Paul's A. M. E. Church, Lexington, Ky., November 26 [1885]," "Report on the Texas State Colored Men's Convention in Houston [1895]," *Colored Conventions Project Digital Records,* https://omeka.coloredconventions.org; *The Daily Citizen* (Asheville, NC), February 7, 1890; see articles by Sanderfer, Johnson, Ramey Berry, and Thibodeux in Foreman et al., eds., *The Colored Conventions Movement,* 275–329.

10. Foner, *Reconstruction,* 77; Charles Stearns, *The Black Man of the South, and the Rebels: Or, The Characteristics of the Former, and the Recent Outrages of the Latter* (New York, 1872), 187; Union Republican Congressional Committttee, *Emancipation! Enfranchisement! Reconstruction! Legislative Record of the Republican Party During and Since the War* [1868].

11. *Official Journal of the Constitutional Convention of the State of Alabama* (Montgomery, 1868), 61; *Proceedings of the State Convention of Maryland to Frame a New Constitution* (Annapolis, 1867), 29; *Report of Select Committee of the Constitutional Convention of the State of Mississippi* (Jackson, 1868); *Proceedings of the Constitutional Convention of South Carolina,* 2 vols. (Charleston, 1868), 41, 48, 64, 71, 87, 113–18, 125–31, 146–47, 196–97, 396–98, 400–404, 417–24, 688–704, 838; *Proceedings of the Florida Convention, March 31, 1868,* Fortieth Congress, 2d Session*; Journal of the Proceedings of the Constitutional Convention of Georgia* (Augusta, 1868), 143; *Journal of the Constitutional Convention of the State of North Carolina* (Raleigh, 1868), 33, 162–63, 216, 235–38; *Journal of the Constitutional Convention of the State of Virginia* (Richmond, 1867), 92, 210; *Official Journal of the Proceedings of the Convention, For Framing a Constitution of the State of Louisiana* (New Orleans, 1867–1868), 110, 115, 224, 285, 293–94, 315; *The Constitution of the State of South Carolina, with*

the Ordinances Thereunto Appended (Charleston, 1868), 3, 7, 26–28; *Constitution and Ordinances of the State of Mississippi* (Jackson, 1868), 2–6, 11, 26; *Statement and Memorial in Relation to Political Affairs in Texas* (Washington, 1869), 14–17; Richard L. Hume and Jerry B. Gough, *Blacks, Carpetbaggers, and Scalawags: The Constitutional Conventions of Radical Reconstruction* (Baton Rouge, 2008); Foner, *Reconstruction,* 316–33; Hahn, *A Nation under Our Feet,* 191–215.

12. John R. Lynch, *The Facts of Reconstruction* (New York, 1913), 92–95; Philip Dray, *Capitol Men: The Epic Story of Reconstruction through the Lives of the First Black Congressmen* (New York, 2008); Eric Foner, ed., *Freedom's Lawmakers: A Directory of Black Officeholders During Reconstruction* (New York, 1993), 180–81; *TI*, April 28, 1870; James S. Pike, *The Prostrate State: South Carolina under Negro Government* (New York, 1874); William C. Harris, "Blanche K. Bruce of Mississippi: Conservative Assimilationist," and John Hope Franklin, "John Roy Lynch: Republican Stalwart from Mississippi," in Howard N. Rabinowitz, ed., *Southern Black Leaders of the Reconstruction Era* (Urbana, 1982), 3–58; Lawrence Otis Graham, *The Senator and the Socialite: The True Story of America's First Black Dynasty* (New York, 2006); John R. Lynch, *Reminiscences of an Active Life: The Autobiography of John Roy Lynch*, ed. John Hope Franklin (Chicago, 1970); Vernon L. Wharton, *The Negro in Mississippi, 1865–1890* (Chapel Hill, 1947), chap. 12; Matthew Lynch, ed., *Before Obama: A Reappraisal of Black Reconstruction Era Politicians*, vol. 1: *Legacies Lost* (Santa Barbara, 2012), chaps. 1, 2, 5, 10.

13. David C. Rankin, "The Origins of Negro Leadership in New Orleans during Reconstruction," and Thomas C. Holt, "Negro Legislators in South Carolina during Reconstruction," in Rabinowitz, ed., *Southern Black Leaders of the Reconstruction Era,* 155–90, 223–46; James Haskins, *Pinckney Benton Stewart Pinchback* (New York, 1973); Charles Vincent, *Black Legislators in Louisiana during Reconstruction* (Baton Rouge, 1978); Okon E. Uya, *From Slavery to Public Service: Robert Smalls, 1839–1915* (New York, 1971); Peggy Lamson, *The Glorious Failure: Black Congressman Robert Elliot and the Reconstruction in South Carolina* (New York, 1973); Cyril O. Packwood, *Detour—Bermuda, Destination—U.S. House of Representatives: The Life of Joseph Hayne Rainey* (Bermuda, 1977); Foner, ed., *Freedom's Lawmakers,* 35–36, 176–77; see articles by J. Brent Morris, Linda English, William P. Kladky, Martin A. Parlett, Karen Cook Bell, and Peter J. Breaux in Matthew Lynch, ed., *Before Obama: A Reappraisal of Black Reconstruction Era Politicians*, vol. 2, *The Fifteenth Amendment in Flesh and Blood* (Santa Barbara, 2012).

14. Loren Schweninger, *James T. Rapier and Reconstruction* (Chicago, 1978); Foner, ed., *Freedom's Lawmakers,* 94–95, 136, 113, 214–15; Stephen Middleton, ed., *Black Congressmen during Reconstruction: A Documentary Source Book* (Westport, 2002); Peter D. Klingman, *Josiah Walls: Florida's Black Congressman of Reconstruction* (Gainesville, 1976); Benjamin R. Justesen, *George Henry White: An Even Chance in the Race of Life* (Baton Rouge, 2001); Luis-Alejandro Dinnella-Borrego, *The Risen Phoenix: Black Politics in the Post–Civil War South* (Charlottesville, 2016).

15. John Mercer Langston, *From the Virginia Plantation to the National Capital: The First and Only Negro Representative in Congress from the Old Dominion* (Hartford, 1894); William Cheek and Aimee Lee Cheek, "John Mercer Langston: Principle and Politics," and John Dittmer, "The Education of Henry McNeal Turner," in Leon Litwack and August Meier, eds., *Black Leaders in the Nineteenth Century* (Urbana, 1988), 103–26, 253–72; *Sufferings of the Rev. T. G. Campbell and His Family in Georgia*

(Washington, 1877), 3, 7–10, 25–26; Joseph P. Reidy, "Aaron A. Bradley: Voice of Black Labor in the Georgia Lowcountry," in Rabinowitz, ed., *Southern Black Leaders of the Reconstruction Era,* 281–308; Russell Duncan, *Freedom's Shore: Tunis Campbell and the Georgia Shore* (Athens, 1986); Stephen W. Angell, *Bishop Henry McNeal Turner and African American Religion in the South* (Knoxville, 1992), 82–92; Andre E. Johnson, *No Future in This Country: The Prophetic Pessimism of Bishop Henry McNeal Turner* (Jackson, 2020); Edmund L. Drago, *Black Politicians and Reconstruction in Georgia: A Splendid Failure* (Baton Rouge, 1982).

16. Nell Painter, "Martin R. Delany: Elitism and Black Nationalism," in Litwack and Meier, eds., *Black Leaders in the Nineteenth Century,* 149–71; Willard B. Gatewood, ed., *Free Man of Color: The Autobiography of Willis Augustus Hodges* (Knoxville, 1982), introduction, 83; F. N. Boney, Richard L. Hume, and Rafia Zafar, eds., *God Made Man, Man Made the Slave: The Autobiography of George Teamoh* (Macon, 1990); Foner, ed., *Freedom's Lawmakers,* 84–85, 96–97, 105–6, 174, 226–27; Mifflin Wistar Gibbs, *Shadow and Light: An Autobiography* (Washington, 1902); Carl H. Moneyhon, "George T. Ruby and the Politics of Expediency in Texas," and Howard N. Rabinowitz, "Holland Thompson and Black Political Participation in Montgomery, Alabama," in Rabinowitz, ed., *Southern Black Leaders of the Reconstruction Era,* 249–80, 363–92.

17. *NE,* January 13, 1870; I. Garland Penn, *The Afro-American Press, and Its Editors* (Springfield, MA, 1891), 100–115, 133–38, 158–64, 183–87, 524–37; Emma Lou Thornbrough, *T. Thomas Fortune: Militant Journalist* (Chicago, 1972); Kerri K. Greenidge, *Black Radical: The Life and Times of William Monroe Trotter* (New York, 2020); Ethan Michaeli, *The Defender: How the Legendary Black Newspaper Changed America* (New York, 2016).

18. Hugh Davis, *"We Will Be Satisfied with Nothing Less": The African American Struggle for Equal Rights in the North during Reconstruction* (Ithaca, 2011); Millington W. Bergerson-Lockwood, *Race over Party: Black Politics and Partisanship in Late Nineteenth-Century Boston* (Chapel Hill, 2018); Andrew Diemer, "Reconstructing Philadelphia: African Americans and Politics in the Post–Civil War North," *PMHB* 133 (January 2009): 29–58; Margaret Garb, *Freedom's Ballot: African American Political Struggles in Chicago from Abolition to the Great Migration* (Chicago, 2014); Leslie A. Schwalm, *Emancipation's Diaspora: Race and Reconstruction in the Upper Midwest* (Chapel Hill, 2009).

19. Carol K. Bleser, *The Promised Land: The History of the South Carolina Land Commission, 1869–1890* (Columbia, 1965); Elizabeth Rauh Bethel, *Promiseland: A Century of Life in a Negro Community* (Philadelphia, 1981); Foner and Lewis, eds., *The Black Worker,* 2:140–68, 175–76: Eric Foner, *Nothing But Freedom: Emancipation and Its Legacy* (Baton Rouge, 1983), 90–106.

CHAPTER SIX: THE RECONSTRUCTION OF WOMEN'S RIGHTS

1. Manisha Sinha, *The Slave's Cause: A History of Abolition* (New Haven, 2016), chap. 9; Ellen Carol DuBois, *Feminism and Suffrage: The Emergence of an Independent Women's Movement in America, 1848–1869* (Ithaca, 1978), 31–50.

2. Elizabeth Cady Stanton, Susan B. Anthony, and Matilda Joslyn Gage, eds., *History of Woman Suffrage,* vol. 1, 1848–1861, 2nd ed. (Rochester, 1889), 67–87; Elizabeth Cady Stanton, *Eighty Years and More: Reminiscences 1815–1877* (New York, 1898), 79–84; Lori D. Ginzberg, *Untidy Origins: A Story of Women's Rights in Antebellum New York*

(Chapel Hill, 2005); Lisa Tetrault, *The Myth of Seneca Falls: Memory and the Women's Suffrage Movement, 1848–1898* (Chapel Hill, 2014); Kabria Baumgartner, *In Pursuit of Knowledge: Black Women and Educational Activism in Antebellum America* (New York, 2019), 45–49.

3. Sylvia Hoffert, *When Hens Crow: The Woman's Rights Movement in Antebellum America* (Bloomington, 1995); Paulina W. Davis, *A History of the National Woman's Rights Movement* (New York, 1871), 12–15, 19–20; Kathryn Kish Sklar, ed., *Women's Rights Emerges within the Antislavery Movement, 1830–1870: A Brief History with Documents* (Boston, 2000), 193–96; Helene Quanquin, *Men in the American Women's Rights Movement, 1830–1890: Cumbersome Allies* (New York, 2020).

4. Alice Stone Blackwell, *Lucy Stone: Pioneer of Women's Rights* (Boston, 1930), 59–61; Joelle Million, *Woman's Voice, Woman's Place: Lucy Stone and the Birth of the Woman's Rights Movement* (Westport, 2003), 69–71; Sally G. McMillen, *Lucy Stone: An Unapologetic Life* (New York, 2015); Carol Lasser and Marlene Deahl Merrill, *Friends and Sisters: Letters between Lucy Stone and Antoinette Brown Blackwell, 1846–93* (Urbana, 1987), 255, 263; Leslie Wheeler, ed., *Loving Warriors: Selected Letters of Lucy Stone and Henry B. Blackwell, 1853 to 1893* (New York, 1981), 135–37.

5. Ida Husted Harper, *The Life and Work of Susan B. Anthony . . . In Two Volumes* (Indianapolis, 1898), 1:59–71, 87–102; Kathleen Barry, *Susan B. Anthony: A Biography of a Singular Feminist* (New York, 1988); Lynn Sherr, *Failure Is Impossible: Susan B. Anthony in Her Own Words* (New York, 1995), chap. 1; Stanton, *Eighty Years and More,* 20–23, 187–88; Anthony to Stone, August 2, 1857, Blackwell Family Collection, Schlesinger Library, HU; Lori D. Ginzberg, *Elizabeth Cady Stanton: An American Life* (New York, 2009); Elisabeth Griffiths, *In Her Own Right: The Life of Elizabeth Cady Stanton* (New York, 1984).

6. Edward A. Hinck, "The *Lily,* 1849–1856: From Temperance to Woman's Rights," in Martha M. Solomon, ed., *A Voice of Their Own: The Woman Suffrage Press, 1840–1901* (Tuscaloosa, 1991), 30–47; Nell Irvin Painter, *Sojourner Truth: A Life, A Symbol* (New York, 1996), 187; Joanne E. Passet, *Sex Radicals and the Quest for Women's Equality* (Urbana, 2003), chap. 1; Barbara Leslie Epstein, *The Politics of Domesticity: Women, Evangelism and Temperance in Nineteenth Century America* (Middletown, 1981).

7. Stanton, Anthony, and Gage, eds., *History of Woman Suffrage,* 1:114–17, 276, 567–68; *The Proceedings of the Woman's Rights Convention, Held at Akron, Ohio, May 28 and 29, 1851* (Cincinnati, 1851), 6; Painter, *Sojourner Truth,* chap. 18; Margaret Washington, *Sojourner Truth's America* (Urbana, 2009), 221–29; Carla L. Peterson, *"Doers of the Word": African American Women Speakers and Writers in the North (1830–1860)* (New Brunswick, 1995), chap. 2; *Proceedings of the Woman's Rights Convention, Held at the Broadway Tabernacle, in the City of New York* (New York, 1853), 76–77; Roslyn Terborg-Penn, *African American Women in the Struggle for the Vote, 1850–1920* (Bloomington, 1998), 14–18.

8. Melba Joyce Boyd, *Discarded Legacy: Politics and Poetics in the Life of Francis E. W. Harper, 1825–1911* (Detroit, 1994); Bettye Collier-Thomas, "Frances Ellen Watkins Harper, Abolitionist and Feminist Reformer, 1825–1911," in Ann Gordon et al., eds., *African American Women and the Vote, 1837–1965* (Amherst, 1997), 41; Johanna Maria Ortner, "Whatever Concerns Them, as a Race, Concerns Me": The Life and Activism of Frances Ellen Watkins Harper" (PhD diss., University of Massachusetts, Amherst, 2021); Dorothy Sterling, ed., *We Are Your Sisters: Black Women in the Nineteenth Century* (New York, 1984), 159–75; Jane Rhodes, *Mary Ann Shadd Cary: The*

Black Press and Protest in the Nineteenth Century (Bloomington, 1998); Peterson, *"Doers of the Word,"* 98–110, 120–35.

9. Stanton, Anthony, and Gage, eds., *History of Woman Suffrage,* 1:672–74, 688–737; Stanton, *Eighty Years or More,* 215–25; Ellen Carol DuBois, " 'The Pivot of the Marriage Relation': Stanton's Analysis of Women's Subordination in Marriage," in Ellen Carol DuBois and Richard Candida Smith, eds., *Elizabeth Cady Stanton: Feminist as Thinker* (New York, 2007), 82–92; Sue Davis, *The Political Thought of Elizabeth Cady Stanton: Women's Rights and American Political Traditions* (New York, 2008), 79–85; Holly Jackson, *American Radicals: How Nineteenth Century Protest Shaped the Nation* (New York, 2019).

10. Lee Ann Whites, *The Civil War as a Crisis in Gender: Augusta, Georgia 1860–1890* (Athens, 1995); Elizabeth D. Leonard, *Yankee Women: Gender Battles in the Civil War* (New York, 1994); Nina Silber, *Daughters of the Union: Northern Women Fight the Civil War* (Cambridge, 2005); Elizabeth Cady Stanton, Susan B. Anthony, and Matilda Joslyn Gage, eds., *History of Woman Suffrage* (New York, 1882), 2:23.

11. L. D. Brockett, M. D. Vaughan, and Mrs. Mary C. Vaughan, *Woman's Work in the Civil War: A Record of Heroism, Patriotism and Patience* (Boston, 1867), 58, 558; Frank Moore, *Women of the War: Their Heroism and Self-Sacrifice* (Hartford, 1867), 571–96; Mrs. A. H. Hoge, *The Boys in Blue or Heroes of the "Rank and File"* (New York, 1867), 15; Joan Waugh, *Unsentimental Reformer: The Life of Josephine Shaw Lowell* (Cambridge, MA, 1998); Ednah Dow Cheney, *Memoirs of Lucretia Crocker and Abby W. May* (Boston, 1888), 13–18; Carol Faulkner, *Women's Radical Reconstruction: The Freedmen's Aid Movement* (Philadelphia, 2006), 34–35; Melinda Lawson, *Patriot Fires: Forging a New American Nationalism in the Civil War North* (Lawrence, 2002), chap. 1; Jeannie Attie, *Patriotic Toil: Northern Women and the American Civil War* (Ithaca, 1998); Judith Ann Giesberg, *Civil War Sisterhood: The U.S. Sanitary Commission and Women's Politics in Transition* (Boston, 2000); Mary A. Livermore, *My Story of the War: A Woman's Narrative of Four Years Personal Experience* (Hartford, 1889), 157; *Catalogue of the Department of Arms and Trophies Donated and Exhibited at the Northwestern Sanitary Fair* (Chicago, 1865); Wendy Hamand Venet, *A Strong Minded Woman: The Life of Mary Livermore* (Amherst, 2005); Jane Stuart Woolsey, *Hospital Days* (New York, 1868), 34, 53–61.

12. *TCR,* January 14, April 22, December 9, 1865, April 14, June 20, 1866; Lynn M. Hudson, *The Making of "Mammy Pleasant": A Black Entrepreneur in Nineteenth-Century San Francisco* (Urbana, 2003); Receipts from Ladies Sanitary Fund to Mrs. M. A. Brown, May 4, June 12, 1865, Brown Family Papers, AAS; Ella Forbes, *African American Women during the Civil War* (New York, 1998), chaps. 5–6; Judith Giesberg, *Army at Home: Women and the Civil War on the Northern Home Front* (Chapel Hill, 2009), 92–118, 163–67.

13. Moore, *Women of the War,* 347–72; Lori D. Ginzberg, *Women and the Work of Benevolence: Morality, Politics, and Class in the 19th Century United States* (New Haven, 1990); Theda Skocpol, *Protecting Soldiers and Mothers: The Political Origins of Social Policy in the United States* (Cambridge, 1992), 102–51, 314–539; Alison M. Parker, *Articulating Rights: Nineteenth Century American Women on Race, Reform, and the State* (DeKalb, 2010).

14. Brockett and Vaughan, *Woman's Work in the Civil War,* 62, 99–132, 172–84, 334–42; Walt Whitman, "Female Nurses for Soldiers," *Specimen Days & Collect* (Philadelphia, 1882–83), 61; Thomas J. Brown, *Dorothea Dix: New England Reformer* (Cambridge,

1998); *Life of Abigail Hopper Gibbons Told Chiefly through Her Correspondence* (New York, 1897), 2:5–6; Margaret Hope Bacon, *Abby Hopper Gibbons: Prison Reformer and Social Activist* (Albany, 2000); *Memoir of Emily Elizabeth Parsons Published for the Benefit of the Cambridge Hospital* (Boston, 1880); Jane E. Schultz, *Women at the Front: Hospital Workers in Civil War America* (Chapel Hill, 2004); Anne Austin, *The Woolsey Sisters of New York: A Family's Involvement in the Civil War and a New Profession* (Philadelphia, 1971); Woolsey, *Hospital Days,* 41–42; Thavolia Glymph, *The Women's Fight: The Civil War Battles for Home, Freedom, and Nation* (Chapel Hill, 2020), 193–94; Leslie A. Schwalm, *Medicine, Science and Making Race in Civil War America* (Chapel Hill, 2023).

15. Stephen B. Oates, *A Woman of Valor: Clara Barton and the Civil War* (New York, 1994); Leigh Fought, *Women in the World of Frederick Douglass* (New York, 2017), chap. 9; Stanton, Anthony, and Gage, eds., *History of Woman Suffrage,* 2:23; Alice Kessler-Harris, *Out to Work: A History of Wage-Earning Women in the United States* (New York, 1982), 75–83.

16. Jim Downs, *Maladies of Empire: How Colonialism, Slavery, and War Transformed Medicine* (Cambridge, MA, 2021); Carolyn Skinner, *Women Physicians and Professional Ethos in Nineteenth-Century America* (Carbondale, 2014); Theresa Kaminski, *Dr. Mary Walker's Civil War: One Woman's Journey to the Medal of Honor and the Fight for Women's Rights* (Guilford, 2020); Mary E. Walker, MD, *Hit: Essays on Women's Rights* (1871; reprint, Amherst, 2003); Gerald Schwartz, ed., *A Woman Doctor's Civil War: Esther Hill Hawk's Diary* (Columbia, 1984), introduction; Rebecca Crumpler, MD, *Book of Medical Discourses in Two Parts* (Boston, 1883), 3; Adele Logan Alexander, *Homelands and Waterways: The American Journey of the Bond Family, 1846–1926* (New York, 2000), 286–87.

17. Lyde Cullen Sizer, *The Political Work of Northern Women Writers and the Civil War, 1850–1872* (Chapel Hill, 2000), 101, 154, 168; Alice Fahs, *The Imagined Civil War: Popular Literature of the North and South, 1861–1865* (Chapel Hill, 2001); Sarah Gardner, *Blood and Irony: Southern White Women's Narratives of the Civil War, 1861–1867* (Chapel Hill, 2004); *Notes of Hospital Life From November, 1861 to August, 1863* (Philadelphia, 1864); Adelaide W. Smith, *Reminiscences of an Army Nurse during the Civil War* (New York, 1911); Whitman, "The Real War Will Never Get into the Books," *Specimen Days*; Hannah Ropes, *Civil War Nurse: The Diary and Letters of Hannah Ropes,* ed. John R. Brumgardt (Knoxville, 1980).

18. L. M. Alcott, *Hospital Sketches* (Boston, 1863), 47–52, 81; Alice Fahs, ed., *Hospital Sketches* (Boston, 2004), vii, 14, 70; Whitman, "Burial of a Lady Nurse," *Specimen Days*; Woolsey, *Hospital Days,* 109.

19. L. Maria Child, *A Romance of the Republic* (Cambridge, 1867); Sarah Elbert, ed., *Louisa May Alcott on Race, Sex, and Slavery* (Boston, 1997); Nina Silber, *The Romance of Reunion: Northerners and the South, 1865–1900* (Chapel Hill, 1993); Frances E. W. Harper, *Iola Leroy or Shadows Uplifted* (Philadelphia, 1892).

20. J. Matthew Gallman, *America's Joan of Arc: The Life of Anna Elizabeth Dickinson: The Story of a Remarkable Woman, the Civil War, and the Struggle for Women's Rights* (New York, 2006); Sarah P. Remond, "The Negroes of the United States of America," *JNH* (April 1942): 216–18; Matthew J. Clavin, *Toussaint Louverture and the American Civil War: The Promise and Peril of a Second Haitian Revolution* (Philadelphia, 2010), 94; *TL*, April 8, 1864; Faulkner, *Women's Radical Reconstruction,* 70–71.

21. Catherine Clinton, *The Other Civil War: American Women in the Nineteenth Century*

(New York, 1984), 90; *Proceedings of the Meeting of the Loyal Women of the Republic, Held in New York, May 14, 1863* (New York, 1863), i–iv, 4; WNLL to Brown, June 20, 1863, Anthony to Brown, Sept. 17, 1863, Olympia Brown Papers, Schlesinger Library, HU; Mattie Griffith Browne to Phillips, October 5, 1863, Stanton to Phillips, June 6, September 29, 1863, Wendell Phillips Papers, Houghton Library, HU; Stanton, *Eighty Years and More,* 234–42; Stanton, Anthony, and Gage, eds., *History of Woman Suffrage,* 2:81–87, chap. 16; Wendy Hamand Venet, *Neither Ballots nor Bullets: Women Abolitionists and the Civil War* (Charlottesville, 1991), 102–22, 131–48; Beverly Wilson Palmer, ed., *Selected Letters of Lucretia Coffin Mott* (Urbana, 2002), 339; Wheeler, ed., *Loving Warriors,* 195, 199.

22. John Stuart Mill, *The Subjection of Women* (London, 1869), 1–13, 50–53, 62–68, 78–90, 96–97, 174–77; *TWJ,* January 29, June 11, 1870; Elizabeth Crawford, *The Women's Suffrage Movement, 1866–1928: A Reference Guide* (London, 1999); Sophia A. van Wingerden, *The Women's Suffrage Movement in Britain, 1866–1928* (London, 1999).

23. Mott to Phillips, April 17, 1866, Wendell Phillips Papers, Houghton Library, HU; *Proceedings of the Eleventh National Woman's Rights Convention, Held at the Church of the Puritans, New York* (New York, 1866), 3, 5–6, 10–11, 13, 45–49, 52, 77–78; *CG,* 39th Congress, 1st Session, May 8, 1866, 2459; Stanton, Anthony, and Gage, eds., *History of Woman Suffrage,* 2:315; DuBois, *Feminism and Suffrage,* 66–68; Christopher Densmore et al., eds., *Lucretia Mott Speaks: The Essential Speeches and Sermons* (Urbana, 2017), 151; Palmer, ed., *Selected Letters of Lucretia Coffin Mott,* 357, 371.

24. *Proceedings of the First Anniversary of the American Equal Rights Association, Held at the Church of the Puritans, New York, May 9 and 10, 1867* (New York, 1867), 3, 5–6, 8, 13–15, 17, 20, 26, 37–40, 44–45, 68–69, 71–72; Densmore et al., eds., *Lucretia Mott Speaks,* 165; Palmer, ed., *Selected Letters of Lucretia Coffin Mott,* 381–84, 390–91; Olympia Brown, *Acquaintances, Old and New, Among Reformers* (1911), 41; Du Bois, *Feminism and Suffrage,* 70; Faye E. Dudden, *Fighting Chance: The Struggle over Woman Suffrage and Black Suffrage in Reconstruction America* (New York, 2011), 90; Stanton, Anthony, and Gage, eds., *History of Woman Suffrage,* 2:89, 94–95; Painter, *Sojourner Truth,* 224–30; Terborg-Penn, *African American Women in the Struggle for the Vote,* 25.

25. Stanton, Anthony, and Gage, eds., *History of Woman Suffrage,* 2:102–51, 309–12; *CG,* 39th Congress, 1st Session, February 14, 1866, 829; *NASS,* February 3, 1866; *Woman Suffrage in New Jersey. An Address Delivered by Lucy Stone before the New Jersey Legislature* (Boston, 1867), 12–13, 16–19; Wheeler, ed., *Loving Warriors,* 215–19, 269–70; Henry B. Blackwell, *What the South Can Do: How the Southern States Can Make Themselves Masters of the Situation. To the Legislatures of the Southern States* (New York, 1867); Blackwell to Brown, May 30, June 8, 12, 1867, Stone to Brown, May 30, 1867, Garrison to Brown, July 13, 1868, Olympia Brown Papers, Schlesinger Library, HU; Stanton to Phillips, April 7, 15, June 15, no year, Wendell Phillips Papers, Houghton Library, HU; Brown, *Acquaintances,* chap. 8; Terborg-Penn, *African American Women in the Struggle for the Vote,* 28–31; Laura Free, *Suffrage Reconstructed: Gender, Race, and Voting Rights in the Civil War Era* (Ithaca, 2015), 142–61; Dudden, *Fighting Chance,* chaps. 5–6; Du Bois, *Feminism and Suffrage,* 94; *TWJ,* May 24, 1890.

26. Brown, *Acquaintances,* 74–79; Stanton, Anthony, and Gage, eds. *History of Woman Suffrage,* 2:320–27, 334–40, 407–8, 411–18, 478, 501–5, 514, 518–22, 545–50, 613, 633–41, 645–46, 715, 801–4, 826; George Washington Julian, *Political Recollections,*

1840–1872 (Chicago, 1884), 324–25; William H. Barnes, *History of the Thirty-Ninth Congress of the United States* (New York, 1868), 490–95; Gordon, ed., *Selected Papers*, 2:194–98; Stone Blackwell, *Lucy Stone,* 195–96, 201–2, 253; Wheeler, ed., *Loving Warriors,* 227–28, 244–45; *TWJ,* October 19, 1872; Stanton, *Eighty Years and More,* 289, 300; *An Account of the Proceedings on the Trial of Susan B. Anthony on the Charge of Illegal Voting* (Rochester, 1874); Nancy A. Hewitt, *Radical Friend: Amy Kirby Post and Her Activist Worlds* (Chapel Hill, 2018), 266–70; Rhodes, *Mary Ann Shadd Cary,* 194–96; DuBois, *Feminism and Suffrage,* chap. 6; *Minor v. Happersett,* 88 US 162 (1875); Free, *Suffrage Reconstructed,* 162–63; Rebecca J. Mead, *How the Vote Was Won: Woman Suffrage in the Western United States, 1868–1914* (New York, 2004), chaps. 2–3; Virginia Scharff, "Broadening the Battlefield: Conflict, Contingency, and the Mystery of Woman Suffrage in Wyoming, 1869," in *Civil War Wests: Testing the Limits of the United States,* eds. Adam Arenson and Andrew R. Graybill (Oakland, 2015), 202–23; Sarah Barringer Gordon, *The Mormon Question: Polygamy and Constitutional Conflict in Nineteenth-Century America* (Chapel Hill, 2021).

27. Stanton, Anthony, and Gage, eds., *History of Woman Suffrage,* 2:378–406, 411, 418, 435, 539; *TWJ,* January 8, April 2, 9, 16, 23, May 28, June 11, August 13, 1870; Anthony to Brown, July 20, 1868, Blackwell to Brown, October 18, 1869, Stone to Brown, April 2, 1870, Celia Burleigh to Brown, October 25, 1871, Olympia Brown Papers, Schlesinger Library, HU; Stone Blackwell, *Lucy Stone,* chap. 15; Griffith, *In Her Own Right,* 111; Dudden, *Fighting Chance,* 10; Wheeler, ed., *Loving Warriors,* 228–30; Lasser and Merrill, eds., *Friends and Sisters,* 175–77; Palmer, ed., *Selected Letters of Lucretia Coffin Mott,* 398–99, 414; Carol Faulkner, *Lucretia Mott's Heresy : Abolition and Women's Rights in Nineteenth Century America* (Philadelphia, 2011), 215–16.

28. Stanton, Anthony, and Gage, eds., *History of Woman Suffrage,* 2:315–17, 332, 516–17, 527–28, 532–33, 542, 756–67, 804–6, 811–13, 841, 851, 854, 857–58; *TWJ,* February 12, October 22, December 3, 1870, January 7, 1871, June 1, 1872; *NASS,* August 28, 1869; Elizabeth Cady Stanton, Susan B. Anthony, and Matilda Joslyn Gage, *History of Woman Suffrage in Three Volumes,* vol. 3, *1876–1885* (Rochester, 1886), 8–16, 58–60, 75–104; Stone Blackwell, *Lucy Stone,* 248–51; Wheeler, ed., *Loving Warriors,* 251; Brown, *Acquaintances,* 37–38; Du Bois, *Feminism and Suffrage,* ch. 5; Dudden, *Fighting Chance,* 3, 80–81.

29. *Proceedings of the Constitutional Convention of South Carolina* (Charleston, 1868), 836, 838; Terborg-Penn, *African American Women in the Struggle for the Vote,* 44–48; Tetrault, *The Myth of Seneca Falls,* 77–86; Noralee Frankel, *Freedom's Women: Black Women and Families in Civil War Mississippi* (Bloomington, 1999); Elsa Barkley-Brown, "To Catch the Vision of Freedom: Reconstructing Southern Black Women's Political History, 1865–1880," in Ann D. Gordon et al., eds., *African American Women and the Vote, 1837–1965* (Amherst, 1997), 73–88; Nancy Bercaw, *Gendered Freedoms: Race, Rights and the Politics of the Household in the Delta, 1861–1875* (Gainesville, 2003); Nell Irvin Painter, "Voices of Suffrage: Sojourner Truth, Frances Watkins Harper, and the Struggle for Woman Suffrage," in Jean H. Baker, ed., *Votes for Women: The Struggle for Suffrage Revisited* (New York, 2002), 35–42; *TWJ,* July 12, 1873, May 9, 1874; "The Texas Reconstruction Convention Considers Woman Suffrage (1868–1869)," in Ruth Winegarten and Judith N. McArthur, eds., *Citizens at Last: The Woman Suffrage Movement in Texas* (College Station, 1987); *Debates and Proceedings of the Arkansas Constitutional Convention* (Little Rock, 1868), 88–91, 113–17, 363–88, 391–94, 489–510, 514–16, 699, 701–24.

CHAPTER SEVEN: THE WANING OF RECONSTRUCTION

1. Douglas R. Egerton, *The Wars of Reconstruction: The Brief, Violent History of America's Most Progressive Era* (New York, 2014); John Patrick Daly, *The War after the War: A New History of Reconstruction* (Athens, 2022); George C. Rable, *But There Was No Peace: The Role of Violence in the Politics of Reconstruction* (Athens, 1984); Ted Tunnell, *Crucible of Reconstruction: War, Radicalism, and Race in Louisiana, 1862–1877* (Baton Rouge, 1984), 6.

2. *NASS*, September 19, 26, October 3, 1868; *NNE*, October 15, 1874; Carole Emberton, *Beyond Redemption: Race, Violence, and the American South after the Civil War* (Chicago, 2013); Mitchell Snay, *Fenians, Freedmen, and Southern Whites: Race and Nationality in the Era of Reconstruction* (Baton Rouge, 2007), 13–14; Peggy Lamson, *The Glorious Failure: Black Congressman Robert Brown Elliot and the Reconstruction of South Carolina* (New York, 1973), 130; Alrutheus Ambush Taylor, *The Negro in the Reconstruction of Virginia* (New York, 1926), 206–62.

3. Alrutheus Ambush Taylor, *The Negro in Tennessee, 1865–1880* (Washington, 1941), 53–101; Thomas B. Alexander, *Political Reconstruction in Tennessee* (Nashville, 1950); *NNE*, January 26, February 2, 9, 23, 1871; Michael Perman, *The Road to Redemption: Southern Politics, 1869–1879* (Chapel Hill, 1984); Eric Foner, *Reconstruction: America's Unfinished Revolution, 1863–1877* (New York, 1988), 412–25; Elizabeth Studley Nathans, *Losing the Peace: Georgia Republicans and Reconstruction, 1865–1871* (Baton Rouge, 1968); *NASS*, December 25, 1869.

4. *NASS*, July 11, 18, 25, August 8, 15, September 5, 12, 19, November 7, 14, 1868, January 23, 1869; *Horrible Disclosures: A Full and Authentic Expose of the Ku-Klux Klan* (Cincinnati, 1868), 25–36, 77, 100; James Melville Beard, *K.K.K. Sketches, Humorous and Didactic, Treating the More Important Events of the Ku Klux Klan Movement in the South* (Philadelphia, 1877); Allen W. Trelease, *White Terror: The Ku Klux Klan Conspiracy and Southern Reconstruction* (New York, 1971); Rable, *But There Was No Peace,* chaps. 5–7; Elaine Frantz Parsons, *Ku-Klux: The Birth of the Klan during Reconstruction* (Chapel Hill, 2015), 6; Scott Reynolds Nelson, *Iron Confederacies: Southern Railways, Klan Violence, and Reconstruction* (Chapel Hill, 1999); *CG*, 42nd Congress, 1st Session, April 1, 1871, 392; John A. Leland, *A Voice from South Carolina* (Charleston, 1879), 101–5; Gladys-Marie Fry, *Night Riders in Black Folk History* (Knoxville, 1975), chaps. 4–5; Kwando Mbiassi Kinshasa, *Black Resistance to the Ku Klux Klan in the Wake of the Civil War* (New York, 2008); *The Masked Lady of the White House; or the Ku-Klux Klan* (Philadelphia, 1868); Kidada Williams, *They Left Great Marks on Me: African American Testimonies of Racial Violence from Emancipation to World War I* (New York, 2012), 1–48.

5. *Horrible Disclosures,* 38–40, 69–88, 92–98, 103–4; *Report of Evidence Taken before the Military Committee in Relation to Outrages Committed by the Ku Klux Klan in Middle and West Tennessee* (Nashville, 1868), 10–15, 17–33, 35–40, 44–49, 53–57, 60–62, 72–74; *Report of Joint Committee on Outrages* (Montgomery, 1868), 12–13, 16–58, 61–70, 76–77; *Testimony Taken by the Joint Select Committee to Inquire into the Condition of Affairs of the Late Insurrectionary States. Alabama* (Washington, 1872), 1:77–78, 112–28; Trelease, *White Terror,* 45, 175, 194–95, 226–73; Michael W. Fitzgerald, *Reconstruction in Alabama: From Civil War to Redemption in the Cotton South* (Baton Rouge, 2017).

6. Rev. H. W. Pierson, *A Letter to Hon. Charles Sumner with "Statements" of Outrages upon Freedmen in Georgia* (Washington, 1870); *NNE*, January 19, 26, May 25, 1871;

Beard, *K.K.K. Sketches,* 110; *Report of the Joint Select Committee to Inquire into the Condition of Affairs in the Late Insurrectionary States* (Washington, 1872), 1; Robert J. Kaczorowski, *The Politics of Judicial Interpretation: The Federal Courts, Department of Justice, and Civil Rights, 1866–1876* (1985; reprint, New York, 2005); William-james Hull Hoffer, *To Enlarge the Machinery of Government: Congressional Debates and the Growth of the American State, 1858–1891* (Baltimore, 2007), 103–8; Williams, *They Left Great Marks on Me,* 51; Gene L. Howard, *Death at Cross Plains: An Alabama Reconstruction Tragedy* (University, AL, 1984), 91, 109.

7. *Testimony Taken by the Joint Select Committee to Inquire into the Condition of Affairs of the Late Insurrectionary States. Georgia* (Washington, 1872): 1:182–89, 193–233; *Testimony Taken by the Joint Select Committee to Inquire into the Condition of Affairs of the Late Insurrectionary States. Georgia* (Washington, 1872), 2:695–707; *Testimony Taken by the Joint Select Committee to Inquire into the Condition of Affairs of the Late Insurrectionary States. Miscellaneous and Florida* (Washington, 1872), 3–14, 75–101, 144–56, 165–84, 385–99; Powell Clayton, *The Aftermath of the Civil War, in Arkansas* (New York, 1915), 56–166, 175–206; *Message of the President of the United States, Communicating, in Compliance with the Resolution of the Senate of the 16th of December, 1870, Information in Relation to Outrages Committed by Disloyal Persons in North Carolina and Other Southern States* (Washington, 1871); *Report on the Alleged Outrages in the Southern States, by the Select Committee of the Senate* (Washington, 1871); Zirui (Jerry) Chen, "The Great North Carolina Ku Klux Trials: Habeas Corpus, Due Process, and the Southern Redemption of the Fourteenth Amendment, 1870–1871," undergraduate History thesis, Columbia University, 2023; *Testimony Taken by the Joint Select Committee to Inquire into the Condition of Affairs of the Late Insurrectionary States. North Carolina* (Washington, 1872), 1:13–31, 31–51, 86–100, 102–201, 417–22, 453–56, 470–93; *Address to the Colored People of North Carolina* (Raleigh, 1870); *Proclamations by the Governor of North Carolina Together with the Opinion of Chief Justice Pearson and the Reply of the Governor* (Raleigh, NC, 1870); *NNE,* January 12, 1871; *Trial of William Holden, Governor of North Carolina, Before the Senate of North Carolina, On Impeachment by the House of Representatives for High Crimes and Misdemeanors,* 3 vols. (Raleigh, 1871); *Report of the Joint Select Committee,* 22–24, 44–47, 289, 554–59; Trelease, *White Terror,* 140–74, 205–42, 311–12, 334–48, 397–98.

8. *Testimony Taken by the Joint Select Committee to Inquire into the Condition of Affairs in the Late Insurrectionary States. South Carolina* (Washington, 1872), 1:4, 36–39, 86–91, 289–97, 316–26, 365–73, 446–520; *Testimony taken by the Joint Select Committee to Inquire into the Condition of Affairs in the Late Insurrectionary States. South Carolina* (Washington, 1872), 1:632–51; *Testimony taken by the Joint Select Committee to Inquire into the Condition of Affairs in the Late Insurrectionary States. South Carolina* (Washington, 1872), 3:1406–15, 1463–87, 1599–1606; *The Great Ku Klux Trials. Official Report of the Proceedings before U. S. Circuit Court, Hon. Hugh L. Bond, Circuit Judge, Presiding, and Hon. George S. Bryan, District Judge, Associate, Held at Columbia, S.C., November Term 1871* (Columbia, 1872), 3–7, 55–58, 140–41, 183–84, 207–8, 220–24; *Proceedings in the Ku Klux Trials, at Columbia, S.C. in the United States Circuit Court, November Term, 1871* (1872; reprint, New York, 1969), 20–32, 68–88, 139–45, 435–57, 460–605, 764–89; Budiansky, *The Bloody Shirt,* 119–45; *A Statement of Dr. Bratton's Case, Being Explanatory of the Ku Klux Prosecutions in the Southern States* (London, Ontario, 1872); W. H. Gannon, *The G. A. R. vs. The Ku-Klux—A Few Suggestions Submitted for the Consideration of the Businessmen and the Working*

Men of the North (Boston, 1872); Trelease, *White Terror,* 349–80, 401–8; Parsons, *Ku-Klux,* chaps. 6–7; Lou Falkner Williams, *The Great South Carolina Ku Klux Klan Trials, 1871–1872* (Athens, 1996); Richard Zuczek, *State of Rebellion: Reconstruction in South Carolina* (Columbia, 1996), chap. 5.

9. *NNE,* January 19, April 27, May 4, August 17, December 7, 1871; *TI,* January 4, May 9, 1872; *TC,* September 25, 1875, September 16, 1876; Andrew L. Slap, *The Doom of Reconstruction: The Liberal Republicans in the Civil War Era* (New York, 2006); Douglas R. Egerton, *Heirs of an Honored Name: The Decline of the Adams Family and the Rise of Modern America* (New York, 2019); John G. Sproat, *"The Best Men": Liberal Reformers in the Gilded Age* (New York, 1968); Nancy Cohen, *The Reconstruction of American Liberalism, 1865–1914* (Chapel Hill, 2002).

10. *NNE,* January 12, April 6, 13, 27, May 18, 1871, September 12, October 31, November 14, 21, December 5, 1872; *TI,* June 23, December 22, 1870, March 16, 30, April 6, 13, 27, May 11, July 13, 1871, January 4, April 4, 28, May 9, June 6, 13 27, July 18, 25, August 8, September 12, October 24, 31, November 7, 21, 28, 1872, January 2, 9, 23, February 6, 20, March 6, 1873; Edward L. Pierce, *Memoir and Letters of Charles Sumner,* vol. 4, 1860–1874 (Boston, 1893), 375, 426–96, 514–34, 550–55; *The Works of Charles Sumner* (Boston, 1883), 14:94–131, 168–249, 306–9, *The Works of Charles Sumner* (Boston, 1883), 15:95–185; *William Lloyd Garrison: The Story of His Life Told by His Children,* vol. 4, 1861–1879 (New York, 1889), 259–60; Slap, *The Doom of Reconstruction,* 117, 220; David W. Blight, *Frederick Douglass: Prophet of Freedom* (New York, 2018), 536–45; Joan Waugh, *U.S. Grant: American Hero, American Myth* (Chapel Hill, 2009), 114–44; Ron Chernow, *Grant* (New York, 2017), chap. 33; Nicholas Guyatt, "America's Conservatory: Race, Reconstruction and the Santo Domingo Debate," *JAH* 97 (March 2011): 974–1000; Lorgia García Peña, *Translating Blackness: Latinx Colonialities in Global Perspective* (Durham, 2022); William Gillette, *Retreat from Reconstruction, 1869–1879* (Baton Rouge, 1979).

11. *TC,* October 9, 1875; Nicolas Barreyre, *Gold and Freedom: The Political Economy of Reconstruction* (Charlottesville, 2015); Jonathan Levy, *Freaks of Fortune: The Emerging World of Capitalism and Risk in America* (Cambridge, MA, 2012), esp. chap. 4; Virginia Traweek and Malcolm Wardlaw, "Societal Trust and Financial Market Participation: Evidence from the Freedman's Saving Bank" (October 2020), in *Freedmen's Bank Research: Collected Data and Records Information on the Freedmen's Savings and Trust,* https://freedmansbank.uga.edu/; *NNE,* May 7, 1874; Blight, *Frederick Douglass,* 545–49; Carl R. Osthaus, *Freedmen, Philanthropy, and Fraud: A History of the Freedmen's Savings Bank* (Urbana, 1976); Mehrsa Baradaran, *The Color of Money: Black Banks and the Racial Wealth Gap* (Cambridge, MA, 2017), chap. 1.

CHAPTER EIGHT: THE COUNTERREVOLUTION OF 1876

1. *TI,* January 9, February 27, March 6, May 29, 1873; *NNE,* March 26, July 16, 1874; Leeanna Keith, *The Colfax Massacre: The Untold Story of Black Power, White Terror, and the Death of Reconstruction* (New York, 2008); Charles Lane, *The Day Freedom Died: The Colfax Massacre, the Supreme Court, and the Betrayal of Reconstruction* (New York, 2008); Tom Barber and Jeff Crawford, "Removing the White Supremacy Marker at Colfax, Louisiana: A 2021 Success Story," *Muster: How the Past Informs the Present Blog of the JCWE,* July 6, 2021; James K. Hogue, *Uncivil War: Five New Orleans Street Battles and the Rise and Fall of Radical Reconstruction* (Baton Rouge,

2006); Stephen Budiansky, *The Bloody Shirt: Terror after Appomattox* (New York, 2008), 149–76; Otis A. Singletary, *Negro Militia and Reconstruction* (Austin, 1957), 66–80; Henry Clay Warmoth, *War, Politics and Reconstruction: Stormy Days in Louisiana*, with a new introduction by John C. Rodrigue (Columbia, 2006); Adam Fairclough, *The Revolution That Failed: Reconstruction in Natchitoches* (Gainesville, 2018); *TC*, January 9, 23, 30, February 6, 1875; Ted Tunnell, *Edge of the Sword: The Ordeal of the Carpetbagger Marshall H. Twitchell in the Civil War and Reconstruction* (Baton Rouge, 2001).

2. *NNE*, June 25, July 2, September 3, 10, 17, 24, 1874; Chris Myers Asch & George Derek Musgrove, *Chocolate City: A History of Race and Democracy in the Nation's Capital* (Chapel Hill, 2017), chap. 6; Kate Masur, *An Example for All the Land: Emancipation and the Struggle for Equality in Washington, DC* (Chapel Hill, 2010), 194–256; Carl H. Moneyhon, *Republicanism in Reconstruction Texas* (Austin, 1980); Loren Schweninger, *James T. Rapier and Reconstruction* (Chicago, 1978), 143–47; Michael W. Fitzgerald, *Reconstruction in Alabama: From Civil War to Redemption in the Cotton South* (Baton Rouge, 2017); Powell Clayton, *The Aftermath of the Civil War, in Arkansas* (New York, 1915), 343–53; Thomas A. DeBlack, *With Fire and Sword: Arkansas, 1861–1874* (Fayetteville, 1998); Singletary, *Negro Militia and Reconstruction,* 50–65, 81–99; Michael Perman, *The Road to Redemption: Southern Politics, 1869–1879* (Chapel Hill, 1984), part 2.

3. *NNE*, June 25, July 2, September 3, 10, 17, 24, 1874; *TC*, January 9, 1875, August 19, September 9, 1876; Henry W. Warren, *Reminiscences of a Mississippi Carpet-bagger* (Holden, 1914), 37–38, 44–45, 69–90; Budiansky, *The Bloody Shirt,* 64–105, 183–217; *Yazoo; Or, on the Picket Line of Freedom in the South. A Personal Narrative by A. T. Morgan* (Washington, 1884), 122, 133; Nina Mjakij, ed., *Portraits of African American Life Since 1865* (Wilmington, 2003), 1–12; George C. Rable, *But There Was No Peace: The Role of Violence in the Politics of Reconstruction* (Athens, 1984), chap. 9; William Charles Harris, *The Day of the Carpetbagger: Republican Reconstruction in Mississippi* (Baton Rouge, 1979), 635–88; Nicholas Lehman, *Redemption: The Last Battle of the Civil War* (New York, 2006); John Hope Franklin, ed., *Reminiscences of an Active Life: The Autobiography of John Roy Lynch* (Chicago, 1970), 166–67, 174–77; Blanche Ames, *Adelbert Ames: Broken Oaths and Reconstruction in Mississippi* (New York, 1964).

4. *NNE*, September 7, 1871, January 4, 18, 25, November 28, December 5, 1872, January 15, March 17, April 9, 23, May 7, 28, June 11, 18, 25, July 9, 23, 30, August 13, 1874; *TI*, May 9, 1872, April 24, 1873; *CR Forty-Third Congress, First Session* (Washington, 1874), 337–41, 382–83, 406–10, 455–58, 565–67, 901–3, 945–51, 1311–14, 4116–68, 4782–95, *Forty-Third Congress, Second Session*, 943–47, 981–82, 1001–2, 1005–9; Henry Wilson, *History of the Rise and Fall of the Slave Power in America* (Boston, 1877), 3:692–96; Edward L. Pierce, *Memoir and Letters of Charles Sumner, 1860–1874* (Boston, 1893), 4:499–504, 598; *The Works of Charles Sumner* (Boston, 1874), 14:277–82, 357–473, 15:286–90, 301–14; Amy Dru Stanley, "Slave Emancipation and the Revolutionizing of Human Rights," in Gregory P. Downs and Kate Masur, *The World the Civil War Made* (Chapel Hill, 2015), 269–303; Alexander Stephens, *A Constitutional View of the Late War Between the States*, 2 vols. (Philadelphia, 1868–70); "Civil Rights Act of 1875," in John H. Bracey Jr. and Manisha Sinha, eds., *African American Mosaic: A Documentary History from the Slave Trade to the Twenty-First Century*, vol. 1, to 1877 (Upper Saddle River, 2004), 366–67; Edward McPherson, *A Hand-Book*

for Politics in 1876: Being a Record of Important Political Action, National and State (Washington, 1876), 12–13; Peggy Lamson, *The Glorious Failure: Black Congressman Robert Brown Elliot and the Reconstruction in South Carolina* (New York, 1973), 176–85; Budiansky, *The Bloody Shirt,* 2–5; Robert Zuczek, *State of Rebellion: Reconstruction in South Carolina* (Columbia, 1996), 129–30; *TC,* January 23, February 13, 27, March 6, 1875, November 4, 1876; Elizabeth D. Leonard, *Benjamin Franklin Butler: A Noisy, Fearless Life* (Chapel Hill, 2022); James M. McPherson, "Abolitionists and the Civil Rights Act of 1875," *JAH* (December 1965): 493–510; Christopher W. Schmidt, *Civil Rights in America: A History* (Cambridge, 2021), chap. 1.

5. *NNE,* August 31, 1871; John A. Leland, *A Voice from South Carolina* (Charleston, 1879), 153–83; Zuczek, *State of Rebellion,* 135–87; Budiansky, *The Bloody Shirt,* 51–64, 221–54; *TC,* July 15, 22, 29, October 21, 28, 1876; Lamson, *The Glorious Failure,* 237–89; Mark M. Smith, "'All Is Not Quiet in Our Hellish Country': Facts, Politics, and Race: The Ellenton Riot of 1876," *SCHM* 95 (April 1994): 142–55; Stephen Kantrowitz, *Ben Tillman and the Reconstruction of White Supremacy* (Chapel Hill, 2000); Singletary, *Negro Militia and Reconstruction,* 136–44; Wilton B. Fowler, "A Carpetbagger's Conversion to White Supremacy," *NCHR* 43 (July 1966): 286–304; *Education at the South: Address of D. H. Chamberlain* (New Haven, 1884); James Green, *Personal Recollections of Daniel Henry Chamberlain* (Worcester, 1908).

6. *TC,* January 9, 1875, January 29, June 10, July 8, September 9, 30, October 28, November 4, 11, 18, 25, December 2, 16, 30, 1876, January 13, 20, February 10, 17, 24, March 3, 10, 17, 24, 31, April 7, 14, 21, 28, May 12, 26, September 22, December 8, 1877; John Roy Lynch, *The Facts of Reconstruction,* ed. William C. Harris (Indianapolis, 1970), 172–90; Vernon Lane Wharton, *The Negro in Mississippi, 1865–1890* (Chapel Hill, 1947), 200–201; Rable, *But There Was No Peace,* chap. 10; Gordon B. McKinney, *Zeb Vance: North Carolina's Civil War Governor and Gilded Age Political Leader* (Chapel Hill, 2004); Jerrell H. Shofner, *Nor Is It Over Yet: Florida in the Era of Reconstruction, 1863–1877* (Gainesville, 1974); Paul Ortiz, *Emancipation Betrayed: The Hidden History of Black Organizing and White Violence in Florida from Reconstruction to the Bloody Election of 1920* (Berkeley, 2005); Zuczek, *State of Rebellion,* chap. 9; Hogue, *Uncivil War,* chap. 7; Adam Fairclough, *Bulldozed and Betrayed: Louisiana and the Stolen Elections of 1876* (Baton Rouge, 2021); Michael A. Bellesiles, *1877: America's Year of Living Violently* (New York, 2010), chap. 2; Michael F. Holt, *By One Vote: The Disputed Presidential Elections of 1876* (Lawrence, 2008); Leland, *A Voice from South Carolina,* 145–53; Carol Gelderman, *A Free Man of Color and His Hotel: Race, Reconstruction and the Role of the Federal Government* (Washington, 2012); Robert Rydell, *All the World's a Fair: Visions of Empire at American International Expositions, 1876–1916* (Chicago, 1984); Paul Leland Haworth, *The Hayes-Tilden Presidential Election of 1876* (Cleveland, 1906); C. Vann Woodward, *Reunion and Reaction: The Compromise of 1877 and the End of Reconstruction* (Boston, 1951); Eric Foner, *Reconstruction: America's Unfinished Revolution, 1863–1877* (New York, 1988), 575–82; Erik B. Alexander and Rachel Sheldon, "The Electoral Count Act Is Broken: Fixing It Requires Knowing How It Became Law," *The Washington Post,* Oct. 28, 2021; Victor de Santis, "Rutherford B. Hayes and the Removal of Troops and the End of Reconstruction," in J. Morgan Kousser and James McPherson, eds., *Region, Race and Reconstruction: Essays in Honor of C. Vann Woodward* (New York, 1982); Gregory P. Downs, *After Appomattox: Military Occupation and the Ends of War* (Cambridge, MA, 2015), 91, 153, 189, 232; Ari Hoogenboom, *The Presidency of Rutherford B. Hayes* (Lawrence, 1988);

David W. Blight, *Frederick Douglass: Prophet of Freedom* (New York, 2019), 582–87; Rayford Logan, *The Betrayal of the Negro: From Rutherford B. Hayes to Woodrow Wilson* (London, 1954); Warren, *Reminiscences of a Mississippi Carpet-bagger,* 107–8.

7. *TC*, January 16, February 13, 20, March 27, November 13, 27, December 18, 1875, October 7, 1876, March 31, April 7, November 10, 1877; *William Lloyd Garrison: The Story of His Life Told by His Children,* vol. 4, 1861–1879 (New York, 1889), 250–58, 261–62, 293–94; Wilson, *History of the Rise and Fall of the Slave Power* 3:740; Clayton, *The Aftermath of the Civil War,* 168–69, 186–93, 353–68; Steven Hahn, "Class and State in Postemancipation Societies: Southern Planters in Comparative Perspectives," *AHR* 95 (February 1990): 75–98; Paul E. Herron, *Framing the Solid South: The State Constitutional Conventions of Secession, Reconstruction, and Redemption, 1860–1902* (Lawrence, 2017), chap. 6; Foner, *Reconstruction,* 587–97; Nicolas Berreyre, *Gold and Freedom: The Political Economy of Reconstruction* (Charlottesville, 2015), 227; Gerald David Jaynes, *Branches without Roots: Genesis of the Black Working Class, 1862–1882* (New York, 1986); Jay Mandle, *The Roots of Black Poverty: The Southern Plantation Economy after the Civil War* (Durham, 1978); Jay Mandle, *Not Slave, Not Free: The African American Economic Experience since the Civil War* (Durham, 1992); Douglas A. Blackmon, *Slavery by Another Name: The Re-enslavement of Black Americans from the Civil War to World War II* (New York, 2008); David M. Oshinsky, *"Worse Than Slavery": Parchman Farm and the Ordeal of Jim Crow Justice* (New York, 1992); Talitha L. LeFlouria, *Chained in Silence: Black Women and Convict Labor in the New South* (Chapel Hill, 2015); Harold D. Woodman, *King Cotton and His Retainers: Financing and Marketing the Cotton Crop of the South, 1800–1925* (Lexington, 1968); C. Vann Woodward, *Origins of the New South, 1877–1913,* vol. 1, *A History of the South* (Baton Rouge, 1964); Edward L. Ayers, *The Promise of the New South: Life after Reconstruction* (New York, 1992); Natalie J. Ring, *The Problem South: Region, Empire, and the New Liberal State, 1880–1930* (Athens, 2012).

8. *Slaughter-House Cases,* 83 U.S. 36 (1873), *United States v. Reese Et Al.,* 92 U.S. 214 (1876), *United States v. Cruikshank Et Al.,* 92 U.S. 542 (1876), in Christian G. Samito, ed., *Changes in Law and Society During the Civil War and Reconstruction* (Carbondale, 2009), 260–85; Robert J. Koczorowski, *The Politics of Judicial Interpretation: The Federal Courts, Department of Justice, and Civil Rights, 1866–1876* (New York, 2005), chaps. 7–9; Ronald M. Labbe & Jonathan Lurie, *The Slaughterhouse Cases: Regulation, Reconstruction, and the Fourteenth Amendment* (Lawrence, 2003); *TC*, November 13, 1875; Robert M. Goldman, *Reconstruction and Black Suffrage: Losing the Vote in Reese and Cruikshank* (Lawrence, 2001); John R. Howard, *The Shifting Wind: The Supreme Court and Civil Rights from Reconstruction to Brown* (Albany, 1999); Pamela Brandwein, *Reconstructing Reconstruction: The Supreme Court and the Production of Historical Truth* (Durham, 1999), chaps. 1–4; Eric Foner, *The Second Founding: How the Civil War and Reconstruction Remade the Constitution* (New York, 2019), 130–48.

CHAPTER NINE: THE CONQUEST OF THE WEST

1. Frederick Jackson Turner, *The Frontier in American History* (New York, 1920), 2, 16–31; John Mack Faragher, *Rereading Frederick Jackson Turner: "The Significance of the Frontier in American History" and Other Essays* (New York, 1994), introduction.

2. Elliot West, "Reconstructing Race," *Western Historical Quarterly* 34 (2003), 6–26;

Brian DeLay, *War of a Thousand Deserts: Indian Raids and the US–Mexican War* (New Haven, 2008); Patricia Nelson Limerick, *The Legacy of Conquest: The Unbroken Past of the American West* (New York, 1987); Heather Cox Richardson, *West from Appomattox: The Reconstruction of America after the Civil War* (New Haven, 2007); Dee Brown, *Bury My Heart at Wounded Knee: An Indian History of the American West* (New York, 1970).

3. A. G. Hopkins, *American Empire: A Global History* (Princeton, 2018).

4. Francis Jennings, *The Invasion of America: Indians, Colonialism, and the Cant of Conquest* (New York, 1976); David E. Stannard, *American Holocaust: The Conquest of the New World* (New York, 1992); Jean M. O'Brien, *Firsting and Lasting: Writing Indians out of Existence in New England* (Minneapolis, 2010); Richard White, *The Middle Ground: Indians, Empires, and Republic in the Great Lakes Region, 1650–1815* (Cambridge, 1991); Roxanne Dunbar-Ortiz, *An Indigenous Peoples' History of the United States* (Boston, 2014); Claudio Saunt, *Unworthy Republic: The Dispossession of Native Americans and the Road to Indian Territory* (New York, 2020); Jeffrey Ostler, *Surviving Genocide: Native Nations and the United States from the American Revolution to Bleeding Kansas* (New Haven, 2019); Andres Resendez, *The Other Slavery: The Uncovered Story of Indian Enslavement in America* (New York, 2016); Micahel Witgen, *An Infinity of Nations: How the Native New World Shaped Early North America* (Philadelphia, 2012); Pekka Hämäläinen, *Indigenous Continent: The Epic Contest for North America* (New York, 2022); Kathleen DuVal, *The Native Ground: Indians and Colonists in the Heart of the Continent* (Philadelphia, 2006); Philip J. Deloria, *Indians in Unexpected Places* (Lawrence, 2004).

5. Patrick J. Jung, *The Black Hawk War of 1832* (Norman, 2007); Gary Clayton Anderson, *Massacre in Minnesota: The Dakota War of 1862, the Most Violent Ethnic Conflict in American History* (Norman, 2019); Jameson Sweet, "Native Suffrage: Race, Citizenship, and Dakota Indians in the Upper Midwest," *JER* 39 (Spring 2019), 108–9; David Nichols, *Lincoln and the Indians: Civil War Policy and Politics* (Columbia, 1978); Michael S. Green, *Lincoln and Native Americans* (Carbondale, 2021), 84; "Massacre of Cheyenne Indians," in *Report of the Joint Committee on the Conduct of the War at the Second Session Thirty-Eighth Congress* (Washington, 1865), i-iv, 3–108; *The Works of Charles Sumner* (Boston, 1874), 9:198; Ari Kelman, *A Misplaced Massacre: Struggling over the Memory of Sand Creek* (Cambridge, MA, 2013).

6. Natalie Joy, "The Indian's Cause: Abolitionists and Native American Rights," *JCWE* 8 (June 2018): 215–42; John Ross to Abraham Lincoln, September 16, 1862, Abraham Lincoln Papers, LC; Fay A. Yarbrough, *Choctaw Confederates: The American Civil War in Indian Territory* (Chapel Hill, 2021); Gregory D. Smithers, *The Cherokee Diaspora: An Indigenous History of Migration, Resettlement, and Identity* (New Haven, 2015); Tiya Miles, "Beyond a Boundary: Black Lives and the Settler-Native Divide," *WMQ* 76 (June 2019): 417–26; Claudio Saunt, "The Paradox of Freedom: Tribal Sovereignty and Emancipation during the Reconstruction of Indian Territory," *JSH* 40 (February 2004): 63–94; *TI*, April 11, 1872; David A. Chang, *The Color of the Land: Race, Nation, and the Politics of Landownership in Oklahoma, 1832–1929* (Chapel Hill, 2010); Kendra Taira Field, *Growing Up with the Country: Family, Race, and Nation after the Civil War* (New Haven, 2018); Alaina E. Roberts, *I've Been Here All the While: Black Freedom on Native Land* (Philadelphia, 2021).

7. Ned Blackhawk, *Violence over the Land: Indians and Empires in the Early American West* (Cambridge, MA, 2006); Pekka Hämäläinen, *The Comanche Empire* (New

508

NOTES

Haven, 2008); Kevin Waite, *West of Slavery: The Southern Dream of a Transcontinental Empire* (Chapel Hill, 2021); Megan Kate Nelson, *Three-Cornered War: The Union, the Confederacy, and Native Peoples in the Fight for the West* (New York, 2020); Robert Wooster, *The American Military Frontiers: The United States Army in the West, 1783–1900* (Albuquerque, 2009); Robert M. Utley, *The Indian Frontier of the American West, 1846–1890* (Albuquerque, 1984), 107; Benjamin Madley, *An American Genocide: The United States and the California Indian Catastrophe, 1846–1873* (New Haven, 2017); Gary H. Whaley, *Oregon and the Collapse of the Illahee: U.S. Empire and the Transformation of an Indigenous World, 1792–1859* (Chapel Hill, 2010); Brigham D. Madsden, *The Shoshoni Frontier and the Bear River Massacre* (Salt Lake City, 1985); Peter Cozzens, *The Earth Is Weeping: The Epic Story of the Indian Wars for the American West* (New York, 2016).

8. Robert Wooster, *The Military and the United States Indian Policy, 1865–1903* (New Haven, 1988); Utley, *The Indian Frontier,* 100, 106; *TC,* June 5, 1875, August 26, 1876; Dunbar-Ortiz, *An Indigenous Peoples' History,* 144–45; Richard G. Hardorff, ed., *Washita Memories: Eyewitness Views of Custer's Attack on Black Kettle's Village* (Norman, 2006); Cozzens, *The Earth Is Weeping,* 112.

9. *TI,* April 11, 1872, May 15, July 31, 1873; Robert A. Williams Jr., *The American Indian in Western Legal Thought: The Discourses of Conquest* (New York, 1990); Francis Paul Prucha, *American Indian Treaties: The History of a Political Anomaly* (Berkeley, 1994); Maggie Blackhawk, "Federal Indian Law as Paradigm within Public Law," *Harvard Law Review* 132 (May 2019): 1787–1848.

10. C. Joseph Genetin-Pilawa, *Crooked Paths to Allotment: The Fight over Federal Indian Policy after the Civil War* (Chapel Hill, 2012), chaps. 3–5; *Fourth Annual Report of the Board of Indian Commissioners to the President of the United States* (Washington, 1872); Paul R. Wylie, *Blood on the Marias: The Baker Massacre* (Norman, 2016); April Rubin, "Massacre Leader's Name Is Removed from Yellowstone Mountain," *NYT,* June 13, 2022; Cozzens, *The Earth Is Weeping,* 153; *TI,* March 31, June 23, 1870, April 27, September 7, November 30, 1871, January 18, April 11, 1872, April 24, June 5, 19, October 23, 1873; Karl Jacoby, *Shadows at Dawn: A Borderlands Massacre and the Violence of History* (New York, 2008); Robert Aquinas McNally, *The Modoc War: A Story of Genocide at the Dawn of America's Gilded Age* (Lincoln, 2017); *NASS,* February 26, 1870; S. C. Gwynne, *Empire of the Summer Moon: Quanah Parker and the Rise and Fall of the Comanches, the Most Powerful Indian Tribe in American History* (New York, 2010).

11. Jeffrey Ostler, *The Plains Sioux and U.S. Colonialism from Lewis and Clark to Wounded Knee* (Cambridge, 2004); Adam Arenson, "John Gast's American Progress: Using Manifest Destiny to Forget the Civil War and Reconstruction," in Virginia Scharff, ed., *Empire and Liberty: The Civil War and the West* (Oakland, 2015), 122–39; Alrutheus Ambush Taylor, *The Negro in Tennessee, 1865–1880* (Washington, 1941), 61; *TC,* July 8, 1876; Elizabeth B. Custer, *"Boots and Saddles" or Life in Dakota with General Custer* (New York, 1885), 262–70; Nathaniel Philbrick, *The Last Stand: Custer, Sitting Bull, and the Battle of the Little Bighorn* (New York, 2010); T. J. Stiles, *Custer's Trials: A Life on the Frontier of a New America* (New York, 2015); Carol Reardon, *Pickett's Charge in History and Memory* (Chapel Hill, 1997); Shirley A. Leckie, *Elizabeth Bacon Custer and the Making of a Myth* (Norman, 1993), part 2; Vine Deloria Jr., *Custer Died for Your Sins: An Indian Manifesto* (New York, 1969); Robert M. Utley, *Sitting Bull: The Life and Times of an American Patriot* (New York, 1993); Peter

Nabokov and Lawrence Loendorf, *Restoring a Presence: American Indians and Yellowstone National Park* (Norman, 2004); Megan Kate Nelson, *Saving Yellowstone: Exploration and Preservation in Reconstruction America* (New York, 2022); Frederick E. Hoxie, *Parading through History: The Making of the Crow Nation in America, 1805–1935* (Cambridge, 1995).

12. Elliott West, *The Last Indian War: The Nez Perce Story* (New York, 2009), 87, 241, 282, 292; "Nez Perce Stage Blessing Ceremony on Traditional Homeland," Associated Press, July 30, 2021; Robert M. Utley, *Frontier Regulars: The United States Army and the Indian, 1866–1891* (Lincoln, 1973); *TC*, October 28, November 9, 1876.

13. Edwin R. Sweeney, *From Cochise to Geronimo: The Chiricahua Apaches, 1874–1886* (Norman, 2010); Stephen M. Barrett, *Geronimo's Story of His Life* (Wentworth, 2016); James McLaughlin, *My Friend the Indian* (Boston, 1910), dedication, preface, chap. 12; William S. E. Coleman, *Voices of Wounded Knee* (Lincoln, 2000); Ostler, *The Plains Sioux and U.S. Colonialism,* part 3; Brown, *Bury My Heart at Wounded Knee,* 416–45; Heather Cox Richardson, *Wounded Knee: Party Politics and the Road to an American Massacre* (New York, 2010); James Mooney, *The Ghost-Dance Religion and the Sioux Outbreak of 1890,* in *Fourteenth Annual Report of the Bureau of Ethnology to the Secretary of the Smithsonian Institution 1892–93,* by J. W. Powell, Director, part 2 (Washington, 1896), 886; John Taliaferro, *Great White Fathers: The Story of the Obsessive Quest to Create Mount Rushmore* (New York, 2002); Pekka Hämäläinen, *Lakota America: A New History of Indigenous Power* (New Haven, 2019); David Grua, *Surviving Wounded Knee: The Lakotas and the Politics of Memory* (New York, 2016).

14. William H. and Shirley A. Leckie, *The Buffalo Soldiers: A Narrative of the Black Cavalry in the West* (1967; rev. ed., Norman, 2012); Charles L. Kenner, *Buffalo Soldiers and Officers of the Ninth Cavalry, 1867–1898: Black and White Together* (Norman, 1990); William T. Hagan, *Indian Police and Judges: Experiments in Acculturation and Control* (New Haven, 1966; reprint, Lincoln, 1980).

15. Brig. Gen. R. H. Pratt, *The Indian Industrial School, Carlisle, Pennsylvania: Its Origin, Purposes, Progress and Difficulties Surmounted* (Carlisle, 1908), 7–9, 18–21, 36–37; Richard Henry Pratt, *Battlefield and Classroom: Four Decades with the American Indian, 1867–1904,* ed. Robert M. Utley (Norman, 1964); Cristina Snyder, *Great Crossings: Indians, Settlers, and Slaves in the Age of Jackson* (New York, 2019), chap. 12; Frederick E. Hoxie, *A Final Promise: The Campaign to Assimilate the Indians, 1880–1920* (Lincoln, 1984); Ward Churchill, *Kill the Indian, Save the Man* (San Francisco, 2004); David Wallace Adams, *Education for Extinction: American Indians and the Boarding School Experience, 1875–1928* (Lawrence, 1995); Margaret D. Jacobs, *White Mother to a Dark Race: Settler Colonialism, Maternalism, and the Removal of Indigenous Children in the American West and Australia, 1880–1940* (Lincoln, 2009); Thomas Babington Macaulay, "Minute" (February 2, 1835), in H. Sharp, ed., *Selections from Educational Records,* part 1, 1789–1839 (Calcutta, 1920), 107–17; Catherine Hall, *Macaulay and Son: Architects of an Imperial Britain* (New Haven, 2012).

16. Sidney L. Harring, *Crow Dog's Case: American Indian Sovereignty, Tribal Law, and United States Law in the Nineteenth Century* (Cambridge, 1994); Blackhawk, "Federal Indian Law as Paradigm within Public Law," 1811–15; Chang, *The Color of the Land*; Philip J. Deloria, "American Master Narratives and the Problem of Indian Citizenship in the Gilded Age," *Journal of the Gilded Age and Progressive Era* 14 (2015), 3–12; Cathleen D. Cahill, *Federal Fathers and Mothers: A Social History of the United States*

Indian Service, 1869–1933 (Chapel Hill, 2013); Stephen J. Rockwell, *Indian Affairs and the Administrative State in the Nineteenth Century* (Cambridge, 2010), 1, 246–328.

17. *NYT*, November 29, 1862; *NASS*, January 1, February 26, 1870; Joy, "The Indian's Cause," 215–42; John Beeson, *A Plea for the Indians; with Facts and Features of the Late War in Oregon* (New York, 1857), 10, 14–17, 23–30, 32–56, 100–15, 124–33; John Beeson, *Are We Not Men and Brethren? An Address to the People of the United States* [1859]; John Beeson, *The Calumet*, New York (February 1860), 29; John Beeson *To the American Public*, Fort Gibson, Indian Territory (January 12, 1874).

18. Lydia Maria Child, *An Appeal for the Indians* (New York, 1868): 3–8, 10, 14; Linda K. Kerber, "The Abolitionist Perception of the Indian," *JAH* 62 (September 1975): 271–95; Helen Hunt Jackson, *A Century of Dishonor: A Sketch of the United States Government's Dealing with Some of the Indian Tribes* (Boston, 1881); Kate Phillips, *Helen Hunt Jackson: A Literary Life* (Berkeley, 2003); Valerie Sherer Mathes, ed., *Indian Reform Letters of Helen Hunt Jackson, 1879–1885* (Norman, 2015).

19. Genetin-Pilawa, *Crooked Paths to Allotment*, chap. 6; *Preamble, Platform, and Constitution of the National Indian Defense Association* (Washington, 1885); Eileen Pollack, *Woman Walking Ahead: In Search of Catherine Weldon and Sitting Bull* (Albuquerque, 2004); Utley, *The Indian Frontier*, chap. 7; Francis Paul Prucha, *American Indian Policy in Crisis: Christian Reformers and the Indian, 1865–1900* (Norman, 1977); *TIW*, January 25, April 26, 1873; William T. Hagan, *The Indian Rights Association: The Herbert Welsh Years, 1882–1904* (Tucson, 1985); Thomas C. Battey, *The Life and Adventures of a Quaker among the Indians* (Boston, 1875), 41, 58–59, 64–70, 90–92, 101–4, 123–28, 180–83.

20. Daniel to Caroline Grant, Arkansas City, June 4, 1872, Grant-Burr Family Papers, AAS; *The Colorado Miner*, January 18, 1872; *The Philadelphia Inquirer*, September 15, 1908; *Baltimore American*, April 18, 1909. Thanks to Hunt Howell for tracing the possible afterlives of this poem.

CHAPTER TEN: THE REIGN OF CAPITAL

1. Jack Beatty, *Age of Betrayal: The Triumph of Money in America, 1865–1900* (New York, 2007); H. W. Brands, *American Colossus: The Triumph of Capitalism, 1865–1890* (New York, 2010); Douglass C. North, *The Economic Growth of the United States, 1790–1860* (New York, 1966); Bruce Laurie, *Artisans into Workers: Labor in Nineteenth-Century America* (New York, 1989); Gunther W. Peck, *Reinventing Free Labor: Padrones and Immigrant Workers in the North American West, 1885–1930* (Cambridge, 2000).

2. Eric Foner, *Reconstruction: America's Unfinished Revolution, 1863–1877* (New York, 1988), chap. 10; Heather Cox Richardson, *The Death of Reconstruction: Race, Labor, and Politics in the Post–Civil War North, 1865–1901* (Cambridge, MA, 2005).

3. *WCW*, May 21, December 3, 1870, January 21, 28, February 4, March 11, 18, April 1, 1871, January 6, 1872; *TI*, June 29, 1871, June 13, 1872; Foner, *Reconstruction*, 460–88; James C. Sylvis, *The Life, Speeches, Labors and Essays of William H. Sylvis* (Philadelphia, 1872), 82, 284–95, 319–29; David Roediger, "Ira Steward and the Anti-Slavery Origins of American Eight-Hour Theory," *LH* 27 (Summer 1986): 410–26; *NNE*, January 19, February 16, 1871; David R. Roediger and Philip S. Foner, *Our Own Time: A History of American Labor and the Working Day* (Westport, 1989), chaps. 5, 6; David Montgomery, *Beyond Equality: Labor and the Radical Republicans, 1862–1872* (New

York, 1967), 123–24, 447; Alex Gourevitch, *From Slavery to the Cooperative Commonwealth: Labor and Republican Liberty in the Nineteenth Century* (Cambridge, 2015); Richard White, *Railroaded: The Transcontinentals and the Making of Modern America* (New York, 2011).

4. [Karl Marx], *Defence of the Paris Commune. Address of the General Council of "The International" to the Working Men of Europe and America* (Washington, 1871), 3, 6–15; *NNE*, June 1, 8, 1871; *TI*, April 20, May 18, August 24, 1871; *WCW*, December 3, 1870, December 9, 16, 30, 1871, January 6, April 27, 1872, March 22, May 10, 1874; Mark A. Lause, "The American Radicals & Organized Marxism: The Initial Experience, 1869–1874," *LH* 33 (1992): 55–80; Philip M. Katz, *From Appomattox to Montmarte: Americans and the Paris Commune* (Cambridge, MA, 1998); Timothy Messer-Kruse, *The Yankee International, 1846–1876: Marxism and the American Reform Tradition* (Chapel Hill, 1998).

5. *NNE*, April 20, 1871; *TI*, November 23, 1871, December 25, 1873; Kevin Kenny, *Making Sense of the Molly Maguires* (New York, 1998), 180–81; Mitchell Snay, *Fenians, Freedmen, and Southern Whites: Race and Nationality in the Era of Reconstruction* (Baton Rouge, 2007), chaps. 3–5; Eric Foner, "Class, Ethnicity, and Radicalism in the Gilded Age: The Land League and Irish America," in *Politics and Ideology in the Age of the Civil War* (New York, 1980), 150–200.

6. James D. McCabe, *The History of the Great Riots: Being A Full and Authentic Account of the Strikes and Riots on the Various Railroads of the United States and in the Mining Regions* (Philadelphia, 1877); *TC*, July 28, August 4, 1877; Philip S. Foner, *American Labor Songs of the Nineteenth Century* (Urbana, 1975), 133; Philip S. Foner, *The Great Labor Uprising of 1877* (New York, 1977); *WCW*, November 19, 1870; Michael A. Belleisles, *1877: America's Year of Living Violently* (New York, 2010), chap. 5; Nick Salvatore, *Eugene V. Debs: Citizen and Socialist* (Urbana, 1984), chaps. 3–4; Walter Johnson, *The Broken Heart of America: St Louis and the Violent History of the United States* (New York, 2020), 155–61.

7. Chad E. Pearson, *Capital's Terrorists: Klansmen, Lawmen and Employers in the Long Nineteenth Century* (Chapel Hill, 2022); *NLT*, June 27, 1874.

8. *TC*, December 23, 1876, January 13, 20, February 3, March 3, 10, May 5, August 4, 11, 18, October 13, 1877; *William Lloyd Garrison, 1805–1879. The Story of His Life Told by His Children*, vol. 4, 1861–1879 (New York, 1889), 248–49; Steven B. Leikin, *The Practical Utopians: American Workers and the Cooperative Movement in the Gilded Age* (Detroit, 2005); James T. Kloppenberg, *Uncertain Victory: Social Democracy and Progressivism in European and American Thought, 1870–1920* (New York, 1986); Daniel T. Rodgers, *Atlantic Crossings: Social Politics in a Progressive Age* (Cambridge, MA, 2000).

9. Henry George, *Progress and Poverty: An Inquiry into the Cause of Industrial Depressions and of Increase of Want with Increase of Wealth . . . The Remedy* (New York, 1979 centennial ed.), xxviii, xxx, 12–13, 50–70, 117–28, 166–68, 260, 274–75, 282–88, 328–57, 405–7, 440–46, 530–45; Laurence Gronlund, *The Cooperative Commonwealth* (Boston, 1984); Edward T. O'Donnell, *Henry George and the Crisis of Inequality: Progress and Poverty in the Gilded Age* (New York, 2015).

10. *NLT*, November 4, 1876; Mark A. Lause, *The Civil War's Last Campaign: James B. Weaver, the Greenback-Labor Party & the Politics of Race & Section* (Lanham, 2001); Sylvis, ed., *The Life, Speeches, Labors and Essays of William H. Sylvis,* 82, 341, 344; *WCW*, July 9, 1870, September 20, 1873; Philip S. Foner and Ronald L. Lewis, eds.,

The Black Worker: A Documentary History from the Colonial Times to the Present, vol. 2, *The Black Worker During the Era of the National Labor Union* (Philadelphia, 1978), 2–4, 32–33, 36–74, 101–8, 242–50, 287; Nikki M. Taylor, *America's First Black Socialist: The Radical Life of Peter H. Clark* (Lexington, 2013).

11. T. V. Powderly, *Thirty Years of Labor. 1859 to 1889* (Columbus, 1889), 135–38, 147–60, 309–27, 412–33, 493–508, 527–58, 651–62; Leon Fink, *Workingmen's Democracy: The Knights of Labor and American Politics* (Urbana, 1983); *The Path I Trod: The Autobiography of Terence V. Powderly*, ed. Harry J. Carman, Henry David, and Paul N. Guthrie (New York, 1940), vii–xi, 114–62; Foner, *American Labor Songs,* 158, 228; Craig Phelan, *Grand Master Workman: Terence Powderly and the Knights of Labor* (Westport, 2000); Susan Levine, "Labor's True Woman: Domesticity and Equal Rights in the Knights of Labor," *JAH* 70 (September 1983): 323–39; Theresa A. Case, *The Great Southwest Strike and Free Labor* (College Station, 2010); Melton McLaurin, *The Knights of Labor in the South* (Westport, 1978); Roediger and Foner, *Our Own Time,* chap. 7; George Frederic Parsons, "The Labor Question," *The Atlantic Monthly* 58 (July 1886): 97–113; James Green, *Death in the Haymarket: A Story of Chicago, the First Labor Movement, and the Bombing That Divided Gilded Age America* (New York, 2006); Jacqueline Jones, *Goddess of Anarchy: The Life and Times of Lucy Parsons, American Radical* (New York, 2017), 112–38; John DeSantis, *The Thibodaux Massacre: Racial Violence and the 1887 Sugar Cane Labor Strike* (Charleston, 2016); Julie Greene, *Pure and Simple Politics: The American Federation of Labor and Political Activism, 1881–1917* (Cambridge, 1998).

12. T. Thomas Fortune, *Black and White: Land, Labor, and Politics in the South* (New York, 1884), preface, 235; Emma Lou Thornbrough, *T. Thomas Fortune: Militant Journalist* (Chicago, 1972); Robin D. G. Kelley, "Abolition Democracy's Forgotten Founding Father," *Boston Review,* April 19, 2022; Edward Bellamy, *Looking Backward, 2000–1887* (Boston, 1888), 78–80, 97–99, 119, 201–20, 260–74, 287, 353–55; Edward Bellamy, *Plutocracy or Nationalism—Which?* (n.p., 1889), 3–11; Edward Bellamy, *Equality* (New York, 1897); Foner, ed., *American Labor Songs,* 130; Henry Demarest Lloyd, *Wealth against Commonwealth* (New York, 1894), 2–7, 432, 510–15; Richard Digby-Junger, *The Journalist as Reformer: Henry Demarest Lloyd and Wealth against Commonwealth* (Westport, 1996); John Thomas, *Alternative America: Henry George, Edward Bellamy, Henry Demarest Lloyd and the Adversary Tradition* (Cambridge, MA, 1983); Sidney Fine, *Laissez Faire and the General-Welfare State: A Study of Conflict in American Thought, 1865–1901* (Ann Arbor, 1956).

13. David Montgomery, *The Fall of the House of Labor: The Workplace, the State, and American Labor Activism, 1865–1925* (Cambridge, 1987); Leon Fink, *The Long Gilded Age: American Capitalism and the Lessons of a New World Order* (Philadelphia, 2015), 36–53; Foner, ed., *American Labor Songs,* 243, 246; Paul Krause, *The Battle for Homestead, 1880–1892: Politics, Culture, and Steel* (Pittsburgh, 1992); Salvatore, *Eugene V. Debs,* part 2; Almont Lindsey, *The Pullman Strike: The Story of a Unique Experiment and a Great Labor Upheaval* (Chicago, 1943); Henry Vincent, *The Story of the Commonweal* (Chicago, 1894), 11, 125–73, 194–95; Benjamin F. Alexander, *Coxey's Army: Popular Protest in the Gilded Age* (Baltimore, 2015); Jerry Prout, *Coxey's Crusade for Jobs: Unemployment in the Gilded Age* (DeKalb, 2016); Mathew E. Stanley, *Grand Army of Labor: Workers, Veterans, and the Meaning of the Civil War* (Urbana, 2021); James Weinstein, *The Corporate Ideal in the Liberal State, 1900–1918* (Boston, 1968); Gabriel Kolko, *The Triumph of Conservatism: A Reinterpretation of American History, 1900–1916* (New York, 1963); Christopher L. Tomlins, *The State and the*

Unions: Labor Relations, Law, and the Organized Labor Movement in America, 1880–1960 (Cambridge, 1985); Martin J. Sklar, *The Corporate Reconstruction of American Capitalism, 1890–1916: The Market, the Law, and Politics* (Cambridge, 1988).

14. Eric Arnesen, *Brotherhoods of Color: Black Railroad Workers and the Struggle for Equality* (Cambridge, MA, 2001); David R. Roediger, *The Wages of Whiteness: Race and the Making of the American Working Class* (New York, 1991); Alice Kessler-Harris, *Out to Work: The History of Wage-Earning Women in the United States* (1982; reprint, New York, 2003); William H. Harris, *The Harder We Run: Black Workers since the Civil War* (New York, 1982); Herbert Hill, *Black Labor and the American Legal System: Race, Work and the Law*, vol. 1 (Washington, 1977); Herbert G. Gutman, *Work, Culture & Society in Industrializing America* (New York, 1966), chap. 3.

CHAPTER ELEVEN: AMERICAN EMPIRE

1. Harvey J. Kaye, *Thomas Paine and the Promise of America* (New York, 2005), introduction; Perry Miller, *Errand into the Wilderness* (New York, 1956); Abram Van Engen, *City on a Hill: A History of American Exceptionalism* (New Haven, 2020).
2. Don E. Fehrenbacher, *The Slaveholding Republic: An Account of the United States Government's Relations to Slavery* (New York, 2001); Samantha Seeley, *Race, Removal, and the Right to Remain: Migration and the Making of the United States* (Chapel Hill, 2021); Paul Frymer, *Building an American Empire: The Era of Territorial and Political Expansion* (Princeton, 2017); Walter Nugent, *Habits of Empire: A History of American Expansion* (New York, 2008).
3. Michael H. Hunt, *The American Ascendancy: How the United States Gained and Wielded Global Dominance* (Chapel Hill, 2007); Frank Ninkovich, *The Global Republic: America's Inadvertent Rise to World Power* (Chicago, 2014).
4. Gunther Peck, *Reinventing Free Labor: Padrones and Immigrant Workers in the North American West, 1880–1930* (Cambridge, 2000); Kris Manjapra, *Colonialism in Global Perspective* (Cambridge, 2020), 114–22; Moon Ho-Jung, *Coolies and Cane: Race, Labor, and Sugar in the Age of Emancipation* (Baltimore, 2006); Andres Resendez, *The Other Slavery: The Uncovered Story of Indian Enslavement in America* (New York, 2016); Pete Daniel, *The Shadow of Slavery: Peonage in the South, 1901–1969* (New York, 1972); *Anti-Slavery Reporter* 20, January 1, 1876, 14–15, April 1, 1876, 46, September 1, 1876, 130–39, November 1, 1876, 158–59, March 1, 1877, 216–18; Madhavi Kale, *Fragments of Empire: Capital, Slavery, and Indian Indentured Labor Migration in the British Caribbean* (Philadelphia, 1998); Mrinalini Sinha, "The Anatomy of a Politics of a People," in Manu Goswami & Mrinalini Sinha, eds., *Political Imaginaries in 20th Century India* (London, 2022), 31–50; Joel Quirk, *The Anti-Slavery Project: from the Slave Trade to Human Trafficking* (Philadelphia, 2011).
5. Mae Ngai, *The Chinese Question: The Gold Rushes and Global Politics* (New York, 2021); Lucy E. Salyer, "Reconstructing the Immigrant: The Naturalization Act of 1870 in Global Perspective," *JCWE* 11 (September 2021): 382–405; Lucy E. Salyer, *Under the Starry Flag: How a Band of Irish Americans Joined the Fenian Revolt and Sparked a Crisis over Citizenship* (Cambridge, MA, 2018); Kevin Waite, *West of Slavery: The Southern Dream of a Transcontinental Empire* (Chapel Hill, 2021), chap. 8; Stacey L. Smith, *Freedom's Frontier: California and the Struggle over Unfree Labor, Emancipation, and Reconstruction* (Chapel Hill, 2011); *CR*, Forty-Third Congress, Session 2 (March 3, 1875), chap. 14.

6. *TC*, July 1, August 12, 1876, September 1, 22, 1877; *TI*, March 3, July 21, August 25, 1870, July 20, 1871; *William Lloyd Garrison, 1805–1879: The Story of His Life Told By His Children, 1861–1879* (New York, 1889), 4:293–304; *NYT*, March 2, 1882; G. B. Densmore, *The Chinese in California: Description of Chinese Life in San Francisco, Their Habits, Morals, and Manners* (San Francisco, 1880); Alexander Saxton, *The Indispensable Enemy: Labor and the Anti-Chinese Movement in California* (Berkeley, 1971); Najia Aarim-Heriot, *Chinese Immigrants, African Americans, and Racial Anxiety in the United States, 1848–1882* (Urbana, 2003); Edlie L. Wong, *Racial Reconstruction: Black Inclusion, Chinese Exclusion, and the Fictions of Citizenship* (New York, 2015); Beth Lew Williams, *The Chinese Must Go: Violence, Exclusion, and the Making of the Alien in America* (Cambridge, MA, 2018); *The Wasp*, January 7, 16, March 31, 8–9, June 9, 16, 1888; Robert Moore, "He Won a Landmark Citizenship Case at the US Supreme Court. El Paso Tried to Deport Him Anyway," *El Paso Matters*, July 4, 2022; Erika Lee, *At America's Gates: Chinese Immigration during the Exclusion Era, 1882–1943* (Chapel Hill, 2003); Mae M. Ngai, *Impossible Subjects: Illegal Aliens and the Making of Modern America* (Princeton, 2004); William Lloyd Garrison Jr., "Chinese Exclusion," *The Advocate of Peace* (February 1902), 35–39; Matthew Frye Jacobson, *Barbarian Virtues: The United States Encounters Foreign Peoples at Home and Abroad, 1876–1917* (New York, 2000).

7. Evelyn Atkinson, "Slaves, Coolies, and Shareholders: Corporations Claim the Fourteenth Amendment," *JCWE* 10 (March 2020): 54–80; Christopher L. Tomlins, *Law, Labor, and Ideology in the Early American Republic* (New York, 1993); Manisha Sinha, "First as Farce, Then as Tragedy," *Jacobin*, December 4, 2018; Thomas Hartmann, *Unequal Protection: How Corporations Became "People"—And How You can Fight Back* (San Francisco, 2009).

8. Christian G. Samito, ed., *Changes in Law and Society During the Civil War and Reconstruction* (Carbondale, 2009): 285–309; Pamela Brandwein, *Rethinking the Judicial Settlement of Reconstruction* (Cambridge, 2011); John H. Bracey Jr. and Manisha Sinha, eds., *African American Mosaic: A Documentary History from the Slave Trade to the Twenty-First Century* (Upper Saddle River, 2004), 1:379; Rebecca J. Scott, "Discerning a Dignitary Offense: The Concept of Equal 'Public Rights' during Reconstruction," *Law and History Review* 38 (August 2020): 519–53; *Justice and Jurisprudence: An Inquiry Concerning the Constitutional Limitations of the Thirteenth, Fourteenth, and Fifteenth Amendments* (Philadelphia, 1889), i–ii; Eric Foner, *The Second Founding: How the Civil War and Reconstruction Remade the Constitution* (New York, 2019), chap. 4; Blair L. M. Kelley, *Right to Ride: Streetcar Boycotts and African American Citizenship in the Era of Plessy v. Ferguson* (Chapel Hill, 2010); Melissa Milewski, *Litigating Across the Color Line: Civil Cases Between Black and White Southerners from the End of Slavery to Civil Rights* (New York, 2018).

9. Jane Dailey, *Before Jim Crow: The Politics of Race in Postemancipation Virginia* (Chapel Hill, 2000); Eric Anderson, *Race and Politics in North Carolina, 1872–1901: The Black Second* (Baton Rouge, 1980); Gordon B. McKinney, "Southern Mountain Republicans and the Negro, 1865–1900," *JSH* 41 (November 1975): 493–516; Lawrence Goodwyn, *Democratic Promise: The Populist Moment in America* (New York, 1976); Mathew Hild, *Greenbackers, Knights of Labor, and Populists: Farmer-Labor Insurgency in the Late Nineteenth-Century South* (Athens, 2007); Omar H. Ali, *In the Lion's Mouth: Black Populism in the New South, 1886–1900* (Jackson, 2010); Charles

Postel, *The Populist Vision* (New York, 2007); Michael Kazin, *A Godly Hero: The Life of William Jennings Bryan* (New York, 2006).

10. J. Morgan Kousser, *The Shaping of Southern Politics: Suffrage Restriction and the Establishment of the One-Party South, 1880–1910* (New Haven, 1974); Dorothy O. Pratt, *Sowing the Wind: The Mississippi Constitutional Convention of 1890* (Jackson, 2017); Michael Perman, *Struggle for Mastery: Disfranchisement in the South, 1888–1908* (Chapel Hill, 2001); *Speeches at the Constitutional Convention, by Gen. Robt. Smalls with the Right of Suffrage Passed by the Constitutional Convention. Compiled by Miss Sarah V. Smalls* (Charleston, 1896), 8–9; Henry Cabot Lodge, "The Federal Election Bill," *North American Review* 151 (September 1890): 257–63; Henry Cabot Lodge, "Obstruction in the Senate," *North American Review* 157 (November 1893): 423–29; Richard E. Welch Jr., "The Federal Elections Bill of 1890: Postscripts and Prelude," *JAH* 52 (December 1965): 511–26; J. Jenkins and J. Peck, "The Blair Education Bill: A Lost Opportunity in American Public Education," *Studies in American Political Development* 35 (April 2021): 146–70; Samito, ed., *Changes in Law and Society*, 310–21; Steve Luxenberg, *Separate: The Story of Plessy v. Ferguson, and America's Journey from Slavery to Segregation* (New York, 2019); Mark Elliot, *Color-Blind Justice: Albion Tourgee and the Quest for Racial Equality from the Civil War to Plessy v. Ferguson* (New York, 2006).

11. Helen G. Edmonds, *The Negro and Fusion Politics in North Carolina, 1894–1901* (1951; reprint, Chapel Hill, 2013); H. Leon Prather Sr., *We Have Taken a City: The Wilmington Racial Massacre and Coup of 1898* (1984; reprint, New York, 2006); David S. Cecelski and Timothy B. Tyson, eds., *Democracy Betrayed: The Wilmington Riot of 1898 and Its Legacy* (Chapel Hill, 1998); LaRae Sikes Umfleet, *A Day of Blood: The 1898 Wilmington Race Riot* (2009; revised, Raleigh, 2020); David Zucchino, *Wilmington's Lie: The Murderous Coup of 1898 and the Rise of White Supremacy* (New York, 2020); Bracey and Sinha, eds., *African American Mosaic*, 1:393–94.

12. Charles W. Chesnutt, *The Marrow of Tradition* (Boston, 1901), 25, 37–38, 91–92, 192. I am flipping the script of James C. Scott, *Seeing Like a State: How Certain Schemes to Improve the Human Condition Have Failed* (New Haven, 1998); Jack Thorne, *Hanover; or, The Persecution of the Lowly. Story of the Wilmington Massacre*, e-edition, https://docsouth.unc.edu/nc/thorne/thorne.html 4–5; David Cecelski, "The Sons and Daughters of North Carolina," blogposts, https://davidcecelski.com; Alfred Moore Waddell, *Some Memoirs of My Life* (Raleigh, 1908), 242–43.

13. Edward A. Pollard, *Black Diamonds Gathered in the Darkey Homes of the South* (New York, 1859); *The Lost Cause: A New Southern History of the War of the Confederates* (Baltimore, 1866); *The Lost Cause Regained* (New York, 1868), 14; Alexander H. Stephens, *A Constitutional View of the Late War Between the States . . . in Two Volumes* (Philadelphia, 1868, 1870); Jefferson Davis, *The Rise and Fall of the Confederate Government*, vols. 1–2 (New York, 1881); K. Stephen Prince, *Stories of the South: Race and the Reconstruction of Southern Identity, 1865–1915* (Chapel Hill, 2016); Nina Silber, *The Romance of Reunion: Northerners and the South, 1865–1900* (Chapel Hill, 1993); Brook Thomas, *The Literature of Reconstruction: Not in Black and White* (Baltimore, 2017); David W. Blight, *Race and Reunion: The Civil War in American Memory* (Cambridge, MA, 2001); W. Fitzhugh Brundage, *The Southern Past: A Clash of Race and Memory* (Cambridge, MA, 2005); Caroline Janney, *Remembering the Civil War: Reunion and the Limits of Reconciliation* (Chapel Hill, 2013); Barbara A. Gannon, *The Won Cause: Black and White Comradeship in the Grand Army of the Republic* (Chapel

Hill, 2011); Karen L. Cox, *Dixie's Daughters: The United Daughters of the Confederacy and the Preservation of Confederate Culture* (Gainesville, 2003); Adam H. Domby, *The False Cause: Fraud, Fabrication, and White Supremacy in Confederate Memory* (Charlottesville, 2020); Sarah Gardner, *Blood and Irony: Southern White Women's Narratives of the Civil War, 1861–1937* (Chapel Hill, 2004); Bruce Baker, *What Reconstruction Meant: Historical Memory in the American South* (Charlottesville, 2007); John David Smith, *An Old Creed for the New South: Proslavery Ideology and Historiography, 1865–1918* (Westport, 1985).

14. Manisha Sinha, "Of Scientific Racists and Black Abolitionists: The Forgotten Debate over Slavery and Race," in *To Make Their Own Way in the World: The Enduring Legacy of the Zealey Daguerreotypes*, ed. Ilisa Barbash, Molly Rogers, Deborah Willis (Cambridge, MA, 2020): 235–58; Hinton Rowan Helper, *Nojuque: A Question for a Continent* (New York, 1867); Albion Tourgee, *A Fool's Errand* (New York, 1876), 120; Henry Louis Gates Jr., *Stony the Road: Reconstruction, White Supremacy, and the Rise of Jim Crow* (New York, 2019), chaps. 2–3; Richard Hofstadter, *Social Darwinism in American Thought* (Boston, 1944); William Graham Sumner, *What Social Classes Owe to Each Other* (New York, 1883); W.E.B. Du Bois, *The Souls of Black Folk* (New York, 1903).

15. Jimmy M. Skaggs, *The Great Guano Rush: Entrepreneurs and American Overseas Expansion* (New York, 1994); Nugent, *Habits of Empire*, 238–53; Walter LaFeber, *The New Empire: An Interpretation of American Expansion, 1860–1898* (Ithaca, 1963); Walter Johnson, *River of Dark Dreams: Slavery and Empire in the Cotton Kingdom* (Cambridge, MA, 2013).

16. Robert E. May, *Slavery, Race and the Conquest of the Tropics: Lincoln, Douglas, and the Future of Latin America* (Cambridge, 2013); Evan C. Rothera, *Civil Wars and Reconstructions in the Americas: The United States, Mexico, and Argentina, 1860–1880* (Baton Rouge, 2022); Edward L. Pierce, *Memoir and Letters of Charles Sumner*, vol. 4, 1860–1874 (Boston, 1893), 416; Gregory P. Downs, *The Second American Revolution: The Civil War–Era Struggle over Cuba and the Rebirth of the American Republic* (Chapel Hill, 2019); Christopher Schmidt-Nowara, *Empire and Antislavery: Spain, Cuba and Puerto Rico, 1833–1874* (Pittsburgh, 1999); Ada Ferrer, *Insurgent Cuba: Race, Nation, and Revolution, 1868–1898* (Chapel Hill, 1999); Rebecca J. Scott, *Slave Emancipation in Cuba: The Transition to Free Labor, 1860–1899* (Princeton, 1986); James M. Shinn Jr., "The 'Free Cuba' Campaign, Republican Politics, and Post–Civil War Black Internationalism," in *Revolutions and Reconstructions: Black Politics in the Long Nineteenth Century*, eds. Van Gosse and David Waldstreicher (Philadelphia, 2020), Angela Alonso, *The Last Abolition: The Brazilian Antislavery Movement, 1868–1888* (Cambridge, 2022); Celso Thomas Castilho, *Slave Emancipations and Transformations in Brazilian Political Citizenship* (Pittsburgh, 2016); Isadora Mota, "On the Imminence of Emancipation: Black Geopolitical Literacy and Anglo-American Abolitionism in Nineteenth Century Brazil," PhD diss., Brown University, 2017; Samantha Payne, "The Last Atlantic Revolution: Reconstruction and the Struggle for Democracy in the Americas, 1861–1912," PhD diss., Harvard University, 2022.

17. David M. Wrobel, *Global West, American Frontier: Travel, Empire, and Exceptionalism from Manifest Destiny to the Great Depression* (Albuquerque, 2013), 22–27; John David Smith and J. Vincent Lowery, eds., *The Dunning School: Historians, Race, and the Meaning of Reconstruction* (Lexington, 2013); Silber, *The Romance of Reunion*, 181; Mark Elliot, "The Lessons of Reconstruction: Debating Race and Imperialism in

the 1890s," in *Remembering Reconstruction: Struggles over the Meaning of America's Most Turbulent Era*, eds. Carole Emberton and Bruce E. Baker (Baton Rouge, 2017), 139–72; Marilyn Lake and Henry Reynolds, *Drawing the Global Color Line: White Men's Countries and the International Challenge of Racial Equality* (Cambridge, 2008), chap. 2; Murat Halstead, *The Story of the Philippines and Our New Possessions* (Chicago, 1898), 11, 58–59, 92–101, 166; Philip S. Foner, *The Spanish-Cuban-American War and the Birth of American Imperialism*, vol. 1: 1895–1898, vol. 2: 1898–1902 (New York, 1972); Jesse Hoffnung-Garskof, *Racial Migrations: New York City and the Revolutionary Politics of the Spanish Caribbean* (Princeton, 2019); William B. Gatewood Jr., *"Smoked Yankees" and the Struggle for Empire: Letters from Negro Soldiers, 1898–1902* (Urbana, 1971), 8; Amy Kaplan, *The Anarchy of Empire in the Making of U.S. Culture* (Cambridge, MA, 2002), chap. 4; Kristin Hoganson, *Fighting for American Manhood: How Gender Politics Provoked the Spanish-American-Philippine-American Wars* (New Haven, 1998); Jodi A. Byrd, *The Transit of Empire: Indigenous Critiques of Colonialism* (Minneapolis, 2011); David J. Silbey, *A War of Frontier and Empire: The Philippine-American War, 1899–1902* (New York, 2007); Nugent, *Habits of Empire*, 265–73; Paul A. Kramer, *The Blood of Government: Race, Empire, the United States and the Philippines* (Chapel Hill, 2006); William Manchester, *American Caesar: Douglas MacArthur, 1880–1964* (Boston, 1978).

18. Noam Maggor, *Brahmin Capitalism: Frontiers of Wealth and Populism in America's First Gilded Age* (Cambridge, MA, 2017); Eric Hobsbawm, *The Age of Empire, 1875–1914* (New York, 1989); Tom Coffman, *Nation Within: The Story of America's Annexation of the Nation of Hawaii* (Kenmore, 1998); Noenoe K. Silva, *Aloha Betrayed: Native Hawaiian Resistance to American Colonialism* (Durham, 2004); Nugent, *Habits of Empire*, 256–65, 287–304; *Hawaii's Story by Hawaii's Queen Liliuokalani* (Boston, 1898), 368–69, 371; Ronald T. Takaki, *Pau Hana: Plantation Life and Labor in Hawaii, 1835–1920* (Honolulu, 1984); E. Berkeley Tompkins, *Anti-Imperialism in the United States: The Great Debate, 1890–1920* (Philadelphia, 1970); Philip S. Foner, *Mark Twain: Social Critic* (New York, 1958); *Address Adopted by the Anti-Imperialist League, February 10, 1899* [Boston]; George S. Boutwell, *Reminiscences of Sixty Years in Public Affairs* (New York, 1902), 2:331–34; Eric T. L. Love, *Race over Empire: Race and Imperialism, 1865–1900* (Chapel Hill, 2004); Daniel Immerwahr, *How to Hide an Empire: A History of the Greater United States* (New York, 2019); Kaplan, *The Anarchy of Empire*, 7, 10; Sven Beckert, "American Danger: United States Empire, Euroafrica, and the Territorialization of Industrial Capitalism, 1870–1950," *AHR* 122 (October 2017), 1137–70; A. T. Mahan, "The United States Looking Outward," *The Atlantic Monthly* (December 1890): 816–24; Bartholomew H. Sparrow, "The Public Response to Controversial Supreme Court Decisions: The Insular Cases," *Journal of Supreme Court History* 30 (November 2005): 204; Sam Erman, *Almost Citizens: Puerto Rico, the U.S. Constitution, and Empire* (Cambridge, 2018).

19. Kaplan, *The Anarchy of Empire*, chap. 6; W.E.B. Du Bois, *Darkwater: Voices from Within the Veil* (New York, 1920).

CHAPTER TWELVE: THE LAST RECONSTRUCTION AMENDMENT

1. Aileen S. Kraditor, *The Ideas of the Woman Suffrage Movement, 1890–1920* (New York, 1965), chap. 7; Louise Michele Newman, *White Women's Rights: The Racial Origins of Feminism in the United States* (New York, 1999).

2. Elizabeth Cady Stanton, Susan B. Anthony, and Matilda Joslyn Gage, eds., *History of Woman Suffrage, 1876–1883* (New York, 1886), 3:62; *TWJ*, May 27, 1876.

3. Jane Addams, *Twenty Years at Hull House* (New York, 1912), esp. chaps. 6–7; Louise W. Knight, *Citizen: Jane Addams and the Struggle for Democracy* (New York, 2005); Victoria Bissell Brown, *The Education of Jane Addams* (Philadelphia, 2003); Lillian D. Wald, *The House on Henry Street* (New York, 1915); Lillian D. Wald, *Windows on Henry Street* (Boston, 1934), 24, 31–32, 49–50, 74–109, 128–29; Claire Coss, *Lillian D. Wald: Progressive Activist* (New York, 1989); Doris Gershon Daniels, *Always a Sister: The Feminism of Lillian D. Wald* (New York, 1989); Wendy L. Rouse, *Public Faces, Secret Lives: A Queer History of the Women's Suffrage Movement* (New York, 2022); Meredith Tax, *The Rising of the Woman: Feminist Solidarity and Class Conflict, 1888–1917* (New York, 1980); Linda Gordon, "'Intersectionality,' Socialist Feminism and Contemporary Activism: Musings by a Second Wave Socialist Feminism," *Gender and History* 28 (August 2018): 340–57.

4. Kathryn Kish Sklar, ed., *The Autobiography of Florence Kelley: Notes of Sixty Years* (Chicago, 1986); Florence Kelley *Woman Suffrage in Relation to Working Women and Children* (n.p., n.d.); Florence Kelley, *Some Ethical Gains Through Legislation* (London, 1902); Dorothy Rose Blumberg, "'Dear Mr. Engels': Unpublished Letters, 1884–1894, of Florence Kelley to Frederick Engels," *Labor History* 5 (1964): 103–33; Kathryn Kish Sklar, *Florence Kelley and the Nation's Work: The Rise of Women's Political Culture, 1830–1900* (New Haven, 1995); Alice Kessler-Harris, *Out to Work: The History of Wage-Earning Women in the United States* (New York, 1982), chap. 7; Wald, *Windows on Henry Street,* 330–32; Lara Vapnek, *Breadwinners: Working Women and Economic Independence, 1865–1920* (Urbana, 2009).

5. August Bebel, *Woman under Socialism*, trans. Daniel De Leon (New York, 1904), 320, 354; Frederick (Friedrich) Engels, *The Origin of the Family, Private Property and the State* (Chicago, 1902): 70–99; Florence Kelley, *Modern Industry in Relation to the Family, Health, Education, and Morality* (London, 1914).

6. Elizabeth Cady Stanton, *The Matriarchate or Mother-Age* (n.p., 1891); Elizabeth Cady Stanton, *Solitude of Self: Address Delivered by Mrs. Stanton before the Committee of the Judiciary of the United States Congress, Monday, January 18, 1892* (n.p., n.d.); Elisabeth Griffith, *In Her Own Right: The Life of Elizabeth Cady Stanton* (New York, 1984), 203–6; Vivian Gornick, *The Solitude of Self: Thinking about Elizabeth Cady Stanton* (New York, 2006).

7. Stanton, Anthony, and Gage, *History of Woman Suffrage*, 3:v, 28–35, 122–23, 272–75, 312–15, 922; Susan B. Anthony and Ida Husted Harper, eds., *The History of Woman Suffrage*, vol. 4, *1883–1900* (Rochester, 1902), chaps. 6, 12; Elizabeth Cady Stanton, *Eighty Years and More: Reminiscences, 1815–1877* (New York, 1898), 310–18, 323–29, 336; *Declaration of Rights of the Women of the United States by the National Woman Suffrage Association, July 4, 1876* (n.p., n.d.); *NYT*, February 13, 1884; *TWJ*, April 5, 12, 1884, January 24, 1885, March 20, 1886, September 10, 1887, April 14, May 5, December 1, 1888, February 22, March 1, 1890; *The History of Woman Suffrage, Review by Rev. William Henry Channing from the Inquirer, London,* November 5th, 1881 (n.p., n.d.); R. G. Foster to Brown, June 7, 1888, Anthony to Brown, March 11, 1888, Clara Colby to Brown, February 6, 1891, Ida Husted Harper to Brown, December 28, 1917, Olympia Brown Papers, Schlesinger Library, HU; Lisa Tetrault, *The Myth of Seneca Falls: Memory and the Women's Suffrage Movement, 1848–1898* (Chapel Hill, 2014), chap. 4; Carol Lasser and Marlene Deahl Merrill, eds., *Friends and Sisters: Letters*

between Lucy Stone and Antoinette Brown Blackwell, 1846–93 (Urbana, 1987), 243, 253–55; Leslie Wheeler, ed., *Loving Warriors : Selected Letters of Lucy Stone and Henry B. Blackwell, 1853 to 1893* (New York, 1981), 313–14, 330; Alice Stone Blackwell, *Lucy Stone : Pioneer of Women's Rights* (Boston, 1930), 94, 229, 236–43, 252–53, 260, 281, 286; Stone Blackwell to Emma Lawrence Blackwell, September 23, 1893, Blackwell Family Papers, Schlesinger Library, HU; Lynn Sherr, *Failure Is Impossible: Susan B. Anthony in Her Own Words* (New York, 1995), xxi; Sally G. McMillen, *Lucy Stone: An Unapologetic Life* (New York, 2015), 251.

8. Anthony and Harper, eds., *The History of Woman Suffrage,* 4:124–42, 182, 230, 246, 263–64, 311–13, 332–33, 435–39, 1053–54; Stanton, Anthony, and Gage, *History of Woman Suffrage,* 3:105; Rachel Foster Avery, ed., *Transactions of the National Council of the Women of the United States* (Philadelphia, 1891), 9–11, 50, 57, 80–91, 214–16, 229–30; Meera Kosmabi, ed., *Pandita Ramabai's American Encounter: The Peoples of the United States (1889)* (Bloomington, 2003); *The National Citizen and Ballot Box,* May 1878; *TWJ,* May 29, 1886; Charlotte Perkins Stetson [Gilman], *Women and Economics: A Study of the Economic Relation between Men and Women as a Factor in Social Evolution* (Boston, 1898); Mrs. J. C. Croly, *The History of the Woman's Club Movement in America* (New York, 1898), 1:193–208; Ian Tyrrell, *Woman's World/Woman's Empire: The Woman's Christian Temperance Union in International Perspective, 1880–1930* (Chapel Hill, 2014); Allison L. Sneider, *Suffragists in an Imperial Age: U.S. Expansion and the Woman Question, 1870–1929* (New York, 2008); Stone Blackwell to Sarah Ellen Blackwell, March 6, 1894, Blackwell Family Papers, Schlesinger Library, HU; Stanton to Brown, May 8, 1888, Olympia Brown Papers, Schlesinger Library, HU; Wheeler, ed., *Loving Warriors,* 290–91; Stanton, *Eighty Years and More,* 318, 381–93.

9. *The Woman's Bible Part I. Comments on Genesis, Exodus, Leviticus, Numbers and Deutoronomy* (New York, 1895); *The Woman's Bible Part II Comments on the Old and New Testaments* (New York, 1898), preface; Kathi Kern, *Mrs. Stanton's Bible* (Ithaca, 2001); *Woman as Inventor by Mrs. M. E. Joslyn Gage* (Fayetteville, NY, 1870), 32; Matilda Joslyn Gage, *Woman, Church and State: A Historical Account of the Status of Woman through the Christian Ages with Reminiscences of the Matriarchate* (Chicago, 1893); Leila R. Brammer, *Excluded from Suffrage History: Matilda Joslyn Gage, Nineteenth Century American Feminist* (Westport, 2000); Sherr, *Failure Is Impossible,* 200, 326; Tetrault, *The Myth of Seneca Falls,* 177–86.

10. Anthony and Harper, eds., *The History of Woman Suffrage,* 4:236–51, 280–82, 430; Ida Husted Harper, ed., *The History of Woman Suffrage in Six Volumes,* vol. 5, 1900–1920 (New York, 1922), chap. 3; *TWJ,* November 2, 1889, May 21, 1903; Kraditor, *The Ideas of the Woman Suffrage Movement,* chap. 7; Paul E. Fuller, *Laura Clay and the Woman's Rights Movement* (Lexington, 1975); Adele Logan Alexander, *Princess of the Hither Isles: A Black Suffragist's Story from the Jim Crow South* (New Haven, 2019); Crystal Feimster, *Southern Horrors: Women and the Politics of Rape and Lynching* (Cambridge, MA, 2009), chaps. 5, 7; Melanie Susan Gustafson, *Women and the Republican Party, 1854–1924* (Urbana, 2001); Jane Turner Censer, *The Reconstruction of White Southern Womanhood, 1865–1895* (Baton Rouge, 2003); Marjorie Spruill Wheeler, *New Women of the New South: The Leaders of the Woman Suffrage Movement in the Southern States* (New York, 1993), 119; Anya Jabour, *Sophonisba Breckinridge: Championing Women's Activism in Modern America* (Urbana, 2019); Martha S. Jones, *Vanguard: How Black Women Broke Barriers, Won the Vote, and Insisted on Equality for All* (New York, 2020), 160, 166–69.

11. Roslyn Terborg-Penn, *African American Women in the Struggle for the Vote, 1850–1920* (Bloomington, 1998), 134; Janice Sumler-Edmond, "The Quest for Justice: African-American Women Litigants, 1867–1890," in Ann Gordon et al., eds., *African American Women and the Vote, 1837–1965* (Amherst, 1997), 100–19; Alfreda M. Duster, ed., *Crusade for Justice: The Autobiography of Ida B. Wells* (Chicago, 1970), 62, 227–30, 415; Ida B. Wells, *Southern Horrors: Lynch Law in All Its Phases* (New York, 1892); Ida B. Wells, *A Red Record: Tabulated Statistics and Alleged Causes of Lynching in the United States 1892–1893–1894* (Chicago, 1895), chaps. 1, 7; Patricia A. Schechter, *Ida B. Wells-Barnett and American Reform, 1880–1930* (Chapel Hill, 2001); Paula Giddings, *Ida: A Sword Among Lions: Ida B. Wells and the Campaign against Lynching* (New York, 2008); Mia Bay, *To Tell the Truth Freely: The Life of Ida B. Wells* (New York, 2009); Sarah L. Silkey, *Black Woman Reformer: Ida B. Wells, Lynching, and Transatlantic Activism* (Athens, 2015).

12. *Ida B. Wells in England. An Address Adopted by a Mass-Meeting of Afro-American Citizens of St. Paul Minnesota, June 11, 1894 Under Auspices of Ladies Home Circle* (n.p., n.d.); Steve Kramer, "Uplifting our 'Downtrodden Sisterhood': Victoria Earle Mathews and New York City's White Rose Mission, 1897–1907," *JAAH* 91 (Summer 2006): 243–66; Hallie Quinn Brown, *Homespun Heroines and Other Women of Distinction* (Xenia, 1926), 111–17, 152–55, 209–18; Elizabeth Lindsay Davis, *Lifting as They Climb* (District of Columbia, 1933), 20–30, 49–50, 217–18, 230–32, 291–92, 299–302, 307–10, 340, 403–4; Stone Blackwell to Emma Lawrence Blackwell, October 27, November 12, 1901, March 30, 1902, Blackwell Family Papers, Schlesinger Library, HU; Deborah Gray White, *Too Heavy a Load: Black Women in Defense of Themselves, 1894–1994* (New York, 1999), chaps. 1–3; Brittney C. Cooper, *Beyond Respectability: The Intellectual Thought of Race Women* (Urbana, 2017), chaps. 1–2; Beverly Guy-Sheftall, *Daughters of Sorrow: Attitudes towards Black Women, 1880–1920* (Brooklyn, 1990); Floris Barnett Cash, *African American Women and Social Action: The Clubwomen and Voluntarism from Jim Crow to the New Deal, 1896–1936* (Westport, 2001); Anthony and Harper, eds., *History of Woman Suffrage*, 4:1043; Jane Rhodes, *Mary Ann Shadd Cary : The Black Press and Protest in the Nineteenth Century* (Bloomington, 1998), 199–200; Evelyn Brooks Higginbotham, *Righteous Discontent: The Women's Movement in the Black Baptist Church, 1880–1920* (Cambridge, MA, 1993); Bettye Collier-Thomas, *Jesus, Jobs, and Justice: African American Women and Religion* (New York, 2010).

13. Mary Church Terrell, *A Colored Woman in a White World* (Washington, DC, 1940): 5, 316–17, 427, chaps. 16, 17, 20, 39; Mary Church Terrell, *The Progress of Colored Women: An Address Delivered Before the National American Women's Suffrage Association* (Washington, 1898), 8; Alison M. Parker, *Unceasing Militant: The Life of Mary Church Terrell* (Chapel Hill, 2020); Joan Quigley, *Just Another Southern Town: Mary Church Terrell and the Struggle for Racial Justice in the Nation's Capital* (New York, 2016); Davis, *Lifting as They Climb*, 213–19, 243–44, 251–52, 262–63, 349–50, 362–66; Anthony and Harper, eds., *History of Woman Suffrage*, 4:1051; Harper, ed., *History of Woman Suffrage*, 5:105–6; Brown, *Homespun Heroines*, 120–27, 177–79, 221–22, 226–32; White, *Too Heavy a Load,* 133–41, 148–57; Joyce Ann Hanson, *Mary McLeod Bethune and Black Women's Political Activism* (Columbia, 2003).

14. Ula Yvette Taylor, *The Veiled Garvey: The Life and Times of Amy Jacques Garvey* (Chapel Hill, 2002); Anna Julia Cooper, *A Voice from the South by a Woman of the South* (Xenia, 1892), 19–23, 28–31, 36–37, 51–60, 73, 87–105, 117–26, 130–42, 163–74, 188–223, 282–83; Vivian M. May, *Anna Julia Cooper, Visionary Black Feminist: A Critical Introduction* (New York, 2007); Paula Giddings, *When and Where I Enter:*

The Impact of Black Women on Race and Sex in America (New York, 1984); Patricia Hill Collins, *Black Feminist Thought: Knowledge, Consciousness and the Politics of Empowerment* (New York, 2009); Carol B. Conaway and Kristin Waters, eds., *Black Women's Intellectual Traditions: Speaking Their Minds* (Lebanon, 2007); Joy James, *Seeking the Beloved Community: A Feminist Race Reader* (Albany, 2013); Mia Bay et al., eds., *Toward an Intellectual History of Black Women* (Chapel Hill, 2015), part 2; Kimberle Crenshaw, *On Intersectionality: Essential Writings* (New York, 2017).

15. Bertha Rembaugh, *The Political Status of Women in the United States: A Digest of Laws Concerning Women in the Various States and Territories* (New York, 1911), xii–xiii, 87–88; Rebecca J. Mead, *How the Vote Was Won: Woman Suffrage in the Western United States, 1868–1914* (New York, 2004); Laurel Thatcher Ulrich, *A House Full of Females: Plural Marriage and Women's Rights in Early Mormonism, 1835–1870* (New York, 2017); Rebecca Edwards, *Angels in the Machinery: Gender in American Party Politics from the Civil War to the Progressive Era* (New York, 1997); *TWJ*, September 1, 1888; Anthony and Harper, eds., *History of Woman Suffrage,* 4:1012–41; Harper, ed., *The History of Woman Suffrage,* 5:624–25; Ida Husted Harper, ed., *The History of Woman Suffrage in Six Volumes,* vol. 6, 1900–1920 (New York, 1922), 713–871; Stone Blackwell to Emma Lawrence Blackwell, December 9, 1894, March 30, 1902, Stone Blackwell to Isaac Hourwich, October 15, 1905, Stone Blackwell to George Kennan, April 1, 13, 1911, Stone Blackwell to Blackwell, June 4, 10, 1896, June 1, 1898 Blackwell Family Papers, "Present Status of Woman Suffrage," 1914, Olympia Brown Papers, Schlesinger Library, HU; Sneider, *Suffragists in an Imperial Age,* chap. 5; Kristin Hoganson, "'As Badly Off as the Filipinos': US Women Suffragists and the Imperial Issue at the Turn of the Twentieth Century," *Journal of Women's History* 13 (Summer 2001): 17; Cathleen D. Cahill, *Recasting the Vote: How Women of Color Transformed the Suffrage Movement* (Chapel Hill, 2020); Leila J. Rupp, *Worlds of Women: The Making of an International Women's Movement* (Princeton, 1997); Keisha N. Blain, *Set the World on Fire: Black Nationalist Women and the Global Struggle for Freedom* (Philadelphia, 2018); Nancy F. Cott, *The Grounding of Modern Feminism* (New Haven, 1987); Dorothy Sue Cobble, *For the Many: American Feminists and the Global Fight for Democratic Equality* (Princeton, 2021).

16. Harper, ed., *The History of Woman Suffrage,* 5:536–37, 545–49, 562–93, 625–55, 675–82; Rembaugh, *The Political Status of Women in the United States,* 29; Carrie Chapman Catt and Nettie Rogers Shuler, *Woman Suffrage and Politics: The Inner Story of the Suffrage Movement* (New York, 1923), 89, 462–88; Susan Goodier and Karen Pastorello, *Women Will Vote: Winning Suffrage in New York State* (Ithaca, 2017); J. D. Zahniser and Amelia R. Fry, *Alice Paul: Claiming Power* (New York, 2014); Kraditor, *Ideas of the Woman Suffrage Movement,* chap. 2; Ellen Carol Du Bois, *Suffrage: Women's Long Battle for the Vote* (New York, 2020); Susan Ware, *Why They Marched: Untold Stories of the Women Who Fought for the Right to Vote* (Cambridge, MA, 2019); Elaine Weiss, *The Woman's Hour: The Great Fight to Win the Vote* (New York, 2018); Corrine M. McConnaughy, *The Woman Suffrage Movement in America: A Reassessment* (Cambridge, 2013); Parker, *Unceasing Militant,* 150; Lisa G. Materson, *For the Freedom of Her Race: Black Women and Electoral Politics in Illinois, 1877–1932* (Chapel Hill, 2009); Liette Gidlow, "The Sequel: The Fifteenth Amendment, the Nineteenth Amendment, and Southern Black Women's Struggle to Vote," *Journal of the Gilded Age and Progressive Era* 17 (July 2018): 433–49; Rebecca DeWolf, *Gendered Citizenship: The Original Conflict over the Equal Rights Amendment, 1920–1963* (Lincoln, 2021).

CONCLUSION: THE NADIR

1. *Lessons of the Hour: Hon. Frederick Douglass, Metropolitan A.M.E. Church, Washington, D.C.* (Baltimore, 1894), 5, 14, 20, 23–24, 31, 36; Nan Elizabeth Woodruff, *American Congo: The African American Freedom Struggle in the Delta* (Cambridge, MA, 2003).

2. August Meier, *Negro Thought in America, 1880–1915: Racial Ideologies in the Age of Booker T. Washington* (Ann Arbor, 1963); Shawn Leigh Alexander, *An Army of Lions: The Civil Rights Struggle before the NAACP* (Philadelphia, 2011); Michael Rudolph West, *The Education of Booker T. Washington: American Democracy and the Idea of Race Relations* (New York, 2006); Andrew Zimmerman, *Alabama in Africa: Booker T. Washington, the German Empire, and the Globalization of the New South* (Princeton, 2010); Kerri K. Greenidge, *Black Radical: The Life and Times of William Monroe Trotter* (New York, 2020); Adam Ewing, *The Age of Garvey: How a Jamaican Activist Created a Mass Movement and Changed Global Black Politics* (Princeton, 2014); David Levering Lewis, *W.E.B. Du Bois: A Biography, 1868–1963* (New York, 2009).

3. Equal Justice Initiative, *Lynching in America: Confronting the Legacy of Racial Terror*, 3rd ed. (Montgomery, 2017); Gregory Mixon, *The Atlanta Riot: Race, Class, and Violence in a New South City* (Gainesville, 2005); Roberta Senchal, *The Sociogenesis of a Race Riot: Springfield, Illinois, in 1908* (Urbana, 1990); Elliot M. Rudwick, *Race Riot in East St. Louis* (Carbondale, 1964); Robert Whitaker, *On the Lap of Gods: The Red Summer of 1919 and the Struggle for Justice That Remade a Nation* (New York, 2008); Claire Hartfield, *A Few Red Drops: The Chicago Race Riot of 1919* (New York, 2018); Randy Krehbiel, *Tulsa, 1921: Reporting a Massacre* (Norman, 2019); Edward Gonzalez-Tennant, *The Rosewood Massacre: An Archeology and History of Intersectional Violence* (Gainesville, 2018); Cameron McWhirter, *Red Summer: The Summer of 1919 and the Awakening of Black America* (New York, 2011); Herbert Shapiro, *White Violence and Black Response: From Reconstruction to Montgomery* (Amherst, 1988); Charisse Burden-Stelly, *Black Scare/Red Scare: Theorizing Capitalist Racism in the United States* (Chicago, 2023); Kim A. Wagner, "'Calculated to Strike Terror': The Amritsar Massacre and the Spectacle of Colonial Violence," *Past & Present* 233 (November 2016): 185–225; Patricia Sullivan, *Lift Every Voice: The NAACP and the Making of the Civil Rights Movement* (New York, 2009); Margaret A. Burnham, *By Hands Now Known: Jim Crow's Legal Executioners* (New York, 2022); Isabel Wilkerson, *The Warmth of Other Suns: The Epic Story of America's Great Migration* (New York, 2010); Martha Biondi, *To Stand and Fight: The Struggle for Civil Rights Postwar New York City* (Cambridge, MA, 2003); Thomas J. Sugrue, *Sweet Land of Liberty: The Forgotten Struggle for Civil Rights in the North* (New York, 2008).

4. Rev. William Barber II, *The Third Reconstruction: How a Moral Movement Is Overcoming the Politics of Division and Fear* (New York, 2016); Manisha Sinha, "The Case for a Third Reconstruction," *The New York Review of Books,* February 3, 2021; Peniel E. Joseph, *The Third Reconstruction: America's Struggle for Racial Justice in the Twenty-First Century* (New York, 2021); W.E.B. Du Bois, *Black Reconstruction in America: An Essay Toward a History of the Part Which Black Folk Played in the Attempt to Reconstruct Democracy in America, 1860–1880* (New York, 1935), 346; Nancy Fraser, *Cannibal Capitalism: How Our System Is Devouring Democracy, Care, and the Planet and What We Can Do About It* (New York, 2022).

INDEX

Ku Klux Klan and, 239
labor organizing and, 373, 384, 385, 429
See also abolitionist feminists; black
   women; black women's activism;
   female abolitionists; women's rights;
   women's suffrage; *specific women*
Women's Christian Temperance Union
   (WCTU), 373, 426, 434, 444
women's club movement, 434–35, 445
women's conventions, 195–96, *200*, 212–13
Women's International League of Peace and
   Freedom, 447
Women's Political Union, 454
Women's Relief Corps, 35
women's rights, 193–230
   abolitionists and, 195–97, 198–99, 434
   American Equal Rights Association and,
     213–14
   black abolitionists and, 198–99
   Civil War work and, 200–207, *203*
   dress reform and, 197–98
   grassroots reconstruction and, 125
   as intrinsic to Reconstruction, xvi, xvii
   transnational context, 211–12
   women's conventions and, 195–96, *200*,
     212–13
   Worcester convention (1850), 196, 198
   See also women's suffrage
women's suffrage, xvi, xvii, xviii, xxv
   American Equal Rights Association and,
     213–14
   AWSA strategies, 224–25
   black abolitionists and, 199
   black officeholders and, 187, 227–28, 455
   black political mobilization and, 227–28
   black women's late nineteenth-century
     activism and, 442–43, 445, 447, 448
   elitism and, 215, 219, 435–36
   Fifteenth Amendment and, 113, 194
   Fourteenth Amendment and, 213, 221,
     222, 439
   imperialism/colonialism and, 436–37, 453
   Indians and, 435–36
   literacy requirements and, 437–38
   National Woman's Party, 448, 454
   nativism and, 226
   NAWSA, 425, 433–34, 436–37, 438,
     439–40, 441, 447–48, 454

New England Woman Suffrage Association, 219
Nineteenth Amendment, xxv, 94, 220,
   229, 425, 441–42, 448, 455
progressive constitutionalism and,
   221–22, 225, 227
Progressive era strategies, 454
racism and, 440–41, 444
Reconstruction legacy and, 425–26
Reconstruction overthrow and, 194, 222,
   226, 348, 425, 435–36
Reconstruction state constitutional conventions and, 218, 227, 228–29
segregation and, 425
Seneca Falls convention (1848), 195, 196,
   197, 432, 433, 434
settlement house movement and, 426–27
sixteenth amendment proposal, 225
socialism and, 429–30
southern strategy, 218, 226, 438–42, 451
Supreme Court and, 222, 305
Thirteenth Amendment proposals and,
   49
transnational implications, 434, 452–53
voting attempts, 221, 227
western states, 222–23, 452
White House picketing, 448, *448*, 454–55
women's Civil War work and, 210
women's club movement and, 434–35
See also women's suffrage movement
   split
women's suffrage movement split, 194–95,
   214–21
   AWSA and NWSA and, 223, 224–26, 425,
     432, 433
   election of 1872 and, 218, 220–21
   Fifteenth Amendment and, 194, 219,
     221–22, 223–24, 432, 439
   Fourteenth Amendment and, 213
   as lost opportunity for interracial
     democracy, 230
   "New Departure" tactics and, 221, 223
   racism and, 215, 219, 226–27, 425
   rapprochement, 425, 431–34
   southern strategy and, 438
   state campaigns and, 215–16, 218–19
   Wells and, 444
Women's Trade Union League, 427